The Ties That Bind

We've fought wars together and together kept the peace. That makes for ties that bind.

George Bush
Canberra, 30 April 1982

The ties that bind
Now you can't break the ties that bind
You can't foresake the ties that bind

© *1979, 1980 Bruce Springsteen*
Used by permission

The Ties That Bind

Intelligence Cooperation between the UKUSA Countries — the United Kingdom, the United States of America, Canada, Australia and New Zealand

Jeffrey T. Richelson and Desmond Ball

Boston
Allen & Unwin
London Sydney

© Jeffrey T. Richelson and Desmond Ball 1985

This book is copyright under the Berne convention. No reproduction without permission. All rights reserved.

First published in 1985
Allen & Unwin Australia Pty Ltd
8 Napier Street, North Sydney NSW 2060 Australia

Allen & Unwin (Publishers) Ltd
18 Park Lane, Hemel Hempstead, Herts HP2 4TE England

Allen & Unwin Inc.
8 Winchester Place, Winchester, Mass 01890 USA

Library of Congress Catalog Card Number 84-72494

British Library Cataloguing in Publication
Richelson, Jeffrey T.
  The ties that bind: intelligence cooperation between the UKUSA countries — United Kingdom, the United States of America, Canada, Australia and New Zealand.
  1. Intelligence service — International cooperation 2. Intelligence service — United States 3. Intelligence service — Great Britain
  I. Title II. Ball, Desmond
327.1′2 JF1525.I6
ISBN 0-04-327092 1

Typeset is 10/11.5 Times by Setrite Typesetters, Hong Kong
Printed by Bright Sun (Shenzhen) Printing Co Ltd., China

Contents

Acknowledgments	vii
Acronyms and abbreviations	viii
1 Introduction	1

I The UKUSA security and intelligence communities

2 The British security and intelligence community	13
3 The Australian security and intelligence community	30
4 The New Zealand security and intelligence community	67
5 The Canadian security and intelligence community	82
6 The United States security and intelligence community	96

II The UKUSA community in operation

7 The mechanics of cooperation and exchange	135
8 The signals intelligence connection	174
9 Ocean surveillance	198
10 Other areas of cooperation	228
11 Discord, non-cooperation and deceit within the UKUSA community	239
12 Organization and performance	269
13 Dissent and the UKUSA security services	283
14 Conclusion	301

III Appendixes

1 The UKUSA SIGINT network	315
2 Heads of the principal UKUSA security and intelligence agencies and organizations	340
Notes	343
Index	393

Acknowledgments

The authors are grateful to the numerous people who granted interviews, engaged us in extremely useful conversations, or otherwise provided us with information and material, and suggestions and criticisms. Many of these people are current or former members of the UKUSA security and intelligence agencies and, for obvious reasons, prefer not to be identified.

Those who we can publicly thank are William Pinwill, Brian Toohey, the late George Munster, Bill D'Arcy, Jann Little and Billie Dalrymple in Australia; William Arkin, James Bamford, Richard Fieldhouse and Scott Armstrong in the United States; Stuart McMillan in New Zealand; Barry Kay in Canada; Duncan Campbell in Britain; and Nils Petter Gleditsch in Norway. We are especially grateful to Duncan Campbell for his assistance with the location of the Government Communications Headquarters (GCHQ) facilities and to William Arkin for the preparation of the penultimate draft of the section on US Signals Intelligence (SIGINT) facilities in Appendix I.

Acronyms and abbreviations

A-2	Air Force Intelligence
AATTV	Australian Army Training Team Vietnam
ABCA	America, Britain, Canada, Australia
ABM	Anti Ballistic Missile
ACLU	American Civil Liberties Union
ACOUSTINT	Acoustical Intelligence
ACPs	Allied Communications Publications
ACSA	Allied Communications Security Agency
ACSI	Assistant Chief of Staff for Intelligence
ADCOS	Aerospace Defense Combat Operations Staff
AEDS	Atomic Energy Detection System
AFAR	Azores Fixed Acoustic Range
AFB	Air Force Base
AFIS	Air Force Intelligence Service
AFP	Australian Federal Police
AFSA	Armed Forces Security Agency
AFSS	Air Force Security Service
AFTAC	Air Force Technical Applications Center
AIB	Allied Intelligence Bureau
AIM	American Indian Movement
ALLO	All Other
ALP	Australian Labor Party
ANA	Arab News Agency
ANZUK	Australia, New Zealand, United Kingdom
APLQ	Agence Presse Libre du Quebec
ARC	Acoustic Research Center
ARIA	Advanced Range Instrumentation Aircraft
ASA	Army Security Agency

ASEAN	Association of South East Asian Nations
ASIO	Australian Security Intelligence Organisation
ASIS	Australian Secret Intelligence Service
ASO	*Australia's Security Outlook*
ASW	Anti-Submarine Warfare
AUSTEO	Australian Eyes Only
AUTEC	Atlantic Undersea Test and Evaluation Center
AWACS	Airborne Warning and Control System
BAKIN	Indonesian State Intelligence Coordination Body
BBC	British Broadcasting Corporation
BIAS	Bureau of Intelligence Analysis and Security
BIOT	British Indian Ocean Territory
BLO	British Liaison Officer
BMEWS	Ballistic Missile Early Warning System
BOSS	Bureau of State Security
BRUSA	Britain–United States Agreement
BSC	British Security Coordination
C^3	Command, Control and Communications
CB	Central Bureau (Australia)
CBNRC	Communications Branch National Research Council
CBW	Chemical and Biological Warfare
CCB	Combined Communications Board
CCCC	Centralised COMINT Communications Center
CCRC	COMINT Communications Relay Center
CCS	Chairman, Chiefs of Staff
CCSE	Canadian Communications Security Establishment
CD	Combat Development
CDA	Combined Development Agency
CDAA	Circularly Disposed Antenna Array
CGS	Chief of General Staff
CHOGRM	Commonwealth Heads of Government Regional Meetings
CIA	Central Intelligence Agency
CIB	Australian Commonwealth Investigation Branch
CID	Criminal Investigative Division
CIET	Campaign for an Independent East Timor
CIG	Current Intelligence Groups
CIS	Counter Intelligence Staff
CND	Campaign for Nuclear Disarmament
COI	Coordinator of Information
COINTELPRO	Counter Intelligence Program
COMINFIL	Communist Infiltration
COMINT	Communications Intelligence
COMIREX	Committee on Imagery Requirements and Exploitation
COMOR	Committee on Overhead Reconnaissance
COMSAT	Communications Satellite

COMSEC	Communications Security
CONUS	Continental United States
CORE	Congress on Racial Equality
COS	Chief of Station
CPBWs	Charged Particle Beam Weapons
CPC	Combined Policy Committee; Crisis Policy Centre
CPUSA	Communist Party of the United States of America
CRO	Japanese Cabinet Research Office
CSE	Communications Security Establishment
CSIS	Canadian Security Intelligence Service
CSO	Commonwealth SIGINT Organisation; Composite Signals Organisation
CSS	Central Security Service; Commonwealth Security Service
CSS ('C')	Chief of Secret Service
CX	British HUMINT Reports
DAFIS	Directorate of Air Force Intelligence and Security
DCD	Domestic Collection Division
DCI	(Thai) Department of Central Intelligence; (US) Director of Central Intelligence
DCIA	Director of Central Intelligence Agency
DDCJIO	Deputy-Director Civilian Joint Intelligence Organisation
DDMJIO	Deputy-Director Military Joint Intelligence Organisation
DDRS	Declassified Documents Reference System
DEA	Drug Enforcement Agency
DEI	Directorate of Economic Intelligence
DES	Data Encryption Standard
DEW	Distant Early Warning
DF	Direction Finding
DGI	Director General of Intelligence
DGSS	Director General Security Service
DIA	Defense Intelligence Agency
DIES	Defence Intelligence Estimates Staff
DIN/DSSCS	Digital Network/Defense Special Security Communications System
DIRNSA	Director of National Security Agency
DIS	Defence Intelligence Staff
DMI	Directorate of Military Intelligence
DMIPS	Directorate of Military Intelligence Planning Staff
DMS	Defence Market Survey
DMSI	Directorate of Management and Support of Intelligence
DNI	Director of the Office of Naval Intelligence
DNIS	Directorate of Naval Intelligence and Security
DoD	Department of Defence

DOE	Directorate of Organization and Establishment
DP	Directorate of SIGINT Plans
DPRS	Directorate of Programme and Research Support
DSB	Defence Security Branch; Defence Signals Bureau
DSCS	Defense Satellite Communications System
DSD	Defence Signals Directorate; Defence Signals Division
DSDLO	Defence Signals Directorate Liaison Officer
DSI	Directorate of Service Intelligence
DSP	Defense Support Program
DSS	Domestic Security Section
DSTI	Directorate of Scientific and Technical Intelligence
ECMs	Electronic Counter Measures
EDP	Electronic Data Processing
EEC	European Economic Community
EEZ	Exclusive Economic Zone
EHF	Extremely High Frequency
EIB	External Intelligence Bureau
ELINT	Electronic Intelligence
EOB	Electronic Order of Battle
EPDS	Evaluation, Plans and Designs Staff
EPL	Emitter Program Listings
ESC	US Air Force Electronic Security Command
EW	Early Warning
FBI	Federal Bureau of Investigation
FBIS	Foreign Broadcast Information Service
FBM	Fleet Ballistic Missile
FECB	British Far Eastern Command Bureau
FIS	Foreign Intelligence Staff
FISINT	Foreign Instrumentation Signals Intelligence
FLQ	Fronte Libre du Quebec
FLTSATCOM	Fleet Satellite Communications
FOSIC	Fleet Ocean Surveillance Information Center
FRD	Foreign Resources Division
FSD	Foreign Service Directorate
FTD	Foreign Technology Division
FY	Financial Year
FYRP	Five Year Rolling Program
G-2	Army Intelligence
GCCS	Government Code and Cipher School
GCHQ	Government Communications Headquarters
GCSB	New Zealand Government Communications Security Bureau
GDIP	General Defence Intelligence Program
GHQ	General Headquarters
GID	General Investigative Division
GIUK	Greenland–Iceland–United Kingdom

GPS	Global Positioning System
GRU	Soviet Military Intelligence
HART	Halt All Racist Tours
HF-DF	High Frequency–Direction Finding
HILEV	High Level Intelligence
HMAS	Her Majesty's Australian Ship
HMNZS	Her Majesty's New Zealand Ship
HOCI	Head of Office of Current Intelligence
HUMINT	Human Intelligence
IAC	Intelligence Advisory Committee
ICBM	Intercontinental Ballistic Missile
IEE	Institute of Electronic Engineers
ILC	International Licensed Carrier
INR	Bureau of Intelligence and Research
INSCOM	Army Intelligence and Security Command
INTELSAT	International Telecommunications Satellite
IOC	Initial Operational Capability
IPC	Intelligence Policy Committee
IRA	Irish Republican Army
IRD	Information Research Department
IRSIG	International Regulations on SIGINT
ISA	Intelligence Support Activity
ITSS	Integrated Tactical Surveillance System
J-2	Joint Intelligence Staff
JCEC	Joint Communications — Electronics Committee
JCS	Joint Chiefs of Staff
JIB	Joint Intelligence Bureau
JIC	Joint Intelligence Committee
JIO	Joint Intelligence Organization
JIS	Joint Intelligence Staff
JRRU	Joint Reports and Research Unit
JSS	Joint Surveillance System
JTLS	Joint Technical Language Service
KGB	Committee for State Security
LF	Low Frequency
LRMP	Long Range Maritime Patrol Aircraft
LRTS	Long Range Technical Search
LSIB	London Signals Intelligence Board
LSIC (D)	London Signals Intelligence Committee (Defence)
MAD	Magnetic Anomaly Detection
MBFR	Mutual and Balanced Force Reduction
MDPPQ	Movement Pour la Defense des Prisoniers Politiques du Quebec
MEIO	Malaysian External Intelligence Organization
MENS	Mission Element Needs Statement
MIAG	Military Intelligence Advisory Group

MIRV	Multiple Independently-Targetable Re-entry Vehicle
MI-5	British Security Service
MI-6	British Secret Intelligence Service
MI-9	Military Intelligence Section 9
MOL	Manned Orbital Laboratory
MO9	Australian Secret Intelligence Service
MRBM	Medium Range Ballistic Missile
NAACP	National Association for the Advancement of Colored People
NAS	National Assessments Staff
NASA	National Aeronautics and Space Administration
NATO	North Atlantic Treaty Organization
NATP	National Anti-Terrorist Plan
NAVALEX	Naval Electronic Systems Command
NAVCOMMs	Naval Communications
NAVSPASUR	Naval Space Surveillance System
NCSS PO	Naval Command Support System Project Office
NFAC	National Foreign Assessment Center
NFIB	National Foreign Intelligence Board
NFIP	National Foreign Intelligence Program
NFOIO	Naval Field Operational Intelligence Office
NIC	Naval Intelligence Command; National Intelligence Committee
NICA	Philippine National Intelligence Coordination Agency
NID	Naval Intelligence Department
NIE	National Intelligence Estimate
NIOs	National Intelligence Officers
NIPE	National Intelligence Programs' Evaluation
NISC	National and International Security Committee
NITC	National Intelligence Tasking Centre
NOFORN	No Foreign Dissemination
NOIC	Navy Operational Intelligence Center
NORAD	North American Air Defense
NOSIC	Naval Ocean Surveillance Information Center
NOSIS	Naval Ocean Surveillance Information System
NOSS	Naval Ocean Surveillance System
NPIC	National Photographic Interpretation Center
NRC	National Research Council
NRL	Naval Research Laboratory
NRO	National Reconnaissance Office
NSA	National Security Agency
NSAM	National Security Action Memorandum
NSC	National Security Council
NSCID	National Security Council Intelligence Directive
NSG	Naval Security Group
NTK	Need-to-know

NZDDI	New Zealand Directorate of Defence Intelligence
NZIC	New Zealand Intelligence Council
NZJIB	New Zealand Joint Intelligence Bureau
NZSIS	New Zealand Security Intelligence Service
OACS/I	Office of the Assistant Chief of Staff for Intelligence
OCI	Office of Current Intelligence
OEIC	Overseas Economic Intelligence Committee
OEL	CIA Office of Electronic Intelligence (ELINT)
OJCS	Office of the Joint Chiefs of Staff
ONA	Office of National Assessments
ONI	Office of Naval Intelligence
OPC	Office of Policy Coordination
OPEC	Organization of Petroleum Exporting Countries
OSCD	Operational Strategy Coordination Division
OSI	Office of Scientific Intelligence; Office of Special Investigations
OSIC	Ocean Surveillance Information Center
OSIS	Ocean Surveillance Information System
OSO	CIA Office of SIGINT Operations; Office of Special Operations
OSS	Office of Strategic Services
OTH	Over the Horizon
OTH-B	Over the Horizon Backscatter radar system
OTS	Oakhanger Tracking Station; Office of Technical Services
OWI	Office of War Information
'P' Directorate	Protective Policing Directorate
PAM	Personal Assessments Manual
PAWS	Phased Array Warning System
PBW	Particle Beam Weapon
PCG	Permanent Coordination Group
PFIAB	President's Foreign Intelligence Advisory Board
PI	Photographic Interpretation
PMV	Politically Motivated Violence
PNGIC	Papua New Guinea Intelligence Committee
PNUTS	Possible Nuclear Underground Test Site
POWs	Prisoners of War
PQ	Parti Quebecois
PRC	People's Republic of China; Policy Review Committee
PROD	National Security Agency Office of Production
PSCC	Protective Services Coordination Centre
PSIS	Permanent Under Secretaries Committee on Intelligence Services
QSTAGs	Quadrapartite Standardization Agreements
QWG	Quadrapartite Working Group
QWG/EW	Quadrapartite Working Group on Electronic Warfare
R&D	Research and Development

RAAF	Royal Australian Air Force
RADINT	Radar Intelligence
RAF	Royal Air Force
RAN	Royal Australian Navy
RANRL	Royal Australian Naval Research Laboratory
RCMP	Royal Canadian Mounted Police
RDSS	Rapidly Deployable Surveillance System
REWSON	Reconnaissance, Electronic Warfare, Special Operations and Naval Intelligence
RFPs	Requests for Proposals
RLPA	Rotatable Log Periodic Array
RMC	Royal Military College
ROCCs	Regional Operations Control Centers
R/T	Radio-Telephonic
RUSI	Royal United Services Institute
RV	Re-entry Vehicle
S&T	Science and Technology
SAC	Security Advisory Committee; Strategic Air Command
SAC-PAV	Standing Advisory Committee on Commonwealth/State Cooperation for Protection Against Violence
SALT	Strategic Arms Limitation Talks
SAM	Security Assessments Manual; Surface-to-Air Missile
SAMOS	Satellite and Missile Observation System
SAR	Synthetic Aperture Radar
SAS	Special Air Service
SASR	Special Air Service Regiment
SBS	Special Boat Squadron
SCA	Service Cryptological Authorities
SCC	Special Coordination Committee
SCF	Satellite Control Facility
SDS	Satellite Data System; Students for a Democratic Society
SEALS	US Navy Special Warfare Unit
SEATO	South East Asia Treaty Organization
SHF	Super High Frequency
SI	Special Intelligence
SIA	Secret Intelligence Australia
SIB	Security Intelligence Bureau
SIDC-PAV	Special Interdepartmental Committee on Protection Against Violence
SIG−I	Senior Interagency Group−Intelligence
SIGINT	Signals Intelligence
SIOP	Single Integrated Operational Plan
SIPRI	Stockholm International Peace Research Institute
SIS	British Secret Intelligence Service; US Army Signals Intelligence Service; US Special Intelligence Service
SITF	Special Incidents Task Force

SLAR	Side-Looking Airborne Radar
SLBM	Submarine-Launched Ballistic Missile
SMOS	Special Minister of State
SNIE	Special National Intelligence Estimate
SOE	Special Operations Executive
SOG	Special Operations Group
SOSUS	Sound Surveillance System
SPA	Socialist Party of Australia; Special Political Activity
SPADATS	Space Detection and Tracking System
SPARG	Security Planning and Research Group
SPASUR	Space Surveillance System
SPECATS	Special Categories
SSA	US Signal Security Agency
SSAs	Single Service Advisers
STAR	Special Tasks and Rescue
SUKLO	Senior United Kingdom Liaison Officer
SURTASS	Surveillance Towed Array Sensor System
SUSLO	Special United States Liaison Officer
SWOS	Special Weapons and Operations Squad
T/A	Traffic Analysis
TAG	Tactical Assault Group
TCP	Technical Cooperation Program
TDI	Target Data Inventory
TELINT	Telemetry Intelligence
TEREC	Tactical Electronic Reconnaissance
TEXTA	Technical Extracts of Traffic
TIWG	Travelling Intelligence Working Group
TK	Talent-Keyhole
TRI-TAC	Tri-Service Tactical Communications
TTCP	The Technical Cooperation Programme
UKUSA	UK–USA Security Agreement
URDF	Unidentified Research and Development Facility
USAF	United States Air Force
USAFSS	US Air Force Security Service
USIB	United States Intelligence Board
USNS	United States Navy Ship
USSR	Union of Soviet Socialist Republics
VHF	Very High Frequency
VHFS	Vint Hill Farms Station
VLF	Vancouver Liberation Front; Very Low Frequency

Hansard (House of Representatives), 19 April 1977, p. 990

Electronic Intercept Stations in Australia
(Question No. 113)

Mr Hayden asked the Prime Minister, upon notice, on 9 March 1977:

(1) Is Australia a signatory to the United Kingdom — United States of America Agreement.

(2) Is it a fact that under the Agreement NSA operates electronic intercept stations in Australia.

(3) Does any other form of station operate in Australia under the Agreement. If so, is it operated by an Australian or an overseas authority or is it operated under some sort of joint authority.

(4) Will he identify the participating country or countries in any such arrangement.

Mr Malcolm Fraser — The answer to the honourable member's question is as follows:

(1) to (4)

The policy of Australian governments has been not to provide information that might confirm or deny speculation about this subject. This remains the policy. I therefore do not propose to answer the honourable member's question.

NATIONAL SECURITY AGENCY
CENTRAL SECURITY SERVICE
FORT GEORGE G. MEADE, MARYLAND 20755

Serial: N9439
7 DEC 1982

Dr. Jeffrey Richelson
The American University
Massachusetts & Nebraska Avenues, N.W.
Washington, DC 20016

Dear Dr. Richelson:

This responds to your Freedom of Information Act request of 22 November 1982 in which you request any documents from 1947 outlining United States-United Kingdom-Australian-Canadian-New Zealand cooperation in Signals Intelligence. You also request a copy of the International Regulations on SIGINT.

We have determined that the fact of the existence or non-existence of the materials you request is a currently and properly classified matter under criteria set forth in Section 1.3 of Executive Order 12356 and paragraph 2-202 of Department of Defense (DoD) Regulation 5200.1-R, which implements Executive Order 12356 for all DoD agencies. Thus, your request is denied pursuant to 5 U.S.C. 552(b)(1).

In addition, this Agency is authorized by law to protect certain information concerning its activities. Title 5 U.S.C. 552(b)(3) exempts matters that are specifically protected from disclosure by statute. The appropriate statutes in this case are: 18 U.S.C. 798; 50 U.S.C. 403(d)(3); and Public Law 86-36. Thus, your request is also denied because any information encompassed by your request, if it existed, would be exempted under 5 U.S.C. 552(b)(3) as specifically protected from disclosure by statute.

As the information you request, if it existed at the NSA/CSS, is denied to you, you are hereby advised of this Agency's appeal procedures.

Any person denied access to information may, within 30 days after notification of the denial, file an appeal to the NSA/CSS Freedom of Information Act Appeal Authority. The appeal shall be in writing addressed to the NSA/CSS FOIA Appeal Authority, National Security Agency, Fort George G. Meade, MD 20755. The appeal shall reference the initial denial of access and shall contain, in sufficient detail and particularity, the grounds upon which the requester believes release of the information is required. The NSA/CSS Appeal Authority shall respond to the appeal within 20 working days after receipt.

Sincerely,

EUGENE F. YEATES
Director of Policy

1

Introduction

The US–British military alliance in the Second World War necessitated a high degree of cooperation with respect to intelligence activities. As the main Allied combatants in the European and Pacific theatres it was imperative that the US and Britain establish a coordinated effort in the acquisition of worldwide intelligence, its evaluation and its distribution. This required coordination in the areas of human intelligence, signals intelligence, ocean surveillance, photographic aerial intelligence and in the production of intelligence estimates.

The cooperation and coordination that resulted between the United States and Britain were expanded to include the other 'Anglo-Saxon' countries — Canada, Australia and New Zealand — covering all areas of intelligence activity. More importantly, they have continued beyond the Second World War to the present day, and indeed play a major part in determining the current intelligence activities of each nation.

History

Of all the areas of intelligence collaboration it was in the areas of signals intelligence and ocean surveillance that the most important and vital cooperation took place. Cooperation began in the spring of 1941 when four American representatives (two from the Navy and two from the Army) delivered a model of the Japanese PURPLE machine — used by Japan to encipher diplomatic communications — to British code-breakers at Bletchley Park. In return the British gave the US representatives an assortment of advanced cryptological equipment, including the Marconi–Adcock high-frequency direction-finder (HF-DF).[1]

Further cooperation involved both exchange of personnel and a division of labour. A small American mission was sent to the Combined Bureau at Singapore for the purpose of cooperation in signals intelligence and ocean surveillance while a British naval officer trained in Japanese and experienced in cryptanalysis was introduced into the American signal intelligence station on Corregidor in the Philippines. A secret channel of communication was established between Corregidor and Singapore for the direct exchange of cryptanalytical material. Meanwhile, it was agreed that the British would break Tokyo–London traffic while the Americans broke Tokyo–Washington traffic. The results of the US code-breaking effort that were considered of possible use to Britain in its war with Germany were passed to London via the British Ambassador in Washington.[2]

US entry into the war expanded the scope of the US–British signals intelligence cooperation. Both US and British commanders in the field (whether directing solely US forces, solely British forces or joint forces) required the most up-to-date intelligence available on the enemy Order of Battle and plan of action — exactly the type of information that could best be provided by intercepts of military wireless traffic. Thus, in addition to the intercepts of diplomatic traffic being widely exchanged it was necessary to broaden the exchange of intercepted military traffic and arrangements for a coordinated attack on such traffic. Britain's production of such intelligence was labelled ULTRA.[3]

While ULTRA information was made available to American and British military commanders via Special Liaison Units, initially, the exact nature of its acquisition was obscured. It was not until April 1943 that the British revealed to US military intelligence officials the secret — that Britain's code-breaking organization could break the ciphers produced by the German ENIGMA machine that was used for much of the German military communications.[4]

During the same visit to Bletchley Park at which British officials revealed the ULTRA secret to the US military intelligence officials, a formal agreement of cooperation was concluded between Britain and the US — the Britain–United States Agreement (BRUSA). The agreement did several things. It established high level cooperation on Signals Intelligence (SIGINT) matters. Specifically, it covered exchange of personnel, joint regulations for the handling of ULTRA material and procedures for its distribution. The joint regulations included strict security regulations that applied to all British or American recipients of ULTRA material.[5]

The BRUSA Agreement was the second formal agreement between British and US intelligence agencies. In 1942, a joint agreement between the US Office of Strategic Services (OSS) and the British Special Operations Executive (SOE) and Secret Intelligence Service (SIS) had been worked out to provide for the coordination of secret intelligence, covert action and sabotage operations. This agreement was intended to:

avoid confusion resulting from the operation of independent organizations in the same country, it [being] agreed in general that the areas of the world would be divided into British or American areas run by SOE or OSS, with the other service stationing a smaller mission or liaison staff subordinate to the controlling agency.[6]

Thus, India was to be a British sphere with the OSS sending liaison officers to New Delhi while China, on the other hand, was to be an OSS responsibility. The SOE was given responsibility for most of Europe while the OSS was made responsible for North Africa, Finland, and eventually Bulgaria, Romania and Northern Norway.[7]

Along with the increased cooperation between Britain and the United States there was also increased involvement by the Anglo-Saxon members of the British Commonwealth — Canada, Australia and New Zealand — in a variety of intelligence activities. US–Canadian cooperation began in October 1941 when the Canadians offered the US Federal Communications Commission free access to the product of Canadian monitoring activities. In return the US provided Canada with technical Direction-Finding (DF) data that were 'invaluable for pinpointing the location of a transmitter'.[8]

Canadian DF stations subsequently made significant contributions to the Allied North Atlantic signals intelligence/ocean surveillance network.[9] The Canadian code-breaking agency was also successful in intercepting and decoding German espionage control messages to and from agents in South America, Canada, Hamburg and Lisbon.[10] Messages to and from the Vichy delegation in Ottawa were also intercepted and decoded.[11] Further, the peculiarities of radio wave propagation resulted in Canadian monitoring facilities being able to intercept military transmissions originating in Europe that were inaccessible to equipment based in Britain.[12]

It was with respect to Japan, however, that SIGINT and ocean surveillance cooperation among all five nations reached its highest level. Monitoring stations in Canada, particularly the major one at Halifax, gathered large quantities of coded Japanese transmissions.[13] In April 1942 a combined Allied signals intelligence agency for the Pacific, the Central Bureau of the Allied Intelligence Bureau (AIB) was activated in Melbourne with a US Chief and an Australian deputy chief.[14]

The extent of cooperation is particularly highlighted by the situation in Australia with respect to intercept stations. Some sixteen stations were operational in Australia at various periods during the Second World War: in addition to nine Australian stations, there was a US intercept station at GHQ Brisbane, a US Army station at Townsville, a US Navy intercept unit in Melbourne, the US Army's 138th Signal Company intercept and DF group near Darwin, a British DF station at Darwin and a British post in Brisbane for the interception and distribution of Japanese radio communications,[15] and on 18 May 1945 a Canadian Special Wireless Group arrived in Darwin to assist in the task of intercepting.[16]

The New Zealand contribution in the signals intelligence ocean surveillance field included passing intercepted messages concerning the presence of Japanese submarines off Sydney Harbour to Australian intelligence officials. New Zealand naval authorities intercepted Japanese wireless transmissions on 23 May, 26 May and 30 May 1942.[17] After the 23 May interception the New Zealand Naval Board informed Australian naval officials of a probable submarine operating 1127 kilometres east of Sydney. On 26 May the Naval Board also informed the Australian Naval Intelligence Directorate of an intercepted (but not decoded) signal indicating the close proximity of Japanese submarines off Sydney. At 6.00 p.m. on 30 May a signal was intercepted by the Naval Board and at 7.10 p.m. the Board notified the Australian Naval Intelligence Directorate of the presence of an enemy unit, probably a submarine, approximately 65 kilometres east of Sydney.[18]

In addition to the crucial cooperation in the signals intelligence and surveillance areas there was also a considerable contribution by Australia and Canada to the secret intelligence and special operations efforts. Australian participation was channelled through offshoots of the respective British agencies — Special Operations Australia (later the Services Reconnaissance Department) of the Allied Intelligence Bureau and Secret Intelligence Australia (SIA).[19] The Services Reconnaissance Department launched a successful attack on Japanese shipping in Singapore Harbour as well as carrying out raids along the coasts of Malaya, the Netherlands East Indies, Portuguese Timor, Borneo and New Guinea.[20]

Similarly, there was a significant Canadian contribution to the operations of the Special Operations Executive and Military Intelligence Section 9 (MI-9) — the latter being the branch of the Military Intelligence Department concerned with Escape and Evasion matters. In Burma, an Anglo-Canadian organization, the Sea Reconnaissance Unit, charted the shoals and depths of the Irrawaddy River.[21] In Canada, several Canadians were interviewed and accepted to work in Europe for MI-9.[22] Additionally, a Canadian–American Special Service Force was trained for commando raids in Norway.[23] In Chapter 7 we discuss in more detail the historical aspects of the UKUSA intelligence cooperation that are most relevant to the present situation.

The UKUSA Agreement

The intelligence relationship between Australia, Britain, Canada, New Zealand and the United States that was forged by the Second World War did not end with the war. Rather, it became formalized and grew stronger. In 1946, William Friedman, America's premier cryptographer, visited the British cryptographers to work out methods of post-war consultation and collaboration. A US Liaison Office was set up in London and schemes were devised for avoiding duplication of effort. It was agreed that solved material was to be exchanged between the two agencies. In addition, an exchange program was started under which personnel from each agency would work for two or three years with the other.[24]

In 1947 an event took place which set the stage for the post-Second World

Introduction 5

War intelligence cooperation that continues to this day — this was the formulation and acceptance of the UKUSA Agreement, also known as the UK–USA Security Agreement or 'Secret Treaty'. The primary aspect of the Agreement was the division of SIGINT collection responsibilities among the First Party (the United States) and the Second Parties (Australia, Britain, Canada and New Zealand).[25] The world was divided into areas of responsibility, with each nation having the primary responsibility for SIGINT collection in a particular area.

In addition to specifying SIGINT collection responsibilities the Agreement also concerns access to the collected intelligence and security arrangements for the handling of the data. Standardized codewords (e.g. UMBRA for Top Secret signals intelligence), security agreements that all employees of the respective SIGINT agencies must sign, and procedures for storing and disseminating codeword material are all part of the implementation of the Agreement.[26] Thus, in a memo concerning the agreement dated 8 October 1948, the US Army Office of the Adjutant General advised the recipients of the memo that:

The United States Chiefs of Staff will make every effort to insure that the United States will maintain in the military security classifications established by the United Kingdom authorities with respect to military information of UK origin, and the military security classifications established by the UK–US Agreement with respect to military information of joint UK–US origin.[27]

Similarly, in 1967 the 'COMINT Indoctrination' declaration which all British COMINT-cleared personnel had to sign included the statement (in the first paragraph) that:

I declare that I fully understand that information relating to the manner and extent of the interception of communications of foreign powers by H.M. Government and *other co-operating Governments*, and intelligence produced by such interception, known as Communications Intelligence (COMINT) is information covered by Section 2 of the Official Secrets Act 1911 (as amended).[28] [Emphasis added.]

These requirements for standardized codewords, security agreements and procedures for the handling and dissemination of SIGINT material are apparently all detailed in a series of 'International Regulations on SIGINT' (IRSIG). As of 1967 the IRSIG was in its third edition.

Despite numerous references to the Agreement in print, officials of some of the participating nations have refused to confirm not only details of the Agreement but even its existence. Thus on 9 March 1977 the Australian Opposition Foreign Affairs Spokesman asked the Prime Minister:

(1) Is Australia a signatory to the UK–USA agreement?
(2) Is it a fact that under this agreement, NSA [National Security Agency] operates electronic intercept stations in Australia?
(3) Does any other form of station operate in Australia under the agreement; if so,

is it operated by an Australian or an overseas authority or is it operated under some sort of joint authority?
(4) Will he identify the participating country or countries in any such arrangement?

The Prime Minister refused to answer and referred to a previous response where he said the Government would not confirm or deny speculation in this area.[29] And the Australian D notice on 'Ciphering and Monitoring Activities' requests newspapers, magazines etc. to refrain from publishing material on 'Australian Collaboration with Other Countries in Monitoring Activities'.

The Canadian Government has been somewhat more forthcoming. The Canadian Minister of State for Science and Technology in 1975, C.M. Orvry, admitted Canadian participation in the Agreement (with the UK and US) and stated that its purpose was 'to ensure effective collaboration between these three countries in security matters'.[30]

Just as the intelligence relationship among the UKUSA nations in the Second World War had signals intelligence at its core but involved more than signals intelligence so the post-war relationship concerns more than signals intelligence. A major area of cooperation, as in the Second World War, is ocean surveillance — its objectives being the location of foreign (particularly Soviet) surface ships and submarines. Such surveillance may be conducted via satellite, surface ship, submarine or ground station. This area of cooperation is a highly formalized one with the output from UKUSA facilities feeding directly into the US Naval Ocean Surveillance Information System (NOSIS).[31] A third formal relationship is the US–British division of the world for the purposes of monitoring foreign radio broadcasts — functions performed by the Central Intelligence Agency's (CIA) Foreign Broadcast Information Service (FBIS) and the British Broadcasting Corporation's (BBC) Monitoring Service.[32]

In addition to the above areas of formalized cooperation the UKUSA nations cooperate in other aspects of intelligence activities — human intelligence collection, covert action, counter-intelligence and security operations as well as the preparation of joint estimates. Additionally, several of the UKUSA nations have provided the US with the necessary facilities (or the opportunity to construct the necessary facilities on their territory) for the conduct of overhead reconnaissance — both photographic and electronic — including bases in the case of aircraft reconnaissance systems, and ground stations in the case of satellite systems.

The Agreement in perspective

The UKUSA intelligence relationship is of major importance to all the participants. The relationship determines the allocation of resources for the intelligence activities of each participant. It gives each nation access to intelligence information it would not otherwise be able to acquire. It also may result in the compromise of a nation's secrets due to a security lapse in a cooperating UKUSA intelligence service — an event which has occurred numerous times in the past and most recently in the case of Geoffrey Arthur Prime.

At the same time it is also important to note that the UKUSA relationship is not the only intelligence relationship in which the United States, Britain, Canada, Australia and New Zealand are involved — although it is the most important one in which they are jointly involved. The US, for example, exchanges intelligence information with a number of other nations, including many NATO (North Atlantic Treaty Organization) partners and Israel. It also has signals intelligence facilities in Europe, the Middle East and Asia. Some of these facilities may be of greater significance in the US strategic intelligence collection effort than some of the UKUSA sites. This would certainly have been true of the facilities in Iran prior to their closing: from these the US could monitor crucial phases of Soviet missile telemetry. This may also be true of present sites in Turkey and Norway as well as sites in China.

An arrangement that presumably includes all the UKUSA members except the United States is the Commonwealth SIGINT Organization (CSO), with Britain as the senior partner. Australian participation in this organization was approved by the Chifley Government in a Cabinet decision of 12 November 1947.[33] As well as membership in the CSO, Australia has close contacts with the intelligence and security organizations of regional neighbours such as Singapore and Malaysia as well as some contact with the Thai and Philippine organizations. The relationship with Malaysia and Singapore extends to SIGINT collection. Thus, the Eighth and Ninth ANZUK (Australia, New Zealand, United Kingdom) Signals Regiments included elements from Defence Signals Directorate (DSD) and its British and New Zealand counterparts, as well as from the Singapore and Malaysian SIGINT organizations.[34]

It is also important to note that the UKUSA Agreement is a tiered treaty in which the US is designated as the First Party, with the other nations designated as Second Parties, and thus the United States (and specifically the NSA) is recognized as the dominant party. This represents a reversal of the US — British SIGINT relationship that existed during the Second World War and further represents Britain's ceding to the United States the dominant role in the Western Alliance.

The reversal in the SIGINT relationship is well-illustrated by the change from British to US control of security procedures. In early 1941 the British strictly limited the number of Americans with ULTRA clearances and the names of all those indoctrinated were required to be reported to the Government Code and Cipher School.[35] Today, it is the United States that controls the clearances and determines indoctrination requirements.

The dominance of the United States is due to a variety of factors. The US has a far greater signals intelligence collection capability than any of the other UKUSA participants. As a result it collects the greatest quantity and highest quality (in sum) of intelligence. Further, the US subsidizes, to a great extent, both British and Australian signals intelligence activities and, presumably, those of Canada as well.[36]

A second factor contributing to US dominance has undoubtedly been the US military dominance among Western nations. In as much as the US was (and possibly still is) the only Western power that could effectively deter and fight the Soviet Union, one would expect the US to be able to exert significant influence in determining collection priorities.

The US thus sits at the node of the information distribution process. According to one former NSA officer, '[all] information comes to the United States, but the United States does not totally reciprocate in passing all the information to the other powers'.[37]

Preview

This book examines the various facets of the UKUSA intelligence relationship. In Part I we examine the structures of the intelligence communities of the participant countries. In addition to examining the particular agencies, services and offices involved in intelligence activities we consider the management structure which is used to exert executive command and control over the agencies. A picture of the organization and structure of each nation's intelligence community is a necessary prelude to an appreciation of the extent of intelligence cooperation among the UKUSA participants. In many ways the chapters which constitute Part I represent the first comprehensive treatment of each nation's intelligence community.

In Part II we examine the actual forms of intelligence cooperation that take place and the effects of this cooperation. Chapter 7 examines the exchange and liaison relationship between the participant nations. It describes the extent of information sharing — what information is shared, what information is withheld and the rationale for so doing — as well as the procedures involved in exchange and dissemination of intelligence. Additionally, we consider the liaison arrangements — the physical presence of representatives from some of the UKUSA nations at the stations and headquarters of other UKUSA nations.

The next two chapters of Part II concern themselves with cooperation in signals intelligence and ocean surveillance. Chapter 8 examines the varieties of signals intelligence and associated collection systems and the ground stations within or run by each of the UKUSA participants. The picture developed is one of an extensive worldwide network dedicated to a massive collection effort. Chapter 9 is concerned with the varieties of ocean surveillance — underwater surveillance systems, High Frequency-Direction Finding (HF-DF), ocean surveillance satellites, airborne ocean surveillance and special Navy operations such as DESKTOP, HOLYSTONE, and JENNIFER.

Chapter 10 describes the range of other forms of intelligence cooperation, including human intelligence gathering, monitoring of public radio broadcasts, covert actions, security investigations and the production of joint intelligence estimates.

Chapter 11 is concerned not with cooperation but rather, with non-cooperation, discord and deceit within and among the UKUSA security and intelligence communities.

Chapter 12 is concerned with the relationship between the organization of the various UKUSA intelligence communities and their performance in various areas — intelligence analysis, collection and security. To a large extent the present structures of these communities have arisen from a combination of historical, budgetary and bureaucratic factors. However, there have been attempts in recent years — primarily in Australia and the United States — to reform those intelligence structures in accordance with a particular philosophy of intelligence organization.

In Chapter 13 we examine the treatment of dissent and dissenters by the UKUSA security services. In recent years the activities of these security services have helped stimulate governmental inquiries into intelligence activities. The pattern of activities revealed is a disturbing one, in that the security services appear to be unable or unwilling to distinguish between legitimate dissent and subversion.

The conclusion, Chapter 14, describes both the benefits of participation and its costs — such as the extent to which participation in the agreements alters the intelligence collection priorities of the participants, the expense involved in participation, and the threats posed by the presence of major US intelligence facilities on the territory of the other participants. Finally, it argues that there is a need for much firmer government oversight of the activities of the UKUSA security and intelligence agencies, and for informed public debate about these agencies and their activities.

I

The UKUSA security and intelligence communities

2

The British security and intelligence community

While the origins of British Secret Service activity are often dated at 1573, during the tenure of Sir Francis Walsingham as Secretary of State to Queen Elizabeth I, the origins of the present British intelligence and security services are of more recent vintage — the early 1900s.[1]

The core of the present British security and intelligence community consists of a small number of organizations whose duties are relatively sharply divided amongst intelligence collection, analysis and covert action; counter-espionage and security; signals intelligence; and defence intelligence. Additionally, there are several other units which perform intelligence functions such as the monitoring of foreign public radio broadcasts and conducting black or grey propaganda activities. There are also security services at both the ministerial and military service level.

Despite a legally enforceable penchant for secrecy on the part of the British intelligence and security services their activities have been partially brought into public view by a variety of factors including a series of penetrations by the Soviet intelligence services. Thus, the 1950s and 1960s saw the penetrations of Kim Philby and George Blake into the Secret Intelligence Service revealed, while 1980 brought the exposure of the past penetration of the Security Service by Anthony Blunt.[2] In that same year accusations were also made that the Security Service had been penetrated up to the level of Director-General.[3] Additionally, charges were made alleging corruption in the signals intelligence establishment.[4]

The five agencies which can be considered to constitute the major members of the British security and intelligence community are discussed below, as are other units with intelligence functions. The major members are the Secret Intelligence Service, the Security Service, the Government Communications Headquarters, the Defence Intelligence Staff and the Special Branch of the Metropolitan Police (Scotland Yard).

Secret Intelligence Service (MI-6)

While British Secret Service activity may indeed date back to 1573, the origins of the Secret Intelligence Service date back to 1907 when the Committee on Imperial Defence discovered that Britain did not have a single agent on the European Continent and, as a result, established the Secret Service Bureau in 1909. The Bureau, divided into a Home Section and a Foreign Section, was placed under the control of the War Office.[5] It had three functions:

(1) to be a screen between the Service departments and foreign spies;
(2) to be the intermediary between the Service departments and British agents abroad; and
(3) to take charge of counter-espionage.

Previously, counter-espionage duties had been performed by the Special Duties Division of the Military Operations Directorate.[6]

In 1910 the two Sections were placed under the control of different agencies — the Home Section being placed under War Office control while the Foreign Section was placed under control of the Admiralty. In 1916, the Foreign Section was returned to War Office control and named MI-1(c) — that is, its cover was as section 1(c) of the Military Intelligence Department. By the end of the war the Foreign Office had assumed control of the Foreign Section, by then renamed the Secret Intelligence Service (SIS).[7] It was not until 1921, however, that the SIS assumed responsibility for espionage on an inter-service basis, adding the Home Office, Colonial Office, India Office and Air Ministry to the Foreign Office, War Office and Admiralty as customers. At the same time it retained a 'military cover', that is MI-6.

The SIS has both internal and external functions. Internally, it seeks to spot, assess and recruit foreigners residing in the United Kingdom for employment as agents when they return to their native countries. Externally, it conducts a wide range of activities, including the collection of intelligence by clandestine means, counter-intelligence operations, covert action and clandestine communications support. Naturally, it furnishes elements of the Government with the products of its intelligence collection and analysis efforts.

Among the SIS's first covert activities were those directed at overthrowing the Bolshevik regime in Russia. These activities began during the latter part of the First World War and continued into the mid-1920s. British agents Sidney Reilly and Bruce Lockhart were involved in providing financial aid to apparent anti-Bolshevik groups.[8]

In the 1950s and 1960s the SIS was heavily involved in covert operations in the Middle East. For example, the SIS financed the Sharg al-Adna broadcasting station (later named the Near East Arab Broadcasting Corporation) to carry out pro-British propaganda. The SIS was also behind the Arab News Agency (ANA) which had been set up during the Second World War to engage in anti-Nazi propaganda.[9]

The SIS was heavily involved in the overthrow of Iranian Prime Minister

Mossadeq in 1953 and his replacement by the Shah. It was Mossadeq's nationalization of the Anglo-Iranian Oil Company which led Britain to seek his overthrow. George Kennedy Young, the Deputy Director of the SIS, played a leading role in the day-to-day planning and liaison with the American Central Intelligence Agency (CIA) in the effort codenamed 'Ajax'. Additionally, British agents played a significant role in day-to-day operations. When Mossadeq replaced the pro-American Chief of Police in April 1953 with a new chief and assigned him the task of purging pro-Americans, SIS agents kidnapped and killed the newly appointed police chief. Additionally, the British-controlled Iranian news media initiated a barrage of anti-Mossadeq propaganda.[10]

Subsequently Young called a joint meeting with the CIA in the beginning of April 1956. CIA representatives included Cairo station chief, James Eichelburger, and Wilbur Crane Eveland, Allen Dulles's personal representative in the Middle East. Young informed Eichelburger and Eveland that the SIS had decided the Governments of Egypt, Saudi Arabia and Syria all threatened Britain's survival and had to be subverted or overthrown.[11]

The SIS's anti-Nasser effort involved use of both Sharg al-Adna and the Arab News Agency as propaganda outlets. Sharg al-Adna broadcast anti-Nasser propaganda while the ANA provided pro-British coverage through its intensive news-gathering network. The ANA also provided cover for SIS agents.[12]

In the mid-1960s Iraq was also a target of SIS inspired propaganda. The service stationed an experienced propagandist in Beirut to organize the publication of anti-government pamphlets for circulation inside Iraq. In Yemen in the 1950s and 1960s the SIS was involved in British military activities directed against Egyptian-backed insurgents and anti-royalists. Imam Ahmad of North Yemen was overthrown by Nasser-backed nationalists in 1962. This led to a British attempt, with Israeli help, to tie down and harass large numbers of Egyptian troops. SIS officers aided Special Air Service soldiers in their operations.[13]

The SIS is headed by the Chief of the Secret Service, also known as 'C' or CSS. As opposed to the CIA, Chiefs of the SIS have had fairly long tenures with only eight chiefs in 70 years: Admiral Sir Mansfield Cummings (1911–23), Admiral Sir Hugh Sinclair (1923–39), Maj.-Gen. Sir Stewart Menzies (1939–53), Maj.-Gen. John Sinclair (1953–56), Sir Dick Goldsmith White (1956–69), Sir John Rennie (1969–73), Sir Maurice Oldfield (1973–78), Sir Arthur Franks (1978–82), and the present Chief, Colin Figures (1982–).

Traditionally, the name of the Chief of the SIS was considered a state secret. However, revelations in both the foreign and then the British press have tended to undermine this practice. Thus, Sir Dick Goldsmith White was named in 1967 in a book by American journalists David Wise and Thomas B. Ross.[14] Sir Maurice Oldfield was named by *Newsweek* shortly after his appointment and Sir Arthur Franks was named in several British publications.

The second-ranking official in the SIS is the Director, who supervises its

16 *The Ties That Bind*

day-to-day operations. Under the Director are four directorates and a group of controllers for supervision of foreign operations. The four directorates are the Directorate of Personnel and Administration; the Directorate of Special Support, which provides technical support for SIS activities; the Directorate of Counter-intelligence and Security, which handles both SIS internal security and offensive counter-intelligence operations; and the Directorate of Requirements and Production, which is responsible both for determining intelligence collection requirements as well as producing intelligence analyses and estimates.[15]

'Foreign' operations of the SIS are under the supervision of seven controllers: Controller/UK, Controller/Europe, Controller/Soviet Bloc, Controller/Africa, Controller/Middle East, Controller/Far East and Controller/Western Hemisphere. The Controller/UK is responsible for spotting and recruiting foreigners residing in Britain to serve as agents in their native lands.[16] An organizational chart of the Secret Intelligence Service is shown in Figure 2.1.

Figure 2.1 Organization of the British Secret Intelligence Service (MI–6)

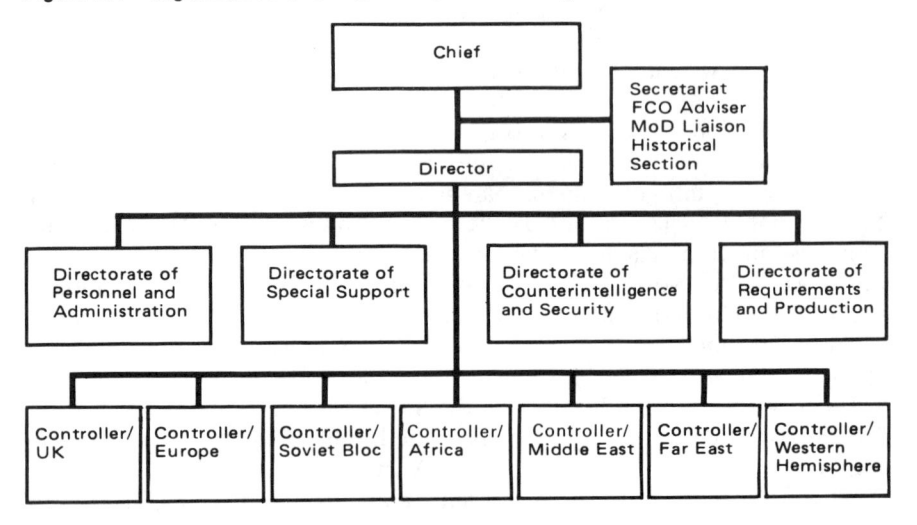

```
                            ┌──────────┐
                            │  Chief   │
                            └────┬─────┘
                                 │         ┌──────────────┐
                                 │         │ Secretariat  │
                                 │         │ FCO Adviser  │
                                 │         │ MoD Liaison  │
                                 │         │ Historical   │
                            ┌────┴─────┐   │ Section      │
                            │ Director │   └──────────────┘
                            └────┬─────┘
      ┌──────────────┬───────────┴──────────┬──────────────┐
┌─────┴──────┐ ┌─────┴──────┐ ┌─────────────┴─┐ ┌──────────┴───┐
│Directorate │ │Directorate │ │ Directorate of│ │Directorate of│
│of Personnel│ │of Special  │ │Counterintelli-│ │Requirements  │
│and Admin.  │ │Support     │ │gence & Security│ │and Production│
└────────────┘ └────────────┘ └───────────────┘ └──────────────┘
```

Controller/UK | Controller/Europe | Controller/Soviet Bloc | Controller/Africa | Controller/Middle East | Controller/Far East | Controller/Western Hemisphere

The headquarters of the Secret Intelligence Service are at Century House, 100 Westminster Bridge Road, SE1. Its London Station facility is at 60 Vauxhall Bridge Road, SE1 and its Training Centre is at 296–302 Borough High Street, SE1. Sabotage and demolition are taught at an undercover establishment in Gosport called Fort Monkton. Additionally, it has a joint office with the Security Service at 140 Gower Street, WC1.[17]

The budget and personnel for the SIS are not made public. One unofficial estimate gives the total SIS/Security Service budget at somewhat more than £100 million.[18]

Security Service (MI-5)

Just as the SIS evolved from the Foreign Section of the Secret Service Bureau, the Security Service evolved from the Bureau's Home Section. As noted above the Home Section remained within the War Office when the Foreign Section was transferred to the control of the Admiralty. In 1916, when the War Office created the Military Intelligence Department, the Home Section became part of the department as MI-5.[19]

The Security Service is still best known by its MI-5 designation despite the fact that it has not been part of the Military Intelligence Department for over 30 years. In 1951 it was responsible directly to the Prime Minister. At that time the Secretary of the Cabinet, Sir Norman Brook, recommended that the responsibility be transferred to the Home Secretary.[20] Shortly afterwards, the Home Secretary, Sir David Maxwell Fyfe, issued a directive to the Director-General making the Security Service responsible to the Home Secretary. As the directive also serves as the charter of today's Security Service it is worth quoting in full:

(1) In your appointment as Director General of the Security Service, you will be responsible to the Home Secretary personally. The Security Service is not, however, a part of the Home Office. On appropriate occasions, you will have right of direct access to the Prime Minister.
(2) The Security Service is part of the Defence Forces of the country. Its task is the Defence of the Realm as a whole, from external and internal dangers arising from attempts at espionage and sabotage, or from actions of persons and organizations whether directed from within or without the country, which may be judged to be subversive of the state.
(3) You will take special care to see that the work of the Security Service is strictly limited to what is necessary for the purposes of this task.
(4) It is essential that the Security Service should be kept absolutely free from any political bias or influence and nothing should be done that might lend colour to any suggestion that it is concerned with interests of any particular section of the community, or with any other matter than the Defence of the Realm as a whole.
(5) No enquiry is to be carried out on behalf of any Government Department unless you are satisfied that an important public interest bearing on the Defence of the Realm, as defined in paragraph 2, is at stake.
(6) You are your staff will maintain the well-established convention whereby Ministers do not concern themselves with the detailed information which may be obtained by the Security Service in particular cases, but are furnished with such information only as may be necessary for the determination of any issue on which guidance is sought.[21]

Despite its undeniable status as a government agency (as indicated by the Fyfe directive) the Security Service is not recognized by law. As the 1963 Denning Report on MI-5 stated, 'The Security Service in this country is not established by Statute nor is it recognized by Common Law. Even the Official Secrets Act does not acknowledge its existence'.[22] The Report went on to note that:

18   The Ties That Bind

The members of the Service are, in the eye of the law, ordinary citizens with no powers greater than anyone else. They have no special powers of arrest such as the police have. No special powers are given to them. They cannot enter premises without the consent of the householder even though they may suspect a spy is there. If a spy is fleeing the country, they cannot tap him on the shoulder and say he is not to go. They have, in short, no executive powers.[23]

With the exception of conducting liaison operations with Commonwealth and other security services through offices abroad, the primary functions of the Security Service are internal. These functions include conducting counter-intelligence and counter-espionage operations, supervising the security investigations of all employees with access to sensitive information, and monitoring domestic movements and organizations for possible subversive elements. The Security Service is also in charge of counter-sabotage activity and the surveillance and control of resident and visiting foreign nationals, including diplomatic missions.

There are two exceptions to the generalization that Security Service activities are conducted on UK territory: the first being territories and colonies still under British control, such as Hong Kong, and the second, certain Commonwealth countries where intelligence activities are still conducted by the Security Service. Under the Attlee Government (1945–51) there were demarcation agreements with the SIS which gave the Security Service the right to operate unimpeded in British or former British territories.[24]

The Security Service is organized into six directorates. Directorates A (Intelligence Resources and Operations), B (Staff Office and Administration and Finance) and S (Support Services, Registry, Computer Centre, Training Office) are primarily administrative and evaluation directorates. Basic security service operations are carried out by Directorates C (Protective Security), F (Domestic Subversion) and K (Counter-espionage). These directorates are further divided into sections and sub-sections.[25]

Some of the activities of Directorate F will be discussed in Chapter 13. Directorate K has two sub-sections of particular interest — K7 and K9. K7 is responsible for counter-intelligence within the British intelligence services, while K9 investigates people who unexpectedly resign or retire from sensitive postions.[26] Directorate C is responsible for both personnel security and document security. An organization chart of the Security Service is shown in Figure 2.2.

Headquarters for the Security Service are located at Curzon Street House, Curzon Street, W1. Other offices include those at 14–17 Great Marlborough Street, W1; 71–72 Grosvenor Street, W1; 41 South Audley Street, Mayfair, W1; and Leconfield House, Curzon Street, W1.[27]

As with the SIS, the Security Service has had relatively few Directors General: Vernon Kell (1909–40), David Petrie (1940–46), Sir Percy Sillitoe (1946–53), Sir Dick Goldsmith White (1953–56), Sir Roger Henry Hollis (1956–63), Sir Edward M. Furnival-Jones (1963–72), Sir Michael Hanley (1972–79), Sir Howard Trayton Smith (1979–81), and the present incumbent, Sir John Lewis Jones.[28]

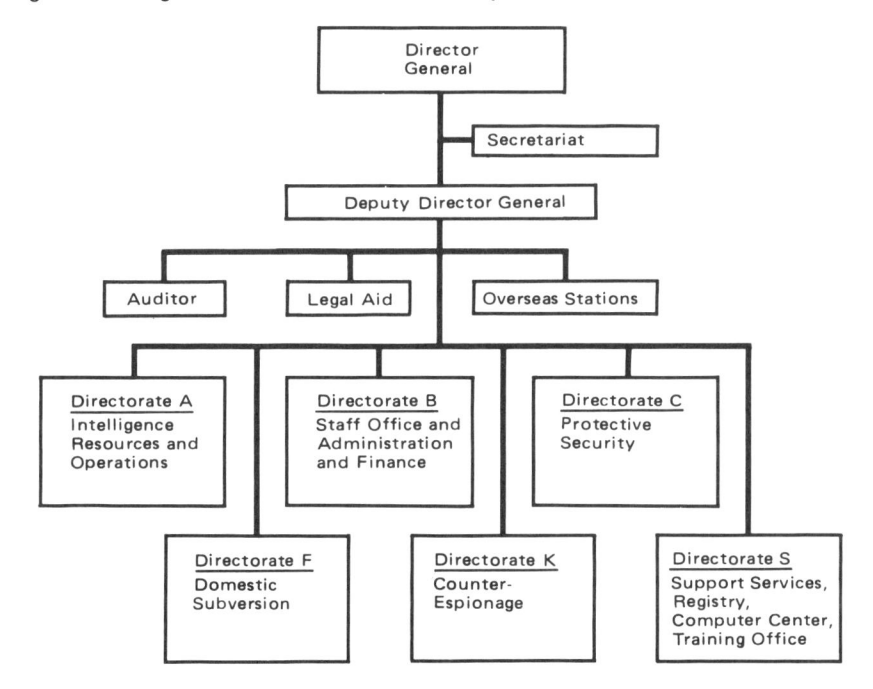

Figure 2.2 Organization of the British Security Service (MI–5)

```
                        Director
                        General
                           |
                      Secretariat
                           |
                  Deputy Director General
                           |
        ┌──────────────────┼──────────────────┐
     Auditor           Legal Aid        Overseas Stations
        |                  |                  |
  ┌─────────────┐   ┌─────────────┐   ┌─────────────┐
  Directorate A    Directorate B    Directorate C
  Intelligence     Staff Office and Protective
  Resources and    Administration   Security
  Operations       and Finance
        |                  |                  |
  ┌─────────────┐   ┌─────────────┐   ┌─────────────┐
  Directorate F    Directorate K    Directorate S
  Domestic         Counter-         Support Services,
  Subversion       Espionage        Registry,
                                    Computer Center,
                                    Training Office
```

Government Communications Headquarters (GCHQ)

The officially defined mission of the GCHQ is the 'reception and analysis of foreign communications and other electronic transmissions for intelligence purposes'.[29] A more detailed description has been offered by Tony Bunyan: 'GCHQ monitors and decodes all radio, telex and telegram communications in and out of Britain, including the messages of all foreign embassies based in Britain, finance and industrial companies, and individuals of interest to the state agencies'.[30] In addition to such activities conducted within Britain the GCHQ maintains intercept stations at various overseas locations, including major stations in Hong Kong, Cyprus and West Germany. Minor stations are located in Malta, Mauritius, Turkey, and Ascension Island.[31] The full extent of the GCHQ network is detailed in Chapter 8 and Appendix I.

In addition to its signals intelligence activities, the GCHQ also 'has the responsibility for developing codes and procedures to safeguard British Government communications'.[32] A specialist unit of the GCHQ, the Diplomatic Telecommunications Maintenance Service, has the responsibility for the debugging of Whitehall offices, outstations and British embassies.[33]

The origins of the GCHQ can be traced back to the First World War and the two military code-breaking bureaus — Room 40 of the Naval Intelligence Division and MI-1(b) of the Military Intelligence Department. In

1919 the remnants of those organizations were set up as the Government Code and Cipher School (GCCS). Initially, the GCCS was under the control of the Admiralty. In 1923, the Secret Intelligence Service took control, with the Chief of SIS being redesignated Chief of the Secret Service and Director of the GCCS. In 1943, the Foreign Office assumed control, by which time the GCCS had been renamed the Government Communications Headquarters (GCHQ).[34]

At the top of the present structure of the GCHQ is the Director, subordinate to whom are four principal directorates — the Directorate of SIGINT Plans (DP), the Directorate of Organization and Establishment (DOE), the Directorate of SIGINT Operations and Requirements, and the Directorate of Communications Security. Attached to the Director is a Staff Officer representing the London Signals Intelligence Board and the London Signals Intelligence Committee (Defence) [LSIC(D)] which are discussed below. Figure 2.3 shows the organizational structure of the GCHQ.

Fig. 2.3 Organization of the Government Communications Headquarters (GCHQ)

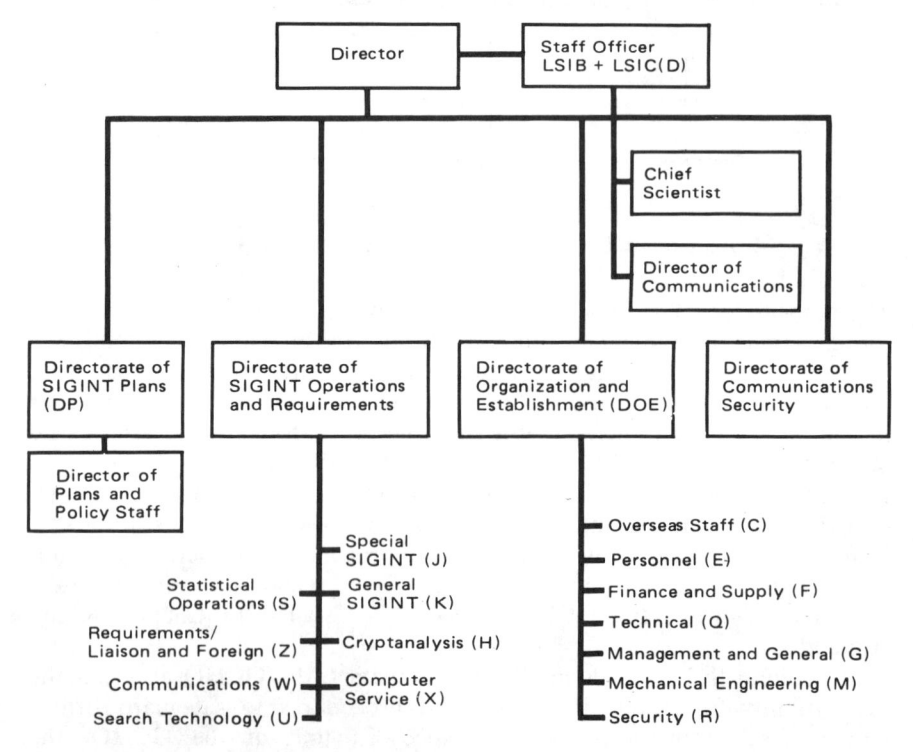

```
                    ┌──────────┐      ┌──────────────┐
                    │ Director │──────│ Staff Officer│
                    └────┬─────┘      │ LSIB + LSIC(D)│
                         │            └──────────────┘
                         │            ┌──────────┐
                         ├────────────│ Chief    │
                         │            │ Scientist│
                         │            └──────────┘
                         │            ┌──────────────┐
                         ├────────────│ Director of  │
                         │            │Communications│
                         │            └──────────────┘
    ┌────────────┬───────┴────────┬────────────────┬─────────────────┐
    │Directorate │ Directorate of │ Directorate of │ Directorate of  │
    │of SIGINT   │ SIGINT         │ Organization   │ Communications  │
    │Plans (DP)  │ Operations     │ and Establish- │ Security        │
    │            │ and Requirements│ ment (DOE)    │                 │
    └─────┬──────┴────────┬───────┴────────┬───────┴─────────────────┘
  ┌───────┴──────┐        │                │
  │ Director of  │        │                ├─ Overseas Staff (C)
  │ Plans and    │        ├─ Special       ├─ Personnel (E)
  │ Policy Staff │        │  SIGINT (J)    ├─ Finance and Supply (F)
  └──────────────┘        ├─ General       ├─ Technical (Q)
     Statistical          │  SIGINT (K)    ├─ Management and General (G)
     Operations (S)       ├─ Cryptanalysis(H)─ Mechanical Engineering (M)
     Requirements/        ├─ Computer      └─ Security (R)
     Liaison and Foreign (Z)│ Service (X)
     Communications (W)
     Search Technology (U)
```

The Directorate of SIGINT Operations and Requirements is central to GCHQ activities and is subdivided into eight divisions: Statistical Operations (S), Requirements/Liaison and Foreign (Z), Special SIGINT (J),

General SIGINT (K), Communications (W), Cryptanalysis (H), Computer Services (X), and Search Technology (U). It is through Z Division that detailed UKUSA as well as other SIGINT requirements are determined. Z Division receives target requests from the Ministry of Defence, the Foreign Office and the military services as well as from the trade and economic ministries. It also maintains liaison with the US, Canadian, Australian and New Zealand SIGINT agencies.

J Division concentrates on the interception of Soviet bloc signals and is hence one of the largest in the GCHQ. Given the sophistication of Soviet encryption techniques and procedures, however, it is doubtful whether the efforts of J Division generally produce much high-level intelligence. K Division deals with all other geographical areas as well as with intercepted commercial messages. The actual code-breaking activity is the responsibility of H Division, while X Division operates the GCHQ computer system.[35] Among the computers employed is a US-built computer known as 'Tandem Nonstop' which analyses the data collected at the GCHQ intercept stations.[36]

The Search Technology Division (U) is concerned with the means of locating a signal rather than its interception — an activity known as Long Range Technical Search (LRTS). This activity is intended to counter the attempts by Soviet and other foreign communications bureaus to give an additional dimension of protection beyond encryption to their communications by concealing the very existence of the signal — either by spreading the signal so thinly across a range of frequencies that it becomes indistinguishable from the background noise or by burying it within other transmissions.[37]

According to James Bamford:

LRTS operators search for any unusual signal above 30 megahertz. Once they discover one which has not previously been logged they photograph it, take it down to the intermediate frequencies, and pass it through various specialized filters ... The 'complete picture' of the signal is then studied ... in order to develop equipment to better capture it and extract usable intelligence from it.[38]

The Statistical Operations Division (S) is also not concerned with decryption but rather, with traffic analysis: that is, S Division studies the 'externals' of a message — its source, destination, priority, etc. — as a means of obtaining information even from unencrypted messages. Such 'externals' can provide information on such questions as troop movements and the imminence of an attack or other military operations. The Communications Division (W) is responsible for delivering the signals intelligence to its final consumer.[39]

The second most important directorate of the GCHQ is the Directorate of Communications Security. Until 1969, the functions of this Directorate were performed by a separate agency, the London Communications Security Agency, which operated under 'cover' as the Communications-Electronic Security Department of the Foreign Office. In 1969, however, the decision was made to merge this agency into the GCHQ, partly as a means of ending the bitter and recurrent feuds between the two organizations.[40]

The Directorate of Organization and Establishment is the administrative directorate. As such, it is responsible for Personnel (E Division), Mechanical Engineering (M), Finance and Supply (F), Management (G), and Security (R). It is also responsible for the Overseas Staff (C), the division which assigns intercept operators to clandestine listening posts within British embassies. The Directorate of SIGINT Plans consists solely of the Plans and Policy Staff, and is responsible for long-range planning for intercept stations and other SIGINT activities.[41]

Finally, subordinate to the GCHQ is the Joint Technical Language Service (JTLS), which consists of translators of a wide range of languages who can transcribe the intercepted voice conversations resulting from various UKUSA COMINT activities.[42] The conversations may include, for example, those of Soviet pilots and army commanders on manoeuvres or of oil ministers of the OPEC countries.

As with the NSA, the GCHQ directs the activities of all Army, Air Force and Navy monitoring stations. In 1963 the GCHQ won the battle to take control of these stations and set up the Composite Signals Organization (CSO) to administer them.[43]

The GCHQ has had a number of recent security problems, the most noteworthy of which concerned Geoffrey Prime, a former GCHQ translator and section chief who was arrested in 1982 for having provided GCHQ material to the Soviet Union for fourteen years.[44] Earlier, it had been charged that numerous classified documents had disappeared from the GCHQ's station at Little Sai Wan in Hong Kong.[45] In addition, it appears that codeword documents, classified TOP SECRET UMBRA, disappeared in 1981 from the Stanley Fort Satellite Station in Hong Kong, a station especially built to intercept signals from Chinese space and missile launches.[46] According to one former GCHQ official, the lost documents contained details of how to detect, follow and understand radio signals from Chinese missiles and satellites — information which could be used by China to avoid such monitoring.[47]

The headquarters of the GCHQ are at Cheltenham, Gloucestershire, and a London office is maintained at 2–8 Palmer Street, SW1.[48] The budget of the GCHQ has been estimated at $200 million and its personnel at 20 000 (5000 at headquarters and 15 000 at the SIGINT stations).[49] The present Director of GCHQ is Peter Marychurch.

Defence Intelligence Staff (DIS)

The year 1946 marked the beginning of a trend with respect to British military intelligence organization. A small coordinating unit, known as the Joint Intelligence Bureau (JIB), was created and headed by Kenneth Strong. The scope of the JIB went beyond providing analysis based on

The GCHQ, Oakley, Priors Road, Cheltenham, Gloucestershire, UK.

military considerations; rather it was to cover political, economic and psychological factors connected with the national interest.[50]

This trend toward centralization culminated in 1964 when the JIB was replaced by the Defence Intelligence Staff (DIS). In addition to performing as a coordinating mechanism for military intelligence, DIS actually absorbed the intelligence branches of the individual services — the Military Intelligence Department, the Naval Intelligence Division and Air Intelligence.[51]

At the head of the DIS is the Director-General of Intelligence (DGI). The Deputy to the DGI is also the Deputy Chief of the Defence Staff (Intelligence). Thus, in addition to his role as deputy he reports directly on general and current intelligence matters to the Chief of the Defence Staff, the Chiefs of Staff Committee and to other staffs in the Ministry of Defence.[52]

The DIS is subdivided into four directorates — the Directorate of Management and Support of Intelligence (DMSI), the Directorate of Scientific and Technical Intelligence (DSTI), the Directorate of Service

Intelligence (DSI) and the Directorate of Economic Intelligence.

The DMSI provides the central staff support for the DGI and Deputy Chief of the Defence Staff (Intelligence) [DCDS (I)] in handling substantive intelligence business (except current intelligence). It coordinates intelligence reporting required by DIS customers as well as the DIS input into the Joint Intelligence Committee (discussed below). DMSI is also responsible for DIS long-term studies on such matters as US—Soviet relations and the Strategic Arms Limitation Talks (SALT).

The DSTI is responsible for producing intelligence concerning electronics, chemical and biological weapons, missiles, atomic energy and the basic sciences, while the DSI is responsible for producing intelligence on broad military aspects of the defence forces and policies of foreign countries and also produces the coordinated DIS output of intelligence for the Assessment Staff.

Figure 2.4   Organization of Defence Intelligence Staff (DIS)

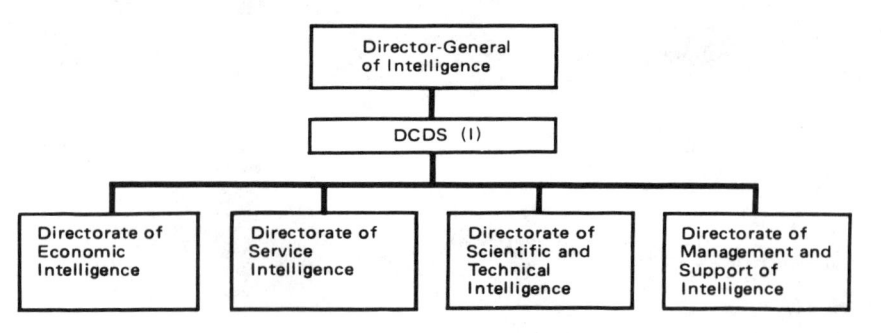

```
            Director-General
            of Intelligence
                  │
              DCDS (I)
    ┌─────────┬────┴────┬─────────┐
Directorate  Directorate Directorate Directorate
of Economic  of Service  of Scientific of Management
Intelligence Intelligence and Technical and Support of
                        Intelligence   Intelligence
```

The Directorate of Economic Intelligence is responsible for studying the general economic developments in the communist countries; armaments production and supporting industries worldwide; and the military and economic aid activities of the communist countries.

The Director-General of Intelligence is Vice-Admiral Sir Roy Halliday. An organization chart of the DIS is shown as Figure 2.4.

Special Branch, Scotland Yard

Scotland Yard, or more properly the Metropolitan Police, performs a wide range of police activities throughout Britain. The Special Branch is a sub-department of the 'C' (Crime) Department. It was formed as the Irish Special Branch in 1883 to combat Fenian bombing in London. The bombings ended on 31 January 1885; but by 1888 it was clear that the scope of Branch activities went beyond the Irish, and the word 'Irish' was dropped from its title.[53]

The responsibilities of the Special Branch include the guarding of royalty, ministers and visiting public dignitaries, the watching of ports and airports (for travellers of security interest), the watching and guarding of embassy buildings, the surveillance of subversive organizations, the monitoring of aliens entering the country and the vetting of applications for naturalization, the preparation of lists of potential internees in cases of war and the investigation of offences against the Official Secrets Act.[54] In the area of counter-espionage the Special Branch serves as the Security Service's executive agent, making arrests at the appropriate times. It also assists in the last stages of surveillance, prepares evidence for court proceedings and provides witnesses at trials.[55]

Special Branch headquarters are located on the top floor of Scotland Yard on Victoria Street. It also operates from offices around London. Organizationally, the Special Branch is divided into three sections — Ports, Administration, and Operations. Protection for royalty and others is provided by the Special Branch Personal Protection Squad.[56] Of 1000 full-time Special Branch officers about 500 are stationed at headquarters, two-thirds of these officers being in the Ports and Administration sections.[57] The Special Branch budget, circa 1975, was estimated at £5–6 million.[58]

Other units

Other British government organizations involved in security and intelligence work include the Foreign Office's Overseas Information Department, the BBC's Monitoring Service, the Post Office and two commando units — the Special Air Service (SAS) and Special Boat Squadron (SBS).

The Overseas Information Department is the successor to the covert Information Research Department (IRD) which operated between 1947 and 1977. The IRD resulted from a memo from Christopher Mayhew to Foreign Secretary Ernest Bevin in 1947 proposing a covert 'propaganda counter offensive' against the Soviet Union.[59] In its 30-year life it operated mainly against communism in Third World countries. The Soviet section in the 1950s employed more than 60 people. Additionally, embassies had IRD men working undercover planting material with local journalists and opinion-formers. A typical IRD operation would have been to study Eastern bloc press reports of drunkenness and produce an article emphasizing how rife alcoholism was under communism.[60]

The department was cut back in 1964 and again in 1968 and 1970. In around 1970 the department was told to stop concentrating so heavily on communism and to promote other British interests. Among other changes, the IRD set up a counter-subversion unit to deal with the Irish Republican Army (IRA).[61]

In May 1977 the IRD was abolished and the Overseas Information Department was formed. It was smaller than the IRD and had a radically different structure.[62]

The BBC Monitoring Service monitors selected news and other broadcasts in various areas of the world from a network of overseas stations. This network includes a remotely controlled listening station on the rooftop of the Vienna embassy to monitor VHF radio and television from Hungary and Czechoslovakia, as well as posts in Accra in Ghana, and Abidjan in the Ivory Coast. A major customer of the BBC Monitoring Service was the IRD.[63]

The Monitoring Service is funded by an £84.4 million Grant-in-Aid from the Foreign Office. Headquarters for the Monitoring Service are at Caversham Park, Reading. The present chief is John Rae.[64]

Three units of the Post Office apparently are involved in security and intelligence work — the R12 Special Investigation Division, the Investigation Division and the Operational Strategy Coordination Division (OSCD). The Investigation Division, which has a 'Special Section', opens mail while the OSCD (formerly the Equipment Strategy Division) is in charge of the national telephone tapping service, known as 'Tinkerbell'. OSCD's offices are located at 93 Ebury Bridge Road, SW1. The equipment at Ebury Bridge Road was designed by the GCHQ.[65]

In addition to performing commando/combat functions, both the army's Special Air Service and the Royal Marine's Special Boat Squadron perform intelligence functions. The Defence Ministry's 1969 Land Operations Manual listed 'collection of information on the location and movement of insurgent forces' and 'border surveillance' among the functions of the SAS. SAS officers also staff the Joint Services Interrogation Unit.[66]

The Special Boat Squadron, headquartered at the Amphibious Warfare Training Centre in Poole, Dorset, consists of approximately 300 men.[67] As with the SAS, the SBS is primarily a commando unit trained in land, sea and air operations, frogman techniques and marksmanship. In the British invasion of South Georgia Island the SBS acted as a reconnaissance squad, hiding by day and scouting by night. The teams mapped out the positions of the Argentine troops, their guns and mortars and their radio posts. The SBS decided where British helicopters should land. Information collected by the SBS was recorded in ten minutes on tape, then 'burped' out by a radio that compressed it into a single second of sound.[68] A permanent intelligence related function of the SBS is to check on the Britain-to-Iceland portion of the Sound Surveillance System (SOSUS) underwater submarine detection system.[69]

Management structure

The management structure of the British intelligence community consists of the Permanent Under Secretaries Committee on Intelligence Services (PSIS), the Coordinator of Intelligence and Security in the Cabinet Office and several committee structures — the Joint Intelligence Committee (JIC), the Overseas Economic Intelligence Committee (OEIC), the Ad Hoc Ministerial Group on Security, the Official Committee on Security, and the London Signals Intelligence Board (LSIB).

The PSIS supervises the budgets of the intelligence organizations, exercises broad supervision over the British intelligence community as a whole, and approves interdepartmentally recommended intelligence priorities.[70] The Secretary of the Cabinet, presently Sir Robert Armstrong, is the Chairman of the PSIS. Other members are the Permanent Under Secretaries of the Foreign and Commonwealth Office, Defence, Treasury, Trade and Industry, and the Chief of the Defence Staff. The Coordinator is an ex-officio member.[71]

The office of the Coordinator of Intelligence and Security was created in 1970 although that function had been performed by various individuals in previous administrations. Thus, the functions performed by the present-day Coordinator were performed in the early 1960s by George Wigg, with the title of Paymaster-General. The Coordinator is an adviser who provides guidance on intelligence priorities and resources and is appointed on the basis of long experience in intelligence. Two previous Coordinators were Sir Dick Goldsmith White (former head of MI-5 and MI-6) and Sir Leonard Hooper (former head of the GCHQ). The present Coordinator is Sir Anthony Duff.[72] The Co-ordinator's basic responsibilities are to:

(1) prepare an annual review of intelligence for presentation to the PSIS. The review looks at intelligence in the previous 12 months and suggests the broad line of future requirements and priorities and proposes any necessary action;
(2) scrutinize the annual financial estimates and five-year forecasts of the individual intelligence agencies and present them to the PSIS with his recommendations;
(3) conduct enquiries on various intelligence subjects which he, the Secretary of the Cabinet or the PSIS may deem necessary; and
(4) generally advise and encourage the intelligence community, particularly the machinery within the Cabinet Office.[73]

Staff support for the Coordinator is provided by the Joint Intelligence Committee Secretariat (see below).

While the Coordinator is an adviser who provides general guidance, the Chairmen of the JIC and of the OEIC are responsible for the production of national intelligence and the day-to-day management of the intelligence community. The JIC and its subordinate elements are charged with the responsibility of ensuring efficiency, economy and adaptation to changing requirements. They are also responsible for assembling and evaluating national intelligence for presentation to the Cabinet, individual ministers and the Chiefs of Staff. The JIC was set up in 1936 under the Chiefs of Staff and transferred to the Cabinet Office in 1957. The rationale for the JIC's assessments function is to have final intelligence estimates and evaluations being made by a body independent of the foreign and defence policy-making bureaucracies.[74]

Subordinate to the JIC is an Assessment Staff and a number of Current Intelligence Groups (CIGs), which collectively constitute the Joint Intelligence Organization (JIO).[75] The Assessment Staff is responsible for preparing both short- and long-term assessments in support of government policy. In performing this function it utilizes the output of various agencies both within and outside the intelligence community. Worldwide coverage of current intelligence is maintained by the CIGs, each of which has its own geographical area of responsibility. Each CIG is chaired by a member of the Assessment Staff.

Membership of the JIC consists of two Foreign and Commonwealth Office representatives, one (a Deputy Under Secretary) as Chairman, the Chief of SIS, the Director-General of Intelligence, the Director-General of the Security Service, the DCDS(I), the Director, GCHQ and the Chairman and Deputy Chairman of the Assessments Staff.[76] In addition, liaison representatives from New Zealand, Australia, the US and Canada attend JIC meetings.

In January 1983 the Franks Committee made several criticisms of the performance of the Joint Intelligence Organization in the period preceding the Argentine invasion of the Falkland Islands, as a result of which a full-time Chairman of the JIC is to be appointed from within the Cabinet Office and given direct access to the Prime Minister.[77]

While the JIC is concerned primarily with diplomatic and military intelligence the OEIC concentrates on economic and non-military scientific and technical intelligence.[78] The Chairman of the OEIC is a representative of the Treasury. Membership includes representatives of a variety of civil departments with an interest in overseas economic matters as well as the heads of the intelligence-producing agencies.

In addition to the JIC and the OEIC a third committee — the London Signals Intelligence Board — monitors the activities of the GCHQ. The LSIB was created in 1942 to increase the level of supervision of SIGINT activities. The Board was presided over by 'C' and attended by the Directors of Intelligence of each of the services and the Director of GCCS.[79] Apparently, a subcommittee of the LSIB, the London Signals Intelligence Committee (Defence) [LSIC(D)], deals with military signals intelligence matters.

The highest level committee for the supervision of security matters is the Ad Hoc Ministerial Group on Security, chaired by the Prime Minister. Subordinate to the Ad Hoc Group is the Official Committee on Security, headed by Sir Robert Armstrong, which supervises the Security Service. The Official Committee has three subordinate committees: the Security, Policy and Methods Committee is a civil service group responsible for dealing with declassification policy and the physical security of documents and buildings; the Personnel Security Committee supervises the 'positive vetting' system; while the recently created Electronics Security Committee is concerned with the protection of sensitive information stored in computer networks.[80]

Figure 2.5 shows the management structure of the British security and intelligence community.

Figure 2.5 Management structure of the British security and intelligence community.

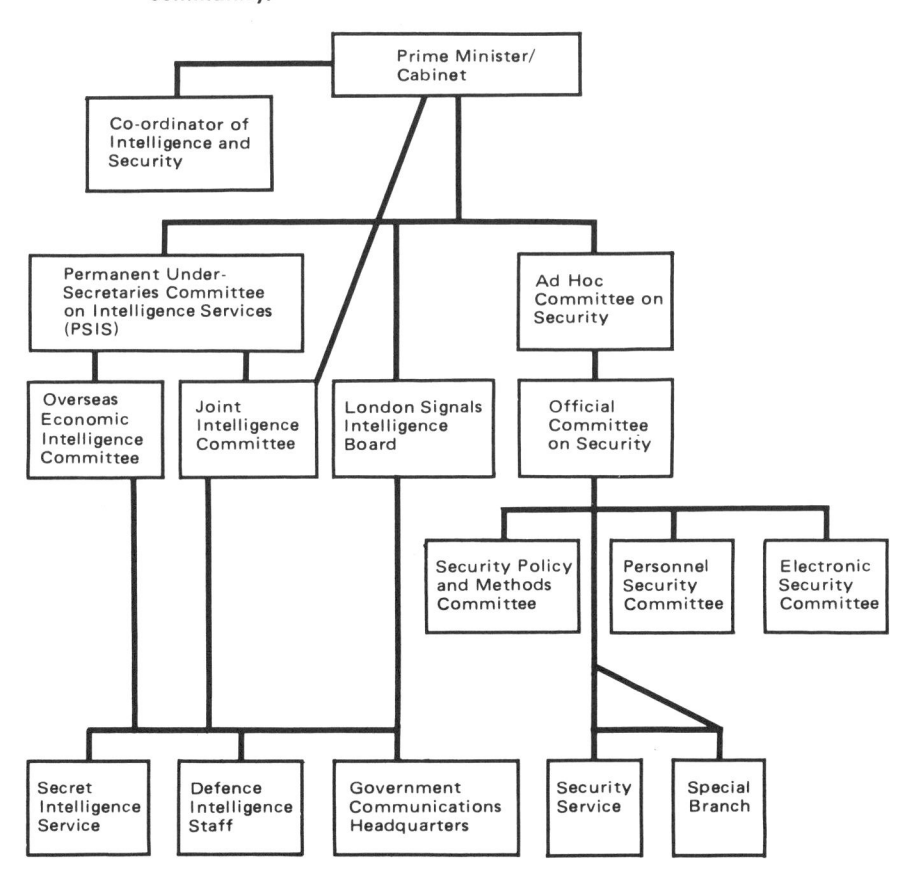

3

The Australian security and intelligence community

The Australian security and intelligence community consists of more than a dozen major collection, assessment and user organizations, deeply intertwined with their respective range of British and US organizations under the UKUSA arrangements. There are agencies concerned with external intelligence and others with internal security matters and counter-terrorist operations. There are agencies concerned with the collection of intelligence by technical means, and others with collection by more classical espionage techniques. Each of the military services has also found it necessary to establish its own intelligence and security organization.

These agencies form a 'community' in the strict sense that there is some identity of professional character and interest. There are numerous interconnections between them, with many having formal liaison offices within other agencies. In addition, there is a great deal of personnel transfer between the agencies. For example, Commander T.E. Nave, the 'father' of Australia's SIGINT operations, worked with the Directorate of Naval Intelligence, Allied Intelligence Bureau (AIB), Secret Intelligence Australia (SIA, the Australian war-time counterpart to Britain's SIS or MI-6), Central Bureau (the war-time SIGINT agency), the Defence Signals Division (DSD, the successor to Central Bureau), and served as Deputy Director of the Australian Security Intelligence Organisation (ASIO) for ten years.[1] Major-General Alan Stretton served in the Directorate of Military Intelligence (DMI), the Joint Intelligence Staff (JIS), the Joint Intelligence Bureau (JIB), and was later Deputy Director (Military) of the Joint Intelligence Organisation (JIO).[2] Other officers have served in both the DSD and the Australian Secret Intelligence Service (ASIS). The present Director-General of ASIO was formerly Deputy Director-General of ASIS. The first head of the Protective Services Coordination Centre (PSCC), A.P. Fleming, had been the first Director of the Joint Intelligence Bureau (1947−48) and was later Controller of Joint Intelligence within the Department of Defence (1948−49). His successor as Director of the JIB, Walter Cawthorn, was later Director-General of ASIS (1960−68). Fleming's successor as the second head of the PSCC, W.T. Robertson, had played a key role in the planning and development of ASIS, was a Deputy Director of ASIS from 1957 to 1968, and was Director-General from 1968 until the termination of his appointment on 7 November 1975. Some members of the Office of National Assessments (ONA) have previously worked with ASIO and the JIO. The first Director-General of ONA, R.W. Furlonger, had also been the first Director of JIO (1969−72).

Many of the current intelligence agencies have a direct historical lineage back to the Second World War, when there operated from Australia more than twenty disparate Allied organizations involved in intelligence activities.[3] Numerous reorganizations have taken place since then, so that the post-war history of the Australian intelligence community is littered with titles that are no longer applicable — such as the Defence Signals Bureau (DSB), the Defence Signals Division (DSD), the Joint Intelligence Bureau (JIB), the Joint Intelligence Staff (JIS), the Joint Intelligence Committee (JIC), the National Intelligence Committee (NIC), the National Assessments Staff (NAS), etc.

The formation and development of many of Australia's security and intelligence agencies were particularly influenced by their counterpart British services. For example, the creation of ASIO was due very much to British and, less directly, American pressure. And as noted in Chapter 7, the relationship between ASIS and the SIS (MI-6) is still so close that ASIS officers continue to refer to the London headquarters of SIS as the 'Head Office' and the Melbourne headquarters of ASIS itself as the 'Main Office'. In the case of the Defence Signals Directorate (DSD), the British Liaison Officer (BLO) is also the Special Assistant to the Director.

The size of the Australian intelligence community is difficult to determine with exactitude. Part of the problem is definitional — a number of organizations have individual officers or even sections whose day-to-day activities clearly fall within the scope of the intelligence community, even though the principal functions of those organizations lie elsewhere; other organizations might normally have minimal connection with the intelligence community except on particular occasions when their involvement is both direct and extensive. Moreover, except in the case of the ONA, the establishment figures of the agencies which make up the Australian intelligence community have never been officially disclosed. However, the total figure for ONA, ASIO, the Services Intelligence Directorates, the JIO, ASIS and the Defence Signals Directorate (DSD) is about 2500 persons.

This makes it, on a population basis, a relatively large security and intelligence community. It is, for instance larger than the Canadian community even though Australia's population is only two-thirds that of

Canada. And it is about ten times as large as the New Zealand security and intelligence community, even though Australia's population is less than five times that of New Zealand.

Estimating the aggregate amount spent for the intelligence activities of the Australian Government is also difficult. The budgets for the JIO, the DSD and certain other units within the intelligence and security community are classified. The Federal Budget brought down in August 1983 provided $A36.8m for ASIO (of which $8.4m is budgeted for construction of ASIO's new headquarters building in Canberra), $12.6m for ASIS, and $2.4m for ONA.[4] No figures are given for Australia's other security services (such as the Protective Services Coordination Centre) although security operations have expanded rapidly in recent years; and the figures for the JIO, the DSD and the Service Intelligence Directorates are not separated out from the overall defence vote. The budget for the JIO is probably about $15m. Determining the budget for the DSD is a more difficult exercise; on the one hand, the manpower establishment for the DSD is greater than that of the other agencies, with about half of this establishment paid by the services hosting the various DSD intercept stations; on the other hand, the capital and maintenance costs of DSD operations — the monitoring facilities and the cryptographic computers — are much higher than those of the other agencies. The DSD's total annual cost is probably fairly close to $30m. This would bring the overall budget for the Australian intelligence community to somewhat more than $100m — an increase of some 100 per cent since 1978 (when the overall figure was about $50m).

The Office of National Assessments (ONA)

The Office of National Assessments (ONA) is Australia's newest but also its most senior intelligence agency. The decision to establish ONA was announced by Prime Minister Malcolm Fraser in a Ministerial Statement on Intelligence and Security Arrangements on 5 May 1977.[5] This decision was a direct and perhaps the single most important product of the Royal Commission on Intelligence and Security conducted by Mr Justice Hope in 1974–77.

The functions of ONA, as set out in the Office of National Assessments Act of 1977 (s5[i]), are:

(a) to assemble and correlate information relating to international matters that are of political-strategic or economic significance to Australia and –
  (i) to prepare reports in relation to such of those matters as are of current significance; and
  (ii) from time to time as circumstances require, to make assessments in relation to such of those matters as are of national importance;
(b) to furnish reports prepared, and assessments made, in accordance with paragraph (a) to appropriate Ministers and other appropriate persons;
(c) to ensure that international developments of major importance to Australia are assessed on a continuing basis; and

(d) to keep under review the activities connected with international intelligence that are engaged in by Australia and to bring to the notice of relevant Departments and Commonwealth authorities any inadequacies in the nature, the extent, or the arrangements for coordination, of those activities that become apparent from time to time and suggest any improvements that should be made to remedy those inadequacies.

The title of the new organization suggests three of its principal characteristics. First, it is an Office, not a Government department or a division of any department. It is an autonomous body, founded by an Act of Parliament, under which it reports directly to the Prime Minister. As its first Director-General noted, 'it has no role in recommending policy although it does — and should — make judgments that are highly relevant to the formation of policy'.[6] Second, it is *national*, in the sense that it concerns itself with external issues of national importance, with 'national' having been defined by the Prime Minister in his Second Reading speech as including:

matters affecting the responsibility of more than one Minister, department or authority
or being of a level of importance warranting cabinet reference
or being of importance to basic government policy.[7]

Third, it is concerned with assessments, in the sense, as outlined by its first Director-General, that

it is occupied with the analytical task of estimating or assessing situations as distinct from gathering information about them. This means it is not an intelligence organisation in the popular sense of gathering information from delicate sources, but of course it handles a certain amount of such information. That material of covert origin is in volume (though not always in value) slight compared to the immense amount of published information, both journalistic and scholarly, as well as diplomatic reports, on which ONA bases its assessments. Essentially its task is to coordinate knowledge from all sources into the best estimate.[8]

One other aspect of ONA's charter is especially noteworthy — namely, Section 5(i)d of the Act, which gives ONA the responsibility for overseeing the total intelligence effort, including the non-secret intelligence gathering programs of various departments dealing with external policy, and for suggesting improvements.

ONA has had two Directors-General. The first, R.W. Furlonger, who headed the Office from its inception until his retirement in April 1981, had also been the first Director of the Joint Intelligence Organisation (1969—72). His successor, Michael Cook, had previously been the Chief Executive Officer in the Prime Minister's Office (1979—80) and a Deputy Secretary in the Department of Foreign Affairs (1980—81).

The staff of ONA, which consists of 34 analysts and a total establishment of about 60 people, is divided into four major groups. There are two divisions, Economic and Political/Strategic, each headed by a Deputy

34   *The Ties That Bind*

Figure 3.1   Office of National Assessments (ONA)

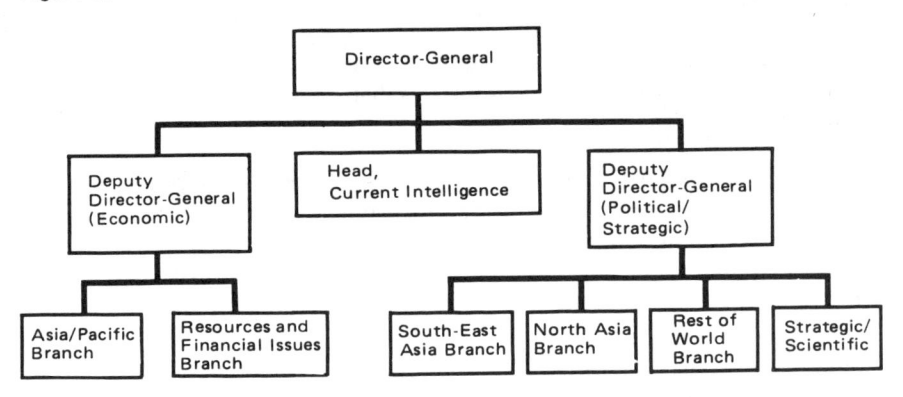

```
                         ┌─────────────────┐
                         │ Director-General│
                         └─────────────────┘
              ┌─────────────────┼─────────────────┐
    ┌─────────────────┐ ┌─────────────────┐ ┌─────────────────┐
    │ Deputy          │ │ Head,           │ │ Deputy          │
    │ Director-General│ │ Current         │ │ Director-General│
    │ (Economic)      │ │ Intelligence    │ │ (Political/     │
    │                 │ │                 │ │ Strategic)      │
    └─────────────────┘ └─────────────────┘ └─────────────────┘
       ┌────┴────┐              ┌───────────┬──────┴────┬────────────┐
  ┌─────────┐┌─────────┐  ┌─────────┐┌─────────┐┌─────────┐┌─────────┐
  │Asia/    ││Resources││  │South-   ││North    ││Rest of  ││Strategic│
  │Pacific  ││and      ││  │East     ││Asia     ││World    ││/        │
  │Branch   ││Financial││  │Asia     ││Branch   ││Branch   ││Scientif-│
  │         ││Issues   ││  │Branch   ││         ││         ││ic       │
  │         ││Branch   ││  │         ││         ││         ││         │
  └─────────┘└─────────┘  └─────────┘└─────────┘└─────────┘└─────────┘
```

Director-General; a Current Intelligence Unit; and a Management Services Section. (See Figure 3.1.)

The Current Intelligence Unit, which has a staff of only three officers, is the smallest group. It is formally tasked with research into and analysis of current international developments of national importance, and has taken over the functions of the former Office of Current Intelligence (OCI) in the JIO, although it is rather smaller than the OCI used to be. The Current Intelligence Unit is responsible for the preparation of a *Current Report*, a *Current Situation Analysis*, a *Weekly Summary*, and a *Watch Report*. The *Weekly Summary* provides a vehicle for publishing items on developments that warrant relatively more detailed reporting than is possible in the *Current Report* and the *Current Situation Analysis*; despite its title, it is not restricted to developments that have occurred in the previous week but is normally limited to periods of a few months. The *Watch Report* is a vehicle for close and detailed reporting on particular crises. The Current Intelligence staff is greatly assisted by assessment officers from the functional divisions in the preparation of these appreciations.

The largest group in ONA is the Political/Strategic Division, which has a staff of about twenty officers, divided into four branches — South East Asia, North East Asia, the Rest of the World, and Strategic/Scientific. This division is responsible for producing assessments, reports and appreciations of international, political and strategic matters of national importance. This includes such wide-ranging matters as nuclear proliferation, the future importance of Antarctica, Soviet attitudes towards US installations in Australia, the global strategic balance, the chances and likely consequences for Australia of global nuclear war, international terrorism, Eurocommunism, political developments in the Middle East, Vietnamese intentions in South East Asia, the prospects for Strategic Arms Limitation Talks (SALT), leadership strains in Indonesia and their implications, etc. Most importantly, the Political/Strategic staff have been centrally involved in the preparation of *Australia's Security Outlook* (ASO), the basic assessment of

Australia's strategic environment produced in 1979 and 1982.

The third group in ONA, the Economic Division, is responsible for assessments on economic matters of national importance, and has a staff of twelve officers divided into two branches — the Asia/Pacific Branch and the Resources and Financial Issues Branch. The subjects covered by this division include the likely long-term evolution of foreign demands for Australia's export products, potential competitive suppliers of those commodities, economic conditions in Australia's principal export markets such as Japan and the EEC (European Economic Community), the future of the international monetary system, and economic and financial developments in Papua New Guinea and the ASEAN (Association of South East Asian Nations) countries.

Finally, there is the Management Services Section which consists of about 25 people and which provides the support staff for the functional groups. This section is also responsible for security within ONA. In March–April 1980 there were allegations that documents had been leaked from ONA, and it was discovered that a Top Secret ASIO document entitled *The Threat to the Internal Security of Australia* had been lost entirely from the Office, and a subsequent ASIO investigation recommended major changes to ONA's security procedures. In 1981 staff were added to the Management Services Section to keep a complete register of all secret files, to issue entry passes to ONA premises, and to conduct 'detailed security checks of restricted areas'.[9]

ONA assessments are ordinarily (that is, unless urgency dictates otherwise) considered by one of two boards — either the Economic Assessments Board or the National Assessments Board. These boards are chaired by the Director-General of ONA (or, in his absence, the relevant Deputy Director-General of ONA) and consist of officers drawn from interested departments. The Economic Assessments Board includes senior officers drawn from the Department of the Treasury or the Department of Finance, along with officers from the Department of Foreign Affairs and from other economic departments, and the civilian element of the JIO as appropriate. The National Assessments Board includes a senior officer from the Department of Foreign Affairs, the senior civilian and the senior military officer from the JIO and an officer from one of the economic departments. For both Boards, senior officers may also be coopted, as appropriate, from other departments and authorities with a contribution to make to the subject under assessment. In dealing with a draft ONA assessment, the Director-General and the Board are expressly asked to 'endeavour to reach agreement'. However, 'there is no obligation to produce an agreed text: ONA can send forward its own assessment but, in doing so, must record significant dissent by individual board members'.[10]

ONA has a 'front office' in the Department of the Prime Minister and Cabinet but, as recommended by the Royal Commission on Intelligence and Security, the establishment is located within the Department of Defence complex at Russell Hill. Although it was initially situated in the JIO building itself (Building L), it now occupies separate premises in Building M. ONA and the JIO jointly run a Watch Office to alert Ministers and senior officials to important current developments.[11] In crisis situations a Joint Crisis Centre is also activated within the JIO building, close to terminals for the receipt of secret source material (especially SIGINT), in order to keep events under the closest possible watch. Such a Centre was activated on 9 February 1979, for example, when ONA had decided that a Chinese invasion of Vietnam was likely in the near future. (The Chinese attack followed eight days later.[12])

The quality and perspicacity of ONA's assessments vary quite markedly, which is perhaps not surprising given the breadth of subjects which must be covered by such a relatively small organization. At least until 1982, the Middle East assessments were considered to be of very high quality. The assessment of the Soviet invasion of Afghanistan, however, was plagued by bureaucratic and political considerations, although the Prime Minister's derogatory comment that 'ONA is a complacent organisation' was not justified.[13] An internal review of ONA's performance during the build-up to the Chinese invasion of Vietnam in 1979 concluded that it was 'poor' — although it 'compared well' with that of the CIA and the British and Canadian intelligence authorities with respect to the judgment 'of the likely nature, scale and duration of the attack'.[14] The weakest ONA assessments, unfortunately, have been the contributions to the reports on *Australia's Security Outlook*. These have been too general and their judgments far too conditional to be of any substantial assistance to Australia's strategic and defence policy planners.

The Defence Signals Directorate (DSD)

The Defence Signals Directorate (DSD) is described in the *Commonwealth Government Directory* as an organization within the Department of Defence 'responsible for defence signals and communications security'. Although there had been occasional references in the press to an Australian signals intelligence (SIGINT) organisation, the existence of the DSD was not officially acknowledged until the Prime Minister's statement on the Royal Commission on Intelligence and Security in the House of Representatives on 25 October 1977, when Mr Fraser stated:

> The Defence Signals Division is an organisation concerned with radio, radar and other electronic emissions from the standpoint both of the information and the intelligence that they can provide and of the security of our own Government communications and electronic emissions. It is an agency which serves wide national requirements in response to national priorities.[15]

The history of the DSD can be traced back to 1939–40, when three signals intercept stations were established — HMAS Harman, near Canberra; Coonawarra, near Darwin; and at Park Orchards in Melbourne.[16]

A small cryptographic or 'special intelligence' organization began operation in early 1940, and the establishment of a Special Intelligence Organisation was formally approved by the Defence Committee on 28 November 1941. This capability was greatly expanded during the Second World War. The number of signals intercept stations was increased to more than a dozen and a variety of new SIGINT and cryptographic groups were established, the most important of which was Central Bureau, which was set up on 15 April 1942.[17] Central Bureau was officially disbanded in late 1945, but the capability was retained. According to Lieutenant Colonel A.W. Sandford, who was Assistant Director of Central Bureau, in a letter dated 16 November 1945, 'the affairs of this Unit are being wound up very satisfactorily ... I am going to Melbourne in the near future to assist in the formation of the post-war organisation'.[18] Initially called the Defence Signals Bureau (DSB), it later became the Defence Signals Division (DSD). In October 1977, the Prime Minister disclosed that it was to be restyled as the Defence Signals Directorate 'in recognition of the enhanced status that the Royal Commission [on Intelligence and Security] recommends should be accorded to the agency'.[19]

The DSD has two basic missions. The first is the protection of Australian defence, diplomatic and intelligence communications from foreign intelligence exploitation and from unauthorized disclosure — the communications security (COMSEC) mission. The second is to exploit foreign signals, communications and other electronic emissions to provide intelligence for other Australian agencies — the SIGINT mission. This mission involves the interception, processing, analysis, and dissemination of information derived from foreign electronic communications and other signals. In addition, the DSD also assists ASIO and ASIS in special SIGINT operations.

The headquarters of the DSD, which had been at Albert Park Barracks in Melbourne since 1947, was transferred to Victoria Barracks in Melbourne in 1979. (The principal reason for the transfer was that other Defence elements were moved from Albert Park in the mid-1970s, leaving the DSD, as the principal remaining occupant, much more conspicuous and exposed; the overseas connections complained that they had less confidence in the protection the DSD could give to classified material in this situation. The move was also necessary to accommodate the new Control Data Corporation CDC 2600 computer which the DSD acquired in 1978 as a replacement for the obsolete CDC 2400 acquired in the early 1960s.)

The Director of DSD is currently Mr T. James, who was formerly the head of the COMSEC Branch of Q Group (COMSEC and Communications), and who succeeded R.D. Botterill in 1982. Mr Botterill became Director in 1978, following the retirement of R.N. Thompson, who had headed the DSD for more than fifteen years.

The DSD is organizationally divided into five groups, each headed by an Assistant Director. (See Figure 3.2.) C Group (SIGINT Operations and Production) is responsible for the operation and maintenance of the

Figure 3.2. Defence Signals Directorate (DSD)

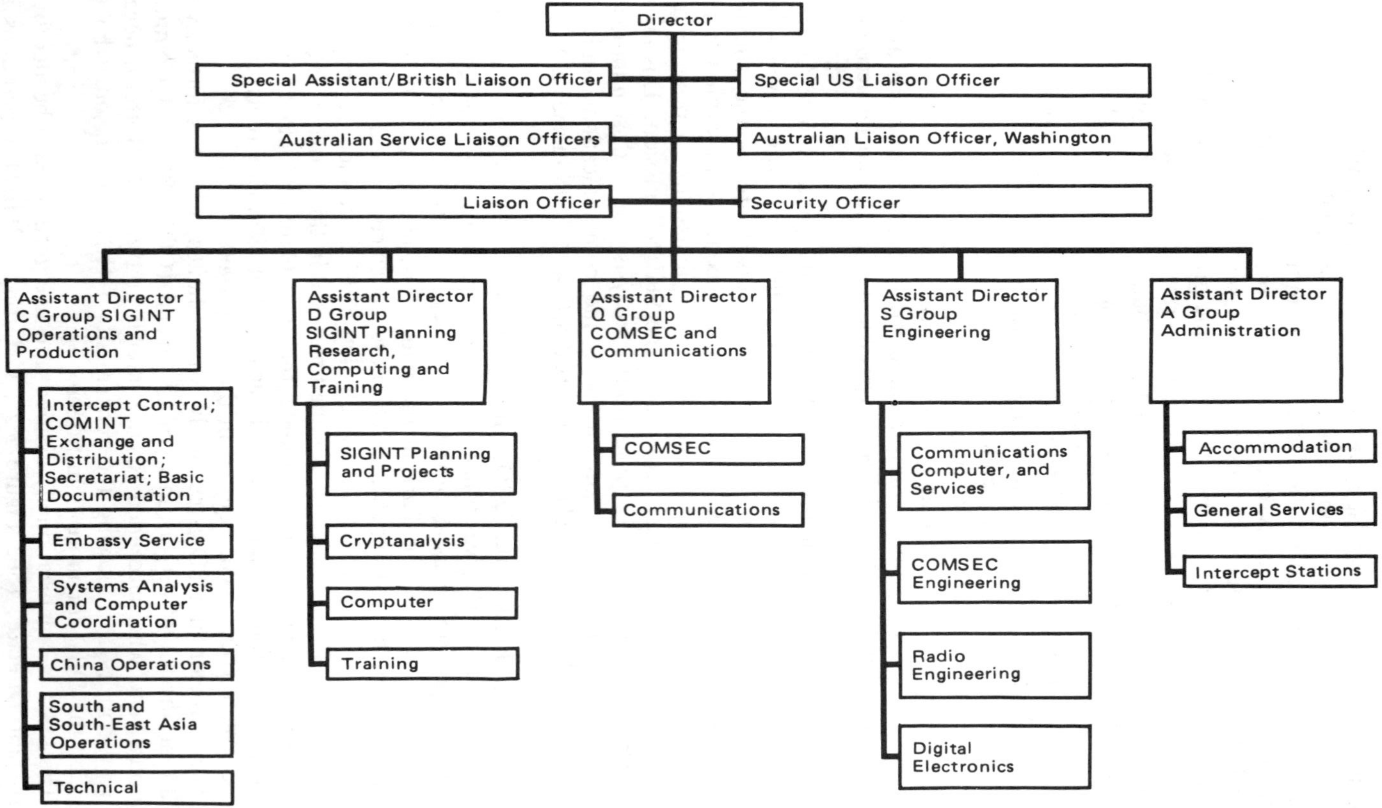

intercept stations; for the coordination of intercept activities with the British GCHQ, the US National Security Agency (NSA), and the New Zealand Government Communications Security Bureau (GCSB); for the exchange and distribution of the signals intelligence; for the secretariat; and for the production and maintenance of basic documentation. Its China Branch has three service sections (Ground Forces, Air and Air Defence, and Navy) and a Cryptanalysis Section, while its South and South East Asia Section is concerned with Indonesia (both Service and diplomatic signals) and 'all other' (ALLO) South and South East Asian signals. The Technical Branch has sections devoted to Electronic Intelligence (ELINT), COMINT Technical Search, and Technical Aids, the responsibilities of which include TEXTA — which stands for 'technical extracts of traffic', a computer-generated digest of intelligence collected from every communications facility in the world (call signs, frequencies, contents of messages, designated recipients, etc.) and is known as 'the Bible of the [UKUSA] SIGINT community'.[20]

D Group, which is responsible for SIGINT planning, research, and computing has sections concerned with Indonesia, other South and South East Asian countries, mathematical research, cryptanalysis and decryption. Q Group is responsible for communications and COMSEC; it is currently headed by B.R. Vale. S Group, the Engineering organization, is responsible for the development and maintenance of computers, test equipment, COMSEC systems and TEMPEST operations (that is, techniques to ensure that equipment such as radios and teletype sets do not radiate communications over other than authorized or prescribed circuits). A Group is concerned with administration, including that at both the Victoria Barracks headquarters and the various DSD intercept stations.

While some initial collation and analysis of the signals intelligence is done in Melbourne, the DSD is essentially a collection agency; assessment of the intelligence is the responsibility of ONA, the JIO and the Strategic Policy and Force Development Organisation of the Department of Defence.[21] The DSD has a small staff in the JIO building at Russell Hill, headed by the DSD Liaison Officer (DSDLO), and there is liaison at both senior and desk levels. The Director of DSD also reports frequently on major matters of organization and intelligence policy concurrently to the Director-General of ONA and Deputy Secretary B, Department of Defence.

The DSD is the largest Australian security or intelligence organization. As at 30 June 1981, it had 512 civilian personnel — an increase of about 20 per cent since 30 June 1973, when there were 420 DSD civilians. About 350 of these civilians work at the DSD headquarters. In addition, there is an equivalent number of military personnel, who operate and maintain the intercept stations themselves, bringing the DSD's total staff to just over 1000 people.

The locations of the DSD stations have long been a matter of public record.[22] The DSD operates five major stations in Australia. HMAS Harman, the only one remaining of the three stations originally established in 1939–40, is the smallest of these; its equipment is obsolete and plans are currently in preparation for its relocation somewhat further out of Canberra. Shoal Bay, near Darwin, is run jointly by the Royal Australian Navy (RAN) and a detachment of 7 Signal Regiment, and was set up in 1973–74 as both a replacement for Coonawarra and a partial replacement for the Singapore station which the DSD had operated from 1949 to 1973. The station at Pearce Air Force Base, outside Perth, has been run by the Royal Australian Air Force's No. 3 Telecommunications Unit since 1946. The station at Cabarlah, near Toowoomba, Queensland, commenced operations on 3 February 1947 under 101 Wireless Regiment, which was redesignated 7 Signal Regiment on 22 December 1964.[23] The station at Watsonia Barracks, north-east of Melbourne was established in 1960 and, with its receiver station at Rockbank, is a direct descendant of the original Park Orchards station.[24] Watsonia is now also the site of a new satellite communications terminal, designated Project 'Sparrow', which was officially declared operational on 1 July 1981; the terminal is operated by a unit of 6 Signal Regiment, and provides direct and secure satellite communications between the DSD headquarters and the NSA headquarters at Fort Meade, Maryland, as well as with the DSD operations in Hong Kong.[25]

Hong Kong remains the location of the DSD's most important overseas facilities. Originally established in 1949, the DSD now has facilities both on the New Territories and on Hong Kong island itself. This latter facility, which is operated jointly with the GCHQ, has recently been moved from Little Sai Wan to a location in the south of the island.[26] In May 1983 it was revealed that the Hong Kong operation includes a 'state of the art' communications intercept project directed against China, called 'Kittiwake', the data from which are sent via a special satellite link back to the Sparrow terminal at Watsonia.[27] Other overseas DSD operations include a system known as 'Reprieve', which consists of extremely sophisticated intercept equipment located in the Australian High Commission in Port Moresby,[28] and similar operations at the Australian embassies in Bangkok and Jakarta.[29] There may also be small DSD facilities remaining in Singapore and at Butterworth in Malaysia (a detachment of 8 Signal Regiment).[30] The DSD also maintains 'tactical' units which have been deployed (for example) to Phuoc Tuy in Vietnam from 1966 to 1971,[31] to Borneo from 1964 until 1966, in Singapore and Malaya during the Communist Emergency from 1951 to 1959,[32] in New Guinea during the period preceding the Indonesian take-over of West Irian, and which were used in Direction-Finding (DF) operations in attempts to locate the source of transmissions from transceivers operated by the Campaign for an Independent East Timor (CIET) outside Darwin and used to communicate with the East Timorese forces (Fretelin) following the Indonesian invasion of East Timor in December 1975.[33]

The DSD provides the Australian intelligence community with substantial

Joint DSD-GCHQ station at Little Sai Wan, Hong Kong.

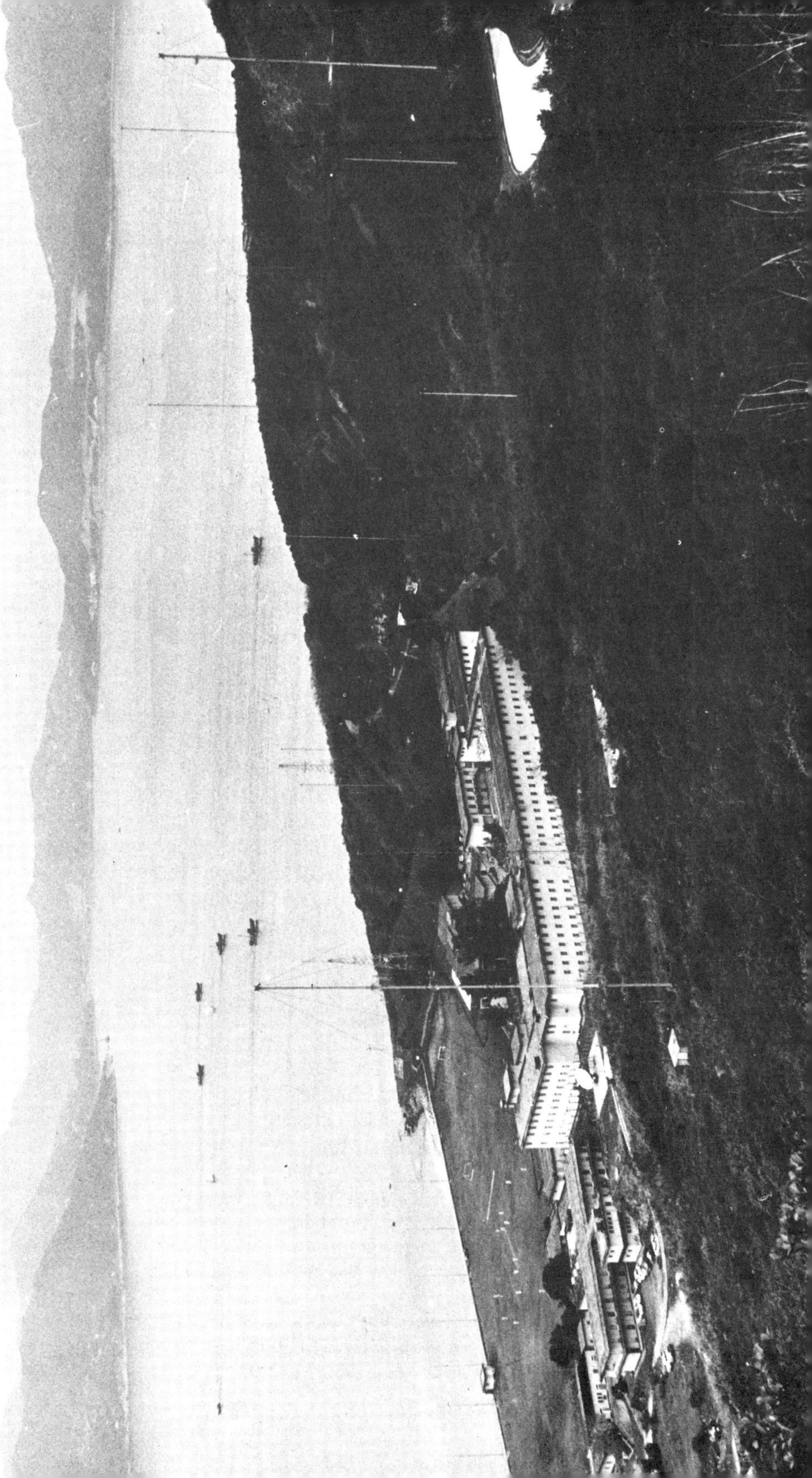

qualities of extremely valuable intelligence. Some examples, taken from the *Annual Report of the Joint Intelligence Organisation, 1974*, include South Korean diplomatic traffic, Pakistani diplomatic traffic after the Indian nuclear test, information on armed incidents between liberation movements and security forces in southern Africa, fighting on the Iran/Iraq border, French nuclear testing and pre-knowledge of detonations, the Indonesian order of battle in Irian Jaya and Timor, as well as diplomatic messages concerning world currency problems and national responses, diplomatic messages relating to the Law of the Sea Conference, Japanese diplomatic messages in general and in particular those with economic content, and 'diplomatic messages emanating from a number of foreign missions in Canberra'.[34] Other examples which have been reported include intelligence on the Indonesian invasion of Timor in October 1975; on Chinese nuclear, advanced weapon, and space-testing activities; on the Middle East, especially the Israeli–Egyptian–Syrian War of October 1973 and the involvement of the superpowers in that war; on Soviet naval activities in the Indian and Pacific Oceans; on Indonesian views on and activities against dissident groups on the Papua New Guinea/Irian Jaya border; on the Vietnamese invasion of Kampuchea in December 1978, and on the subsequent Chinese invasion of Vietnam.[35]

The report of the Royal Commission on Intelligence and Security in 1977 paid tribute to the work of the DSD and recommended that its status be enhanced. It stated: 'DSD is a very capably managed agency and believed to be so by most of its staff and others who deal with it'.[36] This is certainly the assessment of the Canberra consumers of the DSD's material. If there is any criticism, it is that the DSDs collection activities are too wide-ranging and too indiscriminate, producing much intelligence of only marginal strategic significance. The foregoing examples of intelligence provided by the DSD suggests that the DSD is guided more by the requirements of the Western SIGINT community in which it is a major participant rather than by the more delimited requirements of Australian security.

The Australian Secret Intelligence Service (ASIS)

The Australian Secret Intelligence Service (ASIS, also known as M09), is Australia's overseas intelligence and espionage organization. Although it was established in May 1952, its existence was not officially acknowledged until October 1977, when Prime Minister Fraser stated:

The Government [has decided] that ASIS should be publicly acknowledged.
The main function of ASIS is to obtain, by such means and subject to such conditions as are prescribed by the Government, foreign intelligence for the purpose of protection or promotion of Australia or its interests.[37]

The decision to establish ASIS was made at a meeting of senior Ministers on 24 May 1950, following a series of proposals by Alfred D. Brookes and a visit to Australia in April–May 1950 by Colonel C.H. Ellis, the senior SIS officer in the Indo-Pacific area. It was also decided at this same Ministerial meeting that Brookes and W.T. Robertson should go to the UK to make use of SIS facilities offered by Ellis and should then submit a report to the Prime Minister. Brookes and Robertson arrived in London in early August 1950, and were joined by Lieutenant-Colonel R.D. Hearder, whose brief was specifically concerned with Special Operations, on 14 October 1950. All three shared an office in SIS headquarters. Their initial report to the Prime Minister was submitted on 17 April 1951, and a further modified report was submitted on 18 October 1951. This latter report, which recommended that the new Service be responsible for both the collection of secret intelligence by clandestine means and the planning and conduct of special operations, was approved by Prime Minister Menzies in November 1951.[38]

ASIS was established on 13 May 1952, when Brookes was appointed Director by an Executive Council Minute and the Prime Minister issued a Charter which set out the Director's responsibilities and the functions of the Service. This Charter was revised and reissued on 15 December 1954, and again on 15 August 1958.

The 1958 Directive, which remains the basic instruction to the Director, describes the role of ASIS as follows:

You are charged with the conduct of an organization for promoting Australian security by obtaining clandestine intelligence relating to other countries; by planning for clandestine operations in war; and by carrying out such special political action in other countries as may be approved in accordance with this Directive.

This general statement of the role of ASIS is elaborated in a later section of the Directive which sets out the detailed functions. These can be summarized in terms of four principal activities:

(1) The collection of information by clandestine means. This is ASIS's main function. As Mr Justice Hope reported in 1977, 'We are talking here about espionage. ASIS exists to run spying operations in the Australian interest. We should not allow any euphemism to cover that essential point.'
(2) Counter-intelligence, involving the study of subversion and the activities of foreign services in foreign countries. Mr Justice Hope estimated in 1976 that about 9 per cent of ASIS's activities were devoted to this function.
(3) Liaison, involving the maintenance of contact and the exchange of views and information with the intelligence services of friendly countries.
(4) Clandestine or covert activities, involving the conduct of special political action (SPA) and the planning and preparation for all forms of clandestine activity in war or emergency. ASIS has undertaken six SPA operations, all during the period from 1958 to 1964, and all directed against Indonesia.

ASIS is formally responsible to and under the control of the Minister for Foreign Affairs, although for operational purposes it is essentially an independent agency. The size of the organization has never been officially disclosed, but it probably has more than 200 officers and support staff. The current Director is Brigadier Jim Furner, who was appointed in March 1984 and who had previously been Director of the Joint Intelligence Organ-

Figure 3.3 Australian Secret Intelligence Service (ASIS)

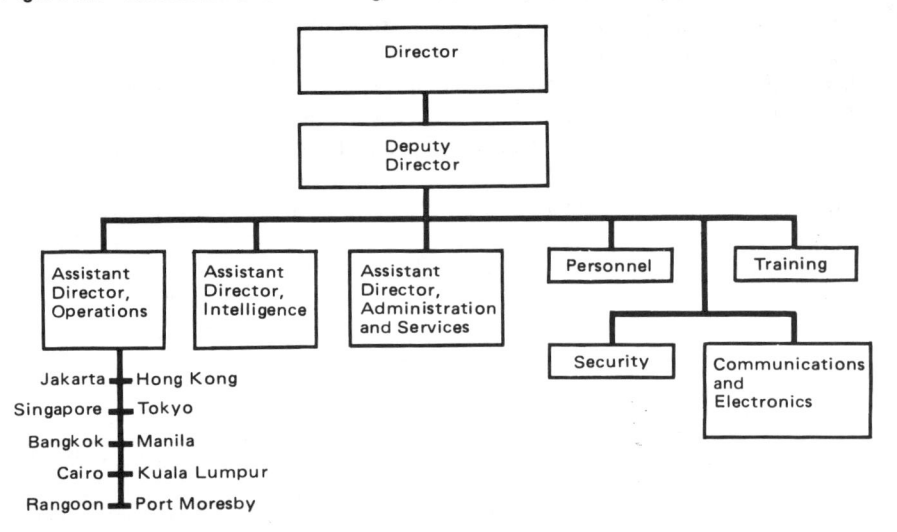

```
                        ┌──────────┐
                        │ Director │
                        └────┬─────┘
                             │
                        ┌────┴─────┐
                        │  Deputy  │
                        │ Director │
                        └────┬─────┘
    ┌──────────┬────────────┼────────────┬──────────┐
┌───┴────┐ ┌───┴────┐ ┌─────┴─────┐ ┌────┴────┐ ┌───┴────┐
│Assistant│ │Assistant│ │ Assistant │ │Personnel│ │Training│
│Director,│ │Director,│ │ Director, │ └────┬────┘ └────┬───┘
│Operations│ │Intelligence│ │Administration│  │           │
└────┬────┘ └─────────┘ │ and Services │ ┌───┴────┐ ┌────┴──────┐
                        └──────────────┘ │Security│ │Communications│
                                         └────────┘ │and           │
                                                    │Electronics   │
                                                    └──────────────┘
```

Jakarta — Hong Kong
Singapore — Tokyo
Bangkok — Manila
Cairo — Kuala Lumpur
Rangoon — Port Moresby

ization. The organizational structure of ASIS is shown in Figure 3.3.

Despite the fact that ASIS is formally under the control of the Minister of Foreign Affairs, it has been headquartered since its inception in Victoria Barracks, Melbourne, and indeed, from 1952 to 1973 its cover title was 'Central Plans Section, Department of Defence'. In 1977, Mr Justice Hope recommended that ASIS should be moved to Canberra and collocated with the Department of Foreign Affairs in the Administrative Building, with a Foreign Affairs cover title. This move was planned to take place in 1984.

In addition to its headquarters, ASIS maintains four other facilities in Australia — a 'Sydney station', which was established in 1962 and which has operated since 1975 under Foreign Affairs cover, and three facilities operated under Defence cover. These are, first, an ASIS Special Communications Laboratory, responsible for the development of chemical and other non-radio secret communications, such as secret inks and photographic microdots, which operates under the cover of an operation of the Defence Science and Technology Organisation. Second, ASIS has 175.6 hectares on Swan Island, near Queenscliff, Victoria, which is used for training in special operations and para-military activities, and which has a staff of sixteen ASIS officers. And, third, ASIS maintains a Radio Communications Station at Kowandi, some 19 kilometres (12 miles) south of Darwin, which became operational in June 1968 and which provides the main communications link between ASIS and the SIS headquarters in London and also serves as the control station for MI-6 and ASIS operations in South East Asia.

ASIS currently maintains ten overseas stations, each of which is manned by from one to three officers, giving a total overseas strength of about twenty officers and about twenty 'operational assistants'. ('Operational assistants' are female members of ASIS who are trained not only to handle the correspondence and cipher communications but also to provide support to the officers in their clandestine or other work in such fields as photography, the handling of clandestine communications, and counter-surveillance procedures. They are also used to maintain contact with important agents in the event of a station officer being absent.) These stations are Jakarta, which was opened on 9 September 1954, and which currently has three ASIS officers and two operational assistants; Singapore, which was opened in 1959, although ASIS officers had served in the SIS station, then the SIS Far East headquarters, since the inception of the Service, and which consists of one officer and one operational assistant; Tokyo, which opened in April 1955 and which until 1976 was primarily used as a base for operations against China; Kuala Lumpur, which was opened in March 1964 and which consists of two officers and two operational assistants; Manila, which was opened in May 1967 and which also represents MI-6 with respect to liaison with the Philippine security and intelligence agencies; Rangoon, which was opened in April 1967, closed in 1974, and recently re-established with one officer and one operational assistant; Bangkok, which was opened in 1969; Hong Kong, which is not really an independent station but rather an integral part of the British SIS station; Port Moresby, which was opened in April 1963, closed on 12 December 1972, and re-opened in 1977 on the direct recommendation of Mr Justice Hope; and Cairo, which was opened in 1981. Mr Justice Hope also recommended in 1977 that ASIS stations should be established in Hanoi, Beijing (Peking) and Moscow. Other ASIS stations which have been maintained from time to time include Dili in East Timor (1960–62), Vanimo in Papua New Guinea (1965–69), Saigon (1970–75), Phnom Penh (1966–75), Santiago in Chile (1972–73), and Baghdad (1977–80).

The reports produced by ASIS include secret material (known as CX) gained by its own efforts as well as material obtained through the exchange arrangements with MI-6 and the CIA. The nature of these reports is indicated in the following excerpt from the JIO *Annual Report* for 1974, in which the Director of JIO stated with respect to ASIS that:

MO9 provided some reporting of primary source material and frequently provided supporting detail. During the period MO9 reporting was found to be useful in the following areas of current interest:
 – Japanese attitudes to economic relations with Australia
 – Khmer insurgent and Vietnamese forces in the Khmer Republic
 – Quality of units and leadership in the forces of the Khmer Republic
 – Internal security in Singapore and Malaysia
 – Internal relationships among the elements of the power grouping in Indonesia
 – The security legal trials in Jakarta
As well as its own reporting, MO9 continued to channel British and US secret reporting to the Australian intelligence community. Though mainly of use as background or supporting information, this has occasionally provided primary-source material on important topics or events, such as:
MI6 – Chinese central government directives as shown in provincial discussions and reactions

- Egyptian government intentions
- Political and economic reporting on India, Bangladesh and Pakistan, including Indo-Soviet relations
- Policy of the Communist Party of Malaya

CIA
- Saigon presidential palace politics and high-level military planning
- Thai military attitudes and involvement in politics
- Malaysian/Indonesian/Philippine discussions about the situation in the southern Philippines
- Chinese central government directives
- Khmer insurgent infrastructure and military strength[39]

Other examples of extremely valuable intelligence obtained by ASIS include official Indonesian Foreign Ministry papers on the 1972 Law of the Sea Conference, which greatly assisted the Australian negotiating team; a Soviet manual on MIG-21 fighter aircraft obtained from Indonesian Air Force sources; and code books and other materials which have greatly assisted the DSD's cryptographic efforts.

Overall, however, there are very real questions regarding the efficiency of the Service and whether or not even the most valuable material it obtains is worth the financial costs and the potential political costs which would be attendant upon disclosure of its activities in countries with whom Australia maintains friendly or at least formal relations. On the one hand, Mr Justice Hope reported in 1977 that ASIS is a 'singularly well run and well managed agency ... right in concept for Australian circumstances'. He recommended 'that the Government accept the continuing need for an Australian Secret Intelligence Service and that ASIS be retained to fulfil that role'.[40]

During his inquiry of 1974–77, Hope received no submission to the effect that ASIS should be disbanded. The Department of Foreign Affairs submitted that 'the Australian Secret Intelligence Service is an asset'. The Department of Overseas Trade stated that some of the material it had received from ASIS had been 'particularly valuable'. The Department of Defence reported, apparently on behalf of the Joint Intelligence Organisation (JIO), that

CX material [secret intelligence] produces a small, but sometimes unique and important, contribution to JIO's total intake of information ... We concluded from a survey conducted within JIO in 1973 that about 15 percent of CX material was 'unique' (meaning that the information was not available from other sources) and 'important'; about 70 percent was 'routine' (of value for background etc., purposes) and the remainder of 'little value'. It must be pointed out that in *any* collection activity items which are both 'unique' and 'important' will be relatively few.

On the other hand, some ASIS activities have been extremely ill-considered; other activities have not been of any direct relevance to Australia's national interests; and many Ministers and senior officials have questioned whether the amount and quality of intelligence have been worth the budget costs or the risk of political and diplomatic embarrassment.

Perhaps the best example of an ill-considered and extremely amateurish

ASIS operation occurred in 1973–76 when ASIS recruited a rather naive and unenthusiastic exchange student to collect secret intelligence in China — without informing either the Department of Foreign Affairs or the Ambassador to China. The agent produced absolutely nothing of value, and became so demoralized that six months after severing his ASIS connection he visited the Chinese Embassy in Canberra and confessed his clandestine activities.[41]

On 16 May 1957, a meeting of Ministers and senior officials decided to terminate ASIS. Unsatisfactory relations had developed between it and the Department of Foreign Affairs, principally because of an increasing concern within Foreign Affairs regarding 'the possible damage to the friendly character of Australian relations with Asia that might arise in the event of publicity being given to the fact that an Australian diplomatic mission or a member of it was engaged in clandestine activities'. This decision was reversed following strong representations from the CIA and the SIS (including a special visit by Sir James Easton, the Vice-Chief of SIS, to Canberra in June 1957). Instead, Brookes was asked for his resignation (on 22 August 1957) and an officer from the Department of Foreign Affairs, R.L. Harry, was appointed as the second Director of the Service.

Former Prime Minister William McMahon has also disclosed that serious consideration was again given to the abolition of ASIS in late 1972. According to McMahon:

Frankly I had very grave doubts in the last year I was Prime Minister whether it was worthwhile keeping that section of the Australian intelligence service [that is, ASIS] going . . .
I did raise that with two of the three most important permanent heads [that is, Sir Keith Waller, Secretary of the Department of Foreign Affairs, and Sir John Bunting, Secretary of the Department of the Prime Minister and Cabinet] but regrettably I raised it only four or five months before December 1972 when we had to go to an election and while I think *the two permanent heads agreed with me that it might be better to abolish it* because the cost was too high and the dividends received were not too good, they both thought that it was an inappropriate time to stir up trouble.[42]

Several Ministers in the former Labor Government have also stated that the contribution made by ASIS does not justify its cost and potential risks. For example, Bill Hayden said in April 1981 that: 'I've yet to be satisfied that the product of ASIS justifies its existence. I put it as toughly as that.'[43] And Alan Renouf, the Secretary of the Department of Foreign Affairs from 1973 to 1976 has also stated that he thought ASIS was of 'doubtful value' and that he saw no reason why the Government 'shouldn't seriously consider scrapping the organisation entirely'.[44]

The Australian Security Intelligence Organisation (ASIO)

The Australian Security Intelligence Organisation (ASIO) was formally established by a directive from Prime Minister Chifley to Mr Justice Reed of the South Australian Supreme Court, appointing him Director-General of Security, on 16 March 1949. From 1938 until the creation of ASIO, internal security was effectively the responsibility of the Army's Directorate of Military Intelligence (DMI); the Commonwealth Investigation Branch (CIB — later the Commonwealth Investigation Service) had nominal responsibility, but it had 'neither the resources nor the expertise to do the job'.[45] Most of ASIO's initial staff were Army personnel, and, of course, the Director-General of ASIO from 1950 to 1970, Brigadier Sir Charles Spry, had been Director of Military Intelligence at Army headquarters for the previous four years.[46]

The creation of ASIO was due very much to British and, less directly, American pressure. The US was reluctant to communicate to Australia certain information about its atomic energy program because of concern about Australia's security arrangements. Moreover, 'American authorities had made it quite clear that they would not pass on to the United Kingdom any information unless it was certain that such information would not be passed to Australia'.[47]

Sir Percy Sillitoe, the Director-General of MI-5 visited Australia in early 1948 and found Australian security arrangements to be quite deficient. The matter was discussed at a meeting between the Prime Minister, Mr Chifley, and the British Cabinet at No. 10 Downing Street on 8 July 1948, and Chifley undertook to institute stricter security arrangements in Australia.[48] As Mr Justice Hope noted, 'the UK Security Service had very strongly urged Mr Chifley to set up a new Service and he eventually agreed'.[49] And Sir Percy Sillitoe has written that 'ASIO ... was set up as a result of my trip'.[50]

The ASIO charter was based on that given to the UK Security Service (MI-5) and defined the task of the organization as 'the defence of the Commonwealth from external and internal dangers arising from attempts at espionage and sabotage, or from actions of persons and organisations, whether directed from within or without the country, which may be judged to be subversive of the security of the Commonwealth'.[51] In 1979, as a result of the Royal Commission on Intelligence and Security, ASIO was given wider responsibility and increased powers. The 1979 Act now requires ASIO to advise the Government on:

(a) the protection of, and of the people of, the Commonwealth and the several States and Territories from —
    (i) espionage;
    (ii) sabotage;
    (iii) subversion;
    (iv) active measures of foreign intervention; or
    (v) terrorism,
whether directed from, or committed within, Australia or not; and
(b) the carrying out of Australia's responsibilities to any foreign country in relation to a matter mentioned in any of the sub-paragraphs of paragraph (a).[52]

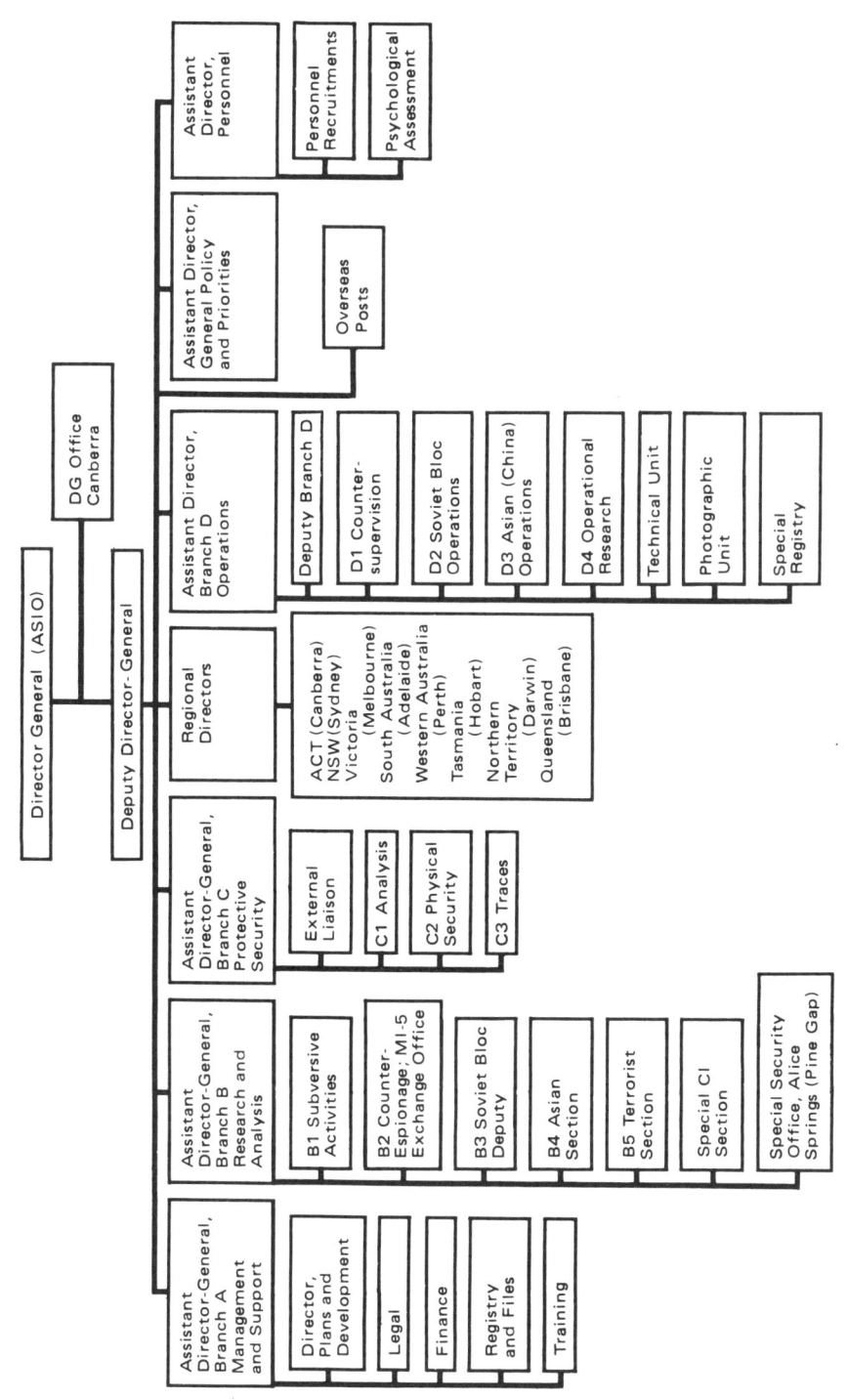

The Australian security and intelligence community 49

Figure 3.4 Australian Security Intelligence Organisation (ASIO)

- Director General (ASIO)
  - DG Office Canberra
  - Deputy Director-General
    - Assistant Director-General, Branch A Management and Support
      - Director, Plans and Development
      - Legal
      - Finance
      - Registry and Files
      - Training
    - Assistant Director-General, Branch B Research and Analysis
      - B1 Subversive Activities
      - B2 Counter-Espionage; MI-5 Exchange Office
      - B3 Soviet Bloc Deputy
      - B4 Asian Section
      - B5 Terrorist Section
      - Special CI Section
      - Special Security Office, Alice Springs (Pine Gap)
    - Assistant Director-General, Branch C Protective Security
      - External Liaison
      - C1 Analysis
      - C2 Physical Security
      - C3 Traces
    - Regional Directors
      - ACT (Canberra)
      - NSW (Sydney)
      - Victoria (Melbourne)
      - South Australia (Adelaide)
      - Western Australia (Perth)
      - Tasmania (Hobart)
      - Northern Territory (Darwin)
      - Queensland (Brisbane)
    - Assistant Director, Branch D Operations
      - Deputy Branch D
      - D1 Counter-supervision
      - D2 Soviet Bloc Operations
      - D3 Asian (China) Operations
      - D4 Operational Research
      - Technical Unit
      - Photographic Unit
      - Special Registry
    - Assistant Director, General Policy and Priorities
      - Overseas Posts
    - Assistant Director, Personnel
      - Personnel Recruitments
      - Psychological Assessment

50 The Ties That Bind

ASIO is headed by a Director-General, of whom there have been five: Mr Justice Reed (1949—50), Brigadier Sir Charles Spry (1950—70), Mr Peter Barbour (1970—75), Mr Justice Woodward (1975—81), and the current head, Mr T.H. Barnett, who joined ASIO from ASIS in 1976. As at 31 October 1980, ASIO had a staff of 700 persons, but there has been a substantial net growth in recent years and the number would most probably have reached 800 persons by 1984, some two-thirds of whom work at the organization's headquarters. This has been located in Melbourne since 1949, but ASIO is to move in 1985 to a new headquarters which is currently under construction in the Department of Defence complex at Russell Hill in Canberra.[53] ASIO offices are located in all eight State and Territory capital cities as well as Alice Springs (which is concerned with the security of the CIA's satellite ground station at Pine Gap). More than 50 officers are located overseas, with responsibilities for liaison with their counterpart services (and most especially MI-5 and the CIA), for the protective security of certain Australian embassies and High Commissions, and for checking visa applications. The organizational structure of ASIO is shown in Figure 3.4.

The allocation of ASIO's staff of 700 officers to its various activities, as at 31 October 1980, is shown in Table 3.1.[54]

Table 3.1 Allocation of ASIO staff members, October 1980

	%
Management	4.5
Administration	16.0
Collection	44.5
Information Management	16.0
Assessment	10.5
Protective Security	1.5
Security Checking	4.5
Liaison	1.5
Training	1.0

Table 3.2 shows the allocation of staff members involved in collection and assessment activities to specific areas of work (55 per cent of total staff, representing 384 officers), while Table 3.3 shows the further division of surveillance work and technical operations among the four target areas.

Table 3.2 Allocation of staff members involved in collection and assessment activities

	%
USSR and Eastern Europe	20.0
Asian Affairs	9.0
Politically Motivated Violence (PMV)	10.5
Subversive Studies	14.5
Surveillance	19.5
Technical Operations	26.5

Table 3.3 Division of staff involved in surveillance work and technical operations in the four target areas

	%
USSR and Eastern Europe	40
Asian Affairs	29
Politically Motivated Violence	16
Subversive Studies	15

ASIO collects its intelligence information by means of a wide range of techniques, including agents, surveillance, interception of telephones and other telecommunications, audio-technical devices (that is, 'bugs', and other listening devices), mail interception, and entry and search (that is, 'black bag jobs'). Of these techniques, the traditional penetration of target organizations by means of agents remains the most widely used. As of 31 October 1981, ASIO was monitoring 58 telephone services; there were two long-term 'audio operations', although listening devices had also been used in the previous year in support of other operational activities; there had been no 'entry and search operations' undertaken in the previous year; and only one mail intercept operation had been carried out in the previous two years.

ASIO operations, with respect to its two principal target areas — USSR/Eastern Europe and Asian Affairs — are mainly concerned with monitoring the activities of Soviet, Eastern European and Chinese intelligence officers within Australia. Its counter-subversive operations are directed mainly against the three major Australian Communist parties, and most particularly the Socialist Party of Australia (SPA); and its concern for politically motivated violence (PMV) extends from Croatian Separatist groups through groups on the extreme right such as the National Front and the League of Rights to newer groups who are '[increasingly willing] to undertake acts of violence and disruption in their protests on certain issues, notably against unemployment and uranium mining'.

With regard to security checking (4.5 per cent of ASIO's resources), ASIO currently conducts about 30 000 security checks a year on persons occupying positions requiring access to classified material. In 1979–80, ASIO conducted 33 862 such security checks (including 17 456 Primary level checks, 14 387 Secret level checks and 2019 Top Secret level checks). However, the number of checks has been progressively reduced over recent years as the employing departments have increased their own responsibilities in this area. The checking process has also now been expedited somewhat by the preparation of two assessment manuals, the Personal Assessment's Manual (PAM) and the Security Assessments Manual (SAM). ASIO is also involved in the security checking of visa applicants, persons seeking a change of visitor status, applicants for citizenship, and some applicants for passports. During 1979–80, some 35 700 visa applications were processed overseas by ASIO officers.

With regard to protective security, ASIO was designated the central reference point for all government departments on protective security matters by Cabinet decision No. 11704 of 22 May 1980. Approximately 200 physical security inspections of government departments and instrumentalities are conducted each year.

As in the case of ASIS, there are some very real questions concerning the efficiency and effectiveness of ASIO. In the first place, it is known to make frequent and sometimes quite consequential errors in its reporting. During its investigation in early 1983 into the relationship between David Combe, the former Federal Secretary of the Australian Labor Party (ALP) and Valeriy Ivanov, a Soviet diplomat and suspected KGB officer expelled in April 1983, ASIO mistakenly reported to the Prime Minister that Mr Combe's wife had had a trip to the Soviet Union paid for her by the Soviet Government and that Mr Combe had met with one of the Prime Minister's closest advisers, Bob Hogg, while Combe was under investigation.[55]

In other instances, ASIO officers have demonstrated an inability to distinguish between subversion and legitimate dissent. This was quite apparent in some of the ASIO reports on groups and individuals opposed to the Vietnam War in the late 1960s and early 1970s, and remains the basis for some of its recent surveillance of groups concerned with unemployment and uranium mining. The Royal Commission on Intelligence and Security also reported in 1977 that ASIO has at times acted both improperly and illegally, although the Royal Commissioner decided against the publication of details of any of its transgressions.[56]

More recently, a former Prime Minister, Sir John Gorton, has described ASIO in the following terms: 'I found ASIO ... to be completely ... well sort of stumblebums. They would tell you things and then say no, its not right, we've got to correct this and then we've got to correct it again, until I gave up relying on them for anything.'[57]

The Joint Intelligence Organisation (JIO)

The Joint Intelligence Organisation (JIO), which is responsible for intelligence collation and assessment within the Department of Defence, was established in 1969 and formally began operation on 2 February 1970.[58] Previously, defence intelligence had principally been the responsibility of the individual Services. A Joint Intelligence Bureau (JIB) had been established within the Department of Defence in Melbourne in 1947, and was supposed to coordinate intelligence from the Department of External Affairs (and, after 1952, from ASIS), and from the Service intelligence groups, but in practice its resources and capabilities were quite limited. There had also been, since the Second World War, a Joint Intelligence Committee (JIC), with an interdepartmental civilian and Service membership, which acted as the principal assessment authority. The JIC was chaired by a Deputy Secretary from the Department of External Affairs and consisted of the three Directors of Service Intelligence and the First Assistant Secretary (Joint Intelligence). The JIC was responsible for 'the preparation of reports and appreciations, as may be required', and had five sub-committees — the Joint Intelligence Staff, Communications Security Committee, Defence Security Sub-Committee, Current Intelligence Sub-Committee, Scientific and Technical Intelligence Sub-Committee.[59] However, to obtain reports and appreciations from these staffs and committees involved a lengthy process of calling meetings and assembling the personnel. In 1968 a committee headed by the Chairman, Chiefs of Staff Committee, General J. Wilton, who was personally 'very unhappy with the lack of a coordinated intelligence view', recommended that a full-time assessment staff be established within the Department of Defence.[60] In addition to absorbing the JIB and some single Service intelligence functions, the Wilton Committee also recommended that a National Assessments Staff (NAS) be created within the JIO for drafting intelligence assessments for a new National Intelligence Committee (NIC). Finally, an Office of Current Intelligence (OCI) was created within the JIO to bring rapidly to the attention of senior policy advisers and relevant agencies external events of probable interest to them. In 1977, the NIC was disbanded and the NAS and OCI transferred to the new Office of National Assessments.

In September 1969, Mr Fraser, then the Minister for Defence, stated that four principles had been adopted in planning the creation of the JIO. These were:

- centralisation and coordination of all relevant inputs;
- greater coordination and increased efficiency in the production of joint service and national intelligence;
- an improvement in the quality and timeliness of intelligence; and
- avoidance of duplication of effort.[61]

The JIO is formally responsible for the preparation of strategic estimates, commentaries and situation reports, both of an immediate and long-term nature, for use by the Defence Department and the Defence Force; for the preparation of papers in response to requests from other departments which have implications for Australia's defence interests; and for continuous monitoring of international developments relevant to Australia's strategic environment. This brief is somewhat less wide than was the case before the creation of ONA.

The JIO is headed by a Director, who is assisted by two Deputy Directors — one civilian (DDCJIO) and the other military (DDMJIO).

The JIO currently consists of seven directorates, with a total establishment of about 338 officers — just over 100 military officers and some 230 civilians. It is located in Building L in the Department of Defence complex at Russell Hill in Canberra. Its organizational structure is shown in Figure 3.5.

Figure 3.5 Joint Intelligence Organisation (JIO)

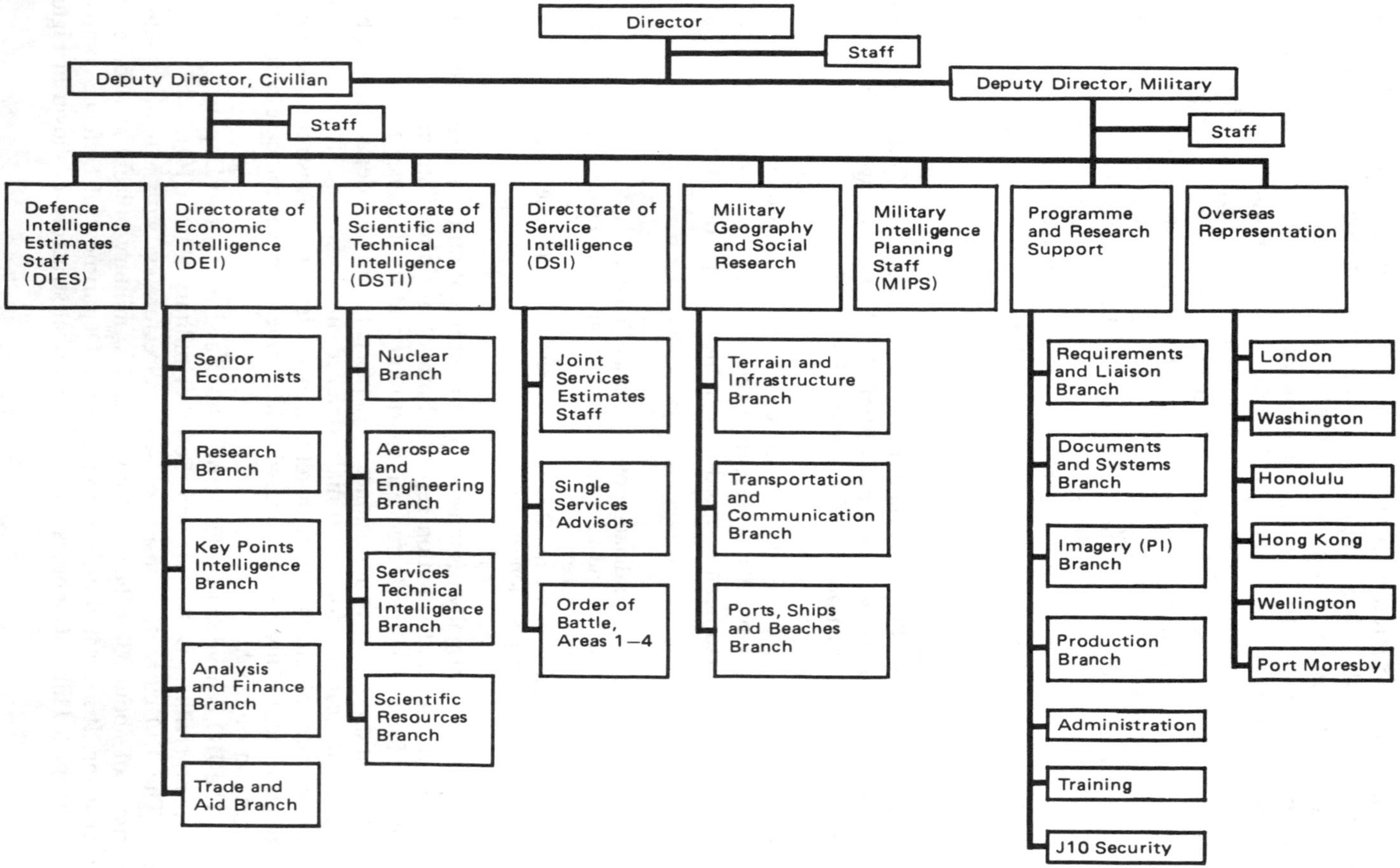

- Director
  - Deputy Director, Civilian — Staff
    - Defence Intelligence Estimates Staff (DIES)
    - Directorate of Economic Intelligence (DEI)
      - Senior Economists
      - Research Branch
      - Key Points Intelligence Branch
      - Analysis and Finance Branch
      - Trade and Aid Branch
    - Directorate of Scientific and Technical Intelligence (DSTI)
      - Nuclear Branch
      - Aerospace and Engineering Branch
      - Services Technical Intelligence Branch
      - Scientific Resources Branch
  - Staff
    - Directorate of Service Intelligence (DSI)
      - Joint Services Estimates Staff
      - Single Services Advisors
      - Order of Battle, Areas 1–4
    - Military Geography and Social Research
      - Terrain and Infrastructure Branch
      - Transportation and Communication Branch
      - Ports, Ships and Beaches Branch
    - Military Intelligence Planning Staff (MIPS)
  - Deputy Director, Military — Staff
    - Programme and Research Support
      - Requirements and Liaison Branch
      - Documents and Systems Branch
      - Imagery (PI) Branch
      - Production Branch
      - Administration
      - Training
      - JIO Security
    - Overseas Representation
      - London
      - Washington
      - Honolulu
      - Hong Kong
      - Wellington
      - Port Moresby

The largest of the analytic directorates is the Directorate of Service Intelligence (DSI), which has more than 60 Service and about 25 civilian analysts, plus a large support staff. The DSI can be regarded as the direct successor to the Joint Intelligence Staff and Joint Intelligence Bureau which existed before the creation of the JIO. The principal responsibility of the DSI is the storage and analysis of strategic intelligence which could be required in military operations by the Australian Defence Forces. The DSI has produced studies on (for example) *The Indonesian Navy, Indonesia's Defence and Security Capability*, and *Structure and Capability of the Malaysian Armed Forces*. These studies examine not only the armed forces and their capabilities, but also the industry, communications, research and development facilities, and government apparatus that could improve existing capabilities and sustain the country in war. More specialised studies have been undertaken on *Civil Telecommunications Networks in Indonesia* and *Airfields in Malaysia, Singapore and Brunei*. The DSI is also responsible for the publication of classified quarterly periodicals on *Order of Battle of the Indonesian Ground Forces* and *Asian Air Orders of Battle*.

With the transfer of the 'national assessment' function to ONA in 1977, the JIO developed a Defence Intelligence Estimates Staff (DIES) to provide a general source of expertise in strategic studies and to prepare assessments on broader strategic developments of interest to Australia — such as developments in the strategic nuclear balance between the United States and the Soviet Union and strategic developments in the Indo-Pacific region. DIES has an establishment of a Director and twelve analysts, together with a small support staff.

The Directorate of Economic Intelligence (DEI) also has a staff of about a dozen analysts, and is concerned with detailed studies of aspects of national economies in the Asian and Pacific region and the maintenance of basic data on their economies, industrial capacities and defence industries. The DEI has continued even since the creation of ONA to review international economic events against the background of the increasing preoccupation of the world with resources (including food) questions, the increasing interdependence of economies as world trade grows faster than additions to world wealth, the energy crisis, the implications of world inflation for international stability, and the concern of many underdeveloped countries at their slow rates of growth and their efforts to obtain a larger share of world product. The DEI produces a *Monthly Review of Economic Intelligence*, on such subjects as *The World Grain Situation, Japan — Defence Procurement, China — Foreign Trade, India — Growing Economic Links with the Soviet Bloc, Indonesian Off-Shore Resources, North Vietnam: Economic Policies and Performance*, and *Some Trends in the Japanese Commercial Shipbuilding Industry*.

The Directorate of Scientific and Technical Intelligence (DSTI) has about 30 analysts, and is concerned with the collation and analysis of information on the defence technology of major countries in the region of Australia's immediate strategic interest as well as with assessment of the implications to

Australia of major global technological developments. DSTI has particular expertise in the broad fields of advanced weapons technology and nuclear technology.

The DSTI has provided intelligence assessments on the preparations for and results of all French nuclear weapons tests in the South Pacific; the nuclear capabilities of near-nuclear countries and the prospects for proliferation; the development of new Soviet strategic missiles; Soviet satellite surveillance programs, including the development of the Soviet ocean surveillance satellite-borne radar system; the activities of Soviet oceanographic research vessels in ocean areas near Australia; developments in Chinese naval technology; and the operational performance and technical characteristics of Chinese and Soviet weapons captured in Vietnam and the Middle East.

The Directorate of Geography and Social Research is a relatively small group concerned with the nature of government and administration, including the role of military and other security forces, in underdeveloped countries suffering population pressures; it also reports on the influences of ethnic and communal groupings on political stability in countries of particular interest such as Papua New Guinea. The Directorate of Military Intelligence Planning Staff (DMIPS) is also a relatively small group, the function of which is to coordinate longer term military estimates within the JIO. Finally, there is the Directorate of Programme and Research Support (DPRS), which is actually the largest section of the JIO. The DPRS provides the support functions and facilities for the six assessment and analytical directorates, such as the control and coordination of external-collection tasking, local and overseas liaison, administration, security, training, coordination and rationalization of computer services, photographic interpretation (PI), printing and drafting services, information storage, distribution and retrieval services, and systems development. The DPRS has a staff of about 120 persons.

The Service intelligence directorates

The single-Service intelligence directorates were much reduced and their functions strictly delimited with the establishment of the JIO. The Wilton Committee saw the Service Directors of Intelligence remaining as intelligence staff officers under command of their respective Chiefs of Staff but having no direct responsibility for the production of joint-Service or national intelligence; only single-Service tactical intelligence was to remain with these directorates.

The army's Directorate of Military Intelligence (DMI), the structure of which is shown in Figure 3.6, has an establishment of more than twenty officers together with a relatively large support staff. The DMI is responsible for formulating army intelligence doctrine and policy for the army in the field; advising the Chief of General Staff (CGS), branches at Army Office,

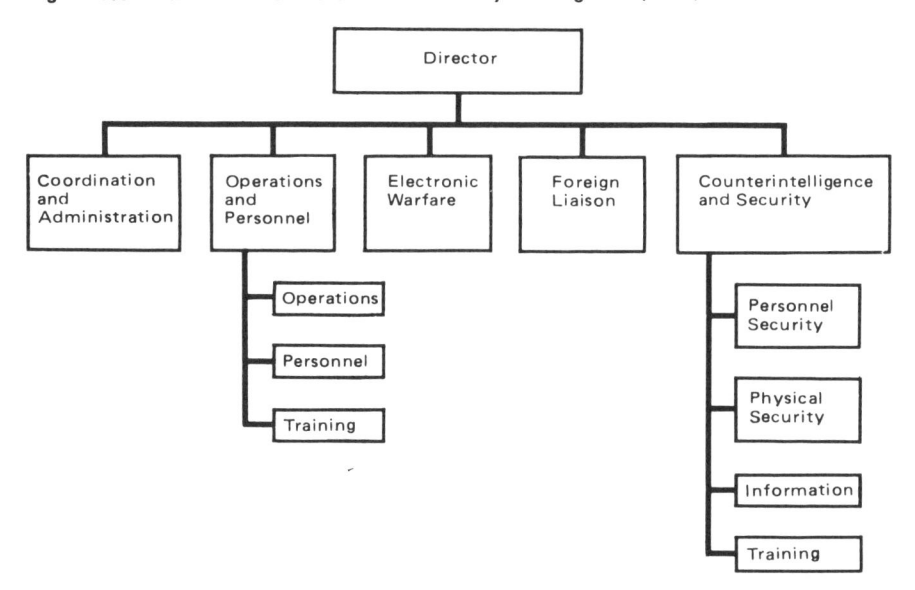

Figure 3.6 Australian Directorate of Military Intelligence (DMI)

commands and military districts on military intelligence matters including counter-intelligence aspects; coordinating army electronic warfare policy and advising on this subject; and performing the Head of Corps function for the Australian Intelligence Corps.

The Directorate of Air Force Intelligence and Security (DAFIS) is responsible for all matters relating to air intelligence concerning the Royal Australian Air Force (RAAF), liaison between the RAAF and foreign intelligence services, the provision of linguists for the DSD operations at Hong Kong and Pearce Air Force Base, and for counter-intelligence, personnel security, and the physical security of RAAF bases and facilities. Its organizational structure is shown in Figure 3.7.

The Directorate of Naval Intelligence and Security (DNIS) is responsible for all aspects of naval intelligence and security, liaison with other Australian and allied intelligence organizations, and for the oversight and coordination of physical and protective security measures at navy establishments. The structure of the DNIS is shown in Figure 3.8

The Service Directors of Intelligence liaise closely and continuously with the Directorate of Service Intelligence (DSI) in the JIO. This is achieved principally through regular meetings of the Military Intelligence Advisory Group (MIAG), which consists of the Director of Service Intelligence and the three Service Directors of Intelligence, and the daily functioning of the three Single Service Advisers (SSAs) in the JIO. There is a two-way flow of information, with the Service Directors feeding in single-Service information and drawing on the JIO for intelligence, information and assessments required for single-Service purposes. Again this is achieved principally

58 *The Ties That Bind*

Figure 3.7 Australian Directorate of Air Force Intelligence and Security (Dafis)

```
                          Director
                 ┌───────────┴───────────┐
        Intelligence                    Security
        Plans and
        Operations
           ├── Intelligence Plans           ├── Police
           ├── Intelligence Operations      ├── Ground Defence Fire Services
           ├── Intelligence Targets         └── Counter-Intelligence
           └── Foreign Liaison
```

Figure 3.8 Directorate of Naval Intelligence and Security (DNIS)

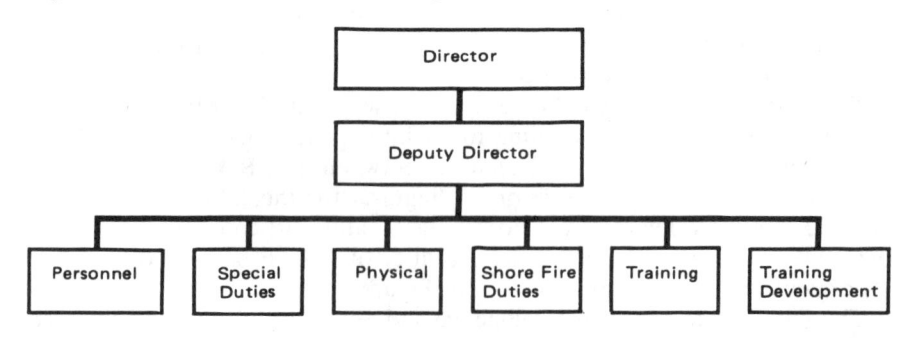

```
                        Director
                           │
                     Deputy Director
   ┌──────────┬─────────┬─────────┬──────────┬─────────┬─────────────┐
Personnel  Special   Physical  Shore Fire  Training   Training
           Duties               Duties                Development
```

through the MIAG and the SSAs, and by the regular dissemination of intelligence through periodic publications and oral briefings.

Another component of the Australian intelligence community relevant here is the Defence representatives and attachés at posts abroad. Training courses for these officers are conducted by the JIO, and a tasking system is run by the Attaché Liaison Officer in the JIO.

The Defence Security Branch (DSB)

The Defence Security Branch, which is part of the Policy Coordination

Figure 3.9 Defence Security Branch (DSB)

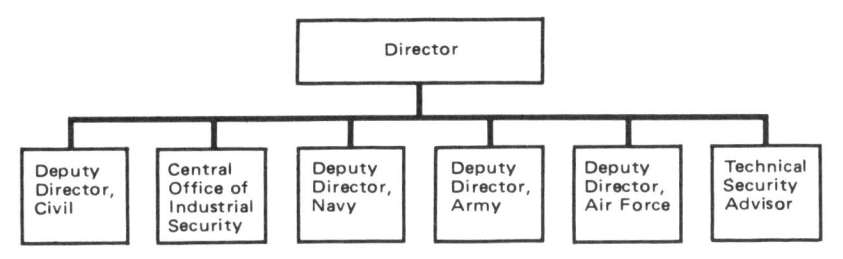

```
                          ┌──────────┐
                          │ Director │
                          └──────────┘
   ┌─────────┬────────────┬─────┴─────┬───────────┬───────────┐
┌────────┐┌────────┐┌────────┐┌────────┐┌────────┐┌──────────┐
│Deputy  ││Central ││Deputy  ││Deputy  ││Deputy  ││Technical │
│Director,││Office of││Director,││Director,││Director,││Security  │
│Civil   ││Industrial││Navy    ││Army    ││Air Force││Advisor   │
│        ││Security ││        ││        ││        ││          │
└────────┘└────────┘└────────┘└────────┘└────────┘└──────────┘
```

Division of the Department of Defence, is formally tasked with the formulation of central security policy and control and the coordination of both civilian and military security measures and practices. The Branch has a Director and four Deputy Directors (see Figure 3.9). The Deputy Director (Civil) is charged with the direction and control of all departmental personnel security operations and procedures including major investigations, the development and maintenance of a centralised records system, and the provision of assessments on adverse personnel security reports; with the defence industrial security program; and with the physical protection of non-Service key locations, including industry. The basic responsibility of departments in matters of personnel security is spelt out in the *Protective Security Handbook*. It says:

Responsibility of Departments
1. Heads of Departments are responsible for determining the areas and matters which are to be regarded as classified; that is, the areas and matters requiring special protection in the interests of national security ... Heads of Departments are also responsible for deciding whether an employee is or is not a suitable person to have access to such classified areas or matter, and for ensuring that effective measures are taken to prevent unsuitable persons obtaining such access.[62]

The three Service Directors of Security — who are simultaneously the Deputy Directors (Security) of the DMI, DAFIS and DNIS — are responsible for security within their respective Services, and for the oversight and coordination of information, training and education, and physical and protective security measures, practices and instructions applicable to the Department of Defence and the Defence Force as a whole.

In many of these functions, the Defence Security Branch liaises very closely with organizations such as ASIO, which has general responsibility for undertaking security checks and advising on security clearances for members of the Department of Defence and the armed services; the Dockyard Police, employed under the Naval Defence Act and responsible for the protection of naval dockyards; and the Special Branches of the State police forces. One particular arrangement here is the Key Points Committee of the Department of Defence, which is responsible for the 'Key Points System'. Key points have been described by the Department of Defence as 'installations and facilities whose functioning is of major importance for a national war effort or for the maintenance of the life of the community and which will, in an emergency, require protection against sabotage and espionage'.[63] These installations and facilities include pumping stations, power plants, communications links, transportation nodes, etc. ASIO and the State Special Branches cooperate with the Defence Security Branch in the vetting of persons employed at these facilities.[64]

Counter-terrorism and protective security

The management and conduct of counter-terrorist and protective security operations in Australia involves a wide variety of Civil Service, police and security agencies, at both State and Federal levels, together with elements of the Australian Defence Force.

The most senior authority in this area is the Standing Advisory Committee on Commonwealth/State Cooperation for Protection Against Violence (SAC-PAV), which was established in 1978 and which consists of senior police and officials from the Federal Government and the eight State and Territory Governments. The function of the SAC-PAV is to propose to Heads of Government's steps to ensure nationwide readiness and co-operation between relevant Commonwealth, State and Territorial Government departments, police forces and when appropriate the Defence Force, for the protection of Australia from terrorism. The SAC-PAV is assisted by a number of working groups on such matters as policy and operational procedures, communications, equipment, legislation and training. Executive support to the SAC-PAV and the coordination of its activities is provided by the Protective Services Coordination Centre (PSCC).[65] The SAC-PAV budget for 1980-81 was $A2.3m.[66]

One of the principal tasks of the SAC-PAV is the preparation and maintenance of the National Anti-Terrorist Plan (NATP), which outlines the arrangements whereby two or more governments within the Commonwealth of Australia can jointly respond to an act of terrorism where actions, threats or demands by the terrorists jointly affect their responsibilities and/or interests. The NATP is not an operational plan, but rather a framework within which governments and police forces prepare detailed plans and operating procedures appropriate to their counter-terrorist roles and responsibilities.[67]

Arrangements outlined in the NATP include the procedures for the activation of a Crisis Policy Centre (CPC) in Canberra as the focal point for the formulation of Commonwealth Government policy and responses in the event of a terrorist incident. The CPC, when activated, has five Groups, made up from representatives from the relevant Government Departments,

The Australian security and intelligence community 61

the Australian Federal Police (AFP), ASIO, and the Australian Defence Force. The five Groups are the Intelligence Group, the Advisory Group, the Response Group, the Media Liaison Group, and the Staff Support.[68]

In addition to the SAC-PAV, there is within the Commonwealth sphere the Special Interdepartmental Committee on Protection Against Violence (SIDC-PAV), which consists of representatives from those Commonwealth departments and authorities which are likely to have responsibilities for various protective or contingency measures for countering terrorism — PSCC (the Head of which chairs the SIDC-PAV), the Department of Prime Minister and Cabinet, the Attorney-General's Department, the Department of Foreign Affairs, the Department of Transport, the Department of Immigration and Ethnic Affairs, the Department of Defence, ASIO and the AFP. The SIDC-PAV has two sub-groups — the Special Incidents Task Force (SITF) and the Travelling Intelligence Working Group (TIWG). It is responsible for coordinating the implementation of Commonwealth Government counter-terrorist policy, for providing the Commonwealth advice to the SAC-PAV, and for the review and consideration of monthly assessments of the level of terrorist threat to Australia.[69]

The PSCC, which is located within the Department of the Special Minister of State, provides the secretariat and serves as the executive agent for both the SAC-PAV and the SIDC-PAV. In addition to its responsibilities for the coordination of the development and the implementation of counter-terrorist measures, it is also responsible for the coordination and monitoring of security arrangements for the protection of Ministers, visiting heads of state, senior military and intelligence officers and other local and visiting persons of high office.[70] It has a staff of about 40 people, and is organisationally divided into three branches, as shown in Figure 3.10.

The actual conduct of anti-terrorist and protective security operations is the responsibility of special police units and elements of the Defence Force. Most of the State and Territory police forces have elite special weapons and tactics groups. For example, the Victorian Police has a Special Operations Group (SOG), which consists of some 30 officers; NSW has a Special Weapons and Operations Squad (SWOS); and South Australia has a Special Tasks and Rescue (STAR) unit.[71]

Figure 3.10 Protective Services Coordination Centre (PSCC)

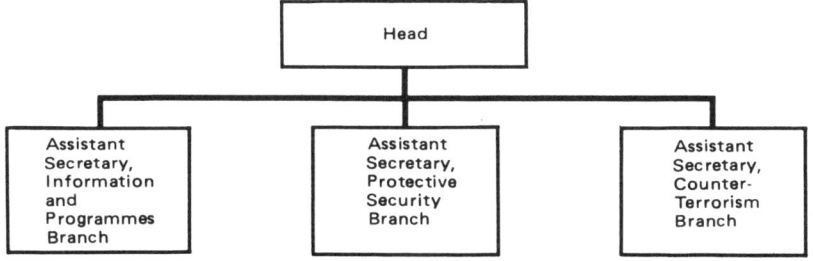

```
                        ┌──────┐
                        │ Head │
                        └──┬───┘
         ┌─────────────────┼─────────────────┐
┌────────┴────────┐ ┌──────┴──────┐ ┌────────┴────────┐
│ Assistant       │ │ Assistant   │ │ Assistant       │
│ Secretary,      │ │ Secretary,  │ │ Secretary,      │
│ Information     │ │ Protective  │ │ Counter-        │
│ and             │ │ Security    │ │ Terrorism       │
│ Programmes      │ │ Branch      │ │ Branch          │
│ Branch          │ │             │ │                 │
└─────────────────┘ └─────────────┘ └─────────────────┘
```

62 The Ties That Bind

In December 1982, following a bombing incident at the Israeli Consulate in Sydney, it was announced that a Commonwealth Protective Security Force was to be established. According to the then Minister for Administrative Services, this force will contain up to 800 police officers and be 'an independent organisation dedicated to the provision of protective security services'.[72] The responsibilities of this force include the guarding and protection of foreign embassies and consulates, the residences of senior officials, government offices, the Australian Atomic Energy Agency's nuclear reactor at Lucas Heights near Sydney, and joint US–Australian defence and intelligence installations such as the ground station for the National Reconnaissance Office/Central Intelligence Agency (NRO/CIA) RHYOLITE SIGINT satellite system at Pine Gap near Alice Springs.[73] In addition, the Australian Federal Police has a Special Branch for counter-terrorist operations.[74] A training centre for the AFP, formally designated a Police Practical Training Complex, is currently being established in the ACT. It will have a wide range of police training facilities, including facilities for training in VIP protection and anti-terrorist activities.[75]

However, it is recognised that any major terrorist operation would rapidly exhaust the capabilities of these State and Federal police organizations, and that only the armed forces can provide the necessary strength to react in any substantial way. Thus in 1978, following a bombing incident outside the Hilton Hotel in Sydney on 13 February 1978 during the Commonwealth Heads of Government Regional Meeting (CHOGRM), Federal Cabinet decided to establish a special army unit organized and trained as a counter-terrorist assault team. Known as the Tactical Assault Group (TAG), this unit is drawn from the Special Air Services Regiment (SASR) based in Perth.[76]

Management structure of the Australian security and intelligence community

The coordination and management of the Australian security and intelligence community is extremely poor. As the Royal Commission on Intelligence and Security concluded in 1977, 'The Australian intelligence community is fragmented, poorly coordinated and organized. The agencies lack proper guidance direction and control. They do not have good or close relations with the system of government they should serve.'[77] There are several reasons for this state of affairs. The formal machinery for management and coordination is weak. There has been a lack of political interest and will at the Ministerial level with respect to guidance and oversight. The disparate physical locations of the various agencies also make coordination and control difficult. As the Royal Commission on Intelligence and Security noted, 'The agencies' isolation from government has not been helped by the collection agencies continuing to have their headquarters in Melbourne, when all the major departments with whom they should relate are located in Canberra'.[78] The situation will perhaps improve with the transfer of ASIO and ASIS to Canberra in 1985 and 1984 respectively.

Australian Ministers have generally been reluctant to become involved in the supervision of intelligence and security activities. As the Royal Commission on Intelligence and Security reported: 'There has been a tendency over the years for ministers to take the intelligence/security business for granted or to leave it to go its own way'.[79]

In the case of ASIS, for example, the Directive of 15 August 1958 stated that a Sub-Committee of Cabinet, consisting of the Prime Minister, the Minister for Defence and the Minister of External Affairs, should be established to determine 'major questions of policy or practice affecting the Service'. However, as the Royal Commission was informed in September 1976, some eighteen years later, 'the sub-committee ... has never met'.[80]

In the case of some particular agencies and operations, it has been impossible for the Minister to exercise any oversight simply because he has been unaware of the subject of his responsibilities. For example, no Minister for the Army was ever briefed on the existence of the DSD, or its facilities and operations, although from 1947 to 1972 many significant aspects of the DSD (such as the station in Singapore) came within the Army portfolio.[81]

Until 1977, the responsibility for providing oversight and guidance to the Australian intelligence community lay with the National Intelligence Committee (NIC), which consisted of the Director of JIO (as Chairman), the First Assistant Secretary of the Defence Division of Foreign Affairs (as Deputy Chairman), the two Deputy Directors of JIO, and the Head of the Office of Current Intelligence (HOCI, JIO); the heads of the DSD, ASIS and ASIO attended meetings of the NIC when matters concerning them were likely to arise. The NIC's terms of reference directed it in respect of intelligence: 'to advise the Defence Committee of any measures considered necessary to increase effectiveness and preparedness, including such advice as will provide a basis for determining the allocation of resources in relation to broad tasks and general priorities'. These terms of reference were supported by Defence Committee Minute No. 9/1973, which read in part:

NIC should be directed to discharge as effectively as possible its responsibilities for reviewing and co-ordinating the working of intelligence and intelligence-gathering bodies as a whole. It should establish the intelligence priorities and rationalize overall tasking for the component agencies.

As a means of providing guidance to the JIO and the collection agencies, the NIC produced a report entitled *Australia's Intelligence Requirements* [NIC 401(75)], dated 14 July 1975. This was a comprehensive list of intelligence aims; it was not a list of intelligence priorities, nor a practical assessment of what might be achieved in a particular period, and was of virtually no use to either the JIO or the other agencies. There was a NIC Standing Group on Intelligence Priorities that was supposed to provide continuing guidance on changes arising from new developments, but it had very little impact and that only in relation to the DSD and the JIO. In 1974 there was also established an Intelligence Programming Group to monitor the Five Year Rolling Program (FYRP) process within the Defence Department, with the aim of 'ensuring that intelligence activities are serving Defence strategic objectives and capability needs with the most efficient use of Defence resources'. This Group's oversight was also limited to those elements of the intelligence community that come under the administrative authority of the Department of Defence, and again its impact was negligible.

The Royal Commission on Intelligence and Security proposed in April 1977 that oversight and guidance be the responsibility of a Ministerial Committee on Intelligence and Security, advised by an Intelligence and Security Committee of senior officials.

In May 1977 the Prime Minister announced that the Government had decided to establish an Intelligence and Security Committee of Cabinet, the formal terms of reference of which were:

to exercise policy control and managerial oversight over the national intelligence community, external and internal, in respect of targets, priorities, activities, organisational requirements, broad allocation of resources, performance and co-ordination and inter-relationships of the various agencies.[82]

However, this Cabinet Committee proved too large and met too infrequently to provide any real working direction to the security and intelligence community. The Committee was chaired by the Prime Minister and had six other members — the Deputy Prime Minister, the Leader of the House of Representatives, the Minister for Foreign Affairs, the Minister for Defence, the Attorney-General, and the Minister for Administrative Services. It met only two or three times a year, and its size and composition meant that when it did meet it was more likely to engage in Cabinet and bureaucratic politics than to formulate any clear guidance. As one observer commented at the time,

Given such a ministerial committee the tendency to attempt to play ministers against each other will be present, an unhealthy situation for the control of intelligence operations. Its very size would be a powerful incentive to more secrecy and not less. The whole scheme might have been deliberately devised to ensure that there was no effective political organisational control and, given the bloody-mindedness of some of the personalities involved, it almost certainly was.[83]

Because of its evident ineffectiveness, this Committee was disbanded by Cabinet in November 1980 and its functions subsumed under the more wide-ranging Foreign Affairs and Defence Committee.

In April 1983, following the election of the new Labor Government, it was decided to establish a National and International Security Committee (NISC) of Cabinet, with much the same responsibilities as the 1977–80 Cabinet Committee. The NISC is chaired by the Prime Minister and has five other members — the Minister for Foreign Affairs, the Minister for

Figure 3.11 The Australian Security and Intelligence Community

- National and International Security Committee (NISC) of Cabinet
  - Permanent Heads Committee
    - National Assessments Board
    - Economic Assessments Board
    - Department of the Special Minister of State (SMOS)
      - Protective Services Coordination Centre (PSCC)
      - Counter-Terrorist Branch Australian Federal Police (AFP)
    - Attorney-General's Department
      - Australian Security Intelligence Organisation (ASIO)
    - Department of Foreign Affairs
      - Australian Secret Intelligence Service (ASIS)
    - Department of Defence
      - Defence Signals Directorate (DSD)
      - Joint Intelligence Organisation (JIO)
      - Defence Security Bureau (DSB)
      - Directorate of Military Intelligence (DMI)
      - Directorate of Air Force Intelligence and Security (DAFIS)
      - Directorate of Naval Intelligence and Security (DNIS)
      - Tactical Assault Group Special Air Services Regiment (TAG/SASR)
    - Office of National Assessments
    - Department of the Prime Minister and Cabinet

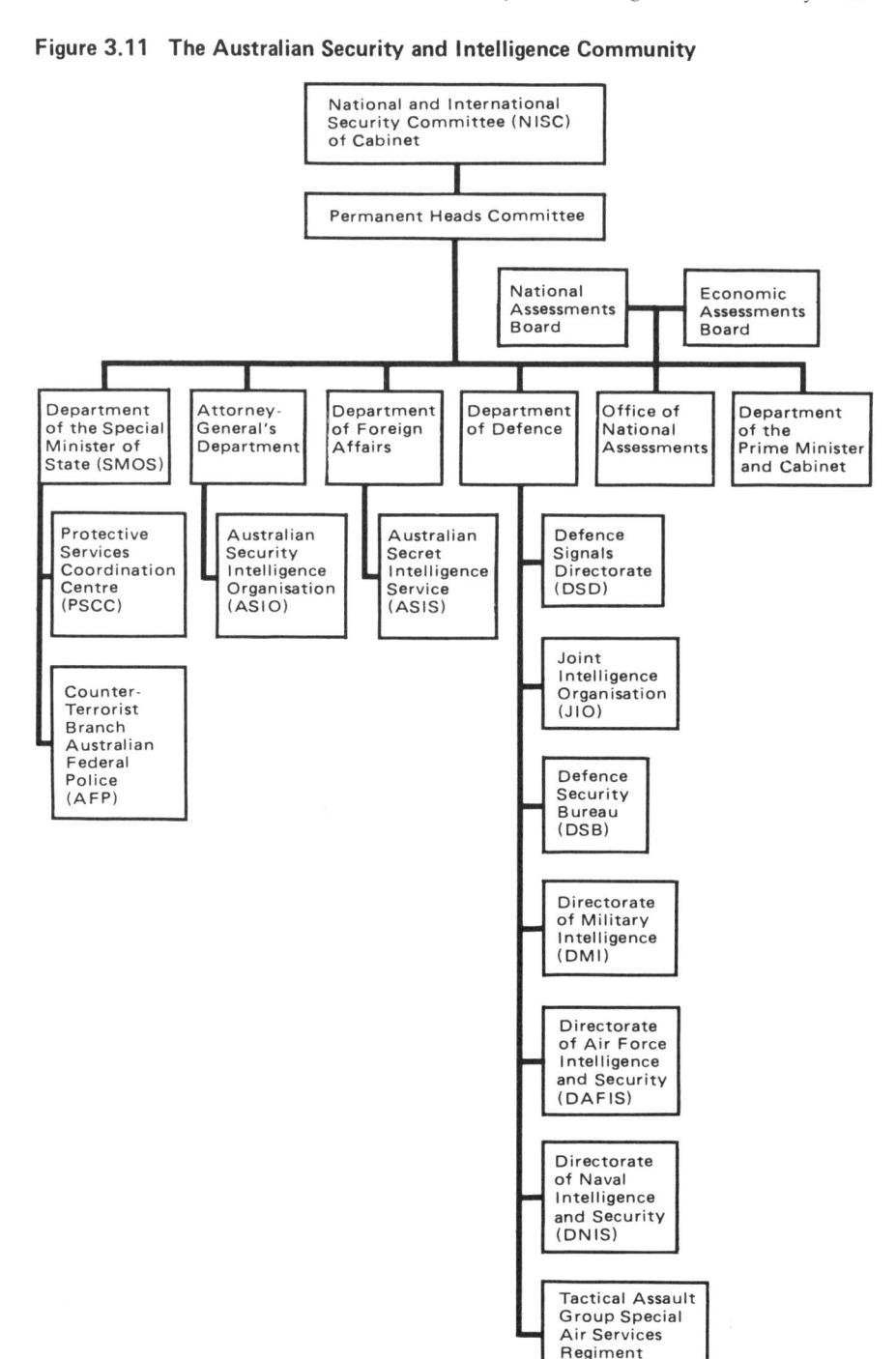

Defence, the Attorney-General, the Deputy Prime Minister and Minister for Trade, and the Special Minister of State.[84] The first decision taken by this Committee (NISC Decision 321) was that of 21 April 1983 which noted that 'the First Secretary at the Soviet Embassy, Mr Valeriy Nikolayevich Ivanov, had acted in a way causing ASIO to assess late last year that he is a professional officer of the Committee for State Security (KGB)' and which instructed the Minister for Foreign Affairs to inform the Soviet Ambassador the next day that Mr Ivanov was 'to leave Australia within seven days'.[85]

The NISC is advised and supported by an Intelligence and Security Committee of Permanent Heads, which was established in 1977 and which comprises the Secretary of the Department of the Prime Minister and Cabinet as Chairman, the Secretary of the Department of Foreign Affairs, the Secretary of the Department of Defence, the Chief of Defence Force Staff, the Secretary to the Treasury, the Director-General of Office of National Assessments and the Director-General of Security. The Secretary of the Attorney-General's Department also attends as a member of the Committee when matters involving ASIO are under consideration. The Committee has met only about fifteen times since its creation in 1977.

Day-to-day oversight and guidance is therefore left to the Director-General of ONA, as per Section 5(i)d of the Office of National Assessments Acted cited above. To assist the Director-General in this capacity, the Royal Commission had proposed 'a small policy and executive staff'. However, the first Director-General, Mr R.W. Furlonger, was unsuccessful in obtaining from the Public Service Board any positions to assist him with his oversight responsibilities, and he and his successor have had to rely on members of their assessments staff for any assistance they required here.[86] In fact, this aspect of the Director-General's responsibilities has effectively languished.

Figure 3.11 shows the management structure of the Australian security and intelligence community.

4

The New Zealand security and intelligence community

The New Zealand security and intelligence community is by far the smallest of those of the five UKUSA partners, with a total membership of about 230 personnel. It also has extraordinarily little independent status; to a far greater extent even than Australia and Canada, the other junior partners in the UKUSA network, it cannot be considered apart from that network. New Zealand has no external intelligence collection agency like the Australian Secret Intelligence Service (ASIS) or MI-6, but relies entirely on its UKUSA partners for the collection of covert or secret intelligence as well as the provision of much of its signals intelligence (SIGINT). The agency responsible for internal security intelligence is the Security Intelligence Service (SIS), which is modelled on the British Security Service (MI-5) and the Australian Security Intelligence Organisation (ASIO) and which was established 'as an integral part of the counter-intelligence defence of the Western democracies'.[1] A SIGINT organisation, entitled the Government Communications Security Bureau (GCSB) was established in 1977, but its activities are directed far more to cooperative operations within the UKUSA SIGINT network than to the satisfaction of New Zealand's particular intelligence requirements. There is a Directorate of Defence Intelligence (NZDDI) and small subsidiary Service intelligence units within the Department of Defence, but strategic and defence assessments, as well as those of more political and economic natures, are the responsibility of the External Intelligence Bureau (EIB) within the Prime Minister's Department. The New Zealand Intelligence Council (NZIC), supported by the Controlling Officals Sub Committee of the NZIC, maintains a general oversight over New Zealand's security and intelligence agencies and activities.

New Zealand Security Intelligence Service (NZSIS)

The New Zealand Security Intelligence Service (NZSIS) is the best known of New Zealand's security and intelligence organizations. It was formally established by an Order-in-Council on 28 November 1956, after some decade and a half of fitful consideration.

In late 1940, at the instigation of the British Government, a Security Intelligence Bureau (SIB) was established as a security and intelligence service responsible directly to the Prime Minister for civil as well as military security; it became operational in February 1941 with the arrival from London of Major Kenneth Folkes to be its head. The SIB was resented by the New Zealand Police, particularly as it was duplicating much of the police's security work, and after a display of gross incompetence it was brought under police control in mid-1942; it was completely disbanded at the end of the war.[2]

In 1948, the British made a second attempt to persuade New Zealand to establish a security and intelligence organization. Sir Percy Sillitoe, Director of the British Security Service or (MI-5) visited New Zealand to put his case to the New Zealand Government. The defection of Igor Gouzenko in Canada in 1945 had persuaded MI-5 that security in the Commonwealth countries was inadequate.[3] Sillitoe was also concerned about industrial troubles in New Zealand, particularly on the wharves, since Britain was highly dependent on New Zealand meat and dairy exports. Although he was rebuffed by Prime Minister Peter Fraser, his visit did lead to the creation of an interdepartmental committee entitled the Advisory Committee on Security. The main meeting of this Committee, to agree on definitive recommendations, took place on 6 December 1951, following a further visit by Sillitoe. MI-5 was represented at this meeting by H. Serpell, Sillitoe's personal assistant, and ASIO, which had been established on 16 March 1949, by D. Hamblen, who was also British. A proposal to establish a small organization modelled on MI-5 and ASIO was accepted by the Committee, but it was temporarily shelved by the new Prime Minister, Sidney Holland.[4]

In 1954, however, Holland was informed by the Australian Prime Minister Robert Menzies that the KGB defector Vladimir Petrov had testified that he had had an unidentified 'contact' in the New Zealand Prime Minister's Department. Doubts had also arisen with respect to the competence of the Special Branch of the New Zealand Police in counter-espionage matters. Hence the decision was made in 1956 to disband the Special Branch and establish the New Zealand Security Service (changed in 1969 to the New Zealand Security Intelligence Service); the MI-5 charter of 1952 was used as the model for NZSIS policy. The Service was headed temporarily by Sam Barnett, the Controller-General of the Police, and then by Dr R.A. Lochore from the Prime Minister's Department.[5] Then, from early 1957, it was headed by the erstwhile Brigadier Herbert E. Gilbert, a graduate of the Royal Military College (RMC) at Duntroon, former Director of Military Intelligence (DMI), and then New Zealand Army

Liaison Officer in London, who remained its head until 20 July 1976.[6] He was succeeded by Mr Paul Loxton Molineaux, also a former graduate of RMC Duntroon who formally took over on 16 August 1976.[7] Mr Molineaux retired on 6 May 1983, and was succeeded on 1 July by Brigadier John Lindsay Smith, who had previously been the Commander of the New Zealand Force South East Asia from 1977 to 1978 and had retired from the Army as Deputy Chief of the General Staff in 1981.[8]

The NZSIS has since its inception been headquartered at Nos 175 and 175A Taranaki Street in Wellington. The two main regional offices are in Auckland and Christchurch.

The total staff of the NZSIS had reached 160 officers as of May 1983,[9] — a more than two-fold increase since the beginning of 1979 when the NZSIS had some 72 officers, of whom 34 were attached to headquarters, fourteen were in the Auckland regional office, eleven in Christchurch, and the rest in the smaller cities.[10] In 1957, Brigadier Gilbert had begun with a staff of nineteen officers, of whom eight were from the New Zealand Armed Forces and most of the others had British or colonial backgrounds.[11] (For example, Major Selwyn Jensen, who came to head the Auckland regional office, had formerly been New Zealand Army Liaison Officer in Australia;[12] others came from Britain, Jamaica, Kenya, Uganda and Australia.)[13] By 1977, some 77 per cent of NZSIS officers were New Zealand born and all but two officers were New Zealand citizens.[14] At the time of Gilbert's retirement in July 1976, about 25 per cent still had some background in the Armed Forces and some 4 per cent had colonial service backgrounds.[15] By 1979, the annual budget of the NZSIS had reached $NZ1 350 000,[16] but given the recent expansion of the Service it is now likely to be more than $NZ3 million.

The NZSIS was given legislative stature in the New Zealand Security Intelligence Act of 11 September 1969. Following a major inquiry into the Service by the Chief Ombudsman, Sir Guy Powles, in 1975–76, it was decided to make some significant changes to its terms of reference, which were given effect in the New Zealand Security Intelligence Service Amendment Act of 16 November 1977. According to these Acts, the functions of the NZSIS are as follows:

FUNCTIONS OF NEW ZEALAND SECURITY INTELLIGENCE SERVICE

(1) Subject to the control of the Minister, the functions of the New Zealand Security Intelligence Service shall be –
   (a) To obtain, correlate, and evaluate intelligence relevant to security, and to communicate any such intelligence to such persons, and in such manner, as the Director considers to be *in the interests of security*;
   (b) To advise Ministers of the Crown, where the Director is satisfied that it is necessary or desirable to do so, in respect of matters relevant to security, so far as those matters relate to Departments or branches of the State Services of which they are in charge;
   (c) To co-operate as far as practicable and necessary with such State Services and other public authorities in New Zealand and abroad as are capable of assisting the Security Intelligence Service in the performance of its functions;

70 The Ties That Bind

  (d) To inform the *New Zealand Intelligence Council* of any new area of potential espionage, sabotage, terrorism, or subversion in respect of which the Director has considered it necessary to institute surveillance.

(2) It shall not be a function of the Security Intelligence Service –
  (a) To enforce measures for security; or
  (b) To institute surveillance of any person or class of persons by reason only of his or their involvement in lawful protest or dissent in respect of any matter affecting the Constitution, laws, or Government of New Zealand.

SECURITY for the purpose of these functions means 'the protection of New Zealand from acts of espionage, sabotage, terrorism, and subversion, whether or not it is directed from or intended to be committed within New Zealand':

  '*Espionage*' means any offence against the Official Secret Act 1951 which could benefit the Government of any country other than New Zealand:
  '*Sabotage*' means any offence against section 79 of the Crimes Act 1961:
  '*Terrorism*' means planning, threatening, using, or attempting to use violence to coerce, deter, or intimidate –
  (a) The lawful authority of the State in New Zealand: or
  (b) The community throughout New Zealand or in any area in New Zealand for the purpose of furthering any political aim.
  '*Subversion*' means attempting, inciting, counselling, advocating, or encouraging –
  (a) The overthrow by force of the Government of New Zealand; or
  (b) The undermining by unlawful means of the authority of the State in New Zealand.

The functions of the NZSIS are described more particularly below.

Liaison with friendly security and intelligence agencies

The principal *raison d'être* of the NZSIS is to act as a conduit for communication of security and intelligence material from friendly agencies and to ensure the protection of the material. According to the statement that the NZSIS submitted to Sir Guy Powles,

The New Zealand Security Service was formed in 1956 on the pattern of the British counterpart, MI5 ... The Service was set up as an integral part of the counter-intelligence defence of the Western democracies. The establishment of an acceptable form of Service was a prerequisite if other countries were to pass intelligence to New Zealand. This reciprocal requirement still applies.[17]

Brigadier Sir Herbert Gilbert stated in a press interview on 17 July 1976, three days before his retirement, 'We depend on our friends abroad for information over a wide variety of fields and they give us this information on the understanding that we will protect it as they do'.[18] And he wrote in October 1977: 'We may not have home-grown military secrets, but we are entrusted with much highly classified material by our friends and allies'.[19] And Sir Guy Powles concluded:

Intelligence material [from overseas] is made available on the clear understanding that it will be afforded in New Zealand substantially the same degree of security as it is afforded in the country of origin. This requirement is quite specific, and is specifically attached in the form of tags and stamps to every piece of written material received. In essence, we are required to maintain and enforce personnel and physical security standards comparable to those of our allies, or we face being excluded from this essential intelligence.[20]

Counter-espionage

A prime function of the NZSIS is the surveillance of known or suspected espionage activities in New Zealand. Much of the effort in this field is directed towards detecting and obtaining information about the activities of the intelligence services of the Soviet Union — the KGB and GRU (Soviet Military Intelligence).

As the Powles report noted: 'Experience overseas has shown that up to 60 per cent of the staff of Soviet diplomatic missions abroad consist of intelligence officers. Soviet diplomatic representation in New Zealand has, over the years, conformed to this pattern'.[21]

In May 1977, New Zealand Prime Minister Mr Muldoon stated that there were KGB agents attached to the Soviet Embassy in Wellington.[22] According to one report, up to sixteen of the 31 staff at the Embassy were, in 1980, believed to be KGB.[23] Another report states that there are 'between 12 and 14' KGB officers at the Embassy.[24]

There are several important examples of NZSIS counter-espionage activity. The NZSIS provided the proof which led to the expulsion in July 1962 of Mr Vladislav Sergevich Andreev, Commercial Counsellor at the Embassy, and Mr Nikolai Ivanovich Shtykov, Second Secretary, at which time Prime Minister Keith Holyoake stated that 'The removal of these two officials was requested because they had been engaged in espionage. Of this the Government has conclusive and irrefutable proof'.[25] The NZSIS co-operated closely with ASIO in the operation in 1960–62 which led to the expulsion on 7 February 1963 of Ivan Fedorovich Skripov, First Secretary at the Soviet Embassy in Canberra.[26] In February 1975, during the trial of Dr William Ball Sutch, the NZSIS disclosed that it had monitored meetings between Sutch, a former Secretary of the Department of Industry and Commerce, and D.A. Razgoverov, First Secretary at the Soviet Embassy in 1974.[27] And the Soviet Ambassador to New Zealand, Mr Vsevolod Sofinsky was expelled in January 1980 after reports from the NZSIS that he was personally involved in passing 'large sums of money' to the Moscow-aligned Socialist Unity Party.[28]

These and other instances notwithstanding, however, the Powles report found that too little attention was being accorded counter-espionage activities by the NZSIS and recommended that it allot a higher priority to them.[29]

Counter-subversion

With regard to counter-espionage and counter-subversion priorities, Sir Guy

Powles was advised by the NZSIS as follows: 'In the matter of threats to New Zealand security, no clear distinction can be drawn between espionage and subversion, as these areas are inter-related and complementary. Both constitute parallel threats and the significance of both is approximately equal.'[30]

The Service also advised him 'that approximately 10 per cent of its work in the field of counter-subversion is concerned with protest groups ... Virtually every form of protest and dissent — not necessarily either very militant or very radical — falls within the Service's net'.[31] The NZSIS has evinced a particular interest in protest groups concerned with racial discrimination, such as the organisation known as Halt All Racist Tours (HART). Indeed, an incident in June 1973 involving the NZSIS bugging of HART headquarters in Christchurch led to the NZSIS making a liar out of Prime Minister Norman Kirk, and showed that the NZSIS does not always tell the truth to its Minister. On the basis of assurances from the NZSIS, Kirk had assured HART that allegations that the NZSIS had installed listening devices at its premises were unfounded, but HART was subsequently able to confirm the bugging operation.[32]

Sir Guy Powles found that 'subversion is no real threat to our national policy' and recommended that the situation in which the number of NZSIS officers engaged on counter-espionage and counter-subversion work was approximately equal be reordered 'in favour of work in the field of counter-espionage'.[33]

Vetting

The vetting of New Zealand Government employees is one of the major functions of the NZSIS. A rationale for vetting was given by Selwyn Jensen at the time of his retirement as head of the Auckland regional office in March 1975: 'If there was no security service, the time would come when subversives would penetrate the Public Service to such a degree that they would ultimately control key Government departments.'[34]

According to the Powles report, over the period from 1969 to 1975 the NZSIS was requested to vet approximately 7000 persons per year.[35] There are four levels of extent and intensity of vetting: name checks; normal vetting; intermediate vetting; and positive vetting (of which there were 650 carried out in 1972).[36] The Powles report found that for all types of Government employee vettings, the NZSIS gave an absolute security clearance in more than 99.5 per cent of the cases: 'There were several tens of thousands of vetting requests received over this period [1969 to 1975 inclusive], and less than one-half of one per cent resulted in adverse or qualified recommendations'.[37]

Screening

The largest number of security checks undertaken by the NZSIS are not concerned with New Zealand citizens but involve the screening of persons wishing to enter New Zealand and persons applying for New Zealand citizenship. The screening of immigrants is normally done at the behest of the Immigration Division of the Department of Labour, while the screening of applicants for citizenship is undertaken at the request of the Citizenship Division of the Department of Internal Affairs. There are thousands of applications for citizenship made each year, and all are vetted by the NZSIS.[38]

Counter-terrorism

There are several organizations in New Zealand with responsibility in the field of counter-terrorism, but primary responsibility for this area of security was given to the NZSIS by the NZSIS Amendment Act of 16 November 1977.

The Powles report found that there were no clear lines of responsibility laid down for the relevant New Zealand agencies concerned with terrorism, and that cooperation between them 'has not been as effective as it should have been'.[39] Powles recommended that the NZSIS, the police and other Government agencies such as the Ministry of Defence and the Ministry of Foreign Affairs consult 'to improve working relationships both generally and specifically in relation to terrorism', and also 'with the object of determining clear lines of responsibility for counter-terrorism'.[40]

In May 1977, Mr Muldoon announced that the Government had set up a Cabinet Committee to examine the problem of potential terrorism in New Zealand, and an Officials Committee had also been established for the same purpose.[41]

The NZSIS Amendment Act of 16 November 1977 included terrorism as an area of security for which the NZSIS was now responsible, and it was disclosed in early 1978 that a Terrorist Intelligence Centre had been established at NZSIS headquarters to coordinate the flow of all external and internal information on possible terrorist threats. The Centre has a staff of three, including the section head. All NZSIS field intelligence in New Zealand on potential terrorism, as well as advice from abroad, is routed to this Centre.[42] The Centre has close liaison with the police, who have executive responsibility for combatting actual or intended acts of terrorism in New Zealand.

An Airport Security Service was also formed in early 1977, and became fully operational in July. According to Prime Minister Muldoon, 'that's all part of the same [counter-terrorist] operation'.[43]

The External Intelligence Bureau (EIB)

From 1964 to 1975 there existed within the New Zealand Department of Defence a Joint Intelligence Bureau (NZJIB) responsible for strategic and defence assessments. (The JIB was originally part of the Prime Minister's Department but was moved to Defence in 1964.)[44] The NZJIB was modelled closely on the Australian JIB, which was established within the Department of Defence in 1947 and disbanded with the creation of JIO in 1969. By the late 1960s and early 1970s, the NZJIB had become increasingly oriented toward general political assessments, producing reports on such subjects as the viability of the Sihanouk regime in Cambodia. In 1974, Prime Minister Norman Kirk directed that a review be undertaken of New Zealand's external intelligence and research services.[45] A senior officer of the JIB visited the JIO in Canberra in 1974 to study Australia's assessment organization, and it was decided by the end of 1974 to establish a more integrated intelligence organization, and one which would have economic and political assessment capabilities in addition to JIB's strategic and defence assessment responsibilities. The formation of the External Intelligence Bureau (EIB) in 1975 was greatly assisted by the JIO.

On 3 February 1975, Prime Minister W.E. Rowling approved the terms of reference of the EIB. The EIB is part of the Prime Minister's Department, and is 'intended to meet the New Zealand Government's requirements for timely, relevant and useful information, intelligence and assessments on developments overseas which are likely to affect New Zealand's interests'. The full terms of reference, as reconfirmed by Prime Minister Muldoon on 21 January 1977, are:

NEW ZEALAND EXTERNAL INTELLIGENCE BUREAU
TERMS OF REFERENCE

(1) The External Intelligence Bureau, which is to be a part of the Prime Minister's Department, is intended to meet the New Zealand Government's requirements for timely, relevant and useful information, intelligence and assessments on developments overseas which are likely to affect New Zealand's interests.

(2) The Bureau is to be headed by a Director who is to be responsible to the Permanent Head, Prime Minister's Department for executive control of the Bureau. The Director is to receive direction and guidance on matters of policy from the New Zealand Intelligence Council. The Director is to be assisted by a Deputy Director who shall act for him in his absence.

(3) The External Intelligence Bureau is to function both as an intelligence research organisation and as a co-ordinating body. It is to assemble, evaluate and present intelligence on political, social, economic, strategic, geographic, scientific and technical subjects as required by the New Zealand Government. The Bureau is to consult with appropriate departments in preparing its assessments.

(4) For its information the External Intelligence Bureau is to draw upon the Ministry of Foreign Affairs, the Ministry of Defence and other appropriate sources within New Zealand. It is also, with the authority of the New Zealand Intelligence Council, to maintain liaison with appropriate organisations overseas.

(5) The External Intelligence Bureau is to provide the Directorate of Defence Intelligence with administrative, library, mapping and cartographic services and is also to provide the New Zealand Intelligence Council with such administrative and secretarial services as it may require.

R.D. Muldoon   21 January 1977.
Prime Minister

The replacement of the JIB with the EIB within the Prime Minister's Department was announced by Mr Rowling on 23 April 1975. He stated that the new bureau would bring together a number of functions formerly undertaken by the Ministers of Foreign Affairs and Defence, and that it would be better equipped to respond to the specific requirements of the Government for information on international developments which could affect New Zealand's interests. These developments were in the economic, scientific and technical fields as well as in the more traditional field of defence. Mr Rowling said the EIB would not have responsibilities in the internal security field and would have nothing to do with the activities of NZSIS.[46] The first Director of the EIB was V.E. Jaynes, who had previously headed the JIB; it is currently headed by R.B. Atkins.

Most of the material from which the EIB derives its assessments is obtained from organizations overseas — most particularly, from the Australian Secret Intelligence Service (ASIS), the Joint Intelligence Organization (JIO), the Office of National Assessments (ONA), and the British Secret Intelligence Service (SIS or MI-6). ASIS itself provides the channel over which its own reports and, by agreement with the British, MI-6 reports, reach the EIB. There is also an economist from the JIO's Directorate of Economic Intelligence (DEI) seconded to the EIB and, in return, there is a specially indoctrinated officer at First Secretary level in the New Zealand High Commission in Canberra responsible for liaison with the JIO and ONA. Liason with other overseas organizations, such as the CIA, is maintained by the NZSIS in support of the EIB.[47]

Directorate of Defence Intelligence (NZDDI)

The Directorate of Defence Intelligence (NZDDI) within the Department of Defence is responsible for the preparation and dissemination of defence intelligence; the coordination of the activities of the small Service intelligence units; and the conduct of the defence intelligence aspects of New Zealand's overseas intelligence connections. The Director of NZDDI is responsible to the Minister of Defence, through the Chief of Defence Staff and the Secretary of the Department of Defence.

The Service intelligence units consist of a small Directorate of Military Intelligence at the New Zealand Army headquarters in Wellington and even smaller intelligence units within the Navy and Air Force. Brigadier Gilbert, the first head of the NZSIS, had previously been Director of Military Intelligence (DMI); and Major Selwyn Jensen had been DMI immediately before he became head of the Auckland regional office of the NZSIS in January 1958.[48]

New Zealand maintains a large number of close and well-established connections with its UKUSA partners in the area of defence intelligence. New Zealand defence intelligence staff meet annually with their counterparts in the US, British, Canadian and Australian defence intelligence agencies to discuss common areas of interest and compare analytical techniques and methodology; at another annual conference the defence intelligence representatives of New Zealand, the United States and Australia produce formal intelligence estimates relating to regional subjects of common concern; and officers of the NZDDI participate in an annual naval intelligence conference attended by defence intelligence staffs from Australia and the United States, with British observers, where particular attention is focused on naval intelligence relating to the Pacific and Indian Ocean areas. Under a 1976 manning agreement, a New Zealand officer occupies an intelligence appointment at the Intelligence Center Pacific in Hawaii and a close relationship exists between the New Zealand Defence Staffs in Washington, London, Ottawa and Canberra with the various relevant defence intelligence agencies in the US, Britain, Canada and Australia.[49]

Government Communications Security Bureau (GCSB)

New Zealand's newest intelligence organization is the Government Communications Security Bureau (GCSB), which was formally established in 1977. The existence of the GCSB was first officially acknowledged in the New Zealand Public Service Official Circular of 16 July 1980, which carried the following notice:

GOVERNMENT COMMUNICATIONS SECURITY BUREAU

This new Bureau has been established within the Ministry of Defence as the national authority for communications and technical security matters. A major function of the Bureau is to establish national communications security standards for application throughout Government. The Bureau also carries out, on request, technical security inspections.
 In carrying out its functions, the Bureau will liaise with all Government departments and agencies which have a communications or security responsibility.[50]

The functions of the GCSB were further adumbrated by the Hon. David Thomson, Leader of the House of Representatives, on 15 August 1980:

Following the recommendations of the Ombudsman's report on the New Zealand Security Intelligence Service, the Government Communications Security Bureau has been set up with the functions of establishing and monitoring national communications and technical security standards. Communications security embraces not only physical encryption of classified messages to prevent their being read by unauthorised persons whilst in transit, but also the physical and radiation security of the cipher and communications equipments used. Technical security calls for the protection of appropriate government offices and installations within New Zealand and missions overseas against eavesdropping. Sophisticated detection equipment and techniques are needed. In carrying out its functions, the Bureau liaises with all government departments and agencies that have a communications or security responsibility; provides advice on questions of communications security, and undertakes technical security inspections when specifically requested to do so by departments or agencies concerned.[51]

However, in addition to being responsible for ensuring the security of official New Zealand communications (the COMSEC mission), the GCSB also operates an intercept facility at Tangimoana which monitors signals emanating from the South and South-west Pacific (the SIGINT mission).

The Tangimoana station was officially opened on 18 August 1982. The antennae at the station consist of a large (150 metre [492-foot] diameter) circularly disposed antenna array (CDAA), two Model 521 Rotatable Log Periodic Arrays (RLPAs), and a Model 540 four-element omni-gain HF/VHF array. About 70 people are employed at the station. The Tangimoana operation is reportedly code-named Project 'Acorn'.[52]

The GCSB facility was originally located at HMNZS Irirangi, near Waiouru, which was established in 1942 as a Naval Wireless Station; although it was only formally given a SIGINT mission in 1977 it is likely that some signals intelligence was received at the station from time to time in the previous 25 years. For example, New Zealand naval authorities intercepted Japanese radio transmissions on 26 and 30 May 1942 concerning Japanese submarine operations close to Sydney, which were passed to the Australian Naval Board by the New Zealand Naval Board.[53]

Until 1977, however, New Zealand relied almost entirely on the Australian Defence Signals Directorate (DSD) for the provision of SIGINT material. Some New Zealanders have been attached to DSD stations (for example, some ten New Zealand officers were attached to the DSD station in Singapore when it was disbanded in 1973);[54] and there are some New Zealanders at the DSD headquarters in Melbourne. DSD assisted with the establishment of the GCSB intercept station, and the DSD headquarters maintains a significant degree of operational control over the facility.

The SIGINT mission of the Tangimoana station is primarily directed towards ocean surveillance. For example, information is collected which assists the policing of New Zealand's Exclusive Economic Zone (EEZ). More generally, the station operates as part of the worldwide HF-DF network of the US Naval Ocean Surveillance Information System (NOSIS). The station concentrates particular attention on signals emanating from the South-west Pacific to South America. (During the Falklands/Malvinas War in April–May 1982, the Irirangi station was able to monitor Argentine naval traffic in the South Pacific, thus providing intelligence which was used by Britain to form a clearer and more comprehensive picture of the Argentine Navy's Order of Battle and its deployments.)

For administrative purposes, the GCSB was established within the New Zealand Ministry of Defence; the Director thus has a responsibility to the Chief of Defence Staff and the Secretary of Defence. However, as part of the New Zealand Intelligence Community, it is subordinate to the New Zealand Intelligence Council and is supervised by the Controlling Officials Sub Committee of the NZIC. The GCSB headquarters, which is located on the 14th floor of the Freyberg Building in Wellington, has a staff of sixteen civilian officers and one service officer, plus about five administrative personnel drawn from the Ministry of Defence. It is financed within the

Defence vote, and its annual cost, including 'salaries, travel costs for inspections, and technical equipment', was officially estimated in 1980 as being 'in the order of $400 000'.[55] It is probably now more than $1 million per year. The current Director of GCSB is Mr C.M. Hansen; the Deputy Director for COMSEC is Mr J. Blackford; and the Executive Officer is Mr B.M. Punnett.[56]

Management structure of the New Zealand security and intelligence community

The political control of the New Zealand intelligence and security community is principally the responsibility of the Prime Minister, although the Directorate of Defence Intelligence is responsible to the Minister of Defence and the GCSB to both the Prime Minister and the Minister of Defence. Section 5(3) of the NZ Security Intelligence Act of 1969 makes the responsibility of the SIS to the Prime Minister quite explicit: 'The Director of Security shall be responsible to the Minister [that is, the Prime Minister] for the efficient and proper working of the Security Intelligence Service.' In addition to the direct line of responsibility from the Director of Security to the Prime Minister, the SIS reports to the Prime Minister through the New Zealand Intelligence Council (NZIC). The EIB also has responsibility to the Prime Minister through the NZIC, while the GCSB is responsible to the Minister of Defence, through the Chief of Defence Staff and the Secretary of Defence, and to the Prime Minister, through both the NZIC and a subsidiary Controlling Officials Sub Committee of the NZIC.

The NZIC is responsible for the general oversight of New Zealand's security and intelligence activities and for ensuring that these are properly coordinated so that the New Zealand Government's requirements in the intelligence field are met effectively. The creation of the NZIC resulted from the same 1974 review which recommended the establishment of the EIB and a greater integration of New Zealand's external intelligence activities.[57] The initial terms of reference of the NZIC, which were approved by Prime Minister W.E. Rowling on 3 February 1975, are set out in full in the Powles report on the NZSIS.[58] The creation of the NZIC was announced by Mr Rowling on 23 April 1975. Mr Rowling stated that the NZIC would be a senior interdepartmental committee responsible to the Prime Minister and under the chairmanship of the Permanent Head of his department, that it would advise the Government on intelligence matters and would ensure that it was provided with timely and useful information on New Zealand's interests overseas, and that it would direct and give policy guidance to the EIB.[59]

Because of the relatively small sizes of the New Zealand security and intelligence organizations, and the fact that they are all headquartered in Wellington, coordination of the activities of these agencies should be relatively easy to achieve. The total number of personnel in the New

Zealand security and intelligence community is only about 230, and the total annual budget for these agencies is unlikely to be more than about $NZ5 million.

However, Ministerial control over the intelligence and security agencies, and cooperation between them, have not always been good. In his report on the NZSIS of 16 July 1976, for example, Sir Guy Powles found that Ministerial responsibility for the NZSIS was inadequate: 'Ministerial responsibility requires a closer relation between the Service and its Minister.'[60] He also found that while the NZSIS must necessarily cooperate with the other organizations concerned with security and intelligence, as well as (because of vetting requests) with almost all other Government departments and agencies, this cooperation was frequently not as close as it should be. For example, Powles reported:

[The work of the NZSIS] overlaps with that of other departments. In the course of my inquiry those most involved have expressed concern that their relationship with the Service is not closer. They consider that they — and they suggest the Service as well — would benefit from closer cooperation. I agree with this view.[61]

Powles recommended that the functions of the NZIC should be widened to include oversight and responsibility for internal security as well as external intelligence activities.[62] As a result, amendments were made to both the NZSIS Act and the NZIC Terms of Reference to involve the Council in the work of the Service.

Section 3(1)(d) of the NZSIS Amendment Act of 16 November 1977 makes the NZSIS responsible to the NZIC in that a function of the NZSIS is now 'to inform the New Zealand Intelligence Council of any new area of potential espionage, sabotage, terrorism, or subversion in respect of which the Director has considered it necessary to institute surveillance'.

The terms of reference of the NZIC were also amended and are as follows:[63]

NEW ZEALAND INTELLIGENCE COUNCIL
TERMS OF REFERENCE

(1) The New Zealand Intelligence Council is to maintain a general supervision of New Zealand's intelligence activities and is to ensure that these are properly co-ordinated so that the New Zealand Government's requirements in the intelligence field are met effectively.
(2) In particular the New Zealand Intelligence Council is:
    (a) to ensure that the New Zealand Government is provided with timely, relevant and useful information and intelligence on developments which are likely to affect New Zealand;
    (b) to advise the New Zealand Government on policy matters relating to intelligence activities;
    (c) to maintain, co-ordinate and generally supervise New Zealand's relations with appropriate intelligence organisations overseas;
    (d) to ensure that there is full co-operation and co-ordination of effort between

80   The Ties That Bind

Government departments and agencies in New Zealand on intelligence matters;
(e) to ensure that the work of the External Intelligence Bureau, the Directorate of Defence Intelligence and the New Zealand Security Intelligence Service is co-ordinated effectively so that there is no unnecessary duplication;
(f) to provide direction and guidance in policy matters to the External Intelligence Bureau and to keep its functions, responsibilities and co-ordinating role under review.
(3) The New Zealand Intelligence Council is to consist of the Permanent Head, Prime Minister's Department, the Secretary of Foreign Affairs, the Secretary of Defence, the Chief of Defence Staff, the Director of Security and the Director of the External Intelligence Bureau (who, in addition, is to be Executive Secretary of the Council). The Council is to meet under the Chairmanship of the Permanent Head, Prime Minister's Department, or, in his absence, a member of the Council designated by the Chairman. The Chairman of the New Zealand Intelligence Council is to report to the Prime Minister on matters concerning the work of the Council.
(4) The Council is to have the authority to form from time to time such working committees and sub-groups as are considered necessary to carry out the functions set out in paragraph 2(a) to (f) above, each committee and sub-group to meet under the chairmanship of an officer designated by the Chairman of the Council after consultation with members of the Council. The Council will be able to consult any person whom it considers could make a useful contribution to its work and in particular, Permanent Heads of other Government departments.

R.D. Muldoon   21 January 1977.
Prime Minister.

The membership of the NZIC was also changed in 1977. The Council is now chaired by the Permanent Head of the Prime Minister's Department, G.C. Hensley, and its membership currently consists of the Secretary of the Department of Foreign Affairs, the Secretary of the Department of Defence, the Chief of Defence Staff, the Director of the EIB, and the Director of the NZSIS. For 'normal and regular working purposes', the members of the Council have designated representatives on their behalf who meet under the chairmanship of an officer of the Ministry of Foreign Affairs nominated, after consultation with the other members of the Council, by the Permanent Head of the Prime Minister's Department. The Director of the EIB serves as the Executive Secretary of the NZIC.[64] In addition, there is now a Controlling Officials Sub Committee of the NZIC which has specific oversight responsibilities with respect to the GCSB.

The management structure of the New Zealand security and intelligence community is shown in Figure 4.1.

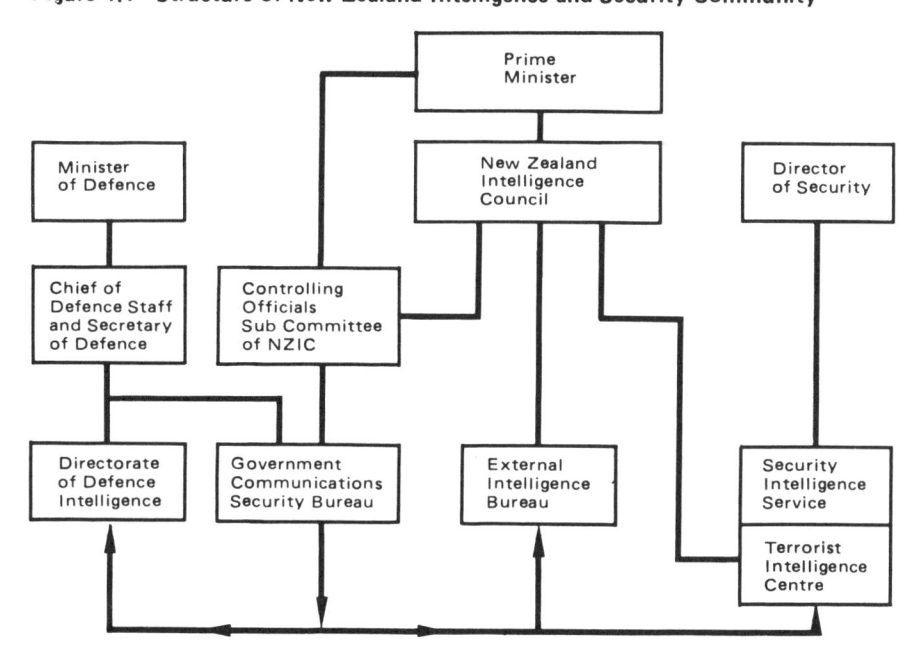

Figure 4.1 Structure of New Zealand Intelligence and Security Community

5

The Canadian security and intelligence community

Canada is generally perceived to be a nation which does not devote a significant amount of resources to security and intelligence activity, especially foreign intelligence activity. The very concept of a Canadian Security and Intelligence Community may thus seem somewhat peculiar. It is probably the case that the vast majority of Canadians, much less non-Canadians, cannot name a single government department with a significant foreign intelligence or internal security function other than the Royal Canadian Mounted Police (RCMP) Security Service. In fact, Canada maintains a wide variety of agencies and bureaus with intelligence and security functions.

This should not be surprising. In addition to its internal security requirements Canada is party to numerous international military and intelligence agreements which give Canada access to significant amounts of strategic intelligence which needs to be protected and analysed. Most prominent among these agreements are the NATO, NORAD and UKUSA agreements.[1] And while Canadian authorities have not previously felt it necessary (with one known exception) to conduct clandestine intelligence collection or covert operations abroad, they do require finished intelligence to aid in the conduct of economic, foreign and defence policy.

Thus, in addition to the Canadian Security Intelligence Service (CSIS) — the successor to the RCMP Security Service — there are several intelligence and security units spread out among various government departments. The major units are the Bureau of Intelligence Analysis and Security and Bureau of Economic Intelligence of the Department of External Affairs, the Office of the Chief, Intelligence and Security and the Communications Security Establishment of the Department of National Defense, and the Police and Security Branch of the Solicitor General's office. Minor units include the Special Investigation Unit of the Department of National Defense, the Director General, Security and Communications Support Services of the Department of Communications, the Security Branch of the Department of Supply and Services and the Enforcement Branch of the Canadian Employment and Immigration Commission.

In addition to the agencies which engage in operational or analytical activities there are several committees which supervise the activities of the Canadian security and intelligence community. As is the case with certain of the British supervisory committees, some of the Canadian committees have a significant role to play in the production of intelligence assessments.

Canadian Security Intelligence Service (CSIS)

Until May 1984, the RCMP Security Service was the agency charged with operational counter-intelligence, counter-subversion and internal security functions. Prior to 1946 these functions were the responsibility of the Intelligence Section of the RCMP Criminal Investigation Branch.[2] In 1946 the revelations of a Soviet defector, Igor Gouzenko, concerning the extent of Soviet intelligence activity in Canada led to the creation of a separate Special Branch to handle such functions. In 1956 the Special Branch was renamed the Directorate of Security and Intelligence, or 'I' Directorate.[3]

As a result of the report of the Mackenzie Commission in 1969, the Directorate was given enhanced status within the RCMP and renamed the Security Service.[4] In 1976 it was given 'National Division' status resulting in more administrative responsibilities being delegated to the Director-General of the Security Service and Security Service headquarters in Ottawa rather than to the heads of the RCMP's geographic divisions. This independence was somewhat curtailed in recent years under RCMP Commissioner Robert Simmonds.[5]

The activities of the Security Service were governed by a directive entitled 'The Role, Tasks and Methods of the RCMP Security Service', issued by the Cabinet on 27 March 1975. The directive authorized the Service to maintain internal security, name, discover, monitor, discourage, prevent and thwart the activities of certain individuals or certain groups in Canada and carry out investigations about them when there are 'reasonable or likely' grounds to believe that they are carrying out or intend to carry out:

(1) spying or sabotage action
(2) activities aiming at gathering information on Canada for the benefit of a foreign power
(3) activities aiming at a change of government in Canada or elsewhere through the use of force, violence or any other criminal action
(4) activities undertaken by a foreign power and related to a real or possible attack against Canada or hostile actions against Canada
(5) activities of a foreign or national group trying to perpetrate acts of terrorism in Canada or directed against Canada
(6) the use or encouragement of the use of force or violence or any other criminal means

(7) the provocation or exploitation of civil disturbances in order to take part in any of the above mentioned activities.[6]

The Security Service was headed by a Director-General (DGSS), the last of whom was J.B. Giroux, who held the rank of Deputy Commissioner, RCMP. Directly responsible to the Director-General were the Audit Unit and the Secretariat as well as three Deputy Directors-General for Operations Service, Operations, and Administration and Personnel.[7]

Subordinate to the Deputy Director-General, Operations Service were five units — E Ops, F Ops, I Ops, J Ops and Automated Information Services. E Ops had responsibility for transcribing wiretapped and bugged conversations for investigators and analysts to study. A special section of E Ops, E Special, was responsible for conducting break-ins to obtain information. F Ops was a highly centralized section responsible for maintaining the files on individuals and groups. A copy of every Security Service report was dispatched to this central storage location where it was indexed, cross-referenced and filed.

I Ops, also known as the Watcher Service, was responsible for following the movements and observing the actions of targeted individuals. J Section planted bugs (but did not engage in wiretapping, which was done by the phone company). In many instances it accompanied E Special members on break-ins.

Under the Deputy Director-General, Operations were five lettered sections and an Intelligence Coordination Unit. A Ops was responsible for security screening — for checking into the backgrounds of individuals who would have access to classified information. The section sought to determine whether the individual is who he or she claimed to be (that is, not an 'illegal' posing as someone who had actually died years earlier) and whether anything in his/her background precluded access to official secrets. Of special concern were 'character weaknesses' (use of drugs, excessive use of liquor, large debts, homosexuality) that might make the individual a target for blackmail, or evidence of extremist political associations and/or disloyalty to the existing political structure.

B Ops was responsible for counter-espionage. Its responsibilities included scrutinizing foreign embassies in Canada, checking the names of immigrants coming to Canada for a possible hostile intelligence service connection and, on occasion, investigating individuals failing A Section screening. B Ops was divided, at the provincial level, into regional desks — including a Russian Desk, Cuban Desk, Czech Desk, Satellite Desk and other desks depending on the particular situation in a given locality.

D Ops handled counter-subversion and was responsible for 'individuals and organizations of subversive interest'. Such individuals and organizations included Maoists, Trotskyites, Quebec separatists, communists and their respective organizations. H Ops was established in 1969 and was responsible for counter-espionage against the People's Republic of China (PRC). L Ops was the informers or 'human source development' section. It was the repository for information on all Security Service informers throughout Canada. Once an informer was recruited, L Ops evaluated the information and decided on the amount of payment as well as when to pay bonuses and what form payment should take.

The Deputy Director-General for Administration and Personnel supervised five sections: Internal Security, Administration, Financial Supply and Services, Staffing and Personnel and Training and Management.

Two RCMP directorates, not under Security Service control, also perform security-related activities — the 'P' (Protective Policing) Directorate and the Foreign Service Directorate. 'P' Directorate, created in 1973, performs counter-technical intrusion activities (which were formerly a Security Service responsibility), airport policing, security engineering, VIP protection and advises the government on physical security questions. The Foreign Service Directorate coordinates all RCMP foreign liaison activity, including the

Figure 5.1 Organization of the RCMP Security Service, 1978

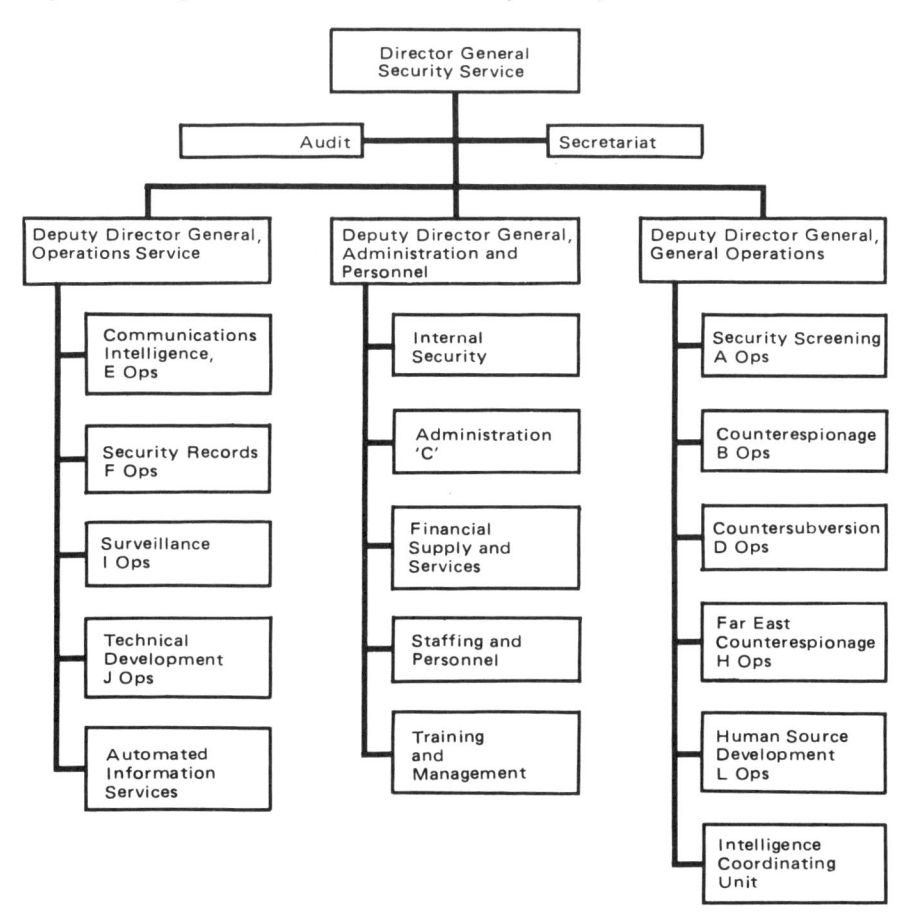

activity of the 28 RCMP liaison officers stationed abroad.[8] The FSD was formed in 1979 and combined Security Service and Criminal Intelligence Branch liaison components under a single commanding officer. This officer reports to the RCMP Commissioner through a committee of senior officials whose membership includes the Director-General Security Service (DGSS). The organization of the Security Service is shown as Figure 5.1.[9]

The idea of a separate civilian (as opposed to RCMP controlled) Security Service had been suggested by the 1969 Mackenzie Commission, but was not adopted by the government of the time, then headed by Prime Minister Trudeau. It was felt by the Mackenzie Commission that RCMP recruitment, training and promotion procedure resulted in a Security Service dominated, in terms of operational decision-making and action, by those who had spent earlier years in conventional police work and gone through training at the RCMP academy in Regina.

Given the composition of RCMP recruits and a policy of recruitment for only the lowest levels of RCMP regular members, it was considered to be unlikely that Security Service members charged with operational duties would have more than a high school education or would be representative of more than a narrow segment of the community. It was suggested that the Security Service needed personnel with broader backgrounds, including university backgrounds, to properly deal with the problems confronting it.

In August 1981, in response to the recommendation of the MacDonald Commission's report on RCMP activities, the Solicitor-General announced that the Security Service would be detached from the RCMP and would become the civilian Canadian Security Intelligence Service.[10] Frederick E. Gibson, the Assistant Deputy Minister of Justice, was named to head the Service but he was replaced by Ted D'Arcy Finn as head of the Security Intelligence Transitional Group and future head of the CSIS.[11] The transitional period extended considerably beyond the intended time. In November 1982 the enabling legislation along with a package of other measures — such as amendments to existing laws to permit mail interception in national security cases — had been before a Cabinet committee for several months.[12]

In May 1983 the Liberal Government introduced Bill C-157 authorizing the establishment of a Canadian Security Intelligence Service (CSIS). The Bill immediately ran into a prolonged storm of criticism over provisions which were considered by many to give the CSIS far too much discretion in the investigation of domestic subversion.

Thus, the Bill would have given the CSIS the authority to seek judicial warrants to conduct intensive surveillance (that is, buggings, wiretaps, break-ins, mail openings) with respect to 'activities within ... Canada directed toward or in support of ... acts of violence ... for the purpose of achieving a political objective within Canada or a foreign state'.[13] Likewise, 'activities ... intended ultimately to lead to the destruction or overthrow of the constitutionally established system of government in Canada' were also a justification for intrusive surveillance.[14]

The first provision could have been used to justify surveillance of groups supporting resistance movements abroad — whether Afghani or Salvadoran. The 'intended ultimately' portion of the second provision could be useful as a pretext for investigating a wide range of non-violent groups whose activities the CSIS might foresee as leading to violence.

In addition to the Canadian Civil Liberties Association, strenuous objections were raised by the Conservative Party and the Provincial attorney-generals. The later group denounced C-157 as a 'massive threat to the rights and freedoms of all Canadians'.[15] The Special Senate Committee on the CSIS recommended a dozen major amendments to the bill.[16] As a result a modified version of the Bill, designated C-9, was subsequently submitted. Despite strong opposition from some groups, C-9 became law in May 1984, thus effecting the creation of the CSIS.

In addition to its composition the CSIS is likely to differ from the RCMP Security Service in several other ways. Unlike the Security Service, the CSIS will not have law enforcement powers, an absence recommended by both the Mackenzie and MacDonald Commissions. Rather, in matters of arrest and seizure, it will cooperate with a special group within the RCMP and with other forces when necessary.[17]

Further, the CSIS will apparently have permission to function abroad to collect information through its own sources for foreign intelligence purposes.[18] While the RCMP did, on occasion, operate abroad it was on an *ad hoc* basis and primarily in pursuit of internal security cases rather than foreign information. A recent case has come to light, however, in which Security Service agents travelled to Basel, Switzerland and New York City in an attempt to recruit a middle-level Soviet trade representative, Anatoly Maximov. These meetings occurred shortly after Prime Minister Trudeau had publicly vowed that the force was engaged in no clandestine operations outside of Canada.[19] The CSIS will not, according to Canadian officials, engage in covert operations abroad that seek to influence or alter the politics of another nation.[20]

Within Canada, the CSIS, can conduct espionage (for example, by means of telephone taps or other forms of electronic surveillance) in order to obtain economic or national security intelligence. Targets could include foreign diplomats, trade officials, foreign business enterprises and foreign visitors.[21]

Another expected difference is that an analytical capability will be established within the CSIS.[22] Whether this will be in relation to domestic security matters only or to both domestic security and foreign intelligence matters is not clear. Presently, intelligence analysis units exist within the Solicitor-General's office as well as the Departments of External Affairs and National Defense.

Despite these probable differences it is likely that, at least initially, the CSIS will bear a strong resemblance to the present Security Service, retaining most of its 2000 members, as well as its functions and organizational structure.

Communications Security Establishment (CSE)

The Communications Security Establishment has a relationship to the Department of National Defense similar to the relationship of the US National Security Agency with the US Department of Defense — as a 'separately organized establishment under general management and direction of the Department of National Defense'.[23]

One function of the CSE is to manage and direct a communications security (COMSEC) program for the entire government. Its second function is to collect communications intelligence (COMINT) and electronic intelligence (ELINT). In addition to its signals intelligence responsibilities under the UKUSA Agreement, the CSE intercepts electronic communications between foreign embassies in Ottawa and their capitals.[24] It is also highly likely that the CSE is heavily involved in anti-submarine warfare and ocean surveillance activities.[25]

The CSE is the successor to several previous Canadian communications security/signals intelligence agencies. In 1941 the Examination Unit of the National Research Council was established to intercept and decode messages to and from the Vichy delegation in Ottawa. Vichy was suspected of propaganda activities in Quebec and interception of the mission's messages appeared to be the best means of determining the nature and extent of these activities.[26] The Unit was established with the help of the American cryptographer Herbert O. Yardley, who was subsequently dismissed — reportedly at the insistence of Winston Churchill.[27]

Subsequently, the Examination Unit added the interception and decoding of the messages to and from German agents in South America to its responsibilities along with ocean surveillance/direction-finding functions. As of 11 January 1942 there were three authorized intercept and D-F stations — one in Ottawa (which was operational), another at Amherst, Nova Scotia (with intercept capability but D-F not yet operational) and a third at West Point Barracks, Victoria (which became operational about April 1942). A fourth station at Riske Creek, British Columbia was authorized in March 1944. According to F.H. Hinsley et al.,

Canadian ... intercept stations and DF organization ... made an indispensable contribution to the Allied north Atlantic Sigint network since the early days of the war. In May 1943, as well as receiving the intelligence summaries issued by Whitehall to the naval commands at home and overseas, the Tracking Room in Ottawa began to receive a full series of Enigma decrypts and from that it carried on a completely free exchange of ideas by direct signal link with the Tracking Room in OIC.[28]

In the aftermath of the war the Examination Unit was saved from probable extinction by the Gouzenko revelations concerning Soviet espionage. In December 1945 it was decided at a meeting of officials from the Department of External Affairs, the Army and the NRC to keep the Unit in operation. By March 1946 plans had been prepared for an establishment of 500 servicemen at 100 high-speed monitoring positions. The initial target was the wireless traffic of the Soviet Embassy, but operations were soon expanded to include radio communications in the northern USSR.[29]

By 1947 at the very latest, the output of the Canadian SIGINT stations had been integrated into the UKUSA network. As Lester B. Pearson, the Under-Secretary of State for External Affairs wrote that year, '[the purpose] of these stations is to intercept traffic upon which the cryptographers here, in London and in Washington work'. The cost at that time was Can$3 million per year, which was hidden in the budget of the Defense Research Board.[30]

Subsequently, the unit was renamed the Communications Branch, National Research Council (CBNRC). On 1 April 1975 the CBNRC was transferred to the Department of National Defense and renamed the Communications Security Establishment.[31] At this time it had approximately 250 to 300 civilian employees and a budget of Can$5 million per year.[32]

Since 1975, the CSE has expanded to some 583 civilian employees.[33] It is presently headed by P.R. Hunt who has three major units subordinate to him — Production, Security, and Administration, each headed by a Director-General.[34] Under the Director-General Administration is a Director, Administration and Finance as well as a Director, Personnel.[35]

Chief, Intelligence and Security

The Chief, Intelligence and Security is responsible to the Vice-Chief of the Defense Staff for defence intelligence production, the conduct of foreign liaison, and military security.

Defence intelligence and liaison functions are performed by three units. These units are supervised by the Director, Defense Intelligence, Director, Foreign Liaison and Director, Scientific and Technical Intelligence.[36] The Director, Defense Intelligence publishes a quarterly journal, the *Canadian Intelligence Quarterly*, at the Secret level.

The Director of Security is responsible for security standards and procedures for the protection of information, the physical security of materials and units, and security clearance of personnel and the supervision of security staffs. Subordinate to the Director of Security are units for Public Operations and Personnel Security.[37]

Bureau of Intelligence Analysis and Security (BIAS)

The Bureau of Intelligence Analysis and Security (BIAS) is one of two intelligence units within the Department of External Affairs and is headed by an Assistant Under Secretary. BIAS is divided into three main units — an Operations Centre, an Intelligence Analysis Division and a Security Division.[38]

The Intelligence Analysis Division has two main functions. One is liaison

90 *The Ties That Bind*

with other departments and governments for the exchange and dissemination of foreign intelligence. Its second function is not completely clear. According to one official source, the division produces current and long-term intelligence assessments.[39] Another official source suggests that it does not prepare assessments but maintains a compendium of information on various areas of the world (based on a variety of information sources) focusing on political, economic and social trends, with some of the information it assembles being distributed to interested government departments (including the RCMP) and to the Intelligence Advisory Committee.[40]

The Security Division is responsible for all matters relating to the security and safety of the department's personnel, property and documents — both in Ottawa and abroad.[41] These functions are the responsibility of the Division's Personnel Security and Physical Security Sections.[42] The National Security Section is responsible for evaluating the activities of foreign diplomats in Canada who are suspected of engaging in 'unacceptable' intelligence activities. It has worked in close liaison with the Security Service — jointly reviewing information pertaining to any expulsion decision. The section is also responsible for granting visas to foreign diplomats.[43]

Directly subordinate to the head of BIAS is the Coordinator of Emergency Preparedness, who is responsible for preparing plans to deal with terrorist attacks on Canadian missions or citizens abroad.[44]

Bureau of Economic Intelligence

The Bureau of Economic Intelligence, previously known as the Joint Intelligence Bureau, is the second intelligence unit within the Department of External Affairs.[45] The Bureau is responsible for the collation, storage and reporting of economic intelligence. It prepares assessments relevant to departments and agencies such as Finance, Industry, Trade and Commerce, Energy, Mines and Resources and the Bank of Canada.[46]

In the past it has also been a requester and consumer of domestic intelligence. For example, in October 1960, as a result of a request from the Joint Intelligence Bureau, the RCMP headquarters directed regional divisions to report on industrial disputes likely to involve a slow-down of production or a strike. The divisions were told that the major concern was 'with Communist-inspired disputes which could have an adverse effect on the Canadian economy'.[47]

In addition to a Current Intelligence Staff, which is directly subordinate to the Assistant Under Secretary who heads the Bureau, are three area divisions — the Africa, Middle East and Western Hemisphere Division, the Asia Division and the Europe Division.[48] Priorities for the Bureau are established by the Economic Intelligence Subcommittee of the Intelligence Advisory Committee.

Police and Security Branch

The Police and Security Branch, in the Office of the Solicitor-General, is somewhere between being a member of the management structure and being an analytical unit. The branch was created in 1971 as the Security Planning and Research Group (SPARG) of the office of the Solicitor-General.[49] In announcing its formation, the Solicitor-General Jean Pierre Goyer stated that its functions would be:

(1) to study the nature, origin and causes of subversive and revolutionary action, its objectives and techniques, as well as the measures necessary to protect Canadians from internal threats;
(2) to compile and analyze information collected on subversive and revolutionary groups and their activities, to estimate the nature and scope of internal threat to Canadians and to plan for measures to counter these threats; and
(3) to advise me on these matters.[50]

SPARG was to have only research, analysis and planning functions — with no field security or operational intelligence duties, which some feared to be among its intended functions.[51] Subsequently, SPARG added law enforcement and police matters to its security functions and became, in December 1972, the Police and Security Planning and Analysis Group. In 1974 it was retitled the Police and Security Planning and Analysis Branch and subsequently the Police and Security Branch.[52]

The initial intention to have SPARG serve as an assessor of RCMP security intelligence reports and perform long-term research was never implemented because of the difficulty of obtaining the required information from the RCMP. By 1974 the Branch had assumed prime responsibility for research and development in relation to the Government's capacity to respond to civil emergencies and natural disasters.[53]

As presently constituted the Police and Security Branch consists of three sections — Security Information Analysis and Contingency Planning, Police and Law Enforcement, and Security Policy.[54] It has approximately twenty analysts and has been headed since 1979 by Michael Shoemaker.[55]

Presently the Branch is responsible for analysing and proposing measures in response to:

(i) threats to the internal security of Canada from organizations, groups and individuals either in Canada or elsewhere;
(ii) policy formulation for the protection of personnel, property and equipment in the federal government, including the security of government information;
(iii) the role of the federal government in law enforcement in Canada;
(iv) contingency planning for Ministry crisis handling in emergency situations.[56]

Implementation of this responsibility has included projects involving:

(1) development of contingency planning procedures in the event of internal security crises such as riots, the hijacking of aircraft, kidnapping and the holding of hostages;
(2) studies to assess Canada's vulnerability to possible acts by international terrorist organizations;
(3) studies on establishing national police research and training capabilities;

(4) formulation of government policy and recommendations on the physical security of information and property; and
(5) studies on the practical implementation of legislation, such as the Protection of Privacy Act.[57]

Other units

The Special Investigation Unit of the Department of National Defense performs functions similar to the US Defense Investigative Service — that is, it conducts clearance investigations as well as investigations concerning espionage, subversion, sabotage and arson within the armed forces.[58]

The Security Branch of the Department of Supply and Services has an Industrial and Protective Programs Division subdivided into an Industrial Security Requirements Section and Protective Services Section.[59] The Industrial Security Section is responsible for the protection of classified information in the hands of Canadian companies undertaking work on behalf of the Canadian or other governments. The Section is subdivided into a number of functional areas: information security, personnel security clearance, electronic data processing security, training and field and industrial security officers.[60] The Protective Services Section is concerned with hardware security and closed circuit television systems in new buildings.[61]

The Intelligence Division of the Enforcement Branch of the Canada Employment and Immigration Commission is concerned chiefly with analysing and reporting on the long-term trends in illegal immigration and in collecting and analysing information on immigrants active in organized crime.[62] The Security Review and Special Categories Division examines applicants for entry to Canada from the point of view of security considerations.[63] In a recent case, a deportation order was issued against Salvadoran journalist Victor Regalado on the basis of intelligence reporting which, according to the Immigration Minister, indicated Regalado would work to overthrow 'a government' while in Canada.[64]

Organizations and individuals concerned with communications security, in addition to CSE, are the Director-General, Security and Communications Support Services of the Department of Communications, the Communications Security Branch of the Telecommunications and EDP Directorate of the office of the Solicitor-General, and the Director, Communications Security under the Director-General, Communications and Electronic Operations in the Department of National Defense.[65]

Management structure

Control and supervision of the Canadian security and intelligence community is exercised at both the ministerial and deputy ministerial level. The most senior supervisory body is the Cabinet Committee on Security and Intelligence, formed in 1963, and chaired by the Prime Minister.[66]

It is likely that the Cabinet Committee exercises only general guidance, dealing extensively only with the most sensitive matters, especially with regard to security policy. This would be consistent with former Prime Minister Trudeau's view that:

the politicians who happen to form the government should be kept in ignorance of the day-to-day operations of the police force and even of security ... It is a matter of stating, as a principle, that the particular minister of the day should not have a right to know what the police are doing constantly in their investigative practices, in what they are looking at and what they are looking for, and in the way they are doing it.[67]

Staff assistance to the Prime Minister is provided by the Privy Council Secretariat for Security and Intelligence. The Secretariat is headed by the Assistant Secretary to the Cabinet for Security and Intelligence.[68] In addition to the Assistant Secretary there were, in 1980, seven officers assigned to the Secretariat. On the security side were a security policy adviser and two officers who are responsible for personnel and physical security within the Privy Council office. In addition there were four intelligence officers seconded from the Departments of External Affairs and National Defense and the RCMP. These officers, under the direction of the Intelligence Advisory Committee, perform staff work involved in collating intelligence reports and participate in working groups that prepare long-term intelligence assessments.[69]

Until 1972, the vehicles for deputy ministerial control of the intelligence community were the Security Panel and the Intelligence Policy Committee. The Security Panel was formed under the auspices of the Privy Council in 1946 and was chaired by the Secretary to the Cabinet. It was established as a result of proposal by Norman Robertson, the Under Secretary of the Department of External Affairs, to create a committee bringing together the representatives of External Affairs, the RCMP, the directors of the intelligence agencies of the armed services and the Director-General of Defense Research for the purpose of directing intelligence and security activities. Robertson's proposal was considered preferable to one put forward by the army's Chief of Staff for a more elaborate intelligence and security organization.[70]

The function of the Security Panel was to formulate security policy, including the security screening process, for approval by the Cabinet. Initial membership included the directors of the military intelligence services and representatives from the Department of External Affairs and the RCMP. Membership was later expanded to include the Departments of Manpower, Immigration, Supply and Services, the Solicitor-General's Office and the Public Service Commission. The military was eventually represented by the Deputy Minister for National Defense and Chief of the Defense Staff. After 1953 all representatives on the Security Panel were of deputy minister rank or its equivalent.[71]

In 1960 the Intelligence Policy Committee (IPC) was formed to determine general intelligence policy. Until 1963 the IPC reported to the Defense Committee of the Cabinet (while Security Panel proposals went to the full

Cabinet).[72] With the formation of the Cabinet Committee on Security and Intelligence both the IPC and the Security Panel were subordinated to that body.

In 1972 the Security Panel and the IPC were merged to form the Interdepartmental Committee on Security and Intelligence, which is chaired by the Secretary of the Cabinet/Clerk of the Privy Council.[73] The primary motivation for the merger was a desire to coordinate the external intelligence function with counter-terrorist activities.[74]

Under the Interdepartmental Committee are two subcommittees — the Security Advisory Committee (SAC) and the Intelligence Advisory Committee (IAC). Membership in the SAC includes the Head, Police and Security Branch, as Chairman, the Director-General, CSIS as Vice-Chairman and the heads of the intelligence units in the External Affairs, National Defense, Supply and Service Departments and the Canada Employment and Immigration Commission. Also included is the Assistant Secretary to the Cabinet for Security and Intelligence.[75] Support staff is provided by the Police and Security Branch.

The SAC has two functions. One is to review the adequacy of policies concerning personnel and physical security in government departments. To aid it in this task the SAC has a network of sub-committees dealing with specific substantive areas — communications and computer security, protection of nuclear materials and crisis management.[76] Its second function is to assess the Canadian situation in weekly reports to the Interdepartmental and Cabinet Security and Intelligence Committees. These reports are based largely on information provided by the Security Service.[77]

The Intelligence Advisory Committee is responsible for external intelligence matters. It collates and disseminates external intelligence weekly as well as preparing periodic assessments on particular subjects. Its Review and Priorities Group has primary responsibility for developing annual intelligence priorities.[78] The IAC is chaired by the Deputy Under Secretary of State (Security and Intelligence) of the Department of External Affairs and consists of the DGSS as well as the heads of the other units concerned with external intelligence.[79]

Supervision of the Communications Security Establishment is the responsibility of a committee of deputy ministers. This committee is in turn overseen by the Clerk of the Privy Council and reports to the Cabinet Committee on Security and Intelligence.[80]

The management structure of the Canadian security and intelligence community is shown in Figure 5.2.

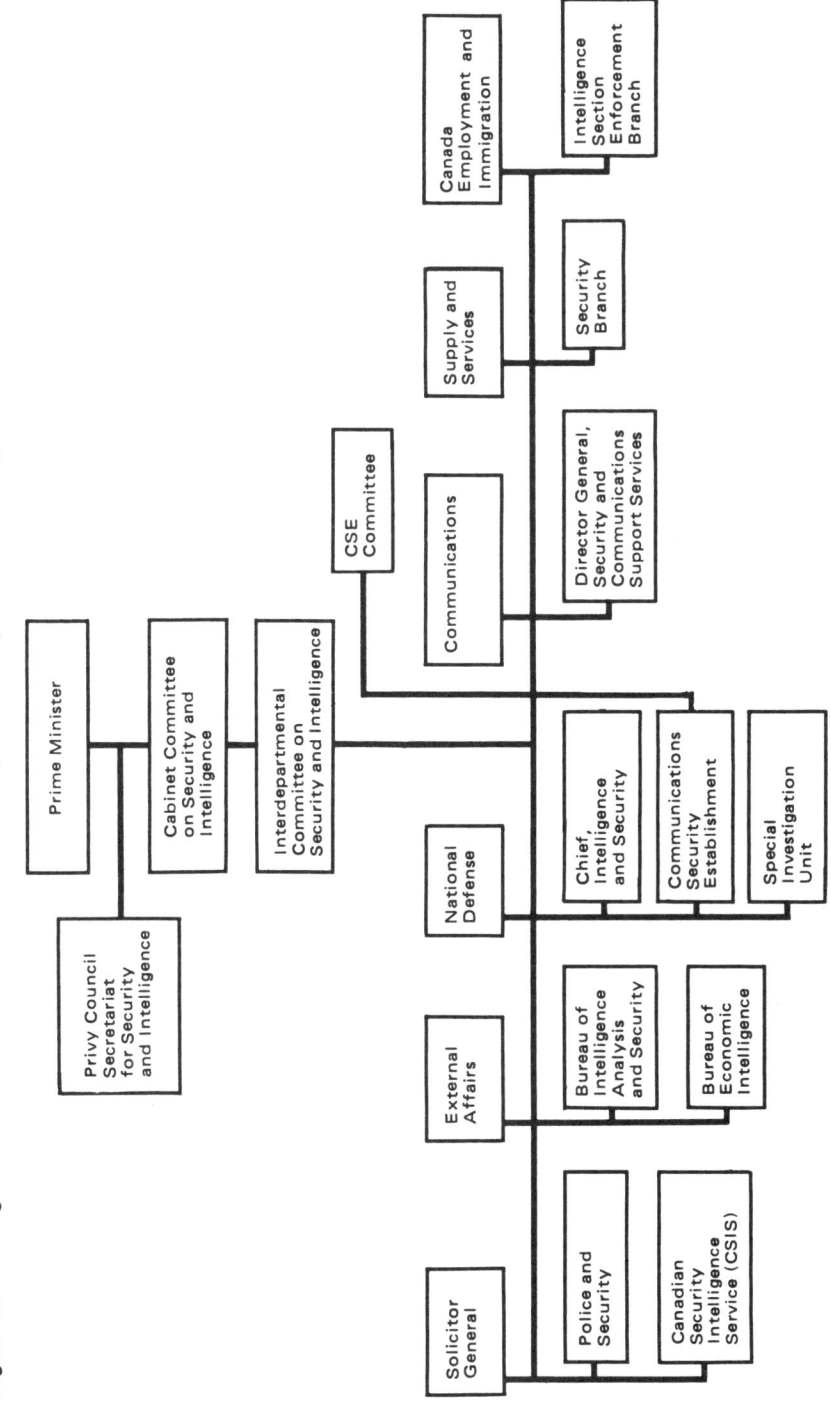

Figure 5.2 Management Structure of the Canadian Security and Intelligence Community

6

The United States security and intelligence community

The activities of the United States intelligence and security services are similar to the activities of the intelligence and security services of many other nations: namely, intelligence collection and analysis, covert action and counter-intelligence (offensive and defensive). However, the extent of these activities and the methods employed, especially with respect to technical intelligence collection, far surpasses those of every other nation except perhaps the Soviet Union.

The United States collects information via reconnaissance satellites, aircraft, ships, signals intelligence intercept stations, radars and underseas surveillance as well as via the traditional overt and clandestine human sources. The total cost of these activities is in excess of US$15 billion per year.

Given this wide range of activity it is not surprising that a plethora of organizations are involved in intelligence and security activities. The exact number of members of the US intelligence and security community is somewhat ambiguous or subjective. Some organizations are clearly members — the Central Intelligence Agency (CIA), the State Department's Bureau of Intelligence and Research and the Justice Department's Federal Bureau of Investigation (FBI). Within the Defense Department are two national level intelligence organizations — the National Reconnaissance Office (NRO) and National Security Agency (NSA) — and several departmental level organizations, including the Defense Intelligence Agency (DIA).

In addition, each of the major military services (Army, Navy, Air Force) has an intelligence community of its own, with several subordinate but distinct organizations reporting to an Assistant Chief of Staff for Intelligence. Further, there are several agencies or offices that constitute marginal members of the intelligence and security community — three such examples are the Treasury Department's Office of Intelligence Support; the

Drug Enforcement Administration's Office of Intelligence; and the Defense Intelligence Division of the Energy Department's Office of the Assistant Secretary for International Affairs.

As might be expected, given the large number of agencies and different branches of the Executive involved in intelligence activities, the management structure for the US intelligence and security community is quite complex. After examining both the fully fledged and marginal members of the community we will focus on that management structure.

National Reconnaissance Office (NRO)

The National Reconnaissance Office manages satellite reconnaissance programs for the entire US intelligence community. These programs involve the collection of photographic and signals intelligence via such satellite reconnaissance systems as the Air Force's KH-8 'close look' and KH-9 'Big Bird' photographic reconnaissance satellites, the CIA's KH-11 photographic reconnaissance and RHYOLITE signals intelligence satellites and the Navy Space Project's WHITE CLOUD ELINT/ocean surveillance satellites.[1]

The NRO has a broad range of functions. It has participated in various policy committees — such as the NSAM 156 Committee established by President Kennedy in 1962 to review the political aspects of US policy on satellite reconnaissance.[2] It has also played a significant role in drawing a curtain of secrecy around the US reconnaissance program. Thus, in a memorandum to President Kennedy concerning the SAMOS II photographic reconnaissance satellite, the Assistant Secretary of Defense for Public Affairs, Arthur Sylvester noted that the material to be made available to newsmen concerning the launch and the program 'represents a severe reduction from what had previously been issued'. Sylvester further stated that 'Dr Charyk [Director of NRO] has reviewed those changes and is satisfied that they meet all his security requirements and those of his SAMOS Project Director, Brigadier-General Greer'.[3]

The NRO is also responsible for the routine operation of the satellites including manoeuvres such as turning them on and off and facing them toward or away from the sun.[4] More importantly, the NRO prepares a reconnaissance schedule which details the assignment of reconnaissance systems to targets.[5] The schedule is several inches thick and filled with hundreds of pages of highly technical data and maps.

While the NRO has existed under the 'cover' of the Under Secretary of the Air Force and the Office of Space Systems, it is, as its name indicates, a national level organization. And, in fact, it is directly supervised by one of two National Executive Committees chaired by the Director of Central Intelligence — the National Reconnaissance Executive Committee.[6]

The NRO came into existence on 25 August 1960 after several months of debate within and among the White House, Department of Defense, Air Force and CIA concerning the nature and duties of such an organization. Its creation was a response to various problems plaguing the early missile and satellite programs.[7] The national-level character of the organization was a major point of importance to those involved in its formation. Thus, George Kistiakowsky, President Eisenhower's Special Assistant for Science and Technology, noted that it was important 'that the organization have a clear line of authority and that on the top level direction be of a national character, including OSD and CIA and not the Air Force alone'.[8] One reason why such a framework was desired was to be certain that the utilization of the photographic 'take' not be left solely in the hands of the Air Force.[9]

The existence of an office known as the National Reconnaissance Office was kept secret from the US public and most of the rest of the government for thirteen years, until 1973. An obscure reference to its creation but not its name, appeared in the 12 September 1960 issue of *Aviation Week*. In that issue it was noted that 'Development of SAMOS is being moved directly under the Secretary of the Air Force ... Brig. Gen. Richard B. Curtin will lead SAMOS development in the new office'.[10]

The first revelation of the NRO's existence came in 1973 as the result of an error made in editing a Senate Committee report. The name National Reconnaissance Office was not deleted from a list of intelligence agencies that the Senate Committee recommended should make their budgets public.[11] The slip led to an article in the *Washington Post* a few months later in which the NRO's functions, budget and 'cover' were discussed.[12] The following year the CIA lost in its attempt to have a similar discussion deleted from Marchetti and Mark's *The CIA and the Cult of Intelligence*.

The NRO is still considered a secret organization and references to it in the Department of Defense *Annual Report* and Executive Orders are merely to offices charged with 'the collection of specialized foreign intelligence through reconnaissance programs'. The closest an Executive Branch document has come to admitting the existence of the NRO was the report of the Murphy Commission, which referred to 'A semi-autonomous office within the Defense Department with the largest budget of any intelligence agency [that] operates overhead reconnaissance programs for the entire intelligence community'.[13]

The headquarters of the NRO is located at 4C−956 in the Pentagon, which is officially the Office of Space Systems and subordinate to the Deputy Under Secretary of the Air Force for Space Systems.[14] Both the Director, Office of Space Systems, and the Deputy Under Secretary are traditionally high ranking officials of the NRO. The Director, traditionally, is the Under Secretary of the Air Force. Thus, the NRO's first Director, Joseph Charyk, held the position at the same time as he was Under Secretary of the Air Force as did Hans Mark in the Carter Administration. The only apparent exception to this rule was the appointment of Robert J. Hermann as successor to Hans Mark as Director, NRO when Hermann was Assistant Secretary of the Air Force for Research, Development and Logistics. This break in tradition was apparently due to the lack of knowledge of Antonia Chayes, Mark's successor as Under Secretary, with respect to reconnaissance satellites.[15] The break with tradition was only temporary as Under Secretary of the Air Force Edward C. Aldridge became Director, NRO with the advent of the Reagan Administration.

As noted above the NRO is responsible for managing the entire satellite reconnaissance effort. At the same time, it is known that the CIA's Directorate of Science and Technology is heavily involved in reconnaissance satellite development through its Office of Development and Engineering and its Office of SIGINT Operations.[16] Specifically, it is these offices which appear to have been responsible for the development of the KH-11 and RHYOLITE satellites.[17] Likewise, development of Navy satellites, including the WHITE CLOUD ocean surveillance satellite, is the responsibility of the Navy Space Project of the Naval Electronics Systems Command (NAVALEX). The NSA's Office of Microwave Space and Mobile Systems is also involved in the development of reconnaissance satellites. These offices are likely to have significant links with the NRO.

Another office that is a subordinate unit of the NRO is the Air Force Special Projects Office, located at the Space Division in El Segundo, California. Thus, in discussing the appointment of a new Special Projects Director to head that office, *Aviation Week and Space Technology* noted that:

the special projects group has the responsibility for gathering satellite strategic reconnaissance data for use by national intelligence organizations. It directs the design, development and procurement of photographic and other types of military reconnaissance satellites and their subsystems, operating under an annual budget of $250 to $350 million. The group is resident ... at the Air Force's [Space Division] but reports directly to the Secretary of the Air Force.[18]

Location of an NRO component in El Segundo allows direct and frequent contacts with the corporations that develop and build reconnaissance satellites — TRW, Hughes and Lockheed — as well as with the Aerospace Corporation. (TRW, Hughes and Aerospace are all only a matter of blocks from the Space Division.) Aerospace, via its Project WESTWING, provides advice to the NRO on satellite proposals.[19]

The NRO's present budget appears to be in the range US$2–$2.5 billion.[20] The number of people employed by the NRO is not known.

National Security Agency (NSA)/Central Security Service (CSS)

After the NRO, the National Security Agency (NSA) is the most secret (and secretive) member of the US intelligence and security community. The predecessor of the NSA, the Armed Forces Security Agency (AFSA), was established within the Department of Defense in 1949.[21] The AFSA took over the strategic communications–intelligence functions and coordination responsibilities of cryptographic units of the military services, leaving them with the responsibility for tactical signals intelligence; the cryptographic units also provided manpower for AFSA-directed strategic collection activities.

On 24 October 1952 President Truman, in a Top Secret seven-page memorandum to the Secretary of State and Secretary of Defense, entitled 'Communications Intelligence Activities', abolished the AFSA and transferred its personnel to a newly created National Security Agency.[22] The Truman memorandum had its origins in a memo sent by the Director of Central Intelligence, Walter Bedell Smith, to National Security Council Executive Secretary James B. Lay on 10 December 1951 stating that 'control over, and coordination of, the collection and processing of communications intelligence have proved ineffective ...' and recommending a survey of communications intelligence activities.[23] This proposal was approved on 13 December 1951 and a report completed by 13 June 1952.[24]

As the change in the agency's title indicated, the new agency's role was to extend beyond the armed forces. Thus, NSA is considered to be 'within the [Department of Defense]' but not part of DOD.[25]

The NSA Headquarters, Fort George C. Meade, Maryland, USA.

The (still classified) charter for the National Security Agency, National Security Council Intelligence Directive No. 6, entitled 'Communications and Electronics Intelligence', was not issued until 15 September 1958.[26] In its revised form — NSCID No. 6 of 17 February 1972, entitled 'Signals Intelligence' — it directs the NSA to produce intelligence 'in accordance with objectives, requirements and priorities established by the Director of Central Intelligence and the United States Intelligence Board'.[27] The Directive also authorizes the Director, NSA 'to issue direct to any operating elements engaged in SIGINT operations such instructions and assignments as are required. All instructions issued by the Director under the authority provided in this paragraph shall be mandatory, subject only to appeal to the Secretary of Defense'.[28]

In regard to the scope of SIGINT activities, which comprise Communications Intelligence (COMINT) and Electronics Intelligence (ELINT) activities, the directive further states that:

COMINT activities shall be construed to mean those activities which produce COMINT by interception and processing of foreign communications passed by radio, wire, or other electromagnetic means, with specific exception stated below and by the processing of foreign encrypted communications, however transmitted. Interception comprises search, intercept and direction finding. Processing comprises range estimation, transmitter operator identification, signal analysis, traffic analysis, cryptanalysis, decryption, study of plain text, the fusion of these processes, and the reporting of the results.

COMINT and COMINT activities as defined herein shall not include (a) any intercept and processing of unencrypted written communications, press and propaganda broadcasts, or (b) censorship.

ELINT activities are defined as the collection (observation and recording) and the processing for subsequent intelligence purposes, of information derived from foreign, non-communications, electromagnetic radiations emanating from other than atomic detonation or radioactive sources. ELINT is the technical and intelligence information product of ELINT activities.[29]

The issuance of the NSA's charter followed a year after its official acknowledgment in the Government Organization Manual of 1957 as 'a separately organized agency within the Department of Defense' for 'the performance of highly specialized technical functions'.[30] Despite the lack of official acknowledgment until 1957, the NSA's existence became known several years earlier. In 1953 its existence was revealed by virtue of plans for the construction of new headquarters at Fort George G. Meade, Maryland (where it remains today).[31] The NSA was again in the news in late 1954 when an NSA employee was caught taking secret documents home, apparently with the intention of transmitting them to the Soviet Union.[32] A far greater breach occurred in 1960, when two cryptographers (William H. Martin and Bernon F. Mitchell) defected to the Soviet Union.[33] And on 22 July 1963, Victor Norris Hamilton, a research analyst at the NSA turned up in Moscow and announced that he was defecting. The next day, Jack E. Dunlap, an NSA employee since 1958, was found dead of carbon monoxide poisoning. It was discovered that Dunlap was a Soviet agent recruited while employed by the NSA in Turkey.[34]

The NSA has two basic missions: Communications Security (COMSEC) and Signals Intelligence (SIGINT). In its COMSEC role the NSA creates, reviews and authorizes the communications procedures and codes of eighteen government agencies including the State Department, Defense Department, the CIA and the FBI.[35] This role includes secure data and voice transmission links on such satellite systems as the Defense Satellite Communications System (DSCS) and the Satellite Data System (SDS).[36] Likewise, FBI agents use a special scrambler phone for sensitive communications that require a different code each day from the NSA.[37] In addition, it is likely that the NSA is responsible for developing the codes by which the President must identify himself in order to authorize a nuclear strike.[38]

The NSA's COMSEC responsibilities also include more mundane activities. One such activity is data processing security — ensuring that unauthorized individuals or governments are not able to tap into data banks. The data banks to be protected from such intrusion include both government and private data banks, regardless of whether they hold classified data. Thus, the NSA has created a Computer Security Center to cooperate with business organizations in evaluating methods for preventing unauthorized access to computer systems.[39]

In addition, the NSA is heavily involved in *tactical* communications security. According to the NSA's Deputy Director for Research and Engineering, Dr William Mehuron, 'most of our COMSEC work is really tactical'.[40] Such tactical COMSEC involves projects like developing equipment for field radio systems and the design and development of the cryptographic portions of the Tri-Service Tactical Communications (TRI-TAC) System switch.[41]

Just as the NSA's communications security role extends far beyond the traditional code-making role, so its SIGINT role extends far beyond the traditional code-breaking role and is directed at gathering foreign military, political and economic intelligence. This intelligence concerns not only the Soviet Union and other hostile nations but also Third World and allied nations.

Signals intercepted may include diplomatic communications, conversations between military personnel and amongst military–political leaders as well as commercial communications. Thus in the early 1970s the NSA managed, both via satellite and embassy listening post, to intercept the radio telephone conversations conducted by Soviet leaders when they were in their limousines.[42] At the same time the NSA is alleged to intercept personal and commercial international communications transmitted via satellite, transatlantic cable and telephone (microwave) — including INTELSAT/ COMSAT and the London–Paris phone links.[43]

In pursuit of military intelligence concerning the Soviet Union and other countries, NSA monitors the electronic emissions of radars (known as RADINT — radar intelligence) and aircraft, the telemetry of missiles (TELINT — telemetry intelligence), the signatures of Soviet submarines and the data transmitted by Soviet spacecraft. Thus, in 1976 the NSA monitored the conversation between Premier Alexei Kosygin and Cosmonaut Vladimir M. Komarov, who had been informed by Soviet ground control that the braking parachutes designed to bring his spacecraft safely to earth were malfunctioning and there was no hope for a safe re-entry.[44]

Clearly, the NSA provides intelligence relevant to a wide range of government activities. COMINT provides data of use in analysing the possible courses of action of foreign governments and in determining negotiating strategy, whether in regard to military or economic negotiations. Thus, the NSA apparently obtained advance warning of the Arab attack on Israel in 1973 as well as knowledge of the Soviet bargaining position in SALT I.[45] ELINT and TELINT help determine the order of battle and capabilities of foreign forces — both conventional and strategic. RADINT is useful in pinpointing the location of radars and in developing electronic countermeasures (ECMs). On the basis of RADINT the NSA prepares Emitter Program Listings (EPL), detailing radar locations and frequencies.[46] Identification of Soviet submarines by their signatures is a significant aid to anti-submarine and underseas surveillance activities. Collection and analysis of seismic data can provide information about possible nuclear detonations.

In recent years, the NSA has become involved in several controversies due to US-based activities. In 1975 two NSA operations, SHAMROCK and MINARET, were revealed. SHAMROCK involved the interception of all private cables leaving the US. In 1945 the Army Security Agency (now INSCOM — Army Intelligence and Security Command — the Army component of the NSA) asked three cable companies (RCA Global, ITT and Western Union) for access to all international cables. The companies complied despite a finding by their lawyers that such activity was illegal. In the early years of the program the cables were processed against a small Watch List geared to provide foreign intelligence. By the late 1960s, 150 000 cables per month were involved. The program was terminated on 15 May 1975.[47] According to Dr Louis Tordella, Deputy Director of NSA from 1958–74, no President after Harry Truman knew of SHAMROCK.[48]

MINARET involved intercepting, reviewing and disseminating the international radio and telephone communications of specific Americans (including Jane Fonda and Benjamin Spock) and American organizations on a Watch List.[49] The primary purpose of the program was to discover foreign links to anti-Vietnam war activity, and civil disturbances. The program was conducted between 1965 and 1973, with the CIA, the FBI, Secret Service, the DIA, Bureau of Narcotics and Dangerous Drugs as well as the NSA contributing to the 1650 names on the Watch List.[50]

Additionally, it was revealed that the NSA Office of Security Services compiled files on about 75 000 American citizens between 1952 and 1974 for the ostensible purpose of maintaining the security of the NSA sources and methods.[51] Any citizen whose name was mentioned in an NSA intercept had a file.

The most recent controversies have involved the NSA's interest in academic research in cryptography and the Data Encryption Standard (DES). The NSA has suggested that unrestricted research and publication by academic cryptographers could imperil national security by making cryptographic techniques available to nations which would not otherwise be able to develop such advanced systems, or inadvertently expose a weakness in a code system now used by the US Government.[52] Under present arrangements some researchers voluntarily submit material to NSA prior to submission to journals. The NSA's role in the efforts of the US National Bureau of Standards to certify a single Data Encryption Standard to be used for all Government and other non-classified data produced allegations of the NSA tampering with the standard.[53] However, a Senate Committee found these to be unsubstantiated.[54]

As noted above the NSA is located at Fort George G. Meade in Maryland. This facility houses somewhere between 20 000 and 24 000 employees.[55]

The NSA is divided into several offices/organizations — the three most prominent being the Office of Signals Intelligence Operations, the Office of Communications Security and the Office of Research and Engineering.[56] The Office of SIGINT Operations has three production units responsible for different geographical areas of the world. A Group is responsible for the USSR and its satellites; B Group's area of responsibility includes China, Korea, Vietnam and the rest of Communist Asia; while G Group is responsible for all other nations — both Third World and allied. Collection of material for the production units is the responsibility of the individual units.

The Office of Communications Security, also known as the S Organization, is responsible for COMSEC with respect to the various forms of communications discussed above — diplomatic communications, sensitive secure phone links, satellite voice and data transmissions and data processing. The Office of Research and Engineering has the responsibility for developing the techniques and equipment necessary for conducting intercept operations, breaking codes and ensuring secure US codes. It is subdivided into three divisions. The Mathematical Research Techniques Division explores code-breaking possibilities. The Intercept Equipment Division, as its name indicates, concentrates on developing the equipment required for the NSA's COMINT and ELINT interception programs. The Cryptographic Equipment Division seeks to develop secure coding machines.

In addition to the three main offices there are several others of importance. The Office of Telecommunications and Computer Service (T Organization) is responsible both for computer support and the functioning of the NSA's communications network — the Digital Network Defense Special Security Communications System (DIN/DSSCS). Information transmitted on this system, via the Defense Satellite Communications System, includes intercepts from overseas stations. The Office of Installations and Logistics (L Organization) is responsible for overseas housing, disposal of classified waste, construction of facilities at Fort Meade and procurement of computers. The Office of Administration (M Organization) has a variety of functions, including personnel matters, training, employment and security — the latter being handled by the Office of Security, M5.

Two other offices of importance are the Office of Plans and Policy and the Office of Programs and Resources. The Office of Plans and Policy serves as a staff office for the Director of NSA with the Deputy Director for Plans and Policy serving as chief of staff. The Office of Programs and Resources is charged with the management and allocation of SIGINT/COMSEC resources — most specifically, with the preparation of the Consolidated Cryptographic Program.

The present Director (DIRNSA) is Lieutenant-General Lincoln G. Fauer. An organization chart of the NSA is shown as Figure 6.1.

The size of the NSA budget has been variously estimated at US$1.2 billion, $3 billion and $10 billion.[57] The disparities may be a function, respectively, of one-time purchase of equipment and the difference between the NSA's headquarters budget and the total NSA controlled SIGINT/COMSEC budget. This latter budget would incorporate the funds spent under the direction of the NSA's other half — the Central Security Service

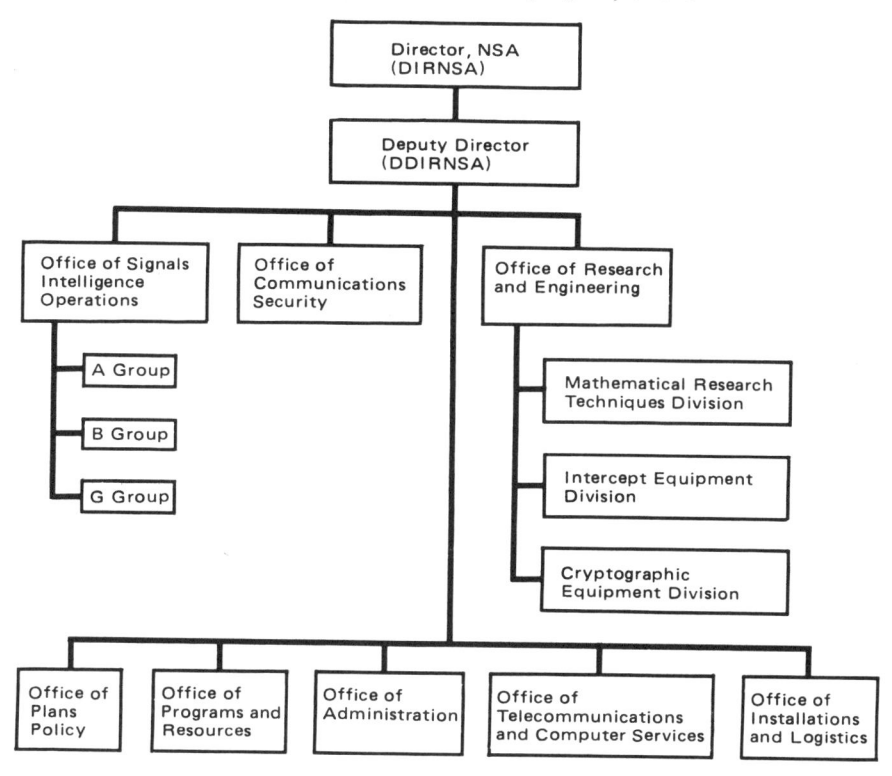

Figure 6.1 Organization Chart, National Security Agency (NSA)

(CSS). The CSS is responsible, in theory, for supervising and directing the activities of the Service Cryptological Authorities (SCA) — the Army Intelligence and Security Command (INSCOM), the Naval Security Group Command (NSG) and the Air Force Electronic Security Command (ESC). The Central Security Service function of the NSA, with the DIRNSA serving as Chief, CSS was established in 1971 in order 'to provide a unified, more economical and more effective structure for executing cryptologic and related operations presently conducted under the Military Departments'.[58]

In addition to performing tactical COMSEC and SIGINT missions, the SCA provides personnel to man strategic SIGINT collection facilities in the US and overseas. The personnel involved may be in the 50 000–100 000 range. When the budgets for personnel and related facilities are added to the NSA's headquarters budget the total may reach US$10 billion.

Central Intelligence Agency (CIA)

In the aftermath of the Second World War the US central intelligence organization which had been created for the conflict was disbanded. Several branches of this organization, known as the Office of Strategic Services (OSS), were distributed among other departments of the government.[59] Thus, the X-2 (counter-intelligence) and Secret Intelligence Branches were transferred to the War Department as the Strategic Services Unit while the Research and Analysis Branch was relocated in the State Department.[60]

Shortly afterwards, however, President Truman found himself deluged by intelligence reports from several government agencies and set up the National Intelligence Authority and its operational element — the Central Intelligence Group (CIG) — to coordinate and collate the reports. The CIG served both as a coordinating mechanism as well as having responsibility for intelligence collection.[61]

As part of the general consideration of national security needs and organization, the question of intelligence was addressed in the National Security Act of 1947. The Act established the Central Intelligence Agency as an independent agency within the Executive Office of the President to replace the CIG. According to the Act, the CIA was to have five functions:

(1) to advise the National Security Council in matters concerning such intelligence activities of the Government departments and agencies as related to national security;
(2) to make recommendations to the National Security Council for the coordination of such intelligence activities of the departments and agencies of the Government as relate to national security;
(3) to correlate and evaluate intelligence relating to the national security, and to provide for the appropriate dissemination of such intelligence within the Government using where appropriate existing agencies and facilities;
(4) to perform for the benefit of the existing intelligence agencies, such additional services of common concern as the National Security Council determines can be more effectively accomplished centrally;

CIA Headquarters, Langley, Virginia, USA.

(5) to perform other such functions and duties related to intelligence affecting the national security as the National Security Council may from time to time direct.[62]

The CIA was to have no domestic role or powers of arrest.

The provisions of the Act left a great deal of room for interpretation. Thus, provision (5) has been cited as authorizing covert action measures. Whatever the intentions of Congress in 1947, the CIA developed in accord with a maximalist interpretation of the Act. Thus, the CIA has become the primary agency of the US Government for intelligence analysis, human intelligence collection and covert action. It also, as noted above, has played a major role in the development of overhead reconnaissance systems, such as the U-2 aircraft and KH-11 and RHYOLITE satellites. Additionally, the Director of the CIA is also the Director of Central Intelligence and is responsible for managing the activities of the entire intelligence community.

Not only did the CIA develop in accordance with a maximalist interpretation of the National Security Act, it strayed beyond those limits. Thus, between 1952 and 1972 it ran a mail-opening program, HTLINGUAL, which involved opening mail being sent to and from the Soviet Union. The operation, which took place mainly at La Guardia and Kennedy International airports in New York, involved over 215 000 letters. As did the NSA, the CIA maintained a Watch List which specified attention for certain groups and individuals, including many with no intelligence connection — such as the American Friends Service Committee, the Federation of American Scientists, and the playwright, Edward Albee.[63]

From 1956 until it was ended in 1972, the HTLINGUAL program was run by the CIA's Counter-intelligence Staff (CIS). The specially created Special Operations Group of the CIS was responsible for Operation CHAOS, which sought to determine the existence of links between the anti-war movement and foreign governments. CHAOS agents 'followed the activities of ... organization's leaders abroad, spied on their meetings, broke into their hotel rooms, and sent thousands of cables back to headquarters detailing their activities'.[64] Personality files were compiled on 13 000 individuals, over 7000 of whom were American citizens.[65] Subject files were opened on 1000 domestic organizations, including the Students for a Democratic Society, American Indian Movement, Women's Liberation Movement, National Mobilization Committee to End the War in Vietnam, Grove Press Inc., and the Youth International Party.[66]

Under the codename MKULTRA the CIA experimented with mind-altering drugs on persons who did not know that hallucinogens were being given to them.[67] Additionally, two programs run by the CIA's Office of Security, ostensibly to protect CIA personnel and property, involved domestic spying. Project RESISTANCE's initial purpose was to provide protection for CIA recruiters on college campuses. Eventually the purpose expanded to involve protection for all government recruiters. The office sought information from college administrations, local police and college newspapers.[68]

Project MERRIMAC was designed to provide advance warning of demonstrations that might threaten CIA personnel or facilities in Washington. Agents were infiltrated into over ten activist organizations, including the Washington Ethical Society, the Black Panthers, CORE (Congress on Racial Equality), War Resister's League and the Women's Strike for Peace. Agents followed prominent leaders home, took pictures of participants in demonstrations and noted down licence plate numbers.[69]

As a result of the exposure of such activities, Executive Orders by Presidents Ford and Carter expressly forbade such activities. President Reagan's Executive Order 12333 has loosened the restrictions somewhat, but much less than originally intended.[70] Under this order the CIA is permitted to collect 'significant' foreign intelligence secretly within the United States if that effort is not aimed at learning about the domestic

The United States security and intelligence community 109

activities of American citizens and corporations. The order also gives the CIA authority to conduct, within the United States, 'special activities' or covert operations, if approved by the President, that are not intended to influence US political processes, public opinion or the media. Additionally, the order permits physical surveillance of American citizens and corporations abroad in any counter-intelligence or significant foreign intelligence investigation that cannot be obtained by other means. The Carter Order limited such surveillance abroad to Americans and United States groups suspected of being agents of a foreign power.[71]

The headquarters of the CIA is in Langley, Virginia, although it has many offices and over 3000 employees scattered around the Washington area. Altogether, the CIA had from 16 500 to 20 000 employees in the Washington area and a budget of US$800 million to $1 billion in 1978.[73] The present Director is William J. Casey and the Deputy Director is John McMahon.

The CIA is divided into four major components, each headed by a Deputy Director and six offices directly subordinate to the Director and the Deputy Director. The six offices are the Office of the General Counsel, Office of the Inspector General, Office of the Comptroller, Office of Equal Employment Opportunity, Office of the Director of Personnel and Office of the Director of Policy and Planning. The major components are the Directorate of Administration, the Directorate of Operations, the Directorate of Science and Technology and the Directorate of Intelligence. The general structure of the CIA is that depicted in Figure 6.2.

Within the Directorate of Administration are nine offices which perform a wide range of administrative services — the Office of Communications, the Office of Logistics, the Office of Security, Office of Training and Education, Office of Finance, Office of Information Services, Office of Data Processing, the Office of Medical Services and the Office of Personnel.[74] The Office of

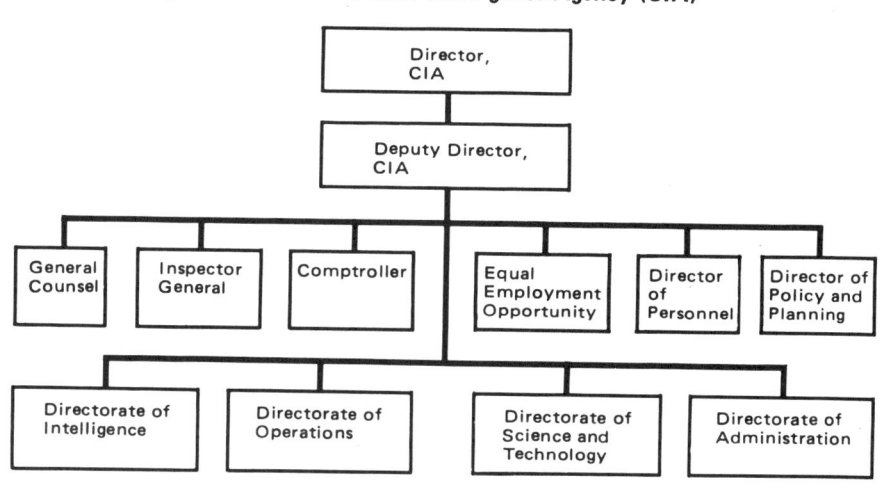

Figure 6.2 Organization of the Central Intelligence Agency (CIA)

Communications, with over 2000 employees, maintains facilities for secret communications between CIA headquarters and overseas bases.[75] This presumably includes control over the CIA PYRAMIDER-type agent communications satellites.[76] The Office of Logistics operates weapons and other warehouses in the US as well as supplying office equipment.[77]

The Office of Security is responsible for the physical protection of CIA installations, overt and covert, at home and abroad. It also administers polygraph tests to applicants and contractor personnel.[78] The Office of Finance maintains field units in Hong Kong, Beirut, Buenos Aires and Geneva with easy access to monetary markets. It is also responsible for payroll and maintaining centralized financial records.[79] The Office of Medical Services provides cleared psychiatrists and physicians to treat agency officers.[80] The Office of Personnel is responsible for recruitment, maintenance of personnel files and with the Office of Training operates CIA training facilities, including the main facility known as 'The Farm' at Camp Peary, Virginia.[81] The Office of Training conducts over 60 courses on world affairs, management theories and techniques, foreign languages and intelligence evaluation and production.[82]

The Directorate of Operations, formerly the Directorate of Plans, is in charge of clandestine collection and covert action (special activities). It is organized into various headquarters staffs, area divisions and support divisions. The major headquarters staffs are the Foreign Intelligence Staff, the Counter-intelligence Staff, the Covert Action Staff, and Staff D.[83] The Counter-intelligence Staff is in charge of offensive counter-intelligence operations — penetration of hostile services, collecting information concerning such services and debriefing defectors. At the height of its influence, under James Angleton, it had about 200 employees.[84] After Angleton's dismissal the Staff was radically reduced in size and assignment to the staff was made a temporary tour of duty. Operational Counter-intelligence responsibility was assigned to the geographic divisions of the Directorate of Operations.[85]

The Covert Action Staff develops the plans for covert action operations which have included:

(1) political advice and counsel;
(2) subsidies to individuals;
(3) financial support and 'technical assistance' to political parties;
(4) support to private organizations, including labor unions and business firms;
(5) covert propaganda;
(6) private training of individuals and exchange of persons;
(7) economic operations; and
(8) paramilitary (or) political action operations designed to overthrow or support a regime.[86]

The Foreign Intelligence Staff (FIS) is responsible for checking the authenticity of sources and information, screening clandestine collection requirements and reviewing the regional division projects, budget infor-

The United States security and intelligence community 111

mation and operational cable traffic. The responsibilities and authority of the FIS were summarized by its former head, Peer de Silva, as follows:

The Foreign Intelligence Staff had a continuing responsibility for monitoring intelligence collection projects and programs carried out abroad. These operations and collection programs were of course controlled and directed by the area divisions concerned; the FI Staff simply read the progress charts on the various projects (or the lack of progress) and played the role of determining which intelligence collection programs should be continued, changed or terminated. With the exception of a few individual operations of special sensitivity, this FI Staff function was worldwide.[87]

Staff D is in charge of bugging and wiretapping in support of CIA and NSA activities. It may also be involved in various cryptological activities. Thus, on one occasion it apparently gave money to a code clerk working in the Washington Embassy of a United States ally for supplying information which assisted in breaking the ally's code.[88] At one time, it also housed the CIA Executive Action capability, ZR/RIFLE.[89]

Actual implementation of staff-planned activities are the responsibility of the area divisions — the Soviet Bloc Division, Western Hemisphere Division, European Division, East Asia Division, Africa Division, Near East Division, Special Operations Division, Foreign Resources Division and Domestic Collection Division.[90] The Special Operations Division handles paramilitary activities. The Foreign Resources Division (FRD) was created in 1963 as the Domestic Operations Division and given the responsibility for the 'clandestine operational activities of the Clandestine Services conducted within the United States against foreign targets'.[91] The present function of the FRD is to locate and recruit foreign nationals residing in the US who are of special interest concerning possible cooperation with the CIA abroad.[92]

The Domestic Collection Division (DCD), known until 1973 as the Domestic Contact Service (and part of the Intelligence Directorate until then), openly collects intelligence from US residents who have travelled abroad. The intelligence concerns a wide variety of subjects, primarily of an economic and technical nature.[93] In the past the DCD has participated in domestic spying on American citizens and collected information on foreign students studying in the US.[94] One of its continuing responsibilities is the resettlement of defectors.[95]

Two additional staff elements are the Evaluations, Plans and Designs Staff (EPDS) and the Central Cover Staff. The EPDS appears to be the successor to the Missions and Programs Staff and does much of the bureaucratic planning and budgeting for the Deputy Director for Operations (DDO). The Central Cover Staff is the apparent successor to the Operational Services Division and sets up CIA proprietary and business cover organizations.[96] An organizational chart of the Directorate of Operations is shown as Figure 6.3.

As of 1973 the Directorate had 6000 employees and a budget of US$440 million. About $260 million was spent on covert action while 4800 employees were located in the area divisions.[97] Cutbacks by CIA Directors James Schlesinger and Admiral Stansfield Turner reduced personnel by

112 *The Ties That Bind*

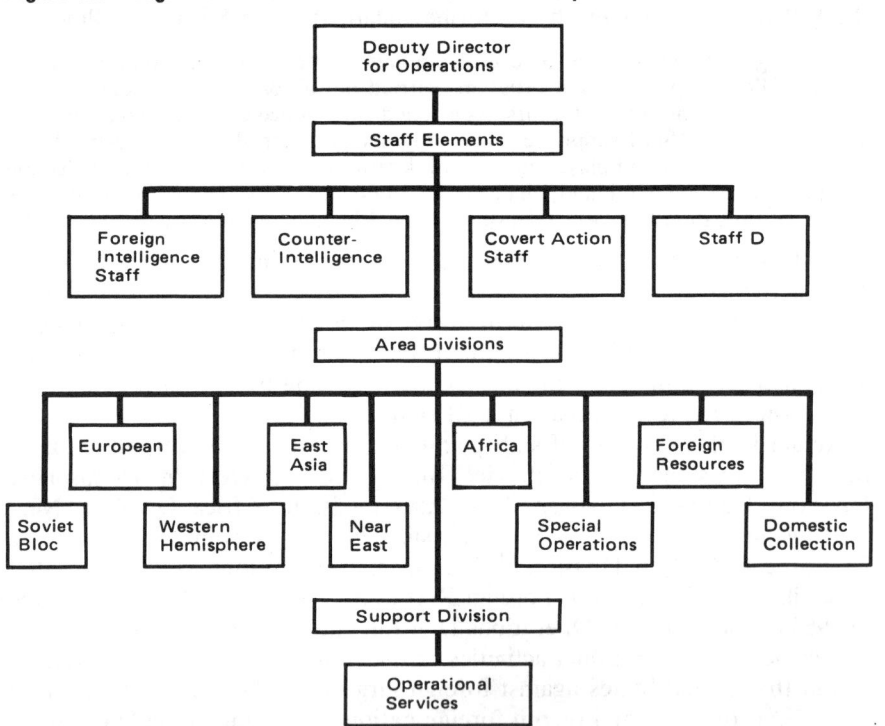

Figure 6.3 Organization of the CIA's Directorate of Operations

```
                    Deputy Director
                    for Operations
                          |
                    Staff Elements
    ┌─────────────────┬───┴───────────────┬─────────────┐
  Foreign          Counter-          Covert Action    Staff D
  Intelligence     Intelligence      Staff
  Staff
                          
                    Area Divisions
    ┌──────────┬──────────┬──────────┬──────────┐
  European   East        Africa    Foreign
             Asia                   Resources
  Soviet    Western     Near      Special      Domestic
  Bloc      Hemisphere  East      Operations   Collection

                    Support Division
                          |
                    Operational
                    Services
```

about 2000, but many of these positions have been restored by the present Director, William Casey. The present Deputy Director for Operations is Clair E. George.[98]

The Directorate of Intelligence, known from 1978 to 1981 as the National Foreign Assessment Center (NFAC), is the primary US government organization for intelligence analysis. As such it is the unit primarily responsible for preparing the various National Intelligence Estimates (NIEs) and Special National Intelligence Estimates (SNIEs). The most important of these is the annual NIE 11-3/8 on 'Soviet Strategic Capabilities and Objectives'.

As shown in Figure 6.4 the present structure of the Directorate includes three staffs (Management and Analysis Support, Arms Control Intelligence, and Collection Requirements and Evaluation), five regional offices and five functional offices. The functional offices — the Office of Global Issues, Office of Imagery Analysis, Office of Scientific and Weapons Research, Office of Central Reference, Office of Current Production and Analytical Support — are, with two exceptions (Global Issues and Current Production and Analytical support), carryovers from the NFAC organizational framework, which was stricly functional. Offices such as the Office of Soviet Analysis were created by grouping together Soviet analysts from all areas of research.

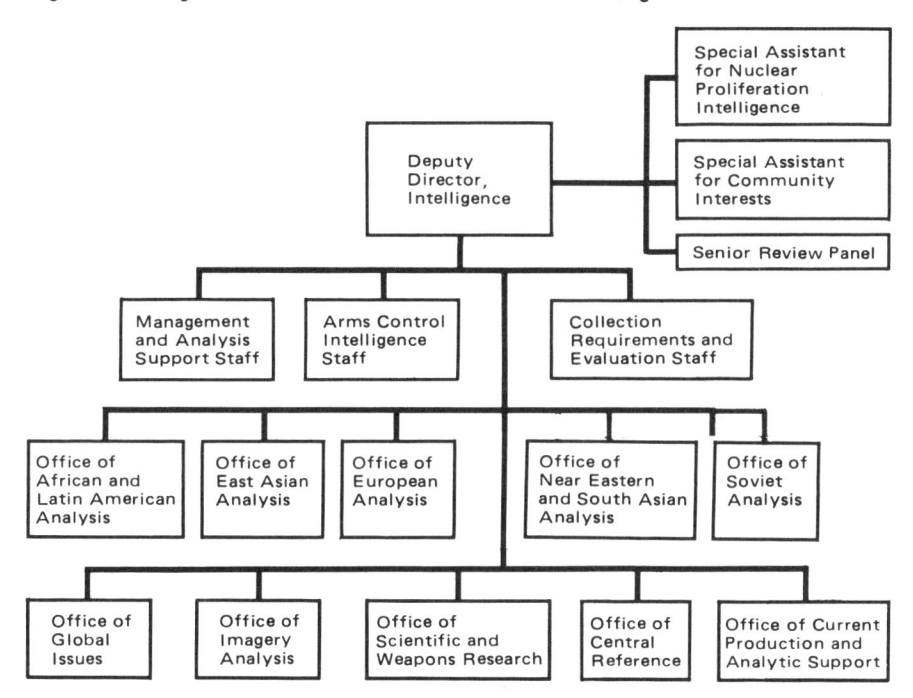

Figure 6.4 Organization of the CIA's Directorate of Intelligence

```
                                    ┌─ Special Assistant for Nuclear Proliferation Intelligence
              Deputy Director,      ├─ Special Assistant for Community Interests
              Intelligence          └─ Senior Review Panel
                   │
   ┌───────────────┼───────────────┐
Management      Arms Control    Collection
and Analysis    Intelligence    Requirements and
Support Staff   Staff           Evaluation Staff

Office of      Office of      Office of      Office of            Office of
African and    East Asian     European       Near Eastern         Soviet
Latin American Analysis       Analysis       and South Asian      Analysis
Analysis                                     Analysis

Office of      Office of      Office of           Office of    Office of Current
Global         Imagery        Scientific and      Central      Production and
Issues         Analysis       Weapons Research    Reference    Analytic Support
```

A more instructive picture of the Directorate of Intelligence's functions and actual output can be obtained by considering its organization as of April 1979, when (as NFAC) it consisted of nine research offices, an Operations Center and a Publications and Presentations Group.[99] The research offices were the offices of Central Reference, Scientific Intelligence, Economic Research, Political Analysis, Strategic Research, Imagery Analysis, Weapons, Intelligence, Geographic and Cartographic Research and Current Operations.

The Office of Central Reference provided (and still provides) data in the form of directories of foreign government officials, lists of organizations and public appearances as well as biographies of individuals of interest. The Office of Scientific Intelligence (OSI) had responsibility for a wide range of scientific analysis, covering both the natural sciences as well as agricultural, medical and psychological questions. Thus, the OSI prepared psychological/personality profiles, and estimated the health of foreign leaders as well as the status of other nations' nuclear power programs. The Office of Imagery Analysis was created to give the CIA its 'own' photo-interpretation unit in addition to the CIA-run National Photographic Interpretation Center which was to serve the entire intelligence community.[100] The Office of Strategic Research was responsible for military intelligence matters. It was primarily concerned, through its Strategic Evaluation Center, with Soviet strategic forces. The Office of Current Operations was apparently responsible for maintaining the CIA Watch Office. The Office of Political Analysis was concerned with all aspects of political activity, including the projected outcome of elections, terrorism, the standing of political parties, the impact of domestic politics on foreign policy, etc. Table 6.1 lists some of the papers produced by these offices as well as by the Office of Economic Research and Office of Geographic and Cartographic Research.

The Directorate of Science and Technology was created in 1962 as the Directorate for Research, to consolidate in one unit various CIA offices dealing with technical intelligence collection.[101] As noted above, the Directorate, through its Office of Development and Engineering and its Office of SIGINT Operations (OSO), has been heavily involved in the development of reconnaissance satellites. It also houses the National Photographic Interpretation Center (NPIC), which is responsible for the interpretation of the 'take' of photographic reconnaissance aircraft and

Table 6.1 Reports produced by NFAC offices

NFAC Office	Title
Political Analysis	Patterns of International Terrorism Profile of Violence: An Analytical Model International Terrorism in 1978 A Guide to Political Acronyms
Strategic Research	Chinese Defense Spending 1965–1979 A Dollar Cost Comparison of Soviet and US Defense Activities 1968–1978 The Egyptian Arms Industry
Central Reference	Dmitriy Ustinov: USSR Minister of Defense The Leadership of the USSR Academy of Science Directory of Officials of the People's Republic of China Directory of USSR Ministry of Defense and Armed Forces Officials
Geographic and Cartographic	Kampuchea: A Demographic Catastrophe The Refugee Resettlement Problem in Thailand Relating Climate Change to its Effects Pakistan: The Ethnic Equation
Scientific Intelligence	Soviet Millimetre Wave Technology and Systems Applications Biological and Environmental Factors Affecting Soviet Grain Quality Foreign Development and Application of Automated Controls for the Steel Industry Plant Breeding and Protection Research for Food Production in China
Economic Research	The World Oil Market in the Years Ahead Arms Flows to LDC's: US–Soviet Comparisons 1974–1977 Korea: The Economic Race Between North and South USSR: The Long Term Outlook for Grain Imports China: In Pursuit of Economic Modernization Soviet Strategy and Tactics in Economic and Commercial Negotiations with the United States

satellites. Under the provision of National Security Council Intelligence Directive Number 8, the NPIC is run by the CIA as a 'service of common concern' serving the entire intelligence community.[102] The NPIC is located in the old Naval Gun Factory along the Annacostia River in Washington.[103]

Additionally, the Directorate has an Office of Research and Development, an Office of Technical Service and houses the Foreign Broadcast Information Service (FBIS). The Office of Technical Service (OTS) is the successor to the Technical Services Division of the Directorate of Operations and was transferred to the Directorate of Science and Technology in 1973. The OTS supplies 'scientific support' such as communications devices, exotic weapons and chemicals.[104] The FBIS monitors the public radio broadcasts of foreign nations and prepares summaries of broadcasts of interest for use by both intelligence analysts and scholars.

Bureau of Intelligence and Research (INR)

As noted above, with the dissolution of the Office of Strategic Services, its research and analysis functions were transferred to the State Department. This function was carried out by the Interim Research and Intelligence Service. Since then it has undergone two name changes and many more reorganizations. It has been designated the Bureau of Intelligence and Research (INR) since 1957.[105]

The Director of the Bureau, who holds rank equivalent to an Assistant Secretary of State, is Hugh Montgomery. The Bureau has a staff of about 300 and a budget of US$20 million.[106] The Bureau engages in no collection activity beyond reporting through normal diplomatic channels and open source collection. While its main function is to provide intelligence support to the Secretary of State and other State Department components, it is also involved in the preparation of NIEs and SNIEs.

In terms of its production functions, the INR 'faces in two directions'. One direction is outward, where it is involved in interagency intelligence production efforts — NIEs and SNIEs. The second direction is inward — toward the State Department internal organization. In this role it prepares a variety of intelligence products. The *Morning Summary* is prepared in collaboration with the Department's Executive Secretariat. It is designed to inform the Secretary of State and his principal deputies of current events and current intelligence. Regional and functional summaries include *Arab–Israeli Developments* (six times a week), *Afghanistan Situation Report* (twice a week), *African Trends, East Asian Highlights, Inter-American Highlights, Soviet Weekly, Politico-Military Analyses*, and *Human Rights Highlights* (each written once a week).[107]

Single subject reports are published under three different titles — *Current Analyses, Assessments and Research* and *Policy Assessments*. Current Analyses papers analyse recent or ongoing events and assess prospects and implications over the following six months. Assessments and Research papers either assess past trends or project the course of events more than six months in the future. Policy Assessments papers analyse the context or results of past policies or assess policy options.[108]

The Director, INR is assisted by four Deputy Assistant Secretaries who directly supervise the INR's sixteen offices. The Deputy Assistant Secretary for Intelligence and Research is the second-ranking individual in the Bureau. He or she supervises the Office of the Executive Director and Office of Intelligence Support. The Office of the Executive Director handles personnel, budget and finance, and general administrative support for the Bureau. The Office of Intelligence Support is the State Department's centre for the receipt of intelligence information, in whatever form, and for its processing and dissemination under security safeguards.[109]

The Deputy Assistant Secretary for Current Analysis supervises six geographical offices and the Office of Politico-Military Analysis. The geographic offices are the Offices of Analysis for Africa, Latin America, East Asia and the Pacific, the Soviet Union and Eastern Europe, Western Europe and the Near East, and South Asia. The primary function of the Current Analysis offices is to produce analyses of developments and issues that are, or will be, of concern to the policymaker. They are responsible for preparing the regional and other special summaries and for preparing INR contributions to community-wide estimates and assessments. Current Analysis analysts also conduct longer range studies and assessments under the direction and guidance of the Deputy Assistant Secretary for Assessments and Research.[110]

The Deputy Assistant Secretary for Assessments and Research has the primary responsibility for the Bureau's long-range analytical studies. He is responsible for the Office of Long Range Assessments and Research, the Office of Economic Analysis, the Office of the Geographer, the Global Issues Staff and the Reports Coordination and Review Staff. The Office of Long Range Assessments and Research prepares its own long-range assessments on selected topics, contributes on occasion to assessments on selected topics and on assessments prepared elsewhere in the Bureau, and commissions contractors and consultants for those topics which cannot be done in the INR. The Office of Economic Analysis produces reports for policymakers on current and longer range issues involving international economic concerns such as foreign economic policies, business cycles, trade, financial affairs, food, population, energy and economic relations between the industrialized countries and the developing nations.[111]

The Office of the Geographer prepares studies of policy issues associated with physical, cultural, economic, and political geography, emphasizing the law of the sea, US maritime issues, and international boundaries and jurisdictional problems. The Global Issues Staff produces finished intelligence on selected transnational, regional and global topics including science and technology, narcotics, human rights and refugees, oceans, and the environment. The Reports Coordination and Review Staff is responsible for the final production of the INR's formal reports. It is responsible for editorial review, format, printing and distribution.[112]

The Deputy Assistant Secretary for Intelligence Coordination supervises the Office of Intelligence Liaison and the Office of Intelligence Resources. The Office of Intelligence Liaison works with intelligence agencies on human collection efforts and coordinates proposals for special political activities. Its basic responsibility in connection with those programs is to ensure 'thorough consideration of their support of and implications for U.S. foreign policy'.[113] The office also processes requests for biographic data and other intelligence agency documents, handles defector cases, and conducts briefings on intelligence matters for State Department officers going to and returning from overseas posts. It also handles liaison with designated foreign intelligence representatives.

The Office of Intelligence Resources provides staff support, representation and coordination for the Department's interests in the National Foreign Intelligence Program and budget. It works with other intelligence community agencies, concerned areas of the Department, and overseas missions in planning, tasking, deploying, and evaluating technical collection activities.[114]

The Office of Intelligence Coordination works with the Defense Intelligence Agency (DIA) and the Federal Bureau of Investigation (FBI). It also represents the Department of State in the coordination and setting of priorities for national intelligence collection and production, and works with other agencies on human source collection programs.

Federal Bureau of Investigation (FBI)

Domestic counter-intelligence and security activity is the responsibility of the Federal Bureau of Investigation (FBI), which is subordinate to the Department of Justice. Such activity is only one of the FBI's responsibilities, which also includes Federal criminal law enforcement. Hence, it is more appropriate to compare the FBI with Scotland Yard than with the British Security Service — not only because it is not solely a counter-intelligence organization but because it *does* have powers of arrest.

Overall the FBI has about 20 000 employees and a budget of over US$500 million.[115] The Intelligence Division, which handles counter-intelligence, has approximately 800 employees and a budget of US$60 million.[116] The present head of the division is Edward J. O'Malley.

As a result of disclosures in 1975 concerning improper FBI domestic activities, primarily in regard to domestic security activity, these functions were reorganized in August and September 1976. Previously the Intelligence Division consisted of a Counter-intelligence Branch and an Internal Security Branch. In the reorganization, the Internal Security Branch was transferred to the General Investigative Division (GID) — later renamed the Criminal Investigative Division (CID) and renamed the Domestic Security Section (DSS). As its name indicated its responsibility was to be confined to subversive activities. More importantly, by placing the DSS within the GID its activities were separated from counter-intelligence activities which involved different circumstances and rules. In April 1977 the DSS was retitled the Domestic Security — Terrorism Section.[117]

The Intelligence Division's only direct interests in a domestic group concern the US Communist Party. Otherwise its role is purely one of foreign counter-intelligence.[118] Within the Division are a Soviet Section and a Sino-Satellite Section which covers all non-Soviet communist intelligence services.[119]

Over the years the FBI has tried to expand its role into the foreign intelligence field. In 1940 President Roosevelt assigned jurisdiction of non-military intelligence in the Western Hemisphere to the FBI, which created a Special Intelligence Service (SIS) for this function. The SIS had approximately 360 agents, mostly in Mexico, Argentina and Brazil.[120] While stripped of this function in 1946, the Bureau maintained representatives as Legal Attachés in ten embassies as of 1970. The attachés' official role was liaison with national police forces on matters of common concern and dealing with Americans who found themselves in trouble with the law. In 1970 the Bureau expanded from ten to twenty the number of embassies with FBI representation and instructed agents to collect foreign intelligence. The expansion was given the codename HILEV — for High Level Intelligence — and particularly interesting material was to be slugged with that designation by overseas agents. Some such material was distributed to high officials — for example, Henry Kissinger — outside normal intelligence channels.[121] In the aftermath of Hoover's death and the revelations of FBI misconduct, this program was (probably) terminated, with FBI representation being reduced to fifteen embassies. However, there has been at least one subsequent instance of an FBI attempt to engage in clandestine collection abroad. During the investigation of the Letelier murder the FBI operated an undercover informer in Chile, code-named 'Gopher'. Gopher told the FBI that the right-wing Partia y Libertad had contracted with Chilean narcotics traffickers to kill Letelier. Gopher turned out to be a former DEA (Drug Enforcement Agency) informant who had been terminated and blacklisted years earlier for double dealing, misrepresentation and moral turpitude.[122]

Despite its failure to acquire a significant *overseas* role in the collection and production of foreign intelligence, the FBI has been heavily involved in domestic activities designed to generate foreign intelligence. Thus provision (c) of section 1.14 of Executive Order 12333 allows the FBI to:

Conduct within the United States, when requested by officials of the intelligence community designated by the President, activities undertaken to collect foreign intelligence or support foreign intelligence collection requirements of other agencies within the intelligence community ...[123]

In the past, such activities have included wiretapping and break-ins. According to Marchetti and Marks, the FBI operates wiretaps against numerous foreign embassies in Washington. FBI agents regularly monitor the phones in the offices of all communist governments represented in Washington. Additionally, the phones in the offices of non-communist governments are tapped — especially when those nations are engaged in negotiations with the US or when significant developments are taking place in these countries.[124] In addition the FBI has conducted break-ins at foreign embassies to obtain cryptoanalytical and other foreign intelligence.[125]

Defense Intelligence Agency (DIA)

The Defense Intelligence Agency was created in 1961 as part of a general movement to centralize many of the functions performed by the individual military services. The DIA was established by a department directive (DoD 5105.21) on 1 August 1961. The directive made the DIA responsible for:

(1) the organization, direction, management, and control of Department of Defense intelligence resources assigned to or included within the DIA;
(2) review and coordination of those Department of Defense intelligence functions retained by or assigned to the military departments. Overall guidance for the conduct and management of such functions as will be developed by the Director, DIA, for review, approval, and promulgation by the Secretary of Defense;
(3) supervision of the execution of all approved plans, programs, policies and procedures for intelligence functions not assigned to DIA;
(4) obtaining the maximum economy and efficiency in the allocation and management of Department of Defense intelligence resources. This included analysis of those DOD intelligence activities and facilities which can be fully integrated and collected with non-DOD intelligence organizations;
(5) responding directly to priority requests levied upon the Defense Intelligence Agency by the USIB (United States Intelligence Board);
(6) satisfying the intelligence requirements of the major components of the Department of Defense.[126]

The creation of the DIA was, according to one analyst, a by-product of the missile gap controversy of the late 1950s:

Faced with the disparate estimates of Soviet missile strength from each of the armed services which translated into what have been called self-serving budget requests for weapons for defense, the United States Intelligence Board created a Joint Study Group in 1957 to study the intelligence producing agencies. In 1960 this panel returned various recommendations, among which are proposals for the consignment of the defense departments to observer rather than member status on the Intelligence Board and creation of a coordinating Defense Intelligence Agency which would represent the armed services as a member of the USIB. Defense Secretary McNamara adopted these proposals.[127]

Since its creation the DIA has undergone numerous reorganizations (four between 1961 and 1970) and has been subjected to severe criticism by numerous commentators. The criticism has been directed at both the quality of the DIA's intelligence output,[128] as well as its inability to effectively supervise and constrain the growth of the service intelligence components.[129] Abolition of the DIA has often been suggested — such a suggestion having been made, for example, by the Pike Committee.[130]

Such an outcome seems unlikely and the DIA continues to serve as the prime intelligence component of the Defense Department with respect to strategic intelligence matters. Thus, the DIA takes part in the formulation of the National Intelligence Estimates and Special National Intelligence Estimates on such topics as Soviet strategic forces and terrorism. It also serves as the validating authority for much of the work done by service intelligence components such as the Air Force Foreign Technology Division. Additionally, it is responsible for production of the Target Data Inventory (TDI), which is a data bank containing all the facilities that US strategic nuclear planners might desire to target. The TDI serves as the data base from which the National Strategic Target List and ultimately the SIOP is drawn.[131] DIA also engages in R&D Test and Evaluation programs related to intelligence technology. In its Fiscal 1982 request to Congress it specified four areas of research — crisis management, scientific and technical intelligence, automated data processing capabilities, and collection management capabilities. Specifically, the DIA requested funding to develop an automated system to 'support timely analysis of Indicator and Warning Intelligence', as well as funding to 'develop methodology and data bases to accomodate added intelligence requirements as a direct result of ... U.S. policy regarding nuclear targeting in PD #59 [Presidential Directive No. 59]'.[132] It also requested US$0.7 million for the development of an Advanced Imagery Requirements and Exploitation System.[133]

Organizationally, the DIA is divided into five directorates and an office of the Deputy for General Defense Intelligence Program.[134] O/GDIP prepares with military service and CIA collaboration the budget estimates of the General Defense Intelligence Program. Further, it tasks organizations under its direction to fulfil GDIP objectives.

The Directorate for Intelligence and External Affairs is the DIA's link to the National Foreign Intelligence Program (NFIP), the rest of the intelligence community and DIA customers outside the intelligence community including negotiating teams (for example, SALT, and Mutual Balanced Force Reduction [MBFR]). It also handles liaison with such organizations as Australia's JIO and Britain's Defence Intelligence Staff.

The Directorate for Resources and Systems provides various support services including security, personnel, communications and information services. The Directorate for Joint Chiefs of Staff (JCS) Support handles liaison with the JCS, the NSA and National Military Intelligence Center (which is subordinate to the National Military Command Center). The Directorate has primary responsibility for all work assigned to the DIA by the JCS and the Office of the Joint Chiefs of Staff (OJCS). It also provides Daily Intelligence Notes, Intelligence Appraisals and the Weekly Intelligence Summary.

The Directorate for Management and Operations levies, manages, and evaluates all Department of Defense intelligence collection and production requirements, including HUMINT, SIGINT and Imagery. Along with the NSA it runs the Defense Special Missile and Astronautics Center at Fort Meade which provides warning of missile and space launches with the objective of allowing US intelligence assets to be targeted on those launches.[135]

The Directorate for Foreign Intelligence is the branch of the DIA responsible for producing finished intelligence. It produces all-source finished military intelligence on orders of battle, military doctrine, strategy and tactics, C^3, equipment and logistics, nuclear energy, weapons systems, strategic defence and space. It is also the DIA branch which prepares the estimates for the Secretary of Defense and is the DIA contributor to the NIEs and SNIEs. The Directorate for Scientific and Technical Intelligence (DSTI) assigns tasks to and evaluates the work of the five service scientific intelligence centers — the Army's Missile Intelligence Agency, Armed Forces Medical Intelligence Center, and Foreign Science and Technology Center, the Air Force's Foreign Technology Division and the Navy's Naval Intelligence Support Center. An organization chart of the DIA is shown as Figure 6.5.

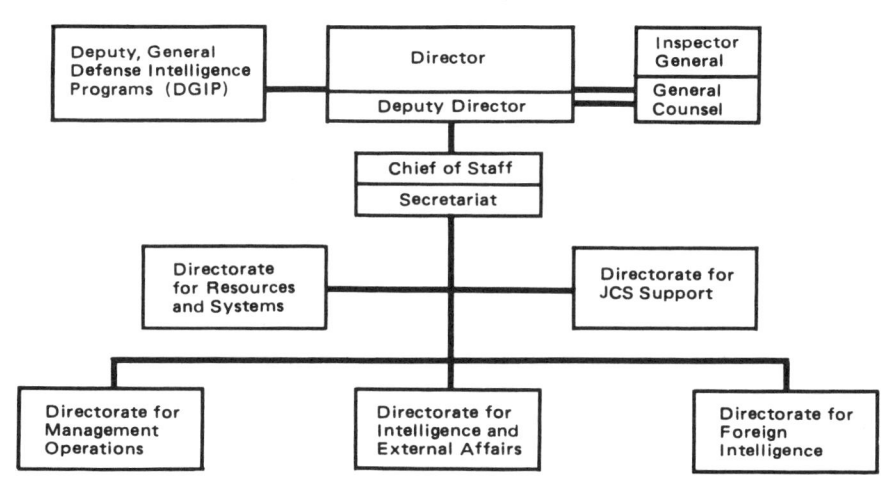

Figure 6.5 Organization of the Defense Intelligence Agency (DIA)

```
┌─────────────────────┐  ┌──────────────────┐  ┌──────────────────┐
│ Deputy, General     │  │     Director     │  │ Inspector        │
│ Defense Intelligence│──┤                  ├──┤ General          │
│ Programs (DGIP)     │  │ Deputy Director  │  │ General Counsel  │
└─────────────────────┘  └────────┬─────────┘  └──────────────────┘
                                  │
                          ┌───────┴────────┐
                          │ Chief of Staff │
                          │  Secretariat   │
                          └───────┬────────┘
              ┌───────────────────┼───────────────────┐
      ┌───────┴────────┐                     ┌────────┴────────┐
      │ Directorate    │                     │ Directorate for │
      │ for Resources  │                     │  JCS Support    │
      │ and Systems    │                     │                 │
      └────────────────┘                     └─────────────────┘
              │                                       │
   ┌──────────┼──────────────────┬────────────────────┘
┌──┴──────────┐  ┌───────────────┴──┐  ┌──────────────────┐
│ Directorate │  │ Directorate for  │  │ Directorate for  │
│ for Mgmt    │  │ Intelligence and │  │ Foreign          │
│ Operations  │  │ External Affairs │  │ Intelligence     │
└─────────────┘  └──────────────────┘  └──────────────────┘
```

As of 1978 the DIA had 4300–5500 employees (including 1000 attachés) and a budget in the US$200–250 million range.[136] The Director of DIA is Lieutenant-General James A. Williams. At the present time DIA has offices at six locations in the northern Washington area — Arlington Hall Station (main headquarters); Cafriz Building, Pomponio Plaza; Washington Navy Yard (possibly NPIC liaison); Annacostia Annex (Defense Intelligence School); and the Pentagon. Construction of new headquarters are underway which would leave the DIA with three sites — the new headquarters, Washington Navy Yard, and the Pentagon.[137]

The Army intelligence community

Unlike Britain, which abolished her service intelligence components with the creation of the Defence Intelligence Staff, the US maintained the individual service components. This was partly because it was felt such components were still needed for tactical intelligence collection. In practice, however, they have provided both tactical and strategic intelligence.

In the years since the DIA's creation the service intelligence components have grown both in terms of personnel and budget. In fact, each service has an intelligence community of its own. The members of the army intelligence community are the Office of the Assistant Chief of Staff for Intelligence (OACS/I), the Army Intelligence and Security Command (INSCOM), the Intelligence Support Activity, the Missile Intelligence Agency, the Armed Forces Medical Intelligence Center and the Foreign Science and Technology Center.

The Office of the Assistant Chief of Staff for Intelligence is at the apex of the Army intelligence community. OACS/I is a headquarters operation (that is, management and supervision rather than operations) charged with overall direction of army intelligence activity. It is the ACS/I who represents the army before the National Foreign Intelligence Board.

OACS/I is divided into six directorates, an Intelligence Automation Management Office and a Plans, Programming and Automation Security Branch. The directorates are the Intelligence Resources Management Directorate, the Program, Budget and Management Directorate, the Foreign Liaison Directorate, the Foreign Intelligence Directorate, the Counterintelligence Directorate, and the Intelligence Systems Directorate.[138]

The Army Intelligence and Security Command, headquartered at Fort Meade, was created by the merger of the Army Intelligence Command and the Army Security Agency in 1976.[139] The former performed counterintelligence duties while the latter was created in 1945 to perform cryptologic duties. INSCOM is responsible to the Assistant Chief of Staff for Intelligence (ACS/I) with respect to all but its cryptologic duties, in which case it is responsible to the Chief, Central Security Service. INSCOM personnel man SIGINT collection facilities at several overseas bases, including several in Japan and Turkey. INSCOM also performs clandestine human collection and analysis activities.[140]

A unit only recently revealed to exist is the Intelligence Support Activity (ISA).[141] The ISA is a clandestine collection and covert operations unit and was apparently created as a result of the seizure of US hostages by Iranian militants and the subsequent rescue mission. According to one account the CIA was not willing to risk its agents to provide equipment or information and ISA was created to fulfil such needs.[142]

Since its creation ISA has been involved in providing intelligence and equipment in support of Lieutenant-Colonel Bo Gritz's search for American POWs thought by some still to be in Laos. In Europe ISA played an unspecified role in the January 1982 rescue of Brigadier General James Dozier. In one nation in which the US has no diplomatic relations, arms and bullet-proof vests were provided to cooperative persons for information about military deployments.[143]

The Missile Intelligence Agency, located in Huntsville, Alabama, is responsible for production of intelligence concerning all foreign missile systems relevant to the Army's missions — tactical ground-to-ground, air-to-ground and ship-to-surface missiles as well as strategic missiles.[144] The Armed Forces Medical Intelligence Center is managed by the Army for the Department of Defense and is responsible for providing intelligence on the medical problems US troops might encounter in foreign nations — particularly those where there are sharply different environments and diseases to those in the US.[145] The Foreign Science and Technology Center, located in Charlottesville, Virginia, is responsible for producing scientific and technical intelligence in support of army R&D programs and identifying flaws in foreign weapons at which US countermeasures can be directed. The Center also manages the US Army program for material exploitation as well as supporting the army's scientific and technical intelligence collection effort.[146]

The US Army Special Forces have performed numerous intelligence and special operations missions. Established in 1952 and headquartered at Fort Bragg, North Carolina, the Special Forces' primary mission is insurgency, and in particular making contact with dissidents behind enemy lines and training them in guerrilla operations, sabotage and terror.[147]

In the late 1950s the CIA began turning to the Special Forces to provide manpower for covert operations around the world. The relationship flourished in South East Asia in the 1960s and 1970s as hundreds of Special Forces troops served in operations supervised by the CIA. During the Vietnam war Special Forces were sent on missions into North Vietnam, Laos and Cambodia to conduct strategic intelligence operations.[148]

It was estimated in 1978 that Army Intelligence had a US$9 million budget and 37 500 personnel.[149] Many of the 37 500 personnel are assigned to G-2 units.[150] The present Assistant Chief of Staff for Intelligence is Major General William Odom.

The Air Force intelligence community

Five organizations comprise the air force intelligence community — the Office of the Assistant Chief of Staff, Intelligence (OACS/I); the Air Force Intelligence Service (AFIS); the Office of Special Investigations (OSI); the Electronic Security Command (ESC); the Foreign Technology Division (FTD) of the Air Force Systems Command; and the Air Force Technical Applications Center (AFTAC).

The OACS/I is organized into two main directorates — the Directorate of Intelligence Plans and Systems and the Directorate of Estimates. The Directorate of Intelligence Plans and Systems consists of an Electromagnetic Combat Intelligence Group and four divisions — system integration, imagery, SIGINT/Technical and Plans. The Estimates Directorate also consists of four divisions — the General Threat Division, the Regional Estimates Division, the Strategic Studies Division and the Weapons, Space and Technology Division.[151]

The OACS/I is primarily a management organization, directing the work of the air force intelligence community. This framework was dictated by a 1971 directive by the Secretary of the Air Force mandating reassignment of Air Staff operating and support functions to other organizations.[152] In response to this mandate the Air Force Intelligence Service (AFIS) was created in June 1972. AFIS responsibilities include production of all-source intelligence on matters that affect air force policies and resources, force deployment and employment; and intelligence on current indications and warning matters. It is also responsible for security and communications management, intelligence data management, attaché and Soviet Affairs studies.[153]

Two subordinate units of the AFIS of particular interest are the Directorate of Evasion and Escape/Prisoner of War Matters and the Air Force Special Activities Center. The Directorate is responsible for all aspects of intelligence support of evasion and escape/prisoner of war matters while the Center 'provides centralized management of all Air Force activities involved in the collection of information from human resources' — including defectors. The Center, headquartered at Fort Belvoir, Virginia, has major subordinate units in the European and Pacific theatres.[154]

The Office of Special Investigations (OSI) has both a counter-intelligence and criminal investigative role. In its counter-intelligence role it both conducts investigations concerning air force personnel and prepares studies of hostile intelligence services.

The Electronic Security Command (ESC), formerly the Air Force Security Service, is headquartered in San Antonio, Texas. The ESC performs cryptographic, cryptanalytic and electronic warfare functions for the air force as well as operating under NSA/CSS direction. In the latter capacity it provides personnel for overseas and domestic strategic intelligence collection.

The Foreign Technology Division (FTD) of the Air Force Systems Command is located at Wright-Patterson Air Force Base in Dayton, Ohio and was formerly known as the Air Technical Intelligence Center. FTD is one of the largest and most important US intelligence units. According to one account:

FTD acquires, evaluates, analyses and disseminates information on foreign aerospace technology in concert with other divisions, laboratories and centers. Information collected from a wide variety of sources is processed on unique electronic data handling and laboratory processing equipment and analyzed by scientific and technical specialists.[155]

The foreign aerospace technology that is the subject of the FTD's analyses includes Soviet Intercontinental Ballistic Missiles (ICBMs) and Submarine-Launched Ballistic Missiles (SLBMs). The FTD has the *primary* responsibility for interpreting communications intercepted from Soviet rocket boosters to their ground controls. Likewise, the FTD conducted the telemetry analysis on the 1968 Soviet SS-9 'triplet' tests, in which three re-entry vehicles were released from the Missile, and developed the thesis that the Mod-4 of the SS-9 might possess some primitive MIRV characteristics.[156]

The Air Force Technical Applications Center, with 1380 personnel and headquartered at Patrick Air Force Base, Florida, operates the United States Atomic Energy Detection System (AEDS). The system employs scientific means to obtain and evaluate technical data on the nuclear energy activities of foreign powers — including whether foreign nations are complying with the Limited Test Ban Treaty and Threshold Test Ban Treaty.[157]

Data are obtained via airborne, underwater, space operations and ground stations. Present aerospace collection assets include U-2s as well as the Vela and DSP satellites. AFTAC's extensive network of US and foreign ground sites and bases include three support squadrons (at McClellan AFB, California; Wheeler AFB, Hawaii; and Lindsey Air Station, Germany), nineteen detachments, six operating sites and fifty equipment locations.[158]

The budget and personnel of the Air Force intelligence community may constitute the largest single block in the US intelligence community. ESC employs 11 000 individuals alone while FTD may employ 20 000 or more.[159] In terms of dollars, the Air Force intelligence community may spend over US$4 billion a year.[160]

The Naval intelligence community

The naval intelligence community is the most complex of the three service intelligence communities, in large part because it has a substantial strategic intelligence *collection* role. At the top of the naval intelligence community is the Assistant Chief of Naval Operations for Intelligence, who is simultaneously the Director of the Office of Naval Intelligence (DNI). The Office of Naval Intelligence (ONI) is a supervisory organization which directs the activities of the various naval intelligence operating agencies.

Directly subordinate to the DNI are the several divisions that constitute the ONI organization — the Security of Military Information Division; the Plans, Policy and Estimate Division; the Special Projects Division and the Plans, Programs and System Architecture Division.

Also subordinate to the DNI are two organizations which are headed by

126 *The Ties That Bind*

Deputy DNIs — the Naval Intelligence Command (NIC) and the Naval Security Group Command.[161] The functions of the NIC include the direction and coordination of intelligence collection, production and dissemination to satisfy Navy Department and national requirements. In addition to numerous management divisions at NIC headquarters, NIC has four subordinate commands — the Naval Investigative Service, the Naval Intelligence Processing Systems Support Activity, the Naval Intelligence Support Center, and the Navy Operational Intelligence Center (NOIC).[162]

The Naval Investigative Service is responsible for naval security and counter-intelligence matters. The Naval Intelligence Processing Systems Support Activity deals with automated naval intelligence processing and communications systems. The Naval Intelligence Support Center is the scientific and technical intelligence branch of the NIC. It is responsible for processing, analysing, producing and disseminating scientific and technical intelligence on foreign naval systems.[163] (See Figure 6.6.)

Figure 6.6 Organization of the Office of Naval Intelligence (ONI)

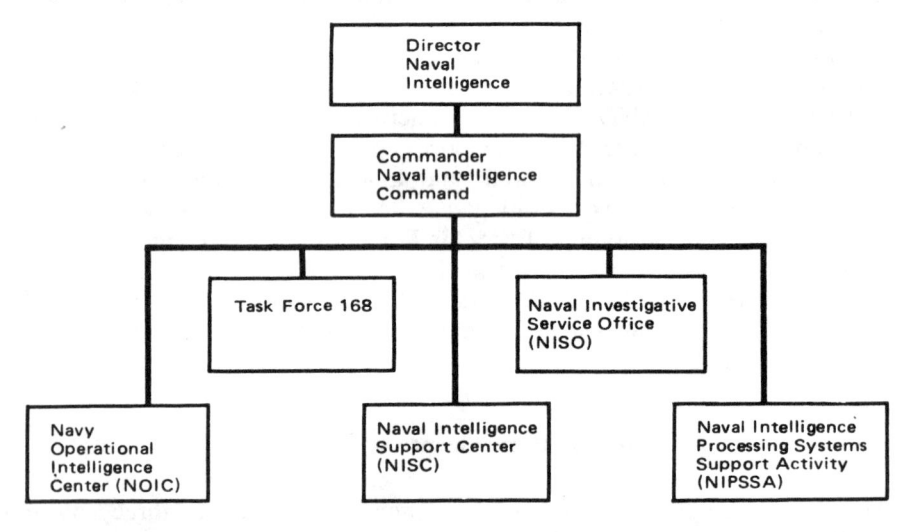

```
                    Director
                    Naval
                    Intelligence
                         |
                    Commander
                    Naval Intelligence
                    Command
                         |
        ┌────────────────┼────────────────┐
                   Task Force 168    Naval Investigative
                                     Service Office
                                     (NISO)
        |                |                    |
    Navy            Naval Intelligence    Naval Intelligence
    Operational     Support Center        Processing Systems
    Intelligence    (NISC)                Support Activity
    Center (NOIC)                         (NIPSSA)
```

The NOIC has functions related to ocean and underseas surveillance. These functions are to:

(1) provide current operational intelligence and ocean surveillance information on a continuous watch basis;
(2) provide current locating information and operational histories of selected foreign merchant and fishing fleets;
(3) provide central data base and intelligence interface for the Current Operations Department;
(4) provide specialized operational intelligence support for U.S. Navy underseas warfare operations.[164]

Information collected is transmitted to one of NOIC's subdivisions in Suitland, Maryland, the Current Operations Department for analysis and processing.[165] (See Figure 6.7.)

The Naval Security Group Command (NSG) performs cryptological and cryptographic activities for the navy. It provides personnel to man the CLASSIC WIZARD ocean surveillance earth terminals as well as providing personnel for NSA activities in the US and abroad. In the US it has been given the responsibility of intercepting the communications of foreign embassies.[166] NSG personnel man SIGINT/ocean surveillance sites at naval bases in Japan, Scotland, Norway and Iceland.

Subordinate to the Commander of NSG is a Deputy Commander and six Assistant Commanders, including Assistant Commanders for Signals Security, Special Operations and Technical Development. Subordinate to each of the Assistant Commanders for Special Operations and Technical Development are Directors for ASW (Anti-Submarine Warfare)/Ocean Surveillance. Subordinate to the Assistant Commander for Signals Security is a Director for Electromagnetic Surveillance.[167]

Another naval organization with a significant intelligence R&D management role is the Naval Electronics Systems Command (NAVALEX), within which are several units of interest, including the Reconnaissance, Electronic Warfare Special Operations and Naval Intelligence (REWSON) Project and the Underseas Surveillance Project.

The REWSON Project includes a Submarine Reconnaissance and Special Operations Division. This division may be responsible for providing the equipment required for the sensitive Special Navy operations such as HOLYSTONE, DESKTOP and SAND DOLLAR that are discussed in Chapter 9. The Underseas Surveillance Project is responsible for several underseas surveillance systems, including SOSUS, RDSS and SURTASS. SOSUS, the Sound Surveillance System, consists of an array of hydrophones attached to the ocean floor to detect submarines. RDSS, the Rapidly Deployable Surveillance System, consists of hydrophones dropped from aeroplanes while SURTASS, the Surveillance Towed Array Sensor System, consists of an array of hydrophones towed by a surface ship.[168]

Finally, there is the Navy Space Command, headquartered at Dahlgren, Virginia, which became operational on 1 October 1983. This Command is responsible for oversight of the Naval Space Surveillance (NAVSPASUR) System and for a wide variety of navy satellite systems — including the Navstar GPS, the Fleet Satellite Communications (FLTSATCOM) system, and the WHITE CLOUD and radar ocean surveillance satellites.[169]

As of 1978 the naval intelligence community had about 17 000 employees and a budget of US$1.2 billion.[170]

Other units

In addition to the multitude of agencies and offices described above there

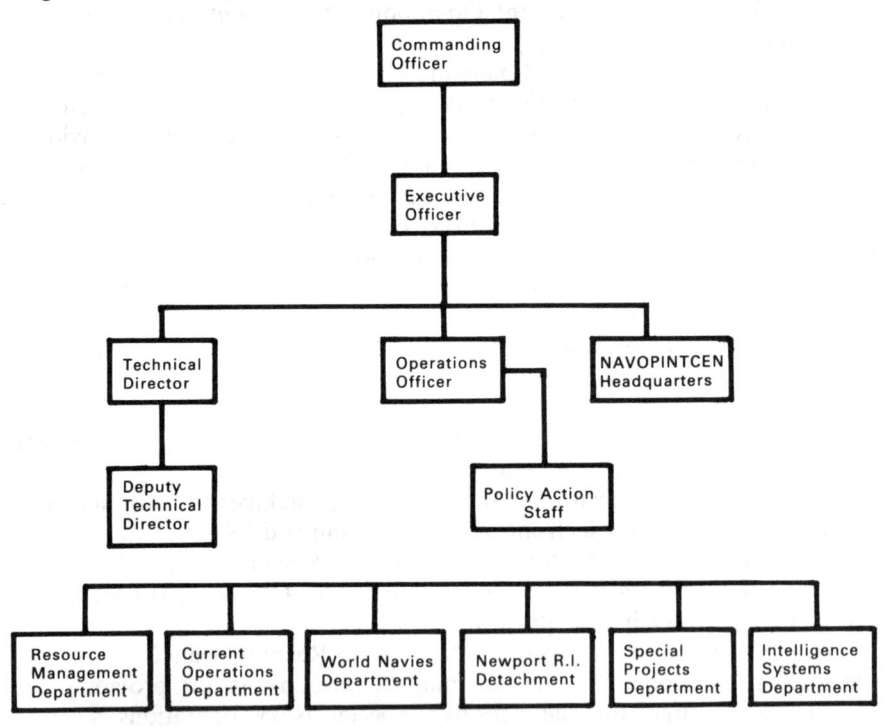

Figure 6.7 Navy Operational Intelligence Center (NOIC)

```
                        Commanding
                         Officer
                            |
                        Executive
                         Officer
          _____|_____
         |              |               |
    Technical      Operations      NAVOPINTCEN
    Director        Officer       Headquarters
         |              |
     Deputy        Policy Action
    Technical        Staff
    Director
```

Resource	Current	World Navies	Newport R.I.	Special	Intelligence
Management	Operations	Department	Detachment	Projects	Systems
Department	Department			Department	Department

are several additional offices and agencies with intelligence functions. These include the Treasury Department's Office of Intelligence Support, the Drug Enforcement Administration's Office of Intelligence, the Office of the Assistant Secretary for International Affairs of the Defense Intelligence Division of the Department of Energy, the Intelligence Division of the Office of Export Enforcement and the Office of Intelligence Liaison in the Commerce Department, and several Department of Defense units — such as the Defense Investigative Service and the Defense Mapping Agency.

The Treasury Department's Office of Intelligence Support provides economic information and analysis to the Secretary of the Treasury while the DEA's Office of Intelligence collects foreign intelligence on the traffic in narcotics. The Defense Intelligence Division of the Office of the Assistant Secretary for International Affairs of the Department of Energy monitors nuclear weapons and foreign energy developments.[171] The Commerce Department's Office of Export Enforcement, particularly its Intelligence Division, is concerned with detecting possible violations of export controls, especially in regard to the shipment of high technology equipment to Soviet bloc countries, while the Office of Intelligence Liaison serves as the departmental link to the intelligence community. Another Commerce Department unit, the Special Projects Office advises US agencies on how to prevent electronic theft of data.[172]

The Defense Investigative Service performs counter-intelligence, security and security clearance functions for the Department of Defense. Using the data produced by reconnaissance and geodetic satellites, the Defense Mapping Agency plays a crucial role in producing intelligence to be used in preparing the SIOP. Among its mapping functions is the specification of the latitude and longitude of targets in the Soviet Union. This is especially crucial since 'on all geographic maps published in the USSR not one Soviet city or town is shown in its current position with relation to its lines of latitude and longitude'.[173]

Management structure

At the apex of the US management structure are the President and the National Security Council (NSC) committees charged with the supervision of intelligence matters. Under the Carter Administration there were two such committees — the Special Coordination Committee (SCC) and the Policy Review Committee (PRC). The SCC had jurisdiction over counter-intelligence matters while the PRC served as the successor to the 54/12 Group, Special Group, 40 Committee, 303 Committee and Operations Advisory Group as the committee charged with approving covert action operations.[174]

Under the Reagan Administration there is apparently a single NSC Committee, the Senior Interagency Group—Intelligence (SIG—I), to deal with all intelligence matters. SIG—I's charter gives it jurisdiction over collection activities and counter-intelligence activities.[175] However, supervision and approval of covert or special activities are functions of the National Security Planning Group — which consists of the President, Secretaries of State and Defense, Director of the CIA and selected presidential aides.[176]

Directly below the NSC is the Director of Central Intelligence/Director of the CIA. Providing advice, counsel and support to the Director of Central Intelligence (DCI) are the National Intelligence Council, Intelligence Community Staff and the National Foreign Intelligence Board. The National Intelligence Council consists of the National Intelligence Officers (NIOs). Each NIO is responsible for producing National Intelligence Estimates with regard to a specific geographic or substantive area. The NIOs draw on resources from the CIA and other intelligence agencies as necessary. There are NIOs for Strategic Forces and Conventional Forces as well as for several geographical areas.[177] The Intelligence Community Staff is responsible for evaluating the performance of the entire community, considering alternative allocations of resources and drawing up the National Foreign Intelligence Program.

The National Foreign Intelligence Board (NFIB) is the successor to the United States Intelligence Board, which was abolished in 1976. The DCI serves as Chairman. Membership of the NFIB includes the Directors of NRO, NSA, INR, DIA, representatives from the FBI, Department of

Energy, and Treasury Department as well as the Deputy Director, CIA as the CIA representative. The chiefs of the service intelligence components sit as observers.[178]

The NFIB provides advice and counsel to the DCI on matters concerning:

(1) production, review and coordination of national foreign intelligence;
(2) the National Foreign Intelligence Program (NFIP) budget;
(3) interagency exchanges of foreign intelligence;
(4) arrangements with foreign governments on intelligence matters;
(5) protection of intelligence sources and methods;
(6) activities of common concern;
(7) other matters referred to it by the DCI.[179]

There are twelve NFIB committees which are involved in carrying out the above tasks as well as providing a means of obtaining interagency consensus on certain matters. These committees are: the SIGINT Committee, Technology Transfer Intelligence Committee, Economic Intelligence Committee, Security Committee, Human Resources Committee, Critical Collection Problems Committee, Scientific and Technical Intelligence Committee, Information Handling Committee, Joint Atomic Energy Intelligence Committee, Weapons and Space Systems Intelligence Committee, Foreign Language Training Committee and the Committee on Imagery Requirements and Exploitation (COMIREX).[180]

The SIGINT Committee was formed in 1962 by the merger of the COMINT and ELINT Committees. It reviews and validates all proposed requirements before they are levied on the NSA.[181] The Security Committee oversees the establishment of security procedures concerning personnel, facilities, documents, dissemination, the release of intelligence to foreign governments and intelligence stored in or processed by computers.[182] The Human Resources Committee was established in 1973 on a one-year trial basis as the Human Sources Committee, to coordinate the various human source collection programs, both overt and clandestine. In 1974 it was accorded permanent status.[183]

The Joint Atomic Energy Intelligence Committee was created to 'foster, develop and maintain a coordinated community approach to problems in the field of atomic energy intelligence, to promote interagency liaison, and to give added impetus and community support to the efforts of individual agencies'.[184] Among other functions the Weapons and Space Systems Intelligence Committee, formerly the Guided Missile and Astronautics Intelligence Committee, assigns designators and codenames for Soviet weapons systems.[185]

The Committee on Imagery Requirements and Exploitation (COMIREX) was formed in 1967 and succeeded the Committee on Overhead Reconnaissance (COMOR) as the USIB Committee responsible for approving the Joint Reconnaissance Schedule and settling disputes over the assignment of reconnaissance priorities. Unlike COMOR, COMIREX also has responsibility for the distribution of imagery obtained from overhead reconnaissance programs.[186] A revision of DCI Directive No. 1/13 in 1973 established the Assistant Chief of Staff for Intelligence (Army), the Director of Naval Intelligence, and the Assistant Chief of Staff, Intelligence (Air Force) as members of COMIREX.[187]

Three additional committees outside the NFIB structure are important in directing COMSEC and reconnaissance programs. The National Communications Security Committee, previously known as the US Communications Security Board, is an interagency committee dealing with a variety of COMSEC issues — including computer and telecommunications security.[188]

The National Reconnaissance Executive Committee, which was created in 1965, consists of the DCI, the Assistant to the President for National Security Affairs and a Department of Defense representative as members. The Committee is responsible for the supervision, budget, R&D program, and structure of the NRO and reports to the Secretary of Defense. If the DCI disagrees with the Secretary's decision he may appeal to the President.[189] One such instance involved the proposed ARGUS or Advanced RHYOLITE satellite which the then Secretary of Defense, James Schlesinger, ruled was unnecessary. DCI William Colby appealed to President Ford who overruled Schlesinger. However, the proposed satellite was not funded by the responsible Congressional committee.[190]

There is a second Executive Committee, probably called either the National Executive Committee for Underseas Surveillance or the National Executive Committee for Special Navy Activities, which provides national level supervision of underseas surveillance activity such as Project HOLYSTONE. As with the National Reconnaissance Executive Committee, it is chaired by the DCI and reports to the Secretary of Defense.[191]

Outside the intelligence community *per se* are two presidential advisory committees. The President's Foreign Intelligence Advisory Board has the authority to review the performance of all agencies in intelligence collection, analysis and execution. It has a full-time staff and consultants to conduct special inquiries. The Intelligence Oversight Board is a three-member committee whose function is to insure the 'legality and propriety' of intelligence activities.[192]

II

The UKUSA community in operation

7

The mechanics of cooperation and exchange

The 1947 agreement on cooperation in the area of signals intelligence (SIGINT) is the most secret and in many ways the most consequential of the myriad of ties which link the five UKUSA countries. However, in addition to the UKUSA Agreement or so-called 'Secret Treaty' of 1947, there are numerous other agreements, both multilateral and bilateral, which govern the exchange of intelligence information between these countries. Moreover, there are unwritten agreements, based on convention and working practice, which in many cases are just as important as the written agreements.

These agreements, conventions and working practices cover, *inter alia*, the arrangements for both the collection of intelligence and the exchange of raw intelligence information and assessments based on that intelligence. They designate the specific national agencies responsible for particular collection activities and the targets of those activities; the mechanisms by which and the conditions under which the various forms of intelligence are exchanged between the participating governments and agencies; and the indoctrination and classification procedures which govern the distribution of the intelligence information.

The UKUSA Agreement, together with many of the other current arrangements, is a direct extension of the cooperation and exchange arrangements established during the Second World War. In the case of Britain and the Dominions — Canada, Australia and New Zealand — close intelligence and security connections can be traced back to the first decade of this century, when the initial variants of many of the current organizations were established. In some instances, the Dominion agencies were essentially branches of the relevant British organizations. For example, Lieutenant Colonel H.E. Jones, the Director of the Australian Commonwealth Investigation Branch (CIB), which existed from 1919 to 1943, reported directly to MI-5 in London, and when the CIB was disbanded on 1 January 1944, following the establishment of the Commonwealth Security Service (CSS), Lt Col. Jones refused to provide the new Director-General of Security the codes and ciphers which he had used in his transactions with MI-5 and without which the new service could not begin to operate.[1]

In the case of British and US security and intelligence agencies, however, although there were substantial informal contacts during the inter-war years, formal relationships were not established until after 15 September 1939, when President Roosevelt wrote to Winston Churchill suggesting that a confidential exchange of information be instituted between Britain and the US.[2] The basis of the five-power special relationship in the field of security and intelligence was established during the next two to three years.

By June 1942, an intricate network of agreements and working arrangements covered cooperation between the five UKUSA countries in the areas of security intelligence, espionage, signals intelligence (SIGINT), ocean surveillance, and special operations.

Following President Roosevelt's suggestion to Churchill in September 1939, the President met privately with Churchill's special envoy, William Stephenson — the 'man called Intrepid' — in April 1940, to discuss a plan for secret cooperation between the FBI and British secret intelligence, and the British Security Coordination (BSC) was set up in New York in June 1940.[3]

The Charter of BSC, as disclosed to the US State Department and FBI, was as follows:

Consequent upon the large-scale and vital interests of the British Government in connection with the purchase and shipment of munitions and war material from the United States, coupled with the presence in this country of a number of British official missions, a variety of security problems has been created, and these, affecting closely as they do the interests of the British Government, call for very close and friendly collaboration between the authorities of the two countries.

Thus, for example, the presence in large numbers of British and Allied ships engaged in loading explosives and other war materials, and the existence of large quantities of similar materials in plants, on railways, and in dock areas throughout the country, presenting as they do a tempting target to saboteurs and enemy agents, constitute in themselves a security problem of considerable magnitude.

With a view to co-ordinating the liaison between the various British missions and the United States authorities in all security matters arising from the present abnormal circumstances, an organization bearing the title *British Security Coordination* has been formed under the control of a Director of Security Co-ordination, assisted by a headquarters staff.[4]

In practice, the BSC was an 'all-encompassing secret security organisation' which represented all the British secret agencies, including the British Secret Intelligence Service (SIS or MI-6), the Security Service (MI-5), the Special Operations Executive (SOE), and the Government Code and Cipher School (GCCS).[5] BSC was described by General William J. Donovan, Director of the US Office of Strategic Services, as 'the greatest integrated, secret intelligence and operations organisation that has ever existed anywhere'.[6]

Cooperation between the US and the UK in the area of signals intelligence (SIGINT) was first discussed, *inter alia*, at the meeting between President Roosevelt and William Stephenson in April 1940. Stephenson informed the President of the progress made by the GCCS at Bletchley toward breaking the German code system and requested that German radio transmissions intercepted by US monitors be passed to Bletchley.[7] On 8 July 1940, the British Ambassador in Washington, Lord Lothian, formally proposed to President Roosevelt that the UK and the US share their technological secrets relating to 'submarine detection and radio interception'.[8] In October 1940, the British learned of the US success in breaking the Japanese high-level J-19 or PURPLE diplomatic code, and in November 1940 Britain and the US signed a highly secret agreement — the direct ancestor of the BRUSA and UKUSA agreements — which provided for 'a full exchange of cryptographic systems, cryptanalytical techniques, direction finding, radio interception, and other technical communication matters pertaining to the diplomatic, military, naval, and air services of Germany, Japan and Italy'.[9]

In January 1941, a small US mission visited Bletchley 'for the purpose of establishing technical co-operation with the British cryptanalytic service'.[10] The mission delivered to the GCCS two PURPLE machines for decoding Japanese diplomatic codes, two RED machines for decoding Japanese naval codes, and a mixed variety of code systems.[11] In return, the US was given an assortment of advanced cryptographic and radio monitoring systems, including the new Marconi–Adcock high-frequency direction-finding (HF-DF) system.[12]

By mid-1941, some six months before Pearl Harbor, cooperation between the UK and the US in SIGINT was, according to the BSC papers, quite unqualified.[13] In the Pacific, for example, the two most important signals intercept and cryptanalysis stations were that of the British GCCS at Singapore and that of the US Navy at Corregidor, and 'it was agreed that anything received by either unit would immediately be exchanged'.[14]

By 1941, the SIGINT cooperation arrangements had also been extended to Canada and Australia. Monitoring stations in Canada (and particularly the major one at Amherst near Halifax) were gathering large quantities of coded Japanese radio transmissions and by 1941 the Canadian SIGINT organisation — the Examination Unit of the Department of External Affairs — was cooperating fully with the British GCCS.[15] By the spring of 1941, a British officer from Halifax was liaison officer for 'special intelligence' in Washington.[16]

In the case of Australia, a small cryptographic organization under the Director of Naval Intelligence had been working with the British Far Eastern Combined Bureau (FECB) in Singapore since the late 1930s. In early 1941, Commander T.E. Nave, who had been working with the FECB in Singapore, began setting up the nucleus of an Australian SIGINT group

138 The Ties That Bind

in Melbourne; the establishment of this group was formalized by the Defence Committee on 28 November 1941.[17]

In late 1940 and early 1941, arrangements were also made for Allied access to Australia's three major radio interception and cryptographic stations — HMAS Harman near Canberra, Coonawarra near Darwin, and at Melbourne. These stations were also substantially expanded at this time.[18]

Congressional testimony concerning the Pearl Harbor attack reveals that Australian intercept stations received the famous Japanese 'Winds' message of 19 November 1941 and the '14 Part' message of 6 December and that these were immediately forwarded to London and Washington.[19] According to that testimony:

The Australians had a small Communications Intelligence Organisation and in December 1941 they were intercepting Japanese diplomatic radio traffic and reading messages in the J-19 system. (The Dutch in Java were also reading J-19, as well as the British in Singapore and London and the US Army and Navy in Corregidor and Washington). The Australian CI Unit had liaison with the Singapore CI Unit, including exchange of translation and keys, except for the Purple and Red Machines. The winds 'set-up' message, dated 19 November 1941, was in J-19. Singapore sent translations to Corregidor and undoubtedly sent these same translations to Australia.[20]

The testimony states that in November and December 1941 (that is, before Pearl Harbor), the following stations were monitoring Japanese radio transmissions on a cooperative basis, in addition to stations in the United States, England, Canada, and China:

Heeia, T.H.	US Navy
Corregidor	US Navy
Singapore	British Intelligence
Australia	Australian Intelligence
Java	NEI Intelligence

On 17 May 1943, Britain and the United States signed the BRUSA Agreement — a formal agreement between the COMINT agencies of the UK and the US. As James Bamford has written:

The significance of the [BRUSA] pact was monumental. It established for the first time intimate cooperation on COMINT of the highest level. It provided for exchange of personnel, joint regulations for the handling of the supersensitive material, and methods for its distribution. In addition, paragraph eight of the agreement provided that all recipients of high-grade COMINT, whether British or American, were bound to the severely strict security regulations that were appended to the document. The cooperation, procedures, and security regulations set out in the BRUSA Agreement serve as landmarks in the history of communications intelligence. Even today, they form the fundamental basis for all SIGINT activities of both the NSA and GCHQ.[22]

The BRUSA arrangements went beyond Britain and the United States to include the code-breaking agencies of Canada and Australia as well. For example, at the Joint Allied SIGINT Conference held under BRUSA auspices at Arlington Hall Station, the headquarters of the US Army Signal Intelligence Service (SIS) on 13 March 1944, the participants included the Chief of the US Signal Security Agency (SSA) and his principal officers; Commander Edward Travis, the Director of GCHQ, Leonard James Hooper, a future Director of GCHQ, and Colonel John H. Tiltman, the GCHQ Liaison Officer to the SSA; Lieutenant-Colonel Edward M. Drake from the Canadian Examination Unit of the Department of External Affairs, Canada's war-time SIGINT organization, who later became the head of CBNRC; and Captain S.R.I. Clark from Australia's Central Bureau (CB).[23]

By 1942, mechanisms of cooperation and exchange had also been established in virtually all other areas of security and intelligence. This was much assisted by the creation of the office of the Coordinator of Information (COI) — the forerunner of the OSS and thence the CIA — by Presidential Executive Order on 11 July 1941.[24] COI was established at the instigation of BSC; the head of COI, General Donovan, was a close friend of William Stephenson; and in its formative stages the COI was entirely dependent on BSC. As Sir William Stephenson has written:

Collaboration began at once. Indeed, together we [Donovan and Stephenson] drew up the initial plans for his agency both as regards establishment and methods of operation ... To secure the closest day-to-day working liaison between BSC and COI, I set up an office in Washington to which I attached experienced officers of all branches, and he in turn established an office in New York.

It is fair to say that if our friend [Donovan] had not been able to rely on BSC's assistance, his organization could not have survived; and indeed it is a fact that before he had his own operational machinery in working order, which was not until several months after Pearl Harbor, he was entirely dependent on it.

The provision of such assistance was the ensuring of COI's full collaboration. To indicate its comprehensive character some points may be enumerated briefly:

(1) The bulk of COI's secret intelligence before Pearl Harbor, and for several weeks thereafter, was supplied by my organization BSC from its various sources.
(2) BSC controlled through its intermediaries two short-wave radio services, one for broadcasts to Europe and Africa, the other for broadcasts to the Far East. These were made available to COI immediately after Pearl Harbor and they were the foundation of all American short-wave radio propaganda.
(3) COI officers of all divisions, as well as COI agents, were in the beginning trained at BSC schools in Canada.
(4) BSC supplied COI with all the equipment which it needed for some period after Pearl Harbor, when such equipment was not yet in production in the United States.
(5) In September 1941 I made arrangements for senior COI officers to spend three months studying all SOE training and operations at first hand.
(6) In January 1942 I had senior officers of SOE sent to set up the Special Operations division of COI.
(7) In October 1941 I arranged for the lecturers in communications in all BI to come to Washington to assist in the establishment of a world-wide system of clandestine communications for COI. The head of my own Communications division, who was probably the most experienced in the field, continued to act as adviser to COI.

These are but a few instances of assistance rendered to the nascent COI. In short, BSC had a considerable part in the up-bringing of the agency of which it was in a sense the parent.[25]

Donovan was later to tell General Walter Bedell Smith, the second Director of the CIA (1951–53) that 'Bill Stephenson taught us everything we ever knew about foreign intelligence operations'.[26]

On 13 June 1942 the COI was abolished and replaced by two new agencies: the Office of War Information (OWI), and the Office of Strategic Services (OSS). BSC again played a critical role in the development of the OSS, of which Donovan remained in charge. At the time the Executive Order creating the OSS was issued, both Donovan and Stephenson were in London 'and it was therefore the occasion for discussions concerning secret collaboration between OSS and its British equivalents'.[27] These discussions resulted in two agreements — one between the OSS and British Intelligence (MI-6) and the other between the OSS and the SOE. These agreements have been described by Sir William Stephenson as follows:

(1) Between OSS and BI it was decided that there should be as free an interchange of information as possible but no integration of OSS with BI. Thus Donovan's organization would be free to adopt its own methods of collating intelligence and would operate independently of BSC. This agreement, which was formalized in an exchange of letters, remained valid for the duration of the war.
(2) Between OSS and SOE for Special Operations the world was divided into various zones, British zones, American zones, and British–American zones. It was decided that in British zones SOE should have command and in American zones OSS should have command, while in the British–American zones such as Germany both organizations would be free to operate independently, although wherever possible activities should be closely co-ordinated. This agreement, known as the London Agreement, was with certain minor alterations subsequently approved on the American side by the US Chiefs of Staff and on the British side by the British Chiefs of Staff and the Foreign Office.

Thus provision was made by OSS and BI for independently pooling their resources in the field of secret intelligence and by OSS and SOE for a working partnership in the field of special operations.[28]

These agreements remain in many ways characteristic of those which subsequently established the post-war regime for cooperation in the areas of 'special intelligence' and covert operations.

By 1942 cooperation was also formalized in the area of security intelligence. In the case of Britain and Canada, cooperation between MI-5 and the RCMP had been established many years before the Second World War.[29] In New Zealand, the Security Intelligence Bureau (SIB) was established in late 1940 at the direct instigation of the British Government and was initially headed by a British officer.[30] In Australia, the two organizations with wartime responsibility for security intelligence — the Army's Directorate of Military Intelligence (DMI) and the CIB/CSS — each had established close relationships with both MI-5 and the FBI before Pearl

Harbor.[31] Cooperation between the FBI and British Intelligence was discussed at the meeting between President Roosevelt and William Stephenson in April 1940. As Stephenson later reported to Churchill, 'The President has laid down the secret ruling for the closest possible marriage between the FBI and British Intelligence'.[32]

Plans for cooperation in security intelligence matters in the Western Hemisphere were discussed at a meeting of senior members of the BSC, the FBI and the RCMP at the FBI headquarters in Washington on 31 December 1941, just three weeks after Pearl Harbor. The agenda for this meeting expressed its purpose as follows:

> The Government of the United States is interested in establishing a more closely correlated and official machinery for handling of investigative activities in the Western Hemisphere. Matters to be considered will include the improvement of existing coverage of subversive groups, the improvement of facilities for the exchange of information, the consideration of establishing liaison representatives at the headquarters of various groups and the establishing of an international body to convene from time to time for the purpose of outlining investigative and operational procedure as joint undertakings and on a Hemisphere basis.[33]

Following the conclusion of the Second World War, with the disbandment of many of the wartime security and intelligence agencies — such as the BSC, the OSS, the SOE and the Allied Intelligence Bureau (AIB) in Australia — some of these wartime agreements, understandings and working arrangements lapsed. In other cases, the wartime agencies were simply reorganized — for example, Central Bureau in Australia was reorganised as the Defence Signals Bureau (DSB) in November 1945; the GCCS at Bletchley was reorganized as the Government Communications Headquarters (GCHQ) in 1946 — and the agreements between them simply adjusted to accord with 'peacetime' circumstances. From 1947 to 1950, with the onset of the Cold War, most of the wartime agencies were re-established in one fashion or another — for example, the CIA, established in 1947, was in many ways a direct successor to the COI and OSS. With only relatively minor reforms and amendments, these agencies and the network of cooperation and exchange arrangements which bind them comprise the current UKUSA community.

There are currently more than a thousand defence and security treaties and agreements in force, both unilateral and multilateral, between the UKUSA countries. (There are about 100 military agreements between the United States and Canada alone.) Several hundred of these treaties and agreements are concerned with cooperation and exchanges in security and intelligence matters.

Signals intelligence

Cooperation and exchange in the area of signals intelligence (SIGINT) is primarily governed by the UKUSA Agreement of 1947, which actually consists of a series of agreements, exchanges of letters and memoranda of common understandings signed in 1947, and which has been described as 'quite likely the most secret agreement ever entered into by the English-speaking world'.[34]

The UKUSA Agreement effectively brought together 'under a single umbrella' the SIGINT organizations of the United States, Britain, Canada, Australia and New Zealand — that is, those organizations currently known as the National Security Agency (NSA), the Government Communications Headquarters (GCHQ), the Communications Security Establishment (CSE), the Defence Signals Directorate (DSD), and the Government Communications Security Bureau (GSCB). Although the 1947 agreement was essentially a reformulation of the BRUSA Agreement of 17 May 1943, it did not in all respects supersede the BRUSA Agreement.

The UKUSA Agreement is a tiered arrangement under which the parties have agreed to cooperate in the collection and exchange of certain intelligence activities, and principally signals intelligence (SIGINT). The NSA and the GCHQ are currently designated as the First Parties to the Agreement, with the CSE, DSD and the GCSB being the Second Parties. The SIGINT agencies of the NATO countries and selected other countries such as Japan and South Korea subsequently acceded to the Agreement as Third Parties. Cooperation and exchange between the First and Second Parties is supposed to be essentially unqualified, although the provisions of the Agreement are reportedly 'much less generous' with respect to Third Parties.[35]

In the case of the US and British agencies, the UKUSA Agreement states that:

The United States Chiefs of Staff will make every effort to insure that the United States will maintain the military security classifications established by United Kingdom authorities with respect to military information of U.K. origin, and the military security classifications established by U.K.–U.S. agreement with respect to military information of joint U.K.–U.S. origin or development; will safeguard accordingly such military information; will not exploit such information for production for other than military purposes; and, will not disclose such military information to a third nation without U.K. consent. The British Chiefs of Staff will make every effort to insure that the United Kingdom will maintain the military security classifications established by the U.S. authorities with respect to military information of U.S. origin, and the military security classifications established by U.K.–U.S. agreement with respect to military information of joint U.K.–U.S. origin or development; will safeguard accordingly such military information; will not exploit such information for production for other than military purposes; and will not disclose such military information to a third nation without U.S. consent.

For the purpose of this agreement the United Kingdom, the British Dominions, and India are considered to be separate nations.[36]

Integration of the Canadian and Australian SIGINT agencies into the UKUSA system was spelled out in the charter of the Commonwealth SIGINT Organisation (CSO), under which the agencies then known as the

CBNRC and DSB were directly tied to the GCHQ. Australian participation in the CSO was approved by the Chifley Government in a Cabinet decision of 12 November 1947.[37] There also exists a CANUSA Agreement which covers certain aspects of SIGINT cooperation between the NSA and the CSE.

Under the UKUSA and CSO pacts, the five nations carved up the earth into spheres of primary SIGINT collection responsibility, with each national SIGINT agency 'assigned specific targets according to its potential for maximum intercept coverage'.[38] The current division of responsibility allocates coverage of the eastern Indian Ocean and parts of South East Asia and the South-west Pacific to the DSD; Africa and the Soviet Union east of the Urals to the GCHQ; the northern USSR and parts of Europe to the Canadian CSE; a small portion of the South-west Pacific to the New Zealand GCSB; and all the remaining areas of interest to the NSA and its component service agencies.

The geographical division of the world is, in practice, of course not as clear-cut as this. The GCHQ maintains joint control (with the DSD) of the SIGINT operations in Hong Kong as a colonial legacy.[39] The GCHQ and NSA operate the SIGINT station on Masirah Island, Oman, as a joint facility.[40] The SIGINT station outside Istanbul is a joint operation of the GCHQ and the US Navy's Naval Security Group (NSG).[41] The station at Leitrim, Canada, has NSG and INSCOM detachments in addition to personnel from the Canadian Communications Security Establishment (CCSE).[42]

The UKUSA Agreement also provides that the participating agencies of the US, Britain, Canada, Australia and New Zealand 'standardize their terminology, codewords, intercept-handling procedures, and indoctrination oaths, for efficiency as well as security'.[43] The basis for this was established by the BRUSA Agreement, the Appendix to which bound both US and British recipients of COMINT to very strict security regulations.[44] As James Bamford has written: 'The cooperation, procedures, and security regulations set out in the BRUSA Agreement serve as landmarks in the history of communications intelligence [COMINT]. Even today, they form the fundamental basis for all SIGINT activities of both the NSA and GCHQ.'[45]

In October 1943, the US War Department issued its formal regulations conforming to the BRUSA Agreement. These included, *inter alia*, the introduction of an entirely new lexicon of common codewords. Three levels of codewords were established for SIGINT material. The agreed codeword for intercepted messages enciphered in the adversary's highest code system was the British ULTRA (the US equivalent of which had been DEXTER); intercept messages of a lesser importance were assigned the codeword Pearl (the US equivalent of which had been 'Corral'); and SIGINT considered to be of the lowest security importance, such as Traffic Analysis (T/A) intelligence, the codeword Thumb (the US equivalent of which had been 'Rabid'). (Pearl and Thumb were reportedly later replaced by the single codeword Pinup.)[46]

144   The Ties That Bind

In addition to the standardization of codewords, the BRUSA/UKUSA Agreements also rationalized the worldwide interception and COMINT relay systems of the UKUSA agencies. By 1956, for example, the NSA had established ten COMINT Communications Relay Centers (CCRCs), with a specific Service SIGINT agency responsible for a designated Center — the Naval Security Group (NSG) was responsible for the CCRCs at Port Lyautey, French Morocco and Wahiawa, Oahu, Hawaii; the Army Security Agency (ASA) was responsible for the CCRCs at Clark Field in the Philippines, Permasans in West Germany, and one in Japan; and the Air Force Security Service (AFSS) was responsible for those at Nan Szu Pu in Taiwan, Karamursel in Turkey, Onna in Okinawa, Elmendorf Air Force Base in Alaska, and Chicksands in the United Kingdom. Each of these Centers was responsible for operating and coordinating the communication of COMINT material from SIGINT facilities in their particular regions — from seven sites in the case of the CCRC at Onna, Okinawa, to 31 sites in the case of Permasans in West Germany. In addition, the NSA headquarters at Fort Meade, Maryland, was directly responsible for COMINT communication from SIGINT sites in the US as well as between itself and the GCHQ at Cheltenham, England, and the CBNRC, Ottawa, Canada.[47] Three particular COMINT distribution sub-systems are shown in Figures 7.1 to 7.3. It is noteworthy that in 1956 it was still considered that 'the BRUSA agreement may necessitate continuation of the term Centralized COMINT Communications Center (CCCC) for the UK facility [at Chicksands]',[48] rather than the newer term COMINT Communications Relay Center (CCRC), even though almost a decade had passed since the UKUSA Agreement had been signed.

The BRUSA/UKUSA and Commonwealth SIGINT Organisation (CSO) agreements are supplemented by a series of 'International Regulations on SIGINT', generally referred to as IRSIGs, and a series of 'COMINT Security Regulations', which together prescribe security procedures, including methods of personnel indoctrination, to which the participating governments have agreed.[49] Both the IRSIGs and the COMINT Security Regulations are quite voluminous; they are regularly up-dated and are usually kept in large loose-leaf binders. The excerpts from Document 1 of the Third Edition of the IRSIG, reprinted below, relate to indoctrination and secrecy oaths demanded of all UKUSA personnel with security clearances allowing access to COMINT material:

145

Figure 7.1 COMINT Teletype Distribution System Fort Meade, Maryland, USA

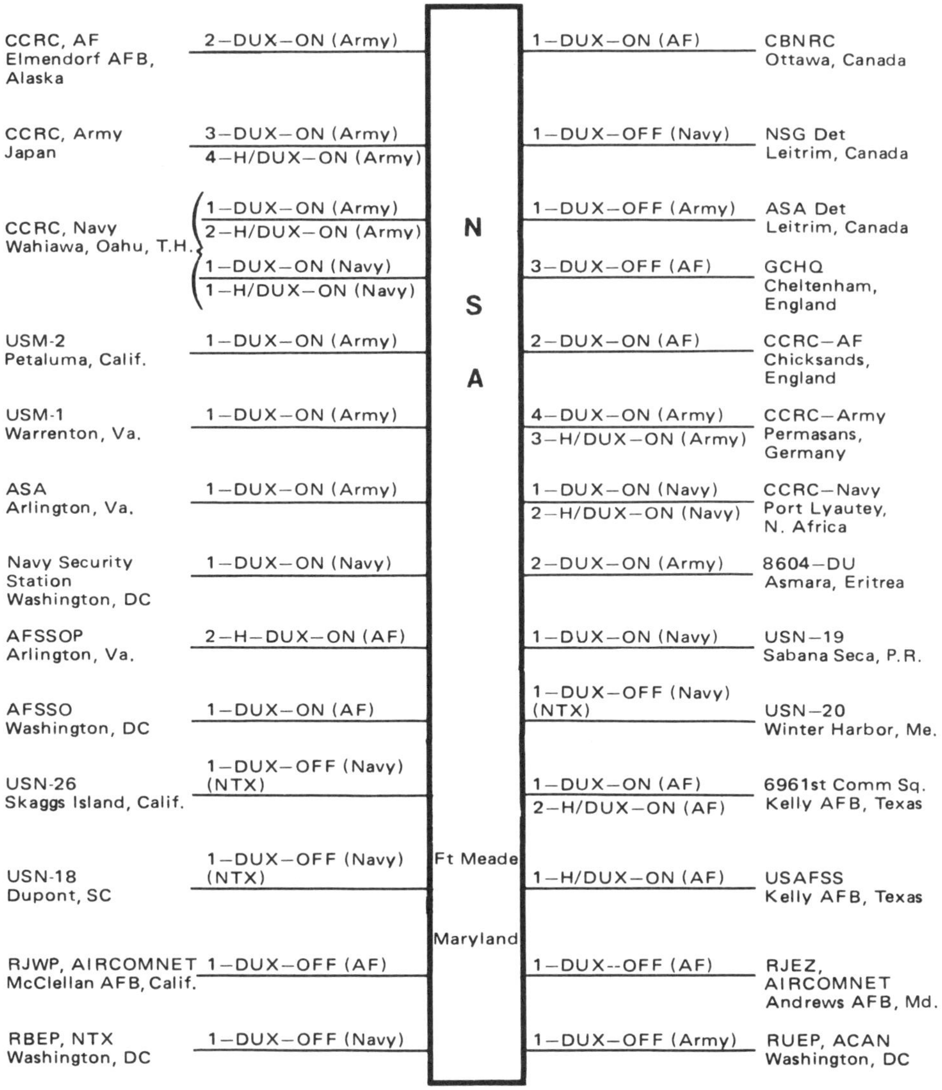

Left Site	Left Link		Right Link	Right Site
CCRC, AF Elmendorf AFB, Alaska	2–DUX–ON (Army)		1–DUX–ON (AF)	CBNRC Ottawa, Canada
CCRC, Army Japan	3–DUX–ON (Army) 4–H/DUX–ON (Army)		1–DUX–OFF (Navy)	NSG Det Leitrim, Canada
CCRC, Navy Wahiawa, Oahu, T.H.	1–DUX–ON (Army) 2–H/DUX–ON (Army) 1–DUX–ON (Navy) 1–H/DUX–ON (Navy)	N S A	1–DUX–OFF (Army) 3–DUX–OFF (AF)	ASA Det Leitrim, Canada GCHQ Cheltenham, England
USM-2 Petaluma, Calif.	1–DUX–ON (Army)		2–DUX–ON (AF)	CCRC–AF Chicksands, England
USM-1 Warrenton, Va.	1–DUX–ON (Army)		4–DUX–ON (Army) 3–H/DUX–ON (Army)	CCRC–Army Permasans, Germany
ASA Arlington, Va.	1–DUX–ON (Army)		1–DUX–ON (Navy) 2–H/DUX–ON (Navy)	CCRC–Navy Port Lyautey, N. Africa
Navy Security Station Washington, DC	1–DUX–ON (Navy)		2–DUX–ON (Army)	8604–DU Asmara, Eritrea
AFSSOP Arlington, Va.	2–H–DUX–ON (AF)		1–DUX–ON (Navy)	USN–19 Sabana Seca, P.R.
AFSSO Washington, DC	1–DUX–ON (AF)		1–DUX–OFF (Navy) (NTX)	USN–20 Winter Harbor, Me.
USN-26 Skaggs Island, Calif.	1–DUX–OFF (Navy) (NTX)		1–DUX–ON (AF) 2–H/DUX–ON (AF)	6961st Comm Sq. Kelly AFB, Texas
USN-18 Dupont, SC	1–DUX–OFF (Navy) (NTX)	Ft Meade Maryland	1–H/DUX–ON (AF)	USAFSS Kelly AFB, Texas
RJWP, AIRCOMNET McClellan AFB, Calif.	1–DUX–OFF (AF)		1–DUX--OFF (AF)	RJEZ, AIRCOMNET Andrews AFB, Md.
RBEP, NTX Washington, DC	1–DUX–OFF (Navy)		1–DUX–OFF (Army)	RUEP, ACAN Washington, DC

Figure 7.2 COMINT Communications Relay Center Chicksands Priory, England

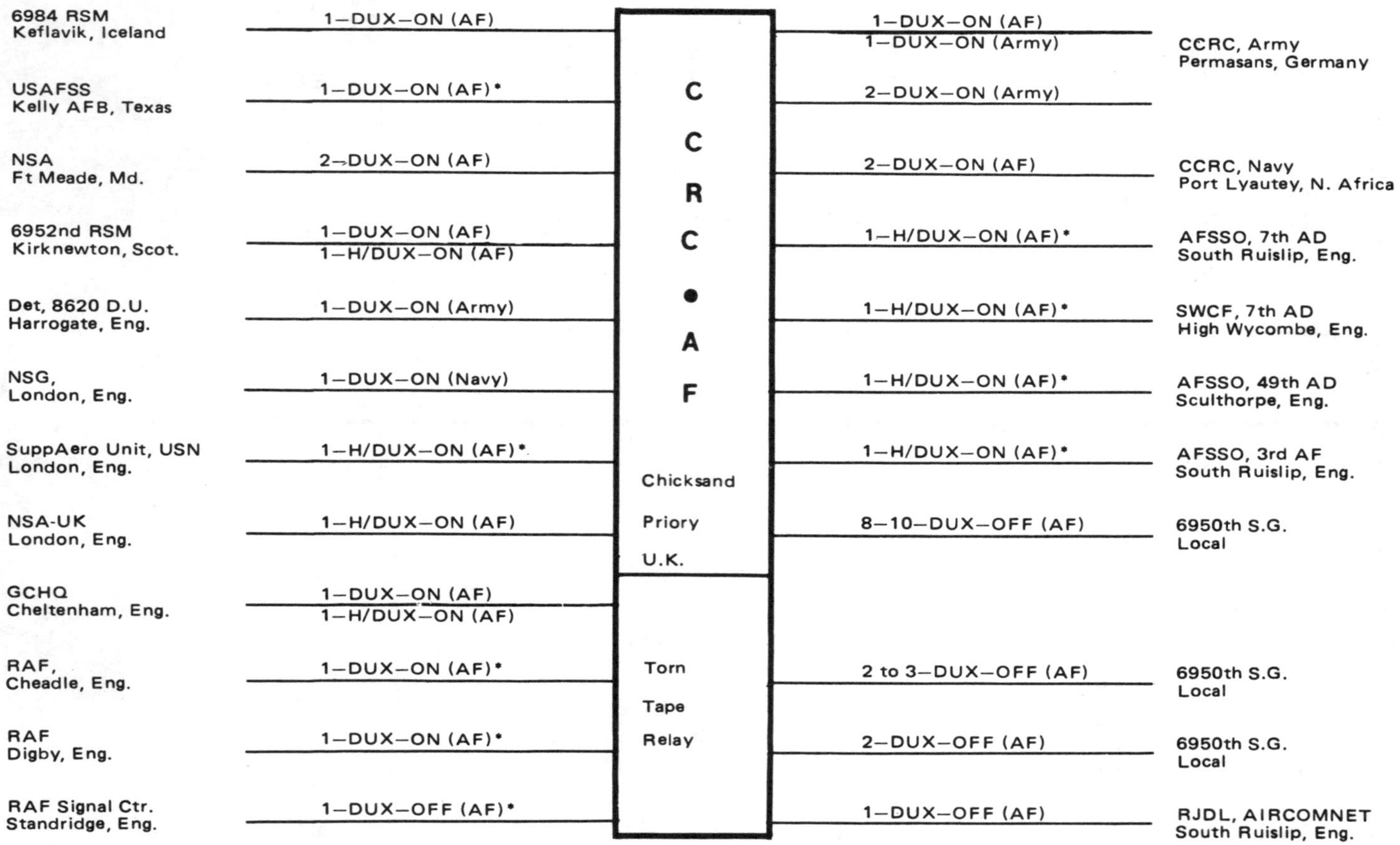

Left Station	Left Line	Center	Right Line	Right Station
6984 RSM, Keflavik, Iceland	1–DUX–ON (AF)		1–DUX–ON (AF)	CCRC, Army, Permasans, Germany
		C	1–DUX–ON (Army)	
USAFSS, Kelly AFB, Texas	1–DUX–ON (AF)*	C	2–DUX–ON (Army)	
NSA, Ft Meade, Md.	2–DUX–ON (AF)	R	2–DUX–ON (AF)	CCRC, Navy, Port Lyautey, N. Africa
6952nd RSM, Kirknewton, Scot.	1–DUX–ON (AF) / 1–H/DUX–ON (AF)	C	1–H/DUX–ON (AF)*	AFSSO, 7th AD, South Ruislip, Eng.
Det. 8620 D.U., Harrogate, Eng.	1–DUX–ON (Army)	●	1–H/DUX–ON (AF)*	SWCF, 7th AD, High Wycombe, Eng.
NSG, London, Eng.	1–DUX–ON (Navy)	A	1–H/DUX–ON (AF)*	AFSSO, 49th AD, Sculthorpe, Eng.
SuppAero Unit, USN London, Eng.	1–H/DUX–ON (AF)*	F	1–H/DUX–ON (AF)*	AFSSO, 3rd AF, South Ruislip, Eng.
NSA-UK, London, Eng.	1–H/DUX–ON (AF)	Chicksand Priory U.K.	8–10–DUX–OFF (AF)	6950th S.G. Local
GCHQ, Cheltenham, Eng.	1–DUX–ON (AF) / 1–H/DUX–ON (AF)	Torn Tape Relay	2 to 3–DUX–OFF (AF)	6950th S.G. Local
RAF, Cheadle, Eng.	1–DUX–ON (AF)*		2–DUX–OFF (AF)	6950th S.G. Local
RAF, Digby, Eng.	1–DUX–ON (AF)*			
RAF Signal Ctr. Standridge, Eng.	1–DUX–OFF (AF)*		1–DUX–OFF (AF)	RJDL, AIRCOMNET, South Ruislip, Eng.

Figure 7.3 COMINT Communications Relay Center Wahiawa, Oahu, Hawaii

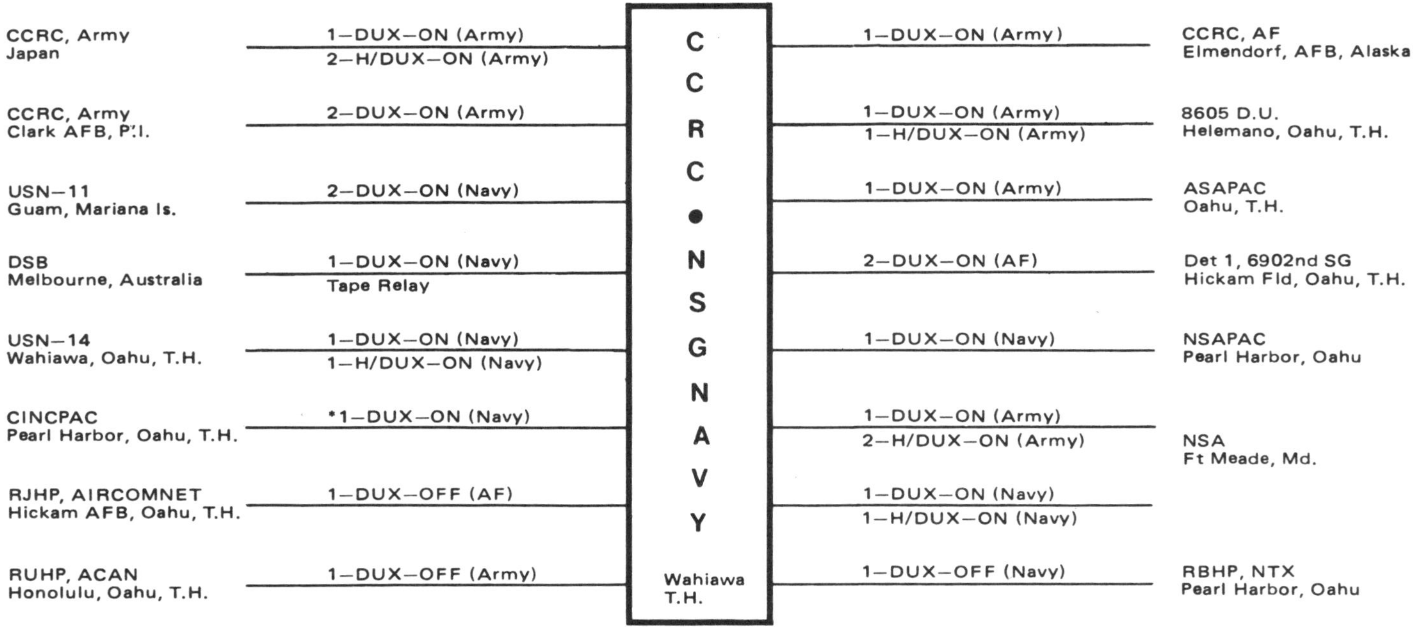

Left Station	Left Circuits	Center	Right Circuits	Right Station
CCRC, Army Japan	1–DUX–ON (Army) 2–H/DUX–ON (Army)	C	1–DUX–ON (Army)	CCRC, AF Elmendorf, AFB, Alaska
CCRC, Army Clark AFB, P.I.	2–DUX–ON (Army)	C	1–DUX–ON (Army) 1–H/DUX–ON (Army)	8605 D.U. Helemano, Oahu, T.H.
USN–11 Guam, Mariana Is.	2–DUX–ON (Navy)	R C	1–DUX–ON (Army)	ASAPAC Oahu, T.H.
DSB Melbourne, Australia	1–DUX–ON (Navy) Tape Relay	• N	2–DUX–ON (AF)	Det 1, 6902nd SG Hickam Fld, Oahu, T.H.
USN–14 Wahiawa, Oahu, T.H.	1–DUX–ON (Navy) 1–H/DUX–ON (Navy)	S G	1–DUX–ON (Navy)	NSAPAC Pearl Harbor, Oahu
CINCPAC Pearl Harbor, Oahu, T.H.	*1–DUX–ON (Navy)	N A	1–DUX–ON (Army) 2–H/DUX–ON (Army)	NSA Ft Meade, Md.
RJHP, AIRCOMNET Hickam AFB, Oahu, T.H.	1–DUX–OFF (AF)	V Y	1–DUX–ON (Navy) 1–H/DUX–ON (Navy)	
RUHP, ACAN Honolulu, Oahu, T.H.	1–DUX–OFF (Army)	Wahiawa T.H.	1–DUX–OFF (Navy)	RBHP, NTX Pearl Harbor, Oahu

HANDLE VIA COMINT CHANNELS ONLY
CONFIDENTIAL
IRSIG — 3RD EDITION
DOCUMENT I. — PART I
OFFICIAL SECRETS ACTS DECLARATION
COMINT INDOCTRINATION

DECLARATION TO BE SIGNED AFTER BRIEFING FOR
COMMUNICATIONS INTELLIGENCE

(1) I declare that I fully understand that information relating to the manner and extent of the interception of communications of foreign powers by H.M. Government and other co-operating Governments, and intelligence produced by such interception, known as Communications Intelligence (COMINT), is information covered by Section 2 of the Official Secrets Act 1911 (as amended).
(2) I further understand that the sections of Official Secrets Acts, set out on the back of this document, cover material published in a speech, lecture, or radio or television broadcast, or in the Press or in Book form. I am aware that I should not divulge any information gained by me as a result of my appointment to any unauthorized person, either orally or in writing, without the previous official sanction in writing of ...... I further understand that I am liable to be prosecuted if I publish without official sanction any information I may acquire in the course of my tenure of an official appointment, or retain without official sanction any sketch, plan, model, article, note or official documents which are no longer needed for my official duties, and that these provisions apply not only during the period of my appointment, but also after my appointment has ceased.
(3) I further declare that I understand that COMINT and all information relating to COMINT may only be discussed with persons whom I know to be COMINT indoctrinated.
(4) I will observe and comply with such provisions of the COMINT Security Regulations as may be brought to my attention either now or in the future and in particular I AGREE not to enter, without the written permission of .... any of the following countries, i.e. Albania, Bulgaria, China, Cuba, Czechoslovakia, Vietnam, Poland, Roumania, Tibet and U.S.S.R; until .... months after I have ceased to be authorized to receive COMINT and have signed Part II of this Declaration (whether I am still in the service or not).
(5) I UNDERSTAND the need for secrecy about COMINT never expires and I will immediately report to the responsible authority any infringement of the COMINT Security Regulations which may come to my notice.

Dated this .... day .... 19 .... at ....

Signature of witness
(who should be an authorized indoctrinating officer).

....
Surname (Block letters)
....
I have explained those parts

Signature ....
Surname (in block letters) ....
Full Christian Name(s) ....
Rank or Grade ....
Appointment held ....
Service number (where applicable) ....

of the COMINT Security
Regulations which he/she
needs to know, and I am
satisfied that he/she
understands.

HANDLE VIA COMINT CHANNELS ONLY
CONFIDENTIAL
PART II
FORM OF DECLARATION TO BE SIGNED ON CEASING TO BE CURRENTLY COMINT INDOCTRINATED

(6) Since it has been determined that I no longer require COMINT in the performance of my duties having today relinquished my appointment as/at .... I realise that I am no longer included on the list of persons authorized to receive information from or in connection with COMINT and that any special privileges, such as access to COMINT establishments, cease forthwith.

(7) I understand that the provisions of the Official Secrets Acts continue to apply to me, notwithstanding the relinquishment of my appointment, and that all information which I have acquired or to which I have had access whilst so employed is information which is covered by Section 2 of the Official Secrets Act, 1911, (as amended); and that the sections of the Official Secrets Acts set out on the back of Part I of this document cover material published in a speech, lecture, radio or television broadcast or in the Press or in book form or otherwise and that I am liable to be prosecuted if, either in the United Kingdom or abroad I communicate, either orally or in writing, including publication or otherwise, to any unauthorized person any information acquired by me as a result of my said appointment, unless I have previously obtained the official sanction in writing of ....

(8) I undertake not to discuss henceforth codeword COMINT or matters pertaining thereto with any person whatsoever unless and until I am specifically freed in writing from this obligation by ....

(9) I also undertake to bring immediately to the notice of .... any breach of COMINT Security Regulations which may come to my notice in the future.

(10) In view of the risk to security that would be involved if I were to be apprehended and subjected to interrogation, I confirm my previous agreement not to travel to any of the Sino-Soviet Bloc countries specified in Clause 4, without the written consent of .... until after .... 19 ....

Dated this .... day .... 19 ....
Signature of witness, (who At ....
should be an authorized
indoctrinating officer). Signature ....
.... Surname (in Block Letters) ....
Surname (Block Letters) Full Christian Name(s) ....
....

These agreements are cemented by the exchange of SIGINT personnel among the US, British, Canadian, Australian and New Zealand agencies, as well as by the joint staffing of many of the major UKUSA SIGINT stations.

The NSA maintains an 'Office of the Special United States Liaison Officer' (SUSLO) near Grosvenor Square in London, while the GCHQ has a 'Senior United Kingdom Liaison Office' (SUKLO) in Washington.[50] There is a GCHQ Liaison Officer at DSD headquarters in Melbourne, where there are also about ten NSA personnel attached to the SUSLO.[51] The New Zealand GCSB is generally represented abroad by the DSD Liaison Officer. Major SIGINT stations at which there is extensive joint staffing include those at Masirah Island, Diego Garcia, Hong Kong, Leitrim, Ascension Island, Istanbul, and Menwith Hill in Yorkshire. The close personal relationship between senior UKUSA personnel is evinced in the letter of 22 July 1969 (reprinted below), from Leonard James Hooper, then the Director of GCHQ, to Lieutenant-General Marshall S. Carter, on the occasion of General Carter's retirement as Director of NSA:[52]

GOVERNMENT COMMUNICATIONS HEADQUARTERS,
OAKLEY, CHELTENHAM, GLOS.
D/8586/1003/11
22nd July 1969

Lieutenant-General Marshall S. Carter,
Director,
NSA

Dear Pat,

Last week you told me that you were relinquishing your post as Director NSA from 1st August and going into retirement. Yesterday I was informed of the name of your successor.

This is simply to tell you how much we in GCHQ have valued your part in our dealings with NSA over the past four years. From the outset, though the extent of our working partnership was new to you, you showed an instinctive feeling for its nature and depth which was a great strengthener to those of us who had worked so long in it, and you have consistently gone out of your way to help us sustain and if possible improve our contribution to it. For this we are very grateful. You have given us practical help whenever we sought it but, more importantly, you have given every encouragement and made us feel that GCHQ really mattered to Director NSA. I think you believe, as I do, that the professional relationship between our two Agencies remains of great importance to our two countries and you have certainly made a very great personal contribution to its present strength and closeness.

You kindly received my senior staff whenever they came to Washington and they, like me, have benefited from your wisdom, kindness and hospitality. There are many who will remember you with respect and affection.

For myself I can truly say that my early years as Director GCHQ were made much easier by knowing that I had so good a friend and so understanding a colleague in the Director of NSA. No one could ask for more.

I do not yet know Admiral Gayler but I look forward to meeting him soon. Please tell him what you have found to be the worthwhile and the difficult parts of the UKUSA relationship and assure him that we in GCHQ will do our best to assist NSA in continuing its great and important mission under his leadership.

Thank you for all you have done, and for your way of doing it. You and your wife take with you into retirement the best wishes of myself and all my colleagues. May you have many years in which to enjoy a well-earned rest.

Yours Very Sincerely,
Joe Hooper

Clandestine intelligence collection

The only UKUSA agencies concerned with covert intelligence collection and production are the British Secret Intelligence Service (SIS), the American CIA, and the Australian Secret Intelligence Service (ASIS). Cooperation between these three agencies, while not covered by any formal agreement comparable to the UKUSA Agreement in the SIGINT area, has nevertheless been extremely close, and many of the mechanisms for cooperation and exchange parallel those operating in the SIGINT area.

Cooperation between the SIS and the CIA was established at the outset of the creation of the CIA in July 1947. Many members of the new US agency, and particularly those with backgrounds in the OSS, had worked during the Second World War under the tutelage of the SIS. CIA and SIS liaison offices were established in London and Washington respectively, and within two years there were 'ten or a dozen' SIS officers in Washington.[53] In September 1949, H.A.R. (Kim) Philby arrived in Washington, ostensibly as a First Secretary in the British Embassy but in reality to head the SIS representation in the US, with a brief to strengthen SIS–CIA relations.[54] As a *Sunday Times* team has written:

It is difficult to exaggerate the importance of this posting. The Central Intelligence Agency had been set up in 1947 and although beginning to feel its strength still tended to regard SIS with some awe. Between the two existed what CIA officers describe as 'a very special relationship', and with it, 'an amazingly free exchange of information' took place. Philby was right in the heart of this. His contacts ranged from the director, a tough ex-army man, General Bedell Smith, down through the ranks. He was privy to CIA planning; he told the CIA what SIS was doing; he was often briefed by Bedell Smith himself on policy and, above all, he knew what the CIA knew about Soviet operations.[55]

During the 1950s and 1960s there were numerous important and extremely sensitive intelligence collection operations run jointly by the CIA and the SIS. For example, from 1954 until its compromise in 1956, the CIA and the SIS jointly operated a telephone tap link at the end of a tunnel some 550 metres (1804 feet) inside East Berlin which tapped the telephone lines connecting East German government offices, the Karlshorst KGB headquarters and the Soviet army command with direct trunk lines to Warsaw and Moscow.[56] And from April 1961 until the end of August 1962, the SIS and CIA jointly ran the Soviet defector-in-place, Colonel Oleg Penkovsky, an officer in

Soviet military intelligence (GRU), who provided Britain and the United States with comprehensive and detailed analyses of the Soviet missile program — intelligence which was critical in the demise of the 'missile gap' myth in 1961.[57]

The CIA station in London, located in the US Embassy at 24–31 Grosvenor Square, is the Agency's largest liaison station. It is staffed by some 40 CIA officers, who work out of five cover offices — the Political Liaison Section; the Area Telecommunication Office, which has a staff of from nine to thirteen CIA employees at any one time; the Joint Reports and Research Unit (JRRU), which has a staff of about 30 officers, most of whom work in Room 388 in the embassy; the Foreign Broadcast Information Service (FBIS); and the Office of the Special US Liaison Officer, most of whose members are NSA officers but some of whom are CIA.[58] The London station is generally headed by a very senior CIA officer. For example, Cord Meyer, who was Chief of Station from July 1973 to July 1976, had previously been the Chief of the International Organizations Division and the Assistant Deputy Director of Plans;[59] his successor Edward Proctor, was Deputy Director for Intelligence from 1971 until 1976;[60] and the current Chief of Station, Richard F. Stolz, who succeeded Proctor in December 1979, has been a member of the CIA for just on three decades.[61]

In the case of the Australian Secret Intelligence Service (ASIS), close relationships with the SIS and CIA also date from its very beginning. Indeed, ASIS was very much an SIS creation. The decision to establish ASIS derived from a visit to Australia by Colonel R.H. Ellis, a senior officer of the SIS, in March–April 1950. Ellis had discussions with the (Australian) Defence Committee on 27 April and subsequently with a meeting of senior Australian Cabinet Ministers (including the Prime Minister, R.G. Menzies; the Acting Minister for Defence, P.A.M. McBride; the Minister for External Affairs, P.C. Spender; and the Minister for Works and Housing, R.G. Casey), and on both occasions argued strongly that Australia establish an external covert intelligence collection and operations service. Cabinet decided to establish ASIS on 24 May 1950, with A.D. Brookes as Director and W.T. Robertson as Deputy Director; Brookes had worked closely with British wartime intelligence and security organizations, and Robertson had held a senior staff position in the British Army.[62]

ASIS is in many respects a branch of the SIS. The original arrangements for cooperation were made through an exchange of letters between the Australian and British Prime Ministers in May 1950, in which the British Prime Minister, after consultation with the Chief of the SIS, agreed 'to provide suitable facilities to assist in the setting up of an Australian organization on a secure and sound basis'.[63] The original Charter of ASIS, issued by Prime Minister Menzies on 13 May 1952, stated: '[ASIS] will establish the maximum degree of co-operation with other Commonwealth intelligence agencies and will maintain effective liaison with appropriate agencies in other countries, in particular with the British Secret Service'.[64]

The relationship between ASIS and the SIS is so close that there has never been seen any need for written agreements or a formal exchange of liaison personnel. As Justice Hope reported in 1977:

Officers seconded from one service to the other are not regarded as liaison officers; they are working as integrated members of the headquarters to which they have been seconded, owe their full allegiance to that headquarters for the time being, and have no direct contact with their parent organization except for personal administration matters.[65]

ASIS officers were initially posted overseas as integral members of SIS stations. (The establishment of the first ASIS overseas station was not begun until September 1954.) In 1954, with the approval of Prime Minister Menzies, it was agreed that ASIS would take over from the SIS about one-third of the SIS clandestine collection effort in the Far East, thus allowing the SIS to redeploy its resources in other areas. ASIS officers were posted as integral members to the SIS stations in Hong Kong and Singapore. In return, ASIS stations in South East Asia have represented the SIS. For example, the ASIS station in Manila, where the SIS has no station, represents the SIS in contacts with the Philippine National Intelligence Co-ordination Agency (NICA) and the Joint Intelligence Staff (J-2) of the Philippine Armed Forces. The SIS has given ASIS free access to its worldwide records. For example, ASIS was given a copy of the whole SIS Far East personality card index for inclusion in the ASIS Central Card Index, making the ASIS records the most complete foreign personality index in Australia. Since the beginning of ASIS, the SIS has provided training to ASIS officers on the same SIS intelligence courses in which their SIS colleagues are trained. By 1976, more than 80 ASIS officers had undergone training on SIS courses many of whom received further 'on the job' experience in the SIS Head- quarters in London and in SIS stations in Hong Kong and Singapore. Since 1972, ASIS has responded by including some SIS officers in ASIS training courses. Liaison between ASIS and the SIS is conducted over a common system of communications which is considered 'unique amongst clandestine services'. Since 1973, for example, the principal radio communication link between ASIS and the SIS has been provided by the joint ASIS–SIS Radio Communications Station at Kowandi outside Darwin. It is thus not surprising that ASIS officers continue to call the London headquarters of the SIS the 'Head Office' and the Melbourne headquarters of ASIS itself the 'Main Office'.[66]

The relationship between ASIS and the CIA is both more circumscribed and more formalized. As Justice Hope reported in 1977:

As with ASIS relationship with SIS, no formal contractual agreement exists between Australian and American Governments concerning co-operation between ASIS and CIA. There are, however, general understandings between the two services covering a number of matters of mutual interest.

ASIS liaison with CIA is harmonious and effective, but different in nature from the ASIS/SIS relationship. For one thing, CIA is much more a 'foreign' intelligence service, and thus treats ASIS with some professional reserve. The Americans expect a more exact *quid pro quo* from ASIS than does SIS. The sheer size of the CIA, and the associated internal communications problems, work against a closer relationship.[67]

Contact with the CIA was established by ASIS, and visits of senior personnel were exchanged, in 1952. On 30 April 1954, the first CIA Liaison Officer arrived at ASIS headquarters in Melbourne, and this posting has been maintained since then — a somewhat more formal arrangement than that which exists between ASIS and SIS.[68]

The ASIS–CIA relationship is also more circumscribed in that 'CIA has not found it acceptable, except in rare instances, to pass to ASIS reports produced in areas where ASIS has no representation', whereas the SIS provides ASIS with reports on countries in the Middle East, Africa, and Europe where ASIS is not represented; with regard to training, although senior ASIS officers have visited CIA training headquarters and held broad discussions with CIA officers on training, the CIA has limited its practical cooperation to the supply of training aids, lecture notes, etc.; and whereas ASIS and the SIS have established machinery for joint clandestine paramilitary action in the event of emergencies — the Joint Clandestine Organization — the CIA has not wished to discuss war or emergency planning matters with ASIS.[69]

A measure of the relationship between ASIS, the SIS and the CIA is the quantity of secret intelligence reports (known as CX material in the case of ASIS and SIS reports, and codenamed 'Remarkable' in the case of CIA reports) which are exchanged between them. The first SIS CX material was passed to ASIS in July 1952. By 1956, ASIS was receiving over 200 reports a month from the SIS and the CIA, of which about 80 per cent were from the SIS. By 1974, ASIS had received over 50 000 secret intelligence reports from the CIA, and 44 000 from the SIS, as compared to about 10 000 ASIS reports passed to both the SIS and CIA. The numbers of reports produced by ASIS and received by ASIS from the SIS and the CIA in 1974 and 1975, are given in Table 7.1.[70]

Table 7.1 Reports produced by ASIS, and received by ASIS from the SIS and CIA, 1974–75

	1974	1975
ASIS	507	516
SIS	697	1211
CIA	588	794

Other treaties and agreements involving intelligence cooperation and exchange

In addition to the BRUSA/UKUSA and related SIGINT agreements and the largely unwritten understandings with respect to covert intelligence collection and production, there are more than a thousand other treaties, agreements, exchanges of letters and memoranda, and unwritten understandings and working relationships, both bilateral and multilateral, concerning the exchange of intelligence information between the UKUSA countries. The most important of these are the ABCA Agreement; various agreements between the NATO countries; agreements concerned with North American air defences; those concerned with ocean surveillance; and various technical cooperation programs.

The ABCA Agreement

ABCA is the agreement whereby the armies of America, Britain, Canada and Australia, with New Zealand as an associate sponsored by Australia, 'cooperate where possible to share information, to achieve operational compatibility and to obtain the maximum economy by use of the combined resources and efforts' of the armies of the five UKUSA countries.[71]

The ABCA Agreement originated from the secret Quebec Agreement of 1946 which in turn was designed to implement the terms of the public Three Power or Tripartite Statement signed by the US, Britain and Canada in November 1945. The Quebec Agreement of 1946 was principally concerned with the exchange of intelligence information relating to research and development in the areas of chemical and biological warfare (CBW), nuclear energy and nuclear weapons and missiles and rockets. Responsibility for the control of the exchange of this information between the US, Britain and Canada was exercised by the Combined Policy Committee (CPC), which in turn had a branch called the Combined Development Agency (CDA), one of the purposes of which was to 'use every endeavour to secure all available [uranium] supplies from the rest of the British Commonwealth and other countries'.[72] In what came to be known as the Anglo–American Modus Vivendi, an unsigned working arrangement was reached between the US, Britain and Canada at a meeting of the CPC in January 1948, in which it was agreed that a limited amount of information could be exchanged with Australia provided that Australia could assure the security of that information[73] — a condition which was met with the creation of the Australian Security Intelligence Organisation (ASIO) in March 1949. The CDA then approached the Australian Government to establish a program for Australian participation in atomic energy research and development, including the exploration for uranium ores and the development of the known and potential resources of those ores. At the same time, agreement was also reached between Australia and the UK with regard to the testing of British rockets in the Woomera region of South Australia.[74] To complete the cooperation in this field, Prime Minister Menzies announced on 18 February 1952 that the UK, 'in close cooperation with the Government of the Commonwealth of Australia', would begin testing atomic weapons in Australia during the course of the year.[75] The Tripartite Agreements of 1945–46 had now become the Quadrapartite Agreements.

156 The Ties That Bind

The Quadrapartite Agreements for the sharing of classified material were later replaced by the ABCA Agreement. At the working level of the ABCA Program are a series of Quadrapartite Working Groups (QWGs), each of which covers a functional area such as Armour, Infantry, Command and Control, Air Defence, Combat Development, and Electronic Warfare. According to an Australian delegate to a meeting of the ABCA QWG on Combat Development (QWG/CD) in 1977:

> The QWGs work mainly by correspondence, but meet at intervals of about 18 months in each country in turn to develop quadrapartite thought and ideas which could influence national R&D programmes, to exchange information on current and future equipment and tactics, to originate Quadrapartite Standardization Agreements (QSTAGs) and to identify areas which could lead to closer cooperation between [the ABCA] Armies.[76]

The QWG on Electronic Warfare (QWG/EW) serves as a forum for the exchange of SIGINT concepts, doctrines, procedures and material requirements between the ABCA partners. The Standing Chairman of the QWG/EW is the Commander of the US INSCOM Combat Developments Activity, who is also the Senior US Delegate to the QWG/EW.[77]

While the ABCA Agreement relates to the exchange of intelligence and other information between the armies of the UKUSA countries, the navies of these countries have also developed arrangements for the exchange of views and information on their requirements for 'communications interoperability', including cryptographic systems and communications security (COMSEC). Again, these arrangements have a direct lineage to those of the Second World War and its immediate aftermath. Even before the war, the British, Canadian, Australian and New Zealand navies used a common Commonwealth *Conduct of the Fleet* book, *Fleet Signalling* book and *Code of Flags*, common radio transmission techniques, and interoperable cryptographic systems. Proposals for a structure to formulate a combined US–British communications policy were exchanged at the beginning of the Second World War, and the first charter of a Combined Communications Board (CCB) was approved by the Combined Chiefs of Staff on 16 July 1942. The membership of the CCB consisted of representatives of the three British services, the US army and navy, and one representative each of Australia, Canada, and New Zealand.[78]

There have been several successor organizations to the CCB, which was dissolved in October 1949. As one account has described:

> The UK and the US agreed that the work previously carried out by the CCB should be continued by the Washington based U.K. Joint Communications–Electronics (C–E) Staff and the U.S. Joint C–E Committee, with representation of Australia, Canada and New Zealand being invited where appropriate. This arrangement continued until early 1951 when Canada joined as a full member of the organization which came to be known as the CAN–UK–US Joint Communications–Electronics Committee (JCEC). On December 18, 1969, Australia became a full member of

the organization which was reconstituted as the 'Australian–Canadian–United Kingdom–United States Military C–E Board' (AUS–CAN–UK–US MCEB). New Zealand became a full member on September 20, 1972 and the title Combined Communications–Electronics Board (CCEB) was adopted.[79]

With the formation of NATO on 4 April 1949, the three UKUSA members of NATO — the United States, Britain and Canada — 'released high grade cryptographic systems for common use by and between the NATO nations' and sponsored the production and adoption of a series of 'Allied Communications Publications'. In 1960, a CAN–UK–US Naval Communications (NAVCOMMs) Board was established, together with a Supervisory Board to oversee the efforts of it and subordinate organizations. Australia became a member in 1966 and New Zealand, which originally had an associate status, in 1980. This formed the present AUS–CAN–NZ–UK–US NAVCOMMs Organization. At the third meeting of the Supervisory Board in 1978, it was also decided to establish an AUS–CAN–NZ–UK–US Naval Command and Control Board responsible for command and control problems that fall outside the purview of the NAVCOMMs Organization and a Permanent Coordination Group (PCG) consisting of Washington-based AUS–CAN–NZ–UK–US representatives to oversee the Command and Control Board.[80]

North American Air Defense

The geographical proximity of the United States and Canada, together with the fact that Canada is located astride the principal great circle routes which would be used by Soviet ICBMs and long-range strategic bombers in the event of a nuclear war with the United States, have led to a particularly close relationship between the US and Canada in the area of air defence intelligence, surveillance and early warning. Most of the dozens of agreements and understandings in this area exist under the umbrella of the North American Air Defense (NORAD) Agreement, which was formalized with an exchange of notes between the US and Canadian Governments on 12 May 1958, although the North American Air Defense Command had itself begun operations on 12 September 1957.[81]

The principal mission of NORAD is to provide warning of attack against North America by bombers or ballistic missiles to the US and Canadian national command authorities. NORAD is also responsible for the surveillance of space, to keep track of manmade objects in orbit around the earth, and for the maintenance in peacetime of a surveillance system in North America capable of detecting and identifying unknown aircraft.[82]

The NORAD command structure links the relevant US and Canadian authorities and agencies along both operational and managerial lines, as shown in Figure 7.4.[83]

NORAD both operates its own surveillance and early warning systems and has access to collection sensors controlled by other agencies. For

158   The Ties That Bind

Figure 7.4 Command Structure of NORAD

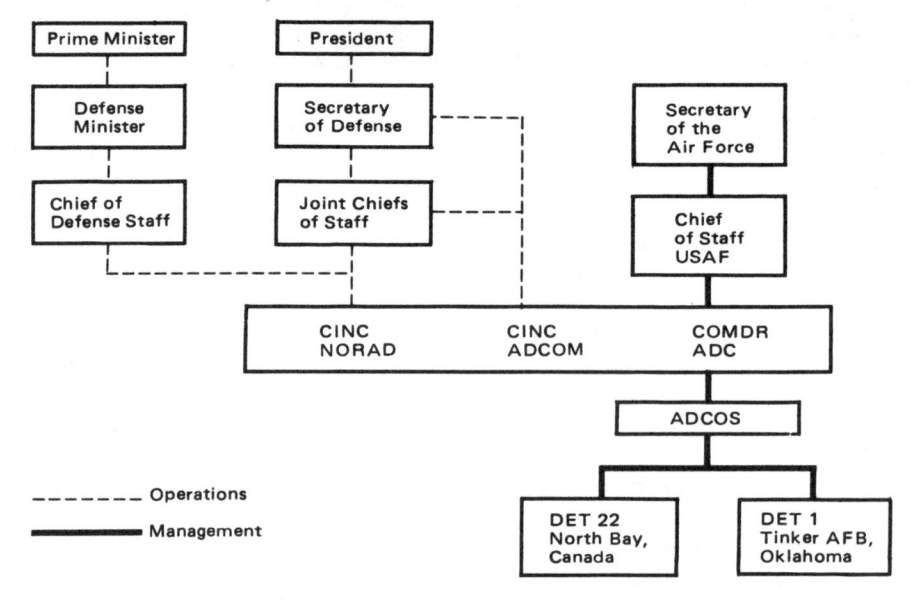

```
┌──────────────┐        ┌──────────────┐
│Prime Minister│        │  President   │
└──────┬───────┘        └──────┬───────┘
       ┆                       ┆
┌──────┴───────┐        ┌──────┴───────┐              ┌──────────────┐
│   Defense    │        │  Secretary   │              │  Secretary   │
│   Minister   │        │  of Defense  │──────────┐   │   of the     │
└──────┬───────┘        └──────┬───────┘          ┆   │  Air Force   │
       │                       │                  ┆   └──────┬───────┘
┌──────┴───────┐        ┌──────┴───────┐          ┆          │
│   Chief of   │        │ Joint Chiefs │──────┐   ┆   ┌──────┴───────┐
│Defense Staff │        │   of Staff   │      ┆   ┆   │    Chief     │
└──────┬───────┘        └──────┬───────┘      ┆   ┆   │   of Staff   │
       └───────────────────┐   ┆              ┆   ┆   │     USAF     │
                           ┆   ┆              ┆   ┆   └──────┬───────┘
       ┌───────────────────┴───┴──────────────┴───┴──────────┴───────┐
       │      CINC                   CINC                  COMDR     │
       │      NORAD                  ADCOM                 ADC       │
       └──────────────────────────────────────────────────┬──────────┘
                                                   ┌──────┴──────┐
                                                   │   ADCOS     │
                                                   └──┬───────┬──┘
                                              ┌──────┴──┐ ┌────┴────────┐
─ ─ ─ ─ ─  Operations                         │ DET 22  │ │   DET 1     │
──────────  Management                        │North Bay│ │Tinker AFB,  │
                                              │ Canada  │ │  Oklahoma   │
                                              └─────────┘ └─────────────┘
```

Command structure on the realigned North American Air Defense Command (NORAD) has two functions, operations (dashed lines) linking the Canadian Prime Minister and US President to the commanders, and management (solid lines), in which NORAD's commander-in-chief is linked from operations to management of the defense forces. The managers are Secretary of the Air Force, US Air Force Chief of Staff, commander, Air Defense Center (ADC), to Aerospace Defense Combat Operations Staff (ADCOS), and then to Detachment 22 at North Bay, Canada, and Detachment 1 at Tinker AFB, Okla., where the Boeing E-3A airborne warning and control system (AWACS) aircraft assigned to NORAD are based.

example, operational control of the three infra-red early warning satellites of the Defense Support Program (DSP), which provides the first warning of any ICBM or SLBM launch, as well as control of the two DSP ground stations at Nurrungar, South Australia and Buckley, Colorado, is the responsibility of the new US Air Force Space Command, although NORAD has direct access to the DSP satellites and ground stations. Secondary warning of ICBM attack is provided by the Ballistic Missile Early Warning System (BMEWS), which consists of three huge radar stations at Thule in Greenland, Clear in Alaska, and Fylingdales in England, and by a new system of three over-the-horizon backscatter (OTH-B) radars at Moscow in Maine and sites on the west and south coasts of the United States. For warning against SLBM attack, the DSP satellites are complemented by the SLBM Phased Array Warning (PAVE PAWS) radar system, of which two sites (at Otis AFB, Massachusetts, and Beale AFB, California) are currently operational, with two more (one at Robins AFB in Georgia, and the other at Goodfellow AFB in south-west Texas) under construction. The AN/FPS85 radar at Elgin AFB, Florida, also performs a detection function against SLBMs launched from south of the US.[84]

For surveillance of satellites, NORAD has operational control of the US

The mechanics of cooperation and exchange 159

Navy's Space Surveillance (SPASUR) system, which consists of a global network of radars and camera systems, including the 3.04 metre (10-foot) tall Baker–Nunn cameras which are capable of photographing an object the size of a basketball at 32 190 kilometres (20 000 miles) out in space. NORAD also controls the six-storey COBRA DANE phased-array radar at Shemya Island, Alaska, just 724 kilometres (450 miles) from the Soviet land mass, which is able to detect an object the size of a basketball at 3219 kilometres (2000 miles), and which can also detect, track and identify some 200 satellites or missiles simultaneously.[85]

For early warning of bomber attack, NORAD controls the Distant Early Warning (DEW) radar chain in Canada; seven Boeing E-3A airborne warning and control systems (AWACS) based at Tinker AFB, Oklahoma; the Seek Skyhook balloon tethered off the Florida Straits for monitoring the south-eastern air approaches to the United States; and the new Joint Surveillance System (JSS), which consists of 48 radars controlled from seven Regional Operations Control Centers (ROCCs) in the continental United States (CONUS), Alaska, and Canada.[86]

Ocean surveillance

As described in detail in Chapter 9, all the five UKUSA countries cooperate extremely closely in the area of ocean surveillance. One of the five ground control stations for the US CLASSIC WIZARD Ocean Surveillance Satellite System is located at Edzell in Scotland, and another is on the British Indian Ocean Territory (BIOT) of Diego Garcia.[87] The US Caesar/SOSUS facility at Brawdy in Wales is the largest SOSUS station outside the

Edzell, near Dundee, Scotland. US Naval Security Group (NSG) CLASSIC WIZARD station, used to monitor naval communications in the North Sea and the Norwegian Sea. It is also a ground control element for the White Cloud Ocean Surveillance ELINT satellites (see page 216).

US. The Naval Atlantic Undersea Test and Evaluation Center (AUTEC) at Andros Island in the Bahamas is operated jointly by the UK and the US, with some participation from Canada and New Zealand.[88] Selected SIGINT sites in all five countries have recently been equipped with new HF-DF antenna arrays and linked together as components of the US Naval Ocean Surveillance Information System (NOSIS). Four of the five UKUSA countries operate variants of the P-3C Orion long-range maritime patrol (LRMP) aircraft, while the UK contributes its Nimrod LRMP aircraft to the joint ocean surveillance mission. Under the Radford–Collins Agreement of 1951, Australia and the US have an agreed division of responsibilities for 'the surveillance and tracking of the Soviet fleet in the Pacific and Indian Oceans'.[8]

Technical cooperation programs

The UKUSA countries are party to hundreds of technical cooperation agreements involving the exchange of technical intelligence relating to new weapons research and development (R&D), including both the R&D undertaken by the Allied countries themselves as well as that which is known of Soviet and Warsaw Pact R&D. Some of the more significant of these are The Technical Co-operation Programme (TTCP), an arrangement between Canada, the UK, the US, New Zealand and Australia designed 'to promote a regular exchange of technical information in areas of current interest in defence research and development'; the Joint Project Agreement between the UK and Australia concerning the development and operation of the Woomera Range in South Australia; the Cooperative Research and Development Project Agreement between the US and Australia 'relating to co-operative research and development in specific defence fields'; the Data Exchange Agreement between the US and Australia 'concerning an exchange of information in specific subject areas not covered by the Cooperative Projects Agreement'; and the Commonwealth Advisory Aeronautical Research Council, which discusses and coordinates research in aeronautics.[90]

Liaison arrangements

The liaison arrangements through which these extensive and close intelligence cooperation and exchange agreements are effected are themselves numerous and varied. They include the exchange of special liaison officers, the use of joint communication channels, the joint manning of important facilities and installations, informal contacts and close personal relationships between senior members of the intelligence agencies of the five UKUSA countries, and an agreed system of security classifications and procedures for protecting exchanged intelligence information.

Liaison personnel

The fundamental mechanism for the exchange of intelligence material is the posting of designated liaison officers to the embassies and High Commissions in the capitals of the cooperating countries and existence of Special Liaison Offices at the headquarters of the cooperating agencies. In Australia, for example, the NSA maintains a Special US Liaison Office and GCHQ a British liaison officer at DSD headquarters at Victoria Barracks in Melbourne; the CIA has a liaison officer at ASIS headquarters in Victoria Barracks; there are two MI-6 officers in the British High Commission in Canberra and two CIA and one DIA officer in the American Embassy responsible for liaison with the JIO and ONA; there is also an accredited representative in Canberra of New Zealand's EIB. In New Zealand there are two CIA liaison officers at the US Embassy in Wellington; there is an FBI liaison officer; there are JIO and ASIO representatives in Wellington; and a senior MI-5 liaison officer is maintained under diplomatic cover at the British High Commission in Wellington.

These liaison officers are responsible for physically handling the exchange of intelligence information and material; for ensuring that the agreed procedures for protecting this intelligence are properly implemented; and for reporting back to their own headquarters on the operational requirements and practices of their host agencies.

Joint communication systems

In addition to the network of liaison officers, which generally use their national communication systems for communicating between their liaison offices, embassies and High Commissions and their own headquarters, there are several important joint communications stations and channels. For example, there is a joint ASIS–MI-6 Radio Communications Station at Kowandi near Darwin;[91] a ground terminal for the US Defense Satellite Communications System (DSCS), at Watsonia Barracks in Melbourne, is used by the NSA and CIA Liaison Offices at Victoria Barracks to communicate with their headquarters at Fort Meade and Langley, as well as by the DSD and ASIO Liaison Offices to communicate back to their Melbourne headquarters; under the BRUSA Agreement, the UK and the US agreed that the US SIGINT station at RAF Chicksands would serve as a Centralized COMINT Communication Center (CCCC);[92] and some UK and Canadian agencies and their field stations use the US AUTODIN and AUTOVON defence communication systems.

Joint manning of facilities

The exchange of intelligence material between the UKUSA countries is greatly expedited by the joint staffing and operation of many of the most important intelligence collection stations. These include the joint US–Australian NRO SIGINT satellite ground station and DSP early warning satellite ground station at Pine Gap and Nurrungar respectively; the joint US–UK Satellite Control Facility at Oakhanger and SIGINT satellite ground station at Menwith Hill; the joint UK–Australia SIGINT facilities in Hong Kong, the joint US–Canadian SIGINT station at Leitrim, and joint US–British SIGINT stations at Teufelsberg in Berlin, Masirah in Oman, and Diego Garcia in the Indian Ocean; and the joint US–British operation of U-2 and SR-71 reconnaissance aircraft from bases such as Lakenheath and Mildenhall in England and the British bases at Akrotiri and Episkopi in Cyprus.

Informal contacts and personal relationships

As a result of the very close working relations established between the intelligence and security agencies of the UKUSA countries since the Second World War, and the formative role of the British SIS (MI-6) and MI-5 in the creation of so many of these agencies, together with the widespread exchange of liaison officers, the joint staffing and operation of many of the most important intelligence collection facilities, and various cooperative covert operations, there have developed extremely close personal relationships between the senior officers of these agencies.

The movements of two particularly interesting individuals — both of whom have come under official suspicion as having worked for the Soviet Union — are illustrative of the close working relationship between personnel of the intelligence agencies of the UKUSA countries. The first, Colonel Charles H. Ellis, was an Australian who was brought up in New Zealand and served in the British Army during the First World War. Ellis joined the British SIS in 1920, and from 1940 to 1944 was William Stephenson's principal MI-6 assistant at BSC headquarters in New York. He was principally responsible for producing 'the original blueprint for OSS', for which he was awarded the American Legion of Merit by President Truman in 1946.[93] Following a brief period at SIS headquarters in London after the Second World War, he was in 1946 appointed field officer in charge of South East Asia and the Far East and posted to Singapore.[94] In 1947, he visited Australia to discuss intelligence matters with Sir Frederick Sheddon, the Secretary of the Department of Defence. He again visited Australia in March/April 1950 as the special representative of Sir Stewart Menzies, Chief of SIS, and in discussions with the Defence Committee and Cabinet was successful in putting the case for the creation of ASIS.[95] In April 1950, he was designated Chief Controller Pacific Area and as such was the senior SIS officer responsible for SIS activity in the area from India to the Americas inclusive.[96] He retired from the SIS in late 1953, emigrated to Australia, and immediately signed a two-year contract with ASIS,[97] although he evidently stayed with ASIS for only a few months. In March 1954 he arrived back in Britain as an ASIS–ASIO courier for the SIS and

MI-5, to which he relayed the information that Vladimir Petrov, a KGB officer in the Soviet Embassy in Canberra was about to defect to the Australian security authorities. He then went back to part-time work with the SIS.[98]

The second person of interest is Leslie James Bennett, whose movements link British, Australian and Canadian intelligence and security agencies. Bennett joined the Royal Corps of Signals in May 1940 and after training as a signals intelligence officer was posted to Malta in August 1940. In 1942 he joined the Army Intelligence Corps and was subsequently responsible for the establishment of a series of signals intercept posts in North Africa. In July 1946 he transferred to the new GCHQ. His first posting abroad with the GCHQ was concerned with the conversion into a GCHQ station of an Army Radio Security Service station in Austria. In October 1947 he was posted to Turkey to expand the GCHQ intercept facilities in Istanbul. He returned to the GCHQ in May 1948 to head the Section responsible for monitoring transmissions between Moscow and Soviet agents abroad, duties which also made him Secretary of the interdepartmental Counter-Clandestine Committee, which consisted of representatives of the GCHQ, MI-6 and MI-5. In early 1950 he was posted to the headquarters of the Australian Defence Signals Bureau (DSB) in Melbourne as GCHQ's Traffic Liaison Officer, and later in 1950 he moved to Hong Kong to establish the joint GCHQ–DSB SIGINT stations at Little Sai Wan and on the New Territories. Bennett returned to the GCHQ in 1952 to become Section head responsible for the Middle East, and then the head of the General Search Section where he again supervised the analysis of intercepted short-wave signals between Moscow and Soviet agents abroad. He retired from GCHQ on 13 March 1954, intending to emigrate to Canada to join the CBNRC, but instead joined the RCMP, for which he worked from 1 July 1954 to 28 July 1972.[99]

Many of the heads of the various security and intelligence agencies of the UKUSA countries have also enjoyed close personal relations. The close friendship between Sir Leonard Hooper and General Marshall S. Carter during the period in which they served as the heads of the GCHQ and the NSA is evinced in the letter reproduced on page 150. The following letter shows that a close and cordial relationship also existed between Brigadier C.C. Spry, former Director-General of ASIO and Mr Allan Dulles, former Director of the CIA:

January 16, 1969.

Dear Allan,

I was so sorry to hear that you were in hospital. I do sincerely trust that you are making a speedy recovery.

I was very disappointed that I missed seeing you on my last trip to the States. I do not feel that any of my visits to the USA are complete without such an honour.

I shall never cease to be grateful to you for the initiation and development of relations between your service and mine. I consider, without any reservations, that this was the turning point which enabled ASIO to reach the level of sophistication which it now enjoys. Jim Angleton and others have continued to assist us. I always

consider you as the No 1 honorary Australian in our organisation and Jim No 2.
We have now moved into our new building (and I hope our final resting place). The Government has been more than generous and we have most opulent surroundings.
I do ernestly [sic] hope that you may come to see us. There could not be a more welcome guest.
May both Kathleen and I wish you all the most healthful good wishes for the New Year.
With warmest regards,

Yours very sincerely,
(signed)   C. CHARLES SPRY.[100]

In addition, there are numerous other close personal relationships at the second levels of agency Deputy and Assistant heads.

Classifications and codewords

The protection of shared information is greatly assisted by the acceptance of a common system of security classifications and codewords throughout the UKUSA countries. As the Powles inquiry into the New Zealand Security Intelligence Service (NZSIS) noted in 1976 with respect to the exchange of intelligence material between New Zealand and its allies:

> This intelligence material is made available on the clear understanding that it will be afforded in New Zealand substantially the same degree of security as it is afforded in the country of origin. This requirement is quite specific, and is specifically attached in the form of tags and stamps to every piece of written material received. In essence, we are required to maintain and enforce personnel and physical security standards comparable to those of our allies, or we face being excluded from this essential intelligence.[101]

These 'comparable standards' extend to the use of the four categories of classification — non-classified, confidential, secret, and top secret: 'These classifications [and associated criteria] are generally in conformity with the classifications and criteria adopted by other Governments with which the New Zealand Government has dealings in this field and from which, therefore, it may obtain, and to which it may provide, documents and information.'[102]

The following definitions of Top Secret, Secret, Confidential and Restricted are taken from the Australian *Protective Security Handbook*, issued in June 1978.[103] They are generally the same as those accepted by the other UKUSA countries, with the exception that the United States does not use the Restricted category:

TOP SECRET
National security information which requires the highest degree of protection, is to be classified TOP SECRET. The test for assigning the classification is whether its

unauthorised disclosure could cause *exceptionally grave damage* to the national security. Very little information in fact belongs in the TOP SECRET category, and the classification should be used with the utmost restraint.

SECRET
National security information which requires a substantial degree of protection is to be classified SECRET. The test for assigning the classification is whether unauthorised disclosure of the information could reasonably be expected to cause *serious damage* to the national security. It should be sparingly used.

CONFIDENTIAL
National security information which requires a decided degree of protection is to be classified CONFIDENTIAL. The test for assigning the classification is whether its unauthorised disclosure could reasonably be expected to *cause damage* to the national security. Most national security information will merit classification no higher than CONFIDENTIAL. All Cabinet documents are also to be classified CONFIDENTIAL unless requiring a higher national security classification.

RESTRICTED
National security information which requires some protection but does not warrant a higher classification is to be classified RESTRICTED. The test for assigning the classification is whether unauthorised disclosure could possibly be *harmful* to the national security.

Until 1952, the UK used the term 'Most Secret' rather than the US term 'Top Secret'. Prime Minister Winston Churchill at one time strongly objected to the American usage:

The American expression 'Top Secret' should not be adopted by us. Secrecy is not to be measured by altitude. If it were so, many might think 'Bottom Secret' would be more forceful and suggestive.

It would be good and correct English to say 'Most Secret'. I hope this may be adopted.[104]

However, according to British Cabinet records his effort proved unsuccessful because agreement had already been reached with the US security and intelligence agencies to use the American term.[105]

These definitions are now also accepted by the NATO countries, with some minor variations. For example, NATO documents are stamped with the term 'NATO' preceding the classification level — such as 'NATO RESTRICTED' or 'NATO SECRET'. In addition, NATO TOP SECRET documents are also marked 'COSMIC' to signify that they are 'subject to special security controls'.[106]

In addition to the four basic levels of security classification there is a system of codewords used to designate particular sorts of intelligence material, usually, but not necessarily beyond TOP SECRET. As US Secretary of Defense Robert McNamara testified in February 1968:

There are a host of different clearances [that is, classifications]. I would guess I have perhaps twenty-five. There are certain clearances to which only a handful of people in the government are exposed. There are others with broader coverage, and overlapping coverage, and it is not really a question of degree of clearance. It is a question of need to know, and need to know clearances apply to certain forms of data.

Now, there is a Top Secret clearance that covers certain kinds of information, and is a rather broad clearance and is related to a level of clearances starting [with] For Official Use Only, rising through Confidential and Secret and Top Secret, and generally speaking, that is a pyramidal clearance. There is another clearance, Q clearance, that relates to certain categories of information.

There is another clearance which is the Special Intelligence clearance ... that relates to intercept information.[107]

The codewords for these special categories (often termed SPECATS) of intelligence information are intended to designate special procedures for the handling and distribution of material — usually where the source or the method of obtaining the intelligence is particularly sensitive. Compartmentalization and the 'need-to-know' principle are applied on the basis of the source of the material, the method of collection, and the particular needs of those requiring access to the information.

In the case of SIGINT material or Special Intelligence (SI), the series of codewords derive directly from the system accepted under the BRUSA Agreement of 17 May 1943, which instituted the three basic SI categories of ULTRA, Pearl and Thumb in descending order of importance.[108] The TOP SECRET designation was subsequently changed to DINAR, which was replaced by TRINE in 1965, which was in turn replaced by UMBRA — always written as TOP SECRET UMBRA.[109] Pearl and Thumb were later replaced by the single codeword Pinup, which was in turn later replaced by SPOKE — always written as SECRET SPOKE.[110]

Other five-letter codewords limit access even beyond TOP SECRET UMBRA. For example, the GAMMA series designates intercept material of the highest sensitivity. GAMMA GUPY designates the intercepted conversations of top Soviet officials, such as those which take place over limousine radio telephones. There are about twenty different designations in the GAMMA series, including GAMMA GILT, GAMMA GOUT, GAMMA GULT, GAMMA GANT, GAMMA GABE and GAMMA GYRO. Although the GAMMA series was originally intended to designate highly sensitive Soviet COMINT, it was later used in 1969 and 1970 to also designate the NSA intercepts of the conversations and communications of Jane Fonda, Dr Benjamin Spock and other leading US anti-Vietnam activists.[111]

The series of DELTA codewords designates a somewhat less sensitive area of Soviet intercepts — those relating to Soviet military operations, such as the location of Soviet submarines or Soviet aircraft operations. Codewords in the DELTA series include DELTA DACE, DELTA DICE and DELTA DENT.[112]

Material collected by means of overhead reconnaissance systems — including both satellites and airborne systems — is designated 'Talent-

Keyhole' or TK.[113] Photographic satellites carry a Keyhole or KH codeword — such as KH-1 for the original SAMOS satellites; KH-4 for the Corona/Discoverer satellites; KH-8 for the current 'close look', low-altitude, film-return, high resolution photographic reconnaissance satellites; KH-9 for the 'Big Bird' medium-altitude, film-return satellites; and KH-11 for the Code 1010 digital imaging photographic reconnaissance spacecraft.[114] Intelligence acquired from satellite photography is designated by the codeword RUFF.[115]

Codewords are also used to compartmentalize intelligence as between the designers and the operators of an intelligence collection system, the processors and the analysts of the intelligence collected, and the managers and administrators of the particular project. Material containing details of the operational characteristics of intelligence collection systems is designated by the codeword BYEMAN. The nature of this classification is illustrated in the following excerpt from a TOP SECRET Request for Proposals (RFP) relating to a 'world-wide covert communication satellite system, codenamed PYRAMIDER', issued by the CIA on 22 November 1972:

This study effort is classified TOP SECRET and has been assigned a code-word designator, 'PYRAMIDER'.

All contractor personnel working on this study effort must have a current TOP SECRET clearance and must be approved by [CIA] Headquarters prior to being briefed on PYRAMIDER.

Contractor personnel proposed for clearance access to this study must qualify by holding a currently valid BYEMAN security access approval.

While this study effort will be conducted within the contractor facilities as TOP SECRET, and while only those personnel holding active BYEMAN access approvals are eligible for consideration, the effort is not a BYEMAN study, but is to be conducted in all aspects of document control, physical security standards, communications within Headquarters, and the like, as if it were BYEMAN.

Security officers will assure documents within the contractor facility are stamped TOP SECRET/PYRAMIDER only, and are not entered into the BYEMAN system.

The highly sensitive nature of this effort cannot be emphasized enough. Personnel submitted for access approval will be submitted via cable message which shall fully outline their need-to-know. No Form 2018 will be submitted to Headquarters. A list of those persons approved for access to PYRAMIDER shall be maintained by Headquarters Security Staff. Cable messages shall be sent via secure TWX and shall be slugged PYRAMIDER on the second line. PYRAMIDER shall enjoy limited distribution within Project Headquarters.[116]

The RHYOLITE and CHALET designations for CIA/NRO SIGINT satellites are examples of BYEMAN codenames.

There are also codewords for particular intelligence operations — such as SAND DOLLAR, a joint CIA and Air Force Intelligence operation concerned with the recovery of the Re-entry Vehicles (RVs) of Soviet ballistic missiles tested over the Pacific Ocean,[117] and HOLYSTONE and DESKTOP, highly sensitive US Navy undersea operations described in Chapter 9.

Distinctions between the UKUSA countries with respect to information sharing

Notwithstanding the extraordinary volume of intelligence information exchanged between the UKUSA countries, and the very high quality and extreme sensitivity of much of this material, there is also an enormous amount which is not fully shared among the five countries.

As the Australian Royal Commission on Intelligence and Security reported in 1977, 'it would be naive to imagine that overseas governments will always tell us everything they know about a particular matter. The position they take is quite natural and we should face up to it realistically'.[118] There are various reasons for withholding information from one or more of the other UKUSA countries, some of which were also cited by the Australian Royal Commission.

In the first place, the Need-to-Know (NTK) principle which results in tight compartmentalization within the security and intelligence community of any given UKUSA country also operates as between the UKUSA countries. In many cases, information might simply not be relevant or important to each of the five countries — for example, there is no evident need for New Zealand to be informed of CIA plans for covert operations in Nicaragua.

Each of the UKUSA countries has certain assets, capabilities and plans which are withheld from Allied eyes. Most particularly, information is withheld which might reveal plans or activities directed against the citizens or interests of Allied countries, or — especially in the case of Britain and the US — the conditions under which the smaller Allies might be abandoned in the case of crisis or conflict.

Information is also withheld from general distribution among the UKUSA countries if it is especially sensitive, or if it might reveal the sources and methods whereby it was obtained. For example, US agencies are required to stamp material WNINTEL NOFORN (that is, Warning Notice: Intelligence Sources and Methods Involved; Not Releasable to Foreign Nationals) where dissemination could reveal sources and methods.[119]

It is also accepted practice to exempt from the exchange arrangements material which bears directly on national interests. As the Australian Royal Commission on Intelligence and Security noted in 1977 with respect to material exchanged between MI-6 and ASIS, 'In general, the only reports not exchanged have been those concerning the Governments of Australia or Britain, or reports affecting their commercial interests'.[120] And with respect to the transfer of intelligence material from the CIA to ASIS, the Royal Commission found that 'Intelligence has not been passed [to ASIS] where it has related to Australian policies or interests'.[121]

In some areas, the exchange of intelligence material is conditional on there being some *quid pro quo*. This is particularly the case with material originating with the CIA. As the Australian Royal Commission reported with respect to the exchange relationship between the CIA and ASIS:

[CIA] treats ASIS with some professional reserve. The Americans expect a more exact *quid pro quo* from ASIS than does SIS ...
CIA has not found it acceptable, except in rare instances, to pass to ASIS reports produced in areas where ASIS has no representation ...
... a noticeable feature of CIA releases to Australia has been ... relatively little or nothing [is forthcoming] in respect of countries where ASIS has no station.[122]

Finally, there is no obligation to pass on information which is received by any UKUSA country under separate arrangements with non-UKUSA countries — and, indeed, there are often strict prohibitions against such transfer. Thus, information which is received by the United States from South Korea, or by Australia from the ASEAN countries or Papua New Guinea, or by Britain from the other Commonwealth countries, might not necessarily be passed to the other UKUSA partners.

Restrictions on the distribution of intelligence material as between the UKUSA countries are reflected in a further set of classification categories. These categories, and the situations in which they are applicable, are perhaps best illustrated by reference to the classification of some exemplary recent and current documents.

Each of the UKUSA countries has a classification category which designates that material so marked is not to be distributed to foreign nationals, including members of UKUSA agencies. In the United States, the relevant designation is NOFORN, indicating that the material is not for foreign dissemination. According to a memorandum on the subject of 'Making Classified Security Information Available to Foreign Nationals', signed by President Eisenhower on 25 May 1953:

United States classified security information is [to be] made available to foreign nationals only under the following conditions:
(a) On a real need-to-know basis.
(b) After determination that the furnishing of such information will result in a net advantage to the interests of the United States.[123]

Examples of documents marked NOFORN include a CIA study, *Israel: Foreign Intelligence and Security Services* (SECRET NOFORN, March 1977); a RAND Corporation paper, *The Maturing Threat: An Overview Briefing* (SECRET WNINTEL NOFORN, February 1978) and a RAND study, *The Effects of Increased Hardening on Weapons Requirements to Destroy Targets in the USSR* (SECRET WNINTEL NOFORN); and a study by the US Air Force's Foreign Technology Division, *USSR Communication Space Systems* (NOFORN, 1976).

In Australia, the comparable marking is AUSTEO, indicating that material so designated is for Australian Eyes Only. For example, the *Fifth Report* of the 1977 Royal Commission on Intelligence and Security, *The Australian Secret Intelligence Service*, is marked OYSTER AUSTEO HANDLE VIA COMINT CHANNELS ONLY. The periodic reviews of *Australia's Security Outlook*, prepared by the Office of National Assessments (ONA) and the Joint Intelligence Organisation (JIO) are classified SECRET AUSTEO.

Between the NOFORN category and full five-power dissemination are numerous combinations of classifications limiting distribution of intelligence material to two, three or four of the UKUSA countries. In the case of the two Australasian partners, documents and material are frequently marked ANZEO (Australian and New Zealand Eyes Only). A similar geographically based bilateral relationship between the US and Canada, especially in the area of North American air defence, results in material limited to US–Canadian distribution — such as NORAD studies entitled *Likely Impact of PRC Leadership Change on Aerospace Research and Development* (1977) and *Soviet Manufacturing Experiments in Space May Result in Superior Space Systems* (1979). There is also some intelligence material which is shared only between the UK and Canada — for example, *The Moscow Antiballistic Missile System* (ACSI, 1976). There are also some areas in which intelligence is shared only between Australia and the United States, especially where it involves early-warning or signals intelligence collected through US satellite ground stations in Australia, or joint US–Australian ASW operations — for example, a report produced by two officers of the Royal Australian Naval Research Laboratory (RANRL) in April 1980, entitled *Study of ASW Forces for Australia in the 1990s*, is classified SECRET AUST–US EYES ONLY.

Cooperation and exchange with non-UKUSA countries

The UKUSA countries do not act in isolation. On the contrary, there are extremely extensive and wide-ranging connections between the security and intelligence agencies of the UKUSA partners and those of numerous other countries. These include, most particularly, the non-UKUSA NATO countries (and especially West Germany, Denmark and Norway), some of the other British Commonwealth countries (such as Malaysia and Singapore), Japan, South Korea, the People's Republic of China, the ASEAN countries, Papua New Guinea, Israel, Taiwan, and, much more circumspectly, South Africa.

A large proportion of the intelligence material collected and produced by the UKUSA countries is shared with the non-UKUSA members of NATO, and especially West Germany, Denmark and Norway. Indeed, these countries, together with Japan and South Korea, comprise the Third Parties to the UKUSA Agreement itself.[124]

West Germany, Denmark and Norway each maintain more than half a dozen SIGINT stations, the operations of which are integrated with those of the UKUSA countries and the intelligence product of which is shared with UKUSA countries. Some of the SIGINT stations in these other NATO countries were in fact originally established by the UKUSA SIGINT agencies and continue to function essentially as UKUSA stations. For example, the major West German SIGINT station at Hof, which operates an AN/FLR-12 antenna system, was originally established by the then CIA Office of ELINT (OEL), now called the Office of SIGINT Operations (OSO), through the US Air Force's Security Service (USAFSS), now the USAF Electronic Security Command (ESC); the Hof collection site was sold to the West German Ministry of Defence in 1969 for US$1 in return for data exchange rights.[125] West Germany also remains the host of NSA headquarters in Europe (Frankfurt), the INSCOM headquarters Europe (Frankfurt and Augsburg), and ESC headquarters Europe (Ramstein Air Base). The two SIGINT stations at Bornholm in Denmark are essential elements of the US Naval Ocean Surveillance Information System (NOSIS) in the Baltic Sea area. And all of the eight SIGINT stations in Norway were established on the initiative of the United States and with US funding.[126] The NATO countries have also established an Allied Communications Security Agency (ACSA), adopted common cryptographic systems and produced a series of Allied Communications Publications (ACPs) designed to coordinate the communications procedures, SIGINT and Electronic Warfare (EW) activities of the UKUSA and NATO countries.[127]

Cooperation with Japan is also extremely close, especially on the part of US and Australian agencies. For example, the NSA Far East headquarters is located in Tokyo, and the NSA currently maintains more than a dozen SIGINT facilities in Japan. With respect to Australian–Japanese intelligence relations, liaison was established between the Australian Secret Intelligence Service (ASIS) and the Japanese Cabinet Research Office (CRO) in 1976, and relations have subsequently been established between the CRO and JIO and ONA as well.

Cooperation with South Korea is principally the domain of US intelligence agencies. The NSA currently maintains more than half a dozen SIGINT facilities in South Korea, including a base for one of INSCOM's two aviation companies. However, cooperation with South Korea is much more circumscribed than it is between the UKUSA countries themselves. Until the late 1960s, for example, South Korean officials were excluded from the main NSA building at Fort Meade, whereas access was permitted British, Canadian and Australian officials.[128]

Cooperation between the United States and Taiwan was particularly close during the 1950s and 1960s, but suffered somewhat with the normalization of relations between the US and the People's Republic of China (PRC) in 1972. In the SIGINT area, the station at Nan Szu Pu was used by the NSA as a COMINT Communications Relay Center (CCRC), while each of the service component units of the NSA — the Army Security Agency, the Navy Security Group and the Air Force Security Service — maintained SIGINT sites in Taiwan.[129] There was also close cooperation between the CIA and the Taiwanese intelligence service, including the joint running of covert operations within the PRC.[130]

In 1979, the United States and the People's Republic of China reached agreement on the establishment of two SIGINT stations — at Qitai and

Korla — in the Xinjiang Uighur Autonomous Region in Western China near the Soviet border. The two stations were built by the CIA's Office of SIGINT Operations (OSO) but are manned by Chinese technicians. The information collected at the two sites includes data on the development of new Soviet missiles tested at Leninsk and Sary Shagan, as well as Soviet military communications, and is shared by both China and the US.[131]

Cooperation with the security and intelligence agencies of the ASEAN countries is mainly the responsibility of Australian agencies, and most particularly ASIS, although the UK retains links with Malaysia and Singapore and the US is well represented in Thailand, the Philippines and Indonesia. ASIS has established formal liaison arrangements with all the ASEAN intelligence services. In the case of Malaysia, liaison was established in 1964 with both the Special Branch of the Malaysian Police and the Malaysian External Intelligence Organization (MEIO). In the case of Singapore, ASIS also established formal liaison arrangements in 1964 with the Internal Security Division of the Singapore Ministry of Home Affairs and with the Security and Intelligence Division (Singapore's external intelligence and research organization) of the Ministry of Defence. In the case of the Philippines, ASIS established a relationship with the National Intelligence Coordinating Agency (NICA) in May 1967, and this was extended in 1970 to also include the Joint Intelligence Staff (J-2) of the Philippines Armed Forces. (The ASIS station in Manila also represents the UK SIS with NICA and J-2.) In the case of Indonesia, liaison between ASIS and BAKIN (the Indonesian State Intelligence Coordination Body) began in 1971, and an ASIS Liaison Officer was appointed to BAKIN in 1977. And in the case of Thailand, a liaison agreement between ASIS and the Thai Department of Central Intelligence (DCI) was signed in July 1974. Intelligence gained by ASIS from the relationships with these ASEAN services is often of benefit not just to Australia but also to the other UKUSA countries. For example, a Soviet manual on MIG-21 fighters obtained from Indonesian Air Force sources by ASIS was well received in Britain and the United States.[132]

Australia also has a very close relationship with the Papua New Guinea intelligence and security agencies. In July 1974, just prior to Papua New Guinea's obtaining independence, agreement was reached for an intelligence exchange between the Joint Intelligence Organization (JIO) and the Papua New Guinea Intelligence Committee (PNGIC), the senior intelligence body in PNG. The PNGIC is chaired by the Secretary of the PNG Defence Department and its membership consists of senior representatives from the Department of the Chief Minister, the Department of Foreign Relations and Trade, the PNG Constabulary, the PNG Defence Forces, the Division of District Development, and the PNG Security and Intelligence Organization. Under the 1974 agreement, each party can ask the other for information on specific subjects at any time. The JIO officer in Port Moresby is formally designated as the liaison officer and channel of communication with the PNGIC.[133]

With respect to Israel, there are some two dozen intelligence-sharing agreements currently in effect between US and Israeli security and intelligence agencies.[134] The most important of these, negotiated in 1953 and 1956–57, established a CIA liaison unit with Mossad, the Israeli Secret Intelligence Service, and made Mossad responsible for gathering intelligence in the Middle East for both services.[135] By 1959, all CIA covert operations in the Middle East were also coordinated with Mossad. For example, Mossad conducted for the CIA the operation in August 1966 in which an Iraqi pilot was persuaded to defect to Israel with a MIG-21 fighter.[136] The CIA and Mossad also collaborated in the establishment of Savak in Iran in the mid-1950s.[137] Following the Six-Day War in June 1967 and the Yom Kippur War in October 1973, additional agreements were negotiated under which the Israelis passed to the US information about Israeli experience with Soviet weapon systems.[138] A further agreement of this sort was negotiated in November 1981, but because of the war in Lebanon it was not implemented until March 1983.[139] Under other agreements, the US operates several SIGINT facilities in Israel.[140]

Finally, there is some circumspect cooperation between the UKUSA countries and South Africa. The major SIGINT facility at Silvermine, some 10 kilometres (6 miles) north of Simonstown, was established in 1973 with the assistance of the NSA and GCHQ.[141] According to official South African briefings, information collected at Silvermine is passed to the UK and the US as well as some countries of the old British Commonwealth, including Hong Kong, Singapore, Australia and New Zealand.[142] The South African security intelligence organization, now named the National Intelligence Service but entitled the Bureau of State Security (BOSS) from 1969 to 1978 and the Department of National Security from 1978 to 1981,[143] is also reported to maintain links with MI-5, MI-6, ASIO, and the NZSIS. For example, according to a former BOSS agent, in the mid-1960s MI-5 passed to BOSS 'the names of all people who voted Communist in British general elections'.[144] In return, BOSS provided MI-5 with information relating to protest activities against South African sporting visits to Britain.[145] Background information on South African emigrants to Britain, Australia and New Zealand has also been provided to MI-5, ASIO and NZSIS.[146] In 1973 the Director-General of ASIO was instructed by Ministerial direction to sever all links with BOSS,[147] but neither the degree of compliance with this instruction nor the current state of relations between ASIO and the South African security intelligence organisation are publicly known. On the US side, however, the former Chief of the CIA's Angola Task Force (1975–77) has written that 'the CIA has traditionally sympathised with South Africa and enjoyed its close liaison with BOSS'.[148]

8

The signals intelligence connection

As indicated by the focus of the UKUSA Agreement of 1947 the core of the UKUSA intelligence relationship is signals intelligence (SIGINT). At the time of the inception of the agreement, methods of SIGINT collection were limited. Since that time there has been a quantum leap in both the technology and methods of signals intelligence collection. The UKUSA relationship has kept pace with these changes, with Australia and Britain becoming heavily involved in US spaceborne and advanced airborne SIGINT activities.

As of 1947 — when space systems and advanced airborne systems did not exist — the most significant aspect of the agreement was to divide the world up into areas of signals intelligence collection responsibility, with each nation being responsible for a particular area of the world. This remains a major segment of the intelligence relationship despite the introduction of satellites and long range reconnaissance aircraft — in part due to the superiority of ground-based sites for certain types of SIGINT collection. Thus, during a 1974 visit to Washington the Director of the Australian Joint Intelligence Organization was told that 'in the SIGINT area, the US was willing to rely for its national intelligence purposes on the contribution of its partners under the shared arrangements'.[1]

Under the present division of responsibility the Australian Defence Signals Directorate is responsible for covering parts of the Indian Ocean, the South Pacific, and South East Asia. The United Kingdom's Government Communications Headquarters is responsible for Africa and the USSR west of the Urals.[2]

Canada is responsible for coverage of the northern Soviet Union and parts of Europe.[3] New Zealand is apparently responsible for a small portion of the South-west Pacific. The United States National Security Agency and its military components are responsible for all remaining areas of interest.

Britain's geographical position gives it a significant capability for long range SIGINT collection against certain targets in the USSR.[4] Meanwhile, Britain's historical role in Africa led to its assumption of SIGINT responsibility for that area. Canada's responsibility for the northern USSR stems from its geographical position, which gives it 'unique access to communications in the northern Soviet Union'.[5] Likewise, as noted earlier, the peculiarities of radio wave propagation mean that receivers in eastern Canada can intercept transmission from portions of Europe which are inaccessible to British-based equipment.[6] The areas of responsibility of Australia and New Zealand clearly result from their geographical location.

Just as the entire UKUSA intelligence relationship is more than an agreement to coordinate separately conducted intelligence activities and share the intelligence collected, the SIGINT aspect of the relationship is also more than that. Rather, it is cemented by the presence of US facilities on British, Canadian and Australian territory, by joint operation of facilities (US−UK, Australian−US, UK−Australian) within and outside UKUSA territory and, in the case of Australia, of UK and US personnel (and some NZ personnel) at the DSD facilities.[7]

Before the particular UKUSA facilities and their functions are described, it is useful to first examine the various types of signals intelligence and SIGINT collection systems.

Types of signals intelligence

Signals intelligence is a term which encompasses a wide variety of technical intelligence. The most general division between types of signals intelligence distinguishes between Communications Intelligence (COMINT) and Electronic Intelligence (ELINT).

COMINT is technical and intelligence information derived from the interception of foreign communications by individuals or groups who are not the intended recipients.[8] COMINT thus includes intelligence acquired by the interception of encrypted *or* unencrypted communications. These communications may include diplomatic, commercial, political and military communications conducted by a variety of means — telephone, radio-telephone, radio or satellite.

The variety of targets reflects the wide scope of intelligence requirements. Diplomatic communications can reveal the intentions of foreign governments — Allied or hostile. Commercial communications can indicate forthcoming actions or situations with significant political-economic impact — for example, a rise in the price of oil or the discovery of uranium. Communications among political activists or military commanders can reveal planning for a coup or other major actions. Military communications can also be exploited to determine the Order of Battle of other nations as well as the readiness of a nation's armed forces.

Such communications are transmitted in a variety of ways, such as landline, microwave relay stations, undersea cables or satellites. As one observer has written with regard to microwave relay stations:

> With modern communications, 'target' messages travel not simply over individually tappable wires like those that connect the ordinary telephone, but as part of entire message streams, which can contain up to 970 individual message circuits, and have voice, telegram, telex and high-speed data bunched together.[9]

Such message streams can be monitored over vast distances by interception equipment with high-gain antennas and low-noise amplifiers.[10]

Satellite transmissions may be intercepted from various ground locations. While the ground stations which send messages to satellites have antennas which can direct the signals to the satellite with great accuracy the satellite antennas are smaller and the signals they send back to earth are less narrowly focused — perhaps covering several thousand square kilometres.[11]

Landlines and undersea cables are less susceptible to interception. Tapping cables requires physical access to the cable and the operation and maintenance of the tapping equipment at the point of access. This may be an unattainable requirement for hardened and protected internal landlines — the type of landline that carries much high priority Soviet command and control communication. Undersea cables are more vulnerable since the messages transmitted by them underwater are then transmitted by microwave relay once the cable reaches land.[12]

Electronic Intelligence (ELINT) — technical and intelligence information derived from foreign non-communications electromagnetic radiations emanating from other than atomic detonation or radioactive sources — also encompasses a wide variety of technical intelligence.[13] One prominent example of ELINT is the intelligence collected by monitoring the electronic emanations of radars of foreign nations, particularly those of the Soviet Union and China. The intelligence derived allows for the mapping of locations and hence targeting of early warning (EW) stations, air defence systems, anti-ballistic missile (ABM) systems, airfields, air bases, satellite tracking and control stations and ships at sea. Recording their frequencies, signal strengths, pulse lengths, pulse rates and other specifications allows for the ability to jam the transmitters in the event of war. Knowing the location of air defence systems would give the US and Allied bomber fleets a better chance of evading those systems en route to their targets. Monitoring Soviet radar systems also has an arms control verification aspect, since the 1972 treaty between the US and USSR on the limitation of ABM systems restricts the use of radars in an ABM mode.

Radar intelligence (RADINT) is intelligence data collected about radar systems. Radar (an acronym for Radar Detection And Ranging) was developed to detect incoming enemy aircraft and thus provide warning of attack — allowing civilians to seek cover and fighter aircraft to intercept the incoming bombers.[14] Radar functions by bouncing a radio beam off an object. The distance between the radar and the object can be determined by the time required for the beam's outward and return pulses. Additional information, such as altitude and size can be deduced from the characteristics of the returning beam pulse. Speed and directional data can be established by repeated observations.[15]

Another subcategory of ELINT is Telemetry Intelligence (TELINT). Telemetry is the set of signals by which a missile, or stage of a missile, or a missile warhead sends back to earth data about its performance during a test flight. The data relates to features such as structural stress, rocket motor thrust, fuel consumption, guidance system performance, and the physical conditions of the ambient environment. Intercepted telemetry can provide intelligence on such questions as the number of warheads carried by a given missile, the range of the missile, its payload and throw-weight and hence the probable size of its warheads, and the accuracy with which the warheads are guided at the point of release from the missile's post-boost vehicle.[16] Such information is valuable to the United States both for monitoring Soviet compliance with SALT agreements as well as for making intelligence estimates of Soviet strategic capabilities.

TELINT is also a subcategory of Foreign Instrumentation Signals Intelligence (FISINT). Foreign Instrumentation Signals are electromagnetic emissions associated with the testing and operational deployment of aerospace, surface and subsurface systems which may have either military or civilian application. FISINT includes, but is not limited to, signals from telemetry, beaconing, electronic interrogators, tracking/fusing/arming/command systems and video data links.[17]

Another type of signals intelligence is Acoustical Intelligence (ACOUSTINT) — intelligence information that is derived from the analysis of acoustic waves radiated either intentionally or unintentionally by the target into the surrounding medium.[18] This includes the underwater acoustic waves from ships and submarines that can be used to develop the 'signatures' of those vehicles.

SIGINT collection systems

Just as there are a wide variety of signals intelligence targets there exist a wide variety of collection systems. Among the most expensive and modern of these collection systems are the satellites run by the US National Reconnaissance Office. The best known of these satellites, which plays a significant role in US−Australian signals intelligence activities, is known as RHYOLITE. RHYOLITE, developed by the CIA and built by TRW, was described in a TRW briefing as being a 'multipurpose covert electronic surveillance system'.[19]

RHYOLITE is capable of being targeted against telemetry, radars and communications. The communications intercept capability against Soviet and Chinese telephonic and radio communications extends across the VHF, UHF and microwave frequency bands.[20] With respect to microwave frequencies, Robert Lindsey has written that the RHYOLITE satellites 'could monitor Communist microwave radio and long-distance telephone traffic over much of the European land mass, eavesdropping on a Soviet Commissar in Moscow talking to his mistress in Yalta or on a general talking to his lieutenants across the great continent'.[21]

In addition, the RHYOLITE intercepts of radio-telephonic (R/T) traffic evidently include early morning stock exchange and other business calls.[22] In the VHF-UHF range RHYOLITE satellites regularly monitor the walkie-talkie traffic generated in Soviet military exercises and the message traffic between aircraft and air traffic controllers.[23]

The highest priority of the RHYOLITE program has always been telemetry interception. In the initial stages of the program RHYOLITE had significant success in the area, for it was not until 1975, when informed of RHYOLITE'S capability by Christopher Boyce and Andrew Daulton Lee, that (according to several sources) the Soviet Union abandoned the conventional wisdom that signals at VHF and higher frequencies could not be intercepted by satellites at geostationary (approximately 35 900 kilometres or 22 300 miles) altitudes — an altitude at which the satellite remains fixed over the same point on earth. However, no attempt was made to encrypt the telemetry data until mid-1977, or six months after the arrest of Boyce and Lee.[24] Presumably, the Soviets feared that encryption might give away Soviet acquisition of material on RHYOLITE. It should be noted, however, that former CIA Director Stansfield Turner, in response to being asked whether the information passed by Boyce and Lee led to Soviet encryption, replied 'probably not'.[25]

According to one account there were, as of May 1979, four RHYOLITE launches — the first being on 6 March 1973, with subsequent launches on 23 May 1977, 11 December 1977 and 7 April 1978.[26] According to this account a pair of the satellites are stationed near the Horn of Africa and another pair farther east, with one of each pair being operational and the other being an in-orbit spare. The satellites stationed near the Horn of Africa are primarily there to intercept telemetry signals transmitted by liquid-fuel ICBM's launched from Tyuratam in a north-easterly direction toward the Kamchatka Peninsula while the satellites stationed farther east are intended to monitor telemetry from the solid-fuel SS-16 and SS-20 missiles launched from Plesetsk in north Russia.[27]

It appears that the 6 March 1973 launch was actually the *second* launch. Christopher Boyce was told at a briefing in late 1974 that the first RHYOLITE satellite had been in operation 'for almost four years'.[28] An Australian computer operator who began work at the CIA/NRO ground station at Pine Gap in November 1970 has stated that the first RHYOLITE satellite had become operational just at the time of his arrival.[29] In addition, a former US intelligence official has stated that RHYOLITE ground facilities were installed in Britain in 1970.[30] The most likely candidate as a RHYOLITE launch in 1970 is the launch of 19 June 1970, designated 1970-46A.[31]

All known RHYOLITE launches have employed an Atlas-Agena D

The signals intelligence connection 179

booster to propel the spacecraft into orbit and have taken place at the Eastern Test Range (Cape Canaveral) — the launch site for all geosynchronous launches. Little is known about the physical characteristics of the RHYOLITE spacecraft, although one source states that the main antenna on the RHYOLITE satellite is a concave dish which is more than 21.34 metres (70 feet) in diameter, backed and supported by a framework grid, to which are also attached a number of other appendages, including large panels of solar cells and several lesser antennas (including one for transmitting the intercepted signals down to Pine Gap and perhaps other ground stations, and one for receiving command and control signals from them).[32]

RHYOLITE is not the only US signals intelligence spacecraft, although it is the only one about which there is significant information available. The existence of a SIGINT satellite codenamed CHALET was revealed in 1979.

CIA/NRO ground station for RHYOLITE SIGINT satellites at Pine Gap, near Alice Springs, Australia.

Although this satellite was apparently conceived as a geosynchronous COMINT collector, it was evidently modified to give it a capability to monitor Soviet missile telemetry.[33] CHALET satellites are most probably launched from the Eastern Test Range on a Titan 3C booster. According to one report, a CHALET satellite was launched on 1 October 1979[34], while other launches apparently occurred on 10 June 1978 and 31 October 1981.

Despite the lack of additional explicit information on US SIGINT satellites other than RHYOLITE and CHALET, examination of satellite launch dates, orbits, boosters and launch sites can provide further clues to the nature of the US SIGINT satellite program. First, it is apparent that the US has used its Defense Support Program (early warning) satellite launches as a cover for launches of SIGINT satellites into geosynchronous orbit employing a Titan 3C booster. The rate at which there have been launches of satellites into geosynchronous orbit employing that booster (used for DSP but no other non-reconnaissance satellites) is excessive for the early warning mission in view of likely operational lifetimes and the requirement of only three operational DSP satellites at any moment. More directly, Congressional testimony indicates that only ten DSP satellites had been launched by the end of 1982, while there had been fourteen Titan 3C launches.[35]

Second, it appears that the US has another SIGINT satellite operating under the cover of the Satellite Data System (SDS) program. The known functions of the SDS include the provision of communications links for Strategic Air Command (SAC) bombers flying over the poles, between the Air Force Satellite Control Facility (SCF) in Sunnyvale and the other SCF tracking stations, and between the KH-11 photographic reconnaissance satellite and its Washington area ground station. (It is this relay to SDS and then on to Washington which permits real-time receipt of the satellite's photography.)[36]

In its highly elliptical orbit, with a perigee of 320 kilometres (200 miles) and an apogee of 38 400 kilometres (24 000 miles), SDS 'hovers' over the northern Soviet Union and Arctic for long periods of time. At those times it is ideally suited to receive and transmit photos from the KH-11 as it orbits over Russia or to communicate with bombers flying over the Arctic.[37]

Unlike other 'white' satellites no picture of SDS has ever appeared in published Congressional hearings (or any other place). More significantly, in 1979, by which time five US spacecraft had been launched into the distinctive SDS orbit since 1975, the Air Force Director of C^3 stated that the fourth and fifth satellites were then in the process of being *manufactured*.[38] The satellites were not *delivered* until 1980.[39] The most likely explanation is that two of these five satellites represent a third variety of SIGINT satellite.

Table 8.1 lists DSP and geosynchronous SIGINT satellite launches.

In addition to high-orbiting SIGINT satellites, the US also has a low-orbiting 'Ferret' satellite with the purpose of mapping Soviet air defence, surface-to-air missile (SAM) and early warning radars. When the Ferret program was initiated in 1962 the Ferret was placed into an orbit with an 82-degree inclination, a perigee of 306 kilometres (190 miles) and an apogee of

The signals intelligence connection 181

637 kilometres (396 miles).[40] This initial type of low-orbiting Ferret satellite continued to be employed until 1972. A second set of 'piggyback' Ferrets was initated in 1963. These are launched with a large satellite and then ejected into their own orbits. The most recent versions have been launched on board KH-9 'Big Bird' satellites into a near circular orbit of 507 kilometres (315 miles) with a 96-degree inclination.[41]

Table 8.1 DSP and geosynchronous SIGINT satellite launches

Designation	Date	Launch site	Perigee (km)	Apogee (km)	Comments
1969–36A	13 Apr. 1969	ETR	32 670	39 270	Early Warning Test Satellite
1970–46A	19 June 1970	ETR	31 680	39 860	Possibly Rhyolite
1970–69A	1 Sept 1970	ETR	31 947	39 855	Early Warning Test Satellite
1970–93A	6 Nov. 1970	ETR	26 050	35 806	Titan 3C booster DSP satellite that failed to achieve proper orbit
1971–39A	5 May 1971	ETR	35 651	35 840	Titan 3C; first functioning DSP
1972–10A	1 Mar. 1972	ETR	35 416	35 962	DSP
1972–101A	20 Dec. 1972	ETR	31 012	40 728	
1973–13A	6 Mar. 1973	ETR	35 679	35 855	Rhyolite
1973–40A	12 June 1973	ETR	35 170	35 786	DSP
1975–55A	18 June 1975	ETR	30 200	40 800	Argus
1975–118A	14 Dec. 1975	ETR	35 671	35 785	DSP
1976–59A	26 June 1976	ETR	35 620	35 860	DSP
1977–07A	6 Feb. 1977	ETR	35 620	35 860	DSP
1977–38A	23 May 1977	ETR	35 679	35 856	Rhyolite
1977–114A	11 Dec. 1977	ETR	35 679	35 855	Rhyolite
1978–38A	8 Apr. 1978	ETR	35 679	35 855	Rhyolite
1978–58A	10 June 1978	ETR	29 929	42 039	Chalet
1979–53A	10 June 1979	ETR	35 712	35 854	DSP
1979–86A	1 Oct. 1979	ETR	30 443	41 497	Chalet
1981–25A	16 Mar. 1981	ETR	35 463	38 527	DSP
1981–107	31 Oct. 1981	ETR	35 366	35 526	Chalet
1982–19A	6 Mar. 1982	ETR	35 776	35 793	DSP

Notes: ETR Eastern Test Range, Cape Canaveral

In addition to these SIGINT satellites, there appear to be at least two other systems which may either have just become operational or which should become operational in the very near future. In 1977, the Air Force Special Projects Office (that is, NRO) requested proposals for building a signals intelligence satellite designated Project No. 980.[42] Likewise, a RHYOLITE follow-on satellite and a new Ferret satellite were supposed to be in the advanced developmental stage as of 1979.[43]

Further, the first of a new generation of SIGINT satellites, codenamed MAGNUM, was launched by the Space Shuttle *Discovery* on 24 January 1985. This satellite was reported to cost $300 million, to weigh 5000 pounds, and to be 'the most important and largest' of all SIGINT satellites launched to date.[44]

In addition to its signals intelligence satellites the United States employs several aircraft for SIGINT collection, most especially the SR-71, U-2, RC-135, EC-135N and RF-4 Phantom. The SR-71 (SR for Strategic Reconnaissance) was known as 'Ox Cart' when it was managed by the National Reconnaissance Office. It performs both photographic reconnaissance and signals intelligence functions. At least 30 of the SR-71s, nicknamed 'Blackbirds' for their black epoxy heat resistant paint, are thought to have been built.[45]

The SR-71 is capable of Mach 3 speed [over 3220 kilometres (2000 miles) per hour]. Built by Lockheed Aircraft, it has a wing span of 16.94 metres (55 feet 7 inches), a length of 32.74 metres (107 feet 5 inches) and a height of 5.64 metres (18 feet 6 inches).[46] The aircraft is equipped with a variety of electronic warfare systems, including a radar detector, and possibly Electronic Counter Measures (ECMs) which allow it to wipe itself off opposition radar screens.[47] The SR-71 SIGINT capability includes equipment for monitoring both radio and radar transmissions.[48] The aircraft are now operated by the First Strategic Reconnaissance Squadron of the 9th Strategic Reconnaissance Wing of SAC and are stationed at Beale Air Force Base, California,[49] as well as two overseas locations — Kadena Air Base in Okinawa and RAF Mildenhall, UK. The SR-71s are used for overflights of North Korea, Cuba, and other countries, as well as for peripheral intelligence missions off the coast of the USSR to determine the locations and characteristics of various early warning and air defence radar systems.[50]

Lockheed also designed and produced the U-2 (known as 'Idealist' when managed by the NRO) which, prior to the deployment of the SR-71, was the primary US strategic reconnaissance aircraft. As with the SR-71 it has both photographic reconnaissance and signals intelligence capabilities. More than 55 U-2s in various versions are believed to have been built.[51] There are currently eight U-2s remaining in the US inventory, and Lockheed is under contract to build at least two more over the next two years.

The U-2R, which is the principal version of the U-2, has a wingspan of 31.39 metres (103 feet), a height of 4.88 metres (16 feet) and a length of 19.20 metres (63 feet). It has a range of some 4830 kilometres (3000 miles) and a maximum speed of 528 knots at an altitude of 12192 metres (40000 feet). Its operational ceiling is more than 21336 metres (70000 feet).[52] In addition to its photo-reconnaissance capability both its COMINT and ELINT capabilities have been upgraded, the latter by addition of the SENIOR RUBY ELINT system.[53] Among the present operating bases for the U-2s are RAF Mildenhall and Akrotiri airfield in Cyprus. The U-2s at Akrotiri are responsible for SIGINT missions in the Mediterranean area.[54]

The EC-135 is a modified KC-135 Stratotanker. The EC-135C is equipped as a flying command post in support of SAC's airborne alert role and is fitted with extensive electronic equipment.[55] Eight EC-135Ns, also known as the Advanced Range Instrumentation Aircraft (ARIA), were equipped as airborne radio and telemetry stations for the Apollo space program and have also been used to monitor Soviet missile tests and space activities.[56]

The RC-135 is a modified Boeing 707 that carries sophisticated electronic equipment designed to monitor communications and radar activities.[57] Presently, there are eighteen in the US inventory.[58] In addition to their home base at Offutt AFB, Nebraska, RC-135s are stationed at Kadena AB, Okinawa, Eielson AFB, Alaska, Shemya Island, Alaska, RAF Mildenhall, UK and Hellenikon AB, Greece.[59]

RC-135s regularly fly from their Alaskan bases in elliptical patterns off the Soviet east coast (Kamchatka Peninsula and the Sakhalin Islands) to monitor Soviet air exercises, voice and electronic communications, and the activities of radar stations. These aircraft are also used to monitor the alert status of Soviet air squadrons and the general level of military activity in the Sakhalin region.[60] In addition, RC-135s are used to monitor Soviet missile tests, which frequently conclude in the Kamchatka area. Thus, on 1 September 1983 when the Soviets evidently mistook a KAL 007 flight for an RC-135, the RC-135 was patrolling off Kamchatka in expectation of an SS-X-25 ICBM test.[61]

The RF-4C Phantom has been used to gather intelligence over East Germany.[62] The plane is a multisensor reconnaissance version of the F-4C Phantom II. Before production ended in December 1983, 505 RF-4Cs were built. The plane has three basic reconnaissance systems — conventional cameras, side-looking airborne radar (SLAR), infra-red line scanner, and a tactical electronic reconnaissance (TEREC) system.[63]

In addition to satellites and aircraft, land- and ship-based systems also provide significant signals intelligence. Indeed, as indicated below, for some purposes land-based facilities are superior to satellites or aircraft. Land-based facilities include the FPS-17 and FPS-79 detection and tracking radars, VHF-UHF-SHF receivers, and HF receivers, as well as Over-the-Horizon (OTH) radars, phased array radars and the AN/FLR-9 and Rhombic array antenna systems.

Among the radars used for intelligence purposes, the most important is the COBRA DANE radar on Shemya Island in the Aleutians. COBRA DANE is a phased array radar (that is, it electronically scans the field of view rather than moving an antenna/dish across the field of view), the phased array portion of which is 28.96 metres (95 feet) in diameter and contains 15 360 active radiating elements.[64]

COBRA DANE was designed to track Soviet re-entry vehicles during ICBM tests and to track foreign satellites. It can detect a basketball-sized object at a range of 3220 kilometres (2000 miles) and simultaneously track more than 100 objects. Processed data on objects being tracked are transmitted in real time to the continental US via satellite and distributed to the NORAD Space Defense Center and the air force's Foreign Technology Division.[65]

Shemya is located some 773 kilometres (480 nautical miles) from Kamchatka Peninsula and the surrounding ocean area. From this position, the COBRA DANE radar is able to obtain data on Soviet missile trajectories, separation velocities, payload manoeuvres, and signature

The AN/FLR-9 COMINT and HF-DF antenna system erected at RAF Chicksands, Bedfordshire, in 1965. Commonly known as 'Elephant Cage', the AN/FLR-9 is the largest SIGINT system in the world, with an outer diameter of some 875 feet. Similar AN/FLR-9 systems are located at Wahiawa, Hawaii; Clark Air Force Base, the Philippines; Misawa, Japan; San Vito dei Normanni Air Station, Brindisi, Italy; Augsburg, West Germany; Karamursel, Turkey; Homestead Air Force Base, Florida; and Torii Station, Sobe, Okinawa, Japan.

phenomena of re-entry vehicles from ballistic missiles launched from both Soviet land-based test facilities and the primary SLBM launch site in the White Sea.[66]

In the event of a missile attack the radar would function as an early warning sensor. In this mode, COBRA DANE can detect and track up to 300 objects simultaneously as well as provide predicted impact points for up to 200 objects.[67]

The AN/FLR-9 antenna system, also known as a Wullenweber system, is the largest of the Circularly Disposed Antenna Array (CDAA) configurations. It is designed to locate and intercept signals in the HF and VHF bands. HF radio traffic includes a wide range of Soviet military communications, while the VHF band includes radio-telephone communications.[68]

The outermost circle of the AN/FLR-9 is the size of about three football fields — approximately 266.7 metres (875 feet). The outermost ring has the shortest antenna of the four rings that constitute the array. This ring consists of 120 equally spaced antenna elements — one for each 3° of azimuth. The second ring consists of VHF band reflector screen which consists of vertical wires suspended from pole-supported horizontal braces. The screen is designed to shield the VHF band antenna from signals emanating from any direction other than the one being monitored.

The third ring, which is taller than the second, is the HF band receiving array. It is made up of 40 equally spaced 'folded monopoles' similar to the first ring. The fourth and innermost ring is the giant HF-band reflector screen, which 'looks like an enormous circle of ten-storey high telephone poles, with thin copper wires stretched vertically between them and suspended from above'.[69]

Each antenna element is connected to a separate buried coaxial cable that terminates inside the operations building located at the centre of the array. A goniometer is used to determine which receiving element was the first to have picked up a signal.[70] In as much as the first receiving element to be struck is the one closest to the transmitting station this will give a vague indication of the location of the station. Specific locational data can be obtained from a number of CDAAs over a wide area.

A highly directional antenna system — one that is employed against specific targets — is the Rhombic array.[71] Each element or antenna of the array consists of a wire several feet off the ground and attached to four posts spaced in the shape of a diamond, with each side being approximately three metres (ten feet) in length. At one end the wire is connected to a coaxial cable that runs underground to a centrally located operations building. The entire array consists of between 30 and 40 structures spread over several hundred hectares.

In some situations ground facilities may provide the best data. This has been particularly true with respect to the interception of Soviet telemetry. The sites located in Iran (and most especially Tacksman I and II) provided almost unique access to all phases of Soviet telemetry, including the telemetry related to the initial phase of the launch. By contrast, the RHYOLITE satellite was able to pick up a far smaller set of signals — specifically, it received 1/1000 of the magnitude obtained in Iran.[72] Additionally, a satellite such as RHYOLITE is faced with the problem of extracting Soviet telemetry signals, most of which are in the very high frequency band, from the large number of VHF signals emitted by many other transmitters within the satellite antenna's field of view.[73]

Nor do aircraft have completely adequate telemetry collection capabilities. In theory, the U-2 with a VHF antenna and flying at 30 480 metres (100 000 feet) over Turkey could collect much of the data on missile performance previously intercepted at the Tacksman sites. And the Carter Administration may have reconfigured some U-2s to accomplish this.[74] However, to be assured of having the aircraft in the air at the required times it would be necessary to have advanced warning of Soviet firings. By contrast, from its location in north-eastern Iran, Tacksman II could monitor launch activities from Tyuratam continuously and receive missile telemetry during boost and midcourse trajectory.[75]

At one time the US also placed great reliance on signals intelligence gathered by ship-based equipment. In the aftermath of the *Liberty* and *Pueblo* incidents the US suspended the use of ships for SIGINT collection.[76] However, the US recently used a Spruance class destroyer equipped with electronic intelligence equipment to collect COMINT relating to El Salvador and Nicaragua.[77]

More significantly, a ship-based phased array radar system, COBRA JUDY, has recently been deployed on the USNS *Observation Island*. With its operational base at Pearl Harbor, COBRA JUDY operates in the Pacific Ocean to complement COBRA DANE. The COBRA JUDY system, designated AN/SPQ-11, was designed to monitor the final near-earth trajectories of Soviet re-entry test vehicles. That portion of flight is not visible to COBRA DANE because of line-of-sight constraints imposed by curvature of the Earth.[78]

US facilities

US facilities in the UKUSA nations (other than those in the US itself) will be discussed in subsequent sections. This section covers US facilities located either in the US or non-UKUSA nations.

NSA and its military components maintain listening posts and related facilities at over 150 locations in the United States.[79] Naval Security Group facilities include those at Winter Harbor, Maine; Washington DC; Sugar Grove, West Virginia; Charleston, South Carolina; Homestead, Florida; Key West, Florida; Sabana Seca, Puerto Rico; San Diego, California; Skaggs Island, California; Adak, Alaska; Anchorage, Alaska; Makalapai, Hawaii; Wahiawa, Hawaii; and Guam in the Mariana Islands.[80]

It has been suggested that in addition to serving as a CLASSIC WIZARD ground terminal the Winter Harbor facility may also be involved in intercepting satellite communications directed at the nearby COMSAT/INTELSAT terminal.[81] The same assertion applies to the Sugar Grove, West Virginia facility which is located near the Etam, West Virginia COMSAT/INTELSAT ground stations.[82] It is also known that the NSG operates an AN/FLR-9 HF and VHF intercept and Direction Finding (DF) system at Wahiawa, Oahu (Hawaii) and an HF/DF net at Skaggs Island.[83]

INSCOM also operates listening posts and facilities at numerous locations in the United States, including Fort Devens, Massachusetts; Washington, DC; Vint Hills Farm Station (near Warrenton, Va.); Fort Knox, Kentucky; Fort Sheridan, Illinois; the Theater Intelligence Center (Pacific) at Fort Shafter, Honolulu; and Fort Richardson, Alaska.[84]

The Vint Hills Farm Station has been described as a 'top secret military and electronics monitoring post'.[85] The Vint Hills facility possesses a Rhombic array and it is heavily involved in Project 'Wideband Extraction'. The Project began at Vint Hills during July 1969 with the objective of extracting signals and messages of intelligence interest from a 'wideband' containing hundreds of thousands of other communications. At its inception the headquarters of Project Wideband Extraction were located at Vint Hills. In 1974 they were moved to a Central Security Operations Station at San Antonio, Texas where over 5000 service and NSA personnel analyse Project Wideband Extraction intercepts.[86]

As with the other military components of the NSA, the Air Force's electronic Security Command (ESC) also maintains facilities spread out across the United States. Locations include the headquarters at San Antonio, Texas; Arlington, Va.; Fort Meade, Maryland; Washington DC; Homestead AFB, Florida; Offutt AFB, Nebraska; Elmendorf AFB, Alaska; and Wheeler AFB, Hawaii.[87]

Two major NSA installations are its Pacific headquarters at Pearl Harbor and a research facility at Kent Island in the Chesapeake Bay. The Kent Island Research Facility, formally known as the NSA Propagation Research Laboratory, was established 'for the conduct of research and evaluations on very-high frequency and microwave antenna systems', and specifically to examine 'anomalous propagation effects and other peculiarities associated with [the] problem of intercept[ing] ... communications'.[88]

The National Security Agency and its military components also maintain a large number of bases outside the US and other UKUSA countries. A major portion of these bases are located in Europe. For example, there are at least four contingents of the Electronic Security Command in Germany: Electronic Security, Europe headquarters at Ramstein Air Base, at Hahn Air Base, at Sembach Air Base and Augsburg.[89]

Augsburg is also host to contingents of the Naval Security Group and Army Intelligence and Security Command (66th Intelligence and Security Group HQ).[90] Augsburg has been described by official US military sources as 'the largest communication intelligence complex in Europe'.[91] The Augsburg station has an AN/FLR-9 antenna system and is also a major site of Project Wideband Extraction activity.[92]

Major SIGINT facilities are also maintained in Italy and Greece. There are at least two SIGINT sites in Italy — one in Treviso and the other at San Vito dei Normanni Air Station, near the coast town of Brindisi. San Vito is host to contingents of both the NSG and ESC (6917th Electronic Security Group).[93] More importantly, there is an AN/FLR-9 antenna system at San Vito, installed in 1964.[94] There are two Electronic Security Squadrons in Greece — one stationed at Hellenikon Air Base and the other at the Iraklion Air Station, Crete.[95] Hellenikon is used as a base for RC-135 aircraft. These aircraft are directed primarily towards countries such as Libya, with only about 10 per cent of the missions directed against NATO-targeted Balkan countries.[96] The Iraklion station may have a VHF-UHF-SHF antenna capable of intercepting telemetry from Soviet missile launches at Kapustin Yar and Tyuratam.[97]

Naval Security Group facilities are located in Iceland, Spain and Denmark. Icelandic locations for NSG are at Keflavik and Stokksnes. The NSG site at Keflavik may be used primarily for ocean surveillance with the

Stokksnes site being primarily an ELINT/COMINT station.[988] At Rota, Spain, there is a CDAA, used primarily (if not exclusively) for ocean surveillance.[99] At Bornholm, Denmark there is a VHF-UHF-SHF receiver which may be used to monitor launches from Plesetsk.[100]

Among the most important US signals intelligence sites in Europe are those located in Norway and Turkey. The NSA network in Norway apparently consists of eight stations, including three in the northern corner of Norway — Vardø, Vadsø and Viksjøfjellet.[101] These facilities are operated for the US by Norwegian technicians.[102] VHF-UHF-SHF receivers at Viksjøfjellet and Vardø intercept the telemetry of missile launches from the Barents Sea, White Sea, and Plesetsk. HF receivers at Vadsø record count-down communications from these same locations.[103]

Intelligence collection sites in Turkey are those at Sinop and Samsun on the Black Sea Coast in north central Turkey, Belbasi in central Turkey, Diyarbakir in south-eastern Turkey and Karamursel in north-western Turkey.[104] The Sinop facility is operated by INSCOM and collects data on Soviet air and naval activities in the Black Sea area. It also has HF receivers to record the telemetry of missiles launched from Kapustin Yar and Tyuratam.[105]

Associated with Sinop is Samsun — a communications site manned by the Air Force ECS.[106] The Diyarbakir site is operated by INSCOM and consists of an FPS-17 detection radar and FPS-79 tracking radar both of which are targeted against missiles launched from Kapustin Yar and Tyuratam.[107] Telemetry from missiles launched from those sites are intercepted by the VHF-UHF-SHF receivers at the Karamursel facilities, which has both NSG and ESC contingents.[108]

In addition to European sites, the NSA and the Service Cryptologic Authorities have numerous sites in Asia. Most prominent and important are two monitoring sites in the People's Republic of China, located in the mountainous region of Xingiang Uighur Autonomous Region in western China, near the Soviet border.[109] These sites allow the US to recover a significant portion of the capability lost with the closure of the Iranian sites. Other nations in Asia which host US monitoring sites include South Korea (at Kanghwa Island), the Philippines (at San Miguel and Clark AFB) and Japan.[110]

Japan is host to numerous sites, the most important being the INSCOM facility at Torii Station, Okinawa. This facility has an AN/FLR-9 HF and VHF intercept and DF system, codenamed 'Kinsfolk'. Other Japanese facilities include NSG facilities at Sobe, Okinawa (with HF-DF and COMSEC functions) and Kamiseya as well as an INSCOM facility at Atsugi and ESC sites at Misawa Air Base, and Kadena AFB, Okinawa.[111] From these facilities the US is able to monitor radar signals from both Soviet ground installations and aircraft. In addition, some antennas at these facilities are tuned to intercept the generally uncoded radio transmissions between Soviet air defence installations and interceptor aircraft.[112]

Over the past fifteen years the United States has lost several monitoring sites, mainly due to political changes in host nations or due to international political realignment. The most serious losses were those of the Tacksman sites in Iran. In addition the US closed down the facility for a phased array radar, COBRA TALON, located in Thailand at the request of the Thai government. In 1967 the US lost its base at Peshawar in Pakistan. From that facility the Air Force Security Service (predecessor of ESC) was able to make tape recordings of Soviet missile countdowns, military conversations, civilian radio-telephone communications, and other electromagnetic signals from Central Asia.[113] In North Africa, facilities at Kagnew in Ethiopia and Sidi Yahia in Morocco have been closed down in recent years.[114]

Canadian facilities

Canadian signals intelligence facilities are located on both coasts as well as in the far northern portions of Canada. As noted earlier, there were at least six Canadian monitoring sites during the Second World War — Ottawa; Amherst, Nova Scotia (Halifax); West Point Barracks, Victoria with a subsidiary detachment at Point Grey; Grand Prairie, Alberta; and Riske Creeke, British Columbia. The Riske Creeke station closed in April 1946.[115]

As of 1956 there were four communications links between the CBNRC and the NSA: the link between Fort Meade and the CBNRC, Ottawa; links between the NSA Fort Meade and the NSG and ASA detachments at Leitrim, Ontario; and an air force link with the 5th Radio Squadron of the Royal Canadian Air Force at Whitehorse, Canada.[116]

Present Communications Security Establishment facilities on the East Coast include the Argentia Naval Station in Newfoundland, the Debert Canadian Forces Station at Nova Scotia and the Gander Canadian Forces Station in Newfoundland.[117] The Argentia Facility is an ELINT/HF-DF station while the Gander Station is the home of the 770th Communications Research Squadron.[118]

More centrally located facilities are those at the Carp Canadian Forces Station, Ottawa and the still operational Leitrim Canadian Forces Station in Ontario. Additionally, the 1st Canadian Signals Regiment is located at Kingston, Ontario.[119] West Coast monitoring stations include those at the Masset Canadian Forces Station in British Columbia and Grand Prairie, Alberta.[120]

Whitehorse is the location for one of four northern region stations and installations of the Canadian armed forces. In addition to Whitehorse in the west, there is Inuvik in the north-west, Frobisher in the east and an Alert Station far north of the Distant Early Warning (DEW) line.[121] Both the Inuvik and Alert Stations host monitoring operations and in all probability so do those at Whitehorse and Frobisher.[122] These are the stations that would be most heavily involved in monitoring the northern Soviet Union. It has been alleged that the US conducted ELINT missions into Soviet airspace from Inuvik, using specially equipped C-130s.[123]

Finally, there is a Canadian 'Communications Research Station' in Bermuda.[124] This may be a joint operation with the United States as there is a US Naval Air Station on Bermuda as well as a listing for 'Bermuda Activities' in the US Department of Defense AUTOVON directory.[125]

Australian/New Zealand facilities

Australian participation in UKUSA signals intelligence collection activity takes several forms, including Australian-operated facilities in Australia and abroad, and a US ground facility for the RHYOLITE SIGINT satellite system.

As noted earlier, the Defence Signals Directorate is responsible for SIGINT collection in parts of the Indian Ocean, South East Asia and the Pacific. In carrying out this mission the DSD has established units in Hong Kong and Papua New Guinea. The DSD also works out of embassies in Bangkok and Jakarta and has small facilities at Butterworth (Malaysia) and Singapore.[126]

The Hong Kong facility, which is a joint operation with Britain's GCHQ and has a contingent of 140 Australian military personnel, was upgraded in 1976 with construction of a huge new complex at Tai Mo Shan in the New Territories. There are two intercept stations presently at Hong Kong. The Composite Signals Organization on Hong Kong Island itself houses administrative, signal recording and cryptographic activities; it was originally located at Little Sai Wan but was moved to a new site on the south coast of Hong Kong Island in 1983, with Britain paying for the move.[127]

The New Territories out-station at Tai Mo Shan has an aerial farm that is even larger than the one formerly at Little Sai Wan. Until the mid-1970s the Hong Kong operation was directed almost entirely against the People's Republic of China, but it is now very much involved in monitoring Soviet naval movements along East Asia from the major naval bases at Vladivostok and Petroplavosk–Kamchatka to Cam Ranh Bay in Vietnam.[128]

The DSD facilities in Australia are located at Victoria Barracks in Melbourne; Watsonia Barracks and Rockbank in the outer suburbs of Melbourne; Shoal Bay outside Darwin; HMAS Harman near Canberra; Pearce Air Force Base near Perth; and Cabarlah near Toowoomba. There is extensive NSA and GCHQ participation in the operations of these facilities. The NSA maintains an office at DSD headquarters at Victoria Barracks headed by the Special US Liaison Officer (SUSLO) and staffed by some ten to twelve NSA officers. The British Liaison Officer at Victoria Barracks serves as the Special Assistant to the Director of DSD. There are US and UK SIGINT personnel at several of the DSD facilities. In addition, there are NSA personnel at the US Embassy in Canberra, at the Pine Gap and Nurrungar RHYOLITE and DSP satellite ground stations, and an NSG Detachment has been reported at the North West Cape Naval Communications Station.[129]

Project Sparrow AN/FSC-78 antenna at Watsonia Barracks, Melbourne, Victoria, provides a direct satellite communications link between DSD Headquarters at Victoria Barracks, Melbourne and DSD-GCHQ facilities at Hong Kong as well as with NSA Headquarters, Fort Meade, Maryland.

Watsonia Barracks is located some 15 kilometres (9 miles) from the DSD headquarters at Victoria Barracks and serves as the signals centre for the Australian defence establishment. It houses the School of Signals, 126 Signal Squadron, 6 Signal Regiment, and 700 Signal Troop. The antennas at Watsonia include two log-periodic LP-1001-K antennas. Since 1950, DSD's actual intercept operations have been conducted from Rockbank, some 60 kilometres (37 miles) west of Watsonia. The antennas at Rockbank — which is operated by 6 Signal Regiment — include a large interferometer array for HF intercept and HF-DF, and four log-periodic LP-1001-K antennas.[130] Watsonia is also the site of a satellite ground terminal, known as Project

192 The Ties That Bind

'Sparrow' and involving an AN/FSC-78 18.29 metre (60-foot) parabolic antenna system, which provides a direct satellite communications link between the Australian intelligence agencies and the CIA and NSA.[131]

The DSD station at HMAS Harman, near Canberra, is both the smallest and the oldest of the DSD stations. It began operations in 1939, and by the end of 1940 had a staff of eight full-time and six part-time operators involved in both radio interception and cryptanalytic work. Although most diplomatic messages to and from Australia were at this time dealt with at Singapore, by at least the middle of 1941 Harman had had some success with intercepting and reading Japanese diplomatic communications.[132]

Harman's principal mission remains the interception of diplomatic traffic to and from the foreign embassies in Canberra, although it is also involved in monitoring transmissions emanating from South East Asia. The station operates closely with Darwin on this — often being able to intercept transmissions that either skip over or are too weak to be monitored at Darwin. There is also an Adcock DF system at Harman for limited ocean surveillance activity.[133]

On the west coast of Australia the RAAF station at Pearce near Perth monitors naval and air traffic over the Indian Ocean. The interception and direction finding capability at Pearce was recently upgraded with installation of a new Plessey CDAA, codenamed 'Pusher'. This system is designed for interception, monitoring, direction finding and analysis of radio signals in the HF band from 1.5 to 3.0 MHz.[134]

On the east coast, at Cabarlah, near Toowoomba, Queensland, DSD monitors radio transmissions throughout the South-west Pacific. During the joint Australian–US Kangaroo II military exercise in October 1976, which was watched by Soviet intelligence-gathering trawlers, Cabarlah was used to monitor the trawler's own messages and movements. As with the facility at Pearce, the Cabarlah station has recently been upgraded with a new Plessey CDAA.[135]

For the purpose of monitoring transmissions throughout South East Asia, the most important DSD station in Australia is the one at Shoal Bay, near Darwin, which has approximately 70 military personnel as well as 30 civilians. Shoal Bay became operational in 1974, replacing the Coonawarra station which had been operational since 1939, and the Singapore station operated by the DSD until 1973. The station's DF capability is currently being upgraded. The use of Shoal Bay as a substitute for Singapore resulted from a series of events which followed the British Government's decision in 1967 to withdraw from east of Suez. In 1968 the Australian Joint Intelligence Committee reviewed the likely effects of the British withdrawal on Australian intelligence interests, and JIC Report No. 13/1968 recommended, inter alia, that signals intelligence facilities should continue to be available to Australia in the Singapore area. In October 1968 the Defence Committee endorsed that recommendation. At a meeting on 23 January 1969 the Committee also requested a further report on possible alternatives after 1971 in the event of a suitable site being no longer available in

Singapore or Malaysia. At this time plans were being made for construction of a new naval communications receiving station at Shoal Bay and studies showed that such a station would also serve as a partial substitute for the Singapore station.[136]

The Shoal Bay station was publicly announced in March 1970. The *Northern Territory News* reported on 12 March 1970 that the new station would replace the receiving section of the navy communications complex at Coonawarra; that the receiving aerials would be built on a disused salt pan at Shoal Bay which the Weapons Research Establishment said could hardly be bettered as a site for radio reception; that the receiver would be linked by land-line with the transmitter station at Coonawarra; that Shoal Bay would operate in conjunction with the Harman station, providing an alternative to Harman when reception there was poor; that it would be staffed by about 100 personnel (which would include about 70 SIGINT officers of the 121 Signals Squadron from Singapore); that the station would operate on a year-round, 24-hours-a-day basis; and that the base facilities would be available to other Commonwealth countries and to the US.[137]

The SIGINT systems at Shoal Bay include a CDAA, which was installed in 1974, and two satellite antennae which became operational in 1979 and which (under Project LARSWOOD) are designed to intercept Indonesian satellite communications.

The single most important facility in Australia, certainly from the point of view of the United States, is the Pine Gap facility, near Alice Springs in Central Australia. Officially known as the Joint Defence Space Research Facility, the facility is in fact a CIA-run installation (codenamed 'Merino') that provides control signals and readout from the RHYOLITE SIGINT satellites stationed over the Pacific.[138]

Pine Gap consists of seven large radomes, a huge computer room and about twenty other support buildings. The radomes are made of perspex and mounted on concrete structures and are designed to protect the enclosed antennas against dust, wind and rain, and to hide some of the operational elements of the antennas from Soviet satellite reconnaissance.

The first two radomes, which were installed in 1968, remain the largest in the complex. In March 1967, the first chief of the Pine Gap facility stated that the largest dish is 30.48 metres ('about 100 feet') in diameter. The second radome has a diameter of about 21.34 metres (70 feet). These two radomes now form the western line of the antenna complex. Construction of the third and fourth radomes began in November 1968 and was completed in mid-1969. The third radome, about 16.76 metres (55 feet) in diameter, is some 60 metres (about 200 feet) east of the largest radome; the fourth is less than 6 metres (20 feet) in diameter and is just north of the second radome. In 1973, the antenna which was originally installed in the third radome was dismantled and replaced by a 10 metre communications terminal designated SCT-35. The fifth radome is less than 12 metres (40 feet) in diameter and was installed in 1971. The sixth dish is about the same size as the fifth and was installed in 1977. The seventh radome, which was built in 1980, houses a second communications terminal, designated SCT-8.[139]

On the northern edge of the complex is a high frequency (HF) antenna which provides a direct communications link with the US base at Clark Field in the Philippines. This is the only non-satellite communications system linking the Pine Gap facility with terminals outside Australia, and before the installation of the SCT-35 antenna in 1973 it was the primary communications link between Pine Gap and the United States.[140]

Pine Gap is strictly under US (CIA) control. Very few Australians are permitted in the Top Secret sector of the station. The Signals Analysis Section of the Computer Room is staffed only by CIA and NSA analysts — it includes no US contractor personnel and no Australian citizens.[141]

The New Zealand SIGINT organization, the Government Communications Security Bureau (GCSB), operates a single SIGINT station at Tangimoana in the north island of the country. It is primarily concerned with monitoring communications and other signals in the South-west Pacific area.[142]

British facilities

Britain is heavily involved in the collection of signals intelligence to be shared by the UKUSA partners. Its involvement is two-fold, operating a large number of signals intelligence installations at home and abroad as well as providing facilities in Britain for US signals intelligence operations.

In addition to UK liaison offices at the CSE Ottawa, the DSD Melbourne and the NSA Fort Meade, Britain's overseas stations include the relocated Little Sai Wan station and the Tai Mo Shan station in Hong Kong, both of which are jointly operated with Australia.[143] On the other side of the world, in West Germany, there are several British signals units — the 13th Signals Regiment at Birgelen, a unit at Jever, the 225 Signals Squadron at Celle and the 226 Signals Squadron at Dannenberg. In addition, the 3rd Squadron, 13th Signals Regiment and 26th Signals Unit are located at Teufelsberg, Berlin.[144]

There are also GCHQ Units at Gibraltar; Masirah Island, Oman; at Sinop, Turkey; at Mount Greco and Mount Olympus, Cyprus; and at Pergamos/Ayios Nikoaos, Cyprus (the 9th Signals Regiment, 33 Signals Unit).[145]

The GCHQ also jointly operates two overseas sites with the NSA — one at Diego Garcia in the Indian Ocean, which was initially opened as a British facility in August 1974, and the other at Two Boats on the Ascension Isles in the South Atlantic. These facilities are primarily concerned with the monitoring of naval communications in the Indian Ocean and the South Atlantic respectively.[146]

The GCHQ also operates listening posts in a number of British embassies, including Moscow, Nairobi, Pretoria, Lilongue and Lusaka, and probably also Warsaw, Budapest, Prague, Cairo, Freetown, and Accra.[147]

At one time the GCHQ operated airborne SIGINT platforms from sites in Iran. From these sites it would fly over the Soviet Union to monitor missile testing activity near the Caspian Sea.[148]

The GCHQ operates more than a dozen intercept stations within the UK. Moving from north to south, there are stations at Brora, Scotland; Hawklaw, near Cupar Fife; Irton Moor, near Scarborough, North Yorkshire, which was also an important SIGINT site during the Second World War; RAF Digby, Lincolnshire, which hosts the 339 Signals Unit; Loughborough (Garrat's Way), which hosts the 224 Signals Squadron; Wymeswold, Leicestershire, which is an Army training and field station; Cheadle, Staffordshire, which reportedly monitors Soviet Air Force communications; RAF Wyton; Shenley Church End, near Bletchley, Buckinghamshire, which has an unmanned Pusher CDAA; Poundon, Buckinghamshire, which has a CDAA and a Loop Antenna Array; Blakehill (Cricklade), Wiltshire; and Culmhead, near Taunton, Somerset. Two stations in Northern Ireland — Gilnahirk and Island Hill, Comber — were closed in the late 1970s.[149]

In addition, the GCHQ maintains a London office at Palmer Street, Westminister, which is evidently the site for the interception of International Leased Carrier (ILC) cable and telex traffic. The GCHQ's Composite Signals Organisation (CSO) maintains a satellite ground station at Morwenstow, near Bude, Cornwall, which may be used, *inter alia*, for the interception of INTELSAT satellite communications. And Her Majesty's Government Communications Centre at Hanslope Park, north-west of London, is used to receive SIGINT traffic from the GCHQ posts at British embassies and High Commissions abroad.[150]

The NSA has four major independent establishments in Britain — at Chicksands in Bedfordshire; at Edzell (Tayside) in Scotland; at Menwith Hill, Harrogate; and at Brawdy, Wales. The installation at Brawdy is an NSG facility concerned with ocean surveillance.

The Chicksands facility is a major listening post run by the 6950th Electronic Security Group. During the Second World War, Chicksands served as the primary ENIGMA intercept station. An AN/FLR-9 antenna was installed at Chicksands at approximately the same time as one was installed at San Vito.[151] According to a former NSA officer, one of Chicksands' prime tasks is to monitor the diplomatic communications of France and other European countries.[152] The Edzell, Scotland outpost is an NSG facility involved in both radio monitoring and ocean surveillance. Among the equipment at Edzell is a Circularly Disposed Antenna Array with 80 vertical supports, each 228.6 centimetres (90 inches) in height.[153]

A major NSA station is located at Menwith Hill, about thirteen kilometres (eight miles) west of Harrogate in Yorkshire. The station is about 227 hectares (562 acres) and consists of a large array of satellite tracking aerials. Eight tracking dishes dominate the Menwith Hill site. Most of the time they are pointed towards satellites operating in the highly elliptical orbit of the Soviet Molniya and US Satellite Data System satellites. Hence,

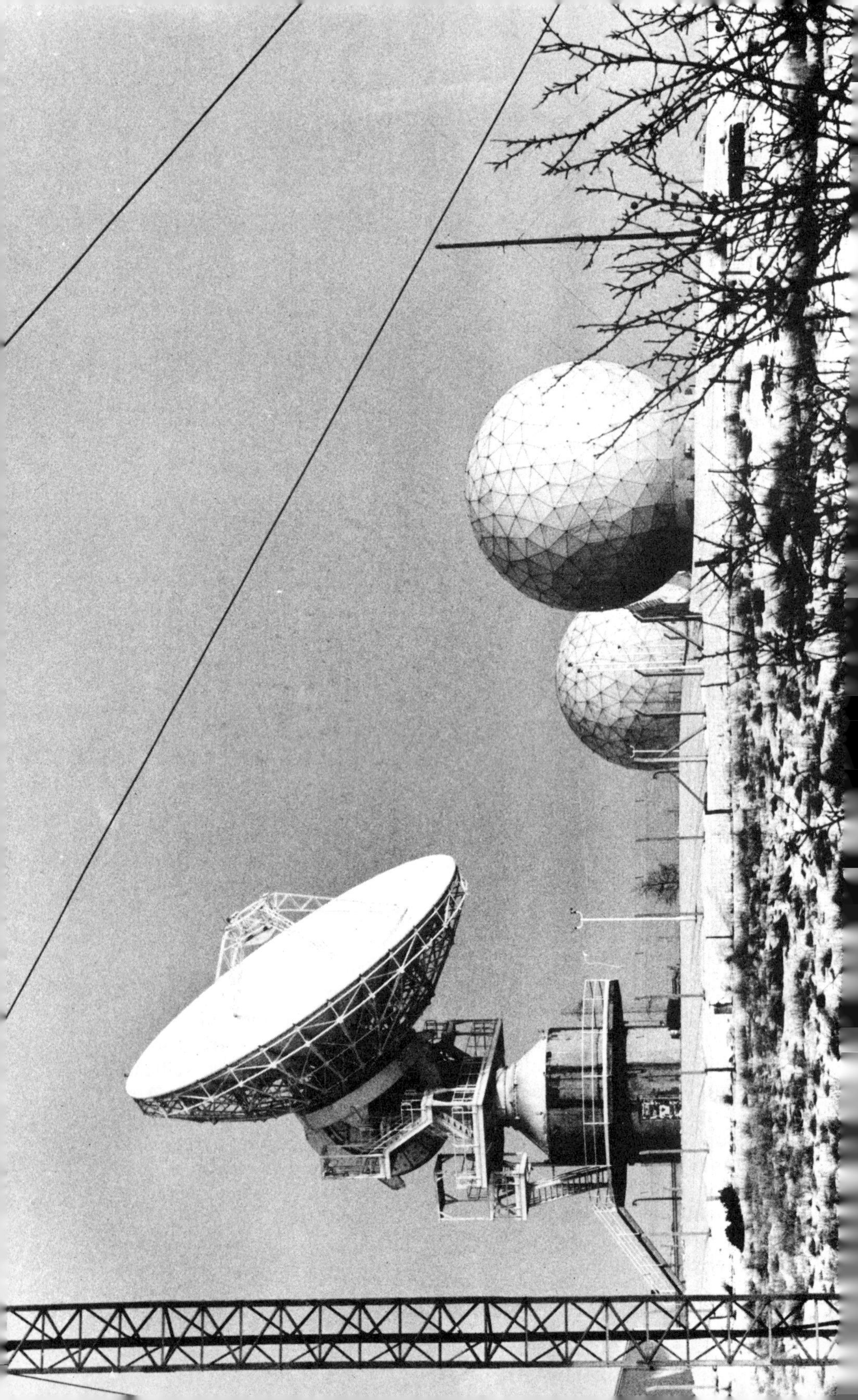

the aerials may be intercepting signals from the former and/or transmitting or receiving signals to or from the latter.[154]

Menwith Hill is also a major COMINT collection site. According to Linda Malvern and Duncan Campbell, Menwith Hill has for fifteen years 'sifted the communications of private citizens, corporations and governments for information of political or economic value to the US'.[155]

The British Post Office has built Menwith Hill into the heart of Britain's national communications system — and Britain occupies a nodal position in the communications of the world, especially those of Western Europe. The first stage of the Post Office microwave network was constructed around Menwith Hill and its operations; at least five high capacity networks feed into the base from all parts of Britain, through the nearby Post Office tower at Hunter Stones.[156]

One former British officer has stated that Menwith Hill intercepts telephone and other communications to and from Europe and the United States. One tap run from Menwith Hill allegedly involves 3600 London to Paris telephone lines. Also, according to a former US official, Menwith Hill provides ground station services for CIA and NSA intelligence satellites.[157] There is also a CDAA and a four-element VHF intercept antenna at Menwith Hill.

Additional satellite tracking stations are located at Croughton and Winkfield.[158]

Finally, at Mildenhall RAF base there is an Electronic Security Squadron which provides personnel to operate the electronic intelligence-gathering equipment which is on several aircraft stationed there. There are two U-2s, two SR-71s, and two RC-135s based at Mildenhall.[159]

NSA SIGINT station and satellite ground station at Menwith Hill, near Harrogate, Yorkshire. Sister station to CIA SIGINT station at Pine Gap. Menwith Hill and Pine Gap are two of the largest satellite ground stations in the world.

9

Ocean surveillance

Within the closed world of military intelligence, naval intelligence services command a special reputation for their extreme secretiveness, the primarily technical character of their operations, and their relative success as compared to those of other military intelligence services. In the UK, the Secret Intelligence Service (SIS or M1-6), the Government Communications Headquarters (GCHQ) and the Signals Intelligence (SIGINT) organization all have direct historical lineages to naval intelligence. When the SIS was first instituted as an independent agency in 1910, as the Foreign Section of the Secret Service Bureau, it was administratively responsible to the Admiralty. During the First World War, the Naval Intelligence Department (NID) was by far the most important of all the British intelligence agencies, as well as the most powerful. Within the NID, Room 40 was given responsibility for the interception and decipherment of enemy signals, and played a vital part in winning the war; its functions were later transferred to the Foreign Office and became the responsibility of the Government Code and Cipher School (GCCS) at Bletchley Park during the Second World War; since then they have been the responsibility of the GCHQ at Cheltenham.

In the United States, the most important Second World War signals intelligence and cryptographic organization was the Navy's OP-20-G, or the G section (Communication Security Section) of the 20th Division (Office of Naval Communications) of the Office of the Chief of Naval Operations; the functions of this organization were later taken over by the Naval Security Group (NSG), the largest component of the US Service Cryptological Authorities. During the Second World War the most critical intelligence successes involved naval operations, including most particularly the Allied operations against German and Japanese submarines.[1]

As noted in Chapter 6, the Current Operations Department of the US Navy Operational Intelligence Center is responsible for the preparation and dissemination of reports on the position and activities of all naval vessels, but particularly Soviet ships and submarines, on a worldwide basis. Data is received at the Current Operations Department from Atlantic, Pacific, and European Fleet Ocean Surveillance Information Centers (FOSICs), which in turn derive their information from a variety of worldwide sources, collectively known as the Ocean Surveillance Information System (OSIS).[2] Directly subordinate to the the Current Operations Department are five major correlation centres which correlate the surveillance information obtained from their assigned geographical areas — Norfolk, Virginia; London, England; Makalapa, Hawaii; Rota, Spain; and Kami Seya, Japan.[3] These centres are evidently operated by the Naval Security Group activity of the NSA.[4] This system is the culmination of the organizational and technical developments in Western naval intelligence of more than half a century.

The surveillance information collected, processed and disseminated through the OSIS is derived from a wide variety of sources, of which the most important are underwater sonar arrays; satellite surveillance systems; high-frequency direction-finding (HF-DF) signals monitoring stations; and numerous other airborne, ship-borne and submarine-borne sensor systems. Integration of the intelligence from these various sources enhances the effectiveness of the OSIS far beyond the particular contributions of its component elements. Participation in this ocean surveillance system involves not merely the five UKUSA partners, but many other Western countries, such as Iceland, Norway, Japan and the Philippines.

Underwater surveillance systems

Underwater surveillance is primarily conducted by means of sonar systems, which sense underwater sound waves reflected from or generated by submarines. The United States, and to a lesser extent the United Kingdom and Australia, have developed a wide range of sonar systems, including large fixed-bottom arrays, towed arrays, rapidly deployable sonars, helicopter-borne dipping sonars, and systems fitted to ships and submarines.

The largest single system is a global network of large fixed sea-bottom arrays of hydrophones that passively listen for sounds generated by submarines. These arrays are individually and collectively known as SOSUS (Sound Surveillance System), although strictly speaking only about two-thirds of the arrays are part of the SOSUS network proper, the other one-third being allied systems. The SOSUS system was described by one US Admiral in 1979 as 'the backbone of our ASW detection capability'.[5]

SOSUS was described by the Stockholm International Peace Research Institute (SIPRI) in 1979 as follows:

Each SOSUS installation consists of an array of hundreds of hydrophones laid out on the sea floor, or moored at depths most conducive to sound propagation, and connected by submarine cables for transmission of telemetry. In such an array a sound wave arriving from a distant submarine will be successively detected by different hydrophones according to their geometric relationship to the direction from which the wave arrives. This direction can be determined by noting the order in which the wave is detected at the different hydrophones. In practice the sensitivity of the array is enhanced many times by adding the signals from several individual hydrophones after introducing appropriate time delays between them. The result is a listening 'beam' that can be 'steered' in various directions towards various sectors of the ocean by varying the pattern of time delays. The distance from the array to the sound source can be calculated by measuring the divergence of the sound rays within the array or by triangulating from adjacent arrays.[6]

Development work on SOSUS began in 1950, at which time the hydrophone arrays were codenamed 'Caesar'. Installation of the first SOSUS/Caesar array was completed on the continental shelf off the east coast of the United States in 1954;[7] subsequent Caesar arrays were installed elsewhere off the east coast, at Brawdy in Wales,[8] and perhaps other locations as well. The Caesar arrays have been progressively up-dated and the technology is now in its fifth generation of development. Caesar uses AN/FQQ-6 and AN/FQQ-9V sonars and AN/VQA-5 spectrum analysers.[9]

The Caesar arrays proved extremely effective during the Cuban Missile Crisis of October 1962, and it was decided to further expand and up-grade this network and to construct variants codenamed 'Colossus' along the Pacific coast of the US. Colossus uses a more advanced form of sonar than Caesar, designated AN/FQQ-10(V).[10] In 1966, the existence of a joint US–Canadian sophisticated detection system, codenamed 'Nutmeg' but similar to Caesar, was reported; it is presumably located at Argentia, Newfoundland.[11] One of the largest underwater hydrophone arrays, codenamed 'Sea Spider', is located off the north coast of Hawaii; it was reportedly this array which monitored and localized the break up of the Soviet submarine which sank north of Hawaii in March 1968 and was subsequently the subject of the CIA/Glomar Explorer recovery effort.[12] In October 1963, the US signed a lease agreement with the UK for the use of a complex of deep underwater facilities, collectively known as the Atlantic Undersea Test and Evaluation Center (AUTEC), in the Bahamas, with the major shore facility on Andros Island; the acoustic range became operational in 1968 and was certified in 1969.[13] In September 1968, construction of a large fixed underwater system known as the Azores Fixed Acoustic Range (AFAR) began off the island of Santa Maria, the southernmost of the Azores group; commissioned by NATO on 19 May 1972, the AFAR system is intended to track Soviet submarines approaching the Straits of Gibraltar or on passage to round the Cape of Good Hope.[14] Other related projects are codenamed 'Barrier' and 'Bronco'.[15]

It was stated in 1974 that there were 22 SOSUS installations located along the east and west coasts of the United States and at various choke points around the world,[16] and the locations of a further fourteen similar installations have also been identified. These 36 facilities are distributed around the world as follows: eight on the east and west coasts of the continental

United States (including one at Cape Hatteras, North Carolina), three in the Bahamas (including the AUTEC facility on Andros Island), two in the United Kingdom (one at Brawdy in Wales and the other in the Shetland Islands), two in Turkey, two in Japan, and one each in Alaska, Hawaii (Sea Spider), Puerto Rico, Bermuda, Barbados, Canada (Argentia, Newfoundland), Norway, Iceland (Keflavik), Santa Maria Island in the Azores (AFAR), Ascension Island, Italy, Denmark, Gibraltar, the Ryukus, Galeta Island in the Panama Canal Zone, the Philippines, Ratidian Point in Guam, Diego Garcia, and in the north-eastern part of the Indian Ocean.[17] Just on half of these facilities are located on the territories or island possessions of the five UKUSA partners.

Data from these shore facilities is transmitted via FLTSATCOM and DSCS satellites to 'a central shore station' at the Acoustic Research Center (ARC) at Moffett Field, California, where it is integrated with data from other sources and processed by the Illiac 4 computer complex to provide a real-time submarine monitoring capability.[18] According to one report, the detection capabilities of SOSUS are sufficient to localize a submarine to within a radius of 80 kilometres (50 miles) at ranges of several thousand kilometres,[19] but other reports suggest that radii of 15 kilometres (9 miles) are now possible.[20] In one test of an array deployed off the coast of Oregon, a submarine was detected off the coast of Japan some 9670 kilometres (6000 miles) away, but ranges up to about half this are more typical.[21] According to testimony submitted to Congress in May 1980:

SOSUS has demonstrated a substantial capability to detect submarines patrolling or transiting through SOSUS areas of coverage ...
Since the first USSR deployment of SSBNs, a large fraction of the SSBN deployed force has been subject to SOSUS detection and tracking.[22]

Other reports have been even more categoric, to the effect that SOSUS has been able to detect all Soviet submarine movements.[23]

The extraordinary capabilities of SOSUS notwithstanding, the US Navy has established requirements for other complementary systems. SOSUS performance is contingent upon sound propagation conditions, which are quite variable, and in some circumstances the performance of fixed arrays is inferior to that of other systems. Moreover, the SOSUS network — the sensors, the cables, and the shore stations — is rather vulnerable.[24] The two most important complementary systems currently under development are a Rapidly Deployable Surveillance System (RDSS) and the Surveillance Towed Array Sensor System (SURTASS).

The RDSS is designed to operate in areas where fixed or manned systems cannot operate safely or reliably. The system consists of large sonobuoys which can be remotely deployed by aircraft and ships (from frigates up) or launched through submarine torpedo tubes, and which moor themselves automatically to the ocean bottom. The RDSS would be particularly useful in monitoring 'such high interest areas as the Dardanelles, Baltic approaches,

Straits of Gibraltar, and the Greenland–Iceland–United Kingdom (GIUK) gap'.[25]

SURTASS is designed to provide a mobile back-up to the SOSUS network. It can be used in areas where SOSUS is unavailable or inoperative, or it can be used to enhance coverage within SOSUS regions.[26] The SURTASS program involves the acquisition of twelve 66 metre (217-foot) ships, designated T-AGOS, which are designed to tow a very long aperture hydrophone array (some 1220 metres [400 feet] long) by a 2000 metre (6561-foot) cable. The T-AGOS ships are designed to operate for up to 90 days on station. Transit speeds are 11 knots and towing speeds must be 3 knots or less, allowing a mission radius of about 4830 kilometres (3000 nautical miles). Data from the hydrophone array are pre-processed on board ship and then sent via FLTSATCOM and DSCS satellites to the Central Shore Station at Moffett Field.[27]

HF-DF signals intelligence

The second principal source of OSIS intelligence is the interception of naval signals by high-frequency direction-finding (HF-DF) stations which are operated around the globe by the NSG component of the NSA, the GCHQ, the DSD, the CSE and other allied SIGINT agencies.

The worldwide intercept and direction-finding network for the US Navy's Ocean Surveillance System is codenamed BULLSEYE. Most of the stations in the BULLSEYE network use the FLR-15 antenna array for the actual signals interception and the MX8550 and OL-125 systems for signal analysis and processing.[28]

The number of UKUSA SIGINT stations involved in ocean surveillance must be somewhere around 40–50. In the Indo-Pacific sub-system alone, for example, there are some twenty stations, ranging from the GCHQ station at Masirah through Diego Garcia and the DSD stations in Australia to the NSG stations in Japan, South Korea, Alaska and California. (See Figure 9.1.) A description of this regional sub-system should serve to both indicate the extensive and intricate nature of the cooperative arrangements of the UKUSA partners as well as illuminating the character of the HF-DF and SIGINT operations in the ocean-surveillance context.

The British SIGINT station at Masirah, an island off the coast of Oman in the Arabian Sea, is located at the former Royal Air Force (RAF) base; although it is operated by the GCHQ, it is evidently financed by the United States.[29] (See Figure 9.2.)

The Diego Garcia station is now probably the most important of the stations in this regional network. Not only is Diego Garcia ideally situated for monitoring naval traffic in the Indian Ocean, but during the 1970s it also acquired many of the functions previously performed by the NSA facility at Kagnew Station at Asmara in Ethiopia.

The Kagnew Station was built by the US Army's Signals Intelligence

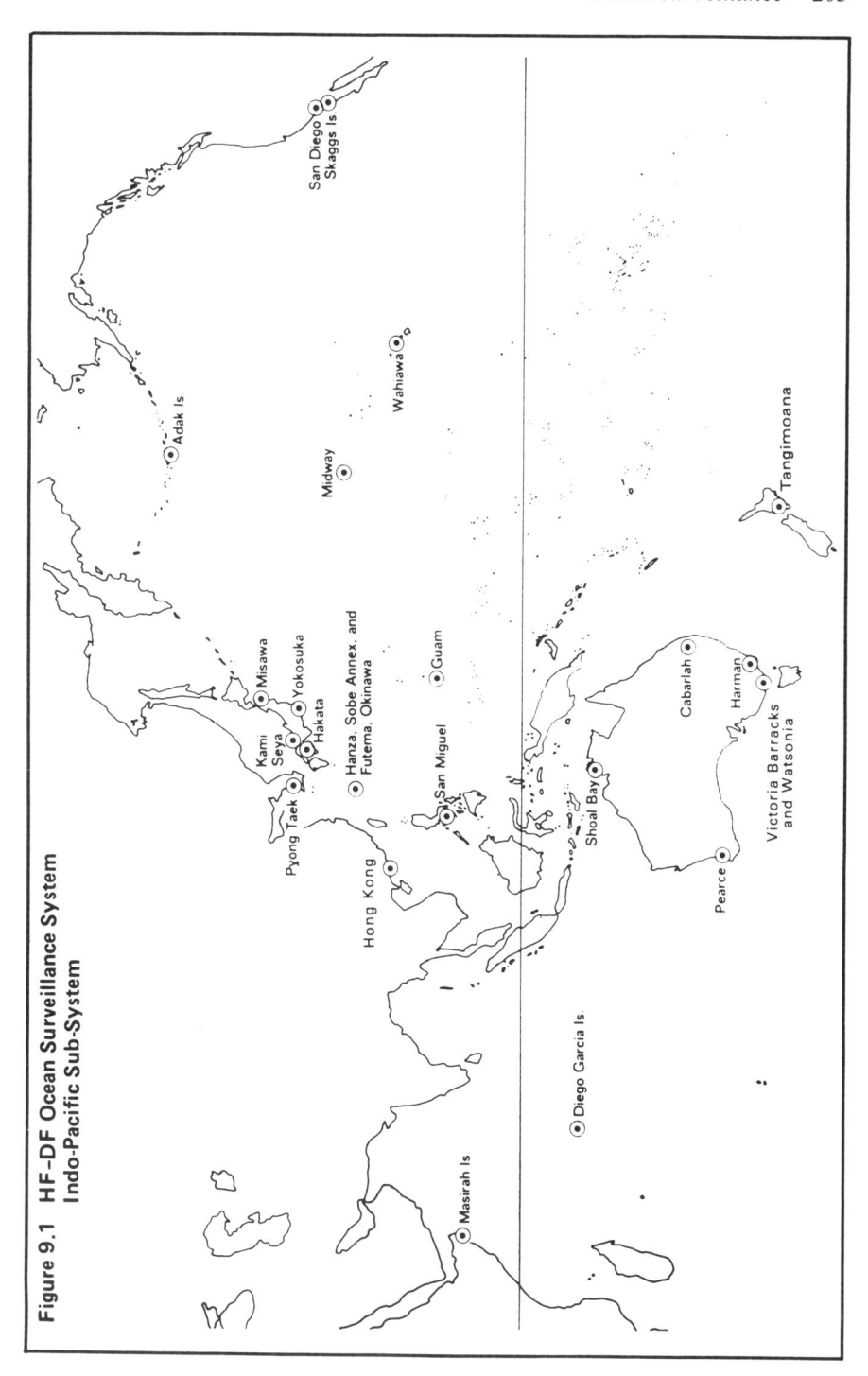

Ocean surveillance 203

Figure 9.1 **HF-DF Ocean Surveillance System Indo-Pacific Sub-System**

204 *The Ties That Bind*

Figure 9.2 Masirah Island, Oman

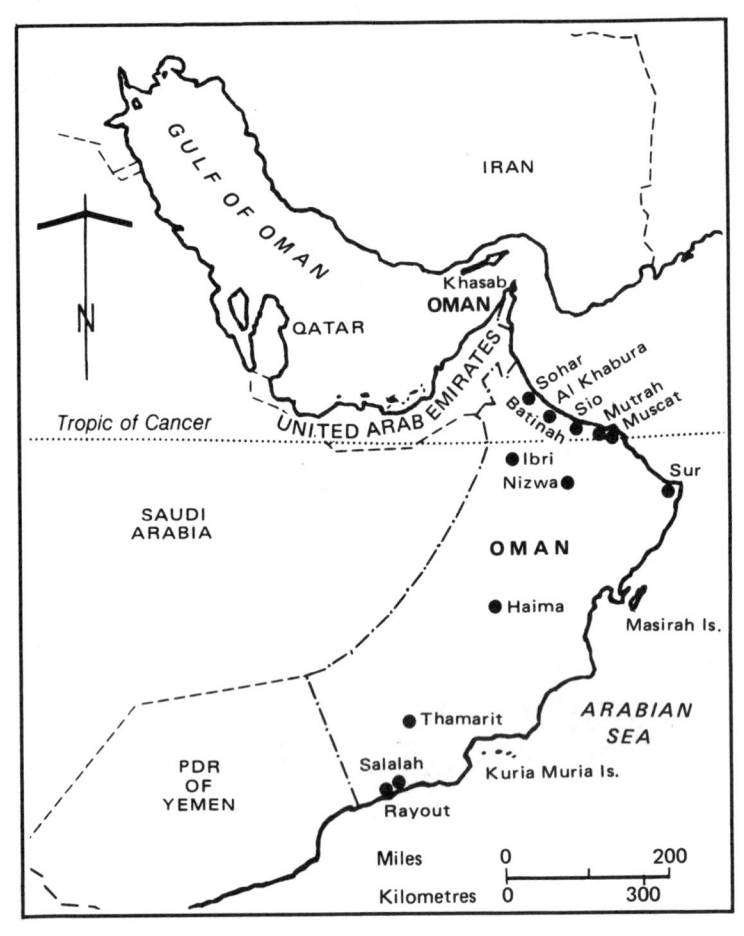

Service in 1942 when it became apparent that the enormous amount of Axis radio communication between Germany and Japan could be monitored by an intercept station in Ethiopia.[30]

It was soon staffed with a team of 300 men, and was further developed in the early post-war period. In the early 1960s, according to the then US Ambassador to Ethiopia, the facility was deemed to be 'strategically vital' to the US, and 'the unhampered use of Kagnew Station' was delineated as the basic US interest in Ethiopia.[31] By the late 1960s, the number of US personnel at Kagnew Station had reached three thousand.[32] However, because of the new revolutionary regime in Ethiopia, and the secessionist insurgency in the coastal province of Eritrea, the US no longer felt that it was wise to keep the facility there, and arrangements were made to move it to Diego Garcia. (The original schedule was to have Kagnew Station closed

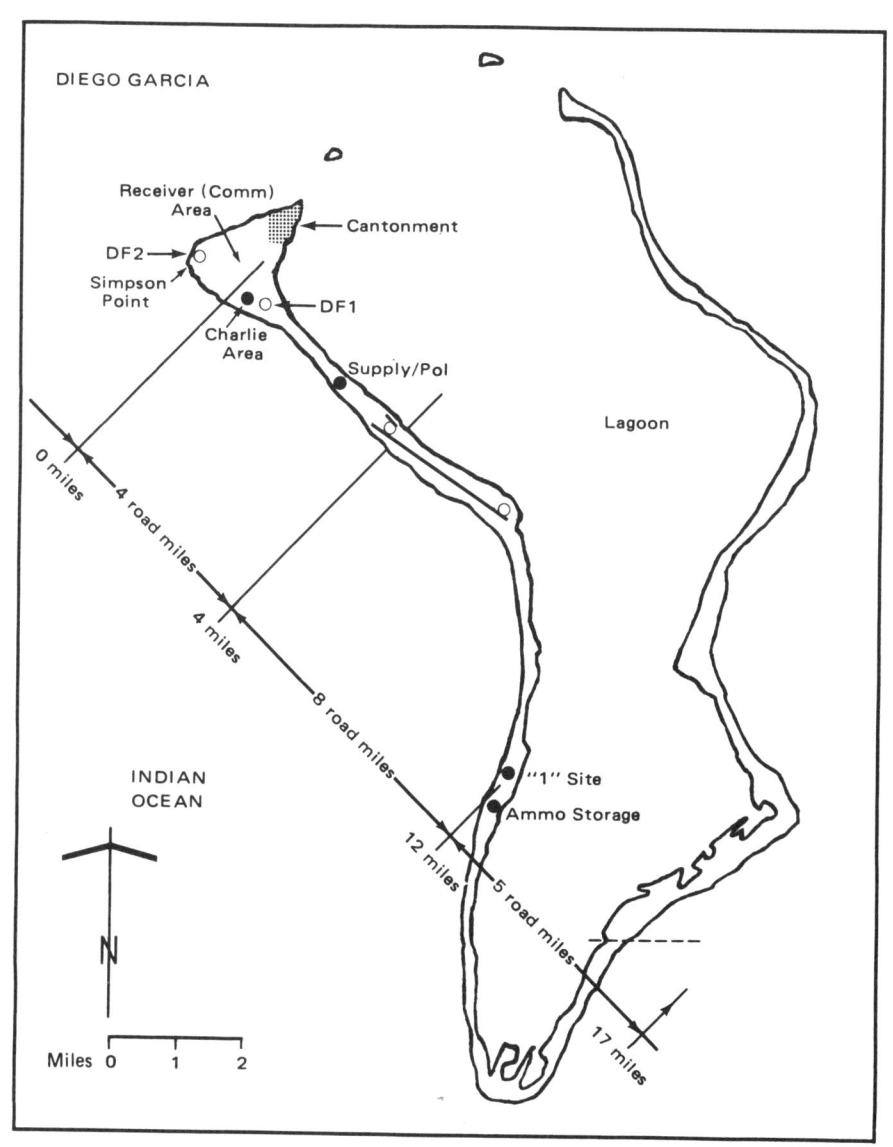

Figure 9.3 Map of Diego Garcia showing the location of the receiver area and the two direction-finder locations (labelled "DF")

by June 1974, but there were still 35 US personnel there in August 1976.)[33]

Diego Garcia is a tiny atoll (78 square kilometres or 30 square miles in area) in the Chagos Archipelago; it lies at 7° 15′ S, just on 1600 kilometres (1000 miles) south of the tip of India and some 3220 kilometres (2000 miles) east of Africa. The atoll is shaped like a distorted horseshoe, 61 kilometres

(38 miles) from one end to the other, and encloses a coral-studded lagoon 11 kilometres (7 miles) wide by 21 kilometres (13 miles) long. The island itself became a British protectorate when Britain set up the British Indian Ocean Territory (BIOT) in November 1965. The military potential of the BIOT was recognised in mutual defence discussions between the UK and the US and on 30 December 1966 a 50-year joint agreement was signed, entitled 'Availability of Certain Indian Ocean Islands for Defense Purposes' (TIAS 6169), making the islands available for the defence purposes of both governments. In December 1970 both governments agreed to the establishment of a communications facility at Diego Garcia, which offered a secure alternative to the Kagnew Station. Funds for the construction of the facility were included in the 1971 Military Construction Appropriation Act; the first construction team arrived on 20 March 1971, and ground was broken at the transmitter site in July and at the receiver site in August. Equipment was moved from Kagnew Station to the island, and the communications facility became operational in 1973. In August 1974 the Diego Garcia station formally opened as part of the HF-DF network of NOSIS, two months after the scheduled date for movement out of Asmara. The station is manned by some 200 US and about 30 British personnel.[34] (See Figure 9.3.)

Although the station is officially described as a 'joint US — British' facility, US officials have testified that normal day-to-day operations are 'conducted simply on the basis of the US military commander on the island informing his British counterpart. That is all that is required.'[35]

The communications receiver area at Diego Garcia is located between Simpson Point and Eclipse Point at the north-west tip of the atoll. There are two HF-DF stations in this area, one of which (DF-1 in Figure 9.3) is also the site of a CLASSIC WIZARD satellite ground station. Intelligence collected at Diego Garcia is sent back to the NSA and the Office of Naval Intelligence by the Defense Satellite Communications System (DSCS); the new DSCS terminal at Diego Garcia is an AN/MSC-61 system similar to that currently being installed at North West Cape.[36]

At the other end of the range of SIGINT stations in this regional subsystem are the stations at Hong Kong, South Korea, Japan, the Philippines, Alaska, Hawaii and California. With respect to the operations at Hong Kong, the British GCCS had operated a listening station at Hong Kong before the Second World War, which was re-established under Australian control in 1949 — although it is actually operated jointly by the DSD and the GCHQ. As noted in Chapter 8, the Hong Kong operation was targeted almost entirely against Chinese signals until the mid-1970s, but it is now very much involved in monitoring Soviet naval movements in the western Pacific Ocean.

On Okinawa, the NSG operates facilities at Hanza, Futema and Sobe. The Hanza station is part of the CLASSIC WIZARD Reporting System.[37] The Futema station has a CDAA system and is part of the BULLSEYE HF-DF system.[38] The facility at Sobe is an annex to the Hanza station and 'is assigned the mission for providing support which consists of HF-DF,

COMSEC and other naval security functions'. The activity at Sobe receives assistance in services and facilities from the nearby Torii Station, which has an AN/FLR-9 HF and VHF intercept and DF system (codenamed 'Kinsfolk') operated by the US Army Intelligence and Security Command (INSCOM) component of NSA.[39]

In Japan itself, the NSG operates facilities at Misawa, Yokosuka, Hakata and Kamiseya. The facilities at Misawa (which has an AN/FLR-9 CDAA) and Yokosuka are part of the CLASSIC WIZARD Reporting System.[40] The station at Kamiseya occupies 237 hectares (586 acres) and at 31 December 1969 was staffed by 1652 personnel, of whom 1370 performed 'NSG functions'. The mission of the Naval Security Group Activity at Kamiseya is officially described as being to 'provide direct and timely Naval Security Group Support to the fleet in the Pacific. Primarily this support consists of HF-DF, COMSEC, and other Naval Security Group functions'.[41]

The NSG station at Adak, Alaska, had 539 personnel as at 30 September 1980. The current HF-DF system at Adak is a SISSZULU system similar to that at the NSG station at Rota, Spain; according to recent Congressional testimony, this SISSZULU system 'is being phased down and replaced with the more capable CLASSIC WIZARD system'.[42] In California, there are NSG stations at San Diego, which is part of the CLASSIC WIZARD Reporting System,[43] and at Skaggs Island, which is described in official testimony as a 'high frequency direction finding (HF-DF) net control station'.[44] In Hawaii, the NSG operates an AN/FLR-9 HF and VHF intercept and DF system at Wahiawa, Oahu. Further south, Soviet naval traffic entering either the South-west Pacific or the South China Sea is monitored by the NSA stations on Guam and the Philippines. Guam was used by the US as a listening station before the Second World War and is now also a station for the CLASSIC WIZARD ELINT and cryptographic system.[45]

The Philippines was also an important US pre-war listening site, with major SIGINT stations at Cavite and then Corregidor. (This station, codenamed 'Cast' and under the command of Commander R.J. Fabian, USN, moved to Melbourne in February 1942.)[46] There are currently two major NSA stations in the Philippines. The first, operated by the 6922nd Security Squadron of the US Air Force Electronic Security Command (ESC) and equipped with an AN/FLR-9 VHF and HF intercept and DF system, is part of the USAF 466L SIGINT program, another worldwide network for the collection, processing, distribution and transmission of electronic intelligence data to a variety of user organizations.[47]

The second, of more direct relevance to NOSIS, is the NSG station at San Miguel, near the Subic Bay naval base. (San Miguel is the station which first collected the intelligence on the so-called 'Tonkin Gulf incident' in 1964.)[48] This station had 1050 NSG personnel in 1971, of whom 950 were military (850 communications technicians and 100 support personnel) and 100 were US civilians in support roles. The station occupies 1060 hectares (2620 acres), with the receiver and DF areas located at the northern end of the base.[49] (See Figure 9.4.)

Figure 9.4 NSG Activity, San Miguel, The Philippines

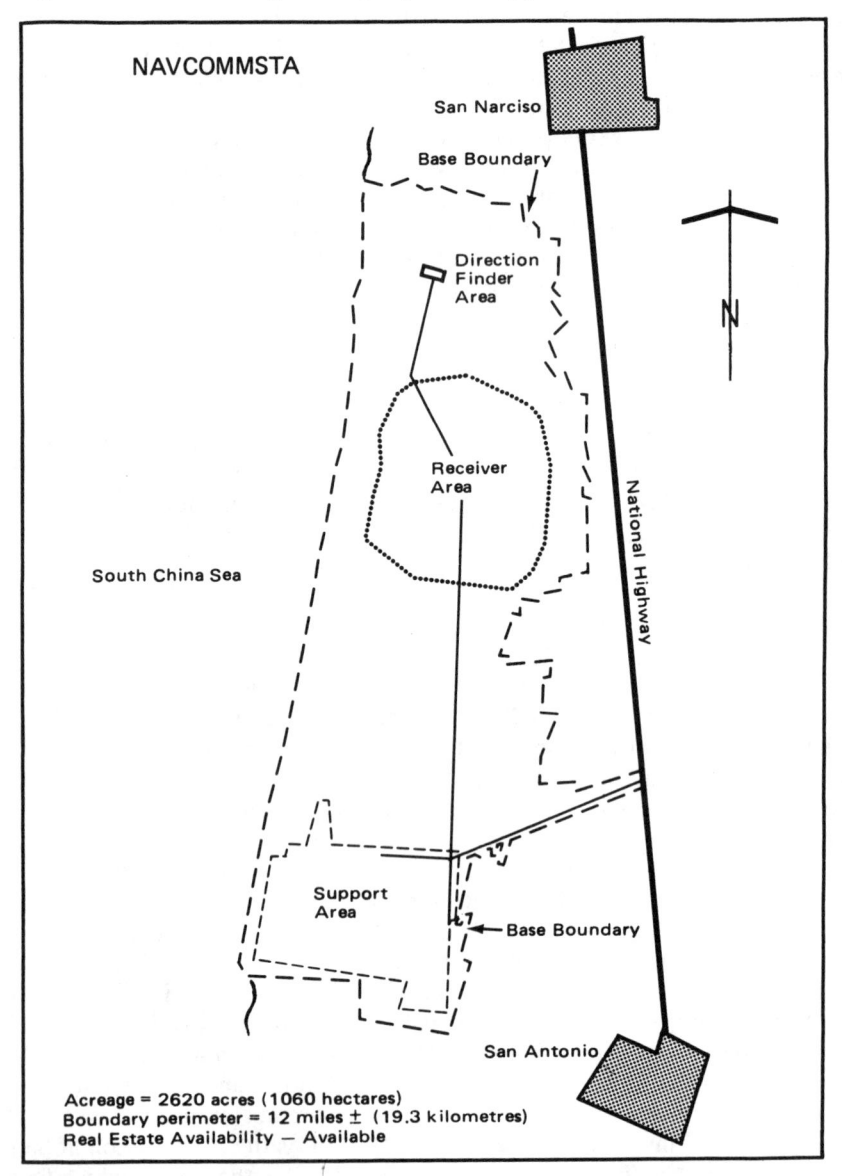

However, the geographical weight of the Indo-Pacific NOSIS sub-system is provided by the DSD stations in Australia — at Pearce, WA, Cabarlah, Qld, Harman, ACT, and Shoal Bay, NT. Australian participation in the NOSIS HF-DF network began in 1973 with the activation of a DF facility at the DSD station at Pearce RAAF Base, WA. This participation is now directed by the Naval Command Support System Project Office (NCSS PO) in Building A, Department of Defence, Canberra, which was established in 1980.

The principal purpose of the DSD station at Pearce is the monitoring of naval and air traffic over the Indian Ocean, while the station at Cabarlah is principally concerned with monitoring radio transmissions throughout the South-west Pacific. As noted in Chapter 8, the interception and DF capabilities at Pearce and Cabarlah were recently up-graded with the installation of new Plessey CDAA systems, codenamed 'Pusher', at these stations. The Pusher system is designed for the interception, monitoring, direction-finding and analysis of radio signals in the HF band from 1.5 to 30 MHz. The main elements of the system are the PVS1120A multiple beam HF receiving antenna system and the PVS860 Series DF equipment. The PVS1120A antenna array consists of two circular sets of 24 equally spaced monopoles. The outer ring (PVS8904) covers the band 1.5 to 10 MHz and the inner (PVS880A) the band 8 to 30 MHz. Sets of feeder cables carry the antenna signals to beam-forming networks at the centre of the circle, and the net effect of the array is 360° cover in azimuth and 24 simultaneous 15°- wide beams. Each of these beams can be fed to a number of monitor receivers. The addition of the PVS860 Series HF-DF system to the multi- beam antenna array provides accurate information on the azimuthal direction of arrival of any given signal.[50] (See Figure 9.5.)

The DSD station at HMAS Harman outside Canberra has only a limited DF capability. The DF system is a four-element Adcock direction-finder; it has four aerials some 10 metres, high spaced about 6 metres apart in the north-south and east-west directions. The elements are base-fed monopoles, and the central wire aerial for sense determination is supported from them by insulated guys (triatics). Two inductive goniometers, one for 1.5 to 6 MHz and the other for 6 to 21 MHz are mounted on a common shaft; the approximate direction of a signal is determined by rotating the goniometer to obtain a signal maximum. This system, of Second World War vintage, is unlikely to have a DF accuracy of better than about 8° and would be of little use to NOSIS.[51]

The DSD station at Shoal Bay near Darwin is concerned with monitoring transmissions throughout South East Asia. This station originally had only a very limited DF capability, but contracts were let in mid-1981 for the procurement of modern DF equipment to enable Shoal Bay to participate fully in NOSIS.

These DSD stations in Australia, together with the Hong Kong operations, are controlled operationally from the DSD headquarters at Victoria Barracks in Melbourne. The DSD headquarters also houses the Special US Liaison Office which consists of about ten NSA officers,[52] and the GCHQ Liaison Officer;[53] these personnel are responsible for integrating the DSD operations into the global systems of the NSA, GCHQ and other associated agencies.

Finally, the New Zealand SIGINT station at Tangimoana is primarily

210 *The Ties That Bind*

Figure 9.5 Diagram of Plessey CDAA code-named 'Pusher', recently installed at Pearce and Cabarlah

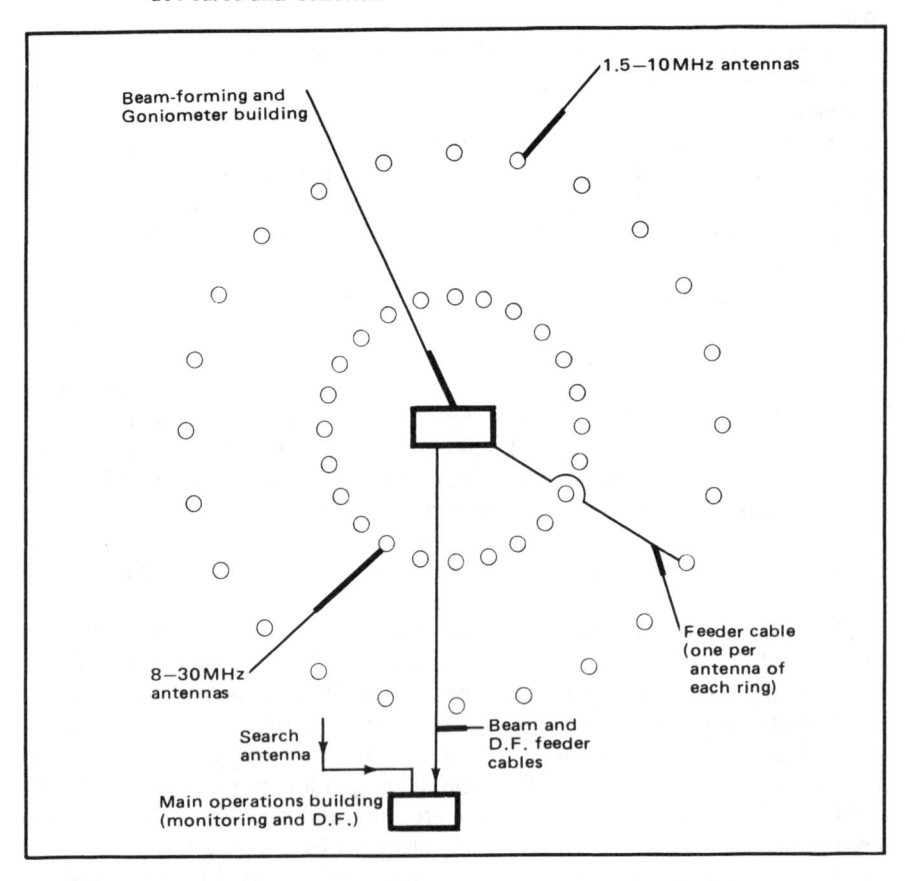

responsible for monitoring traffic over the South-west Pacific and across to Latin America.

The global network of land-based HF-DF stations is supplemented by the CLASSIC OUTBOARD system of ship-based HF-DF equipment. The CLASSIC OUTBOARD (or AN/SSQ-72) system consists of hull- and mast-mounted antenna arrays, the AN/SRD-19 Diamond HF and VHF-DF system, and the AN/SLR-16 communications intercept and analysis receiver. The system is designed to provide over-the-horizon (OTH) detection and indentification of surface ships for targeting purposes, and is to be deployed on 24 US guided missile frigates, destroyers and cruisers, to provide SIGINT, early warning and OTH targeting capabilities to two surface vessels accompanying each US Navy carrier force.[54]

Ocean surveillance satellites

Satellite observation is the most recent source of ocean surveillance intelligence available to the UKUSA partners. The US Navy began to take a serious interest in the possibility of satellite-based ocean surveillance systems in the mid-1960s, when satellite surveillance technology had matured to the point where it seemed that a variety of sensor systems might be effectively applied to the ocean surveillance mission. However, operational ocean surveillance satellite systems did not become available until the mid-1970s.

The first study contracts and requests for proposals for satellite ocean surveillance systems were issued by the Navy in 1968.[55] In 1969, studies were conducted by the Planning Research Corporation, and Hughes Aircraft and a General Electric/Westinghouse team were reportedly selected to conduct parallel program definition studies of a satellite surveillance system using side-looking radar to track ship movements, and other sensors to detect enemy submarines.[56]

It was revealed in Congressional testimony in 1973 that the Navy had begun to use imagery from modified US Air Force reconnaissance satellites in 1971 to gain operational experience and evaluate different types of sensors as an aid to determining its own satellite requirements. In response to a question about cooperative Navy–USAF ocean surveillance efforts, the Acting Assistant Secretary of the Navy for Research and Development testified that experiments were conducted in 1971 which 'took advantage of data which was being supplied by a surveillance satellite to us. It wasn't a Navy satellite.'[57] The Navy later supplied the following information:

The details of the interactions between the Air Force and Navy on ocean surveillance sensor systems are beyond the secret classification ...
All satellite launches are performed by the Air Force and many of the satellites and sensors result from other space programs. The USAF satellite control facilities are used for housekeeping in orbit.[58]

The US Air Force satellites evidently used by the Navy were Lockheed Agena-D spacecraft which had originally been designed for photographic reconnaissance, but they were refitted by the Navy with other sensors, including infra-red scanners operating in the 8–14 micron band and probably phased-array radars to give them an all-weather capability. Among the US Air Force satellites used by the Navy were those launched on 1 September 1972, 21 December 1972, 16 May 1973, 13 February 1974, 6 June 1974, 14 August 1974, and 18 April 1975.[59]

The infra-red scanner deployed on these satellites was reportedly similar to the one supplied by Hughes Aircraft for use on the NASA ERTS-1 earth resources satellite, which was able to discern small pleasure boats on the Potomac from an altitude of approximately 965 kilometres (600 miles). From a reconnaissance satellite altitude of 160 kilometres (100 miles), which would enhance resolution six-fold, large naval vessels would have been readily apparent.[60]

Other sensors tested in the 1970s were designed to detect submarines. The detection of underwater submarine trails may be accomplished by detecting a trail of dead micro-organisms caused by the submarine's passage through

Table 9.1 US ocean surveillance satellites

Satellite	Launch site & vehicle	Launch date	Orbital inclination (deg)	Period (min)	Perigee (km)	Apogee (km)	Comments
USAF/USN (1971–110A)	WTR Thorad/AD	14 Dec. 1971	70.02	104.93	983	999	Quadruple launch designed to demonstrate concept of launching multiple satellites to monitor electronic signals generated by naval vessels.
USAF/USN (1971–110C)	WTR Thorad/AD	14 Dec. 1971	70.01	104.93	983	999	
USAF/USN (1971–110D)	WTR Thorad/AD	14 Dec. 1971	70.01	104.90	982	997	
USAF/USN (1971–110E)	WTR Thorad/AD	14 Dec. 1971	70.01	104.89	981	997	
NASA/GEOS–C (1975–27A)	WTR Delta	10 April 1975	114.96	101.82	839	853	Geodynamic Experimental Ocean Satellite; the satellite was used to calibrate and to determine positions of NASA and other agency C-band radars, and to perform a satellite-to-satellite tracking experiment with ATS-5 spacecraft using an S-band transponder system.
USN/NOSS–1 (1966–38A)	WTR Atlas	30 April 1976	63.4	107.47	1092	1128	US Navy's first operational WHITE CLOUD ocean-surveillance satellite, carried three small sub-satellites. Sensors include infra-red and microwave radiometers and RF antennas for ELINT.
USN/SSU–1 (1976–38C)	WTR Atlas	30 April 1976	63.44	107.49	1093	1129	
USN/SSU–2 (1976–38D)	WTR Atlas	30 April 1976	63.43	107.5	1093	1130	
USN/SSU–3 (1976–38J)	WTR Atlas	30 April 1976	63.45	107.49	1083	1139	
USN/NOSS–2 (1977–112A)	WTR Atlas F	8 Dec. 1977	63.4	107.5	1054	1169	US Navy's second White Cloud ocean-surveillance satellite and sub-satellites.
USN/NOSS–2 (1977–112C)	WTR Atlas F	8 Dec. 1977	63.4	107.5	1054	1169	
USN/NOSS–2 (1977–112D)	WTR Atlas F	8 Dec. 1977	63.4	107.5	1054	1169	

Name	Launcher	Date	Inclination	Period	Perigee	Apogee	Notes
USN/NOSS-2 (1977-112E)	WTR Atlas F	8 Dec. 1977	63.4	107.5	1055	1168	
Seasat A	WTR Atlas–Agena D	27 June 1978	108.02	100.63	776	800	Experimental ocean survey satellite. Sensors included microwave radiometer, radar altimeter, scanning radar scatterometer, infra-red radiometer, and side-looking synthetic aperture radar (SAR).
NOSS-3 (1980-19A)	WTR Atlas F	3 Mar. 1980	63.03	107.12	1035	1150	Third White Cloud Navy ocean-surveillance satellite and SSU sub-satellites.
NOSS-3 (1980-19C)	WTR Atlas F	3 Mar. 1980	63.49	107.4	1048	1166	
NOSS-3 (1980-19D)	WTR Atlas F	3 Mar. 1980	63.49	107.4	1048	1166	
NOSS-3 (1980-19E)	WTR Atlas F	3 Mar. 1980	63.49	107.4	1048	1166	
NOSS-4 (1983-08A)	WTR Atlas F	9 Feb. 1983	63.43		1070	1192	Fourth WHITE CLOUD Navy Ocean Surveillance satellite and sub-satellites.
SSD (1983-08B)	WTR Atlas F	9 Feb. 1983	63.39		1054	1192	
SSA (1983-08E)	WTR Atlas F	9 Feb. 1983	63.44		1059	1175	
SSB (1983-08F)	WTR Atlas F	9 Feb. 1983	63.44		1059	1175	
SSC	WTR Atlas F	9 Feb. 1983	63.44		1059	1175	
NOSS-5 (1983-56A)	WTR	10 June 1983	63.34		1954	1175	Fifth WHITE CLOUD Navy Ocean surveillance satellite and sub-satellites.
GB1 (1983-56C)	WTR Atlas	10 June 1983	63.43		1957	1179	
GB2 (1983-56D)	WTR Atlas	10 June 1983	63.44		1957	1179	
GB3 (1983-56G)	WTR Atlas	10 June 1983	63.45		1957	1179	

Note: WTR Western Test Range

the water, radiation leaks, disturbances in existing phosphorescence, low-frequency signals from the screws, or metallic particles sloughed off from the hull.[61] A US satellite once reportedly detected an American submarine through the trail of disturbed water (the 'submerged wake') which ultimately rises to the surface.[62] Satellite-borne infra-red devices have been developed which can detect the slightly increased temperature in a submarine's wake caused by the discharge of water used to cool the nuclear power plants.[63] Special photographic techniques have also been developed to record water depth, making it possible to detect the presence of a submarine on patrol by a change in the colour record of a given ocean area.[64]

Two distinct ocean surveillance satellite programs had emerged by the end of the 1970s — officially designated the CLASSIC WIZARD/WHITE CLOUD and CLIPPER BOW programs. Both are managed for the National Reconnaissance Office (NRO) by the Navy Space Project in Room PME 106E at the Naval Electronic Systems Command Headquarters.[65] (Table 9.1 gives details of the US ocean surveillance satellites.)

CLASSIC WIZARD/WHITE CLOUD

The US Naval Ocean Surveillance Satellite (NOSS) system achieved an initial operational capability (IOC) with the successful launching of a cluster of WHITE CLOUD NOSS satellites on 30 April 1976. The WHITE CLOUD satellites, which are part of the CLASSIC WIZARD ocean surveillance system, are primarily designed for electronic intelligence (ELINT) missions, although they also carry other sensor systems in addition to their RF receivers.

The concept of launching multiple satellites to monitor electronic signals (radar emissions and communications) in order to detect and locate naval vessels was demonstrated with the launch of a 'mother' satellite and three sub-satellites on 14 December 1971. These satellites were designed and built by the Naval Research Laboratory (NRL), which then proceeded to build the set launched on 30 April 1976 and a further set launched on 8 December 1977.[66]

In June 1977 it was reported that subsequent WHITE CLOUD satellites were being produced by Martin Marietta, under the direction of the US Air Force's Special Projects Office in Los Angeles (the cover for the West Coast office of the NRO), with technical assistance provided by the NRL, and with E-Systems Inc. providing the electronic intelligence (ELINT) receivers and antennas for the satellites.[67] The first launch of the Martin Marietta satellites occurred on 3 March 1980.[68]

The WHITE CLOUD satellites are generally placed in near circular orbits at an altitude of about 1000 kilometres (620 miles) with orbital inclinations of about 63.5 degrees and periods of about 105 minutes. The altitude is high enough to provide a long orbital life yet low enough to permit the ELINT receivers to monitor and record signals of modest power levels. The orbital period of about 105 minutes provides a displacement of approximately 3000

215

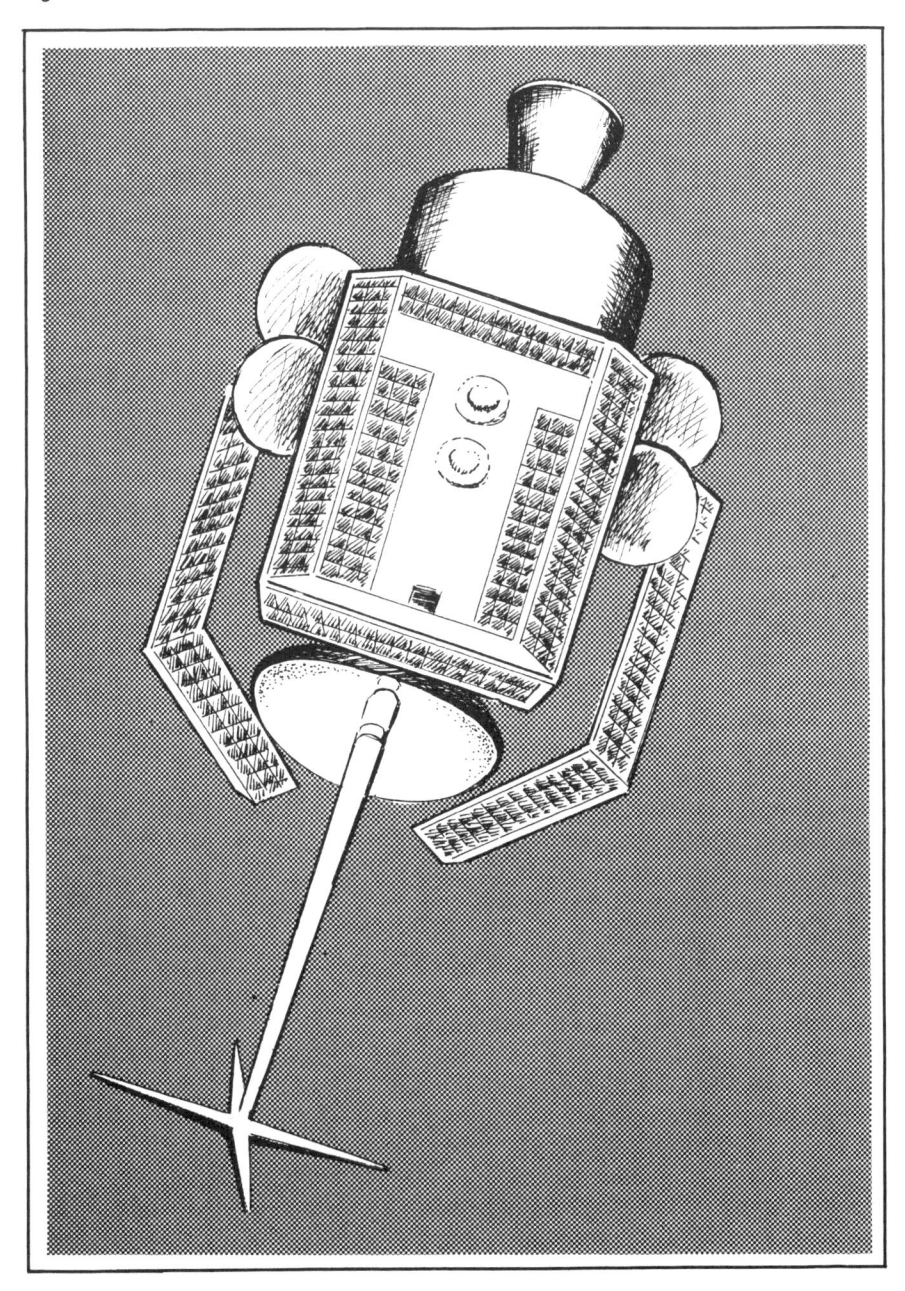

Figure 9.7 US White Cloud Naval Ocean Surveillance Satellite

kilometres (1866 miles) between each orbit; given that at an altitude of 1000 kilometres (621 miles) the spacecraft can receive signals from about 3540 kilometres (2200 miles) away, there is a comfortable overlapping coverage on successive orbits. The three sub-satellites are generally dispensed about 40 to 48 kilometres (25 to 30 miles) apart, which allows the use of interferometry techniques to pinpoint the location of Soviet or other vessels of interest.[69]

The WHITE CLOUD satellites (Figure 9.6) themselves are relatively small, measuring 90 × 240 × 30 centimetres (3 × 8 × 1 feet). The largest surface area on one side is covered by solar cells while the opposite side contains an array of antennas. Four spherical objects, containing passive infra-red and millimetre-wave radiometers as well as other sensors are deployed on the end of metal booms.[70]

The infra-red radiometer is basically a very sensitive thermometer designed to respond to electromagnetic radiation of wavelengths between 8 and 14 microns emitted from the surface of the ocean. It provides high resolution images of the ocean surface and of coastal features, and can show the temperature gradients along the surface of the ocean together with ocean currents and eddies.[71]

The microwave radiometer is used to measure the ocean surface temperature under all weather conditions, with accuracies of 1°C or better; and by sensing the brightness of the foam it can determine ocean surface wind speeds of up to 50 metres (164 feet) per second.[72] These data can be extremely useful in the process of filtering out 'noise' in efforts to detect and track submarines.

The collected intelligence is transmitted by each of the three sub-satellites at slightly different frequencies: 1430·2 MHz, 1432·2 MHz, and 1434·2 MHz, using approximately 1 MHz of bandwidth. The wide bandwidth and rapid modulation indicate that the satellites are transmitting enormous amounts of information and/or recorded radar pulses. Narrow-band telemetry transmissions are made at frequencies of 1427·23 MHz, 1427·43 MHz and 1427·63 mhz.[73]

The ground component of the CLASSIC WIZARD program consists of five major ground stations, co-located with the NSG facilities at Guam (described by one source as the 'master station' for the CLASSIC WIZARD system),[74] Diego Garcia, Adak (Alaska), Winter Harbor (Maine) and Edzell (Scotland). Each of these stations was recently equipped with a new Ocean Surveillance Building and ground terminals for the WHITE CLOUD satellites (at costs of US$3–4m per building/terminal), with Edzell also receiving 'five additional computers'.[75] In addition to these five stations there is a CLASSIC WIZARD 'research' facility at San Diego which probably has some operational capability.[76] The two principal pieces of processing equipment at the CLASSIC WIZARD sites are designated AN/FYK-11A and AN/FSQ-111. The AN/FYK-11A processing system was designed by the Naval Research Laboratory and the Naval Electronics Systems Command and produced by TRW Inc.; it is described as a 'data processing set' for 'telemetric data', and was first fielded in 1975. The AN/FSQ-111 was designed and produced by NRL and is described as a 'digital data set' for the generation, transmission and reception of 'special telemetry signals'; it was first fielded in 1981.[77]

CLIPPER BOW/Integrated Tactical Surveillance System (ITSS)

The second major US Navy ocean surveillance satellite program involves the use of active radar for the detection of surface ships and aircraft. In the late 1960s, the US experimented with a side-looking radar satellite system, Code 770, which involved fitting a long, narrow antenna along the length of an Agena-D rocket upper stage. The radar could 'see' through heavy clouds and plot terrain in great detail.[78] Subsequent radar surveillance satellites have been developed by the US Air Force and 'other [intelligence] agencies', presumably the NRO and/or CIA, but these do not satisfy the Navy's ocean surveillance requirements.[79] These agencies were evidently responsible for the side-looking radars reportedly carried on some Code 467 'Big Bird' surveillance satellites.[80]

SEASAT-A, an experimental ocean survey satellite launched on 27 June 1978, was equipped with a side-looking synthetic aperture radar (SAR). Because the radar resolution of a side-looking radar is proportional to beam width, which is in turn inversely proportional to the length of the antenna, the resolution of a normal side-looking radar that can be carried by a satellite is necessarily quite limited. This problem is overcome by the SAR, in which a relatively short antenna is made to behave like a very long antenna with a narrow beam by taking advantage of the motion of the satellite in its orbit.

Stockholm International Peace Research Institute (SIPRI) has described the operating principle of the SAR as follows:

As the satellite progresses along its orbit, the short antenna of its radar transmits pulses of radiation at regular intervals towards the Earth. As the satellite approaches an object on the Earth, for example, the beam of the antenna falls upon, moves across, and finally leaves the object. During this time it reflects the microwave pulses received from the radar antenna back to the antenna. The greater the distance between the object and the antenna, the longer the object remains in the beam. Seen from the object, therefore, the radar antenna appears much larger than it is and this apparent length will depend on the distance between the object and the real antenna.
The effective length of the antenna is, therefore, proportional to the range of the object. Since resolution is proportional to the length of the antenna, but inversely proportional to the range, the two effects compensate for each other in a synthetic aperture radar and the resolution of the image remains almost the same at all ranges. High-resolution images of the Earth's surface can thus be obtained from great distances.[81]

The SAR aboard the SEASAT-A satellite employed a 2.1 × 10.7 metre (7 × 35-foot) deployable planar antenna and was capable of covering a 100 kilometre (62-mile) swath. The radar provided all-weather photographs of ocean waves and ice fields. It detected icebergs, ice leads (openings in sea ice) and ships and other objects longer than 25 metres (82 feet).[82] Although SEASAT was a NASA program, its operation was controlled by a committee that included Defense Department representation; it was partly financed out of the Defense budget; and data received at the five ground stations able to receive SAR data (Goldstone, California; Fairbanks, Alaska; Merritt Island, Florida; Shoe Cove, Newfoundland, Canada; and Oakhanger in the UK) were sent by communications satellite to the US Navy's Fleet Numerical Weather Control Center in California.[83]

In early 1977, the Navy distributed requests for proposals (RFPs) for design studies for the CLIPPER BOW high-resolution radar ocean surveillance satellite system.[84] The radar operates in the L-band and was developed by Hughes Aircraft and Westinghouse. (See Figure 9.7.) In mid-1978, four companies were still conducting program definition studies for the Navy — Lockheed Missiles and Space Co.; Martin Marietta; McDonnell Douglas; and TRW Systems.[85]

In 1977, the US Navy officially described the CLIPPER BOW project as follows: 'Clipper Bow [sic] will provide Navy commanders at sea (with) all-weather/day-night, active global coverage for surveillance and targeting of hostile ships in the critical area around the task force'.[86]

In testimony to Congress in 1978, Navy spokesmen went to some length to justify the Navy's need for a radar surveillance satellite program separate to that of the Air Force and the 'other [intelligence] agencies':

Clipper Bow was from its inception and is today intended to be a tactical support satellite, no more and no less. It is not intended to supply or to provide, except as a completely adjunct capability, national intelligence or surveillance that is primarily useful on a national scene.

What it is intended to do is to provide the tactical force commander with information that is necessary for his own protection, for his deployment, and movement of his own resources and assets, to provide him with, so to speak, eyes over the horizon, to warn him of the presence of other approaching or attacking battle groups, to provide him the targeting information he would need to fire or vector his assets at enemy targets well beyond the horizon range.

It is not in that sense really intended to be an all-purpose surveillance system as much as it is to be a kind of tactical support capability.

It is intended to be low risk and low cost ... as compared with much more capable, much more sophisticated satellites which are intended to provide much higher resolution information, and consequently require a much higher level of technology, such as the Air Force satellites. The Navy kind is expressly and specifically intended to limit its resolution to no more than is required to locate and provide course information on ships ... for targeting purposes, and to provide in effect the task force commander with a view of the ocean into which he is moving.

It is not intended to provide high resolution information but it is intended to provide him with a fairly continuous information, and as a consequence there is a major difference in terms of how power is used, budgets are used, the kind of resolution requirements that are imposed, and a whole host of other factors ...

The Clipper Bow program has to search limited areas of some kind, whereas ... other [Air Force and intelligence agency] systems are designed to look at fixed points.[87]

Ocean surveillance 219

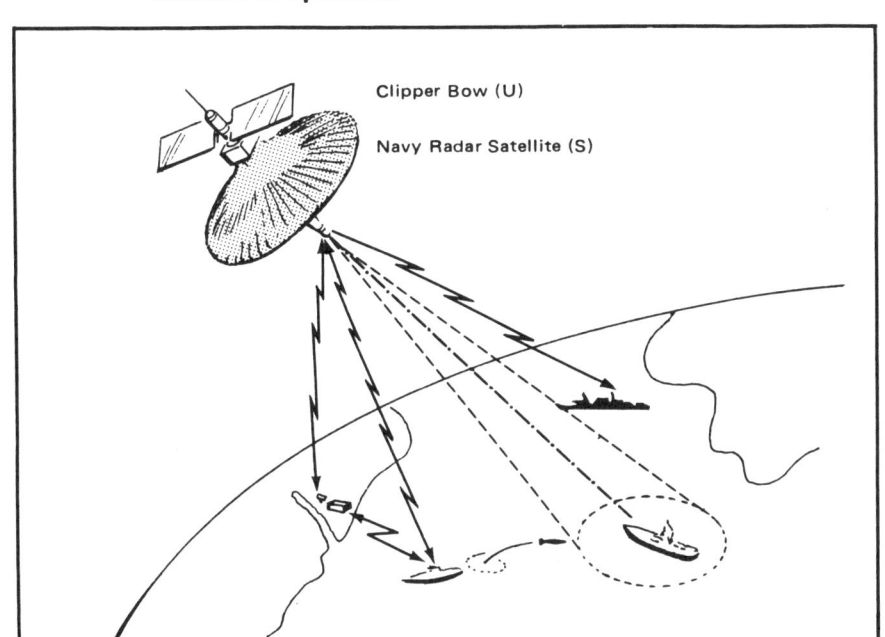

Figure 9.7 Artist's conception of CLIPPER BOW Radar Ocean Surveillance Satellite in operation

When the CLIPPER BOW program was initiated in 1977, it was expected that full-scale engineering development of the satellites would begin in 1979 and that the first satellite would be launched in 1983 and the second in 1984.[88] However, the system as originally designed lacked the capability to track high-speed aircraft such as the Soviet Backfire bomber, and the program was reassessed in 1979–80. On 8 January 1981, a Mission Element Need Statement (MENS) was approved for an Integrated Tactical Surveillance System (ITSS), which involves the development of an ocean surveillance satellite to provide surveillance of both ocean-going ships and high-speed aircraft. Engineering development of the ITSS is expected to begin in FY 1985 or FY 1986, and the first ITSS satellite should be operational by the end of the decade.[89]

The ITSS was described by the Director of the Navy Space Systems Division in March 1982 as:

an amalgamation of all systems that will provide the Navy an all-weather, day and night, worldwide, survivable surveillance capability, as well as the ability to transmit resulting intelligence and information via secure links, and to have processed and correlated information readily available so that tactical decision-makers can make informed decisions.[90]

220   *The Ties That Bind*

Airborne ocean surveillance

The UKUSA countries operate some half dozen aircraft specifically developed or modified for ocean surveillance purposes. These include the Lockheed P-3 Orion, the British Nimrod, modified versions of the B-52 and U-2, and US Navy carrier-based SH-3 helicopters and S-3A anti-submarine aircraft.

The P-3 Orion is the basis of the airborne anti-submarine warfare capability of each of the UKUSA countries except the UK, which operates its own Nimrod long-range maritime patrol aircraft. According to the US Navy, the Orion 'remains unsurpassed in its anti-submarine-warfare and ocean-surveillance capabilities'.[91]

The Orion is a four-engined aircraft capable of flying 2500 kilometres (1550 miles), patrolling for four hours, and returning to base. It has undergone continuous improvements since it first became operational with the US Navy in 1962. It is now equipped with a variety of submarine detection systems, including sonobuoys, an infra-red detection system, a Magnetic Anomaly Detection (MAD) system, and advanced navigation and communication systems. With respect to armament, the bomb bay can accommodate one Mark 25/39/55/56 bomb, three Mark 36/52 mines, three Mark 57 depth bombs, eight Mark 54 depth bombs, and eight Mark 43/44/46 torpedoes, or a combination of two Mark 101 nuclear depth bombs and four Mark 43/44/46 torpedoes; additional mines can be carried on underwing pylons. Current P-3Cs are also being equipped with the Harpoon missile.[92]

Some 648 Orions have been produced. The US Navy has taken delivery of 524, of which 216 are in active service and 117 in reserve. Australia has taken delivery of ten P-3Bs and ten P-3Cs, and has ordered a further ten P-3Cs for delivery in 1985–86. New Zealand acquired five P-3Bs in 1966. In July 1976, the Canadian Government announced its decision to purchase eighteen special versions of the P-3C. Designated the CP-140 Aurora, the new aircraft combines the airframe, engines and basic aircraft systems of the P-3C with the avionics and data processing capabilities of the Lockheed S-3A ASW aircraft. The last of these eighteen aircraft was delivered in April 1981. In addition to these UKUSA countries, Orions are now in service in Spain (six P-3As), Norway (seven P-3Bs) and the Netherlands (thirteen P-3Cs). Japan has announced a firm decision to procure 45 P-3Cs, with a further 45 likely later in the 1980s.[93] (See Table 9.2.)

The US Orions are based worldwide at some sixteen major bases, including Clark Air Force Base in the Philippines, Misawa and Kadena (Okinawa) in Japan, Alaska, Iceland, Hawaii, Guam, Spain, Italy, Ascension Island, Diego Garcia, Lajes air base on Terciera Island in the Azores, California, Canada, Bermuda and Puerto Rico. Assuming a normal operating range of 2300 kilometres (1440 miles), the US Orions are able to cover an area of about 51.5 million square kilometres (32 million square miles), including all ocean areas in which Soviet missile submarines are likely to be found. In addition, US allies operate Orions from Edinburgh in

South Australia, Whenuapai in New Zealand, Andoya in Norway, and Kanoya, Atsugi, Hachinohe and Iwo Jima in Japan. Moreover, to provide occasional surveillance in remote areas, the US Navy has initiated a program to provide an in-flight refuelling capability for its P-3Cs.[94]

Table 9.2 P-3 Orion production: total orders as at December 1980

US Navy	
P-3A	157
P-3B	124
P-3C	243
Australia	
P-3B	10
P-3C	20
Canada	
CP-140 Aurora	18
Japan	
P-3C	45
The Netherlands	
P-3C	13
Norway	
P-3B	7
Spain	
P-3A	6
New Zealand	
P-3B	5
Total	648

The UK Royal Air Force, which has four squadrons (with a total of 28 aircraft) of Nimrod long-range maritime aircraft, has responsibility for airborne ocean surveillance in the Greenland–Iceland–United Kingdom (GIUK) area. The Nimrod is substantially based upon the airframe of the Hawker Siddeley Comet 4C. It has four Spey engines and has a typical ferry range of about 7240 to 8050 kilometres (4500 to 5000 nautical miles) and an endurance of about twelve hours. Its surveillance systems include an EMI Searchwater radar, a twin Marconi AQS-901 acoustics system, a Loral ESM system, sonobuoys, photographic cameras, and a Magnetic Anomaly Detection (MAD) array. Its weapons bay can carry up to six lateral rows of ASW weapons, accommodating up to nine torpedoes as well as depth charges, or varying numbers of different-sized mines and bombs. Two of the four Nimrod squadrons are based at St Mawgan and the other two at Kinloss.[95]

The US Navy also operates two U-2 long-range, long-loitre aircraft specially equipped with a Westinghouse high-resolution side-looking radar, an infra-red scanner, and ELINT and COMINT receivers designed for ocean surveillance purposes. The Navy plans to use these aircraft in close

222 *The Ties That Bind*

conjunction with its Integrated Tactical Surveillance System (ITSS) radar satellites. The satellites are to provide a broad area of coverage and the satellite data used to alert the U-2s to areas of interest; the aircraft would then be directed to these areas to obtain more detailed information.[96]

In the mid-1970s, the US conducted major exercises to test the concept of employing B-52s with multiple in-flight refuelling on long-range, ocean surveillance and sea-control missions, with operations in the Pacific/Indian Ocean region the primary objective.[97] Although there was some opposition from the Navy to the Air Force undertaking these missions, the Air Force B-52s based on Guam began regular ocean surveillance flights in mid-1976.[98]

On 11 March 1981, the Australian and United States Governments reached agreement on the terms and conditions governing US Air Force B-52 staging flights through RAAF Base Darwin. The Agreement provides that the B-52 flights shall be for sea surveillance in the Indian Ocean area and for navigation training; that the agreement of the Australian Government would need to be obtained before the facilities at Darwin can be used in support of any other category of operations; that the B-52 aircraft on surveillance flights will be supported by KC-135 tanker aircraft for aerial refuelling and the operations shall consist of periodic deployments of up to three B-52 and six KC-135 aircraft; and that about 100 US Air Force personnel and associated equipment will support the staging operations and some of these may be stationed at RAAF Base Darwin.[99]

The first B-52 in this operation arrived in Darwin on 5 May 1981, a day after the first KC-135 landed.[100] Six further B-52 staging operations through Darwin occurred in 1981, making an average of approximately one per month (Table 9.3).[101]

Table 9.3 B-52 staging operations RAAF Base, Darwin, 1981

1	5 May	5	14 September
2	19 June	6	28 September
3	20 July	7	10 November
4	17 August		

Special navy activities

The US Navy in cooperation with the NSA, CIA and/or other US intelligence agencies frequently conducts special intelligence operations which are of extraordinary strategic and political sensitivity and technical complexity. Some of the more noteworthy of these special Navy activities are the HOLYSTONE, DESKTOP, PRAIRIE SCHOONER, SAND DOLLAR and JENNIFER projects. At least since the mid-1970s, the oversight of these operations has been the responsibility of a National Executive Committee for Special Navy Activities, chaired by the Director of Central Intelligence (DCI).

The HOLYSTONE Undersea Surveillance Program

According to official US Navy testimony, the nuclear-powered attack submarine 'is considered to be our most effective single antisubmarine platform'.[102] It is particularly effective against other deep-diving nuclear-powered submarines, including Fleet Ballistic Missile (FBM) submarines, and it is the only platform 'that can operate where the enemy controls the air and the surface'[103] — such as waters near the USSR!

The US currently has a total force of 77 attack submarines, including ten new SSN-688 or Los Angeles-class submarines, with the Navy's goal being 90 submarines.[104] These submarines carry a wide range of sensors and weapons systems. In the case of the SSN-688s, the heart of the detection capability is its 15 tonne AN/BQQ-5 sonar system, which has a digital signal processor of unprecedented complexity and performance. According to one US Congressional report, 'the result of US superiority in digital computer technology and electronics may be an SSN capability to trail Soviet submarines without their knowledge, and if detected to maintain trail against even a determined and uncooperative Soviet commanding officer'.[105]

One of the most interesting, not to say dangerous and provocative, submarine surveillance and intelligence operations is a program which has been codenamed at various times HOLYSTONE, PINNACLE, BOLLARD, and most recently, BARNACLE.[106]

This program, which is controlled from Office M-34 at the Atlantic Fleet Command headquarters at Norfolk, Virginia, involves the use of at least four SSN-637 or Sturgeon-class attack submarines specially outfitted with sophisticated electronic equipment operated by special units from the NSA, which gather intelligence either inside or just outside Soviet territorial waters. The program was authorized during the Eisenhower Administration and placed under the direct control of the Chief of Naval Operations. In the mid-1970s, the schedule of HOLYSTONE missions was approved every month by the 40 Committee.[107]

The HOLYSTONE submarines are reported to engage in a wide range of intelligence operations, including close-up photography of the undersides of Soviet submarines and other vessels; plugging into Soviet underwater communication cables to intercept high-level military and other communications considered too important to be sent by radio or other less secure means; electronic observation of Soviet SLBM tests to monitor the various computer checks and other signals which precede test launchings; and the recording of 'voice autographs' of Soviet submarines, which consist of tape recordings of the noises made by submarine engines and other equipment.[108]

The HOLYSTONE submarines generally operated within the 19.3 kilometre (12-mile) territorial limit claimed by the Soviet Union, and often within the 4.8 kilometre (3-mile) limit. For example, one HOLYSTONE submarine is reported to have collided with an E-class submarine in Vladivostok Harbour in the mid-1960s when photographing the underside of the Soviet vessel.[109] On one occasion in November 1969 the USS *Gato* is reported to have operated as close as 1.6 kilometres (one mile) off the Soviet coast; later on the same patrol the *Gato* collided with a Soviet submarine 24–40 kilometres (15–25 miles) off the entrance to the White Sea, in the Barents Sea off northern USSR.[110] And another HOLYSTONE collision occurred in May 1974 in Soviet waters off the port of Petropavlovsk on the Kamchatka Peninsula.[111] HOLYSTONE collisions also occurred on at least six other occasions between 1961 and 1975.[112]

DESKTOP

DESKTOP is a US underwater intelligence activity which evidently involves surveillance of 'a mysterious Soviet undersea operation'.[113] The only official statement ever released about the project states that it is 'an extremely sensitive analysis program dealing with foreign activity'.[114] However, the nature of neither the analysis program nor of the foreign activity has ever been disclosed.

PRAIRIE SCHOONER

According to official US Navy testimony, the PRAIRIE SCHOONER program is an undersea activity which 'supports intelligence collection operations conducted by US submarines. This intelligence is collected through installation of sophisticated, multispectral intelligence collection equipment ... which are operated by fleet commanders as directed by higher authority'.[115]

There are four categories of intelligence collection equipment employed in the PRAIRIE SCHOONER program. The first category consists of acoustic equipment and includes both standard acoustic detection devices and 'additional acoustic devices to further the safe and efficient collection of acoustic intelligence [which] are developed and installed as directed by the Director of Naval Intelligence'.[116] The second category consists of electromagnetic collection equipment which includes numerous and diverse COMINT and ELINT receivers and recorders. The third category consists of electro-optical intelligence collection equipment and includes devices which sense the real-time radiations and reflections in the visible light and infra-red portions of the electromagnetic spectrum. These devices also include systems which record these radiations and reflections for subsequent viewing and analysis. The fourth category consists of recording and reporting equipment designed for the efficient analysis of the collected intelligence and its correlation with other intelligence. This includes 'a capability for the commanding officer to evaluate, at least to a limited extent, his collection efforts on board in order to decide whether further collection effort on a specific target is warranted'.[117]

SAND DOLLAR

Since the early 1960s, the US has maintained a capability for deep-sea search and recovery of relatively small objects from the ocean floor. The USS *Mizar*, for example, is a Navy deep-sea reconnaissance vessel which is equipped with highly sophisticated sonar devices, lights and cameras for still-film and television photography, devices for producing acoustical holographs, a system for magnetic grappling, and a winch capable of raising substantial weights from thousands of metres below the ocean surface. The *Mizar* was used to locate the hull of the sunken US nuclear attack submarine, USS *Thresher*, in May 1964; it assisted in locating and recovering the US H-bomb lost off Palomares, Spain, in 1966; it found the remains of the hull of another US nuclear attack submarine, USS *Scorpion*, which sank near the Azores in May 1968; and it has used its winch and cable to raise the US Navy's *Alvin* submersible vehicle from a depth of more than 1540 metres (5000 feet).[118]

In April 1962, a company known as Ocean Science and Engineering Inc., proposed to the US Air Force and the CIA a technique for recovering Soviet ballistic missile re-entry vehicles (RVs) from deep waters in the Soviet missile testing areas in the Pacific Ocean. Although this proposal was rejected, the Air Force signed a contract with Global Marine Inc. for a similar system later in 1962. This project for the recovery of Soviet RVs was subsequently designated SAND DOLLAR.[119]

Although these RVs do not carry nuclear warheads, their successful recovery would produce intelligence of enormous value. Analysis of the structural dimensions of the nose-cones would indicate the size of their payloads and hence likely yields of the warheads, while analysis of the nose-cone materials, engineering, and ablative techniques would provide intelligence on the technical qualities of the Soviet missile design bureaus and production plants.

AZORIAN/JENNIFER/MATADOR

Soviet ballistic missile RVs typically weigh less than a tonne and measure less than 1.8 metres (6 feet) in diameter. The JENNIFER Project, which in its initial phases was code-named AZORIAN, was concerned with the recovery of an object of an entirely different magnitude — a Soviet Golf (GII)-class Fleet Ballistic Missile (FBM) submarine, with a dead-weight of about 4000 tonnes and a length of some 97.5 metres (320 feet), equipped with three SS-N-5 Serb Submarine Launched Ballistic Missiles (SLBMs), which sank in some 5180 metres (17 000 feet) of water about 1200 kilometres (750 miles) northwest of Oahu, Hawaii, on 11 April 1968.[120]

The project, which is estimated to have cost some US$350m,[121] is probably the most complex and expensive single intelligence mission ever undertaken. It involved the Office of Naval Intelligence, the CIA, the NSA and the NRO, many of the most sophisticated US technical intelligence collection systems, and the use of Howard Hughes' Summa Corporation as a 'cover' for the operation.

The departure of the submarine from its home port at Vladivostok in February 1968 was monitored by US surveillance satellites. Subsequently, the submarine was tracked by the Sea Spider acoustic detection system, a 2092 kilometre (1300-mile) diameter circle of hydrophones deployed around the Hawaiian Islands and reporting to a naval intelligence station at Pearl Harbor. On 11 April 1968, the Sea Spider system detected and recorded the sound of an explosion aboard the submarine, as well as the noises generated as the vessel sank to the ocean floor — including the sound of the implosion as the hull plates were rent apart by the increasing pressures as the submarine descended to the bottom.[122] In June–August 1968, working from data derived from Sea Spider records and navigational information from the Transit navigation satellites, the USS *Mizar* was able to locate and photograph the sunken submarine and report on the prospects for its recovery.[123]

Proposals for the recovery of the submarine were considered by the Navy, the CIA and the NSA through 1968–69, and the project was approved by the NRO and the 40 Committee in 1970. Operational planning of the project was the responsibility of the CIA's Directorate of Science and Technology under Dr Carl Duckett, with the project being funded by the NRO.[124] Contracts were negotiated in 1970–71 between the CIA, Hughes Tool Company (soon to become the Summa Corporation) and Global Marine Inc. for the construction of the *Hughes Glomar Explorer, Hughes Marine Barge* (HMB-1), and associated recovery equipment; the *Glomar Explorer* was launched in November 1972, had its first sea trials in February–March 1973, and was fully operational as from October 1973.[125]

The actual recovery effort was undertaken from 4 July to 12 August 1974. Considerable misinformation has been published about the relative success of the effort, with some reports claiming that little of value was recovered. In fact, however, the effort was evidently extremely successful. Large sections of the submarine were recovered, including the crushed and battered centre segment containing the three SS-N-5 missiles. Also recovered were two nuclear-armed torpedoes, radio equipment, the submarine's navigation system and, reportedly, the code machine and associated code books.[126] This material would have extraordinary intelligence value. Analysis of the hull plates would reveal the state of Soviet metallurgy and welding techniques and the operational depths and speeds of the submarine, and provide a basis for judgments about future designs and metal qualities. Recovery of one or more of the SS-N-5 missiles, together with the fire control system, would provide an enormous amount of intelligence about Soviet missile and warhead technology. The code machine and code books would permit the decryption of reams of previously intercepted and recorded Soviet naval communications, while examination of the machine would determine its design logic and hence facilitate future codebreaking efforts.[127]

The authorization of the JENNIFER Project in 1970 has been followed by approval for several subsequent deep-sea recovery projects. Later in 1970, for example, the US reportedly recovered a nuclear weapon from a Soviet aircraft which crashed in the Sea of Japan. In 1971, the electronic eavesdropping equipment was recovered from a sunken Soviet SIGINT trawler. In 1972, the electronic equipment from a crashed Soviet aircraft was recovered from the North Sea.[128] And in May 1975 the *Hughes Glomar Explorer* undertook its second and final intelligence mission — the recovery of a package of electronic sensing devices which a Soviet submarine had dropped near the US Navy's weapon-testing facility off San Clemente Island, California.[129]

10

Other areas of cooperation

While signals intelligence and ocean surveillance activities form the core of the UKUSA intelligence arrangement — in terms of the level and constancy of cooperation, the importance of the information collected and the resources involved — the relationship does not end there. Just as cooperation during the Second World War extended to all areas of intelligence activity so does present-day cooperation. This chapter looks at cooperation with regard to monitoring of radio broadcasts, covert action and assassination, human intelligence, overhead reconnaissance, production of intelligence estimates, and conduct of security investigations and training.

Radio broadcast monitoring

In addition to the highly formalized signals intelligence and ocean surveillance cooperative arrangements there is a third arrangement of a highly formalized nature in regard to intelligence collection. This is an agreement between the United States and Britain to divide, on a geographic basis, the responsibility for the monitoring of *public* radio broadcasts — mainly news and public affairs broadcasts. These broadcasts can provide valuable political intelligence — particularly because in so many nations the media, particularly radio and television, are under government control. Monitoring of public radio broadcasts can yield intelligence concerning domestic political conflict and the propaganda line a government is taking internally as well as its pronouncements concerning foreign policy and international events. It also allows the US or Britain to judge the effectiveness of their own propaganda operations.

The specific organizations involved in the arrangement are the British Broadcasting Corporation's Monitoring Service and the US Central Intelligence Agency's Foreign Broadcast Information Service (FBIS). Together, the organizations monitor most of the world's significant news and other broadcasts. Both the BBC Monitoring Service and the FBIS have a network of overseas stations, operated with varying degrees of secrecy, to gather their raw material.[1]

The BBC Monitoring Service and the FBIS began in 1948, as an openly acknowledged arrangement. Thus, the BBC Annual Report for 1948–49 noted that:

> There [is] close co-operation between the BBC's Monitoring Service and its American counterpart the Foreign Broadcast Information Branch of the United States Central Intelligence Agency, and each of the two services maintained liaison units at each other's stations for the purposes of a full exchange of information.[2]

The CIA/FBIS liaison unit is located at Caversham Park.

The area of responsibility for the Monitoring Service is roughly equivalent to the GCHQ's area of responsibility for SIGINT collection — Europe, Africa and Western USSR. Thus, the Monitoring Service maintains a remotely controlled listening post on the rooftop of its Vienna Embassy to monitor VHF radio and television broadcasts originating in Hungary and Czechoslovakia. It also maintains listening posts in Accra in Ghana and Abidjan in the Ivory Coast.[3] In 1976–77 the BBC Monitoring Service turned over responsibility for monitoring Far East broadcasts to the FBIS. To compensate, it had to provide additional coverage of Eastern Europe.[4] In 1974–75 it also had to step up its reporting of the events in Portugal and Spain to meet CIA requirements.[5]

The value of the monitoring arrangement has been summed up by Ray Cline, former CIA Deputy Director for Intelligence:

> While [radio broadcast monitoring] is overt intelligence collection, it is a technically complex and costly undertaking. By roughly dividing the world between them and exchanging the materials recorded the U.S. and Great Britain have always saved themselves a great deal of money and trouble.[6]

Covert action and assassinations

With the general decline in covert action activity by the United States (at least until recently) and the divergent views between the US and European countries, including Britain, concerning appropriate reaction to left-wing movements abroad, there has been a corresponding decline in cooperative covert action activities. In the early 1950s, however, cooperation was close and often involved major operations — including the attempted overthrow of the Albanian government and the successful coup that restored the Shah of Iran to the throne.

In April 1950 an army of 500 Albanian émigrés was recruited in Greece. After being armed and trained the army was sent across the border into

Albania with the object of overthrowing the communist-led government. The invading force was met by Albanian troops armed with machine guns, mortars and artillery who ambushed them at exactly the points they had been assured would be open for passage. Of the 500 only 180 made it back to Greece. Two hundred were killed in the fighting while 120 were captured and executed.[7]

Day-to-day planning of the invasion as well as its conduct had been a joint US–British operation, specifically a State Department, CIA, SIS and Foreign Office operation. The Committee of Four responsible for day-to-day planning included Robert Joyce, the State Department Balkan expert, Earl Jellicoe from the British Foreign Office and Frank Lindsay from the CIA's Office of Policy Coordination. Unfortunately for whatever chance the operation might have had of success, the representative from the Secret Intelligence Service was H.A.R. 'Kim' Philby, a Soviet 'mole'.[8]

A more successful operation, in the short term, was Operation 'Ajax'. Ajax was the US–British response to the 1951 nationalization of the Anglo–Iranian Oil Company by Iranian Prime Minister Mossadegh and the subsequent failure of the Shah's military to remove Mossadegh, leading to the Shah's flight into exile. Ajax — the plan for toppling Mossadegh — was first proposed to the British Government by the Anglo–Iranian Oil Company nine months after the nationalization.[9]

The SIS then approached the CIA with the plan in November 1952. The plan ultimately involved the organization of pro-Shah gangs armed with clubs, knives and occasionally a rifle or pistol.[10] CIA representative Kermit Roosevelt was approached by the Anglo–Iranian Oil Company and met the SIS spokesman for Ajax, the Deputy Director of SIS — General John Sinclair.[11] It was explained to Roosevelt that Ajax involved the overthrow of Mossadegh and it was desired to begin the operation immediately.[12]

SIS officials travelled to Washington in December 1952 and February 1953.[13] The first meeting involved purely operational discussions while the February 1953 delegation attended a series of formal planning meetings at which CIA Director Allen Dulles was also present.[14] At these meetings the British 'described the high capability of their principal agents, repeated their assessment of the Army — and of the loyalty of the people at large'.[15] Dulles gave his support to Ajax and plans were developed to attain the Ajax objective with the British government and SIS as the 'driving force'.[16]

While the SIS was the driving force, Kermit Roosevelt was selected as overall commander of the operation — at British suggestion.[17] In conducting the operation Roosevelt relied on both American as well as British agents turned over to Roosevelt by the SIS to implement the operation.[18] Indeed, the majority of the agents was probably British. Thus, in a letter to Leonard Mosley, Kim Philby remarked that 'What is not so generally known is that the British were also heavily involved and felt some resentment when the Americans (a) blew the affair and (b) grabbed all the credit'.[19]

Possibly the most significant form of present US–British cooperation concerning covert operations is in regard to the provision of a British base from which US Army, Navy and Air Force special warfare units can conduct commando raids, sabotage and transport agents in the event of a European conflict. Thus, the Army Special Forces, Navy Special Warfare Unit (SEALS) and Air Force Special Operations Forces are all represented in the United Kingdom.

A regular visit of Army Special Forces, code-named 'Flintlock', has occurred every May for the last several years.[20] More significantly, a new base for US unconventional warfare operations has come into operation at Machrihanish, on the Kiotyre Peninsula on the West Coast of Scotland. The new unit is the Naval Special Warfare Unit 21, and is only the second such US unit stationed abroad.[21] In addition to naval representation there is a Combat Talon aircraft which is equipped to pick up agents in hostile territory without landing.[22] Combat Talon aircraft are painted totally black and carry folding arms in front of the cockpit which can extend and catch a balloon cable attached to the agent on the ground. The agent is then lifted off the ground and winched up into the aircraft.[23]

The unit has been conducting invasion and infiltration exercises along the west Highland coastline. These exercises are probably training for activities on the Baltic coasts of the USSR and Eastern Europe — specifically, the planting of explosives to sink ships, sabotage of harbour operations and infiltration to destroy facilities located inland.[24] Cooperative exercises were held by Special Forces troops at English airbases in Upper Heyford and Lyneham in February 1982. Another exercise was held in mid-November 1981 at the British Special Air Services training base at Pontrilas, near Hereford.[25]

The United States and Australia also engaged in cooperative covert action and unconventional warfare activity during the Vietnam war. An Australian journalist, Denis Warner, has noted the role of some Australian advisers during the war:

Some of the advisers ... when they first went there under [Brigadier] Ted Serong in the early 1960's did in fact go on training teams or ... establishments and teach but a good many others of them were sent out to ... take command or second in command of irregular forces which were working with and under the American Special Forces which were being directed and set up by the Central Intelligence Agency.[26]

According to Brigadier Serong, who went to Vietnam as the first commander of the Australian Army Training Team Vietnam (AATTV) in July 1962:

The war when I came into it was largely a CIA war and I believed then, and I believe now, that that is the way that it should have stayed. They were running a good operation ... I liked that operation. I was pleased to see my people work with the American Special Forces who were themselves working under the overall direction of the CIA at that time. They were military people working in a military context but the overall backing, the financing, the policy direction was coming out of the CIA, and they fitted in — our people — fitted in very well to that.[27]

From its arrival in Vietnam in July 1962, the AATTV 'contributed eight years of unbroken service to special projects of the CIA'.[28] Beginning with two officers, the number of advisers serving with the CIA increased to eleven in 1964–67, then was reduced to four in December 1969 and to one in April 1970; the last officer ceased work with the CIA in July 1970.[29] Activities undertaken by these Australian officers for the CIA included the training of Montagnard tribesmen for operations against the Viet Cong infrastructure in the Highlands, the collection of intelligence on the Viet Cong infrastructure, and participation in the 'Phoenix' program (1967–70), which was described by William Colby in 1971 as an 'essential element of Vietnam's defence against VCI [Viet Cong Infrastructure] subversion and terrorism'.[30] The Phoenix program began to be scaled down in 1969, principally because of criticism about the brutalities, excesses and other abuses which had been committeed in its name. The 'Counter-Terror' operations were especially brutal. As the official history of the AATTV states, the '"Counter Terror Teams" ... were reputedly as ugly as their title. With the task of assassinating the assassins, they were as deadly as their Viet Cong counterparts if not always as discriminating in their selection of victims.'[31] As Brigadier Serong has stated:

We found that the only counter to terror is counter-terror and our job then was to organize special groups who would behave towards the opposition as the opposition were behaving to our people. It was not a very salubrious operation. I suppose it comes under the heading of fighting fire with fire, or as I said to my own people at the time, this is a gutter fight and the only way you fight a gutter fight is to get down in the gutter.[32]

The Australian officers working for the CIA had to swear to tell neither their own colleagues nor the Australian Government the details of their activities with the CIA.[33]

While the United States has been unwilling to discuss with Australia the subjects of emergency war planning and special operations, Australia and Britain have been jointly involved in the preparation for such wartime activities for 30 years. In November 1953 the Australian Defence Minister approved for planning purposes the concept of joint ASIS–SIS action in all spheres of clandestine activity, including special operations, in the event of war or emergency in the ASIS area of operation.

The British SIS has positioned in Australia quantities of operational stores and equipment. This material is under ASIS control and available for unilateral Australian use in the case of war. Further, joint ASIS–SIS special operations exercises were conducted, with government approval, in southern Malaysia in 1970 and Papua New Guinea in 1972.[34]

Overhead reconnaissance

While none of the UKUSA countries other than the United States possesses

Other areas of cooperation 233

advanced means of airborne photographic intelligence collection, the United Kingdom has played a significant role in US collection efforts. Britain and its Royal Air Force became involved in the US U-2 program soon after its inception. The involvement stemmed from the basing of a U-2 unit at Lakenheath. It was decided by the US that the best way to maximize their chances of obtaining permission for an overflight of Soviet territory was to convert to joint Anglo–American control, with either the President or Prime Minister's approval being sufficient to conduct an overflight.[35] The idea was accepted by Britain and a number of RAF pilots were brought to the US and trained, becoming part of the U-2 operation in Turkey. On at least two occasions British Prime Minister Anthony Eden authorized the overflight of Soviet territory using RAF pilots.[36]

This cooperation helped facilitate the receipt of valuable intelligence by the British during the Suez invasion of 1956. On 31 October 1956 a U-2 flying out of Adana in Turkey passed over Egypt in the course of its sweep along the Eastern Mediterranean. Normal practice involved making a 270° turn when passing over a target and flying over it for a second time before proceeding to the next part of the flight.[37]

The target involved was the principal military airport outside Cairo. The first set of photographs taken showed Egyptian military aircraft intact on the ground while the second set showed hangars and installations burning fiercely. In the intervening ten minutes the RAF had destroyed them.[38] The CIA telephotoed the pictures to the RAF and received the return message 'WARM THANKS FOR THE PIX. IT'S THE QUICKEST BOMB DAMAGE ASSESSMENT WE EVER HAD'.[39]

Britain has also provided base support for SR-71s in their photographic as well as ELINT roles. The SR-71 is believed to have carried out missions over South East Asia, China, the Middle East, South Africa and Cuba. One of 'Ox Cart's' earliest missions involved the photographing of sites that were feared to be Chinese medium range ballistic missile (MRBM) deployments. Missions from British airbases, as an aspect of Anglo–American cooperation, received the codename 'Poppy', and SR-71s from British bases in Cyprus obtained important photographic coverage of events in the 1967 and 1973 Arab–Israeli wars.[40] This cooperation paid off for Britain — early in the Falklands crisis the US apparently flew a special SR-71 mission from California over Argentina and the Falklands at British request.[41]

Additionally, Britain also aids US satellite reconnaissance efforts. The Oakhanger Tracking Station (OTS), located at Borden Hauts near London, is part of the US Air Force Satellite Control Facility (SCF). The SCF has five functions — Tracking, Telemetry, Command, Recovery and Radiometric Testing — and consists of eleven Remote Tracking Stations, including four double stations. The SCF performs these functions for a wide range of military satellites, but is especially important with respect to photographic and ferret satellites since such low altitude satellites require relatively frequent transmissions of command messages every revolution in addition to support from an average of 1.5 tracking stations for each earth orbit.[42] Funds were recently requested by the Air Force in order to add a computer capability at Oakhanger for a 'new classified satellite program'.[43]

Human intelligence

While there are formal arrangements among the UKUSA countries with respect to signals intelligence, ocean surveillance and radio monitoring no such agreement exists with respect to human clandestine intelligence collection activities. Thus, there is no overall arrangement for the division of human intelligence collection activity. However, while no formal arrangement exists there is still significant cooperation among the three nations with clandestine human intelligence collection capabilities — that is the US, Britain and Australia.[44]

Both the British SIS and the US CIA have sought Australian cooperation in areas where it has been easier for ASIS to deploy and operate. In the US case, ASIS has provided significant assistance in Chile, Thailand, Indonesia and Cambodia. Thus, in 1976, the Director of the CIA, William Colby, stated that:

> ASIS reporting has naturally been of most value in areas where our own coverage is limited, including the following:
> (a) Reporting on Portuguese Timor and North Vietnam;
> (b) Reporting from Indonesian sources;
> (c) Operations and reporting on Chile; and
> (d) Unique operations and reporting on Cambodia.
> ... During the period we were not present in Chile the service was of great help in assisting us to maintain coverage of that country's internal developments. For example, two of our Santiago Station assets were turned over to ASIS for handling and produced 58 disseminated reports during the period January, 1972 through July, 1973. The effective and professional handling of these assets by ASIS made possible continued receipt of this very useful information. The same basic comments apply to the case of Cambodia.

An ASIS station in Phnom Penh was approved by the Department of Foreign Affairs on 5 February 1965 and subsequently opened later in the year with one officer and one operational assistant. A second officer slot was added in 1970 but eliminated in 1972. The opening of the station coincided, approximately, with the withdrawal of the United States Mission in Cambodia.

The CIA had strongly supported the ASIS proposal to open a new station and upon withdrawal turned over to ASIS a network of agents, some of whom were still operating when Australia withdrew from Cambodia in 1974, following the fall of the government. Information collected by the ASIS–CIA network was made available to the CIA.

The presence of the Australian Secret Intelligence Service in Chile can be traced back to a CIA request for ASIS support, received in early November 1970. It appeared to the US Government that the Allende Government might sever diplomatic relations with the United States. The CIA in anticipation of such a move sought the opening of an ASIS station in the Australian Embassy in Santiago to take over at least a portion of the CIA network.

The proposal was supported by the Secretary of the Department of Foreign Affairs and approved by the Minister. The justification was not in terms of the ability of a Santiago station being able to produce intelligence important to Australia, but rather as reciprocation for the large amount of intelligence made available to Australia by the United States.

Actual agent-running operations did not begin until early 1972, after a five-month period during which embassy cover was established, the operational climate was assessed and sufficient language fluency obtained. Details concerning three agents were passed to ASIS by the CIA for approval. After ASIS was satisfied that the agents were trustworthy approval was given to begin operations.

In March 1973 the Minister requested a review of the station in Chile and in April decided that it should be closed. This decision was communicated to the CIA and active operations were halted on 1 May 1973, with the agents being handed back to the CIA. For cover purposes the ASIS officer remained in Santiago until July and the operational assistant until October 1973.

According to the findings of the Hope Report, ASIS activities in support of the CIA in Cambodia and Chile were strictly confined to intelligence gathering and did not involve covert action (destabilization) activities. Thus, according to Justice Hope, 'at no time was ASIS approached by CIA, nor made aware of any plans that may have been prepared to affect the internal political situation in Chile. The ASIS station in Santiago was concerned only with intelligence gathering via the agents handed over to it'.

Australian–British cooperation with respect to human intelligence collection has been more extensive than Australian–US cooperation — in terms of longevity and depth. Cooperation began in 1954 when it was agreed that ASIS would take over from SIS some general areas of responsibility for clandestine intelligence collection and thus allow SIS to redeploy resources in other areas — specifically, away from South East Asia and towards Europe and the Middle East.

In areas where both SIS and ASIS officers are deployed they maintain a 'close but discreet' relationship. They exchange and discuss field intelligence reports and other aspects of the local situation. The names of persons of operational interest may be cross-checked in the indices held by the other station. In Manila, where there is an ASIS but no SIS station, ASIS acts as a point of contact with the local intelligence authorities for the SIS.

Estimates

The production of intelligence estimates with respect to Soviet guided missiles is another area in which there has been close US and British cooperation. The two countries produced a joint estimate on the subject in 1949, the Joint Anglo–American Study, using information available as at 31 December 1948. A second early study was a joint Army–Navy–Air Force examination of the Soveit missile program that was coordinated by the British in 1949.[45]

A 369-page estimate entitled *A Summary of Guided Missile Intelligence* (US/UK GM4-52) and published on 20 July 1953 was initially prepared by the US Guided Missiles Working Group. The group consisted of Army, Navy, Air Force and CIA guided missiles intelligence specialists. The initial document prepared by the US Working Group was presented at the Joint US/UK Conference on Soviet guided missiles that took place in Washington, DC, on 8–26 September 1952. As a result of the conference, modifications in the original documents were agreed to and incorporated into the final document by the CIA.[46]

The estimate focused on a variety of subjects related to Soviet missiles — surface-to-surface missiles, surface-to-air missiles, air-to-surface missiles, air-to-air missiles, guided missile testing facilities, guidance and control, propulsion and fuels, production, and Soviet guided missile trends. A major focus of the document was Soviet exploitation of the German guided missile program. The document also included a list of personalities known or suspected to be connected with Soviet guided missiles. The list included nationality, location and specialty plus additional pertinent information.[47]

US–Canadian joint estimates produced in the late 1950s focused on Soviet capabilities and likely actions in the event of a major Soviet attack on North America. Thus, *Soviet Capabilities and Probable Courses of Action Against North America in a Major War Commencing During the Period 1 January 1958 to 31 December 1958*, as well as a similarly titled document for the period 1 July 1958 to 30 June 1959, prepared by the Canadian–US Joint Intelligence Committee, assessed the Soviet threat to North America. Factors considered included: communist bloc political stability and economic support; the internal threat to North America; Soviet nuclear, radiological, biological and chemical weapons; aircraft, including bombers, transport aircraft and tanker aircraft; guided missiles; naval weapons; electronics; ground, naval and surface strength and combat effectiveness; Soviet worldwide strategy; and the Soviet capabilities to conduct air and airborne missile, naval, amphibious and internal operations against North America.[48]

More recently, the chiefs of the analytical branches of the Australian, British, Canadian and United States intelligence communities have held meetings every four years to discuss substantive and methodological issues of interest. These meetings apparently are no longer being held.[49]

However, cooperation among those countries in the defence intelligence area remains strong. The Defense Intelligence Agency maintains liaison units at the Australian, British, Canadian defence intelligence organizations.

In addition to continuous liaison there are periodic conferences dealing with a wide range of scientific and defence intelligence matters. Thus, in

1974 the US participated in the Annual Land Warfare Intelligence Conference, the International Scientific Intelligence Exchange, the Quadrapartite Intelligence Working Party on Chinese Guided Missiles and the Tripartite Defense Intelligence Estimates Conference. Held in London in May 1974, the Annual Land Warfare Intelligence Conference involved as participants the US, British, Canadian and Australian defence intelligence organizations, who gathered to discuss the armaments used by communist armies.[50]

The Third International Scientific Exchange, involving US, British, New Zealand and Australia defence intelligence organizations, was held in Canberra from 18–27 June 1974. Initially established to discuss Chinese scientific development, particularly with respect to nuclear weapons, the 1974 meeting also focused on technical developments in India and Japan, nuclear proliferation in Asia, development and military applications of lasers, and application of peaceful nuclear explosives.[51]

The Quadrapartite Intelligence Working Party on Chinese Guided Missiles met in London in 1974. The panel, consisting of representatives from the US, British, Australian, and Canadian defence intelligence agencies, focused on both Chinese guided missiles and satellite launch vehicles.[52]

The United States, New Zealand and Australia constitute the participants in the Tripartite Defense Intelligence Estimates Conference. The 1974 conference, held in Wellington, New Zealand, involved 'the exchange of military estimates and assessments' among the countries.[53]

Security intelligence and counter-intelligence

A further area of significant cooperation among UKUSA nations is with respect to security intelligence and counter-intelligence. Both the CIA and the British Security Service played fundamental roles in the creation and development of the Australian Security Intelligence Organisation and the New Zealand Security Intelligence Service. Cooperation involves the exchange of information on known or suspected Soviet and Eastern European agents, and this forms the basis for counter-intelligence operations. Thus, former CIA Deputy Director for Intelligence, Ray Cline, has noted the existence of 'crucial' US–British exchanges in the counter-espionage and counter-intelligence field.[54]

Additionally, UKUSA security services may from time to time conduct investigations concerning the activities of a national of another UKUSA nation at the request of that other nation. Thus, the British Security Service, at the request of the Nixon White House, attempted to determine if Daniel Ellsberg had any contact with the KGB while attending Cambridge University.[55] It is highly likely that the British Security Service's investigation of Philip Agee's activities while he was in Britain was at least partially at the behest of the CIA.

In a similar vein, a security service may turn over the product of its investigations into domestic matters to a 'friendly' foreign intelligence service. Thus, it has been alleged that Robin Bourne, when head of the Canadian Police and Security Planning and Analysis Group, let the CIA Canadian Chief of Station, Cleveland Cram, read files on Canadian unionists, politicians, academics and journalists.[56]

Training, seconding and equipment

In addition to operational cooperation there has been significant cooperation in the areas of training, seconding and equipment. Since ASIS was first established, the SIS has accepted ASIS officers as students on its professional intelligence courses. ASIS officers assigned to SIS courses have been treated exactly as SIS officers would be and included in all aspects of the training. Over 80 ASIS officers have been trained in this manner. Included are some ASIS technical members who have received access to sensitive British Technical Intelligence collection equipment. In some cases the equipment itself was made available at reasonable cost. A number of these ASIS officers were subsequently attached to SIS headquarters in London and an SIS Asian station. Since 1972 ASIS has included some SIS officers in ASIS training courses.[57]

The CIA has trained NZSIS officers and advised the service on operational matters.[58] CIA involvement in the training of ASIS personnel has been limited — restricted to items such as training aids and lecture notes.

11

Discord, non-cooperation and deceit within the UKUSA community

The UKUSA security and intelligence community consists of more than twenty major agencies, concerned with such roles and missions as security intelligence, protective security, counter-intelligence, covert operations, espionage, technical collection operations, and intelligence analysis and assessment. There is inevitably much duplication of resources and effort and much concomitant competition between many of these agencies. Moreover, each of these agencies has, to greater or lesser extents, different interests, perspectives, and goals, as well as different bureaucratic traditions and imperatives, which inevitably produce rivalry and conflict among them. There are particular conflicts between the military and civilian elements of the community, between intelligence collection and counter-intelligence agencies, between agencies concerned with internal security intelligence and those concerned with external intelligence, and between intelligence collectors and intelligence analysts. More generally, each of the agencies has confidence in and dependence on its own secret sources, and is suspicious of and often deprecating towards those of other agencies. Indeed, the cult of secrecy is itself a principal cause of inter-agency rivalry. As two former British intelligence officers have noted, intelligence services 'like to work in a dense fog of security, in which the germs of inter-secret service jealousy breed fast'.[1] The 'need-to-know' principle, which is accepted as an important and useful security device within the UKUSA community and is legitimised in numerous agreements and working practices, is also frequently used to deny intelligence to rival agencies which actually have a legitimate need for it. It should thus not be surprising that, notwithstanding the close and wide-ranging relationships which bind it together, the UKUSA community is plagued by discord, non-cooperation and deceit.

Each of the five UKUSA countries suffers rivalry and non-cooperation among its security and intelligence services. According to Admiral Rufus

Taylor, a former Director of US Naval Intelligence and a former Deputy Director of the CIA, the US intelligence community closely resembles a 'tribal federation'.[2] Victor Marchetti and John Marks, a former Executive Assistant to the Deputy Director of the CIA and a former Staff Assistant to the Intelligence Director of the State Department's Bureau of Intelligence and Research (INR) respectively, have described it as a:

> community which ... is made up of fiercely independent bureaucratic entities ... All the members except the CIA are parts of much larger governmental departments, and they look to their parent agencies for guidance, not to the DCI [Director of Central Intelligence]. While all participants share the same profession and general aim of protecting the national security, the intelligence community has developed into an interlocking, overlapping maze of organizations, each with its own goals.[3]

And William C. Sullivan, former Assistant Director of the FBI, has said that each US security and intelligence agency has erected barriers around itself which has 'led to a condition of total isolation for each organization ... All of these little empires in the intelligence community — the FBI, State Department, NSA, and the others — had built fences around themselves. I had never seen anything like it. We wouldn't share our information with anyone, and no other agency would give us anything.'[4] And one former Australian intelligence officer has stated that 'the term "intelligence community" is a gross misnomer; it is really a collection of warring sects'.[5]

Non-cooperation also extends from time to time beyond the rivalries of the various national agencies to non-cooperation among the agencies of one UKUSA country and those of another, and even to the conduct of covert operations against the government or agencies of another UKUSA country. Instances of such activity are discussed in the second part of this chapter.

Rivalry and non-cooperation among the national agencies

Bureaucratic rivalry among many of the security and intelligence agencies within the UKUSA countries goes back to their very beginnings. It is rare for a new organization to be established without some opposition from the extant agencies. Any new organization with parallel or intersecting terms of reference is invariably regarded by them as a threat to their budgets, relative status, prospects for growth, and operational freedom.

In the United States, for example, an extremely bitter and long-lasting conflict was occasioned by President Truman's decision to establish the CIA in 1947, at which time he also instructed the FBI to close down its overseas offices (except those in London, Paris, Rome, Ottawa and Mexico City, which were to confine their activities to the international aspects of domestic cases and to engage in neither the collection of foreign intelligence nor the running of informants). The FBI Director, J. Edgar Hoover, was so furious that he issued specific instructions to all his overseas offices that under no circumstances were they to provide any documents or information to the newly established CIA. Hoover's refusal to meet legitimate and authorized requests from the CIA led the then Director of the Agency, General Bedell Smith, to write to Hoover as follows: 'Whether you, Mr. Hoover, like me or not has nothing to do with the cooperation between two government agencies and it is mandatory for you to give the CIA full cooperation within your limits. If it is not done, if you want to fight this, I'll fight you all over Washington.'[6] Although Hoover backed down to Bedell Smith on this occasion, the liaison between the FBI and the CIA was always tenuous during his tenure, and was at times (such as from 1970 to 1972) severed completely.[7]

In Australia, the setting up of the Office of National Assessments (ONA) in 1977–78 was bitterly resented by senior officers within the Department of Defence and its Joint Intelligence Organization (JIO). The Report of the Royal Commission on Intelligence and Security had recommended that 'the greater part of JIO be transferred' to the new office, including the office of Current Intelligence (OCI) and 'those parts of JIO which are clearly national' — that is, the National Assessments Staff (NAS) of the JIO.[8] However, the Secretary of the Department of Defence, Sir Arthur Tange, immediately began a rearguard action to ensure that the Department retained its own strategic assessment capability. As Sir Arthur stated in a letter to the Secretary of the Department of Foreign Affairs:

The Department of Defence and all statutory offices associated with it (that is, the Chiefs of Staff) and the non-statutory CCS [Chairman, Chiefs of Staff] expect JIO — a unique blending of military and civilian expertise — to satisfy the requirements of the Defence Force for appreciated intelligence. This is a fundamental requirement of any Defence Force, and if it does not have an adequate voice in setting priorities and in the staffing and organisation, it will necessarily have to create a new organisation of its own.[9]

Hence, when the NAS was disbanded and its functions formally transferred to ONA, a Defence Intelligence Estimates Staff (DIES) was established within the JIO to replace it. According to a former member of the NAS, the DIES occupies the same offices, has a staff structure 'which looks remarkably like the old national assessment staff', and is publishing assessments that have 'a remarkable similarity' to those of the NAS.[10]

The early relationship between the JIO and ONA was really not the best. As Fedor Mediansky observed:

The teething process for ONA was prolonged by its dependence on Defence for premises and on JIO for data and expertise so that there was about a three-month slippage before ONA could begin its operations.
The problem was a technical one — it was largely at the insistence of the Defence Department and to the discomfort of ONA.
Defence insisted that before co-operation with ONA could begin, Sir Arthur Tange as permanent head would have to be satisfied that the establishment of ONA within the Defence complex would in no way compromise Sir Arthur's responsibility for the overall security of the defence complex.

This requirement needed agreement on limitations to the movement of ONA personnel within the Defence complex generally and, more importantly, within JIO.

Again, access to JIO's data bank and expertise was not forthcoming until Sir Arthur Tange, as permanent head, was satisfied as to the ONA staff's 'need to know'.

According to security regulations a security clearance does not entitle any individual to information — the individual has to establish a 'need to know'. This provision retarded ONA's access to JIO material until the need to know requirements for each officer were established.

While Defence's technical requirements slowed the establishment of ONA they did not, in themselves, impair its long-term capabilities.

Whether the exercise did much to further cheerful co-operation is of course another matter.[11]

Conflict is especially endemic within agencies concerned with security intelligence and between them and the other agencies with whom they must work. Within the security intelligence agencies, there are fundamental differences of approach between the military, police and other civilian elements of which they are typically comprised. For example, Richard Hall has described the civil–military rivalry associated with the creation of the wartime security service in Australia:

When the war broke out [in 1939] there was a bitter dispute between IB [the Investigation Branch of the Commonwealth Attorney-General's Department] and the military, the latter unsuccessfully demanding the former's records. Through the early months of 1940 the battle raged and in June, the month of Dunkirk, a cabinet decision appeared to give victory to the military but the Attorney-General's Department fought back with a counter-proposal for a Ministry of Civil Security. It was March 1941 before the situation was resolved with the establishment of a Security Service in the Attorney-General's Department with [Colonel] Longfield Lloyd of the IB as its first director. But, as with so many bureaucratic decisions, it was a compromise. The services retained responsibility for Western Australia and the Northern Territory as well as power to arrest and intern in all states. The Security Service could only investigate and recommend.[12]

A similar situation developed following the creation of the Australian Security Intelligence Organization (ASIO). As Hall has also noted, 'the early years of ASIO were ... marked by rivalries and differences between members with a civil police background and those from military intelligence.'[13]

More generally, there are typical differences of perspective and approach between counter-intelligence and counter-espionage agencies on the one hand and police and law enforcement agencies on the other, and between these counter-intelligence and counter-espionage agencies and those concerned with intelligence collection and analysis. The Security Service of the Royal Canadian Mounted Police (RCMP), for example, contained an uncomfortable juxtaposition of police and law enforcement functions and counter-intelligence and counter-espionage responsibilities. As one observer of the RCMP Security Service has noted, each of the law enforcement and security intelligence elements 'has its own values and priorities with little in common with the other. They have much in conflict.'[14] Those on the police and law enforcement side are inbred (at least ideally) with the concept that they are the servants of the law and are pledged to uphold the law regardless of the identity of the transgressor and the nature of the transgression. On the other hand:

Any Mountie who moves into the Security Service must unlearn those very principles to become a good counterintelligence officer. No longer is he the servant of the law. He now works for the political benefit of the country, and his objectives are now set by the political masters. No longer can he take action when observing illegal acts, for he no longer is a law-enforcement officer and lacks the police powers of search, seizure, and arrest. Even if he could take legal action, the country's foremost interest might be best served if he did nothing and allowed the illegality to continue. The concept of justice goes out the window. The aim is no longer rightness but effectiveness.[15]

The Canadian experience indicates that it is very difficult for officers to make the transition from police work to counter-espionage operations. As Leslie James Bennett, who headed the RCMPs counter-intelligence activities for almost two decades, is reported to have frequently complained, 'some of the flat-footed Mounties he had to work with were useless, or worse, for counterespionage work'.[16]

In New Zealand, the Powles report on the Security Intelligence Service (NZSIS) also found that cooperation was quite deficient between the NZSIS, which lacks any function to enforce measures for security, and the police, who are responsible for the enforcement of such measures. This was especially the case with respect to intelligence about terrorist organizations:

The Police were of the opinion that ... they were not receiving from the Service all relevant or sufficient information in respect of terrorist organizations. The Service was passing information to the Police on the basis of what the Service considered the Police 'needed to know'. This was 'not good enough' — the Police needed all the information the Service had in order to make their own assessment.[17]

A similar situation has occurred in the relations between MI-5 and the Special Branch in the United Kingdom, where on one occasion, for example, the FBI had passed to the Special Branch information concerning a Soviet agent within the British Labour movement, and Special Branch had withheld it from MI-5 — 'a symptom of the notorious rivalry between [them]'.[18]

In the United States, the responsibility for counter-espionage is shared between the CIA and the FBI, which also has a law enforcement responsibility. As Marchetti and Marks have written:

Primary responsibility for U.S. internal security rests with the FBI, but inevitably there has been friction between the agency and the bureau in their often overlapping attempts to protect the nation against foreign spies. In theory, the CIA cooperates with the FBI in counterespionage cases by handling the overseas aspects and letting the bureau take care of all the action within the United States. In actual fact, the agency tends to keep within its own control, even domestically, those operations which are designed to penetrate opposition intelligence services; the basically defensive task of preventing the Soviets from recruiting American agents in the United States is left to the FBI. While the FBI also on occasion goes on the offensive by trying to recruit foreign intelligence agents, the bureau's first inclination seems to be to arrest or deport foreign spies rather than to turn them, as the CIA tries to do, into double agents. This fundamental difference in approach limits the degree of FBI–CIA cooperation in counterespionage and confirms the general view within the agency that FBI agents are rather unimaginative police-officer types, and thus incapable of mastering the intricacies of counterespionage work. (The FBI, on the other hand, tends to see CIA counterintelligence operators as dilettantes who are too clever for their own good.)[19]

The conflict between counter-intelligence and law enforcement is not simply a manifestation of bureaucratic rivalry but, rather, derives from a number of basic dilemmas pertaining to this type of security operation. Some fundamental decisions must be made, for instance, whenever a foreign agent is discovered: is the agent to be used or punished and, if the former, how is he to be used? The FBI will generally argue in favour of arrest and trial, both because it is an extremely publicity-conscious agency as well as because of the potential deterrent effect of public capture, arrest, trial and sentencing. On the other hand, other security agencies typically feel that the less said about the discovery of an agent the better.[20] For one thing, to punish an agent is usually to forgo the possibility of receiving a cooperative debrief which, at a minimum, would be valuable in ascertaining the extent of the damage caused by the agent, a necessary step preceding any attempt at rectification. Further, a captured agent whose masters are unaware of his capture can be used for the dissemination of 'disinformation'. Indeed, it is sometimes possible to use 'controlled' or 'turned' agents on such a scale as to move beyond tactical disinformation to the deception of a whole government on a strategic level, as occurred with the British 'Double-Cross' operation during the Second World War — in which British intelligence totally penetrated and practically ran Nazi Germany's spy network within the British Isles.[21] Of course, the credibility of a 'controlled' enemy agent generally requires that genuine and important information be compromised, and this is invariably resisted by some security branches. A difference in perspective and approach between the CIA and the FBI came to a head in the late 1960s when Czechoslovakian intelligence operatives in the United States 'recruited' a State Department employee (who really worked for the FBI) and instructed him to plant a microphone-transmitter in a State Department office that handled Czech affairs. Although this was 'a wonderful opportunity to ... feed the Czech intelligence service misleading information', Hoover was 'more interested in the headlines than the work we were supposed to be doing' and, despite opposition from CIA Director Richard Helms, he persisted in having the State Department declare the Czech operatives *persona non grata*. As William Sullivan (who on this occasion supported the CIA's preferred course of action) has noted, 'We lost an opportunity, but Hoover got his headlines'.[22] Finally, counter-intelligence agencies are frequently opposed to arrests and trials because of the possibility that intelligence sources and methods might be compromised. For example, in 1977 the CIA opposed the trial of David Truong, a Vietnamese anti-war activist who was receiving information from a source in the State Department and passing it to Hanoi, on the grounds that a public trial would blow the cover of a valuable agent (code-named 'Keyseat') who had provided the conduit between Truong and the Hanoi Government.[23]

Just as there are fundamental differences of approach and perspective between counter-intelligence and enforcement agencies, there are also compelling and endemic reasons for conflict between counter-intelligence and intelligence collection agencies and between counter-intelligence and intelligence analysis and assessment agencies. As one study of Kim Philby's career has noted, in terms not too dissimilar from the discussion of the preceding paragraphs, there is a basic difference in attitudes between MI-5 and the Secret Intelligence Service (MI-6):

Security, the task of MI5, is a defensive operation concerned with catching spies and locking them up where they can do no further harm. In contrast the main task of the SIS is offensive: the collection of secret information in a wide variety of clandestine ways. Invariably there is a certain conflict in the practice of these two activities: MI5's duty is to close breaches in British defences as soon as they are detected, even if this involves letting the enemy know he has been detected, and thus drying up a potential source of further information about him. SIS's instinct, on the other hand, is to protect its sources of information about the enemy, so as to keep open the channels to him, even at the risk of a continuing leak. The basic clash, then, is between rival attitudes towards secret information.[24]

The mutual antagonism between MI-5 and MI-6 was evident in several aspects of the Philby case. Although MI-5 had become persuaded that Philby was a Soviet 'super agent' soon after the defection of Donald Maclean and Guy Burgess to the Soviet Union in May 1951, Philby continued to receive support and protection from his MI-6 colleagues, who 'regarded the [MI-5] suspicion as quite unjustified and essentially an expression of MI-5s overall distrust of its sister service'.[25] MI-6 was anxious to ensure that any investigation of Philby was kept within its own confines. However, MI-5, 'then to some extent in rivalry and not unhappy to see its sister outfit in trouble', insisted over MI-6 objections that Philby should be subjected to a secret 'trial', which took place in 1952 and which proved inconclusive.[26] MI-5 continued to believe that Philby was a traitor, but despite its warnings MI-6 re-employed Philby in the Middle East, a circumstance which assisted his defection to Moscow in January 1963.

In addition to the basic difference in professional attitudes between counter-intelligence agencies and intelligence collection and assessment agencies, there is a tendency for counter-espionage agencies to be inordinately concerned about the degree of security within their sister agencies. When it became known during the trial of William Kampiles in November 1978 that thirteen copies of the *System Technical Manual* for the CIA's KH-11 photographic reconnaissance satellite were missing from CIA headquarters, for example, the FBI believed that its view of loose internal security within the CIA was confirmed.[27]

This view was taken to extreme lengths by James Jesus Angleton, who for two decades headed the Counter-intelligence Staff of the CIA. Angleton was eccentric, compulsive, secretive and conspiratorial, and on the basis of information provided by a Soviet defector, Anotili Golitsin, in 1962, came to believe that there was a Soviet 'mole' operating at the highest levels within the CIA. Angleton's single-minded search for the 'mole' completely estranged relations between the Counter-intelligence Staff and the other branches of the CIA, virtually paralysed the CIA's operations against the Soviet Union, and crippled relations between the CIA and several friendly intelligence services.[28]

There are good examples in Australia of the conflict between counter-intelligence and intelligence assessment agencies. There has been particular bad blood between ASIO and the JIO. As Richard Hall has noted, 'on occasions, ASIO has placed JIO staff under surveillance, in particular for evidence of unauthorised press or academic contacts'.[29] More seriously, ASIO apparently took exception to the appointment in 1972 of Gordon Jockel as Director of JIO. According to one report, the Director-General of ASIO recommended against the appointment:

Peter Barbour's recommendation against Jockel made the head of defence, Arthur Tange, dig in his heels. Tange had been head of foreign affairs between 1954 and 1965 and knew all there was to know about Jockel. It was Tange who supposedly had the last word. Barbour went to the prime minister of the day, Billy McMahon, but without success and Jockel's appointment was announced.[30]

This episode could hardly have made for the best relations between ASIO and the JIO over the ensuing few years, particularly since ASIO continued to float rumours about Mr Jockel's private life and supposed indiscretions. ASIO operatives have also spread rumours that JIO officers have been responsible for various 'leaks' from the defence establishment — even though this seems in fact not to have been the case.[31]

ASIO has also been concerned about security within the Office of National Assessments (ONA). In March 1980 it was reported that at least three incidents involving leaks of intelligence information had occurred within the previous month, and during the subsequent investigation it was claimed by a former ASIO operative who had joined ONA soon after it was formed in 1977 that security within ONA was extremely lax, that ONA had been taken over by 'Foreign Affairs left-wingers', that SIGINT documents obtained from the DSD and the NSA and held by ONA had been provided to two business consultancy firms dealing with China and the Republic of Korea, and that it was his 'professional belief that security in ONA was so inadequate that a KGB or "friendly" penetration was most likely'.[32] It was also revealed in the press on 3 April 1980 that a copy of a highly sensitive document entitled *The Threat to the Internal Security of Australia*, produced by ASIO in November 1979, had disappeared from ONA, and on 4 April the Director-General of ONA, R.W. Furlonger, announced that he had already, on 1 April, invited the Director-General of ASIO to investigate the matter and 'at the same time ... to review general security procedures in the office.'[33] The ASIO report on its investigation, which was completed in mid-June, found that the missing document could not be located, that there had been irregularities in the handling of Top Secret material within ONA, and that there had been some falsification of records controlling the distribution of Top Secret documents in ONA.[34]

Another source of conflict within the national security and intelligence agencies of the UKUSA countries lies in the rivalry between those agencies concerned with the collection of foreign intelligence and those involved in covert operations in foreign countries. For example, the CIA has objected to the existence of the US Army's Intelligence Support Agency (ISA), which was established in 1980 to covertly prepare for the attempt to rescue the American hostages held in the occupied US Embassy in Teheran. According to Army intelligence officials, the CIA was reluctant to use its agents in Iran to check out the embassy and nearby helicopter landing areas on the grounds that it would compromise their utility for other human intelligence (HUMINT) operations, and, more generally:

The agency [CIA] people were preoccupied with keeping their cover and could not provide equipment or information for the [rescue] operation. They had enough to do covering their skins. The military decided that they needed their own outfit to collect intelligence on areas where they are asked to fight.[35]

On the other hand, Admiral Stansfield Turner, who was Director of the CIA at the time the ISA was established has said that:

It [the Army's ISA] is not a good idea. First, I don't think that the military is very adept at this kind of clandestine, covert activity. Second, it's a bad idea to set up a competition in this activity. They [the ISA and CIA agents] are likely to run into each other in back alleys overseas. They will be bidding against each other [for information and agents]. There's not room for two agencies to compete for clandestine resources.[36]

There are also several interesting instances of differences in bureaucratic interests and operational purposes between those agencies involved in covert operations and those concerned with the collection of intelligence by technical means. In particular, covert or clandestine operations can often disrupt or impair more long-term technical collection efforts. In 1943, for example, an operation by the OSS led to the complete disruption of one of the most productive SIGINT sources available to the Allies. As General George C. Marshall wrote in a note to the Republican Presidential candidate, headed 'TOP SECRET (FOR MR. DEWEY'S EYES ONLY)' and dated 25 September 1944, in an attempt to explain the delicacy of US SIGINT activities:

As a further example of the delicacy of the situation, some of Donovan's people (the OSS), without telling us, instituted a secret search of the Japanese Embassy Offices in Portugal. As a result the entire military attache Japanese code all over the world was changed, and though this occurred over a year ago, we have not yet been able to break the new code and have thus lost this invaluable source of information, particularly regarding the European situation.[37]

A conflict between US technical intelligence operations and covert political operations also arose in Australia in 1967-68, the two parties being Richard L. Stallings, the head of the NRO-CIA RHYOLITE satellite ground station at Pine Gap, and Ray Villemarette, the CIA's Chief of Station (COS) in Canberra. According to a close friend and former CIA colleague, Stallings was angry about certain clandestine political activity being undertaken in Australia by Villemarette and directed against the Anti-Vietnam War movement and the Australian Labor Party (ALP):

He was very much bothered by some of the activities that were going on simultaneously with his work at Pine Gap. They were being conducted by the CIA Station in Canberra under the auspices of a CIA Station Chief. He was very angry about that ... It was some sort of clandestine activity of an internal nature in Australia, and he felt that this was wrong and that it was endangering a legitimate intelligence project [at] Pine Gap, [i.e.] the collection of information on our potential adversaries.[38]

More specifically, according to another account, 'Stallings was worried that Villemarette's efforts were so clumsy that they might become public and wreck Labor Party acceptance of Pine Gap'.[39] Stalling's complained to CIA headquarters about Villemarette's activities, but 'was told to mind his own business'.[40]

More recently, a conflict developed between a covert FBI operation and a US technical collection operation in the Bahamas. Since 1972 the FBI has been investigating the Bahaman activities of the fugitive financier, Robert Vesco, including his links with Bahaman officials involved in illegal drug-smuggling, and once wanted to set up a 'sting operation' to catch the Bahaman officials taking bribes. However, the CIA Station Chief in the Bahamas successfully opposed this operation on the grounds that it might jeopardize the continued use by the US of the Atlantic Undersea Test and Evaluation Center (AUTEC) at Andros Island in the Bahamas, which includes one of the largest sea-bottom arrays in the US global submarine surveillance system.[41]

Other recurrent sources of conflict and non-cooperation within the security and intelligence agencies of the UKUSA community derive from the different interests and perspectives of the civilian and military elements of these agencies. Civil-military disagreement and rivalry are particularly strong within the SIGINT organizations of the UKUSA countries. SIGINT stations are frequently located within military bases (such as RAF Digby, Leicestershire; HMAS Harman, ACT; Agentia Naval Station, Newfoundland; Schofield Barracks, Hawaii; and Homestead Air Force Base, Florida); the great majority of intercept positions, including those at stations not located within military establishments, are manned by military personnel; and a large amount of work and effort which goes into the collection and production of SIGINT 'is the product of Service personnel and equipment which are also engaged in other duties and functions'.[42] The services are naturally primarily interested in the collection of tactical intelligence, such as the determination of the electronic order of battle (EOB) of potential adversaries, and hence in the monitoring of military traffic and, most particularly, the traffic of the same Service of the adversary countries.[43] On the other hand, the civilians who predominate in the central headquarters, cryptographic, and analytic branches, and who are generally more empathetic to the requirements and demands of the national intelligence consumer agencies, are more interested in the collection and production of strategic and diplomatic SIGINT. Although there has been a distinct and overwhelming trend since the Second World War towards centralization and civilian dominance within the UKUSA SIGINT agencies, this has only occurred despite intense resistance from the military. As the Director of the NSA from 1965 to 1969 later recalled, 'I was fighting, the whole four years I was there; I was fighting to keep the military from taking over NSA'.[44] The operation and development of the SIGINT station at Menwith Hill, near Harrogate in Yorkshire, one of the largest stations in the UKUSA SIGINT network, illustrates the conflict of interest between the NSA's Service components and its 'national' or strategic mission. Menwith Hill was formally established as the 13th US Army Security Agency Field Station on 15 September 1960. However, the ASA used the station primarily for the collection of tactical intelligence, and refused to allocate sufficient intercept positions and resources to sources of strategic intelligence such as diplomatic and economic communications. According to Frank Raven, a former chief of G Group of the NSA's Office of Signals Intelligence Operations, 'the Army fought like hell to avoid intercepting it'.[45] In particular, the ASA refused to devote any of the station's resources to the interception of newer forms of communications such as satellite microwave transmissions. As a result, the NSA moved to take direct charge of Menwith Hill on 1 August 1966. ASA personnel were replaced by civilian NSA employees, some eight satellite ground terminals have been installed, and Menwith Hill is now a major site for the collection of strategic and diplomatic communications.[46]

The Australian experience provides examples of a different arena of civil–military hostility. Elements of the Australian military intelligence agencies have resisted all attempts to enhance the national or strategic intelligence effort. According to General Sir John Wilton, who chaired the committee which recommended the creation of the Joint Intelligence Organization (JIO) in 1968–69, the proposal met 'tremendous opposition from the Service intelligence directors'.[47] The most vociferous opponent of the proposal was the then Director of Military Intelligence, Brigadier J.G. Hooton, who later complained publicly that 'the present intelligence organization [JIO] is now dominated by public servants and the various Service inputs are fragmented'.[48] There was also military opposition to the creation of ONA. The Royal Commission on Intelligence and Security had recommended that officers of the Defence Force should be attached to and perform tasks in ONA 'in much the same way as they have done in JIO' and that 'a senior position in [ONA], possibly as deputy to the Director-General, be available for occupation by a serving officer of the Defence Force of at least two-star rank'.[49] The military resisted the transfer of the service intelligence sections of JIO to ONA, and even of individual military personnel, and currently there is not a single military officer attached to ONA.

There are numerous other instances of civil—military conflict within UKUSA intelligence organizations concerned with the management of technical collection systems and the production of intelligence estimates and assessments, but this conflict cannot be wholly explained simply in terms of civil—military rivalry. The fact that within these particular organizations there are conflicts between the military elements and between the civilian elements themselves and that these are just as frequent and of an essentially similar character to those between the civilian and military elements suggests that there are more general bureaucratic political imperatives involved.

With respect to the management of technical collection systems, there has been lively competition between the Services for responsibility for monitoring signals in certain geographic areas and/or transmitted on certain frequencies, and for dominance in the national cryptographic effort. Until the entry of the United States into the Second World War in December 1941, the Army's Signal Intelligence Service and the Navy's Code and Cipher Section engaged in intense rivalry; each Service jealously guarded its work in Japanese military ciphers, and 'whenever an important message was read, each Service would immediately rush to the White House a copy of the translation, in an effort to impress the Chief Executive'.[50] (When it became obvious that some rationalization was necessary, an 'odd-and-even day' arrangement was agreed whereby the Services would alternate daily in reading the Japanese traffic, and the Navy would disseminate the results to the President and the Army to the State Department.)[51] After the war, the Air Force Security Service (AFSS) and the Army Security Agency (ASA) competed in the Far East and West Pacific, with the consequence that certain traffic that was urgently needed but which could not be obtained with the limited facilities possessed by either Service was not collected, until the ASA discontinued its duplicative operations in March 1952.[52] In another field entirely, the US Navy has had to fight on several occasions to retain control of its Space Surveillance system (SPASUR), an 'electronic fence' of radar stations deployed across the United States in an east-west direction over the southern portion of the country, which was established in 1958 and subordinated to the Air Force-dominated NORAD Space Detection and Tracking System (SPADATS) in February 1961. In Australia, there has been an intermittent struggle between the RAN and the RAAF for control of the Orion P-3 ocean surveillance and ASW aircraft, which currently belong to the Air Force, whereas in the US they are operated by the Navy.

Although National Security Council Intelligence Directive (NSCID)-6 of 17 February 1972 directs that the NSA is the principal US SIGINT agency, both the CIA and the FBI have retained approved responsibilities in regard to SIGINT operations which sometimes bring them into competition with the NSA. In particular, the CIA's Office of SIGINT Operations (OSO), formerly the Office of ELINT (OEL), has responsibility for the operational control of those US SIGINT stations primarily concerned with the collection of intelligence on the capabilities of Soviet strategic nuclear delivery systems by the monitoring of telemetry transmitted during the testing of those systems — such as Hof in West Germany (transferred to the West German *Amt fuer Fernmeldewessen Bundeswehr* in May 1962), the seven CIA/OSO stations maintained in Iran until 1979, the Pine Gap RHYOLITE satellite ground station in Australia, and the two new SIGINT stations in China.[53] The NSA has resented the CIA's control of these operations because of the duplication of effort involved, because many NSA officers believe that the NSA could perform the mission at least as well as the CIA's OSO, and because of a nagging suspicion that the CIA does not keep the NSA sufficiently informed of the details of some of these operations. (Some members of the former Labor Government continue to believe that one of the reasons the CIA became so upset with the revelations in Australia in October–November 1975 concerning its operations at Pine Gap was that the Agency had not been fully forthcoming with the NSA and feared that public debate about the facility would attract closer scrutiny from the NSA.)

There has also been a lack of cooperation between the NSA and the FBI, which, like the CIA, is accorded some 'unique [SIGINT] responsibilities' by NSCID-6.[54] On the one hand, the FBI has its own highly secret Cryptanalytical and Translation Section in the Technical Evaluation Unit of the FBI Laboratory which generally attempts to break whatever code or cipher systems it encounters without first informing the NSA, and which frequently finds that the NSA is not prepared to cooperate if it believes that its involvement might be discovered.[55] On the other hand, the FBI has several times refused to assist the NSA in operations where the electronic surveillance of foreign embassies in Washington required the physical emplacement of electronic devices within the embassies. At a meeting of the President's Foreign Intelligence Advisory Board (PFIAB) on 5 February 1971, for example, it was noted that the NSA was urging the FBI to extend its 'black bag' or physical entry operations and that 'NSA and FBI Director Hoover are having a running battle on this very point'.[56]

Many of the most advanced and expensive US technical collection systems, such as those involved in 'overhead reconnaissance', have been the subject of intense jurisdictional struggles between the CIA and the US Air

Force. Management of these systems not only provides access to enormous budgetary resources and pools of skilled personnel, but 'control over the collection of information can be a crucial means of influencing the whole estimating process' since the 'sort of data that is fed into the process helps to determine the final output'.[57] The first major conflict between the CIA and USAF in this area concerned the U-2 reconnaissance aircraft. The U-2 was designed and developed by the CIA (with Richard Bissell as the principal progenitor), but the CIA lacked the capacity to effectively manage the program and had to delegate much of the management responsibility to the Air Force. Although the CIA recognized the operational necessity of this delegation, it was also concerned that the USAF would direct the U-2 program primarily towards the collection of tactical intelligence, requiring high-resolution photography, rather than the long-range strategic intelligence which interested the CIA and which required cameras able to cover large areas with relatively lower resolution. This potential conflict of interest was resolved in three ways: first, by the development of two distinct versions of the U-2, each accommodating the particular sensor needs of the CIA and USAF respectively; second, through the establishment of the Committee on Overhead Reconnaissance (COMOR) in 1960 to determine the targets for reconnaissance and the frequency with which targets would be photographed; and, third, through the sheer expansion of satellite reconnaissance, which made it easier to meet most of the reconnaissance requirements of both the CIA and the USAF.[58] That these means were not completely successful became evident during the Cuban Missile Crisis in 1962, when rivalry between the Air Force and CIA for responsibility for U-2 overflights of Cuba was the principal reason for the ten-day delay between 4 October 1962, when COMOR authorized a U-2 flight over the western end of Cuba, and 14 October, when a U-2 provided the first photographs of the Soviet development of MRBMs and IRBMs in Cuba. At the COMOR meeting of 4 October, the State Department and the Defense Department noted that a U-2 had been shot down over mainland China on 9 September; the Defense Department argued that the possibility of this recurring meant that the pilots of U-2 aircraft overflying Cuba should be officers in uniform rather than CIA agents, so the Air Force should have responsibility for the U-2 flights over Cuba. The CIA argued to the contrary, that this was an intelligence operation and thus within its jurisdiction; moreover, the CIA's U-2s had been modified in certain ways which gave them better SAM avoidance capabilities than those of the Air Force. The CIA and the Air Force 'engaged in territorial disputes', until 9 October, when COMOR gave the mission to the Air Force. However, the Air Force pilots were to fly the CIA aircraft, which required some training, and hence the overflight did not take place until 14 October. This ten-day delay could have been enormously consequential in terms of the outcome of the Cuban Missile Crisis, since it was in this period that the first of the Soviet MRBMs actually became operational.[59]

The CIA and the USAF also competed in the development of the first US photographic reconnaissance satellites. The CIA contender was the 'Corona' or KH-4 program, which involved a recoverable photographic capsule system. Corona was developed under the cover of the Air Force's 'Discoverer biosatellite program', and achieved its first successful launch and recovery with Discoverer 14, launched on 19 August 1960 and recovered the next day. On the other hand, the Air Force believed that a capsule recovery system was too problematical, and instead developed the Satellite and Missile Observation System (SAMOS), retroactively designated KH-1, which involved a radio-transmission system whereby the film was processed on board the satellite, converted into digital signals and transmitted upon command to several ground stations and then converted back to imagery.[60] Both the CIA and the USAF have continued to develop separate photographic satellite systems, with the USAF currently operating the 'Big Bird' KH-9 system (code-named 'Hexagon') and the CIA the KH-11 real-time photographic reconnaissance system.[61]

Further conflict between the CIA and USAF occurred over the SR-71 reconnaissance aircraft, which the CIA had originally developed as a successor to the U-2 but which was 'captured' by the Air Force in 1967.[62] Partly in retaliation for this, CIA Director Richard Helms refused to give his approval for the Air Force's proposed Manned Orbital Laboratory (MOL), which the USAF was promoting as being, *inter alia*, an intelligence collection system. Without the endorsement of the Director of Central Intelligence (DCI), the Air Force was unable to convince the White House of the need for the project, and the MOL was cancelled in 1969.[63]

A final example of conflict with respect to overhead reconnaissance systems involves those agencies concerned with overhead SIGINT collection as opposed to those concerned with photographic intelligence. In 1974, the CIA's OSO proposed a new generation of geostationary satellites to replace the RHYOLITE system. Codenamed ARGUS (for Advanced RHYOLITE), the expensive new system was opposed by the CIA's photographic specialists. As former CIA Director William Colby has recorded:

'Carl Duckett [Deputy Director of the CIA] for Science and Technology said that tomorrow's meeting of the Executive Committee of the National Reconnaissance Office (which I would chair) would see a big fight over whether to delay an electronic sensor system [that is, Argus] in order to find the funds to keep one of our photo systems functioning at peak schedule with the increased costs that inflation had brought.[64]

Although Colby and the NRO approved the ARGUS project, it was vetoed by the new Secretary of Defense, James Schlesinger, Colby's predecessor as Director of the CIA, on the grounds that land-based SIGINT facilities (and most particularly the stations in Iran) made it unnecessary. Colby subsequently exercised his prerogative under NRO procedures to take the matter directly to the President, Gerald Ford, with the recommendation that the NSC review the issue. However, although Ford agreed and the NSC gave full endorsement to ARGUS, the House Appropriations Committee, noting the disagreement over the need for ARGUS and its enormous cost, refused to fund the program.[65]

Many of the same patterns of rivalry and conflict are evident within those UKUSA agencies concerned with intelligence analysis, assessments and estimates. In Australia, for instance, there has continued to be much competition and disagreement on subjects of common interest between the ONA and the JIO, the former a wholly civilian organization and the latter comprised of a fairly even balance of civilian and military officers. As Fedor Mediansky reported in August 1978, not long after ONA began producing assessments, 'Some differences of judgment have already emerged. On a recent South-East Asian study the ONA and the Foreign Affairs Department have continued to disagree, with JIO supporting Foreign Affairs.'[66] Other differences between ONA and the JIO became apparent at the time of the Vietnamese invasion of Kampuchea in late December 1978 and the subsequent Chinese invasion of Vietnam. According to one report, desk-level officers in ONA had predicted in early December the Vietnamese invasion of Kampuchea was likely and the arguments were:

included in the first draft of a situation paper. But it drew so much flak from the Joint Intelligence Organisation that ONA director-general Bob Furlonger refused to back it.

The final draft, which went to ministers in mid December, did not predict the December 25 Vietnamese offensive.[67]

Despite great scepticism from the JIO and the Department of Foreign Affairs, ONA also suggested that the Chinese invasion of Vietnam in February 1979 was likely.[68]

In the United States, the disputes between the various agencies concerned with the production of intelligence estimates are legion. These disputes have been the basis of the 'bomber gap' fears of the mid-1950s, the 'missile gap' fears of the late-1950s, the concern in the mid-1960s that the Soviet Union had embarked on a massive anti-ballistic missile (ABM) program, the concern in the late 1960s that the Soviet Union had developed a MIRVed ICBM, the controversy over the capabilities of the Soviet Backfire bomber in the early 1970s, the assertion that the Soviet Union had developed Charged Particle Beam Weapons (CPBWs) in the mid-1970s, and the controversy over the level of Soviet defence expenditure in the late 1970s. In each of these instances the positions of the Service agencies have been heavily influenced, if not determined, by the implications of the estimates for the budgets and missions of their parent Services.

In the case of the 'bomber gap', Air Force Intelligence and SAC Intelligence prepared estimates of Soviet heavy bomber developments in 1954–55 which projected that by 1959 the Soviet Union would have 400 Mya-4 Bison and 300 Tu-95 Bear bombers, a much larger force than was planned for the SAC for 1959. This estimate was accepted without dissent by the other intelligence agencies in NIE 11–3–55 of 16 May 1955. In the NIE of August 1956, however, which predicted 470 Bisons and Bears by mid-1958 and 800 for mid-1960, both the Army's G-2 and the Navy's Office of Naval Intelligence (ONI) recorded strong dissents. By the time of the 1957 estimate, NIE 11−4−57 of 12 November, the CIA, G-2 and ONI had formed a dominant coalition against the Air Force and the NIE predicted only 150−250 Bisons and Bears for mid-1958 and 400−600 for 1960, with the Air Force's A-2 recording its dissent from this downgrading. As it happened, the Soviet Union had only produced 190 Bison and Bear bombers by early 1961, when Soviet heavy bomber deployment reached its highest level.[69]

In the case of the 'missile gap', a Special National Intelligence Estimate (SNIE) was prepared in December 1957, in the wake of Sputniks I and II, and approved on 5 January 1958, which predicted a nominal Soviet ICBM force of perhaps ten missiles by mid-1958 and 100 ICBMs by mid-1960. By June 1958, however, a revised NIE had been prepared which predicted that the Soviet Union would have up to 100 ICBMs operational in 1959, 500 in 1960, and 1000 by 1961! At this time, according to a CIA officer, 'to the Air Force every flyspeck on film was a missile'. The CIA, G-2 and the ONI began to take issue with the Air Force and the SAC projections, and in the latest NIE prepared during the Eisenhower Administration, NIE 11−4−60 of 1 December 1960, which found that there was still no evidence of any ICBMs actually operational in the Soviet Union, the Army and Navy reckoned that there would be no more than 50 SS-6 Sapwood ICBMs deployed by mid-1961 whereas the Air Force projected more than 200. In an SNIE of 7 June 1961, SNIE 11−8−61, the Air Force actually estimated that some 300 SS-6s would be operational by the end of the month, whereas the CIA and G-2 predicted 125 to 150, the State Department's Bureau of Intelligence and Research (INR) estimated 160, and the Navy reckoned only ten. Four successful recoveries of Corona KH-4 film capsules were made on 16 June, 7 July, 30 August and 12 September, and two further NIEs were approved on 24 August (NIE 11−4−61) and 21 September 1961 (NIE 11−8/1−61). The NIE of 21 September was the last of the 'missile gap' estimates. It stated that the Soviet Union had less than ten to twelve SS-6 ICBMs operational, and for the first time in many years the Air Force accepted the consensual judgment. (SAC Intelligence remained adamant that the Soviet Union had hundreds of SS-6s deployed, but the SAC had no separate representation on the USIB.) As it happened, the Soviet Union only ever deployed four SS-6 missiles![70]

In 1963, the US intelligence community became concerned that the deployment of SA-5 Griffon high-altitude surface-to-air missiles (SAMs) and associated radars near Tallinn in Estonia represented the foundation of a massive ABM system, and although there was some scepticism within the CIA and the Navy, the 1963 NIE reflected this judgment. In NIE 11−4−64, however, the CIA, Navy and the DIA argued successfully that the Tallinn system was intended primarily for use against aircraft (such as the Air Force's proposed RS-70) rather than ballistic missiles, although this judgment was not accepted by the Air Force and Army. In 1965 the DIA reversed its position on the Tallinn system and supported the Army and Air Force against the CIA and Navy, and these positions were maintained in NIE 11–3–66 of 17 November 1966. By 1968, however, it was generally agreed that the SA-5 missiles and the Tallinn system as a whole had essentially no ABM capability.[71]

The concern that the Soviet Union might have developed a MIRVed ICBM ahead of the United States first arose within the Air Force's Foreign Technology Division (FTD), which argued in 1968–69 that analysis of telemetry intercepted during 'triplet' tests of the SS-9 Mod 4 Scarp ICBM suggested that this was a true MIRVed missile. This analysis was accepted within the Air Force generally and by the DIA. However, the CIA believed that the SS-9 Mod 4 carried not MIRVs but only MRVs, that is, three warheads capable of hitting only a single target rather than being independently targeted.[72] The issue went to the USIB on 4 September 1969 and, following severe pressure from the White House, the CIA acceded in the judgment that the Mod 4 was in fact a MIRV, with only the INR dissenting. As the Senate report on US intelligence activities of April 1976 reported, this was a 'stark, and perhaps exceptional', example of White House and Defense Department pressure on the Director of Central Intelligence, but it 'illustrate[s] the kinds of buffeting with which the DCI must contend'.[73] As it happened, the SS-9 Mod 4 was never deployed in any form by the Soviet Union.

Another disagreement occurred with respect to the capabilities of the Soviet Backfire bomber. In 1971, when the Backfire was still being flight tested at Kazan and Ramenskoye, the Air Force concluded that it had sufficient range for intercontinental attack, and this was accepted by the CIA and DIA in the 1971 NIE. By 1973, however, when the first Backfire unit became operational, the CIA and DIA had decided that its range was insufficient for intercontinental missions and that it was primarily intended as a peripheral attack system.[74] Air Force Intelligence again came into conflict with the majority of the US intelligence community over the question of Soviet development of a particle-beam weapon. In 1975–76, the Air Force's Foreign Technology Division became persuaded that large amounts of gaseous hydrogen with traces of tritium which had been detected within the upper atmosphere by the particle detectors on the USAF/TRW 647 DSP early warning satellites controlled from Nurrungar, South Australia, and Buckley, Colorado, were caused by underground nuclear tests at a facility at Semipalatinsk in Kazakhstan related to the generation of power for particle beam weapon (PBW) systems. The Air Force designated this facility a Possible Nuclear Underground Test Site (PNUTS). However, the CIA and DIA refused to accept the FTD assessment and took the position that there was no hard evidence of work on PBWs at Semipalatinsk and the facility there was of questionable application. The CIA designated the site URDF-3, for Unidentified Research and Development Facility–3. The head of Air Force Intelligence, Major-General George Keegan, retired in protest in early 1977 at the refusal of the CIA and DIA to accept the Air Force's evaluation.[75]

Finally, there has been a major disagreement between the CIA and the DIA with respect to the level of Soviet military expenditure and the appropriate techniques for estimating that expenditure. Whereas the CIA employs a direct costing methodology involving the use of fixed vintage parametric dollar cost estimating relationships, the DIA uses variable vintage parametric cost estimating equations. The CIA methodology provides an estimate for Soviet military expenditure which is substantially below that of the DIA, and which undoubtedly underestimated Soviet defence expenditures throughout the 1960s and 1970s.[76] Beginning in 1970, the DIA has simply refused to use the CIA estimates of Soviet weapons costs and defence spending.[77]

Differences of opinion and a certain degree of competition within the intelligence assessment agencies are not always unhealthy phenomena. They can, for example, lead to the clarification of clashing alternatives and to the forceful presentation of opposing cases. Arguments for and against particular positions can be explicated and a more reasoned appreciation might ultimately emerge.

The situation would be less than healthy, however, if the differences were based on entrenched and self-interested bureaucratic lines rather than the evidence available, and if the process for resolving these differences involved factors other than the cogency and wisdom of the respective arguments. Unfortunately, the preceding discussion suggests a 'community' characterized more by parochialism, rivalry and obstruction, and the exercise of bureaucratic/political power rather than a community cooperating to produce an agreed 'truth' for consumption by decision-makers.

Non-cooperation and deception among the UKUSA countries

Regardless of how friendly two nations may be, and no matter how closely their security and intelligence services may cooperate, they are nevertheless never completely forthcoming with respect to their more sensitive activities and sources of information. As Justice Hope noted in his report in 1977 on the Australian intelligence and security community, 'it would be naive to imagine that overseas governments will always tell us everything they know about a particular matter'.[78] And as the biographer of the Dulles family noted, 'neither SIS nor CIA ever told each other everything. The Americans, for instance, were extremely reticent about their dealings with the Gehlen unit, and the British kept silent about many of their activities in the Far East'.[79]

There are numerous reasons for witholding information from other UKUSA governments or their agencies, some of which are explicitly set forth in agreed documentation and others implicitly recognized in working practices and conventions accepted by the UKUSA partners. As discussed in Chapter 7, the need-to-know (NTK) principle operates just as much between the UKUSA countries as within the security and intelligence community of any given UKUSA country. The greater the number of individuals who have access to particular intelligence information the greater the chance of leaks or betrayal. When the information is considered especially vital to national security, there is a natural reluctance to distribute it to any foreign nations.

However, there are a variety of other reasons for withholding information which are rather less legitimate and which, although perhaps commonly practised, are not endorsed in either UKUSA documentation or convention. For example, when shared material is compromised, there is an understandable tendency to minimize, if not hide altogether, the extent of the compromise from the nation that provided the information for fear that such information might be lost in the future. Thus, British intelligence agencies were reluctant to provide the relevant US authorities with a complete account of the damage done by Geoffrey Arthur Prime during the nine years (1968-77) in which he worked as a Soviet agent inside the GCHQ.[80]

In many cases, non-cooperation is explicable only in terms of the personalities involved. This was especially the case when J. Edgar Hoover was Director of the FBI (1924-72). Hoover was conservative, racist, wrathful, and frequently contemptuous of other intelligence and security agencies. As one of his Assistants later noted, 'Hoover's domestic policy of non-cooperation with other US intelligence agencies extended to non-cooperation with other countries'.[81] He seemed to have a particular dislike of the RCMP. As one account of the RCMP Security Service states, 'Hoover was a proud and inflexible man and cut off the flow of security information whenever he felt slighted, and his interpretation of an offense could be whimsical'.[82] According to William Sullivan, for instance, Hoover withheld, from the RCMP, copies of some extremely important Soviet intelligence communications for ten years until 1954, when Sullivan was sent to Ottawa 'to cut them in on the Soviet material'.[83] Sullivan has also written that 'Hoover didn't like the British, didn't care for the French, hated the Dutch, and couldn't stand the Australians. He wouldn't meet with the director of British intelligence, even as a courtesy'.[84]

Hoover was responsible for a rift between the FBI and ASIO which lasted from 1954 until 1966. According to Sullivan, this breach stemmed from the defection of Vladimir Petrov in Australia in April 1954:

When we learned that Petroff [sic] was telling everything he knew, we wrote to the Australians asking them to send us any information he gave them concerning the United States. It was a common request, and there was nothing out of the ordinary about the reply we got from Sir Charles Spry, director of Australian intelligence. 'We will be glad to comply with your request,' Sir Charles wrote, 'but that will take a while longer, as we are still interrogating the subject about matters concerning Australian security.'

'This is a brush-off', said Hoover, and he wrote 'Have absolutely NOTHING to do with the Australians' right on the bottom of the letter from Sir Charles. And so, single-handedly, Hoover broke off intelligence relations between the FBI and Australia, rather like a sovereign who could make or break relations with any country at will. Behind Hoover's back I personally maintained good relations with

Sir Charles, and whenever Sir Charles came to visit Washington, I would send a memo in to Hoover, begging him to relent and meet with the Australian. But Hoover always said no. 'I don't want to see Spry,' he would write on the bottom of my memos, 'he gave me the brush-off in the Petroff case.'

Finally, twelve years after the 'brush-off', Hoover gave in and agreed to see him ... and we resumed 'official' intelligence relations again with Australia.[85]

Counter-intelligence agencies are particularly prone to non-cooperation, since they have a natural tendency to fear that other agencies are insecure. As Philip Agee noted in his *CIA Diary*, 'the two most basic principles of Liaison operations from the counter-intelligence point of view are: first, there is no such thing as a friendly intelligence service, and, second, all liaison services are penetrated by the Soviets or by local revolutionary groups'.[86]

The fear — invariably more imagined than real — that the Australian Government or its intelligence and security agencies might be penetrated has led to frequent threats by the US to cut off the intelligence flow to Australia. Such threats were made in the late 1940s,[87] for example, and again, at least three times, during Labor's term of office from 1972 to 1975.[88] Whether or not any cuts were actually made is a matter of some dispute. On the one hand, in the Annual Report of the Joint Intelligence Organization for 1974, the Director of JIO specifically stated:

The Chairman [of the National Intelligence Committee, i.e., the Director of JIO] continued to keep watch on the volume and nature of intelligence material received by JIO and collection agencies from overseas cooperating agencies. No diminution was detected in the flow of material from British or US agencies.[89]

And according to James Angleton, Chief of CIA Counter-intelligence at the time, severance of the intelligence relationship was considered but the US 'received assurances' from the Australian Government that certain attitudes, actions and policies would not be continued.[90]

On the other hand, a senior ASIO officer reportedly told the *Bulletin* in mid-1976 that the flow of intelligence to Australia was in fact disrupted some time in 1973.[91] And Frank Snepp, who was a senior CIA operative and analyst in the US Embassy in Saigon from 1969–71 and 1972–75, has also stated that at least some intelligence flow to Australia was severed in 1973:

There was a complete alteration of our attitudes towards the Australians when the Whitlam government came into power. I began to sense it around the time of the cease fire in 1973. Orders came down from the front office and from Washington, from Ted Shackley's office in Washington — Ted Shackley was taking over as Chief for the Far East Division of the C.I.A. — that we should have no dealings whatsoever — we as the C.I.A. — with the Australians. Well this was a stunning diktat because although before we had kept our distance and been on friendly but reserved terms with the Australians, we certainly had been willing to take their intelligence and to share our intelligence with them. There was a trade off on intelligence about Vietnam or intelligence about the Chinese and the Soviets which bore on Vietnam or

260 *The Ties That Bind*

South East Asia. After the Shackley diktat — after the Whitlam government came into power — there was an utter severance in our relations on that basis and very frankly I was told by my superiors that the Australians might as well be regarded as North Vietnamese, as North Vietnamese collaborators.[92]

Christopher Boyce has stated on several occasions that the CIA withheld from Australia both information collected from the RHYOLITE SIGINT satellites at Pine Gap as well as its plans for a more advanced SIGINT satellite to replace the RHYOLITES. In a television interview in May 1982, for example, Boyce stated that:

> When the Rhyolite project was first put into place, the Executive Agreement [between Australia and the US] meant that all information was to be shared ... and along came Mr. Whitlam.
> When I went to work for the project, at the initial security briefing that I had, I was told that we weren't in fact going to live up to that agreement and that we hadn't been.
> And [I was told] that there was information that was being withheld and also that the Argus project, which was the advanced Rhyolite project, was to be hidden from Australians.[93]

Former staff at Pine Gap have confirmed that much of the material analysed in the Signals Analysis Section at the station (a Section from which Australians are excluded) is never passed on to the Australian officers, and have stated that this included (for example) voice intercepts obtained from China and Vietnam during the period of the Whitlam Labor Government.[94] More recently, in May 1980, at the time ONA was being investigated by ASIO for allegedly inadequate security procedures, it was reported that the CIA was withholding some of its more sensitive reports and assessments from ONA.[95]

In some cases, information is withheld from a UKUSA partner as a result of its failure to undertake some *quid pro quo*. As described in Chapter 7, for example, the CIA has refused to pass to Australia information relating to areas where ASIS has no representation and hence is unable to offer any directly comparable information in return. Another example, concerning Canadian access to information at NORAD, came to light in 1982 following the Canadian Government's rejection of a US invitation to participate in the development of laser and other satellite weapons in space. According to a Canadian military spokesman at NORAD, Canadian military personnel were consequently 'frozen out of certain sensitive jobs and information at the new US Space Command, which is also centred at NORAD headquarters in Colorado Springs and uses much the same computer information'.[96]

A final example of withholding relates to a situation where certain techniques of intelligence collection are so arcane that they are not shared between partners involved in even the most sensitive operations. In 1949, for example, MI-6 was successful in tapping into the communications links between the headquarters of the Soviet occupation forces in Vienna and the

Soviet Command in Moscow, by means of a 21.34 metre (70-foot) tunnel from the basement of a listening post in the Vienna suburb of Schwechat to the Soviet underground cables. The CIA's Office of Communications was informed of this in 1951, and it was subsequently conducted as a joint operation. In the meantime, however, the Office of Communications had discovered that enciphered Soviet communications could be read because the cipher system produced faint echoes of the clear text which travelled along landlines with the enciphered message. The British were not let in on this secret, even though MI-6 had dug the tunnel and installed the actual taps.[97]

Monitoring the electronic communications of UKUSA partners

Nevertheless, reticence to share extremely sensitive information, deception of an ally regarding the compromise of shared information, and withholding of information from agencies suspected of insecurity are relatively benign aspects of uncooperative activity engaged in by the intelligence services of the UKUSA countries. Much more serious, and in more unequivocal violation of the UKUSA SIGINT arrangements, is the practice of monitoring the communications and other electronic transmissions of the UKUSA partners.

There have been numerous revelations concerning instances where the United States has monitored the communications of its UKUSA partners — including both Second and Third parties to the Agreement — as well as those of its other Allies and neutral countries.

With respect to Third parties, for example, an NSA cryptographic expert, Joseph S. Petersen, was arrested in 1954 for passing secrets to the Dutch Government — among them the fact that NSA had broken the Dutch codes and was engaged in monitoring Dutch diplomatic communications.[98] In 1956, a British Member of Parliament asserted that the US had cracked the British, French and Israeli military and diplomatic communications and thus had been reading their secret traffic during their attack on Egypt in October–November 1956.[99] In 1972, a former NSA officer also wrote that the NSA had monitored Israeli and French communications during the Six-Day War in the Middle East in June 1967.[100]

In September 1960, two NSA defectors to the Soviet Union, Bernon F. Mitchell and William H. Martin, declared that 'the United States successfully reads the secret communications of more than 40 nations, including its own allies', that 'both enciphered and plain-text communications are monitored from almost every nation in the world, including the nations on whose soil [the NSA] intercept bases are located', and that the countries whose communications were monitored by NSA included such NATO allies as Italy, Turkey, and France.[101] In 1963, a former NSA cryptanalyst, Victor N. Hamilton, also defected to the Soviet Union, and in a press statement published in *Izvestia* declared that the Near East Sector of the ALLO [All Other countries] Division of the NSA's Office of Production (PROD), with which he had worked from 1957 to 1959, was concerned with monitoring and deciphering the communications of some fourteen countries, including NATO allies (Turkey and Greece) and other allies which at that time hosted important NSA SIGINT stations (Ethiopia, Morocco and Iran).[102]

In June 1977, Juanita M. Moody, who had worked for the NSA for 33 years and at the time of her retirement in February 1976 was head of PO5, the NSA's consumer staff liaison office through which passes both watch lists and collected intercepts, testified to the Ethics Committee of the House of Representatives that the NSA had intercepted cable traffic between the South Korean Government in Seoul and its Embassy in Washington during 1974 (which indicated that some Congressmen had received cash and gifts from the South Korean Government in exchange for 'influence').[103] In October 1982, it was reported that NSA electronic listening posts in Bremerhaven, Frankfurt, Augsburg, Zweibrucken, West Berlin and Darmstadt in West Germany were engaged in monitoring thousands of West German telephone calls a day, in an attempt to gather information on the Soviet natural gas pipeline project.[104] And in 1983, Seymour Hersh revealed that in 1969 the NSA had intercepted transmissions between Japan (a Third Party to the UKUSA Agreement and the host of some two dozen NSA SIGINT facilities) and the Japanese Embassy in Washington concerning the Okinawa reversion negotiations.[105]

There is also no question that the United States monitors the communications and other electronic transmissions of its closest UKUSA partners. As a former NSA officer stated in 1972, with specific reference to the UKUSA Agreement, 'we violate it even with our Second Party allies [Great Britain, Canada, Australia and New Zealand] by monitoring their communications constantly'.[106] This officer went on to describe how this practice was indirectly allowed, at least in part, by the need to monitor compliance with communications security (COMSEC) procedures: 'In part, we're allowed to do it for COMSEC purposes ... that's communications security. There's supposed to be a random checking of security procedures.'[107]

However, the NSA's monitoring of its UKUSA partners goes well beyond the COMSEC mission. As the same former NSA officer also stated in 1972: 'I know we also monitor their diplomatic stuff constantly. In England, for instance, our Chicksands installation monitors all their communications, and the NSA unit in our embassy in London monitors the lower-level stuff from Whitehall.'[108]

An authoritative discussion of NSA's operations against British military and diplomatic communications is to be found in a biography of Colonel William E. Friedman, America's greatest cryptographer. In 1946 Friedman visited the GCHQ at Cheltenham; one of his main tasks was 'to ensure that the British should be kept away from American work on breaking British cyphers'.[109] Friedman paid a further visit to the GCHQ in 1957. As noted above, it had become apparent following the Suez crisis in 1956 that the US had been reading British diplomatic communications, along with those of France and Israel, and Friedman, who was then the Special Assistant to the Director of NSA, was dispatched to mollify his British colleagues.[110] In

1976, the NSA reportedly stated to the author of Friedman's biography that it was reading the secret messages of all its NATO allies (that is, those of Britain and Canada as well as those of the other NATO countries) on a daily basis.[111] Friedman finally left the NSA with serious moral doubts regarding his role in these operations.

According to an unpublished Congressional report, prepared for the Government Operations Subcommittee of the House of Representatives in 1975 but considered too sensitive to be made public, the monitoring of British communications was a primary mission of the NSA's Vint Hill Farms Station (VHFS), located near Warrenton, Virginia, and then operated by the Army Security Agency. The report stated:

NSA monitors the traffic of specific countries, including Great Britain, our closest ally. The monitoring of government traffic has been confirmed by a former employee of Vint Hill Farms station. [The station] had a whole bank of machines [and] a whole team of men whose only job was to read and process intercepted British communications.[112]

In August 1976, a British MP accused the NSA of using its installations at Chicksands, Edzell, and Menwith Hill near Harrogate in Yorkshire, to monitor commercial communications to and from Britain.[113] And a lengthy and detailed article in the *New Statesman* in July 1980 also argued that one of the principal targets of the NSA Menwith Hill station was British international and domestic telecommunications.[114]

US SIGINT activities against Canada are also allegedly commonplace. One former NSA officer has claimed that the NSA monitors not only Canada's communications to and from its embassy in Washington, but also virtually every means of communication used by the Canadian Government.[115] And William H. Kelly, a former director of the RCMP Security Service has stated, much more equivocally, that 'It would be rather stupid of any Canadian authority to think that if NSA covers the rest of the world that they would make an exception of this country. I think you have to work on the assumption that they do.'[116] It was also alleged in 1982 that the US had broken the Canadian diplomatic code and is routinely 'peeking' at dispatches between Ottawa and the Canadian Embassy in Washington.[117]

It also seems that Australian communications are regularly monitored by the US. In February 1973, for example, the Deputy Secretary B of the Australian Defence Department, Gordon Blakers, was informed that a recent telephone conversation between himself and the CIA's Director of Science and Technology, Dr Carl Duckett, had been monitored by the NSA and found wanting with regard to proper security procedures.[118] According to other reports, the US goes beyond COMSEC operations and also monitors internal Australian radio communications. For example, documents obtained by the *New York Times* in April 1979 revealed that Australian communications were included in the electronic intelligence intercepted by the RHYOLITE SIGINT satellites controlled from Pine Gap.[119] According to a former CIA Chief of Station in Canberra, John

Denley Walker, the intercept capability of the RHYOLITE system is used only against non-Australian military communications: 'It is not remotely its mission to collect personal conversations; if by hazard it picked up domestic conversations, it would get no further than the responsible Australian desk officer'.[120] However, the interception of domestic transmissions in the VHF through millimetre frequencies would not be an accidental hazard for the system; the problem would be a continuous one of having to separate these transmissions from the Soviet radar emissions, telemetry signals, VHF and microwave communications and an enormous range of other radio emanations also 'sucked up' by the RHYOLITE satellites. (This extraction problem is suggested by the code-name of the project: Rhyolite is a volcanic rock containing colourful pieces of quartz and glassy feldspar embedded in a mass of tiny crystals.)[121] The question is really one of what happens to the recordings of any Australian transmissions once they are sorted out — are they destroyed, or passed back unread to the Australian intelligence and security agencies, or are they retained and those of interest read and analysed by the CIA and the NSA? It is most likely that the latter possibility was what Christopher Boyce was referring to when he stated during his trial that the CIA was deceiving Australia 'on a daily basis'.[122]

The NSA and the CIA are evidently not the only US agencies involved in hostile operations against allied telecommunications. For example, in July 1983 the FBI released confidential correspondence between a former FBI officer, David L. Castleberry and FBI Director William H. Webster which revealed that the FBI had secret units in New York, San Francisco and Washington which wiretapped the telephones of the trade missions of US allies.[123]

However, US agencies are apparently not the only ones which conduct SIGINT operations against their allies. It has been alleged, for instance, that the Canadian SIGINT agency monitors the communications between all the diplomatic missions in Ottawa and their home governments, specifically including Britain and the other countries of the European Community.[124] It has also been alleged that the GCHQ monitors US communications. Thus, a former intelligence official who worked at one of London's phone-tapping centres has described the targets of intelligence and bugging and tapping as including 'Embassies, all of them ... including the Americans'.[125]

Covert action in UKUSA countries

Even more serious than the conduct of signals intelligence operations against other UKUSA governments are the allegations of covert activities directed against them. Espionage against one's allies is of course not a new phenomenon. Between the end of the First World War and the beginning of the peace negotiatons, for example, the third priority of British intelligence was the United States, which was suspected of making preparations for chemical warfare.[126] And in 1942, a BSC operative in New York was discovered attempting to 'get the dirt' on Adolf A. Berle, an Assistant Secretary in the State Department, so as to force his removal from that Department.[127]

Most post-war allegations of covert activities directed against allied countries concern US manipulation of British, Canadian and Australian politics. In the case of Britain, the evidence is not very authoritative. It has been alleged, however, by a defector from the South African Bureau of State Security (BOSS) that Peter Bessell, an MP from 1964–70, was an agent of the CIA — that he was recruited by the CIA in 1967, that he collected information about British politicians for the CIA and that he carried out special assignments for the CIA overseas and in the US.[128]

Allegations concerning CIA activities in Canada concern alleged infiltration of the RCMP, attempts to influence provincial elections, infiltration of the Conservative Party as well as support of western Canadian separatist movements by US agents. Svend Robinson, a member of the New Democratic Party, has alleged that five members of the RCMP Security Service, including some who are still on the force, were ready to provide evidence of CIA infiltration of that force.[129]

Robinson has also charged that the CIA financed specific election campaigns and designated political candidates in five provincial elections between 1970 and 1976 — the provinces being Quebec, British Columbia, Alberta, Manitoba and Saskatchewan.[130] This assistance, according to Robinson, included assistance to two successful Social Credit candidates in the 1975 British Columbian election.[131] Robinson has also charged that the CIA financed western Canadian separatist movements and infiltrated the Conservative Party while clandestinely supplying it, through front men, with information on the RCMP.[132]

Allegations made by Robinson were the result of allegations made to him by John Meier, a former executive assistant to Howard Hughes, who was facing extradition to California on the charge of having arranged in 1974 the murder of a Vancouver businessman.[133] Meier's allegations were investigated in the late 1970s by a Toronto lawyer commissioned to conduct a secret investigation. According to Attorney General Robert Kaplan the charges were found to be without substance. According to one account 'informed officials also said that Canada is one of two countries with which the CIA has an agreement to conduct no covert activities that are not supported by the host government — and that it scrupulously clears everything it does with the RCMP'.[134] Similarly, one RCMP Superintendent stated that the RCMP and CIA have a very close relationship and that 'it would be ludicrous to think that the totality of that cooperation would be risked by them trying to introduce some covert program directed at the RCMP'.[135] And a CIA source suggested that 'we would never run a clandestine agent in Canada ... If such an agent were caught the political implications would be tremendous.'[136]

At the same time it should be noted that the two CIA agents named in Philip Agee's *Inside the Company* — Emilio Garza and Virginia Gonzales —

left Canada when identified in 1975. The Canadian Government admitted afterwards that it had been utterly unaware of their real duties in Canada.[137]

Allegations with respect to CIA intervention in Australian politics concern alleged CIA funding of the Australian National Country Party (since 1982 the National Party), infiltration of Australian trade unions, and a CIA role in the fall of the Whitlam Government in 1975. Accusations concerning CIA funding of the National Country Party were made by Australian Prime Minister Gough Whitlam (of the Labor Party) on 2 November and 6 November 1975. On 6 November, Whitlam stated that he knew of two instances in which the CIA had attempted to influence domestic Australian politics.[138] (One instance subsequently described by Whitlam occurred in 1974, when CIA operatives in Perth evidently attempted to persuade union employees at Perth airport to ground aircraft which could be used to fly out a Russian violinist, Georgi Ermolenko, who had sought asylum in Australia but then later changed his mind.)[139]

By far the most serious allegation, but one which also remains unproven, concerns the involvement of elements of the US intelligence community in the fall of the Whitlam Government in November 1975. There is no doubt that some of the actions of the Whitlam Government aroused deep hostility within some of the US agencies. For example, the reaction of the CIA to the 'raid' by the Attorney-General on ASIO headquarters in Melbourne in March 1973 has been described by James Angleton, then the Chief of CIA Counter-intelligence, as follows:

We ... entrusted the highest secrets of counter-intelligence to Australian services and we saw the sanctity of that information being jeopardised by a bull in a china shop ... How could we stand aside without having a crisis, in terms of our responsibilities as to whether we would maintain relationships with the Australian intelligence services ...

Everything worried us. You don't see the jewels of counter-intelligence being placed in jeopardy by a party that has extensive historical contacts in Eastern Europe ...[140]

The CIA was even more concerned about the possibility of the Labor Government compromising the functions and capabilities of the RHYOLITE SIGINT satellite system controlled by the CIA from its ground station at Pine Gap near Alice Springs in central Australia. In early November 1975, it was reported in the Australian press that the first head of the Pine Gap facility, Richard Lee Stallings, and his two successors, Harry Fitzwater and Lou Bonham, were CIA officers.[141] Official briefings to Government Ministers had consistently omitted the fact that Pine Gap was a CIA operation, but inquiries from the Prime Minister to the Departments of Foreign Affairs and Defence in October 1975 indicated that he had discovered this fact through unofficial means. These disclosures and inquiries were profoundly disturbing to some members of the US intelligence community. At this time, the existence of the RHYOLITE project and the capabilities of the RHYOLITE satellites were known to only a very few people in the UKUSA (and perhaps Soviet) intelligence communities. In as much as the RHYOLITE system provided massive amounts of signals intelligence, including the telemetry generated by Soviet missile tests, any activities — direct or indirect — that could lead to the compromise of the program were regarded as being of the gravest consequence. Indeed, the disclosure that Pine Gap was a CIA operation was reportedly described by Sir Arthur Tange, the Secretary of the Australian Department of Defence, as 'the gravest risk to the nation's security there has ever been'.[142]

The CIA and a special secret naval intelligence unit, Task Force 157, apparently adopted two courses of action. One involved the passing of information considered to be detrimental to Whitlam on to the Australian intelligence agencies which in turn passed it on to the Australian press. Thus, according to Ray Cline:

when Whitlam came to power there was a period of turbulence to do with Alice Springs ... the CIA would go so far as to provide information to people who would bring it to the surface in Australia ... say they stumbled onto a Whitlam error which they were willing to pump into the system so it might be to his damage...if we provided a particular piece of information to the Australian intelligence services, they could make use of it.[143]

Secondly, the CIA exerted indirect pressure through the Australian intelligence community, and especially ASIO, by suggesting that the entire US–Australian intelligence relationship was in jeopardy. Thus, the ASIO liaison officer in Washington telexed ASIO headquarters on 8 November that 'CIA feels that everything possible has been done on a diplomatic basis and now on an intelligence liaison link they feel that if this problem cannot be solved they do not see how our mutually beneficial relationships are going to continue'.[144]

On 11 November 1975, the Governor-General, Sir John Kerr, dismissed the Whitlam Government — using an archaic legal provision that had never been used before. It is impossible to determine the extent to which the Governor-General was moved by the 'security crisis'. Sir John himself has written that 'My decision of November 11, 1975, to dismiss Whitlam was exclusively my own, made upon my sole and full responsibility as governor-general. No one else produced it. The CIA had no part in it'.[145] The constitutional crisis engendered by the Government's inability to secure passage of Supply through the Senate clearly demanded resolution, and the apparent failure of the Government's economic policies together with various Ministerial improprieties could undoubtedly have been enough to cause the Governor-General to resolve the issue against the Government. But Sir John's denial cannot be accepted as the last word. Sir John was involved in extensive liaison with British and US intelligence agencies during the Second World War; he was an active member of CIA cultural front organizations in the 1950s and 1960s; despite his denials that as Governor-General he received briefings on the 'security crisis', there is no doubt that he was informed by senior Defence Department officials of their concerns that the Government was endangering the security relationship with the United States; and he need not necessarily have been aware of the origins of some of the 'leaks' and fabrications which embarrassed the Government and which did influence his decision.[146] In the end, the evidence does not allow any categoric judgment. As the Assistant Secretary of State for East Asia and the Pacific, Richard Holbrooke, stated in 1978, 'I cannot vouch for the fact that nothing improper was done by the CIA during the Whitlam government. I can't be sure'.[147]

12

Organization and performance

The organizational structure for the conduct of intelligence activities is a subject that has attracted much attention among Western governments and scholars, including several of the UKUSA governments. In the United States in 1975 the Commission on the Organization of the Government for the Conduct of Foreign Policy (the Murphy Commission) examined some alternative organizational structures that the United States intelligence community might adopt.[1] Similarly, the 1977 Australian Royal Commission on Intelligence and Security (the Hope Commission) devoted a significant amount of attention to the question of organizational structure and how such structure could influence performance.[2] Several of the Hope Commission's recommendations were adopted, significantly altering the structure of the Australian intelligence and security community. And while the basic focus of the Canadian Commission of Inquiry was on RCMP activities it did consider some issues relating to intelligence structure and performance overall.[3]

In addition to governmental attention there has been significant discussion in the academic and journalistic communities concerning the proper organizational arrangement for the conduct of intelligence activities.[4] These discussions have focused on questions concerning intelligence analysis as well as collection and covert action.

This chapter is concerned with the manner in which the various UKUSA intelligence and security communities have been organized for the performance of intelligence activities and the possible effects of that organizational structure on performance. Five specific areas of issues are considered — the separation of analysis and collection activities, the separation of collection and covert action activities, the determination of intelligence priorities and requirements, organizing for analysis, and the external–internal intelligence relationship.

Before we proceed to explore these issues it is important to note that the issues considered here are not the only ones that are relevant to the quality of intelligence performance, especially in regard to the area of intelligence analysis. Thus, Andrew Marshall, Director of Net Assessment in the Department of Defense has stated that:

The quality of analysis produced by the Community is not primarily determined by the general way in which it is organized, but by the analysis programs and the environment within the major organizational elements. You have to attract intelligent and able people, and provide them with both incentives and an appropriate organizational context within which to work... A commitment of upper level managers to the quality of analysis is also required.[5]

Likewise, analysts must be able to maintain independence from vested interests while their agencies maintain their independence from senior policymakers in order for quality intelligence to be produced. Hence, a persistent problem with respect to the US Defense Intelligence Agency has been the awareness of analysts that when their tour with the DIA ended they would be returning to their parent service — and that analysis produced at the DIA that had an unfavourable impact on their parent service could be detrimental to their career prospects.[6] And recently it has been charged the CIA has been too willing to shade its assessments so as to satisfy policymakers.[7] Finally, if national leaders are unwilling to accept the results of intelligence assessments or do not act on them — in the belief that 'it can't happen' — then the futility of the enterprise will soon become apparent, possibly with disastrous effects, as in the cases of Pearl Harbor, Operation Barbarossa and the October 1973 War.[8]

With these factors in mind it is still important to examine the more tangible forms of intelligence organization and the potential effect on the conduct of intelligence activities.

Separating analysis and collection activities

It has been suggested by John Bruce Lockhart that a basic principle concerning the organization of intelligence activities is that the responsibility for intelligence analysis should be housed in a different agency (or agencies) than the one (or ones) responsible for collection.[9] Several reasons have been suggested, by Lockhart and others, why conforming to such a principle is advantageous.

In nations that engage in covert action such activity is usually performed by the same agency that conducts clandestine collection activities — two prominent UKUSA examples being the CIA and British SIS. In such a case the intelligence analysis produced by that agency with respect to any country will be used in evaluating that agency's proposals for covert action operations. Thus a potential conflict of interest exists.

Theoretically, even if an agency conducts all three activities — that is, analysis, covert collections and covert action — such a conflict may be avoided if the analytic and operational branches of the agency are suitably distinct and the agency's highest officials make objective analysis a priority goal. However, the CIA experience is an example of one in which the operations side of the agency was dominant for a significant number of years and may be on the rise again. The only three CIA Directors to rise from the ranks — Allen Dulles, Richard Helms and William Colby — were members of the Agency's Clandestine Services. Together, their tenure comprises almost half the CIA's 35 years of existence.

In any case, even if covert operations were assigned to another agency, collectors may still be faced with a conflict of interest. When there is significant cooperation between two nation's intelligence services one may provide the other with intelligence concerning its own domestic politics. Such an arrangement will be used to forestall contacts with dissident groups and possibly undesirable conclusions concerning the actual stability of the regime. Such an arrangement may be deemed worthwhile by the nation receiving such intelligence if the extent of cooperation on other matters is deemed vital. Thus, the CIA and the Shah of Iran's SAVAK had such an arrangement — an arrangement which forestalled the CIA from conducting its own investigation into Iranian politics. A similar arrangement is said to exist with respect to Israel.[10] To the extent that the collectors 'control' the analysis/collection agency they are in position to pass judgment on the utility of such an arrangement — a judgment which may emphasize the operational benefits of such an arrangement and de-emphasize the analytical costs.

A third potential justification for separating collection and analysis functions is a perceived need for a hierarchical structure — in which intelligence analysis agencies determine what information they require to produce the intelligence demanded by policymakers and then proceed to task collection agencies. Clearly, such a structural arrangement would be facilitated by a sharp demarcation between collection and analysis agencies.

Finally, it has sometimes been argued, particularly by US scholars (and some intelligence officials) that separating collection and analysis functions would allow for a more open intelligence agency which in turn would make such an agency a more desirable place to work for scholars. Thus, it is argued that such an arrangement would *help* attract the able and intelligent people that Andrew Marshall considered a fundamental requirement of a successful intelligence analysis operation. Further, it is also argued that such an arrangement would allow a broadening of contacts with scholars — scholars who may presently be adverse to dealing with an agency dealing in clandestine and covert activities.[11]

Others have argued that there are some potentially serious drawbacks to such an arrangement which make it undesirable. Such a separation, it has been asserted, places a barrier between analysts and collectors that will be detrimental to the overall intelligence effort. Promoting an awareness of the problems and requirements of each group can be beneficial — that for analysts to understand the conditions under which collectors operate can lead them to define their requirements more sharply and realistically while better knowledge by the collectors of the needs and responsibilities of the analysts can lead to better planning to satisfy the requirements of the analysts.[12] Such an arrangement can be best promoted when both collection and analysis functions are housed under the same organizational roof.

It is also a possibility, according to some, that a purely research intelligence analysis organization can be shunted aside more easily if its reports did not please policymakers — that is, did not tell them what they wanted to hear. Thus, Szanton and Allison note that 'The potential vulnerability of such an agency is that in calling the shots just as it saw them it would make few friends; and without substantial collection programs of its own, or a supervisory responsibility for the rest of the community it might simply be ignored'.[13]

Such a view is not unrealistic — one often gets the impression that many officials, including many in the intelligence community, believe that collection *per se* contributes to national security even if the data collected is never analysed.

The debate on the advisability of separating analysis and collection activities has been conducted with respect to the possible separation of analysis and *clandestine human intelligence collection* — for a variety of reasons. The only agencies with programs in both analysis and collection — the CIA and British SIS (although the analytical functions of the SIS are relatively much less important than those of the CIA) — are those with human collection programs. Further, it is the clandestine human programs which, in the eyes of some, hamper both analytical objectivity and a more open relationship with the scholarly community.

Since neither New Zealand or Canada have yet established clandestine foreign collection programs they have not had to deal with the issue. The US and British approach to the location of clandestine collection and analysis functions differs sharply from the Australian approach. As noted in Chapter 6, the CIA encompasses both analysis and clandestine collection functions via the Directorate of Intelligence and the Directorate of Operations. This concentration of responsibilities is one that has developed since 1947 rather than one that was specifically mandated. Thus, in regard to collection responsibilities, National Security Council Intelligence Directive Number 3 of 13 January 1948 stated that:

There shall be an allocation within certain broad categories of agency responsibility for collection abroad, as follows:

Cultural	Department of State
Political	Department of State
Sociological	Department of State
Military	Department of the Army
Naval	Department of the Navy
Air	Department of the Air Force

Economic
Scientific   Each agency in accordance with its respective needs.[14]

It is noteworthy that no specific collection role was allotted to the CIA. Similarly, the CIA's initial role in analysis was to serve as a coordinating mechanism for the rest of the intelligence community.

Over time the CIA's role evolved to its present form. Although there have been numerous proposals to separate analysis and collection there has probably been only one point in time when there was a serious possibility of such an occurrence — the immediate aftermath of the Bay of Pigs invasion, which seemed to provide a classic example of how commitment to a clandestine project can prevent objective analysis of its likely success.[15] At present there seems to be no chance of any alteration in the CIA structure that would result in the removal of the analysis or collection functions.

As with the CIA, the British Secret Intelligence Service combines analysis, clandestine collection and covert action programs under one organizational roof. As with the CIA, the SIS clandestine collection and covert action programs are run via regional offices headed by a Controller while another branch, the Directorate of Requirements and Production, is responsible for analysis. At the same time, it should be noted that the British system apparently concentrates greater responsibility for producing assessments in the Joint Intelligence Committee/Joint Intelligence Organization and its subordinate units than the US system does in the National Foreign Intelligence Board.

In the case of Australia, clandestine collection and analysis functions have always been separated. As previously noted, national intelligence assessments prior to 1977 were the responsibility of the Defence Department's Joint Intelligence Organization while clandestine collection was the responsibility of the Australian Secret Intelligence Service. As a result of the report of the Royal Commission on Intelligence and Security, a new assessments agency, the Office of National Assessments, was created, with responsibility for national assessments and supervision of the entire intelligence community. The Joint Intelligence Organization was, in theory, to be the Defence Department's assessment organization. The separation between collection and assessment functions was maintained. Thus, the Director-General of ONA described the office's functions as being 'occupied with the analytical task of estimating or assessing situations as distinct from gathering information about them. This means it is not an intelligence organization in the popular sense of gathering information from delicate sources'.[16]

Separating collection and covert action functions

In some discussions concerning the organization of the United States intelligence community it has been suggested that — regardless of whether analysis and collection activities are separated — covert action and collection activities should be conducted by separate organizations.[17] Thus, rather than relying on the same set of individuals and the same organizational infrastructure to perform both activities, two separate organizations would exist, each dedicated to a different activity.

There have been two reasons offered in support of such an arrangement. It has been argued that covert action is a specialty which should be performed by individuals who concentrate their activities in that field. Thus, it could be asserted that the psychological make-up of an individual who can effectively conduct covert action is significantly different from the psychological make-up of the effective clandestine collector. The former must be able to organize and deal with groups of individuals, many of whom have conflicting interests, and motivate them into taking action. Further, he may not need to operate over a long period of time — particularly when the objective of the covert action is to bring about a coup or other dramatic event. The latter is an individual who must be able to function anonymously over a prolonged time span, dealing with individuals in a one-to-one relationship.

Secondly, it has been argued that very different requirements exist for successful covert action as compared to successful clandestine collection. Ideally covert action implies secret sponsorship although the activity sponsored may be one which the government of the nation that it is directed against may be well aware of. Thus, US or Soviet covert support for guerilla forces — whether US support in Angola or Soviet support in Yemen — is directed at aiding an activity that is not being conducted secretly. It is the objective of the covert operators in such cases to help the guerilla forces succeed in their objectives while keeping *their aid* secret. And indeed, in certain situations 'covert' action can be openly conducted without serious consequences — thus US aid to Afghan rebels is well known yet continues.[18]

On the other hand, clandestine collection operations, it can be argued, are of a sharply different nature than covert action operations. For a particular clandestine collection effort to produce significant results the counter-intelligence services of a hostile nation must be unaware of its existence. Otherwise, they can take counter-measures which will either eliminate the source or the flow of information.[19] Thus, an organizational structure which mixes clandestine collectors and covert operators — either by having an intelligence officer perform both functions or by having both functions performed out of the same overseas station — in this view weakens the security of the clandestine collection effort.

Others would argue that the separation of covert action and collection functions would be a serious mistake. Because of competing requirements, differing objectives and scarce resources any clandestine or covert activity being conducted on foreign soil must be conducted by a single organization whose chief officer can balance covert action requirements against clandestine collection requirements. In some instances it may be necessary to assign strict priorities among collection and covert activities in a given country (particularly in wartime) — thus it may be necessary to suspend one type of activity in order to allow for the success of the other.

In addition, separate agencies mean separate infrastructures and separate agent networks abroad — resulting in competition for agents and funding. Further, the requirement for additional staff (both support staff and operators) increases the risk of penetration by hostile intelligence services.

Another potential problem with such an organizational structure has been noted by several scholars and intelligence officials.[20] Commenting on proposals to set up a separate agency for covert action, former Director of Central Intelligence, Turner, suggested that such a situation:

> would be costly and perhaps dangerous. You would end up constructing an organization, with people overseas, just for covert action, whereas today we get dual service out of those people. If there were a separate bureaucracy with good people in it, they would end up promoting covert action — not maliciously, but because they would be energetic. We should be ready to do what we're asked to do, but not be out drumming up business.[21]

In both Britain and the United States, as indicated above, covert action and major clandestine collection are handled by the same organization. In Australia the Australian Secret Intelligence Service conducts clandestine collection and other operations through the Assistant Director, Operations. Thus all three UKUSA nations of concern have opted for a single organization to handle both human collection and covert operations functions.

This state of affairs is not surprising since intelligence officials of all three nations are obviously aware of past US and British experiences with separate collection and covert action agencies. In the Second World War British clandestine collection functions were a province of the Secret Intelligence Service. Covert operations including sabotage, aid to guerilla groups and assassination were the function of the Special Operations Executive. This division led to virtually all the problems suggested above — fierce competition for financial resources and agents and disputes over collection as opposed to action priorities.[22]

Similarly, in the early post-World War II era US clandestine and covert activities were partitioned between the Office of Special Operations (OSO) and the Office of Policy Coordination (OPC). The OSO handled clandestine collection and foreign counter-intelligence while the OPC was responsible for covert action. The OSO was wholly responsible to the CIA while the OPC functioned under joint CIA–State Department guidance. The US experience with separate clandestine collection and covert action agencies paralleled the British experience. Thus, one historian has noted that:

> O.P.C.'s anomalous position in the Agency revealed the difficulty of maintaining two separate organizations for the execution of varying but overlapping clandestine activities. The close 'tradecraft' relationship between clandestine collection and covert action, and the frequent necessity for one to support the other was totally distorted with the separation of functions in O.S.O. and O.P.C. Organizational rivalry rather than interchange dominated the relationship between the two components.
>
> On the operating level the conflicts were intense. Each component had representatives conducting separate operations at each station. Given the related missions of

the two, O.P.C. and O.S.O. personnel were often competing for the same agents and, not infrequently, attempting to wrest agents from each other. In 1952 the outright hostility between the two organizations in Bangkok required the direct intervention of the Assistant Director for Special Operations, Lyman Kirkpatrick. There an important official was closely tied to O.P.C., and O.S.O. was trying to lure him into its employ.[23]

The OPC and the OSO were merged into the Directorate of Plans (now Operations) in 1952.

Determination of intelligence priorities and requirements

In conjunction with the requirement that the collation of intelligence be kept separate from collection, Lockhart has suggested that 'intelligence requirements and priorities must be laid down at the national and political level, and never at the departmental/ministerial level'.[24] This requirement is particularly pertinent with regard to collection requirements and priorities.

Within any government there will be numerous consumers of intelligence information. Obviously the agencies involved in foreign affairs and defence policy will require intelligence as will those involved in international economic matters. The need for distinct analytical products can be met to a large extent by allowing each consumer to maintain an analytical intelligence staff to supplement the analyses produced by whatever national agencies exist.

A far more difficult problem arises with respect to collection. Differing needs for finished intelligence imply differing judgments as to the most important collection targets or objectives. Yet it is unfeasible to allow each consumer to set up his own collection effort for intelligence that cannot be overtly acquired. The problems that would arise from the existence of multiple clandestine collection efforts should be clear from the discussion above. Multiple technical collection efforts would result in a waste of resources and be prohibitively expensive. However, an affordable national effort will not allow complete coverage of all targets — even in the case of the US or USSR. Hence, some judgment has to be exercised in the selection of targets — a judgment that logically needs to be made at 'the national and political level, and never at the departmental/ministerial level'.

Establishing a process whereby such judgments are made at the national level is an only partially achieved objective in the United States and Australia. As noted above, the original intent behind the creation of the Central Intelligence Agency was to establish an organization that would coordinate the intelligence activities of the various other US intelligence components and take the results of their work — in both collection and analysis — and produce a national estimate. While the CIA soon grew beyond this rather limited role it did not achieve anywhere near complete control over other agencies.

The need for a broader role for the Director of Central Intelligence has been a subject of contention for well over 25 years. Thus, in 1956 the President's Board of Consultants on Foreign Intelligence Activities stated that:

Despite his title the Director of Central Intelligence neither by law, directive nor otherwise, is the central director of the total intelligence effort of the government. Actually his control of intelligence *operations* is restricted to those of the Central Intelligence Agency. On the other hand, he does have a broad responsibility for the correlation, evaluation and dissemination of intelligence related to the national security.

But the dominant responsibility for the production of 'Departmental' intelligence ... rests with the head of each of the separate Departments and Agencies represented in the Intelligence Community.

In our judgement this arrangement, with its division of responsibility and despite the elaborate intelligence committee coordinating mechanism which exists, is not any longer adequate — wherever their Department needs are judged by them to be paramount the separate elements of the Intelligence Community are inclined to operate independently. This has resulted in an undue amount of built-in duplication in our national intelligence effort. It has also generated competition and frictions, some long standing, which have impeded the real integration of the intelligence activities of the separate elements of the Intelligence Community.

Thus, it concluded that:

a strong centralized direction, under which the resources of the various elements of the intelligence community would be brought closer together would do much to strengthen our national intelligence effort and to contain its cost.[25]

Attempts to bring such a proposal into operation have met with significant, although not complete or totally successful, resistance. Some 'theoretical' success at enhancing the powers of the DCI was achieved during the tenure of Richard Helms. On 5 November 1971 a number of management changes with respect to the intelligence community were announced. Included was the President's intention that the DCI advise him on community-wide budgetary allocations by serving in a last-review capacity. Helms established the Intelligence Community Staff as a replacement for the National Intelligence Programs Evaluation (NIPE). However, it did little and in order to maintain peace in the intelligence community Helms simply approved department requests.[26]

The most significant confrontation over the establishment of requirements and priorities occurred in the first year of the Carter Administration. Carter's Director of Central Intelligence, Admiral Stansfield Turner sought control over the entire intelligence community, most particularly the Department of Defense's National Reconnaissance Office and National Security Agency. Turner sought both budgetary and 'line' or management control over the NRO and the NSA. Under his plan both would report to the DCI rather than the Secretary of Defense.[27]

Turner argued that it would be a mistake to allow collection requirements and priorities to be dominated by technical military considerations. He further argued that economic and non-military information may be of greater value to the President and other policymakers than tactical military intelligence. The President's Chief Intelligence Officer, not the Secretary of Defense or Chairman of the Joint Chiefs of Staff, should determine the 'targets' given top priority by the National Security Agency and National Reconnaissance Office.[28]

Turner's proposal was opposed by Defense Secretary Harold Brown, who argued that military intelligence should be given first priority in matters of national security — that in the absence of control over the NSA and the NRO, the military would not be able to properly and authoritatively advise the President on military matters.[29] One intelligence official observed that 'the reconnaissance capability is considered the lifeblood of the military, and they are not about to relinquish it without another battle'.[30]

The conflict was partially resolved in President Carter's Executive Order 12036. The DCI was not given 'line' (day-to-day management) control over the NRO and the NSA but did receive substantial powers — at least on paper — over budgeting and tasking. In addition to affirming Turner's control over agency budgets the order created a National Intelligence Tasking Center (NITC) with offices for Photographic Intelligence, Signals Intelligence and Human Intelligence tasking. A deputy of DCI would be Director, NITC and in this manner the DCI could issue collection assignments to the NRO, the NSA and other collection agencies.[31] The NITC was generally ineffective, at least partially due to resistance from the other agencies, and was disbanded at the beginning of the Reagan Administration.

Thus, at present, the DCI has some control over the NRO and the NSA with regard to budgets and the influence that can be exercised on the appropriate NFIB committees but he lacks day-to-day management control. Hence, a significant portion of NRO and NSA collection requirements are determined at the department level.

With regard to Australia, the Office of National Assessments Act of 1977, which created the Office, stated that one function of ONA is to:

keep under review the activities connected with international intelligence that are engaged in by Australia and to bring to the notice of relevant Departments and Commonwealth Authorities any inadequacies in the nature, the extent, or the arrangements for coordination, of those activities that become apparent from time to time and suggest any improvements that should be made to remedy those inadequacies.[32]

While establishing itself as the main source of assessments, although not without competition from the JIO, ONA has not exercised the supervisory role created by law. As a latecomer on the Australian intelligence scene it is highly likely that the agencies with a longer history would be resentful of an ONA which attempted to significantly control their activities. Hence, in order to maintain peace in the Australian intelligence community ONA has largely refrained from attempting detailed supervision. Given the limitation of personnel and funds, detailed supervision is likely to be feasible only with the cooperation of the other agencies or aggressive support by the Prime Minister.[33]

Thus there has been an acknowledgement by some in the US and Australian intelligence communities of the desirability of Lockhart's principle. However the bureaucratic politics of those intelligence communities have imposed limitations on how fully it can be implemented.

Of the other three UKUSA intelligence communities only the British community provides a non-trivial case since both New Zealand and Canada have collection programs that are overwhelmingly dictated by their UKUSA participation and not their own national concerns. In the case of Britain, both the SIS and the GCHQ are under Foreign Office control. However, it is not clear whether the SIS and the GCHQ collection requirements (other than those imposed by the UKUSA arrangement) are predominantly based on Foreign Office needs or are determined by the JIC or its subcommittees.

Organizing for analysis

In his description of the requirements for an effective analytical capability, Andrew Marshall noted that 'intellectual competition, especially through competing analytic groups, is critical'.[34] The thesis that competing centres of analysis are crucial to a high quality intelligence product has become an axiom of many US intelligence observers in recent years.

Most of the advocates of competing centres have related what they consider to be CIA underestimates of Soviet military strength and spending to the absence of such competing centres.[35] In addition to what some see as a CIA predilection for interpreting intelligence in a way that is compatible with arms control and *detente* policies it has been charged that the CIA has a 'stranglehold' on the national estimating process.

It is argued that 'national estimates' often represent one particular viewpoint, not necessarily more valid than that of a department or military service, or a lowest common denominator approach which seeks to accommodate the views of all significant elements of the intelligence community. Thus, one critic has written: 'The "national" products of C.I.A. are characterized by the process which produces them. C.I.A. picks the topic for an estimate and assigns a principal drafter who then tries to write a paper reflecting the views on the topic of every agency in the Community.'[36] A less diplomatic assessment was made by Lieutenant General Daniel O. Graham, former Director of DIA:

The Army and Navy had an opinion that said that the Soviets had deployed few, if any, of these big missiles ...

There was an Air Force estimate that was very much higher, and if you look at those estimates back in those days and you say that the Army–Navy estimate is A, the Air Force estimate is B, you will find that the C.I.A. estimate is A+B over 2. That is not intelligence. That is bureaucratic machination.[37]

The answer to this problem, it is suggested, is to make competition rather than consensus the objective of intelligence analysis. The Team A–Team B episode concerning Soviet capabilities is often taken as a model of what such a competitive framework can accomplish.[38] Under such a framework the estimates of agencies other than the CIA would be treated as being equivalent to those of the CIA — disagreements then would be between coequal estimating institutions.

In apparent contradiction to the competing centres principle is Lockhart's principle that 'Ultimate collation of major matters is undertaken at the national level [while] a small high grade collating staff at national level is a key element in bringing balance to the whole intelligence field'.[39] It is somewhat ironic that of all the UKUSA intelligence and security communities the US community is the closest to satisfying the concept of competing centres while the others tend to conform to Lockhart's principle. Thus, despite the central role assigned to the CIA there are numerous other intelligence agencies capable of producing competing estimates — the INR, the DIA, the FTD — and they often do. Thus, the production of the Special National Intelligence Estimate of 27 May 1981 on *Soviet Support for International Terrorism and Revolutionary Violence* was completed '[a]fter several versions were drafted *alternatively* by C.I.A., DIA and C.I.A. again'.[40] In all instances, dissenting agencies may register dissent from national estimates or inter-agency intelligence memoranda via footnotes.

In some sense the US approach can be seen as a compromise between the competing centres approach (although arising from competing bureaucratic interests and different intelligence needs by various departments rather than by theoretical design) and a desire for a central, national level assessments staff.[41] In the other UKUSA nations competing centres exist to a smaller degree. The entire rationale for ONA's creation is the perceived need for a small high grade collating staff at the national level.[42] (At the same time the continued presence of the JIO serves to ensure a degree of competition. Indeed, one observer has noted that while the JIO no longer has a national assessments staff it does have an intelligence estimates staff which occupies the same offices and is developing a staff structure 'which looks remarkably like the old national assessments staff'.)[43] A similar perception resulted in the Canadian Commission of Inquiry's recommendation for the creation in the Prime Minister's office of a Bureau of Intelligence Assessments.[44]

As noted above, the British system depends heavily on the Assessments Staff attached to the Joint Intelligence Committee in addition to the Directorate of Requirements and Production of SIS. To the extent that the Defence Intelligence Staff's mandate is broad enough the possibility of competition with the JIC arises — assuming, of course, that the Assessments Staff does not simply take the work of the SIS and the DIS on disparate components of an issue and uses those as a basis for a national estimate.

The external-internal intelligence relationship and the structure of internal intelligence

There are several issues relating to links between external and internal intelligence activities as well as between internal security/intelligence functions. Some of the more significant specific issues are:

(1) whether external and internal intelligence (particularly counter-intelligence) functions should be handled by the same or separate organizations;
(2) whether security intelligence functions should be performed by an agency different from the one performing national criminal investigative duties; and
(3) whether within the area of security intelligence activities domestic security/counter-terrorism intelligence activities should be separated from counter-intelligence.

Lockhart suggests that 'in a democracy the internal security service should be kept separate from the external secret service with clearly defined responsibilities to separate Ministers'.[45] There are several arguments in favour of such an approach. Some would argue that the types of individuals required for each type of work are vastly different — in one case individuals who are willingly to accept a great deal of risk, live abroad and break foreign laws, and in the other individuals who see themselves as defenders of their own nation's law.

A related argument is that an agency which must break the law abroad should not be given internal functions, that to expect it to switch from its illegal activities to legal activities — to keep two set of rules in mind — as it crossed the border would be unrealistic.

Third, it has been suggested that a combination of external and internal (counter) intelligence would be a mistake since the excesses of one individual or group would then cover both the domestic and foreign areas.[46] Further, combining these functions would remove the checks and balances that exist when separate agencies handle domestic and foreign intelligence.

Others argue that counter-intelligence work is not divisible by borders, that cases move in and out of the nation's home territory and that an arrangement that requires shifting institutional responsibilities is inherently inefficient. Proponents of such a view recommended that the Reagan Administration create a separate counter-intelligence agency with both domestic and foreign mandates.[47]

At present the US, Britain and Australia all have separate agencies to fulfil their internal and external human intelligence requirements and have had such separate agencies for over 30 years. (While the FBI did conduct foreign intelligence operations in Latin America during the Second World War, and has at times tried to develop a foreign intelligence capability, its external role — in theory and practice — has been negligible.)

Neither Canada nor New Zealand have external human intelligence collection programs at present. As noted in Chapter 5, the Canadian Commission of Inquiry did recommend that the new Canadian domestic security intelligence service have powers allowing it to collect intelligence abroad. However, with different personnel requirements for internal and external intelligence in mind Canadian officials gave serious consideration to the creation of a separate clandestine collection service — one whose existence would not be publicly acknowledged.

With respect to the potential separation of security intelligence and national criminal investigative functions it has been argued that a security intelligence service often 'has' to operate outside the law and hence its duties would be inappropriate for a national police force. Others would suggest that precisely because of the temptation to operate outside the law it is necessary to have individuals who are trained to enforce the law performing internal intelligence functions — particularly with respect to domestic security matters. Thus, Roderick McLeod, the Ontario Assistant Deputy Attorney General asserted that the agency replacing the RCMP Security Service may ultimately employ people lacking the discipline and accountability to senior officers that he believed characterize RCMP investigators.[48]

With the creation of the Canadian Security Intelligence Service, the United States became the only UKUSA nation to combine national criminal investigative functions and primary security intelligence functions in the same agency. The Canadian SIS, NZSIS, British Security Service, and ASIO are all agencies with security intelligence functions only.

The final issue discussed here is the possible separation of domestic security intelligence work from counter-intelligence work. Domestic security intelligence work or 'counter-subversion' is generally directed at political–social groups which are perceived to present a threat to 'society' because of their propensity for violence or ability to obstruct the lawful functioning of government.[49] Counter-intelligence is primarily aimed at preventing the disclosure of classified information to foreign agents, although it may also involve preventing successful foreign covert action. Thus, when a subversive group is supported by a foreign government, domestic security intelligence and counter-intelligence may overlap.

The overwhelming evidence, however, is that, at least in the UKUSA nations, domestic 'subversive' groups have not been funded by foreign sources. Thus, a significant rationale for the separation of domestic security intelligence and counter-intelligence functions might be said to exist. To this point, only the US has effected such a sharp separation. As noted above, in 1977 the FBI separated domestic security/terrorism intelligence activities from counter-intelligence activities, assigning the former to the Criminal Investigative Division and the latter to the Intelligence Division. In Britain the Security Service handles both functions, although maintaining separate directorates, while in Australia different sections within the same directorate are responsible for both functions. The Canadian Security Intelligence Service will be responsible for both activities.

13

Dissent and the UKUSA security services

Individual freedom ceases to exist from the moment the community has reason to believe that every wall has ears, that the expressed opinion, the casual remark, are noted. Security not left within strict limits ceases to be a protector. It becomes an oppressive shadow in the lives of the community. [Editorial, 'Security Can Go Too Far', (*New Zealand*) *Evening Post*, 4 October 1966.]

Within the last decade the activities of the intelligence communities of Australia, Canada, New Zealand and the United States have come under official scrutiny by select governmental investigating bodies. In each case, a major (or the exclusive) reason for the inquiry has been the domestic activities of those intelligence communities and, in particular, of their security services.

In each case, also, the investigating bodies have discovered a wide range of security service activity which would generally be considered either improper or clearly illegal. These activities have been directed against a wide range of individuals and groups. Some of these individuals and groups advocated radical (but non-violent) change in various aspects of the political, economic and social status quo, while others were relatively close to the political mainstream.

The activities directed against such groups have been extensive and varied. In some cases activity has been 'restricted' to the creation of files, collection of information on group political positions and members, and attendance (surveillance) at its public meetings and rallies. Such information may be collected via open sources (for example, group pamphlets, newspapers, open avowals of affiliation) or by more surreptitious means (for example photographing the licence plates of cars parked outside a meeting hall).

In other cases groups may be infiltrated by security service members or their informants. Such infiltrators may be used solely to collect information on the group and its members. Alternatively, infiltrators may attempt to influence the activities of the group. Influence may be exerted in an attempt to prevent violence or, as has often been the case, in an attempt to push the group into illegal activity. An infiltrator who succeeds in provoking illegal and/or violent activity allows the security service or police to invoke legal sanctions and helps to discredit the group in the eyes of the general public.

A third class of activity is mail surveillance and electronic surveillance. Mail surveillance includes both mail cover and mail opening operations. A mail cover operation involves noting either the return address on letters to a targeted individual or group or the address on letters sent by a targeted individual or group. Electronic surveillance includes placing microphones in a residence, hotel, meeting place or business office and interception of phone calls — either by phone tapping or interception of microwave transmissions. The extent to which such surveillance is legal (and the circumstances under which it is) varies among the above-mentioned countries.[1] However, it is generally agreed that such activities are unacceptable when used to monitor non-violent political activity.

Another form of intrusive activity is the break-in (also known as black-bag jobs) — that is, uncontested physical searches or surreptitious entries. Break-ins have been conducted to acquire information as well as to install microphones. In many cases the information acquired from break-ins or electronic surveillance has been used in support of what has been referred to as 'dirty tricks', domestic covert action or disruption activities. The objective of such activity is to damage the effectiveness of a particular individual, group or movement. The objective may be achieved by promoting factionalism within a group, causing or aggravating disputes between groups, or by leaking information to the media which is designed to discredit a particular individual or group.

In this chapter we will first review various instances of such activities by the security services of the United States, Australia, Canada, New Zealand and the United Kingdom. While the latter nation's security service has not been the subject of a recent governmental inquiry, there is substantial reason to believe that its activities have involved the same actions as those of the other nations' security services. Second, we will explore the potential explanations for the similarity between security service activities in all five nations — an especially interesting question given that one supposed aspect of their common heritage is political tolerance. Third, we will consider the consequences of such security service activities — both in terms of their effect on national security and on the domestic political process.

Before we proceed to discuss the security services involved and the activities outlined above, several caveats are in order. No attempt is made to give a full quantitative description of the extent of surveillance, break-ins, etc. Quantitative information is available only in the cases of the United States and Canada. No attempt is made to discuss the differing legal frameworks under which the security services operate. As noted above, while there is some variation in the laws regarding the legality of the use of techniques such as mail openings and phone tappings, it is generally agreed

Dissent and the UKUSA security services 285

that their use to monitor or disrupt non-violent political activity is unacceptable.

Finally, this paper focuses only on the activities of the UKUSA security services and the police and special branches that act as surrogates or executive agents. (In the case of the United States, the domestic activities of the Central Intelligence Agency and National Security Agency are considered in Chapter 6.) We wish to explore the way in which the security services have carried out the 'counter-subversion' duties that are part of their charters. While evidence of improper domestic activity by other agencies without such a domestic mandate merits attention and is certainly disturbing, it is of more interest to examine the activities of those services which have conducted 'counter-subversion' activities for a significant period of time and which will continue to conduct such activities for the foreseeable future. For it is the pattern of their activities which best permits generalizations concerning the rationale for such activities.

Surveillance and monitoring

Surveillance and monitoring of dissent are two activities that have been engaged in by the UKUSA security services. Surveillance may involve attendance at meetings or rallies or photographing participants at them. Thus, it involves observance of individual or group activities as they are being conducted. Monitoring involves collection and analysis of information about individuals and groups of interest. It may involve use of purely public source information (for example, group pamphlets, newspaper and position papers) or the supplementary use of non-public information (for example, membership lists, tax records, permit applications). Since their creation, all of the UKUSA security services have engaged in such activities against political and social dissenters.

Shortly after its formation in 1949, the Australian Security Intelligence Organisation infiltrated Dr Michael Bialoguski into the New South Wales Peace Council. Bialoguski's function was to report on the names, addresses and occupations of those present and the proceedings of the meetings, the agenda, the motions and discussions.[2]

After 1953, the South Australian Special Branch opened files on a wide range of individuals and groups. A 1976 investigation uncovered 300 separate dossiers and 40 000 index cards (28 000 of which referred to individual persons), the greater part of which concerned 'matters, organizations and persons unrelated to genuine security risks'.[3]

The information collected concerned non-communist socialist parties, political files relating to Australian Labor Party personalities and information on Federal, State and municipal elections. Additionally, files were maintained on the Australian Council of Trade Unions, campus activities concerned with the Vietnam war, peace and anti-uranium activities, the Council of Civil Liberties, Eastern and Orthodox church groups, and those advocating workers' participation in industry. Further, homosexuals, antiracial discrimination groups and groups advocating divorce law reform and constitutional reform were also the subject of entries in security records.[4]

During the Vietnam war films were taken in Canberra of demonstrations against the war. These films had special departmental showings, in which senior departmental officers were called in from all departments, not just those with a security connection, to identify any of their staff for the benefit of attending ASIO personnel.[5]

The 1979–80 ASIO Annual Report indicates that monitoring activity is conducted against both left- and right-wing groups. The report suggests that 'small but highly motivated subversive groups outside the communist parties are prepared to undertake acts of violence and disruption in their protests on certain issues, notably unemployment and uranium mining'. Right-wing groups include the various 'Immigration Control' groups whose activities, according to the report, 'while not revolutionary promote division and hatred within the country'.[6]

In the United Kingdom, the Security Service and Special Branch devote a great deal of attention to surveillance and monitoring. In 1948, instructions were issued to Chief Constables throughout the country to compile lists of people believed to be members of the Communist Party and its front organizations. This practice continues today, with the lists being collated nationally by the Special Branch and forwarded to MI-5.[7]

Surveillance and monitoring of trade unions has been a particular concern of the British security agencies. The Attlee Administration of 1945–51 established a separate squad of the Special Branch to investigate communists in the trade unions and report on unofficial strikes.[8] In his memoirs, Harold Wilson notes that in the 1964–70 period the Special Branch kept close watch on the movements of the leaders of the seamen's union and informed him when they were visited by members of the Communist Party.[9]

A more recent instance of monitoring of unionist activity concerns a shop steward who worked in a Carnation Foods factory in Dumfries. The report was prepared by a detective of the Dumfries and Galloway Special Branch in response to a request by the Security Service and stated, in part, that:

Hogg has been described by a *management contact* as being more than usually active in union debates within the factory and is thought of as very left wing. Hogg is thought to be connected with the Socialist Workers Party also, although this cannot be verified at present and is based solely on hearsay information *from inside* the Carnation Foods factory.

Hogg cannot proceed any further within the Carnation Foods factory either in a work capacity or within the union structure at the factory and it's *thought by management* that he may well leave sometime in the near future to take up some of full employment with the TGNU. The situation will obviously be *monitored* and any further development will be reported in due course. [Emphasis added][10]

Aside from union activity, the Security Service and Special Branch monitor others forms of political activity. Thus, the activities of the

Campaign for Nuclear Disarmament (CND) have come under close scrutiny. The Special Branch uses the police forces of local areas to note the names and addresses of those writing letters to local papers in support of CND positions. They also note the registration numbers of cars parked outside meetings. In addition, they take photographs of CND marches in their cities and pass them on to the Special Branch.[11]

The various types of information collected (not only about the CND) by the local police and passed on to the Special Branch include:

- all names of political activists appearing in the press
- all names of those signing petitions to Parliament
- papers, magazines and leaflets of political groups
- names of those who attend or help the defense in certain trials
- information concerning demonstrations and meetings.[12]

In some cases surveillance and monitoring is conducted with respect to a specific event. Thus, the Special Branch Superintendent at Holyhead sent the following Confidential instructions to all stations in Anglesey in 1968:

In connection with proposed investiture of the Prince of Wales at Caernarvon in 1969, the activities of the above mentioned societies [the Welsh Language Society and the Welsh Nationalist Party] are being watched. Please submit to this office full details of all persons presently known to be connected with any of these societies or being sympathizers therewith ... Details of movements or activities in connection with these activities should also be reported.[13]

The capability of the British Security Service to engage in surveillance and monitoring and to retrieve data has been enhanced over the last five years. Its Mayfair based computer has a storage capacity of 20 million files and is connected to a growing network of other government data banks. Information is passed among Inland Revenue, the Department of Health and Social Security, the Department of Employment and the Security Service.[14]

Surveillance and monitoring activities have also been extensively conducted in the United States. FBI files indicate that in the 1946–48 period numerous political dissidents were the subject of FBI investigations. These individuals included actors Frederic March and Edward G. Robinson, prominent New Dealers Edward Condon and David Niles, supporters of Henry Wallace's Progressive Party presidential campaign, and opponents of the House Committee on Un-American Activities.[15] And, more recently, the FBI monitored the activities of the late John Lennon with regard to both his public appearances and his personal life.[16]

By 1975, the FBI was conducting surveillance of 1100 organizations and their subdivisions. In 1974, it had 19 659 domestic intelligence files. Ninety per cent of these involved individual targets investigated because of a suspected relationship (for example, membership or support) to a target group or, in a small number of cases, due to suspected personal involvement in activities such as demonstrations.[17]

That such security service activity may involve monitoring of groups whose activities are in no way related to national security issues is illustrated by the fact that in the spring of 1971, on assignment from the White House, the FBI's Domestic Intelligence Division monitored a nationwide series of Earth Day rallies (National Environment Teach-Ins) sponsored by an environmental protection group, including a group of interested Congressmen.[18]

In Canada a wide range of individuals and groups have been subject to surveillance. Included in the surveillance have been leaders and members of the National Farmers' Union, National Democratic Party, Canadian Association of University Teachers, the Parti Quebecois, the National Indian Brotherhood and the former Waffle faction of the NDP.[19]

It has been asserted that in New Zealand no individuals involved strictly in protest or dissent are placed under surveillance by the Security Intelligence Service.[20] However, according to Chief Ombudsman Sir Guy Powles, 'virtually every form of protest and dissent — not necessarily either very militant or very radical — falls within the Service's net'.[21] This was justified to Powles by the NZSIS on the grounds that the activities of anti-establishment protesters and radical dissent groups could become subversive and have an 'inherent potential' for subversion. Thus, those who supported the 'No Maoris, No Tour' campaign and members of the Citizen's All Black Tour Association were investigated for communist leanings.[22]

As of 1976, about 10 per cent of the NZSIS's counter subversion work was concerned with protest groups although, allegedly, monitoring involved use only of overt sources.[23] Notwithstanding the source of information, 'personal files have been opened on a number of people engaged in political protest activities which suggest they might conceivably in the future become subversive or become the target for subversives'.[24]

Infiltration

Infiltration of dissenting groups, which may be labelled subversive or 'potentially' subversive, may be conducted for several reasons. Infiltration may be considered useful or necessary to conduct surveillance and monitoring — as in the case of Dr Biagoluski's infiltration of the New South Wales Peace Council. In other instances, the security service may seek to infiltrate groups to determine if they have been infiltrated by subversive/communist elements. Finally, the security service may infiltrate individuals to effect the outcome of group decision-making or serve as *agent provocateurs*.

Thus, the New Zealand Security Intelligence Service has 'penetrated both the Socialist Unity Party and Communist Party to their cores', with the object of obtaining information on those groups and all of their members.[25] In the 1950s and 1960s, there was evidence of NZSIS infiltration of college campuses. A security agent was elected secretary of a student left-wing club at Victoria University of Wellington in the early 1950s, and absconded with all the records including membership lists.[26] In 1969, a security officer who had been a student at Victoria University during the two previous years attempted to recruit students at Victoria to spy on outside organizations such as the Committee on Vietnam.[27]

Outside college campuses there have also been instances of attempted NZSIS infiltration of peace groups. In 1964, a security officer, D. Godfrey, allegedly approached a young woman and requested her to become secretary of a peace council and turn over copies of minutes of the council's meetings. In 1972, an NZSIS officer is reported to have asked at least one individual to inform on the Auckland Anti-War Mobilization Committee.[28]

In the United States the FBI has extensively infiltrated the US Communist Party since the 1930s, with the infiltration penetrating to the highest levels of the party.[29] At one point the infiltration was so extensive that there was one informer for every 5.7 members.[30] It has also infiltrated political and social movements to determine if they were 'subversive' or were being infiltrated by subversive elements. Thus, the Women's Liberation Movement was infiltrated to gather information concerning the movement's policies, leaders and members. Despite the conclusion that the movement's purpose was 'to free women from the humdrum existence of being only a wife and mother', it was recommended that the investigation be continued.[31]

Under its COMINFIL (Communist Infiltration) program, the Bureau sought to determine if various organizations had been infiltrated by communists. This program involved Bureau infiltration of such organizations as the Southern Christian Leadership Conference, the National Association for the Advancement of Colored People, the Northern Virginia Citizens Concerned About the ABM, and the National Conference on Vietnam Veterans.[32]

The RCMP Security Service, on several occasions, has infiltrated *agent provocateurs*. In the early 1970s, it infiltrated an officer into the Partisan Party, which had grown out of the Vancouver Liberation Front (VLF). The VLF had its beginnings on the campus of Simon Fraser University as an alliance of radical political groups, black activists, militant feminists, anti-war radicals and US draft evaders, and it adopted a pro-violence position.[33] The Partisan Party renounced this stance in favour of a non-violent posture and concentrated on community-oriented work with the goal of winning popular support. The RCMP infiltrator consistently opposed the party's anti-violence posture. During demonstrations he urged others to kick in windows and engage in other (minor) illegal acts.[34]

In another operation an RCMP agent infiltrated various Black and Indian groups to offer them weapons and training. The alleged objective was 'to determine if such groups were violence prone'.[35] The infiltrator was recruited from the United States with the help of the US Justice Department. A false immigration record was arranged for him in order to enhance his credibility.[36]

Mail surveillance and electronic surveillance

Two of the more intrusive techniques employed by the UKUSA security services are mail surveillance and electronic surveillance. As noted above, mail surveillance involves either noting the addresses on an envelope or opening the envelope and examining its contents, while electronic surveillance may involve planting microphones in a home, office or hotel room or intercepting phone messages (either by phone tapping or microwave interception).

Both the RCMP Security Service and the FBI have engaged in extensive mail surveillance operations. The RCMP program, known as Operation Cathedral, lasted from the 1950s until 1977 and involved mail covers and mail openings. Mail openings were estimated to have been in the hundreds.[37]

In the period between 1970 and 1977, 66 mail opening operations took place. Twenty-one occurred in the 1970–73 period in Quebec and were related to persons known or suspected of Front Libre du Quebec (FLQ) terrorist activity, eleven involved persons known or suspected to be involved in international terrorism, twenty-five involved persons known or suspected to be involved in foreign espionage or foreign covert action, and nine were classified as 'miscellaneous'.[38]

The FBI conducted eight mail opening programs in as many cities between 1940 and 1966, one of which was conducted for all 26 years. FBI programs were intended to aid in the detection of Soviet and Chinese communist agents and hence were limited to communications between the selected US cities and the USSR and the PRC.[39] However, 'information was obtained regarding two domestic anti-war organizations and government employees and other Americans who expressed "pro-Communist" sympathies'.[40] Additionally, between 1958 and 1973, under Project HUNTER, the Bureau received copies of 75 000 intercepted letters from the CIA's mail opening program.[41]

The RCMP Security Service and the FBI have also engaged in various forms of electronic surveillance. Between 1971 and February 1978, the Security Service installed 223 long-term listening devices and 357 short-term devices. In 1972, 42 major installations were carried out — seventeen of these installations were counter-espionage related while 25 were 'counter-subversion' related.[42]

Until 1972, the FBI engaged in extensive warrantless electronic surveillance for both counter-espionage and counter-subversion purposes. The counter-subversion electronic surveillance was directed at both individuals and groups. Thus, the hotel room of one Congressman was bugged, while Dr Martin Luther King, Jr. was subject to extensive electronic surveillance.[43] Additionally, the offices of a wide range of political organizations were subject to electronic surveillance — the Communist Party, the American Civil Liberties Union, the Black Panther Party, the Student Non-Violent Co-ordinating Committee, the Institute for Policy Studies, and the Students for a Democratic Society.[44]

Both the Australian and New Zealand security services have also made use of electronic surveillance. Apparently, an attempt was made to bug the headquarters of the Communist Party of Australia in Dixon Street, Sydney. The CPA found a tie line which led down the wall next door into a telephone junction under the street pavement and exhibited its find to the Australian Broadcasting Corporation. Presumably, the purpose of the bugging was to record meetings at which members would report on overseas congresses they had attended.[45]

In addition, evidence suggests the bugging of Dr Jim Cairns, a former Australian Labor MP. Cairns was able to identify information that allegedly appeared in an ASIO report as part of a conversation he had in his home with a conscientious objector.[46] ASIO's Annual Report for 1980–81 indicated that it was tapping nineteen phones in March 1973 and 58 as of 31 October 1980.[47]

The New Zealand SIS has apparently also been involved in mail openings and electronic surveillance. In the late 1960s, the chief of the NZSIS, Brigadier Gilbert, was quoted as saying that after identifying a 'subversive' person 'we use whatever means are available to us. These obviously vary a great deal'.[48] During the administration of Norman Kirk (1972–74), the Deputy Director of the NZSIS confirmed that the organization had been bugging Trevor Richards at HART (Halt All Racist Tours) headquarters in Rugby Street, Christchurch.[49] Additionally, it has been alleged that in the 1960s the Peace, Power of Politics Conference (which ran counter to the SEATO conference) and John Thew, a Labour Party nominee, were bugged.[50]

Break-ins

As with the techniques discussed above, the use of break-ins or surreptitious entries is not confined to any one of the UKUSA security services. It has been suggested that a series of break-ins into the cars and homes of members of the Agee/Hosenball Defence Committee was the work of the British Security Service and Special Branch. The car of the treasurer of the organization was broken into twice within two weeks. On the first occasion, a handbag with the paying-in and paying-out records of the committee was stolen. Subsequently, the passport, driving licence, diary and cheque book that were in the handbag were returned. In the second instance, papers were rifled through but nothing was taken. Several months later, the home of Aidan White, a member of the Defence Committee, was ransacked, with papers being rifled and files entered but no valuables taken.[51]

In the case of Canada and the United States there is evidence of break-ins having been conducted on a large scale. The MacDonald Commission found evidence of about 400 warrantless break-ins by the entire RCMP.[52] Between 1971 and 1978, 55 break-ins were conducted to install listening devices, while 47 were conducted to search for and/or photograph documents and physical evidence.[53] The latter 47 break-ins involved 34 targets — thirteen being 'hit' twice.[54]

Two specific RCMP Security Service operations involving break-ins were

Operation Ham and Operation Bricole. Operation Ham involved a break-in by the E Special Unit of the Security Service at the offices of a private company holding membership lists and financial data of the Parti Quebecois (PQ). The intent was to remove the PQ computer tapes, copy them in another location, and return them before the night was out.[55]

Operation Ham was allegedly motivated by several factors — a persistent leakage of federal documents into the hands of the PQ which appeared to be the result of a systematic attempt to gather sensitive documents, a report of foreign funding of the PQ, and the fear that there was a movement of extreme nationalists into the PQ with the objective of taking it over.[56] Recently, there have also been allegations of a foreign espionage connection to the PQ in the 1973 time period.[57]

The Security Service wanted to check the membership lists to determine if there were PQ members who had access to the leaked documents and to establish whether there were geographical or other patterns in extremist participation in the PQ. Financial data would be used to determine the existence of any foreign funding. The data were acquired but yielded nothing of value.[58]

Operation Bricole was a cooperative effort among G section of the Security Service, the Montreal Urban Community Police and the Sûreté du Quebec. On 6 October 1972, the building containing the headquarters of two left-wing action groups — the Agence Presse Libre du Quebec (APLQ) and the Movement Pour La Defense des Prisonniers Politiques du Quebec (MDPPQ) — was entered. By 2 a.m. half a tonne of documents had been loaded into a truck outside.[59] The raid had two objectives: to produce intelligence for the police forces and to diminish the effectiveness of the groups by lowering morale and hindering fund-raising capabilities.[60]

In the United States the FBI engaged in break-ins on a massive scale until 1966. The offices of the Socialist Workers Party and its affiliate offices in New York City were burglarized at least 92 times between 1960 and 1966. Ten thousand photographs of documents (correspondence, records and letters) were made. Additionally, two related burglaries were conducted at private homes.[61]

Further, in the early 1970s, break-ins were regularly conducted by the New York City FBI office to obtain entrance to the homes of friends and relatives of Weather Underground fugitives, both to forage for clues to their whereabouts and to plant microphones.[62] Additional break-ins in quest of such information were conducted in Los Angeles and Oregon.[63] An agent from the Chicago office testified to having participated in 238 break-ins and said that 24 agents were assigned to the full-time burglarizing of homes of Communist Party members.[64]

In Australia there is evidence of at least two break-ins conducted by ASIO in 1971–72. One was at the home of Douglas White, a member of the editorial board of a leftist theoretical journal (*Arena*). ASIO had formed the opinion that White was at the centre of New Left protest over Vietnam. Told by an informant that White would be visiting his sick wife on a specific weekend in January 1971, ASIO went in, looked at his books, examined his correspondence and left enough mess to suggest a visitation by local hoodlums.[65]

The second instance involved W. Alexander Boag, an accountant who prepared tax returns for E.G. Hill, chairman of the Communist Party of Australia (Marxist-Leninist). During 1972, ASIO gained repeated access to the records in Boag's office and apparently made photostats of a number of them.[66]

Finally, in 1960, the New Zealand Security Service conducted several break-ins. In April and August the Security Service broke in and entered the Communist Party headquarters in Auckland in order to install radio transmitters.[67] Additionally, a Labour Cabinet Minister, Sir Evera Tirikatena, caught a security officer going through his files at a time when anyone who supported the 'No Maoris, No Tour' movement was considered a security risk.[68]

Dirty tricks

Under the heading of dirty tricks or domestic covert action comes a wide range of activities. These include attempts to ferment factionalism within groups or to create or exacerbate disputes between groups, to disrupt personal relationships, to damage the reputation of individuals or groups by causing actions/intentions to be falsely attributed to them, or by leaking to the media derogatory 'information' concerning an individual.

Prior to 1977, ASIO maintained a Special Projects Section, one of whose functions was to prepare material for 'countersubversive covert spoiling activities'. In one instance a journalist was approached and offered a continuous supply of Special Projects materials as the basis for starting a magazine.[69]

In Canada various types of dirty tricks have been employed by the RCMP Security Service. Such activities date back to at least 1956. In that year the RCMP apparently distributed at least one letter prepared by the RCMP among members of the Labour Progressive Party. The letter was designed to appear to have been written by a member of the party and attacked the Soviet Union on a vital issue and the Soviet Communist Party's post-Stalin leadership in general.[70]

Between 1971 and 1974, a national program of 'disruptive countermeasures' was conducted under the codenames ODDBALL and CHECKMATE by a Special Operations Group at headquarters.[71] CHECKMATE operations included an approach to the employer of a person regarded as a terrorist or a supporter of a 'subversive' group with a view towards persuading the employer to discharge the person. In another two instances, the Security Service spread information, believed to be true, to discredit the leader or other members of political or other organizations to create dissension among subversive groups. On another occasion, the Security Service spread information, known to be false, designed to discredit a leader of an organization regarded as 'subversive'.[72] The Security Service also drafted false letters, filed false tax returns, made threatening phone calls and attempted to immobilize a suspect's car with chemicals. It also used confidential medical files as part of the disruptive tactics against certain groups.[73]

A prime target of the RCMP Security Service dirty tricks was the FLQ. A memo signed by the Director General of the Security Service on 22 February 1971 specified that Disruptive Tactics be employed against the FLQ, including 'Making use of sophisticated and well motivated plans built around existing situations such as power struggles, love affairs, fraudulent use of funds, information on drug use, etc., to cause dissension and splintering of the separatist/terrorist groups'.[74] Specific tactics used against the FLQ included the burning of a barn owned by an FLQ member's relative, that was believed to serve as a meeting place for various groups, as well as issuance of a fake FLQ communiqué urging violence.[75]

The biggest employer of dirty tricks has been the US Federal Bureau of Investigation. The most notorious of its operations was the one directed against Martin Luther King, Jr.[76] Minor dirty tricks involved the passing of information to newspapers on the past communist affiliation of King advisers and attempting to block honorary degrees awarded by Marquette University and Springfield (Mass.) College by notifying school officials of personal material.[77]

The most drastic operation centred around tapes of King's extramarital sexual activities that the Bureau had acquired by bugging King's hotel rooms. At the end of 1963, William C. Sullivan, head of the Domestic Intelligence Division, authored a memo which suggested the removal of King from his 'pedestal' and his replacement by the 'right kind of national Negro leaders . . .'[78]

In November 1964, King was sent an edited tape of the material and a note written (but not signed) by Sullivan. The note said:

KING
In view of your low grade . . . I will not dignify your name with either a Mr. or a Reverend or a Dr. And, your last name calls to mind only the type of king such as King Henry the VIII . . .
King, look into your heart. You know you are a complete fraud and a great liability to all of us Negroes. White people in this country have enough frauds of their own but I am sure that they don't have one at this time that is anywhere near your equal. You are no clergyman and you know it. I repeat you are colossal fraud and an evil vicious one at that. You could not believe in God . . . Clearly you don't believe in any personal moral principles.
King, like all frauds your end is approaching. You could have been our greatest leader. You, even at an early age, have turned out to be not a leader but a dissolute, abnormal moral imbecile. We will now have to depend on our elder leaders like Wilkins, a man of character and thank God we have others like him. But you are done. Your 'honorary' degrees, your Nobel Prize (what a grim farce) and other awards will not save you.

King, I repeat you are done

No person can overcome facts, not even a fraud like yourself ... I repeat no person can argue successfully against facts. You are finished ... And some of them pretend to be ministers of the Gospel. Satan could not do more. What incredible evilness ... King you are done.

The American public, the church, organizations that have been helping — Protestant, Catholic and Jews will know you for what you are — an evil, abnormal beast. So will others who have backed you. You are done.

King, there is only one thing left for you to do. You know what it is. You have just 34 days in which to do it ... You are done. There is but one way out for you. Your better take it before your filthy, abnormal fraudulent self is bared to the nation.[79]

Beyond such operations directed at specific individuals, the FBI conducted a series of Counter-intelligence Programs (COINTELPROs) directed at a wide variety of groups. The first COINTELPRO was initiated in 1956 against the Communist Party (COINTELPRO–CPUSA). Subsequently, other programs were directed against the Social Workers Party (1961–69), White Hate Groups (1964–71), Black Nationalist Hate Groups (1967–71), and the New Left (1968–71).[80] Other COINTELPROs were directed against US-based Puerto Rican independence groups in the US, Yugoslav and Cuban agents in the US, as well as a joint program with the Mexican police to interfere with the relationship between the US and Mexican communist parties. Additionally, Operation Hoodwink was an attempt to disrupt and cause a dispute between the Mafia and the CPUSA.[81] Termination of the COINTELPROs resulted after a raid at an FBI office in Media, Pennsylvania, that threatened to — and eventually did — expose the program.

In each of these cases a wide range of dirty tricks was employed against each group or set of groups. In the case of the New Left COINTELPRO, a large percentage (39 per cent) of all actions attempted to keep the targets from speaking, teaching and writing. Specific tactics used included anonymous letters, contacting employers and funding organizations to get targets fired or funding halted.[82] Thus, in the case of Morris Starsley, an associate professor of philosophy at Arizona State University from 1964–70 and an organizer of anti-war teach-ins and rallies, the Bureau sent an anonymous letter about him to a committee of professors who were reviewing his faculty appointment. The letter accused him of involvement in activities on a par with those of the Nazi or Soviet Secret Police. In what appeared to be a direct result, he lost his teaching post and was unable to find another.[83]

In the case of the Black Nationalist COINTELPRO, attempts were made to encourage gang warfare and falsely label targets as informants. Thus, the Bureau sought to stimulate violence between the Black Panther Party and the United Slaves organization.[84]

The FBI also sought to discredit the American Indian Movement (AIM) and anti-nuclear power activists. In May 1976, the Bureau's Chicago office falsely reported to the Nuclear Regulatory Commission that motorcycle gangs and Indians 'were planning to take over the Zion Station nuclear plant in Illinois'. The report was apparently part of a nationwide attempt to discredit AIM. As part of this campaign, the Bureau sent similar and more extreme reports of planned Indian terrorism to the Justice Department, US Marshal's Office, Secret Service and NRC.[85]

As part of its campaign to discredit anti-nuclear activists, the FBI channelled information to a media source in an attempt to discredit Karen Silkwood. Silkwood, a 28-year-old lab technician, was killed in a mysterious car crash in 1974 while on her way to give a reporter documentary evidence of lax safety regulations at the Kerr-McGee plutonium plant in Oklahoma.[86] Jacques Srouji, a copy editor for the *Nashville Tennessean*, was given access to approximately 1000 pages from the FBI's investigative files on the Silkwood case, including those dealing with her personal life. This material was used in a chapter of Srouji's book on nuclear power, which was in favour of nuclear power.[87] Additionally, the Bureau spread rumours concerning the sexual activities of a Congressman, his aide, a publisher and union official involved in the case in an attempt to discredit them.[88]

Why?

It is striking that the security services of five nations, each of which is supposedly dedicated to democratic freedom and tolerance, should all have engaged in such a wide range of repressive activities. These activities have occurred over a long period of time (not just since the advent of the Cold War) and irrespective of the external threat faced. Thus one must look for some common basis for these activities.

Part of the explanation may lie in a 'policeman's world view' in which those substantially different from the mainstream are considered potential sources of subversion and therefore must be watched — whether their differences are political or cultural. Thus, Sir Harold Scott, Commissioner of the Metropolitan Police from 1945 to 1953, wrote that 'The Special Branch ... is primarily an intelligence department. Its business is to keep watch on any body of people, of whatever political complexion, whose activities seem likely to result sooner or later in open acts of sedition or disorder'.[89] Similarly, the RCMP Security Service described its role with respect to Canadian Indians as:

One of monitoring the tone and temper of the Native population in Canada for the purpose of forewarning government and law enforcement agencies of impending disorder and conflict. Within this context, it is necessary to identify subversive elements (foreign or domestic) striving to influence or manipulate native grievances for ulterior motives.[90]

A second factor may be the espionage version of the 'Lessons of Munich' — the 'lesson' learned as a result of the infiltration of Soviet agents into US and British foreign affairs, defence and intelligence agencies during the 1930s and 1940s.[91] Charles Brennan of the FBI justified the Bureau's investigative programs against Vietnam war opponents with no prior involvement in violence on the basis of future need. Such programs were set up, he said, in order to avoid the 'tragic mistakes' of the 1930s, when college students, moved by the Depression, became involved with communist activities and were subsequently employed in sensitive positions in government which had no records of their earlier communist involvement; 'I do not want a repetition of that sort of circumstance to come about'.[92] A similar justification for such programs could be found in the view expressed to Sir Guy Powles by the New Zealand SIS: 'In the matter of threats of New Zealand security no clear distinction can be drawn between espionage and subversion, as those areas are interrelated and complementary and the significance of both is approximately equal'.[93]

Such a world view may be partially the product of the training and background of SIS members. Thus it has been noted that NZSIS recruits are usually 'young, perhaps with a military service background, right-wing, and jingoistic. Such people find it hard to differentiate between a Communist and a member of the New Zealand Labour Party'.[94]

While such factors as mentioned above can be judged to have had some role in motivating the activities of the security services, they are not sufficient to explain such activities completely. The first, if taken as the major explanation, would imply that the pattern of activities that has emerged over many years in each of the nations has been due mainly to over-zealousness and narrowmindedness of security officials against the wishes of their more 'liberal' political superiors. Despite the FBI's stretching of presidential directives, it is difficult to accept such an explanation with respect to the United States, especially with regard to the use of the FBI under the Kennedy, Johnson and Nixon Administrations.[95] Likewise, a former Director-General of the RCMP Security Service stated that he found it 'very difficult to accept the thesis that ministers were not aware in general terms of the problems of the security service in carrying out their activities of this kind'. And indeed, the Commission of Inquiry (MacDonald Commission) concluded that Prime Minister Trudeau knew that the RCMP was engaged in law-breaking.[96]

The second factor is also not sufficient to explain the breadth of security service activities. When one looks at the organizations subject to surveillance and harassment — the New South Wales Peace Council and anti-Vietnam war demonstrations (Australia), the National Unemployed Worker's Movement and CND (Britain), Black, Indian and separatist groups (Canada), Women's Liberation, NAACP, ACLU, Socialist Workers Party (United States) — it is apparent that a broader explanation is required.

Such an explanation may be that the subversion being combated is not subversion of the state but subversion of the prevailing political–economic social order. The security services have acted as defenders of that order and of those benefiting from it — politically and economically. Thus, one FBI agent, in talking of his disillusionment, stated that he 'came to see the Bureau not as the defender of 'democracy', but as the keeper of the status quo — not as an instrument of orderly change but as the handmaiden of reaction and the tool of retrenchment'.[97]

Groups which challenge *any* aspect of that status quo have been considered, *ipso facto*, subversive. It has been irrelevant whether the groups want radical change in foreign and defence policy, economic policy, the treatment of women, blacks and Indians, or in environmental policy. Thus, a 1972 paper written by the RCMP Security Service, entitled *Black Nationalism and Black Extremism in Canada*, contained the assessment that 'Having become more conscious of their black identity, the danger is that Canadian blacks of nationalist persuasion will become more turned in on themselves and become more willing to protest ... and more likely to take offence at real or imaged discrimination'.[98]

Nor is it the case that only small groups are subject to security service attention. If the opposition party is seeking major changes, that in itself subjects it to attention. Thus, it has been noted that in New Zealand '[the] Security Service clearly equates dissent with disloyalty'[99] and that:

Attitudes adopted by the New Zealand Security Intelligence Service from time to time certainly suggest that it still reflects its origin in the Cold War era; that it sees itself mainly concerned to spy on one sector of our society in the interests of another sector and not to have regard to the attitudes and interests of all New Zealanders.[100]

A paid security informant of the Special Branch in 1955 noted that 'Detective Patterson of the "Special Branch" had frequently questioned him about the Labour Party. The aim of his whole approach seemed to be that he would like to say that the Communist Party, was influencing the policy of the Labour Party ...'[101] Further, Roger Boshier has noted that:

The New Zealand Security Service did apparently attempt to discredit the last Labour Administration and has taken some part in efforts to prevent the return of Labour government since. There is good reason to suggest that Security can undermine a government when it happens to be a Labour government.[102]

To the extent that the activities of any group threaten a significant sector of the political–economic elite they are regarded as dangerous. As Frank Donner has written with respect to the FBI, 'The counterculture of the sixties recognized what was the blood and marrow of the Bureau's heritage, that culture is politics, the first line of defense of the capitalist economic order'.[103]

Consequences

It would be a serious distortion of the evidence to suggest that the security services of the UKUSA nations are 'secret police' organizations of the type to be found in the Soviet bloc and much of the rest of the world.[104] Clearly, they are not — either in terms of the types of measures they employ or the targets of their activity. In addition, it is clear that exposure of the type of activities discussed above can lead to reforms of some consequence.[105] At the same time, it would be naive to suggest that the exposure of such activities has eliminated the possibility of their future occurrence. Several FBI agents told Sanford Ungar that they would still use forbidden procedures 'if necessary to get the job done'. It is worth quoting Ungar at length:

One young agent, discussing the revelations about the Bureau's COINTELPRO activities between 1956 and 1971, said 'These things were great for getting at groups like the Klan and SLA. You have to break their balls any way you can ... Kelly said it won't be done anymore, but I can assure you that it will, informally if not in an official program'. Many agents in security work, he said, would not hesitate to try to have the subjects of their investigations fired from their jobs or evicted from their homes as was sometimes arranged under COINTELPRO. He added that 'If I, as a case agent, have an extremist, I would probably do anything I can to put him in jail. If I have to buy information or read his mail sometimes in order to accomplish that, I would do it. I would conduct a neighborhood investigation just to discredit him, and tell his neighbors about the groups he was affiliated with'.[106]

Such attitudes are not uncommon within the FBI, judging by the show of support given the former senior officials Mark Felt and Edward Miller when they were brought to trial for authorizing illegal break-ins. Indeed, such attitudes seem to be shared by the Reagan Administration as indicated by the presidential pardons issued to Felt and Miller.

More significantly, the Director of the FBI told Congress in June 1982 that guidelines restricting spying on domestic political organizations were going to be eased to let the Bureau keep an eye on 'terrorist' groups. In responding to the Director's testimony, the head of the Senate Judiciary Subcommittee on Terrorism, Senator Jeremiah Denton, suggested that the Socialist Workers Party favoured the overthrow of the Government of the United States by force and violence, while the National Lawyers Guild was an organization that 'seeks to exploit the law in order to bring about revolutionary change'.[107]

Subsequently the Attorney-General's guidelines for domestic security investigations gave the FBI authority to initiate an investigation 'if circumstances indicate that the group is engaged in activities that will involve force or violence in violation of Federal law now or in the future'.[108] As with Bill C-157, the language is permissive enough to allow investigation of non-violent groups based on security service perceptions of where their activities might lead.

In any case, even if the activities of the security services are not in the same league as those of the KGB, they can have serious and detrimental social consequences. These consequences include the consequences to individuals, to the political life of the nation, and to the national security. Obviously, such activities may distort the political life of the nation. Even when activities involve 'only' surveillance and monitoring, they can have a chilling effect on national political life — causing some to alter their public utterances, and causing others to refrain from political activity altogether.

When such activities involve dirty tricks, the course of political life may be substantially altered for a significant time. Candidates who might have been elected may be defeated, parties that might have developed a following may be torn apart by security service activity, and alliances that might have formed may never occur. Finally, individuals who have put faith in the process may see no recourse but violence.

Further, such activities may have a detrimental effect on the national security that the security services are supposed to protect. Such unjustified 'counter-subversion' activities divert time, attention, manpower and money from counter-espionage and protective security efforts that are necessary to protect military plans and facilities, technology and intelligence systems from compromise by hostile intelligence services. Thus, in his report on the NZSIS, Guy Powles noted that 'Subversion is no real threat to our national policy'[109] and that 'As matters now stand the number of officers in the Service engaged in counterespionage and counter-subversion work is approximately equal. I think there should be a reordering of these priorities in favour of work in the field of counterespionage.'[110]

Similarly, some FBI sources insist that the country's counter-intelligence needs would be more than covered merely by shifts of manpower from unnecessary internal security cases.[111] According to Sanford Ungar, the drain of such activities on counter-intelligence requirements was especially evident in the 1960s:

Once an organization or activist, such as Students for a Democratic Society (SDS) and its leaders had been put into the category of a threat, they were pursued with a vengeance almost unknown in FBI annals. Their phones were tapped, their associations and philosophies traced, their meetings infiltrated, their every movement watched in the hope that some basis could be found for charging them with a local or federal crime. The manpower assigned to such domestic intelligence and surveillance responsibilities was sometimes doubled, tripled or quadrupled — even at the expense of the Bureau's responsibilities for genuine counterintelligence efforts against foreign espionage.[112]

14

Conclusion

The UKUSA security and intelligence community, with more than a quarter of a million full-time personnel and a total budget of US$16–18 billion, constitutes one of the largest bureaucracies in the world. As such, it not only wields enormous political power and influence, but also exhibits most of the typical attributes of large bureaucratic organizations, including a tendency to define and pursue bureaucratic political objectives which are not necessarily in complete concordance with the national interests of the five UKUSA countries themselves.

However, the UKUSA security and intelligence community is obviously much different from any normal governmental bureaucracy. In the first place, it is a truly multinational community, with its numerous organizations and agencies bound together by an extraordinary network of written and unwritten agreements, working practices and personal relationships. Secondly, it is able to shroud itself in secrecy and to invoke the mantle of 'national security' to an extent unmatched by even the national defence establishments. And, third, many of its elements have executive and coercive powers, including the right to indulge in extreme and violent practices (such as assassination and 'special political activities') which are generally prohibited in national and international laws.

There is no doubt that these cooperative arrangements and practices greatly enhance the efficiency and effectiveness of the security and intelligence capabilities of the UKUSA countries. To begin with, there are major economic benefits to be derived from international cooperation and exchange. Because of their different geographic circumstances and technical endowments, each of the UKUSA parties has comparative advantages with respect to different intelligence activities.

It would be quite uneconomic, and in some cases economically impossible, for each of the UKUSA parties to attempt to satisfy all their intelligence needs on the basis of their own independent efforts and resources. New Zealand, with an intelligence and security community of only about 230 personnel, obviously must obtain the great bulk of its intelligence information from 'our friends abroad'.[1] There is obviously little sense in New Zealand and Australia duplicating their intelligence collection and assessment efforts, given their close geographical proximity, their similar strategic concerns and interests, and their extremely limited resources. Even in the case of the United Kingdom, which pioneered the development of 'technical means' of intelligence collection, the development and operation of modern overhead systems such as photographic, SIGINT and ocean surveillance satellites is clearly beyond its capacity. Only the United States can afford to deploy the full panoply of modern technical collection systems; for the other parties, access to the intelligence collected by these systems can only be gained through cooperation and exchange arrangements.

Cooperation and exchange is especially fruitful with respect to signals intelligence (SIGINT). Indeed, it is clear from the experience of the Second World War that such cooperation and exchange is necessary if the full strategic potential of SIGINT is to be realized. The exchange of information on German and Japanese codes in 1940–41 and the provision of PURPLE machines by the US Army's Signal Intelligence Service for Britain's Government Code and Cipher School (GCCS) stations at Bletchley and Singapore enormously assisted both the US and British decryption efforts. The greatly increased volume of radio and other electronic material which was made available to the various US, UK, Canadian and Australian analytic units was of great assistance in 'traffic analysis', which remains as productive a source of intelligence as actual decryption. It also assisted cryptanalysis, since analysts had 'more opportunities to detect recurrent names, call signs and technical jargon from which deductions could be made'.[2] Geographical coverage of enemy transmissions was also vastly increased.

There are similar benefits to be gained from cooperation and exchange in the area of ocean surveillance. The effectiveness of a continuous, whole-ocean anti-submarine detection and tracking system, for example, is much greater than the sum of the capabilities of its component elements would suggest. It is obviously much easier for (say) a Canadian CP-140 Aurora ocean surveillance aircraft to find and track a Soviet submarine as it transits from the Norwegian Sea to the north-west Atlantic if the location of the submarine is given to the CP-140 by a British Nimrod that has tracked it since it passed between Iceland and the Faroe Islands, than it would be for the CP-140 to search and find that submarine without such intelligence. Identification is also made much easier. In the case of a submarine detected by an RAAF P-3C Orion south of the Cocos (Keeling) Islands, for example, the possibilities would be that it was American or British, in which case confirmation should be readily forthcoming; or that it belonged to France; one of the littoral countries; or to the Soviet Union — in which case the submarine ports and support facilities would be continuously monitored and attempts made to follow the movements of all submarines leaving those ports and facilities.

In the counter-intelligence and security intelligence areas, the exchange of information obtained from Soviet defectors (such as Igor Gouzenko in Canada in September 1945, Vladimir Petrov in Australia in April 1954, Anatoli Golitsin in the US in December 1961, and Vladimir Kuzichkin in Britain in October 1982), together with the exchange of investigatory material on Soviet diplomats and other embassy staff in London, Washington, Ottawa, Canberra and Wellington, have been of critical importance in the detection of KGB agents and the monitoring of KGB activities in the UKUSA countries. A recent example is the identification of Valeriy Ivanov as a KGB officer in Canberra. Although ASIO had strongly suspected since June 1982 that Ivanov was a KGB officer, the confirmation came 'from an overseas source' in early 1983[3] — evidently MI-5, on the basis of information provided by Kuzichkin.

However, these undeniable benefits which flow from intelligence cooperation and exchange must be balanced against the costs, risks and constraints which are imposed by the UKUSA security and intelligence arrangements. These impositions are particularly significant in the case of the smaller UKUSA countries.

As with any cooperation and exchange arrangement, the benefits do not necessarily accrue to each participant equally. Indeed, it is quite possible for one particular party to be worse off in terms of costs, risks and loss of sovereignty even though there are net benefits to the UKUSA community as a whole. For the benefits to accrue equally, there would need to be some approximate equivalence in resource endowments and comparative advantages as well as some concordance of national interests, neither of which conditions pertain. There are enormous national differences within the UKUSA community with respect to intelligence collection and assessment resources and capabilities. The US security and intelligence agencies account for perhaps 90 per cent of the total budgets and personnel of all the UKUSA agencies, while the British agencies account for about 8 per cent and the Canadian, Australian and New Zealand agencies together only about 2 per cent.

Further, no matter how friendly two countries may be and no matter how closely their security and intelligence agencies may cooperate, their national interests will rarely be in complete concordance. In the Australian case, for example, the former Prime Minister, Malcolm Fraser, stated on 1 June 1976 that 'the interests of the United States and the interests of Australia are not necessarily identical'.[4] And with more direct reference to the UKUSA exchange arrangements, the Royal Commission on Intelligence and Security reported in April 1977 that 'Australia's intelligence interests do not, and cannot, coincide with those of any other country'.[5] The same can of course be said with respect to the intelligence interests of the US, Britain, Canada or New Zealand.

There is the very real possibility, for instance, that the priorities for resource allocation with respect to both intelligence collection and assessment will tend to reflect more the requirements of the UKUSA community as a whole rather than the more delimited security requirements of the individual UKUSA countries. This is especially likely in the case of the smaller countries (Australia, Canada and New Zealand), but there are also several noteworthy instances concerning British intelligence deployments. For example, the GCHQ maintained a major SIGINT station in Singapore for several years after the British Government's decision in 1967 to withdraw from East of Suez, and still maintains a large MI-6 presence there. It would also be difficult to justify the continued (and recently modernized) GCHQ and MI-6 deployments in Hong Kong simply on the basis of Britain's national security requirements. In the case of Australia, the ASIS station in Chile in 1972–73 served only to assist the CIA's destabilization operation against the Allende Government rather than any direct Australian security interests, while much of the SIGINT collected by the DSD is relevant only to US strategic planning. Indeed, the devotion of scarce collection resources to UKUSA requirements has led to serious deficiencies with respect to the determination of the detailed military capabilities of Australia's potential adversaries and the compilation of data bases on the physical aspects of the Australian continent and maritime approaches and the environment of future Australian military operations.

This can, in turn, lead to a distortion of the defence postures and foreign policies of the smaller UKUSA countries. Since the development of a defence force structure is inevitably based at least to some extent on intelligence assessments, a close intelligence relationship in which the priorities for intelligence collection are determined more by the interests of the dominant partners and the resultant intelligence assessments are not always of relevance to the smaller partners can lead to defence postures which are less optimal than those which might have been developed on the basis of more independent assessments. It is also likely that the degree of independence enjoyed by the smaller parties in their foreign relations and foreign policy-making can be constrained by the existence of such close intelligence relationships with larger powers with more global interests.

In times of war or crisis, the demands and obligations of secret agreements and working practices tend readily to conflict with avowed national foreign policies. In October 1973, for example, during the Yom Kippur War in the Middle East, intelligence derived from SIGINT collected at the NRO/CIA satellite ground station at Pine Gap in central Australia was passed to Israel by the United States and was of great assistance in the successful Israeli break through the Egyptian lines in the Sinai; this information was passed on even though the official, declared position of the Australian Government was one of 'even-handedness' in the war. And in April 1982, at the outset of the Falklands war between Britain and Argentina, the US continued to provide Britain with SIGINT (obtained primarily by the NSG station at Galeta Island, Panama), photographic intelligence (obtained from both SR-71 aircraft and KH-11 satellites), and ocean surveillance intelligence (including ELINT obtained by the WHITE CLOUD satellites), even though the avowed US policy was initially one of neutrality. Indeed, for three weeks following the Argentine invasion of 1 April the US attempted to act as an 'honest broker' to mediate a settlement of the conflict.[6]

A risk of an entirely different order is the possibility that a particular UKUSA country could be attacked in a conflict in which another UKUSA country was a belligerent, because of the close intelligence relationship between them, even though the former country was not itself otherwise involved. SIGINT stations, for example, figured as prime targets during the Second World War. In the week preceding D-Day, Allied Air Forces systematically attacked all the German SIGINT stations across the Channel, including the headquarters of the German SIGINT organization in north-western Europe at Ferme d'Urville near Cherbourg.[7] Australian forces successfully attacked Rommel's SIGINT post at Tel-el Eisa in July 1942.[8]

Current Soviet military doctrine rates important intelligence facilities among the highest priority targets to be attacked in the event of a nuclear exchange with the United States.[9] These facilities include critical SIGINT sites (such as Augsburg in Germany), ocean surveillance facilities (such as SOSUS arrays at Brawdy in Wales and Argentia in Newfoundland, Canada), and satellite ground stations (such as the CLASSIC WIZARD/ WHITE CLOUD station at Edzell in Scotland, the photographic satellite ground terminal at Oakhanger in Hampshire, and the NRO/CIA PHYOLITE station at Pine Gap in central Australia). Indeed, it is possible to envisage situations short of an all-out Soviet–US nuclear exchange in which the Soviet Union might attack such intelligence facilities, located outside the US but in other UKUSA countries, in order to demonstrate its resolve and at the same time degrade US strategic intelligence capabilities while avoiding the political and strategic consequences of attacks on similar facilities in the United States itself.[10]

There are other aspects of the UKUSA relationship which are inimical for quite different reasons. One of the outstanding features of the relationship — and, indeed, one of its enduring strengths — is that elements of it frequently come to perceive their ultimate loyalties as lying more with the UKUSA community than with their own governments. This was the implication, for instance, of the statements of the South Australian Commissioner of Police, Harold Salisbury in 1978 to the effect that the duty of Australian security intelligence officers lay 'not to any politically elected Government' but, rather, 'to the West as a whole. There are no national boundaries nowadays.'[11] Australian army officers attached to the CIA in Vietnam from 1962 to 1970 were prepared to swear that they would not divulge details of their activities with the CIA to their nominal Australian commanding officers or the Australian Government.

Some elements of the UKUSA community have also used the ties, obligations and allegiances of the UKUSA relationship to frustrate the intentions and explicit policies of their own Governments and sometimes even to assist in the breach of their own national laws. The relations between senior members of the GCHQ and the NSA, for example, have sometimes been of this nature. In July 1969, the Director of the GCHQ, Sir Leonard Hooper, stated in a letter to the Director of the NSA, Lieutenant-General Marshall ('Pat') Carter that 'I have often felt closer to you than to most of my own staff — indeed closer to you than to any [except perhaps two of my most senior colleagues]'.[12] In the same letter, Hooper recalled his practice of soliciting support from the NSA Director in his lobbying efforts in Whitehall. A particular instance concerned the GCHQ's project to construct two large satellite antennas at Morwenstow, near Bude, in Cornwall, one purpose of which was reportedly to intercept communications between INTELSAT satellites and the INTELSAT ground station at Goonhilly Downs, also in Cornwall. The resistance to the project within the British Government was only overcome when its importance to the UKUSA arrangements were stressed. In thanking Carter and the NSA Deputy Director, Louis Tordella, for their support in this, Hooper wrote: 'I know that I have leaned shamefully on you, and sometimes taken your name in vain, when I needed approval for something at this end. The aerials at Bude ought to be christened "Pat" and "Louis"!'[13]

Included in the closely cooperative activities of the GCHQ and the NSA have also been instances of assistance in illegal operations. For example, the GCHQ assisted the NSA in Operation MINARET, which (as mentioned in Chapter 6) involved the interception of the international aural and non-aural (for example, telex) communications of specific US citizens and organizations between 1965 and 1973. The GCHQ provided the NSA with copies of telexes and cable traffic carried by International Licensed Carriers (ILCs, such as the RCA, the ITT and the Western Union) which it had obtained by its own means.[14]

As described in Chapter 13, elements of the security and intelligence agencies in each of the UKUSA countries have frequently engaged in improper or illegal activities against citizens of their own countries. The actual extent of the various illegalities has varied from country to country according to differences in the provisions of their respective national laws (since what is illegal in Britain or Australia, for example, could well be legal in the United States), but there has been a distinct pattern in the character of these activities in each of the five countries. Although these countries pride themselves on their democratic traditions and their tolerance of dissent, the targets of physical and electronic surveillance, break-ins and 'dirty tricks' have included not only potential 'subversives' and groups and individuals who may be prone to violence, but also those engaged in the non-violent promotion of political, economic and social reform. Indeed, the widespread and persistent nature of repressive activities against those who question the economic and social status quo suggests that many members of the UKUSA security services are unable or unwilling to distinguish between protest and dissent on the one hand, and subversion and disloyalty on the other. As a consequence, the vitality of national political life is diminished and, through the misdirection of relatively scarce resources to 'counter-subversion' activity, the national security effort is degraded.

Participation in the UKUSA cooperation and exchange arrangements thus provides a number of very important benefits and savings, but it also imposes a wide range of extremely serious costs, risks and constraints. Unfortunately, however, there is no simple way of weighing the costs against the benefits so as to produce some sort of net assessment. Many of the variables are uncertain, and the 'bottom line' of any balance sheet depends on subjective judgments about the value of security and intelligence activities rather than any objective calculation of costs and benefits.

In any case, each of the UKUSA governments, regardless of their political colour, considers the benefits of intelligence cooperation and exchange to be clearly overwhelming. It is impossible to envisage any of them giving any serious consideration whatsoever to withdrawing from the UKUSA arrangements. So long as security and intelligence agencies are deemed necessary — and the trends over recent years suggest that the UKUSA governments consider them to be increasingly necessary — then the greatly enhanced effectiveness and efficiency which the cooperative arrangements permit their operations will ensure that cooperation continues.

This means that the relevant subject for discussion is not so much the question of whether any of the UKUSA countries might or should sever their security and intelligence ties but, rather, the conditions of the cooperation arrangements. Some of the costs and risks could be ameliorated by differently configured arrangements. Improved safeguards can be designed to reduce the incidence of hostile action by the security and intelligence agencies of one UKUSA country against the government or citizens of another, and of illegal and improper activities against the citizens of their own countries.

However, there is no way of eliminating the costs and risks altogether. Some inimical practices are simply unavoidable. This is especially the case with regard to technical intelligence collection operations, which are frequently quite indiscriminate — so that many SIGINT collection systems, for example, intercept the signals of allied and friendly countries along with those of potential adversaries. The risk of being subjected to attack because of the hosting of critical intelligence facilities is, in a sense, a function of the importance and utility of those facilities. These costs and risks are the inevitable consequence of the value of the intelligence operations.

What this means is that the costs and risks must be explicitly and specifically acknowledged and mechanisms must be established to limit them to whatever extent is possible. As the Australian Royal Commission on Intelligence and Security found in 1977, 'We ... need constantly to re-assess the benefits to Australia from intelligence relationships with other countries against the costs'.[15] It would be appropriate for each of the UKUSA countries to institutionalize some mechanism for such constant reassessments.

A fundamental condition of the maintenance of security and intelligence agencies and their participation in cooperative arrangements with allied agencies must be, given the extraordinary powers and capabilities of these agencies and the increasingly pervasive nature of their operations, that they be subject to firm, continuous and responsible oversight and direction. Unfortunately, the management structures and processes for the provision of such oversight and direction have proved to be deficient to greater or lesser extents in all of the UKUSA countries. In the United States, for example, the Senate Select Committee to Study Governmental Operations With Respect to Intelligence Activities (that is, the Church Committee) found in 1976 that guidance and direction was deficient at each of the appropriate levels. At the Congressional level, the Committee found 'that Congress has failed to provide the necessary statutory guidelines to ensure that intelligence agencies carry out their missions in accord with constitutional processes. Mechanisms for, and the practice of, congressional oversight have not been adequate'.[16] At the Executive level, the Committee found similarly 'that Presidents have not established specific instruments of oversight to prevent abuses by the intelligence community. In essence, Presidents have not exercised effective oversight'.[17] Further, coordination and guidance was not forthcoming from the Director of Central Intelligence (DCI). The Committee found that:

the DCI in his coordinator role has been unable to ensure that waste and unnecessary duplication are avoided. Because the DCI only provides guidance for intelligence collection and production, and does not establish requirements, he is not in a position to command the intelligence community to respond to the intelligence needs of national policymakers. Where the DCI has been able to define priorities, he has lacked authority to allocate intelligence resources.[18]

In the case of New Zealand, the report by the Chief Ombudsman on the Security Intelligence Service (NZSIS) in 1976 found that cooperation between the New Zealand intelligence and security agencies was poor, that there was a lack of clear lines of responsibility, and that the degree of ministerial control that was exercised over the NZSIS — by far the largest of the New Zealand agencies — was quite limited. According to that report:

the information [provided to the Prime Minister by the NZSIS] is not, on the whole, presented in a way which allows or encourages the [Prime] Minister to take any positive part in the presentation of the Service's programme ... I am concerned that as a result the [Prime] Minister is not in a position to take those actions required of him by his responsibility and that the Service does not have the guidance it constitutionally should.[19]

In the case of Australia, the Royal Commission on Intelligence and Security found in its 1977 report that 'The Australian intelligence community is fragmented, poorly co-ordinated and organized. The agencies lack proper guidance direction and control. They do not have good or close relations with the system of government they should serve'.[20] Although new organizational structures were established as a result of the Royal Commission — and most particularly an Intelligence and Security Committee of Cabinet and an Office of National Assessments, the Director-General of which is responsible for day-to-day oversight and guidance of the Australian security and intelligence community — the fact is that coordination, guidance and control have not been markedly improved.

In the case of Canada, supervision has been similarly deficient. The Commission of Inquiry Concerning Certain Activities of the RCMP (the MacDonald Commission) reported in August 1981 that 'It is clear that by 1965 the RCMP was receiving little direction or guidance at the ministerial level. Nor did it appear to be seeking any ... The RCMP was not dissatisfied with a relationship which enabled them to operate in a semi-autonomous fashion.'[21] Although some changes were made in 1965 (including the transfer of responsibility for the RCMP from the Minister of Justice to the Solicitor General), the situation was scarcely improved. The MacDonald Commission found that the Cabinet Committee on Security and Intelligence, the most senior supervisory body, had met only twenty times between 1972 and mid-1980, that between 1975 and 1980 it had received only two 'annual' reports from the Security Service, and that ministerial responsibility had been particularly 'neglected' in the crucial area of 'policy of operations'.[22]

And in the case of Britain, the Report of the Committee of Privy Counsellors (the Franks Report) of January 1983 found that the machinery for coordination and supervision of the British intelligence community was defective. The Report found that liaison between the Assessments Staff of the Joint Intelligence Committee (JIC), the Foreign and Commonwealth Office and the Ministry of Defence was insufficiently close; that the agencies responsible for the collection of external intelligence (that is, MI-6 and the GCHQ) were insufficiently responsive to the requirements of the JIC; and that the authority of the JIC, which is formally responsible for the day-to-day management of the British intelligence community, is vitiated because its Chairman is neither full-time nor a member of the Cabinet Office.[23] Although there is a Coordinator of Intelligence and Security in the Cabinet Office, his functions are essentially advisory. There is no ministerial committee for the oversight of the British security and intelligence community, and there is no machinery for any parliamentary review or scrutiny of its activities.[24]

The second essential condition for the maintenance of the UKUSA arrangements, in addition to firm, effective and responsible governmental oversight and control of the UKUSA security and intelligence agencies, is that the citizens of the five democracies be officially and fully apprised of the nature and operations of these agencies, and of the consequences (both beneficial and disadvantageous) of the international cooperative arrangements among them — to the extent permitted by the genuine requirements of national security.

There are numerous reasons for providing more information and encouraging greater public debate on the UKUSA community. At the most general level, there is the public's interest in the scrutiny and control of all arms of government, including the security and intelligence agencies. The UKUSA community has now reached enormous proportions in terms of personnel and budgetary resources; its technological capacity is immense; it has its own bureaucratic momentum; and the consequences of its activities affect not only the basic national security interests of the five UKUSA countries but also the civil rights of each of their citizens. Greater freedom of information is therefore also required in order to provide the ordinary citizen with some recourse if he or she believes they have unjustifiably been adversely affected by security and intelligence operations.

Greater public information and debate would not necessarily be harmful to the operations of the security and intelligence agencies. Secrecy has shielded these agencies from full accountability and effective supervision and led to their being less effective and less efficient than they otherwise might be. A clear statement of objectives and of priorities can only be the product of informed public debate. Moreover, as the US Senate's Select Committee's Inquiry into Foreign and Military Intelligence reported, 'secrecy has been a tragic conceit'.[25] The truth inevitably prevails, and operations which have been undertaken on the premise that they could be plausibly denied will in the end only damage the reputation of the UKUSA countries and the faith of their citizens in their governments.

This is not to say, of course, that there are no matters of genuine secrecy. Indeed, secrecy is an essential part of many security and intelligence activities. The effectiveness of these activities can be undermined if the operational and investigative techniques are revealed and the extent of resources and capabilities is disclosed. It is not possible to construct any general or timeless definition of what constitutes a valid national secret, but it would include details about some military activities and the particular characteristics and performance parameters of some weapons systems; some sources and methods of intelligence collection, particularly with respect to technical collection systems; and techniques of analysis, especially where these might be frustrated by an adversary cognizant of them.

In the end, the basic dilemma of how to balance the requirements of secrecy with those of democratic government cannot be resolved absolutely. Rather, it is a matter of continuous judgment about where to draw a satisfactory line. It is most important that some process be devised through which agreement can be reached on what generally constitutes a valid national secret, that the matter can be kept under constant review, and any changes requiring the protection of new types of information can be addressed, understood and agreed on within a framework of democratic decision-making.

As a general principle, the citizens of the UKUSA countries should know as much about the operations of the UKUSA security and intelligence community as do the intelligence agencies of the Soviet Union and other national adversaries.

In any case, the conflict of interest between the requirements of secrecy and the basis of democratic government itself has come to be reconciled in each of the UKUSA countries too far in favour of secrecy. In the United States, the Senate Select Committee was clearly persuaded that the mantle of 'national security' was frequently invoked to conceal illegal, improper and unwise acts from the American people, that much more information about security and intelligence matters could be disclosed without damage to national security, and that the clash between secrecy and open democratic processes had typically been reconciled at the expense of the latter.[26] In New Zealand, the Chief Ombudsman reported in 1976 that 'less secrecy is called for' in regard to certain operations of the Security Intelligence Service (NZSIS) and that it was necessary to remove 'many of the undesirable aspects of the cloak of secrecy which covers the Service'.[27] In Australia, the Royal Commission on Intelligence and Security reported in 1977 that 'although operational secrecy is essential for the effective discharge of their duties by the [security and intelligence] agencies', there has been 'unnecessary secretiveness in some of their activities which need not be secret'.[28] And in Canada, the Commission of Inquiry Concerning Certain Activities of the RCMP reported in 1979 that 'in balancing the interests [between secrecy and democracy] we feel that much more information with respect to security and intelligence can be made available than has been the case in the past'.[29]

The product of increasing the amount of publicly available information about the UKUSA security and intelligence agencies and their interrelationships should be a much more informed public debate on this crucial subject. It is now more than three and a half decades since the UKUSA arrangements formally came into effect, just on four decades since the BRUSA Agreement formally created the SIGINT connection, and some three to four decades since all the principal mechanisms for intelligence cooperation and exchange were established between the UKUSA countries. There have been significant changes in the international security environment, alliance relationships, and the capabilities and practices of the UKUSA security and intelligence agencies during this period. The time is long overdue for an informed public debate on the UKUSA security and intelligence arrangements and for the bases and parameters of UKUSA security and intelligence operations to be established through open democratic processes.

III

Appendixes

1

The UKUSA SIGINT network

This appendix consists of a listing of all US, UK, Canadian, Australian and New Zealand signals intelligence (SIGINT) facilities and stations for which we have been able to find references. Some of the stations are no longer operational, and this is noted whenever we are aware that this is the case. Some Third Party locations are also listed.

It should also be noted that there are significant variations among these facilities and stations — in terms of mission, physical size, personnel and equipment.

The primary sources for the compilation of this appendix were US Congressional *Hearings*; documents declassified under the US Freedom of Information Act; US Department of Defense directories (such as the Defense Communication Agency's *Global Autovon Defense Communications System*); professional journals (such as *INSCOM Journal*, the journal of the US Army Intelligence and Security Command, and *Military Intelligence*, the journal of the US Army Intelligence Center and School, Fort Huachuca, Arizona); press reports; and information provided by Duncan Campbell of the *New Statesman*, London, and William Arkin of the Institute for Policy Studies, Washington, DC.

US SIGNALS INTELLIGENCE FACILITIES — US LOCATIONS

UNIT	LOCATION	COMMENTS
1 NSA HQ Also CCS HQ, INSCOM HQ, NSGA Fort Meade 6940 ESW, Co A, Marine Spt Bn, NSG Det, National Crypto- logic School, CONUS MI Gp (SIGINT/EW)	Fort George C. Meade, Md.	NSA, CSS and INSCOM HQ; 13 745 personnel base population (8558 military, 3896 civilian); Air Force personnel assigned to 6940 ESW/694 ESS (formerly 6470 ABG, 6971 ESS, 6972 ESS, 6973 ESG, 6974 ESS); 886 Navy personnel (875 military, 11 civilian); National Cryptologic School; Defense Special Missile Astronautics Center (DEFSMAC); elements of NSA at Baltimore–Washington Airport (FANX III); INSCOM HQ moved from Arlington Hall Station, VA in 1981–82
2 NSG HQ	Naval Security Station 3801 Nebraska Avenue NW, Washington, DC	739 personnel assigned to NSG HQ (435 military and 304 civilian); 112 personnel assigned to SIGSEC work; 15.38 hectares (38 acres)

315

3 ESC HQ	Kelly Air Force Base, San Antonio, Texas	There are about 3000 ESC personnel at San Antonio. In addition to ESC headquarters, the following units are also located at San Antonio: Air Force Cryptologic Depot; Air Force Electronic Warfare Center; 6960 Air Base Squadron; 6948 Security Squadron (M); 6993 Security Squadron; Air Force Communications Security Center; Joint Electronic Warfare Center
	ALASKA	
4 NSGA; Co I, Marine Spt Bn	Naval Station Adak	HF/DF station at SOSUS Naval Facility; SISS ZULU ocean surveillance system being replaced by CLASSIC WIZARD; 3057 hectares (7553 acres); 'Zeto Point' is collection site; 350 personnel assigned to NSGA; 41 Marines in Co I; formerly USN-13
5 SIGSEC Det	Fort Richardson, Anchorage	SIGSEC support element for 172 Infantry Brigade
6 ESC Alaska; 6981 ESS; NSGA; NSASA/CSS Rep, Alaska (NSAAL)	Elmendorf AFB, Anchorage	Support to Alaskan Air Command and Joint Task Force Alaska (JCS); NSA COMINT Communications Relay Center; 46 personnel assigned to NSGA
7 (Det 3, 6981 RSM)	Attu Island	Former AFSS COMINT station; remote antennas still operated on island
8 6985-ESS; 6 SW	Eielson AFB	24 SRS with 8 RC-135 provides monitoring crews
9 (172 NUD[AS])	Allen AAF, Fort Wainwright Fairbanks	Three OV-1D Mohawk in support of 172 Infantry Brigade. Moved to Hunter AFF, GA in mid-1970s
10 (Det K, 8614 DU)	Gambell	Former ASA station
11 (8607 DU)	Kenai	Former ASA station
12	Kodiak	Former Naval SIGINT station
13 (Det 2, 6981 RSM)	King Salmon	Former AFSS station
14 (Det 1, 6981 RSM)	North-East Cape	Former AFSS station
15 (Det 4, 6981 RSM)	Point Barrow	Former AFSS station
16 6984 ESS; Det 1, 6 SW; OL–FW, 6981 ESS	Shemya AFB	COBRA DANE (AN/FPS-108) precision phased array radar monitoring Soviet missile testing; rotational RC-135 flights from Eielson AFB including 2 COBRA BALL equipped RC-135 on 24-hour alert for missile test monitoring from 1984; ASA from August 1957–April 1975; operations transferred to Bendix Corp 1 April 1975
	ARIZONA	
17 Det 2, ESC Tactical	Davis-Monthan AFB	Tactical support to AF units
18 USAICS; Army Elec Proving Grounds	Fort Huachuca, Sierra Vista	Army intelligence training and test center; systems development of SOTAS, Corps Systems; former ASA T&E Center

		CALIFORNIA	
19	9 SRW	Beale AFB	1 SRS with 9 SR-71; 99 SRS with 5 U-2R; 9 RTS has ELINT/ PHOTINT and other sensor analysis responsibilities
20	601 ASA Co (DS)	Fort Ord	Support to 7 Infantry Division; SIGSEC Spt Det
21	NSG Dept	Imperial Beach	NSG SIGSEC Department at Naval Radio Receiving Facility, Imperial Beach and Naval Radio Transmitting Facility at Chollas Heights; 93 NSG personnel (80 military, 13 civilian)
22	Combat Systems Technical Schools Command	Mare Island Naval Shipyard, Vallejo	Naval cryptologic technical maintenance school
23		McClellan AFB	
24	NSG Det	Monterey	Support to Defense Language Institute and Naval Postgraduate School
25	NSG Dept/NSG FO	Naval Station, San Diego	CLASSIC WIZARD research facility, NSG SIGSEC Department at NCS San Diego and direct support of Pacific Fleet; 106 personnel (97 military, 9 civilian)
26		San Francisco	NSA Station; former HQ, ASA Security Region IV
27	NSGA	Skaggs Island, Sonoma	Alternate net control officer HF-DF net (Pacific); 292 personnel (256 military, 36 civilian); 1339 hectares (3309 acres)
28		Two Rock Ranch Station, Petaluma Station, Petaluma	ASA site closed in 1970, 209 kilometres (130 miles) south of COMSAT/INTELSAT ground station at Jamesburg, Ca
		COLORADO	
29	Aerospace Data Facility	Buckley ANGB, Aurora	DSP ground station (one of two main readout stations, the other being at Nurrungar, Australia); large NSA contingent
30	374 CEWI Co	Fort Carson	Tactical support to 4 Infantry Division
31	NSA/CSS Rep, NORAD	Peterson AFB	Liaison with NORAD HQ
		CONNECTICUT	
32	NSG Det	Naval Submarine Base, New London, Groton	ESM/ELINT support; 26 military personnel at Submarine Base
		DISTRICT OF COLUMBIA	
33		Washington, DC	INSCOM site
34		Washington, DC	AFSS Office cited in 1956
		FLORIDA	
35		Cudjoe Key AFS, Perky	'Seek Skyhook' radar balloon collection site of 671 Radar Squadron; also SIGINT function, satellite facility of NAS Key West; twelve military personnel; 28.33 hectares (70 acres)
36	Det 1, ESC Tactical	Eglin AFB	Support of Air Warfare Development Center

318 The Ties That Bind

37	6947 ES; NSGA; USAFS Key West; Co H, Mar Spt Bn	Homestead AFB	'Seminole Station'; AN/FLR-9 CDAA; Joint Field Station; 345 NSG personnel (295 military, 50 civilian); 330 hectares (815 acres); NSA activity (NDS Site Alpha); formerly Det H, 2nd Radio Bn, USMC
38	OL-HL, ESC Tactical	Hurburt Field	Support of AF Special Operations
39	NSG Det; OL, 6947 ESS	Key West, Boca Chica	Detachment of NSGA Homestead, 28 military personnel. Support of JARCC; ESS has Spanish language SIGINT mission in support of balloon at Cudjoe Key
40	Det 1, 6947 ESS	MacDill AFB	Support to Readiness Command and missile warning radar
41	NSG Det	Naval Station, Mayport	Direct support to Atlantic Fleet ships, including SIGSEC; 14 military personnel
42	NSG FO	Orlando	
43	Det 5, 9 SRW	Patrick AFB	New base for deployments of SR-71 and U-2R
44	Naval Tech Training Center	Corry Station, Pensacola	Naval, Marine Corps and Army SIGINT technical training; Marine Corps students assigned to Co K, Marine Spt Bn; AF students assigned to 6945 School Sqn
		GEORGIA	
45	902 Military Intelligence Gp	Atlanta	INSCOM Counter-intelligence and Signals Security Support Battalion
46	504 CEWI Gp; 224 Military Intelligence Battalion	Hunter AAF, Savannah	HQ for tactical support to FORSCOM units in US including SIGINT, EW and SIGSEC 6 OV-1D of 172 MICAS (moved from Ft Wainwright, AK)
47		Fort McPherson	INSCOM Station; former HQ Security Region II, ASA
48	Det 8, 2762 LS	Robins AFB	'Special Project Senior Year'
		HAWAII	
49	1st Radio Bn	MCAS Kaneohe Bay	Marine Corps tactical SIGINT personnel for Pacific region
50	USAFS Kunia	Kunia, Oahu	NSA remote operations facility opened in 1980, 1400 NSA personnel
51		Helemano, Oahu	Former HQ, USASA Pacific and 8605 DU
52	ESC Pacific	Hickam AFB, Oahu	ESC HQ Pacific; support to PACAF and manning of PACOM ELINT Center; Det 1, 6902 ESG?
53	NSG Dept	Makalapa Heights, Honolulu	Support to Pacific Fleet
54	NSG Det; NSA/CSS Pac (INCPAC); NSG Pacific	Pearl Harbor, Oahu	Support of 3rd Fleet, CINPAC HQ and Intelligence Center Pacific (IPAC), SIGSEC 168 NSG personnel (167 military, 1 civilian)
55		Schofield Barracks	'Tri-service Cryptologic Agency'
56	INSCOM Theater-Intelligence Center-Pacific (TICP)	Fort Shafter	Building T-1504, Fort Shafter

57	372 ASA Co (DS)	Fort Shafter	Tactical support to 25 Infantry Division (possibly at Schofield Bks)
58	NSGD	Wahiawa	AN/FLR-9 HF/DF intercept system; Net Control Officer HF/DF Net Pacific; support to NAVCAMS and TSC; 273 NSG personnel (258 military, 15 civilian); formerly USN-14
59	6924 ESS	Wheeler AFB	
		ILLINOIS	
60		Bannockburn	Former NSGA; call sign 'Nevada Turtle'
61	902 MI Gp	Fort Sheridan	
62	NSG FO	Great Lakes Naval Training Center	Liaison at major naval training center
		INDIANA	
63	NSG Det	Naval Weapons Support Center, Crane	Three NSG personnel; support to Naval Weapons Support Center
		KANSAS	
64	337 ASA Co (DS)	Fort Riley	Tactical support to 1 Infantry Division, Co C, 318 MI Bn
		KENTUCKY	
65	265 CEW Co	Fort Campbell	Countermeasures EW Co in support of 101 Airborne Division (Air Assault)
66	902 MI Gp	Fort Knox	
		LOUSIANA	
67	405 ASA Co (DS)	Fort Polk	Tactical support to 5 Infantry Division
		MAINE	
68	NSG Det	NAS Brunswick	Support to Brunswick TSC; 18 NSG military personnel
69	NSGA	Winter Harbor	CLASSIC WIZARD site; collection facility located 201 kilometres (125 miles) from COMSAT/INTELSAT terminal at Andover, Maine; main station at tip of Schoodic Peninsula; operations site at Corea; 356 NSG personnel (302 military, 54 civilian); 236 hectares (583 acres); formerly USN-20
		MARYLAND	
70	Harry Diamond Labs	Adelphi	SIGINT, EW, Radar and Electro-optics R&D
71		Andrews AFB	
72		Cheltenham	Former NSG site at least partly relocated at Sugar Grove; no Naval personnel
73	NIPSSA	Suitland	NSG support to the Naval Intelligence Support Center; 64 military personnel
		MASSACHUSETTS	
74	402 ASA Det (SOD) (Abn)	Fort Devens, Ayer	INSCOM Training Center and School; tactical support of 10 Special Forces Group
		MISSISSIPPI	
75	ESC School	Keesler AFB	Training school for morse operators and cryptologists

#	Unit	Location	Notes
		NEBRASKA	
76	ESC Strategic; 6949 ESS; 343 SRS	Offutt AFB	Support to SAC; 6949 ESS is mobile support unit to 343 SRS with 8 RC-135A/C/U/V 'Rivet Joint' aircraft; formerly 6944 ESW
		NEVADA	
77	Det 3, ESC Tactical	Nellis AFB	Support to RED FLAG aircraft tactics and electronic warfare training activities
		NEW JERSEY	
78	513 Military Intelligence Group	Fort Monmouth	Army Communications and Electronics Material Readiness Activity; Combat Surveillance and Target Acquisition Lab; EW Lab; PM, SOTAS: PM; REMBASS
		NORTH CAROLINA	
79	2nd Radio Bn	MCB Camp Lejeune	SIGINT support to Atlantic Marine Corps units
80	313 CEWI Bn (Corps)	Fort Bragg, Fayetteville	Tactical support to XVIII Corps (Abn) and 82 Airborne Division; 400 ASA Det (SDD) (formerly 801 MID) support to 5th SFG; 705 MID support to 7 SFG; 1 MIBARS/376 CEWI Co; formerly 358 ASA Co
		OKLAHOMA	
81	OL-TT, ESC Tactical	Tinker AFB	Support to AWACs
		PENNSYLVANIA	
82		Tobyhanna Army Depot	Army Electronics Material Readiness Activity
		SOUTH CAROLINA	
83	NSGA	Charleston	Support to Atlantic Fleet and SIGSEC; 17 NSG personnel (16 military, 1 civilian)
84		Dupont	Former NSG unit (USN-18)
85		Fort Jackson	
86	DL-TS, ESC Tactical	Shaw AFB	
		TEXAS	
87	OL-TB, ESC Tactical	Bergstrom AFB	
88		Ft Bliss	SIGSEC support detachment, 3 Armored Cavalry Regiment; Co C, EW Avn Co (Fwd), 15 MI Bn with 7 RU-21D Guardrail, 2 JU-21A for airborne DF (formerly 156 ASA Co (Avn) (Fwd)); 1 ASA Co (Avn) (R) with 9 RU-21A/B/C also possibly stationed; airborne units at Biggs AAF; 336 ASA Co
89	6906 ESS; 8075 ESS (AFRES)	Brooks AFB	AFSS HQ from May 1949 to July 1953; support to Air Force COMSEC Center; reserve unit activated 1 October 1981
90	303 CEWI Bn; 312 CEWI Bn; 522 CEWI Bn	Fort Hood, Killian	Tactical support of III Corps (303 CEWI Bn, including 375 CEWI Vo), 1 Cavalry Division (312 CEWI Bn), 2 Armored Division (522 CEWI Bn); 312 CEWI Bn formerly 371 ASA Co; 522 CEWI Bn includes former

The UKUSA SIGINT network

91	USAF School of Applied Cryptologic Sciences	Goodfellow AFB, San Antonio	502 MI Co; 522 CEWI Bn with EH–1H Quick Fix (EW/COMINT); Co B, 15 MI Bn with OV–10 Training in cryptography and traffic analysis; 3480 TTG operates school; 97 NSG students
92	ESC HG; 6948 ESS (M); 6993 ESS; USAFS	Kelly AFB, San Antonio	ESC HQ and 'Alamo Station'; also location of Air Force Electronic Center; Air Force Cryptologic Support Center; Central Security Operations Center; Project Wideband Extraction HQ; Joint Electronic Warfare Center
93	6933 ESS; 6948 ESS	Medina Annex, Lackland AFB	Consolidated Security Operations Station?
		VIRGINIA	
94	Intelligence Analysis Group	Arlington Hall Station, Arlington	SIGINT analysis for INSCOM. Former site of INSCOM HQ
95	NIPSSA	The Pentagon, Arlington	NSG support; 27 military personnel
96		Fort Belvoir	
97	NSGA Northwest	Chesapeake	Net Control Officer, HF/DF Net Atlantic; 410 NSG personnel (330 military, 71 civilian); colocated with NAVSATCOMFAC; location of Atlantic Fleet SIGSEC Operations Center
98	NSA Propogation and Research Lab; Naval Experimental Test Facility	Kent Island, Chesapeake Bay (New Kent?)	Propagation and Research Laboratory, 'for the conduct of research and evaluations on very very high frequency and microwave antenna systems'
99	ESC Tactical	Langley AFB	Support to Tactical Air Command
100	VAQ-33	NAS Norfolk	EW training and support with EA-4B/F/J, ERA-3B EC/NC-121K, EA-6A/B
101	NSG Det; NSG Atlantic	Naval Station, Norfolk	Support to Command, 2nd Fleet, Atlantic Fleet, FICEURLANT, LANTCOM ELINT Center, and FOSIC; 120 NSG military personnel
102	Army Signal Warfare Center; Engineering and Maintenance	Vint Hill Farms Station (VHFS), Warrenton	Subordinate to Army Communications and Electronics Material Readiness Activity; integrates EW programs of INSCOM and former EW Lab; EMRA repairs and maintains fixed station antenna systems, facilities and structures; former SIGINT station part of Project 'Wideband Extraction' (24 January 1969–3 July 1974) when project was transferred to San Antonio, Texas; interception of British and other country diplomatic signals; interception of domestic communications during Vietnam war demonstrations; formerly USM-1

322 *The Ties That Bind*

	Unit	Location	Comments
		WASHINGTON	
103		Bainbridge Island	
104	NSG element	Jim Creek Naval Radio Station, Oso	Former NSG facility
105	109 CEWI Bn	Fort Lewis	Tactical support of 9 Infantry Division; formerly 9 MI Co and 335 ASA Co (DS)
106		Marietta	Former NSG activity
107	Yakima Research	Yakima Proving	NSA site located 161 kilometres (100 miles) north of COMSAT/INTELSAT ground station at Brewster
		WEST VIRGINIA	
108	NSG Det	Sugar Grove	Collection facility located near COMSAT/INTELSAT terminal at Etam; double set Wullenweber antennae, 18.29 metre (60-foot) microwave receiving antenna, four satellite antennas (150-, 105-, and 30-foot dishes [45.72, 32, and 9.14 metres]); 79 NSG military personnel

US SIGNALS INTELLIGENCE FACILITIES — OVERSEAS

	UNIT	LOCATION	COMMENTS
		AUSTRALIA	
109	SUSLO (NSA)	Victoria Barracks, Melbourne	NSA liaison to Australian DSD
110	NSG?	North West Cape	Possible NSG monitoring site colocated with major Navy communications station. According to a former NSA officer, this station 'intercepts traffic in the Sunda Straits and in the Indian Ocean'. Although mentioned in Congressional testimony, the existence of NSG at North West Cape is officially denied by the Australian Department of Defence
111		US Embassy, Canberra, ACT	
112	Joint Defense Space Communications Station (JDSCS)	Nurrungar (Woomera)	USAF 5 Defence Space Communications Sqdn operating one of two major grounds stations for DSP satellite early warning system (other at Buckley ANGB, Aurora, Colorado); NSA contingent, function probably COMSEC
113	Joint Defense Space Research Facility (JDSRF)	Pine Gap (Alice Springs)	CIA/NRO operated ground station for RHYOLITE and other SIGINT satellites
		AZORES	
114	NSGA Lajes	Terceira Island	Operations site at Villa Nova
		BAHAMAS	
115	Army Signal Radio Propagation Station	Grand Bahama Island	Former ASA site

The UKUSA SIGINT network

		CANADA	
116		Ottawa	SUSLO
117		Leitrim	NSG and ASA Detachments
118	NSGA	Argentia, Newfoundland	
		CHILE	
119		Easter Island	Abandoned in October 1970, following election of Salvador Allende
120		Unknown location	Located on an offshore island. Also abandoned in October 1970
		CHINA	
121	CIA OSO	Korla, Xinjiang Uighur Autonomous Region	SIGINT site established in 1979 under Project Karakoram-80; operated by CIA Office of SIGINT Operations (OSO)
122	CIA OSO	Qitai, Xinjiang	SIGINT site operated by CIA Office of SIGINT Operations
		CUBA	
123	NSGA/Co L, Marine Spt Bn	Guantanamo Bay	SIGINT station directed against Cuba located at Leeward Point (Formerly Det L, 2 Radio Bn, FMFLANT)
		CYPRUS	
124	OL-OH, 9 SRW	Akrotiri AB	Rotational U-2 flights from British AB since 1973; U-2 crashed on runway during takeoff 7 December 1977
125		Nicosia	Formerly USF-61
126		Karavas	Reopened 1978
127		Mia Milia	Reopened 1978
128		Yerolakkos	Reopened 1978
129		Panayia Aphendrika	New station located between Ayios Philon and Apostolos Andreas in north Cyprus
		DIEGO GARCIA	
130	NSG Dept	Diego Garcia	'Reindeer Station' became operational in 1973. Formally opened as part of NOSIS HF-DF network in August 1973. Equipment includes HF-DF system; CLASSIC WIZARD ground terminal; and DSCS ground terminal
		ETHIOPIA	
131	(NSG; USASAFS)	Asmara, Ethiopia	US operation began with a detachment of the Second Signal Security Service Battallion in 1941. Operated by Army Security Agency (ASA) until September 1972, when it was transferred to NSG. NSG activity until 1976, by which time Diego Garcia NSG activity was fully operational. Completely ceased operations in May 1977
		GREECE	
132	6916 ESS; NSG Det; Det 3, 306 SW; VQ-2 Det Athens	Hellenikon AB, Athens	SIGINT support to rotational RC-135s from Offutt AFB, Nebraska; rotational EP-3B/E from Rota, Spain

133	6931 ESG	Iraklion AS, Crete	Includes telemetry interception; formerly 6938 RSM
134	NSG	Nea Makri	
135		Levkas Island	Sub-station to Nea Makri
		GUAM	
136	VQ-1	NAS Agana	HQ for one of two Navy Fleet Air Reconnaissance Squadrons ('World Watchers') (other at Rota, Spain), with EP-3B/E and EA-3B SIGINT aircraft; squadron flies out of Atsugi, Japan and Cubi Point, Philippines
137	NSG Dept; Co C, Marine Spt Bn	Finnegayan	CLASSIC WIZARD master station, BULLSEYE network station, AN/FLR-15 antenna array, AN/FSQ-11 FYK-111A data/ FYK-111A data equipment specifically designed for 'telemetric data'; also support to NAVCAMS and NAVFAC on Guam; formerly USN-11
		HONDURAS	
138	Detachment of 224 Military Intelligence Battalion	Palmerola	INSCOM activity. Detachment of 224 MI Battalion, from Hunter Army Airfield, Savannah, Georgia, operates 12–16 OV-1 Mohawk and RU-21 Ute aircraft in missions over El Salvador and Nicaragua
139		La Cieba	Two RU-21 Ute aircraft used for SIGINT missions over El Salvador and Nicaragua
		ICELAND	
140		Keflavik	HF-DF and support to NAVFAC TSC; formerly 6984 RSM
141	(NSG)	Stokksnes	Former NSG activities
		ITALY	
142	NSG Det	Naples	Support to 6th Fleet and Allied Forces, Southern Europe (NATO)
143	6917 ESG; NSGA	San Vito dei Normanni AS, Brindisi	Operations unit is 6917 ESS; AN/FLR-9 antenna installed in 1964; formerly 6935 RSM
144	(328 CRC)	Treviso	Former SIGINT operations
145	Det P, 201 ASA Co	Vicenza	SIGSEC support to Southern European Task Force and US Army in Italy
		INDIA	
146		Unknown location	US SIGINT station installed in north India to replace Bada Bier, Pakistan. Monitored Chinese nuclear and missile installations in Xinjiang Province and also activities in Pakistan. Closed
		IRAN	
147		Behshahr	SIGINT station near the south-east corner of the Caspian Sea. Established about 1959. Operated by CIA Office of SIGINT Operations (OSO). Consisted of a command centre; an antenna inside a 30-foot

The UKUSA SIGINT network 325

148		Kabkan	(9.14 metre) radome; a radio-monitoring antenna on a steel tower; and a communications satellite terminal. Used to monitor Soviet missile tests and military communications. One of seven such sites formerly operated by CIA in Iran. Abandoned on 31 January 1979 Located 64.73 kilometres (40 miles) east of Meshad in north-eastern Iran. Operated by CIA's OSO. Direct line of sight to Tyuratam, about 1200 kilometres (746 miles) from the border. Codenamed 'Tacksman II'. Abandoned at the end of February 1979
149		Meshad	Site of another CIA SIGINT facility, separate from that at Kabkan. Closed 1979
150		Klanabad	Located in the middle of the south shore of the Caspian Sea. Site of 2 CIA SIGINT posts. Closed 1979
151		Astara	CIA SIGINT post located on the western shore of the Caspian Sea. Closed 1979
152		Shirabad	Second CIA SIGINT post on western shore of Caspian Sea. Closed 1979
153		Project Ibex	CIA SIGINT system planned for southern Iran. Plan called for 11 ground monitoring posts, 6 airborne units, and several mobile ground units. Abandoned in 1979
		JAPAN	
154	(6922 Radio Group [Mobile])	Ashiya AFB, Kyushu	Former AFSS site, 1100 personnel
155	NSG Det; VQ-1 Det Astugi	Atsugi, Honshu	Rotational EP-3B/E ELINT/SIGINT Aries aircraft from NAS Agana, Guam; former USASA Special Activities Det-1 (SAD-1), deactivated 29 November 1974
156	NSA/CSS Rep Japan	Camp Zama, Tokyo	Colocated with HQ, US Army Japan
157	(8612 DU)	Chitose, Hokkaido	'Location 12', ASA site established 1945, closed 31 March 1971
158	NSA Japan?	Fuchinobe	
159		Fuchu AS	ASC?
160	NSG	Futenma, Okinawa	Site located 16 kilometres (10 miles) North of Naha; part of BULLSEYE HF/DF network, AN/FLR-15 antenna; formerly USN-25
161		Hakata	NSG Det; former ASA Field Station closed June 1972
162	USAFS Okinawa; NSGA; Co D, Marine Spt Bn; Det, 6990 ESS	Hanza, Makiminato, Okinawa	'Torii Station', 'fixed strategic installation of the ASA [INSCOM] engaged in communications

326 *The Ties That Bind*

			intelligence (COMINT) activities'; AN/FLR-9 HF/VHF DF system, Operation 'Kinsfolk'; 1694 personnel (1553 military, 141 civilian) (FY82); 189 hectares (467 acres)
163	(1st Radio Squadron Mobile; 6920 Security Group)	Johnson Air Base	Former AFSS site
164	NSG Det	Kamiseya	Supports the Naval Current Support Group of the Seventh Fleet; 'HF/DF, COMSEC and NSG functions'; manning for FOSIF Westpac; 1370 personnel (December 1969); formerly USN-39
165	(8610 DU)	Kyoto, Honshu	Former ASA site
166	6920 ESG; NSGA; Co E, Marine Spt Bn; USAFS; NSA/CSS Misawa Rep	Misawa AB, Honshu	Largest US SIGINT facility in Japan; AN/FLR-9 CDAA; 1000 Air Force, 600 Navy, 150 Army, 65 Marine Corps personnel (Feburary 1980); formerly 6921 ESW/RSM 6920 SW/ABG/SG
167	(326 CRC)	Momayama	
168		Moriyama	ESC site?
169	NSA Element	Onna, Okinawa	NSA COMINT Communications Relay Center (CCRC)
170	(NSG)	Sakata, Honshu	Site located 4 kilometres (2.5 miles) S of Yamagata
171	(6924 RSM)	Shiroi	Former AFSS site
172	6990 ESS; Det 1, 9 SRW; Co D, Mar Spt Bn; NSA element; NSG element	Kadena AB, Sobe, Okinawa	SR-71/U-2 rotational flights from Beale AFB, California; NSA Joint Sobe Processing Center (JSPC), tri-service facility with Army designated executive agent; HF/DF, and COMSEC functions of NSG; rotational RC-135 flights from Offutt AFB, NB; formerly 313 Air Det, 8603 DU; 3 INSCOM FS; possibly also Det O, 1st Radio Bn
173		Tamara Lane Annex Misawa, Honshu	Operational site of Misawa?
174		Wakkanai AS, Hokkaido	Located 3.21 kilometres (2 miles) south-east of Wakkanai
175	NSA Pacific, Far East	Yokota AB	Liaison with HQ, US Forces Japan and HQ, 5 Air Force; formerly 6007 Radio Gp (AFSS)
176	NSG Det	Yokosuka	CLASSIC WIZARD Reporting System; support to Seventh Fleet HQ and ships homeported at Yokosuka
		KWAJALEIN	
177		Kwajalein	CDAA
		LIBYA	
178	(6934 RSM)	Tripoli	AFSS site, closed
		MIDWAY ISLAND	
179	NSGA	Midway Island	NSG site
		MOROCCO	

180	(USN–12)	Sidi Yahia	NSG site, near Rabat, Morocco. Used for monitoring international telephone and telex signals. Closed in October 1978, but may have been reopened in 1982
181	(5th Air Detachment)	Sidi Slimane	AFSS site
182		Port Lyautey	NSA COMINT Communications Relay Center (CCRC)
183		Kenitra	Joint CIA/NSA SIGINT station. Closed in October 1978, but may have been reopened in 1982
		OMAN	
184		Masirah Island	GCHQ facility, but evidently some NSA involvement. Part of US NOSIS HF-DF system
185		Al Khasab	Reported to be a US SIGINT installation
186		Um Al-Ranam I	Reported to be a US SIGINT installation
		PAKISTAN	
187	(6937 Communications Group)	Bada Bier	AFSS facility, established in 1959. Located near Peshawar, 241 kilometres (150 miles) from the Soviet border. Part of 466L Program. Vacated in January 1970, but NSA presence reportedly re-established
		PANAMA	
188	193 CEWI Co Site A	Fort Clayton	INSCOM site; support of 193 Infantry Brigade; formerly 408 ASA Co/Det
189		Site B	Unmanned INSCOM site operated from Fort Clayton
190	NSGA	Galeta Island	NSG activity. Located 19.31 kilometres (12 miles) south-west of Colon. Antenna is CDAA. 63 personnel (60 military, 3 civilian); 1038 hectares (2566 acres)
		PHILIPPINES	
191	6922 ESS	Clark AB	AN/FLR-9 HF-DF CDAA. Part of 466 L Program. HF communication link with Pine Gap, Australia
192	VQ-1 DET	NAS Cubi Point	Rotational EP-3B/E and EA-3B ELINT/SIGINT aircraft from NAS Agana, Guam
193	NSG Det	Naval Base, Subic Bay	
194	(USN-27)	Sangley Point	NSG activity. May no longer be operational
195		San Miguel	NSG site. Had 950 military personnel and 100 civilian personnel in 1971. Has a HF-DF facility. San Miguel was the station which collected the intelligence on the so-called 'Tonkin Gulf incident' in 1964
		PUERTO RICO	
196	NSGA	Sebana Seca	381 personnel (318 military, 63 civilian); 911 hectares (2251 acres) formerly USN-19

328   *The Ties That Bind*

197		SAUDI ARABIA Jeddah	'Briscoe Cat'
198	332 ASA Co	SOUTH KOREA Chunchon	
199	102 CEWI Bn	Camp Hovey	Tactical support of 2 Infantry Division; formerly 329 ASA Co and 2 MI Co; 'detachments spread out along the DMZ for surveillance, observation and interception'
200	6903 ESS; Det 2, 9 SRW	Osan AB	SR-71/U-2 rotational flights from Beale AFB, California
201	USAFS Korea; NSG Det	Pyongtaek	'Zoecheler Station', includes 332 ASA Co (Ops) (Fwd). CLASSIC WIZARD Reporting system
202	146 CEWI Bn (AE) (Prov)	Camp Humphreys, Pyongtaek	INSCOM Location 177. 6RU-21H Guardrail V, OV-1D; (moved from Taegu AB in 1978–79); 704 MIDAS inactivated 15 May 1979 (with OV-1D); 146 ASA Co. (Avn) incorporated into new Bn Located next to a fixed site, codenamed 'Adventurer', used for 'ground processing activities'
203		Kanghwa-Do, on Kanghwa Island	INSCOM site
204	NSA/CSS Pacific-Korea Rep	Seoul	
205	(329 ASA Co [DS])	Camp Casey, Tongduchon-Ni	Tactical support to 2 Infantry Division; incorporated into 102 CEWI Bn
206	(ASA Pac Korea Det)	Uijongbu	
207	HQ, 502 MI Gp	Camp Coiner, Yongsan	INSCOM HQ for South Korea
208	(6915 RSM; 332 CRC)	SPAIN El Casar Del Talamanca	Former SIGINT activities
209	NSG Dept; Co F, Mar Spt Bn; VQ-1; OL-FR, 6950 ESG	Rota	SISS ZULU, CDAA; Net Control Officer HF/DF Mediterranean Area; Navy Fleet Air reconnaissance squadron (one of two worldwide, the other at NAS Agana, Guam), with EA-3B/E (with Deepwell AN/ALR-60); NSG/Marine Corps units support FOSIF/Sixth Fleet Current Support Group and Aircraft Carrier deployments. 785 NSG personnel in June 1982
210		Torrejon AB	'Olive Harvest Detachment'
211	(327 CRC)	TAIWAN Nan Szu Pu	Former ASA site and NSA COMINT Communication Relay Center (CCRC), closed 1972
212	(NSGA)	Taipei	Former NSG activity (USN-21) and AFSS (AFT-13), closed
213	6937 USA Group	6213 Air Base Station	AFSS site, operational in 1971 but now probably closed
214		ShuLin-Kon Air Station	AFSS site, operational in 1972
215	7th Radio Research Field Station	THAILAND Ramasun, Thailand	INSCOM site, established in 1964, vacated by INSCOM and transferred

216		Chiang Mai, Thailand	to Thai military in 1970. Now operated under supervision of 'US civilian technicians' Closed
217		Ubon, Thailand	Closed
218		Udorn, Thailand	Closed
219	83rd Radio Research Special Operations Unit		INSCOM site. Closed October 1970
220	Detachment 2, 6925 RSM	Bangkok, Thailand	AFSS site. Closed
221		Dong Muang Airfield	AFSS facility, became operational in 1956. Closed
		TURKEY	
222		Adana (Karatus)	Unknown function
223		Agri	Telemetry intercept station
224		Ankara	Formerly USM-49
225		Antalya	Telemetry intercept station
226		Belbasi	Monitors Soviet missile telemetry
227		Diyarbakir	Main site for radars at Diyarbakir and Pirinclik; 326 personnel (158 military, 168 civilian); 5.67 hectares (14 acres); ESC/possibly INSCOM manned; formerly Det 4, 6933 RSM; FPS-17 and FPS-79 early warning and spacetrack radars; formerly COBRA MIST (OTH) radar
228		Edirne	Telemetry intercept station
229	NSG	Istanbul	ELINT unit with AN/FLR-2 and AN/APR-9 antennas
230	INSCOM Det 97	Izmit	INSCOM site
231		Karamursel	Former NSG/ESC site; NSA COMINT Communications Relay Center (CCRC)
232		Kars	Telemetry intercept station
233		Kunia	
234		Pirinclik	Operations radar site for Diyarbakir
235		Samsun	Former ESC SIGINT site, formerly Det 2, 6933 RSM
236		Sile	Formerly Det 3, 6933 RSM
237	USAFS (TUSLOG Det 4); NSGA	Sinop	'Diogenes Station', also known as 'Location 276'; Army operated, jointly manned station; 310 military personnel; 107.24 hectares (265 acres)
238		Trabzon	Formerly AFSS SIGINT site, Det 1, 6933 RSM
239		Yamanlar (Izmir)	Telemetry intercept station
		UNITED KINGDOM	
240	6952 ESS; 10 RTS; Det, 2 MI Bn (AE)	RAF Alconbury	Rotational U-2 ELINT operations; TR-1 deployment starting in 1986; 10 RTS conducts ELINT/PHOTINT and other sensor exploitation and analysis; Army unit (formerly Det C, 2 MIBARS) conducts imagery interpretation (HQ in Kaiserlautern, West Germany)
241	NSG	Brawdy, Wales	NSG site at SOSUS TSC
242	Element of SUSLO, NSA	Cheltenham	Liaison office at GCHQ HQ

#	Unit	Location	Notes
243	6950 ESS; Joint Operations Centre	RAF Chicksands	AN/FLR-9 CDAA; operations unit is 6950 ESS; 1358 personnel (1243 military, 115 civilians); 515 hectares (1273 acres)
244	OL-DA, 6913 ESS	RAF Croughton	Probably SIGSEC support to DCA–UK HQ and major communications node
245	NSGA; Co B, Marine Spt Bn	Edzell, Scotland	CLASSIC WIZARD, AN/FLR CDAA; five additional computers were recently installed as part of CLASSIC WIZARD update; 'mission is to operate a high frequency direction finding facility'; 842 personnel (664 military, 78 civilian); 179 hectares (443 acres)
246	OL-FP, 6950 ESG	RAF High Wycombe	Possibly liaison office to UK Strike Command or support for US at High Wycombe
247	NSA	Holyloch, Scotland	
248	(6952 RSM)	Kirknewton, Scotland	Former Air Force SIGINT station closed in September 1960
249	SUSLO (NSA); NSS Det; NSG Eur	London	NSA liaison with UK GCHQ; Naval support of US Naval Forces Europe HQ and FOSIC London (FOSICLAN)
250	'USAFS/13 USASAFS'; OL-FZ, 6950 ESG	Menwith Hill, Harrogate	Project Wideband Extraction; NSA station with minimal military manning; operates 'Phase III site (AN/FSC-78)'; '355 OL'; formerly 8620 DU
251	6988 ESS; Det 1, 306 SW; Debt 4, 9 SRW; Det 1, 6949 ESS	RAF Mildenhall	Rotational RC-135 SIGINT aircraft and crews from Offutt AFB, NB; SR-71; formerly 6954 ESS; rotational EP-3E aircraft from Rota, Spain
252		RAF Sculthorpe	Former AFSS site, formerly 49th Air Det
253		South Ruislip	Former AFSS site, formerly 7th Air Det
254		RAF Wyton	Former site of intermittent deployment of EP-3 aircraft from Rota, Spain
		USSR	
255	USM-2	Moscow	INSCOM facility in US Embassy in Moscow, intercepts microwave transmissions including telephone conversations
		WEST GERMANY	
256	XXX CEWI Bn; Det K, 201 ASA Co	Bleidorn Kasern Ansbach AAF, Katterbach, Ansbach	Tactical support of 1 Armored Division; CEWI (HQ Bleidorn Ksn) incorporates 501 MI Co and 202 ASA Co (DS) Arm); Co D (SOTAS) Ansbach AAF at Katterbach; formerly elements of 504 MI Co
257	USAFS; NSGA; 6913 ESS; NCEUR Augsburg; OL-FU, 6950 ESG; 502 I&S	Gablingen Ksn/Flak Ksn-Sheridan Ksn, Augsburg	'Largest COMINT complex in Europe'; AN/FLR-9 CDAA; 'Site 300' operations site, 130.3 hectares (322 acres) at Gablingen;

The UKUSA SIGINT network 331

	Bn (EW) 201 ASA Co (Scty); Det T, 201 ASA Co		Administrative elements at Flak and Sheridan Ksn; 326 ASA Co, 307 ASA Bn, Flak Ksn; 1, 2, 3 Ops Bns, 328 ASA Co (C&P), 409 ASA Co (Ops), 302 ASA Bn, Sheridan Ksn; NSGA includes DF and 'Div 21'; 201 ASA Co HQ for all Army SIGSEC elements in Europe
258	6915 ESS; NSA Eur Spd; Det F, USAFS Augsburg ('Southgate')	Bad Aibling	Major NSA facility; 'Wildbore'; 130.3 hectares (322 acres) at QU238075; formerly Det 72, 6950 ESG; satellite terminal installed in 1982; DF Det/CSS Det, Forward Ops Bn, USAFS Augsburg; Wildbore Det/DF Det, Southgate
259	6910 ESG	Bad Hersfeld	
260	Bad K Det, 415 ASA Co; Det E, 201 ASA Co	Bad Kreuznach	Tactical support to 8 Infantry Division
261	401 SOD (Abn)	Bad Toelz	Support to Special Forces Det, Europe
262	(B611 DU)	Baumholder	Former Army SIGINT unit, closed in 1972
263	NCEUR Berlin; Det O, 201 ASA Co	Berlin	Support to US Commander, Berlin
264	Element of 6912 ESS	Marienfelde, Berlin	AF SIGINT operation, called 'ASA Operations Facility' (at UU996083); Streamliner Remote Communications Center
265	6912 ESG/OL–JA, 5911 ESS	Tempelhof AB, Berlin	Operations unit is 6912 ESS; also SIGSEC mission
266	USAFS; element of 6912 ESS	Teufelsburg, Berlin	Major SIGINT station with Army, Air Force and UK personnel; located at UU806180
267	326 ASA Det	Bindlach	
268		Brandhof	Unmanned Army LaFaire Vite Site
269	(6913 RSM; USN-40)	Bremerhaven	Former SIGINT station (NSG and AFSS)
270	(6911 RSM)	Darmstadt	Former AFSS site
271	(6912 RSM)	Dromersheim	Former AFSS site
272	Det 1, 330 EW Avn Co (Fwd); 73 CBTI Co (AS)	Echterdingen AAF, Stuttgart	Airborne SIGINT units with IMINT/ELINT functions, with 15 RV/OV-10 Mohawk; formerly 73 MICAS
273	Det N, USAFS Augsburg	Eckstein Hoher Bogen (Mt Eckstein)	Remote collection site; possibly Co B, Fwd Ops Bn, USAFS Augsburg
274	NCEUR Frankfurt; OL-FA, 6950 ESG	I.G. Farben Building, Frankfurt	NSA Europe Office, Germany, Laboratory (NSA/CSS); formerly Joint Operations Support Activity (JOSAF), European Security Region
275	302 ASA Bn (Corps); Det D, 201 ASA Co	Frankfurt	V Corps support
276	Det G, 201, ASA Co	Drake Ksn, Frankfurt	SIGSEC support
277	533 CEWI Bn; Det S, 201 ASA Co	Michael Bks, Frankfurt	Tactical support of 3 Armored Division; formerly 856 ASA Co (DS) (Arm)
278	340 SIGINT; EW Co, 11 ACR; Det D (Fwd), 201 ASA Co	Sickels AAF, Fulda	Tactical support to 11 Armored Cavalry Regiment

332   The Ties That Bind

279	XXX CEWI Co	Lucius D. Clay Ksn, Garlstedt	Tactical support of 2 Armored Division (Fwd)
280		Giessen AAF	SOTAS/Quick Fix Co, 3 Armored Division
281	Det L, 201 ASA Co	Goeppingen	SIGSEC support to 1 Infantry Division (Fwd)
282	Det Q, 201 ASA Co	Grafenwoehr	SIGSEC support to Seventh Army Training Center
283	OL, 6911 ESS; element 330 ASA Co; element 307 ASA Bn	Gruenstadt	Near Worms?, tactical site
284	6911 (Mobile)	Hahn AB	Mobile tactical support unit
285	Army Cryptologic Spt Gp; OL-FD, 6950 ESG; Det A, 201 ASA	Campbell Bks, Heidelberg	Operational extension of NSA in support of DCSI, USAREUR; Air Force ESC liaison to HQ, USAREUR
286		Heidenheim	Unmanned Army La Faire Vite Site
287	(502 CRG)	Heilbronn	Former ASA site?
288	(8606 DU)	Herzogenaurach	Former ASA station, closed 1972
289		Hof	AN/FLR-12 antennas; transferred to West German control in 1969, US retains data exchange system
290	Det R, 201 ASA Co	Hohenfels	SIGSEC support to Seventh Army Training Center
291	108 CEWI Bn	Idar Oberstein	Tactical support to 8 Infantry Division; incorporating 415 ASA Co (DS)
292	2MI Bn (AE)	Kapaun Bks, Kaiserslautern	HQ or element of HQ for Corps level airborne SIGINT unit; activated 16 May 1979 in consolidation of former 2 MIBARS; includes CBTII Co, 330 Avn Co (EW) (formerly 330 ASA Co), 73 CBTI Echterdingen; systems include Guardrail (airborne tactical COMINT) and Quick Look (airborne passive LOS ELINT/ESM); battalion elements at Ramstein AB, Sembach, Echterdingen, Zweibrucken, and Alconbury, UK
293	851 ASA Co (DS)	Kitzingen	Tactical support to 3 Infantry Division
294	331 ASA Co	Knielingen	
295		Landshut	La Faire Vite Site (at TP 947823)
296	6910 ESW	Lindsey AS	
297	307 ASA Bn (Corps)	Ludwigsburg	VII Corps support
298		Finthen AAF, Mainz	SONTAS/Quick Fix, 108 CEWI Bn
279	Det M, USAFS Augsburg	Mt Meissner	Operational site of USAFS Augsburg element of 302 ASA Bn, remote duty station possibly Co A, Fwd Ops Bn, USAFS Augsburg
300	Det H, 201 ASA Co	Moehringen, (Stuttgart)	SIGSEC support and 'Project Beta'
301	Element of 2 MI Bn (AE)	Muenchweiler	Element of HQs
302	HQ, 66 MI Gp; Det 71, 6950 ESG	McGraw Ksn, Feucht AAF	Major subordinate command of INSCOM in Europe; Air Force liaison office
303		Nurnberg	Aviation elements, XXX CEWI Bn

304	XXX CEWI Bn; Det A, 201 ASA Co	Merril Bks, Nurnberg	Tactical support to 2 Armored Cavalry Regiment; formerly 359 ASA Co
305	Det B, 201 ASA Co	Pirmasens	SIGSEC support and NSA COMINT Communications Relay Centre (CCRC)
306		Praunheim	Det 7, JCF, Radio Eval Spt Office; Det 3, 1100 ABW, OJCF
307	ESC Europe HQ; Flt Ops, 330 Avn Co	Ramstein AB	Air Force SIGINT HQ, colocated with HQ, US Air Forces Europe (USAFE); Army RU-21H Guardrail aircraft also use the airfield; formerly 6910 AFSS Gp
308	(307 CRB; 339 CRO)	Rothwesten	Former ASA field station closed in 1972
309	(8608 DU)	Scheyern	Former ASA site
310	Det A, USAFS Augsburg	Schleswig	Small SIGINT site, 25 personnel, 40.23 kilometres (25 miles) S of Danish border; DF Det; possibly designated Det, Fwd Ops Bn, USAFS Augsburg
311	Det, 326 Ops Co (Fwd)	Mt Schneeberg	Operational site of USAFS Augsburg, remote duty station
312		Schwamberg	Unmanned Army La Faire Vite Site
313	6918 ESS; 330 Avn Co (Fwd)	Sembach AB	Army unit with Guardrail V system
314		Slegelback	
315	NSA/CSS Eur (NCEUR); EUDAC; Det 70, 6950 ESG; JRC EUCOM	Patch Bks, Stuttgart-Vaihingen	Liaison with European Command HQ; European Defense Analysis Center, Joint Reconnaissance Center, Europe
316	Det A, USAFS Augsburg	Todendorf	Remote colection site on 'NATO base'; formerly NSGA; possibly closed in mid-1970s (see also Schleswig)
317	(AFSS)	Wiesbaden AB	Former AFSS site
318	Det K, USAFS Augsburg	Wobeck	Remote ELINT station, part of La Faire Vite network; formerly 4th Platoon, 326 Ops Co (Forward); possibly redesignated Det Wobeck, 307 ASA Bn or Co C, Fwd Ops Bn, USAFS Augsburg
319	Det M, 201 ASA Co	Worms	SIGSEC support and 'Project Scope-Picture-FWD'
320	103 CEWI Bn/Det 1, 201 ASA Co	Leighton Bks, Wurzburg	Tactical support of 3 Infantry Division
321		Wurmburg	La Faire Vite network control center
322	Element of 2 MI Bn (AE)	Zweibrucken AB	Army airborne SIGINT unit; formerly Det B, 2 MIBARS, former AF site (6901 AFSS Gp) closed in 1967

BRITISH SIGNALS INTELLIGENCE FACILITIES — UK LOCATIONS

REF	UNIT	LOCATION	COMMENT
323	GCHQ	Priors Road, Oakley, Cheltenham, Gloucestershire	GCHQ. Also houses Joint Technical Language Service (JTLS)

#	Site	Location	Notes
324	GCHQ	Benhall, Cheltenham, Gloucestershire	
325		Blackhill (Cricklade), Wiltshire	
326	CSO Central Training School (CTS)	Bletchley Park, Buckinghamshire	Headquarters of GCHQ during World War II. Now CSO CTS
327	4 Communications Unit	Boddington, Gloucestershire	Military unit attached to and supporting GCHQ Cheltenham
328		Bower, near Wick, Scotland	Closed
329		Brora, Scotland	CSOS
330		Cheadle, Staffordshire	CSOS. Main RAF W/T monitoring station during World War II; now monitors Soviet Air Force communications
331		Croft Spa	Adcock DF site. Closed
332		Culmhead, near Taunton, Somerset	CSOS
333	RAF 399 and 591 Signals Units	RAF Digby, Leicestershire	Main UK RAF SIGINT site
334	CSOS Earls Court	Empress State Building Earls Court, London	CSOS
335	223 Signals Squadron	Flowerdown, near Winchester, Hampshire	Closed
336	224 Signals Squadron	Garratts Way, Loughborough	Army training and field station
337		Gilnahirk, Northern Ireland	Closed in late 1970s
338	HMG Communications Centre/Diplomatic Telecommunications Maintenance Service (DTMS)	Hanslope Park	Interception site for German Abwehr services signals during World War II. Now communications centre for SIGINT traffic collected at GCHQ posts in British Embassies. DTMS is a debugging/'sweeping' unit CSOS
339		Hawklaw near Cupar, Fife	
340		Irton Moor, near Scarborough, North Yorkshire	CSOS. Was also an important SIGINT site during World War II
341		Island Hill, Comber, Northern Ireland	Closed in late 1970s
342		Morwenstow, near Bude, Cornwall	Satellite ground station with three terminals and further two terminals planned
343		Palmer Street, Westminster, London SW1	GCHQ London Office. Probable station for interception of ILC (International Licensed Carrier) traffic Antennas include CDAA and Loop Antenna Array Unmanned 'Pusher' CDAA
344	Foreign Office Training Establishment	Poundon, Buckinghamshire	
345		Shenley Church End, near Bletchley, Buckinghamshire	
346		Wincombe near Shaftesbury, Dorset	Closed
347	224 Signals Squadron	Wymeswold, Leicestershire	
348		RAF Wyton	Base for SIGINT aircraft

BRITISH SIGNALS INTELLIGENCE FACILITIES — OVERSEAS LOCATIONS

UNIT		LOCATION	COMMENTS
349		Aden	Former major RAF SIGINT site
350		Two Boats, Ascension Island	Operated jointly with US Important SIGINT site during the Falklands war
351		Victoria Barracks, Melbourne, Australia	SUKLO, DSD HQ
352		RAF Bahrain	
353		Francistown, Botswana	Closed
354	9th Signals Regiment	Ayios Nikoaos, Cyprus	
355		Mount Olympus, Cyprus	OTH Radar site located in the Troodos Mountains. ELINT Detachment for Pergamos
356		Akrotiri, Cyprus	British Sovereign Base (BSB) used by U-2, R-1 and SR-71 aircraft. Used to monitor the Camp David Accord
357		Episkopi, Cyprus	Also used to monitor the Camp David Accord
358	33 Signals Unit, RAF	Pergamos, Cyprus	Located within the British Sovereign Base (BSB) at Dhekelia
359		Prague Embassy, Czechoslovakia	Probably used for monitoring
360		Diego Garcia	Joint GCHQ/NSA station. Forms part of NOSIS
361		Cairo Embassy, Egypt	Probably used for monitoring
362		Accra Embassy, Ghana	Probably used for monitoring
363		Gibraltar	COMINT and HF-DF station
364		Stanley Fort Satellite Station, Hong Kong	Built by RAF in 1977. Monitors the Chinese space and missile programs
365		Little Sai Wan, Hong Kong Island	Operated jointly with DSD. Recently relocated in south Hong Kong Island (Chung Hom Kok?)
366		Tai Mo Shan, New Territories, Hong Kong	Operated jointly with DSD.
367		Budapest Embassy, Hungary	Probably used for monitoring
368		Nairobi Embassy, Kenya	Used for monitoring
369		Sigli, Malta	Closed
370		Mauritius	Closed in 1975
371		Lilongwe Embassy, Malawi	Used for monitoring
372		Masirah Island, Oman	GCHQ station operated jointly with NSA. Forms part of NOSIS
373		Warsaw Embassy, Poland	Probably used for monitoring
374		Dahran, Saudi Arabia	Possible GCHQ site
375		Freetown Embassy, Sierra Leone	Probably used for monitoring
376		Pretoria Embassy, South Africa	Used for monitoring
377		Sinop, Turkey	Joint operation with US INSCOM

336 The Ties That Bind

#	Unit	Location	Comments
378		Fort George C. Meade, Maryland, USA	SUKLO, NSA HQ
379		Moscow Embassy, USSR	Used for monitoring
380	3rd Squadron, 13 Signals Regiment and 26 Signals Unit, RAF	Teufelsberg, Berlin, West Germany	
381	291 Signals Unit, RAF	Scharfoldenorf, West Germany	Closed
382	13 Signals Regiment	Birgelen, West Germany	
383	Detachment of 13 Signals Regiment	Jever, West Germany	
384	225 Signals Squadron; 14 Signals Regiment (EW)	Celle, West Germany	
385	226 Signals Squadron	Dannenberg, West Germany	
386		Gorleben, near Hanberg West Germany	Alleged British listening station
387		Lusaka Embassy, Zambia	Major covert South African monitoring station

CANADIAN SIGNALS INTELLIGENCE FACILITIES

#	Unit	Location	Comments
388	CSE HQ	Ottawa, Ontario	Also site of World War II station
389		Amherst, near Halifax, Nova Scotia	World War II station
390		West Point Barracks, Victoria	World War II station
391		Riske Creeke, British Columbia	World War II station
393		Grand Prarie, Alberta Point Grey	Subsidiary detachment to West Point Barracks
394	5th Radio Squadron RCAF	Whitehorse, Canada	Probably involved in monitoring USSR
395	Argentia Naval Station, SWBD	Argentia, Newfoundland	
396	Carp Canadian Forces Station, SWBD	Ottawa	
397	Debert Canadian Forces Station, SWBD	Nova Scotia	
398	770th Communication Research Squadron, Gander Canadian Forces Station, SWBD	Newfoundland	
399	1st Canadian Signals Regiment Co.	Ontario	
400	St Margarets 21st Radio Station	New Brunswick	
401	Inuvik Canadian Forces Station	Inuvik, New Territories	Probably monitors USSR
402	Leitrim Canadian Forces Station	Leitrim, Ontario	

403 Masset Canadian Forces Station, SWB	Masset, British Columbia	
404	Hayes River	
405 Alert Station	Elsmire Island	
406 Bermuda Communications Research Station	Bermuda	

AUSTRALIAN SIGNALS INTELLIGENCE FACILITIES — AUSTRALIAN LOCATIONS

UNIT	LOCATION	COMMENTS
407 DSD HQ	Victoria Barracks, Melbourne	
408	HMAS Harman, ACT	Began operation in 1939. Uses Adcock DF system
409 6 Signal Regiment	Watsonia/Rockbank, Victoria	AN/FSC-78 terminal installed at Watsonia for direct satellite communications with NSA and CIA
410 No. 3 Telecommunications Unit	Pearce Air Force Base, Western Australia	Monitors Naval and air traffic over Indian Ocean. Uses Plessey CDAA
411 7 Signal Regiment	Cabarlah, Queensland	Monitors radio transmission through South-west Pacific. Also uses Plessey CDAA
412 RAN/Detachment of 7 Signal Regiment	Shoal Bay, near Darwin, Northern Territory	Replaced Coonawarra station and Singapore station. Project LARSWOOD

AUSTRALIAN SIGNALS INTELLIGENCE FACILITIES — OVERSEAS LOCATIONS

UNIT	LOCATION	COMMENTS
413	Port Moresby, Papua New Guinea	Project 'Reprieve'
414	Little Sai Wan, Hong Kong Island	Operated with GCHQ. Recently relocated further south on Hong Kong Island (Chum Hom Kok?)
415	Tai Mo Shan, New Territories, Hong Kong	Operated with GCHQ
416	Singapore	Closed in 1975
417	Bangkok Embassy, Thailand	
418	Jakarta Embassy, Indonesia	

NEW ZEALAND SIGNALS INTELLIGENCE FACILITIES

UNIT	LOCATION	COMMENTS
419 GCSB HQ	14th Floor Freyberg Building, Wellington.	
420	Tangimoana	Only NZ SIGINT station. Transferred from HMNZS Irirangi in August 1982. Antennas include CDAA, two rotatable log-periodic systems, and one omni-gain system. Monitors South-west Pacific and across to South America.

SOME THIRD PARTY UKUSA LOCATIONS

UNIT	LOCATION	COMMENTS
	DENMARK	
421	Aflandshage	100 metre (328-foot) CDAA
422	Almindingen, Bornholm	CDAA
423	Dueodde, Bornholm	VHF antenna
424	Gedser	VHF antenna
425	Hjorring	Antennas include Wullenw ber system; horizontal HF antenna; log periodic antenna; loop antenna; AN/MSC-61 DSCS ground terminal
326	Logumkloster	Antennas include CDAA; horizontal HF antenna; log periodic antenna; two loop antennas
	NORWAY	
427	Fauske (Vetan)	VHF SIGINT station
428	Jessheim	25 metre (82-foot) CDAA and Quadratic HF Log Periodic Array
429	Kirkenes/Hessing	NSA site
430	Randaberg	40 metre (131-foot) CDAA
431	Skage (Namdalen)	40 metre (131-foot) CDAA
432	Vadso	Major HF/VHF SIGINT site; 150 metre 492-foot CDAA; monitors radio communications in Kola Peninsula
433	Vardo	20 metre (66-foot) tower with UHF/VHF SIGINT antennas; possibly triangulated with Viksjofellet
434	Viksjofellet	20 metre (66-foot) tower with UHF/VHF SIGINT antennas; telemetry intercept from Soviet missile tests at Plesetsk, White Sea and Barents Sea
	WEST GERMANY	
435	Ahrweiler	SIGINT analysis center at headquarters of Amt fur Fernmeldewesen Bundeswehr (AFmBw), near Bonn
436	Bad Sachsa	Air Force (Luftwaffe) SIGINT site No. 4. Operates AN/QRC-259 system. Also supports French SIGINT activity
437	Braunschweig	Major SIGINT collection site operated by Bundes Nachrichten Dienst (BND). Also operates AN/QRC-259 receiving system and HF/VHF DF equipment
438	Hof	SIGINT site operated by AFmBw. Antenna is AN/FLR-12
439	Kornberg	Army (Heer) SIGINT Site No. 1
440	Luchow	Luftwaffe SIGINT Site No. 3
441	Markleuthen	Army (Heer) SIGINT Site No. 2
442	Neustadt	Luftwaffe SIGINT Site No. 1 and Navy SIGINT site. Operates AN/WLR-1 receiving systems
443	Pullach	BND HQ in Munich. Maintains Braunschweig site

444	Schneeberg	Army (Heer) SIGINT Site No. 3
445	Wachtberg-Werthoven	Institut fur Funk und Elektronik, maintains major facility for SIGINT R&D and analysis
446	Unknown location near Molln	Luftwaffe SIGINT Site No. 2
447	Unknown location near Teuschnitz	Luftwaffe SIGINT Site No. 5

2

Heads of the principal UKUSA security and intelligence agencies and organizations

UNITED KINGDOM
Chiefs, Secret Intelligence Service (MI-6)
Admiral Mansfield Cumming	1911–19
Admiral Sir Hugh Sinclair	1919–39
Major General Sir Stewart Manzies	1939–53
Major General Sir John Sinclair	1953–56
Sir Dick Goldsmith White	1956–69
Sir John Rennie	1969–73
Sir Maurice Oldfield	1973–78
Arthur Franks	1978–82
Colin Figures	1982–

Directors-General, Security Service (MI-5)
Major General Sir Vernon Kell	1909–40
Sir David Petrie	1940–46
Sir Percy Sillitoe	1946–53
Sir Dick Goldsmith White	1953–56
Sir Roger Henry Hollis	1956–65
Sir Martin Furnival Jones	1965–72
Sir Michael Hanley	1972–79
Sir Howard Truyton Smith	1979–81
John Lewis Jones	1981–

Directors, Government Communications Headquarters (GCHQ)
Commander Alastair Deniston	1939–42
Commander Sir Edward Travis	1942–?
Brigadier Richard Gambier-Parry	?–1952
Sir Eric Jones	1952–60
Sir Clive Lochnis	1960–64
Sir Leonard Hooper	1965–73
Sir Arthur Bensall	1973–78
Sir Brian Tovey	1978–83
Peter Marychurch	1983–

Directors-General, Defence Intelligence Staff (DIS)
Major General Kenneth Strong	1964–66
Air Chief Marshal Alfred Earle	1966–73

Admiral Sir Louis Le Paily   1973–75
Marshal John Aiken   1975–
Vice Admiral Sir Roy Holliday   –

AUSTRALIA

Directors-General, Office of National Assessments (ONA)

Robert W. Furlonger	20 February 1978–29 April 1981
Michael Cook	29 April 1981–

Directors, Defence Signals Directorate (DSD)

R.N. Thompson	?–1978
R.D. Botterill	1978–82
T.W.S. James	1982–

Directors, Australian Secret Intelligence Service (ASIS)

Alfred D. Brookes	13 May 1952–22 August 1957
Ralph L. Harry	23 August 1957–1 April 1960
William T. Robertson (Acting Director)	1 April 1960–1 September 1960
Sir Walter Cawthorn	1 September 1960–3 July 1968
William T. Robertson	3 July 1968–7 November 1975
Ian J.S. Kennison	7 November 1975–October 1981
John Ryan (Acting Director)	October 1981–18 December 1983
F. Stuart Fry (Acting Director)	20 December 1983–29 February 1984
James O. Furner	29 Februrary 1984–

Directors-General, Australian Security Intelligence Organisation (ASIO)

Mr Justice Reed	16 March 1949–July 1950
Brigadier Sir Charles C.F. Spry	July 1950–1970
Peter Barbour	1970–September 1975
F.J. Mahony (Acting Director-General)	September 1975–7 March 1976
Mr Justice Woodward	7 March 1976–7 September 1981
T. Harvey Barnett	7 September 1981–

Directors, Joint Intelligence Organisation (JIO)

Robert W. Furlonger	May 1969–February 1972
Gordon A. Jockel	February 1972–30 March 1978
A.W. McMichael	30 March 1978–10 July 1982
N.L. Webb (Acting)	10 July 1982–5 December 1982
Brigadier James O. Furner	6 December 1982–29 February 1984
G.R. Marshall (Acting)	29 February 1984–

Heads, Protective Services Coordination Centre (PSCC)

Allan P. Fleming	25 August 1976–8 May 1978
William T. Robertson	8 May 1978–1 February 1982
Brigadier P. Michael Jeffrey	2 February 1982–16 May 1983
Brigadier John R. Sheldrick	16 May 1983–

NEW ZEALAND

Heads, New Zealand Security Intelligence Service (NZSIS)

Brigadier Herbert E. Gilbert	28 November 1956–20 July 1976
Paul Loxton Molineaux	16 August 1976–6 May 1983
Brigadier John L. Smith	1 July 1983–

Directors, Joint Intelligence Bureau (JIB)/External Intelligence Bureau (EIB)

V.E. Jaynes	31 March 1952–31 March 1975 (JIB); 1 April 1975–23 December 1979 (EIB)
R.B. Atkins	24 December 1979–

Director, Government Communications Security Bureau (GCSB)

C.M. Hansen	1977–

342 The Ties That Bind

CANADA
Directors-General, Royal Canadian Mounted Police (RCMP) Security Service

William Ketty	1964–67
W. Leonard Higgit	1967–69
J.E.M. Barrette	1969–(?)
Michael Dare	1973–81 (?)
J.B. Giroux	1981–

UNITED STATES
Directors, National Reconnaissance Office (NRO)

Joseph V. Charyk	1960–63
Brockway McMillan	1963–65
Norman S. Paul	1965–67
Townsend Hoopes	1967–69
John L. McLucas	1969–73
James W. Plummer	1973–76
Hans Mark	1977–79
Robert J. Hermann	1979–81
Edward C. Aldridge Jr	1981–

Directors, National Security Agency (NSA)

Lieutenant General Ralph Julian Canine, USA	4 November 1952–November 1956
Lieutenant General John Samford, USAF	November 1956–November 1960
Vice Admiral Laurence Frost, USN	November 1960–30 June 1962
Lieutenant General Gordon Blake, USAF	30 June 1962–1 June 1965
Lieutenant General Marshall S. Carter, USA	1 June 1965–1 August 1969
Vice Admiral Noel Gayler, USN	1 August 1969–24 August 1972
Lieutenant General Samuel C. Phillips, USAF	24 August 1972–15 August 1973
Lieutenant General Lew Allen, Jr, USAF	15 August 1973–5 July 1977
Vice Admiral Bobby Ray Inman, USN	5 July 1977–10 March 1981
Lieutenant General Lincoln D. Faurer, USAF	10 March 1981–

Directors, Central Intelligence Agency (CIA)

Real Admiral Roscoe Hillenkoeter, USN	1947–50
General Walter Bedell Smith, USA	1950–53
Allen W. Dulles	1953–61
John A. McCone	1961–65
Vice Admiral William F. Raborn, Jr, USN	1965–66
Richard Helms	1966–73
James R. Schlesinger	1973
William Colby	1973–76
George Bush	1976–77
Admiral Stansfield Turner, USN	1977–81
William J. Casey	1981–

Directors, Defense Intelligence Agency (DIA)

Lieutenant General Joseph F. Carroll, USAF	1961–70
Lieutenant General Donald V. Bennett, USA	1970–73
Vice Admiral Vincent P. De Poix, USN	1973–75
Lieutenant General Daniel D. Graham, USA	1975–76
Lieutenant General Eugene F. Tighe, USAF	1976–77
Lieutenant General Samuel V. Wilson, USA	1977–78
Lieutenant General Eugene F. Tighe, USAF	1978–82
Major General James B. Williams, USA	1982–

Directors, Federal Bureau of Investigation (FBI)

J. Edgar Hoover	1924–72
L. Patrick Gray	1972–73
Clarence Kelley	1973–77
William Webster	1977–

Notes

1 Introduction
1 James Bamford, *The Puzzle Palace: A Report on America's Most Secret Agency* (Houghton Mifflin, Boston, 1982), p 312.
2 Ronald Lewin, *The American Magic: Codes, Ciphers and the Defeat of Japan* (Farrar, Straus, Giroux, New York, 1982), p 46.
3 For accounts of the various apsects of the ULTRA operation see F.W. Winterbotham *The Ultra Secret* (Harper & Row, New York, 1974); Joseph Garlinski, *The Enigma War* (Charles Scribner's, New York, 1980); Gordon Welchman, *The Hut Six Story: Breaking the Enigma Codes* (McGraw Hill, New York, 1982); Peter Calvocoresi, *Top Secret Ultra* (Panthcon, New York, 1980); Ralph Bennett, *Ultra in the West: The Normandy Campaign of 1944–1945* (Charles Scribner's, New York, 1979) and Ronald Lewin *Ultra Goes to War* (McGraw Hill, New York, 1978). With regard to the ocean surveillance/naval intelligence aspect see Patrick Beesly, *Very Special Intelligence: The Story of the Admiralty's Operational Intelligence Centre* (Sphere Books, London, 1977); and W.J. Holmes, *Double Edged Secrets: US Naval Intelligence Operations in the Pacific During World War II* (Naval Institute Press, Annapolis, 1979).
4 Bamford, *The Puzzle Palace*, p 314.
5 ibid.
6 Thomas F. Troy, *Donovan and the CIA: A History of the Establishment of the CIA* (Alethia Books, Frederick, 1981), p 163.
7 Richard Dunlop, *Donovan: America's Master Spy* (Rand McNally, Chicago, 1982), p 355.
8 Bob Elliot, *Scarlet to Green: Canadian Army Intelligence 1903–1963* (Hunter Rose, Toronto, 1981), p 461.
9 F.H. Hinsley, E.E. Thomas, C.F.G. Ransom and R.C. Knight, *British Intelligence in the Second World War, Volume 2* (Cambridge University Press, New York, 1981), p 551n.
10 See p.xv of David Kahn's Introduction in Herbert O. Yardley, *The American Black Chamber*, (Ballantine, New York, 1981); Robert Sheppard, 'Lack of Quick RCMP Action Upset Gouzenko, Papers Say', *Toronto Globe and Mail*, 17 October 1981 p 5; and Elliot, *Scarlet to Green*, p 461.
11 ibid.
12 ibid., p 460.
13 Joint Committee on the Investigation of the Pearl Harbor Attack, *Pearl Harbor Attack* (US Government Printing Office, Washington, DC, 1946), Part 2, p 947.

344   The Ties That Bind

14 D.M. Horner, 'Special Intelligence in the South-west Pacific Area in World War II', *Australian Outlook* (Vol. 32, No. 4), 1978, pp 310–27.
15 Desmond Ball, 'Allied Intelligence Cooperation Involving Australia during World War II', *Australian Outlook* (Vol. 32, No. 4), 1978, pp 299–309.
16 Elliot, *Scarlet to Green*, pp 384–5.
17 Steven L. Carruthers, *Australia under Siege: Japanese Submarine Raiders 1942* (Solus Books, Sydney, 1982), p 19.
18 ibid., pp 19, 64.
19 Ball, 'Allied Intelligence Cooperation Involving Australia During World War II'.
20 Roy MacLaren, *Canadians Behind Enemy Lines 1939–1945* (University of British Columbia Press, Vancouver, 1981), p 183.
21 ibid., p 302.
22 ibid., p 264.
23 ibid., p 95.
24 Richard Clark, *The Man Who Broke PURPLE* (Little, Brown, Boston, 1977), 208.
25 Ball, 'Allied Intelligence Cooperation Involving Australia during World War II'.
26 Duncan Campbell, 'Threat of the Electronic Spies', *New Statesman*, 2 February 1979, pp 140–4.
27 Office of the Adjutant General, 'United States–United Kingdom Security Agreement', (Department of the Army, Washington, 8 October 1948).
28 Emphasis added. See Chapter 7 for the entire document.
29 Paul Kelly, 'NSA, The Biggest Secret Spy Network in Australia', *National Times*, 23–28 May 1977.
30 *Hansard (Canadian House of Commons)* No. 18, 24 March 1975.
31 Desmond Ball, 'The US Naval Ocean Surveillance Information System (NOSIS) — Australia's Role', *Pacific Defence Reporter*, June 1982, pp 40–9.
32 Duncan Campbell and Clive Thomas, 'BBC's Trade Secrets', *New Statesman*, 4 July 1980, pp 13–14.
33 Desmond Ball, *A Suitable Piece of Real Estate: American Installations in Australia* (Hale and Iremonger, Sydney, 1980), p 40.
34 Michael Richardson, 'Two Listening Posts', *Age*, 17 February 1973, p 15.
35 Lewin, *Ultra*, p 46.
36 Ball, *A Suitable Piece of Real Estate*, p 40; Chapman Pincher, *Inside Story: A Documentary of the Pursuit of Power* (Stein and Day, New York, 1979), p 157.
37 Transcript of 'The Fifth Estate: The Espionage Establishment', broadcast by Canadian Broadcasting Company, 1974.

2 The British security and intelligence community

1 For a history of British secret service activities see Richard Deacon, *A History of the British Secret Service* (Taplinger, New York, 1969); and Nigel West, *MI-6: British Secret Intelligence Operations 1909–1945* (Weidenfield and Nicholson, London, 1983).
2 See Bruce Page, David Leitch and Philip Knightley, *The Philby Conspiracy* (Signet, New York, 1968); Andrew Boyle, *The Climate of Treason* (Hutchinson, London, 1980).
3 Chapman Pincher, *Their Trade is Treachery* (Sidgwick and Jackson, London, 1980).
4 Duncan Campbell, 'The Spies Who Spend What They Like' *New Statesman*, 16 May 1980, pp 739 ff; and 'GCHQ: The Cover Up Continues', *New Statesman*, 23 May 1980, pp 774–7.
5 F.H. Hinsley, E.E. Thomas, C.F.G. Ransom and R.C. Knight, *British Intelli-*

gence in the Second World War, Volume 1 (Cambridge University Press, New York, 1979), p 16; and West, *MI-6*, p 4.
6 Hinsley et al., *British Intelligence in the Second World War, Volume 1*, p 16.
7 ibid.
8 Edward Van Der Rhoer, *Master Spy: A True Story of Allied Espionage in Soviet Russia* (Charles Scribner's, New York, 1981).
9 Andrew Weir, Jonathan Bloch and Pat Fitzgerald, 'Sun Sets Over the Other Empire', *The Middle East*, October 1981, pp 39–42.
10 ibid.
11 Donald Neff, *Warriors of Suez: Eisenhower Takes America into the Middle East* (The Linden Press/Simon and Schuster, New York, 1981), pp 215–16; Wilbur Crane Eveland, *Ropes of Sand* (Norton, New York, 1980).
12 Weir et al., 'Sun Sets Over the Other Empire', p 40.
13 ibid.
14 David Wise and Thomas B. Ross, *The Espionage Establishment* (Random House, New York, 1967).
15 Duncan Campbell, 'Friends and Others', *New Statesman*, 26 November 1982, p 6.
16 ibid.
17 Duncan Campbell, 'Big Brother's Many Mansions', *New Statesman*, 8 February 1980, pp 194–7.
18 ibid.
19 F.H. Hinsley et al., *British Intelligence in the Second World War, Volume 1*, p 16.
20 J. Ll, J. Edwards, *Ministerial Responsibility for National Security* (Canadian Government Publishing Centre, Hull, 1980), p 60.
21 Lord Denning's *Report* (Her Majesty's Stationery Office, London, 1963), paragraph 238.
22 ibid.
23 ibid., p 91.
24 'The Honourable Grammar Schoolboy', *New Statesman*, 7 July 1978, pp 12–13.
25 Tony Bunyan, *The Political Police in Britain* (St Martin's, New York, 1976), pp 175–7.
26 ibid.
27 Campbell, 'Big Brother's Many Mansions'.
28 Nigel West, *A Matter of Trust: MI-5, 1945–72*, (Weidenfield and Nicholson, London, 1982), p 13; and 'Thatcher's Leak', *New Statesman*, 7 January 1983, p 5.
29 See Duncan Campbell, 'Threat of the Electronic Spies', *New Statesman*, 2 February 1979, pp 142–5.
30 Bunyan, *The Political Police in Britain*, p 191.
31 Duncan Campbell, 'Threat of the Electronic Spies', p 142.
32 Richard Walsh and George Munster, *Documents on Australian Foreign Policy, 1968–1975* (J.R. Walsh and G.J. Munster, Sydney, 1980) p 96.
33 Chapman Pincher, *Inside Story: A Documentary of the Pursuit of Power* (Stein and Day, New York, 1979), p 32.
34 F.H. Hinsley et al., *British Intelligence in the Second World War, Volume 1*, p 20.
35 Duncan Campbell, 'Inside the "Sigint" Empire', *New Statesman*, 29 October 1982, p 4; and James Bamford, *The Puzzle Palace* (Penguin, New York, 1983), pp 494–500.
36 *Aviation Week and Space Technology*, 1 November 1982, p 4.
37 Bamford, *The Puzzle Palace* (Penguin), p 494.
38 ibid., p 495.
39 ibid.
40 James Bamford, *The Puzzle Palace: A Report on NSA, America's Most Secret Agency* (Houghton Mifflin Company, Boston, 1982), p 335.

41 Campbell, 'Inside the "Sigint" Empire', p 4; and Bamford, *The Puzzle Palace* (Penguin), p 493.
42 ibid.
43 Duncan Campbell and Mark Hosenball, 'The Eavesdroppers', *Time Out*, 21–27 May 1976, p 8.
44 'The Treason of Geoffrey Prime', *The Economist*, 13 November 1982, p 63.
45 Duncan Campbell, 'The Spies Who Spend What They Like', *New Statesman*, 16 May 1980, pp 738–44.
46 Duncan Campbell, 'GCHQ's Lost Secrets', *New Statesman*, 5 November 1982, p 5.
47 ibid.
48 Campbell, 'Big Brother's Many Mansions', pp 194–7.
49 Campbell, 'Threat of the Electronic Spies', p 142.
50 Bunyan, *The Political Police in Britain*, p 186.
51 ibid.
52 Munster and Walsh, *Documents on Australian Foreign Policy, 1968–1975*, pp 95–6. The rest of this section on the DIS is also derived from this source.
53 Bunyan, *The Political Police in Britain*, pp 104–5.
54 ibid., pp 131–2.
55 ibid.
56 ibid., p 134; and Carol Ackroyd, Karen Margolis, Jonathan Rosenhead and Tim Shallice, *The Technology of Political Control* (Pluto Press, London, 1977), p 125.
57 ibid., p 139.
58 ibid., p 134.
59 David Leigh, 'Secret British Propaganda Unit Revealed', *Los Angeles Times*, 17 March 1978, p 7.
60 ibid.
61 ibid.
62 ibid.
63 Duncan Campbell and Clive Thomas, 'BBC's Trade Secrets', *New Statesman*, 4 July 1980, pp 13–14.
64 ibid.
65 Duncan Campbell, 'Big Buzby is Watching You', *New Statesman*, 1 February 1980.
66 Tony Geraghty, *Inside the S.A.S.* (Ballantine, New York, 1982), pp 13, 240.
67 Jon Connell, 'Retaking the Falklands', *Sunday Times* (London), 4 April 1982.
68 'The Cockleshell Heroes', *Newsweek*, 10 May 1982, p 31; 'Britain's Special Boat Squad: A Dirty Bunch', *New York Times*, 20 May 1982, p 10; and William Tuohy, '1st British Wave: Elite Boat Squad', *Los Angeles Times*, 27 April 1982, p 14.
69 'The Cockleshell Heroes', *Newsweek*, 10 May 1982, p 31.
70 Munster and Walsh, *Documents on Australian Foreign Policy, 1968–1975*, p 92.
71 ibid., pp 92–93.
72 Duncan Campbell, 'Unaccountable Empire Building', *New Statesman*, 19 November 1982, pp 8–9; and *The Economist*, 27 November 1982, p 29.
73 Munster and Walsh, *Documents on Australian Foreign Policy, 1968–1975*, pp 93–4.
74 'Britain's Foreign Office', *The Economist*, 27 November 1982, pp 19–26.
75 The Rt Hon. The Lord Franks (Chairman), *Falkland Islands Review: Report of a Committee of Privy Counsellors* (Her Majesty's Stationery Office, London, January 1983), p 94.
76 Munster and Walsh, *Documents on Australian Foreign Policy, 1968–1975*, p 94.
77 Lord Franks, *Falkland Islands Review*, p 86; Robert A. Erlandson, 'Falklands

Report Spurs Change in British Intelligence Network', *Baltimore Sun*, 26 January 1983, p 5; and 'Thatcher to Run Intelligence', *Chicago Tribune*, 27 January 1983, p 5.
78 Munster and Walsh, *Documents on Australian Foreign Policy, 1968–1975*, p 94.
79 Ronald Lewin, *The American Magic: Codes, Ciphers and the Defeat of Japan* (Farrar, Straus, Giroux, New York, 1982), p 121n.
80 Campbell, 'Unaccountable Empire Building'; and 'Making Whitehall Mole-Proof', *The Economist*, 5 June 1982, p 37.

3 The Australian security and intelligence community
1 Letter from T.E. Nave to Desmond Ball, 20 April 1978.
2 Alan Stretton, *Solder in a Storm: An Autobiography* (Collins, Sydney, 1978) pp 69, 111.
3 See Desmond J. Ball, 'Allied Intelligence Cooperation Involving Australia During World War II'; *Australian Outlook*, vol. 32, No. 3, December 1978, pp 300–3.
4 *Budget Statements 1983–84 Budget Paper No. 1* (Australian Government Publishing Service, Canberra, 1983), pp 222–3.
5 *Hansard (House of Representatives)*, 5 May 1977, pp 1630–3.
6 R.W. Furlonger, 'The Role of the Office of National Assessments', *Pacific Defence Reporter*, September 1978, p 63.
7 *Hansard (House of Representatives)*, 15 September 1977, p 1179.
8 Furlonger, 'The Role of the Office of National Assessments', p 63.
9 See Dennis Shanahan, 'ONA Seeks Staff to Tighten its Security', *Sydney Morning Herald*, 5 July 1980; and Dennis Shanahan, 'Security Body Gets Watchman', *Sydney Morning Herald*, 10 January 1981, p 17.
10 See Furlonger, 'The Role of the Office of National Assessments', p 63.
11 ibid., p 64.
12 See Brian Toohey, 'Listening in on Pierre in Paris', *National Times*, 6–12 May 1983, p 6.
13 See Paul Kelly, 'Advisers Accused of Complacency', *National Times*, 24 February–1 March 1980, pp 1, 3.
14 For excerpts from this review of ONA's performance, see Brian Toohey, 'How the Line to America Went Dead', *National Times*, 6–12 May 1983, pp 5–7.
15 *Hansard (House of Representatives)*, 25 November 1977, p 2339.
16 Commander J.B. Newman, 'Memorandum for Discussion at Singapore', (October 1940), Australian Archives Accession No. MP1185/8, File MP 1937/2/415. See also *Canberra Times*, 21 April 1979, p 2; and '6 Signal Regiment', *Signalman*, No. 5, 1980, p 19.
17 See Desmond Ball, *A Suitable Piece of Real Estate: American Installations in Australia* (Hale and Iremonger, Sydney, 1979), pp 31–32, and p 153, note 7.
18 Letter from Lt.-Col. A.W. Sandford to General Berryman, 16 November 1945, in Berryman Papers, Personal Correspondence File, Australian War Memorial.
19 *Hansard (House of Representatives)*, 25 October 1977, p 2339.
20 See Winslow Peck, 'U.S. Electronic Espionage: A Memoir', *Ramparts*, August 1972, p 41.
21 Sir Arthur Tange, *Australian Defence: Report on the Reorganisation of the Defence Group of Departments*, Canberra, November 1973, p 52.
22 See Ball, *A Suitable Piece of Real Estate*, pp 42–44.
23 'A Short History of the Seventh Signal Regiment and Borneo Barracks, Cabarlah', *Signalman*, vol. 1, No. 2, 1978, p 62.
24 '6 Signal Regiment', pp 19–20.
25 ibid., p 22; 'Official Opening and Handover of the Watsonia Satellite Terminal',

348 The Ties That Bind

  Signalman, No. 8, 1981, p 31; 'Project Sparrow Satellite Terminal Progresses', *Signalman*, No. 6, 1980, p 49; and Toohey, 'Listening in on Pierre in Paris', *National Times*, 6–12 May 1983, p 6.
26 'Hong Kong Spy Radio Moves South' *Defense Electronics*, March 1982, p 30.
27 Toohey, 'Listening in on Pierre in Paris', p 6.
28 ibid.
29 John Lombard, 'More Facts About Our Spooks', *Nation Review*, 9–15 December 1976, p 171.
30 Michael Richardson, 'Two Listening Posts: One Secret', *Age*, 17 February 1973, p 15.
31 Peter Young, 'Our Spies Weren't in the Race', *Bulletin*, 19 October 1974, pp 23–4.
32 'A Short History of the Seventh Signal Regiment and Borneo Barracks, Cabarlah', p 62.
33 See for example, 'Fretelin Radio Base Exposed', *C.B. Australia*, vol. 2, No. 3, December 1977, pp 1, 4.
34 Joint Intelligence Organisation, *Fourth Annual Report, 1974*, Canberra, November 1974, Part 2, pp 4–5.
35 See, for example, Warren Beeby, 'Government's Warning Was on Target', *Australian*, 19 February 1979, pp 1, 4.
36 *Hansard (House of Representatives)*, 25 October 1977, p 2339.
37 ibid.
38 The discussion of ASIS in this Section, unless otherwise sourced, is derived from Royal Commission on Intelligence and Security, *Fifth Report* (Australian Government Printer, Canberra, 1977), a *Top Secret* report obtained by the *National Times* in early 1981. See Brian Toohey, 'ASIS', *National Times*, 15–21 March 1981, pp 10–16.
39 Joint Intelligence Organisation, *Fourth Annual Report, 1974*, pp 9–10.
40 *Hansard (House of Representatives)*, 25 October 1977, p 2339.
41 See Stuart Simson, 'The Spy Who Came Out and Apologised', *National Times*, 6 October 1979, pp 34–5.
42 Interview with William McMahon, 'Four Corners' (ABC Television), 17 May 1977, transcript, pp 13–14.
43 See Russell Skelton, 'Hayden Queries Effectiveness of Top Spy Force', *Age*, 8 April 1981.
44 'Renouf Calls for End to Spy Network', *Canberra Times*, 17 March 1981.
45 Stretton, *Soldier in a Storm*, p 69. See also Captain C.D. Coulthard-Clark, 'Australia's War-Time Security Service', *Defence Force Journal*, No. 16, May/June 1979, pp 22–7; and Austin Laughlin, *Boots and All: The Inside Story of the Secret War* (A Colorgravure Publication, Melbourne, 1951), pp 80–83, 104–105.
46 Coulthard-Clark, 'Australia's War-Time Security Service', p 27.
47 *Hansard (House of Representatives)*, 30 September 1948, p 1038.
48 ibid.
49 Royal Commission on Intelligence and Security, *Fourth Report*, vol. 1, pp 1–2.
50 Sir Percy Sillitoe, *Cloak Without Dagger*, (Cassell, London, 1955), p 192.
51 Royal Commission on Intelligence and Security, *Fourth Report*, vol. 11, p 2.
52 *Australian Security Intelligence Organisation Bill 1979*, p 2.
53 'ASIO Building Goes Ahead at Russell', *Canberra Times*, 12 December 1981, p 12.
54 This account of ASIO's activities, unless otherwise sourced, is derived from ASIO's *Annual Report 1979–80*, which was obtained by the *National Times* in 1981. See Mark Plunkett, 'ASIO's Annual Report: Australian Spooks Trail Unemployed and Chinese', *National Times*, 28 June–4 July 1981, p 3.
55 See the Testimony of the Prime Minister, Mr R.J. Hawke, before the 1983 Hope

Royal Commission, in the *Australian*, 4 August 1983, p 4.
56 Royal Commission on Intelligence and Security, *Fourth Report*, vol. 1, pp 70−1.
57 Sir John Gorton, interviewed in *Allies* (A Grand Bay Film, Directed by Marian Wilkinson and Produced by Sylvie Le Clezio, Sydney, 1983), transcript of interview.
58 *Australian*, 12 January 1970; *Australian Financial Review*, 2 February 1970.
59 See T.B. Millar, *Australia's Defence* (Melbourne University Press, Melbourne, 2nd edition, 1969), p 211; and F. Mediansky, *The Military and Australia's Defence* (Longman-Cheshire, Melbourne, 1979), p 24.
60 Interview with General Sir John Wilton, 24 January 1978.
61 *Hansard (House of Representatives)*, 23 September 1969, p 1810.
62 Royal Commission in Intelligence and Security, *Second Report*, p 33.
63 ibid., p 13.
64 See Stuart Cockburn, *The Salisbury Affair* (Sun Books, Melbourne, 1979), p 318.
65 Brigadier J.R. Sheldrick, 'The Vital Installations Program', paper prepared for a Conference on *The Civil Infrastructure in the Defence of Australia: Assets and Vulnerabilities* (Strategic and Defence Studies Centre, Australian National University, Canberra, 28 November−2 December 1983), p 4.
66 Ken Haley, 'The Strategists Who Run the Secret War on Terrorism', *Age*, 10 January 1983.
67 Brigadier Sheldrick, 'The Vital Installations Program', p 5.
68 ibid., p 7; and *Age*, 10 January 1983.
69 Sheldrick, 'The Vital Installations Program', p 7.
70 ibid., pp 3, 7.
71 Major C.O.G. Williams, 'Contained Terrorist Incidents in Australia: Police or Military Problem?', *Australian Defence Force Journal*, No. 28, May/June 1981, p 54.
72 'Crack Security Force to be Established Soon', *Australian*, 23 December 1982, p 1.
73 'Security Force Formed Separate From AFP', *Canberra Times*, 23 December 1982, p 1.
74 ibid.
75 Peter Windsor, Director of Information, Australian Federal Police, Letter to the Editor, *Australian*, 7−8 January 1984, p 10.
76 Frank Cranston, 'Anti-terrorist Force Backed', *Canberra Times*, 4 July 1979, and Major Williams, 'Contained Terrorist Incidents in Australia', pp 53−6.
77 Royal Commission on Intelligence and Security, *Third Report*, p 16.
78 ibid., p 17.
79 ibid., p 23.
80 Royal Commission in Intelligence and Security, *Fifth Report*, paragraphs 313−314 and footnotes 5−108.
81 *Hansard (House of Representatives*, 1 March 1973, p 115.
82 *Hansard (House of Representatives*, 5 May, 1977, p 1631.
83 Richard Hall, *The Secret State: Australia's Spy Industry* (Cassell Australia, Sydney, 1978), pp 159−60.
84 'PM to Head Surveillance Committee', *Canberra Times*, 16 April 1983.
85 Royal Commission on Australia's Security and Intelligence Agencies, *Report on Terms of Reference (C)* (Australian Government Publishing Service, Canberra, December 1983), pp 39−40.
86 *Australian Financial Review*, 7 August 1978.

4 The New Zealand security and intelligence community
1 Sir Guy Powles, *Security Intelligence Service: Report by Chief Ombudsman* (New

350 The Ties That Bind

  Zealand Government Printer, Wellington, 1976), p 18.
2 Michael Parker, *The S.I.S.: The New Zealand Security Intelligence Service* (The Dunmore Press, Palmerston North, 1979), pp 10–13.
3 Sir Percy Sillitoe, *Cloak Without Dagger* (Cassell, London, 1955), pp 190–2.
4 Parker, *The SIS*, pp 9–19.
5 ibid., pp 24–5.
6 Mervyn Cull, 'Goodbye Cloak and Dagger', *New Zealand Herald*, 17 July 1976, Section 2, p 1.
7 'New Chief of SIS a Stickler — But He is Fair', *New Zealand Herald*, 20 July 1976, p 3; and Parker, *The SIS*, p 198.
8 'Mr Smith Takes Over SIS', *New Zealand Herald*, 6 May 1983; 'Terrorism Main Concern of SIS', *Christchurch Press*, 6 May 1983, p 4; and 'Spy Novel Fan Heads SIS', *Dominion*, 6 May 1983.
9 ibid.
10 Parker, *The SIS*, pp 107–9.
11 ibid., pp 46–7.
12 'No Cloak and No Dagger', *New Zealand Herald*, 17 March 1975, p 6.
13 Alister Taylor, 'The Security Axis', *New Zealand Monthly Review*, May 1975, p 8.
14 *Hansard*, 19 October 1977, p 3783.
15 Cull, 'Goodbye Cloak and Dagger', p 1.
16 Parker, *The SIS*, p 109.
17 Powles, *SIS*, p 18.
18 Cull, 'Goodbye Cloak and Dagger', p 1.
19 *NZ Listener*, 15 October 1977, p 15.
20 Powles, *SIS*, p 20.
21 ibid., p 26.
22 'PM Says KGB Agents Work in NZ', *New Zealand Herald*, 3 May 1977, p 3.
23 Dai Hayward, 'Stop Spying or Go Home, NZ Tells Russians', *Australian*, 9–10 February 1980.
24 Parker, *The SIS*, p 172.
25 ibid., p 78.
26 ibid., pp 64–74.
27 'Agent Tells of Meetings Between Sutch [and] Russian', *New Zealand Herald*, 18 February 1975, p 3.
28 *Canberra Times*, 30 January 1980.
29 Powles, *SIS*, p 31.
30 ibid., p 27.
31 ibid.
32 Margaret Hayward, *Diary of the Kirk Years* (Cape Catley and A.H. and A.W. Read, Wellington, 1981), p 142.
33 Powles, *SIS*, pp 27, 31.
34 'No Cloak and No Dagger', p 3.
35 Powles, *SIS*, p 33.
36 Parker, *The SIS*, p 165.
37 Powles, *SIS*, p 38.
38 Parker, *The SIS*, pp 167–9; and Powles, *SIS*, p 47.
39 ibid., p 70.
40 ibid.
41 'Move Against Possible Terrorism in NZ', *New Zealand Herald*, 24 May 1977, p 8.
42 Parker, *The SIS*, p 188.
43 'Move Against Possible Terrorism in NZ', p 8.

Notes 351

44 'New Set-up for Foreign Agency', *New Zealand Herald*, 24 April 1975, p 1.
45 ibid.
46 ibid.
47 'CIA Here But Not Active — PM', *New Zealand Herald*, 23 May 1977, p 1.
48 'No Cloak and No Dagger', p 6.
49 Material provided by New Zealand Defence Headquarters, Wellington, May 1983.
50 Public Service Official Circular No 1980/26, State Service Commission SSC 32/0/0, Wellington, 16 July 1980.
51 *Parliamentary Debates (House of Representatives)*, 15 August 1980, p 2774.
52 Roger Foley, 'Spying on Radio Waves', *New Zealand Times*, 8 April 1984; and David Young, 'Secret Circles', *New Zealand Listener*, 21 April 1984.
53 See Steven L. Carruthers, *Australia Under Siege: Japanese Submarine Raiders 1942*, (Solus Books, Sydney, 1982), pp 19, 133.
54 Fred Brenchley, 'Why Our Troops Are Staying in Singapore', *The National Times*, 12–17 February 1973, pp 1, 3.
55 *Parliamentary Debates (House of Representatives)*, 15 August 1980, p 2774.
56 'Keeping an Eye on the Ears', *New Zealand Herald*, 14 August 1980, p 1; and letter from B.M. Punnett, Executive Officer, Government Communications Security Bureau, Wellington, 29 June 1983.
57 'New Set-up For Foreign Agency', p 1.
58 Powles, *SIS*, p 100.
59 'New Set-up For Foreign Agency', p 1.
60 Powles, *SIS*, p 63.
61 ibid., p 61.
62 ibid., pp 61–4.
63 ibid., p 63.
64 ibid., pp 61–4, 100.

5 The Canadian security and intelligence community
1 Additionally, there is The Technical Cooperation Program (TTCP) and the ABCA Agreement. The TTCP is an agreement between Canada, the UK, the USA, and Australia which involves an exchange of technical information concerning defence research and development. The ABCA Agreement involves consultation of the military forces of those nations on matters 'of military service interest'. These and other relevant agreements are discussed in Chapter 7.
2 Commission of Inquiry Concerning Certain Activities of the Royal Canadian Mounted Police (the MacDonald Commission), *Freedom and Security Under the Law, Volume 1* (Canadian Government Publishing Centre, Hull, 1981), p 62.
3 ibid., p 63. On the Gouzenko revelations see H. Montgomery Hyde, *The Atom Bomb Spies* (Ballantine, New York, 1981).
4 Royal Commission on Security (the Mackenzie Commission), *Report of the Royal Commission on Security* (Abridged) (Ministry of Supply and Service, Ottawa, 1969).
5 Commission of Inquiry, *Freedom and Security ... Volume 2*, p 71.
6 Professor J.L.J. Edwards, *Ministerial Responsibility for National Security* (Canadian Government Publishing Centre, Hull, 1981), p 92.
7 John Sawatsky, *Men in the Shadows: RCMP Security Service* (Doubleday, New York, 1980); Richard French and Andre Beliveau, *The RCMP and the Management of National Security* (Institute for Research on Public Policy, 1979). These references constitute the sources for the description of RCMP organization which follows.
8 Commission of Inquiry, *Freedom and Security ... Volume 1*, p 80.

352 The Ties That Bind

9 French and Beliveau, *The RCMP and the Management of National Security*.
10 'Mounties to Lose National Security Role', *Los Angeles Times*, 26 August 1981, p 4.
11 *Government of Canada Telephone Directory, National Capital Region* (Canadian Government Publishing Centre, Hull, November 1982), p 229E.
12 Jeff Sallot, 'Transition to a Civilian Security Agency Incomplete 15 Months After Promised', *Toronto Globe and Mail*, 23 November 1982, p 9.
13 Canadian Civil Liberties Association, *Submissions to the Special Committee on the Senate on the Canadian Security Intelligence Service* (Toronto, 1983), p 1.
14 ibid.
15 Linda McQualg, 'Insecurities About Security', *Maclean's*, 6 June 1983, p 13.
16 'Controlling the Spies', *Maclean's*, 14 November 1983, pp 23–4.
17 Robert Sheppard, 'Ottawa Yields on Civilian Agency, Other Moves Delayed', *Toronto Globe and Mail*, 26 August 1981, p 3.
18 Henry Giniger, 'Ottawa Pledges Tight Rein on Security Force', *New York Times*, 27 August 1981, p 8.
19 'The Mole that Slipped Away', *Maclean's*, 24 January 1983, p 13.
20 'Restrict Role to Spying, Kaplan Says of Agency', *Toronto Globe and Mail*, 11 September 1981, p 8.
21 Jeff Sallot, 'Spying on Foreign Diplomats Part of Security Bill', *Toronto Globe and Mail*, 23 September 1983, p 4.
22 Commission of Inquiry, *Freedom and Security ... Volume 2*, p 604.
23 Commission of Inquiry, *Freedom and Security ... Volume 1*, p 88.
24 Transcript of 'The Fifth Estate — The Espionage Establishment', broadcast by the Canadian Broadcasting Company, 1974.
25 On Canada's ASW and ocean surveillance role see Colin Gray, *Canadian Defense Priorities: A Question of Relevance* (Clarke, Irwin & Company, Toronto, 1972).
26 J.L. Granatstein, *A Man of Influence: Norman A. Robertson and Canadian Statecraft 1929–1968* (Deneau, Ottawa, 1981), p 180.
27 See David Kahn's 'Introduction', p xv in Herbert O. Yardley, *The American Black Chamber* (Ballantine, New York, 1981); and R. Harris Smith, *OSS: The Secret History of America's First Central Intelligence Agency* (Dell, New York, 1972), pp 245–56.
28 F.H. Hinsley, E.E. Thomas, C.F.G. Ransom and R.C. Knight, *British Intelligence in the Second World War, Volume 2* (Cambridge, New York, 1981), p 551n.
29 J.L. Granatstein, *A Man of Influence*, p 180; Robert Sheppard, 'Lack of Quick RCMP Action Upset Gouzenko, Papers Say', *Toronto Globe and Mail*, 17 October 1981, p 5; Robert Bothwell and J.L. Granatstein (eds), *The Gouzenko Transcripts: The Evidence Presented to the Kellock–Taschereau Royal Commission of 1946* (Deneau, Ottawa, 1983), p 20.
30 ibid.
31 *Minutes of Proceedings and Evidence of the Standing Committee on Miscellaneous Estimates, House of Commons, No. 18*, 24 March 1975, pp 18–20.
32 'Secret Listening Agency Expands its Operations', *Toronto Globe and Mail*, 12 November 1983, p 3.
33 ibid.
34 *Government of Canada Telephone Directory*, p 161E.
35 ibid.
36 ibid.
37 ibid.; Royal Commission on Security, *Report ...*, p.87.
38 *Government of Canada Telephone Directory*, p 98E.
39 *Organization of the Government of Canada, 1980* (Canadian Government Publishing Centre, Hull, 1980) p 202.

Notes 353

40 Commission of Inquiry, *Freedom and Security ... Volume 1*, p 86.
41 *Organization of the Government of Canada, 1980*, p 202.
42 *Government of Canada Telephone Directory*, p 98E.
43 Commission of Inquiry, *Freedom and Security ... Volume 1*, p 86.
44 ibid.
45 Commission of Inquiry, *Freedom and Security ... Volume 2*, p 493.
46 ibid.
47 ibid.
48 *Government of Canada Telephone Directory*, p 98E.
49 French and Beliveau, *The RCMP and the Management of National Security*, p 15.
50 ibid.
51 Chris Belfour, 'Super-Snooper or Security Analyst?', *Toronto Globe and Mail*, 10 September 1971.
52 Commission of Inquiry, *Freedom and Security ... Volume 1*, p 84.
53 ibid., p 83.
54 ibid., p 82.
55 ibid., p 34; C.E.S. Franks, *Parliament and Security Matters* (Canadian Government Publishing Centre, Hull, 1980) p 59.
56 Commission of Inquiry, *Freedom and Security ... Volume 1*, p 84.
57 *Organization of the Government of Canada 1980*.
58 Commission of Inquiry, *Freedom and Security ... Volume 1*, p 87.
59 *Government of Canada Telephone Directory*, p 256E.
60 Commission of Inquiry, *Freedom and Security ... Volume 1*, p 88.
61 ibid.
62 ibid., p 89.
63 ibid.
64 'Kaplan, Axworthy Refuse To Testify on Deportation', *Toronto Globe and Mail*, 11 May 1982, p 3.
65 *Government of Canada Telephone Directory*, pp 164E, 232E.
66 Commission of Inquiry, *Freedom and Security ... Volume 2*, p 845.
67 *Transcript of the Prime Minister's Press Conference in Ottawa* (Prime Minister's Office, Ottawa, 9 December 1977), pp 18–22.
68 Commission of Inquiry, *Freedom and Security ... Volume 2*, p 847.
69 ibid., p 848.
70 Bothwell and Granatstein, *The Gouzenko Transcripts*, p 29.
71 Commission of Inquiry, *Freedom and Security ... Volume 1*, pp 89–90.
72 ibid.
73 ibid.
74 ibid., p 91.
75 ibid., pp 91–2.
76 ibid., p 92.
77 ibid.
78 Commission of Inquiry, *Freedom and Security ... Volume 2*, p 856.
79 Commission of Inquiry, *Freedom and Security ... Volume 1*, p 92.
80 'Secret Listening Agency Expands its Operations', *Toronto Globe and Mail*, 12 November 1983, p 3.

6 The United States security and intelligence community

1 For descriptions of these programs see Robert Lindsey, *The Falcon and the Snowman* (Simon and Schuster, New York, 1979); Philip J. Klass, 'US Monitoring Capability Impaired', *Aviation Week and Space Technology*, 14 May 1979, p 18; 'Space Reconnaissance Dwindles', *Aviation Week and Space Technology*, 6 October 1980, pp 18–20; 'Expanded Ocean Surveillance Effort Set', *Aviation Week and Space Technology*, 10 July 1978, pp 23 ff.

2 Raymond Garthoff, 'Banning the Bomb in Outer Space', *International Security*, vol. 5, 1980/81, pp 25−40.
3 Arthur Sylvester, 'Memorandum for the President, White House: SAMOS II Launch' (Office of the Assistant Secretary of Defense for Public Affairs, Washington, 1961), *Declassified Documents Reference System (DDRS)*, 1979−364B.
4 Philip Taubman, 'Secrecy of US Reconnaissance Office is Challenged', *New York Times*, 29 February 1980, p 10.
5 Victor Marchetti and John Marks, *The CIA and the Cult of Intelligence* (Knopf, New York, 1974), p 332.
6 William Colby and Peter Forbath, *Honorable Men: My Life in the CIA* (Simon and Schuster, New York, 1978), p 370; Philip Agee, 'How the Director of Central Intelligence Projected US Intelligence Activities for 1976−1981', *Covert Action Information Bulletin*, No. 6, 1979, pp 13−24.
7 George B. Kistiakowsky, *A Scientist in the White House: The Private Diary of President Eisenhower's Special Assistant for Science and Technology* (Harvard University Press, Cambridge, Mass., 1976), pp 378−9.
8 ibid., p 382.
9 ibid., pp 394−5.
10 'USAF Strengthens SAMOS Effort', *Aviation Week*, 12 September 1960, p 31.
11 Special Senate Committee on Secret and Confidential Documents, *Report 93−466* (US Government Printing Office, Washington, DC., 1973), p 95.
12 Laurence Stern, '$1.5 Billion Secret in the Sky', *Washington Post*, 9 December 1973, pp 1, 9.
13 Commission on the Organization of the Government for the Conduct of Foreign Policy, *Report* (US Government Printing Office, Washington, DC 1975), p 95.
14 James Canan, *War in Space* (Harper & Row, New York, 1982), pp 110−11; *Department of Defense Telephone Directory* (US Government Printing Office, Washington, DC, August 1982), p 0−103.
15 Canan, *War in Space*, pp 110−11.
16 James Ott, 'Espionage Trial Highlights CIA Problems', *Aviation Week and Space Technology*, 27 November 1978, pp 21−2; Desmond Ball, *A Suitable Piece of Real Estate* (Hale and Iremonger, Sydney, 1980), p 84.
17 ibid.
18 'New USAF Special Projects Director', *Aviation Week and Space Technology*, 11 August 1975, p 51.
19 Canan, *War in Space*, p 89.
20 Taubman, 'Secrecy of US Reconnaissance Office is Challenged', *New York Times*, 29 February 1980, p 10.
21 David Kahn, *The Codebreakers* (MacMillan, New York, 1967), p 675.
22 Senate Select Committee to Study Governmental Operations with Respect to Intelligence Activities, *Supplementary Detailed Staff Reports of Intelligence Activities and the Rights of Americans* (US Government Printing Office, Washington, DC, 1976), p 736.
23 'Proposed Survey of Communications Intelligence Activities', 10 December 1951, *DDRS*, 1980−168B.
24 ibid.; Committee Appointed to Survey Communications Intelligence Activities of the Government, *Report to the Secretary of State and Secretary of Defense*, 13 June 1952.
25 Senate Select Committee to Study Governmental Operations with Respect to Intelligence Activities, *Foreign and Military Intelligence, Book 1* (US Government Printing Office, Washington, DC, 1976), p 326.
26 National Security Council Intelligence Directive No. 6, 'Communications Intelli-

gence and Electronics Intelligence', 15 September 1958, sanitized version published in *DDRS*, 1976–167D.
27 National Security Council Intelligence Directive No. 6, 'Signals Intelligence', 17 February 1972, sanitized version published in *DDRS*, 1976–168A.
28 James Bamford, *The Puzzle Palace: A Report on NSA, America's Most Secret Agency* (Houghton Mifflin Company, Boston, 1982), p 157.
29 National Security Council Intelligence Directive No. 6, 'Signals Intelligence', *DDRS*, 1976–168A.
30 *US Government Organization Manual* (US Government Printing Office, Washington, DC, 1957).
31 'Washington Firm will Install Ft Meade Utilities', *Washington Post*, 7 January 1954, p 7.
32 'US Security Aide Accused of Taking Secret Documents', *New York Times*, 10 October 1954, pp 1, 33.
33 Jack Raymond, 'US Fears two Security Aides have gone behind Iron Curtain', *New York Times*, 6 August 1960, pp 1, 2.
34 Edward J. Epstein, 'The Spy War', *New York Times Magazine*, 28 September 1980, pp 34 ff.
35 Senate Select Committee to Study Governmental Operations with Respect to Intelligence Activities, *Foreign and Military Intelligence, Book 1*, p 354.
36 House Committee on Appropriations, *Department of Defense Appropriations for FY 1982*, Part 8, (US Government Printing Office, Washington, DC, 1981), pp 824–9.
37 Leslie Maitland, 'FBI Says New York is a 'Hub' of Spying in US', *New York Times* 14 November, p 12.
38 Patrick E. Tyler and Bob Woodward, 'FBI Held War Code of Reagan', *Los Angeles Times*, 13 December 1981, pp 1, 27.
39 Walter Sullivan, 'US Seeks to Link Industry on Computer Defenses', *New York Times*, 12 August 1981, p A17.
40 House Committee on Armed Services, *Hearings on Military Posture and H.R. 5968*, (US Government Printing Office, Washington, DC, 1982), Part 5, p 1188.
41 ibid.
42 Seymour Hersh, 'The President and the Plumbers: A Look at Two Security Questions', *New York Times*, 9 December 1973, pp 1, 76.
43 Duncan Campbell and Linda Malvern, 'America's Big Ear on Europe', *New Statesman*, 18 July 1980, pp 10–14; Bamford, *The Puzzle Palace*, pp 172, 173.
44 Winslow Peck, 'US Electronic Espionage: A Memoir', *Ramparts*, August 1972, pp 36–50.
45 'Eavesdropping on the World's Secrets', *US News and World Report*, 26 June 1978, pp 45–9.
46 Harry F. Eustace, 'Changing Intelligence Priorities', *Electronic Warfare/Defense Electronics*, November 1978, pp 30 ff.
47 Morton H. Halperin, Jerry J. Berman, Robert L. Borosage and Christine M. Marwick, *The Lawless State* (Penguin, New York, 1976), pp 173–5; Senate Select Committee to Study Government Operations with Respect to Intelligence Activities, *The National Security Agency and Fourth Amendment Rights* (US Government Printing Office, Washington, DC, 1976), pp 30–4.
48 Halperin, *et al.*, *The Lawless State*, p 174.
49 Bob Woodward, 'Messages of Activists Intercepted', *Washington Post*, 13 October 1975, pp A1, A4.
50 Halperin, *et al.*, *The Lawless State*, p 176; Senate Select Committee, *The National Security Agency and Fourth Amendment Rights*, pp 60–3.
51 Halperin, *et al.*, *The Lawless State*, p 176.

356   The Ties That Bind

52 Evans Witt, 'Advances in Cryptography Press Issues of Compute Privacy', *Los Angeles Times*, 16 May 1981, pp 1 ff.
53 Gina Bari Kolata, 'Cryptography: A New Clash between Academic Freedom and National Security', *Science*, 29 August 1980, pp 995–6; and 'NSA's Cryptic Alliance', *Newsweek*, 24 August 1981, p 51.
54 Senate Select Committee on Intelligence, *Unclassified Summary: Involvement of NSA in the Development of the Data Encryption Standard* (US Government Printing Office, Washington, DC, 1978).
55 Eustace, 'Changing Intelligence Priorities'; and 'Shaping Tomorrow's CIA', *Time* 6 February 1978, pp 10 ff.
56 Except where noted all material on NSA organization is based on Bamford, *The Puzzle Palace*, pp 56–117.
57 *Time*, 6 February 1978, pp 10 ff; Eustace, 'Changing Intelligence Priorities'; and Tad Szulc, 'The NSA — America's $10 Billion Frankenstein', *Penthouse*, November 1975, pp 55ff.
58 Melvin Laird, *National Security Strategy of Realistic Deterrence: Secretary of Defense Melvin Laird's Annual Defense Department Report FY 1973* (US Government Printing Office, Washington, DC, 1972), p 135.
59 For a history of the OSS see R. Harris Smith, *OSS: The Secret History of America's First Central Intelligence Agency* (University of California Press, Berkeley, California, 1972).
60 Senate Select Committee to Study Governmental Operations With Respect to Intelligence Activities, *Supplementary Detailed Reports on Foreign and Military Intelligence, Book IV* (US Government Printing Office, Washington, DC, 1976), pp 4–6.
61 ibid.
62 House Permanent Select Committee on Intelligence, *Compilation of Intelligence Laws* (US Government Printing Office, Washington, DC, 198), p 7.
63 Halperin *et al.*, *The Lawless State*, pp 140–2.
64 ibid., p 153.
65 ibid.
66 US Commission on CIA Activities within the United States, *Report to the President* (US Government Printing Office, Washington, DC, 1975), p 144n3.
67 John Marks, *The Search for the Manchurian Candidate: The CIA and Mind Control* (New York Times Books, New York, 1979).
68 Halperin *et al.*, The *Lawless State*, p 145.
69 ibid., p 146.
70 'Reagan's New Plan for a Tougher CIA', *Newsweek*, 19 October 1981, p 64.
71 Judith Miller, 'Reagan Widens Intelligence Role; Gives CIA Domestic Spy Power', *New York Times*, 5 December 1981, pp 1, 11.
72 Paul Hodge, 'CIA Plans Major New Building', *Washington Post*, 2 October 1981, p B1.
73 Eustace, 'Changing Intelligence Priorities'; and *Time*, 6 February 1978, pp 10 ff.
74 *CIA Fact Book* (US Government Printing Office, Washington, DC, 1980).
75 Marchetti and Marks, *The CIA and the Cult of Intelligence*, p 74.
76 Jeffrey Lenorovitz, 'CIA Satellite Data Task Study Revealed', *Aviation Week and Space Technology*, 2 May 1977, p 25; Arnaud de Borchgrave, 'Space-Age Spies', *Newsweek*, 6 March 1978, p 7.
77 Marchetti and Marks, *The CIA and the Cult of Intelligence*, p 74.
78 ibid., p 73.
79 Marchetti and Marks, *The CIA and the Cult of Intelligence*, p 73; US Commission, *Report to the President*, p 91.

80 Marchetti and Marks, *The CIA and the Cult of Intelligence*, p 74.
81 ibid.
82 US Commission, *Report to the President*, p 92.
83 Marchetti and Marks, *The CIA and the Cult of Intelligence*, pp 57–73; John Stockwell, *In Search of Enemies: A CIA Story* (W.W. Norton, New York, 1978); and David Martin, *Wilderness of Mirrors* (Harper & Row, New York, 1980), pp 121, 127–8.
84 Seymour Hersh, 'The Angleton Story', *New York Times Magazine*, 25 June 1978, pp 13 ff; Henry Hurt, *Shadrin: The Spy Who Never Came Back* (Reader's Digest Press, New York, 1981), p 147.
85 Samuel T. Francis, 'The Intelligence Community', in Charles L. Heatherly, *Mandate for Leadership: Policy Management in a Conservative Administration* (Heritage Foundation, Washington, 1980).
86 Marchetti and Marks, *The CIA and the Cult of Intelligence*, pp 387–8. For accounts of such activity see Joseph Smith, *Portrait of a Cold Warrior* (Ballantine, New York, 1981); Warren Hinckle and William Turner, *The Fish Is Red: The Story of the Secret War Against Castro* (Harper & Row, New York, 1981); Robert Borosage and John Marks (eds), *The CIA File* (Grossman/Viking, New York, 1976); Thomas Powers, *The Man Who Kept The Secrets: Richard Helms and the CIA* (Knopf, New York, 1979); and Kermit Roosevelt, *Countercoup: The Struggle for the Control of Iran* (McGraw Hill, New York, 1979).
87 Peer de Silva, *Sub Rosa: The CIA and the Uses of Intelligence*, (Times Books, New York, 1978), p 291.
88 Bamford, *The Puzzle Palace*, p 142.
89 Martin, *Wilderness of Mirrors*, pp 121, 127–8; '3 Tales of the CIA', *Ramparts*, April 1967, pp 17–21.
90 Marchetti and Marks, *The CIA and the Cult of Intelligence*, pp 70–5; David Wise, *The American Police State* (Vintage, New York, 1976), pp 188–92.
91 ibid., p 188.
92 Senate Select Committee to Study Governmental Operations ..., *Foreign and Military Intelligence, Book I*, p 439.
93 ibid; Wise, *The American Police State*, p 189.
94 Senate Select Committee on Intelligence, *National Intelligence Act of 1980* (US Government Printing Office, Washington, DC, 1980), p 192.
95 Wise, *The American Police State*, pp 70–5.
96 Marchetti and Marks, *The CIA and the Cult of Intelligence*, pp 70–5; House Permanent Select Committee on Intelligence, *Prepublication Review and Secrecy Arrangements* (US Government Printing Office, Washington, DC, 1980), p 10.
97 Marchetti and Marks, *The CIA and the Cult of Intelligence*, pp 70–5.
98 Charles R. Babcock, 'CIA Shift Returns Covert Operation Veteran to Post', *Washington Post*, 29 June 1984, p. A-12.
99 *CIA Fact Book*, Unpaginated.
100 Bamford, *The Puzzle Palace*, p 189.
101 Senate Select Committee to Study Governmental Operations, *Supplementary Detailed Staff Reports, Book IV*, pp 77–8.
102 National Security Council Intelligence Directive Number 8, 'Photographic Interpretation', 17 February 1972, DDRS, 1976–253G.
103 George Wilson, 'N-Pic Technicians Ferret Out Secrets Behind Closed Windows', *Los Angeles Times*, 12 January 1975, p 14.
104 Powers, *The Man Who Kept the Secrets*, p 341, n38.
105 Senate Select Committee to Study Governmental Operations, *Supplementary Reports on Intelligence Activities* (US Government Printing Office, Washington, DC, 1976), pp 271–3.

106 House Committee on Foreign Affairs, *The Role of Intelligence in the Foreign Policy Process* (US Government Printing Office, Washington, DC, 1980), p 57.
107 *INR*, (Department of State, Washington DC, 1980), p 7.
108 ibid.
109 ibid., pp 11–12.
110 ibid., pp 12–13.
111 ibid., p 13.
112 ibid., p 14.
113 ibid.
114 ibid.
115 *Time*, 6 February 1978, pp 10 ff.
116 Eustace, 'Changing Intelligence Priorities', p 38.
117 Comptroller General of the United States, *FBI Domestic Intelligence Operattions: An Uncertain Future* (General Accounting Office, Washington, DC, 1977) p 11.
118 John T. Elliff, *The Reform of FBI Domestic Intelligence Operations* (Princeton University Press, Princeton, NJ., 1979), p 77.
119 Leslie Maitland, 'New York Termed Hub of Foreign Spies in U.S., *New York Times*, 14 November 1981, p 12.
120 Sanford J. Ungar, *The FBI* (Little, Brown, Boston, 1976), p 240.
121 ibid., p 242.
122 Taylor Branch and Eugene M. Propper, *Labyrinth* (Viking, New York, 1982), pp 231, 350, 358.
123 'Text of the President's Executive Order on Intelligence Activities', *New York Times*, 5 December 1981, p 10.
124 Marchetti and Marks, *The CIA and the Cult of Intelligence*, p 204.
125 Douglas Watson, 'Huston Says NSA Urged Break-Ins', *Washington Post*, 3 March 1975, pp A1, 6.
126 Senate Select Committee, *Supplementary Reports on Intelligence Activities* (US Government Printing Office, Washington, DC, 1970), p 266.
127 ibid.
128 Patrick McGarvey, *The CIA: The Myth and the Madness* (Penguin, Baltimore, 1972), p 80.
129 'Defense Intelligence Organization Criticized', *Aviation Week and Space Technology*, 3 August 1970, p 17; Benjamin Schemmer, 'The Slow Murder of the American Intelligence Community', *Armed Forces Journal International*, March 1979.
130 *CIA: The Pike Report* (Spokesman Books, Nottingham, 1977), p 261.
131 Desmond Ball, *Targeting for Strategic Deterrence* (Adelphi Paper No. 185, The International Institute For Strategic Studies, London, Summer 1983), p. 26.
132 House Committee on Armed Services, *Hearings on Military Posture and H.R. 2970*, (US Government Printing Office, Washington, DC, 1981), Part 4, pp 1143–5.
133 ibid.
134 The following description is drawn from *DIA: Organization, Mission and Key Personnel* (US Government Printing Office, Washington, DC, 1980); and *Department of Defense Telephone Directory* (US Government Printing Office, Washington, DC, December 1982), pp 0–11 to 0–13.
135 Bamford, *The Puzzle Palace*, p 190–1.
136 Eustace, 'Changing Intelligence Priorities', p 38; and *Time*, 6 February 1978, p 15.
137 Senate Committee on Appropriations, *Military Construction Hearings FY 1976* (US Government Printing Office, Washington, DC, 1975), p 54.
138 *Department of Defense Telephone Directory*, December 1982, p 0–25.

139 Jules Spry, 'Army Intelligence Unit Moving Headquarters to Meade', *Baltimore Sun*, 3 December 1980, p E2.
140 INSCOM Regulation 10-2, 1 April 1982, released with deletions under the Freedom of Information Act.
141 Jay Peterzell, 'Can Congress Really Check the CIA?', *Washington Post*, 24 April 1983, pp C1, C4; Raymond Bonner, 'Secret Pentagon Intelligence Unit is Disclosed', *New York Times*, 11 May 1983, p A13.
142 Robert C. Tooth, 'White House to Put Limits on Army's Secret Spy Unit', *Los Angeles Times*, 15 May 1983, pp 1, 10.
143 ibid.
144 Army Missile Command Regulation 10-2, Chapter 29, Missile Intelligence Agency, nd.
145 See Department of Defense Directive 6420-1, 'Armed Forces Medical Intelligence Center', 9 December 1982.
146 *US Army Foreign Science and Technology Center* (Charlottsville, FS & TC, n.d.).
147 Richard Halloran, 'Military is Quietly Rebuilding the Special Operations Force', *New York Times*, 19 July 1982, pp 1, 9.
148 Charles Simpson III, *Inside the Green Berets* (Presidio Press, Novato, 1983), pp 88-182.
149 Eustace, 'Changing Intelligence Priorities', p 38.
150 Marchetti and Marks, *The CIA and the Cult of Intelligence*, p 90.
151 *Department of Defense Telephone Directory*, December 1982, p 0-107.
152 'Air Force Intelligence Service', *Air Force Magazine*, May 1982, p 126.
153 ibid.
154 ibid.
155 'Special AFSC Organizations', *Air Force Magazine*, May 1982, p 200.
156 John Prados, *The Soviet Estimate: U.S. Intelligence Analysis and Russian Military Strength* (Dial Press, New York, 1982), p 201.
157 'Air Force Technical Applications Center', *Air Force Magazine*, May 1983, pp 134-7.
158 ibid.
159 ibid.; 'USAF Personnel Strength by Commands, SOA's and DRO's', *Air Force Magazine*, May 1981, p 160.
160 Eustace, 'Changing Intelligence Priorities'.
161 *Department of Defense Telephone Directory*, December 1982, pp 0-90 to 0-91.
162 Charles David Taylor, *An Alternative Method of Information Handling Within the Naval Intelligence Community* (Naval Postgraduate School, Monterey, 1980), p 150.
163 ibid., p 150.
164 ibid., p 151.
165 ibid.
166 Szulc, 'NSA', *Penthouse*, November 1975, pp 55 ff.
167 *Department of Defense Telephone Directory*, December 1982, p 0-91.
168 Thomas S. Burns, *The Secret War for the Ocean Depths* (Rawson Associates Publishers, New York, 1978), pp 158-9.
169 'Navy Activates Space Command', *Defense Electronics*, October 1983, p 30. See also House Committee on Armed Services, *Hearings on Military Posture and H.R. 5068*, (US Government Printing Office, Washington, DC, 1977), Book 1, Part 3, pp 746-51.
170 Eustace, 'Changing Intelligence Priorities', p 38.
171 'U.S. Foreign Intelligence — It's More than the CIA', *U.S. News and World Report*, 1 June, 1981, p 36.
172 Muriel Dobbin, 'Silicon Valley Spies Face Few Obstacles', *Baltimore Sun*,

1 August 1982, pp 1, 7; William Broad, 'Evading the Soviet Ear at Glen Cove', *Science* (vol. 217, No. 3), September 1982, pp 910–11.
173 Leonid Vladimirov, *The Russian Space Bluff: The Inside Story of the Soviet Drive to the Moon* (Dial Press, New York, 1973), p 49.
174 Lawrence J. Korb, 'National Security Organization and Process in the Carter Administration', in Sam C. Sarkesian (ed.), *Defense Policy and the Presidency* (Westview, Boulder, Colorado, 1979), pp 111–37.
175 'Statement by the President: National Security Council Structure', The White Office of the Press Secretary, Washington, 12 January, 1982.
176 David Wise, 'Blurring Its Trail, The CIA Steps Up Covert Action', *Los Angeles Times*, 21 March, 1982, p 3.
177 House Select Committee on Intelligence, *U.S. Intelligence Agencies and Activities: Intelligence Costs and Fiscal Procedures* (US Government Printing Office, Washington, DC, 1975), Part 1, p 389.
178 Taylor, *An Alternative Method of Information Handling Within the Naval Intelligence Community*, p 138.
179 ibid.
180 Letter from L. Strawderman, CIA Information and Privacy Coordinator to J. Richelson, 22 October 1982.
181 Director of Central Intelligence Directive No. 6/1, 'SIGINT Committee', 31 May 1962, *DDRS*, 1980–131D.
182 Director of Central Intelligence Directive No. 1/11, 'Security Committee', 23 August 1974, *DDRS*, 1980–133A.
183 Senate Select Committee to Study Governmental Operations, *Foreign and Military Intelligence, Book I*, p 85.
184 Director of Central Intelligence Directive No. 3/3, 'Production of Atomic Energy Intelligence', 27 January 1959, *DDRS*, 1980–130E.
185 House Committee on Appropriations, *Department of Defense Appropriations for 1978*, Part 2, p 224.
186 Senate Select Committee to Study Governmental Operations, *Supplementary Detailed Staff Reports*, p 75; Director of Central Intelligence Directive No. 1/13, 'COMIREX', 1 July 1967.
187 Director of Central Intelligence Directive No. 1/13, 'Coordination of the Collection and Exploitation of Imagery Intelligence', 2 February 1973, *DDRS*, 1980–132D.
188 See National Communications Security Committee, Working Group on Computer Security, *Computer and Telecommunications Security*, July 1981.
189 Senate Select Committee, *Supplementary Detailed Staff Reports*, p 75.
190 Phillip J. Klass, 'U.S. Monitoring Capability Impaired', *Aviation Week and Space Technology*, 14 May 1979, p 18.
191 Senate Select Committee to Study Governmental Operations, *Foreign and Military Intelligence, Book I*, p 335. A figure indicates the existence of 2 Excoms and 2 Reconnaissance programs, with DCI and Secretary of Defense oversight.
192 Judith Miller, 'Intelligence Advisory and Oversight Units Named', *New York Times*, 21 October 1981, p A27.

7 The mechanics of cooperation and exchange
1 See 'Mr. Jones: Australia's Master Spy', *Canberra Times*, 25 June 1978, pp 13, 16.
2 William Stevenson, *A Man Called Intrepid: The Secret War 1939–1945* (Sphere Books, London, 1977), p 25.

3 ibid., pp 106–10.
4 See H. Montgomery Hyde, *Secret Intelligence Agent* (Constable, London, 1982), pp 266–7.
5 Sir William Stephenson, 'Appendix: The Story of OSS', in Hyde, *Secret Intelligence Agent*, pp 247–8.
6 Cited in Hyde, *Secret Intelligence Agent*, p xviii.
7 Stevenson, *A Man Called Intrepid*, pp 108–10.
8 Ronald W. Clark, *The Man Who Broke PURPLE: The Life of the World's Greatest Cryptologist, Colonel William F. Friedman* (Weidenfield & Nicholson, London, 1977), p 116.
9 See Ladislas Farago, *The Broken Seal* (Random House, New York, 1967), p 253; and James Bamford, *The Puzzle Palace: A Report on NSA, America's Most Secret Agency* (Houghton Mifflin, Boston, 1982), p 311.
10 Clark, *The Man Who Broke PURPLE*, p 119.
11 ibid., pp 119–21; and Bamford, *The Puzzle Palace*, p 312.
12 ibid.
13 Stevenson, *A Man Called Intrepid*, pp 177, 273.
14 US Congress, Joint Committee on the Investigation of the Pearl Harbor Attack, *Pearl Harbor Attack* (US Government Printing Office, Washington, DC, 1946), Part 36, p 50.
15 *Pearl Harbor Attack*, Part 2, p 947 and Part 8, p 3709; and Stevenson, *A Man Called Intrepid*, p 264.
16 *Pearl Harbor Attack*, Part 8, p 3709.
17 'Cryptographic Organisation, 1939–1942', Australian Archives, CRS A816, Item 43/302/18.
18 Commander J.B. Newman, 'Memorandum for Discussion at Singapore', (no date, but probably October 1940), Australian Archives, Accession No. MP 1185/8, File MP 1937/2/415.
19 *Pearl Harbor Attack*, Part 8, pp 3594, 3597.
20 ibid., p 3614.
21 ibid., p 3584.
22 Bamford, *The Puzzle Palace*, p 314.
23 ibid., p 315.
24 Stephenson, 'Appendix: The Story of OSS', p 253.
25 ibid., pp 253–5.
26 ibid., p 248.
27 ibid., p 256.
28 ibid., pp 256–7.
29 John Sawatsky, *Men in the Shadows: The RCMP Security Service* (Doubleday Canada Limited, Toronto, 1980), pp 14–16.
30 Michael Parker, *The S.I.S.: The New Zealand Security Intelligence Service* (The Dunmore Press, Palmerston North, 1979), pp 10–13.
31 The original Australian security intelligence organization was in fact an Australian branch of MI-5. See Frank Cain, *The Origins of Political Surveillance in Australia* (Angus & Robertson, Sydney, 1983), pp 1–2, 241, 279, 281–3.
32 See Stevenson, *A Man Called Intrepid*, p 109.
33 Hyde, *Secret Intelligence Agent*, pp 177–8.
34 Bamford, *The Puzzle Palace*, p 309.
35 ibid., p 315.
36 'United States–United Kingdom Security Agreement', Memorandum from the Office of the Adjutant General, US Army, Washington, DC, 8 October 1948.
37 Memo from R.N. Thompson to Sir Arthur Tange, 'SIGINT Presence in Singapore and New Station at Darwin', 23 February 1973.

38 Bamford, *The Puzzle Palace*, p 309.
39 Duncan Campbell, 'The Spies Who Spend What They Like', *New Statesman*, 16 May 1980, p 739.
40 Don Oberdorfer, 'Behind a New Policy: Oil, Crises and a Year of Deliberations', *Washington Post*, 24 January 1980, p 1; Oswald Johnston, 'U.S. Talks with Britain, Portugal on Use of Bases', *Los Angeles Times*, 25 January 1980, p 1. See also 'New Listening Post?' *Defense Electronics*, November 1979, p 25.
41 Minutes of Meeting of US EUCOM ELINT Technical Sub-Group (Turkey) Conference No. 8, 8 February 1956; and John Sawatsky, *For Services Rendered: Leslie James Bennett and the RCMP Security Service* (Doubleday Canada Limited, Toronto, 1982), pp 23−5.
42 Notes by the Secretaries to the Joint Communications−Electronics Committee, *Revision of Interim Outline Plan for Telecommunications Support of National Security Agency* (JCEC 1371/1, 19 July 1956), Appendix C to Enclosure A, p 1.
43 Bamford, *The Puzzle Palace*, p 309.
44 ibid., p 314.
45 ibid.
46 ibid.
47 Notes by the Secretaries, JCEC 1371/1, 19 July 1956.
48 ibid., p 6.
49 Duncan Campbell, 'Threat of the Electronic Spies', *New Statesman*, 2 February 1979, p 142; and Bamford, *The Puzzle Palace*, p 309.
50 ibid., p 317.
51 See Desmond Ball, *A Suitable Piece of Real Estate: American Installations in Australia* (Hale and Iremonger, Sydney, 1980), p 41; and Brigadier R.M. Bremmer, 'My Visit to the Australian Intelligence Corps, December 1971'. *The Rose and the Laurel*, vol. 8, No. 34, December 1972, pp 57−8.
52 Bamford, *The Puzzle Palace*, p 337.
53 Patrick Seale and Maureen McConville, *Philby: The Long Road to Moscow* (Penguin, Harmondsworth, 1978), pp 243−4.
54 ibid., p 245.
55 Bruce Page, David Leitch and Phillip Knightley, Philby: *The Spy Who Betrayed A Generation* (Penguin, Harmondsworth, 1979), p 210.
56 See E.H. Cookridge, *George Blake: Double Agent* (Ballantine, New York, 1982), pp 149−52.
57 See Oleg Penkovsky, *The Penkovsky Papers* (Ballantine, New York, 1982); and Desmond Ball, *Politics and Force Levels: The Strategic Missile Program of the Kennedy Administration* (University of California Press, Berkeley, 1980), pp 102−3.
58 Philip Agee and Louis Wolf, *Dirty Work: The CIA in Western Europe* (Lyle Stuart Inc., Secaucus, New Jersey, 1978), pp 731−2; and 'Behind the American Eagle', *Time Out*, 28 April 1975, p 5.
59 Cord Meyer, *Facing Reality: From World Federalism to the CIA* (Harper and Row, New York, 1980), Chapter 9.
60 Agee and Wolf, *Dirty Work*, pp 623−4, 732.
61 ibid., pp 669−70; Duncan Campbell, 'New London CIA Chief: It's Dicky', *New Statesman*, 14 March 1980; and *Covert Action Information Bulletin*, No. 8, March−April 1980, p 34.
62 Australian Royal Commission on Intelligence and Security, *Fifth Report* (1977) Appendix 5D, paragraphs 10−44.
63 ibid.
64 ibid., Appendix 5A, paragraph 13.
65 ibid., Appendix 5E, paragraph 7.

66 ibid., Appendix 5E, paragraphs 2–18.
67 ibid., Appendix 5D, paragraphs 76, 217–222.
68 ibid.
69 ibid.
70 ibid., Appendix 5D, paragraphs 211, 219.
71 Major J.F. Koek, 'A Guide for International Military Standardization: ABCA Armies' Operational Concept, 1986–95', *Defence Force Journal*, No. 5, July August 1977, p 51.
72 Margaret Gowing, *Britain and Atomic Energy 1939–1945* (Macmillan, London, 1965), Volume 1, pp 75–7. See also C.R. Dalton, *Without Hardware* (Ochre Press, Towamba, NSW, 3rd edition, 1980), p 73; and Michael Carr, 'Australia and the Nuclear Question: A Survey of Government Attitudes, 1945–1975' (Unpublished MA Honours Thesis, University of New South Wales, 1979) p 49.
73 ibid., p 17.
74 ibid., p 22.
75 ibid., p 42.
76 J.F. Koek, 'A Guide for International Military Standardization', p 51.
77 'EW Meeting', *Hallmark*, June 1975, p 6.
78 Commander Robert Howell, R.N., 'Aus-Can-What?', *Signal*, September 1982, pp 35–7.
79 ibid., p 35.
80 ibid., pp 35–7.
81 North American Air Defence Command (NORAD), *NORAD Fact Sheet* (Peterson Air Force Base, Colorado Springs) pp 1–2.
82 ibid.
83 Herbert J. Coleman, 'NORAD Broadens Operational Horizons', *Aviation Week and Space Technology*, 16 June 1980, p 234.
84 ibid., pp 233–7; and 'Air Force Picks Goodfellow AFB as Fourth Pave Paws Site', *Aerospace Daily*, 21 October 1981, p 279.
85 *NORAD: North American Air Defence Command* (NORAD Briefing Brochure).
86 ibid.; and 'JSS', *DMS Market Intelligence Report* (DMS Inc., Greenwich, Connecticut, January 1981).
87 House Committee on Appropriations, *Military Construction Appropriations for 1981* (US Government Printing Office, Washington, DC, 1980), Part 1, p 1506.
88 'Naval Atlantic Undersea Test and Evaluation Center (AUTEC)', *DMS Market Intelligence Report* (DMS Inc., Greenwich, Connecticut, 1980) p 1.
89 *Bulletin*, 12 January 1982, p 70.
90 Department of Supply, *Weapons Research Establishment Annual Report 1973–74* (Australian Government Publishing Service, Canberra, 1974), p 54.
91 Australian Royal Commission on Intelligence and Security, *Fifth Report*, Appendix 5–D, paragraphs 193–197.
92 Notes by the Secretaries JCEC 1371/1, 19 July 1956, p 6.
93 Hyde, *Secret Intelligence Agent*, p 135.
94 ibid., p 148.
95 Australian Royal Commission on Intelligence and Security, *Fifth Report*, Appendix 5–D, paragraphs 16, 24–30.
96 ibid., footnote 5–D–21.
97 Chapman Pincher, *Their Trade is Treachery* (Sidgwick and Jackson, London, 1981), p 167.
98 ibid.; and Hyde, *Secret Intelligence Agent*, p 149.
99 See John Sawatsky, *For Services Rendered: Leslie James Bennett and the RCMP Security Service* (Doubleday, Garden City, New York, 1982); and David Leigh,

'Soviet Breach Feared at British Code Centre', *Guardian*, 28 January 1980, p 2.
100 *Sydney Morning Herald*, 4 April 1981, p 6.
101 Sir Guy Powles, *Security Intelligence Service: Report by Chief Ombudsman* (New Zealand Government Printer, Wellington, 1976), p 20.
102 ibid., p 35.
103 Commonwealth of Australia, *Protective Security Handbook* (Australian Government Publishing Service, Canberra, 1978), p 2.
104 'A Most Secret Surrender', *Canberra Times*, 4 January 1983.
105 ibid.
106 US Department of Defense, *Industrial Security Manual for Safeguarding Classified Information* (Department of Defense, Washington, DC, DOD 5220.22–M, July 1981), pp 96–8.
107 Senate Foreign Relations Committee, *The Gulf of Tonkin: The 1964 Incidents* (US Government Printing Office, Washington, DC, 1968), pp 35–9.
108 Bamford, *The Puzzle Palace*, p 314.
109 David Wise, *The Politics of Lying: Government Deception, Secrecy, and Power* (Random House, New York, 1973), pp 57–8.
110 Bamford, *The Puzzle Palace*, p 314; and Wise, *The Politics of Lying*, pp 57–8. For a recent example of material classified as 'SECRET SPOKE', see Jack Anderson, 'Syrians Strive to Oust Arafat as PLO Chief', *Washington Post*, 10 November 1982, p D–22.
111 See Bob Woodward, 'Messages of Activists Intercepted', *Washington Post*, 13 October 1975, pp 1, 14.
112 ibid., p 14.
113 Wise, *The Politics of Lying*, p 56; and Seymour M. Hersh, *The Price of Power: Kissinger in the Nixon White House* (Summit Books, New York, 1983), p 92.
114 Robert C. Toth, 'CIA "Mighty Wurlitzer" is Now Silent', *Los Angeles Times*, 30 December 1980, pp 1, 12; and Jeffrey Richelson, 'The Keyhole Satellite Program', *Journal of Strategic Studies*, (vol. 7, No. 2), 1984, pp 121–153.
115 James Ott, 'Espionage Trial Highlights CIA Problems', *Aviation Week and Space Technology*, 27 November 1978, pp 21–2.
116 Robert Lindsey, *The Falcon and the Snowman: A True Story of Friendship and Espionage* (Simon and Schuster, New York, 1979), pp 214–15.
117 Roy Varner and Wayne Collier, *A Matter of Risk* (Coronet, Hodder and Stoughton, Sevenoaks, Kent, 1980), pp 32–3.
118 Royal Commission on Intelligence and Security, *Third Report: Abridged Findings and Recommendations* (Australian Government Publishing Service, Canberra, April 1977), p 16.
119 See, for example, the WNINTEL NOFORN caveats in Central Intelligence Agency, *Israel: Foreign Intelligence and Security Services* (Directorate of Operations Counterintelligence Staff, Central Intelligence Agency, March 1977), p 2.
120 Royal Commission on Intelligence and Security, *Fifth Report*, Appendix 5–E, paragraph 12.
121 ibid., Appendix 5–D, paragraph 219.
122 ibid., paragraph 222; Appendix 5–D, paragraph 219; and Appendix 5–E, paragraph 21.
123 Memorandum from President Dwight D. Eisenhower to Heads of All Departments and Agencies, 'Making Classified Security Information Available to Foreign Nationals', 25 May 1953.
124 Winslow Peck, 'US Electronic Espionage: A Memoir', *Ramparts*, vol. 11, No. 2, August 1972, p 45.
125 'West Germans Eavesdrop on Warsaw Pact Nations', *Electronic Warfare/*

Defense Electronics, November/December 1977, pp 51–2; and 'CIA Develops Accommodation Site in Germany', *Electronic Warfare/Defense Electronics*, January 1979, p 22.
126 Nils Petter Gleditsch and Owen Wilkes, *The Oslo Rabbit Trial* (Defense Campaign for Gleditsch and Wilkes, Oslo, December 1981), p 162.
127 Howell, 'Aus-Can-What?', pp 35–7.
128 Bamford, *The Puzzle Palace*, p 326.
129 Notes by the Secretaries, JCEC 1371/1, 19 July 1956.
130 See, for example, Ralph W. McGehee, *Deadly Deceits: My 25 Years in the CIA* (Sheridan Square Publishers, New York, 1983), p 49.
131 'Spying on Russia, With China's Help', *US News and World Report*, 29 June 1981, p 10; *Far Eastern Economic Review*, 26 June 1981, p 9; and *Washington Post*, 18 June 1981, p 34.
132 Royal Commission on Intelligence and Security, *Fifth Report*, Appendix D, paragraphs 126–161.
133 Joint Intelligence Organization, *Fourth Annual Report, 1974*, (Department of Defence, Canberra, 1974), pp 25–6. For a recent statement to the effect that Australia and Papua New Guinea 'have an arrangement to assist each other on intelligence matters', see the Leader of the PNG Opposition and former Commander of the PNG Defence Force, Mr Ted Diro, cited in *Canberra Times*, 10 May 1983.
134 Richard Halloran, 'US Offers Israel Plan on War Data', *New York Times*, 13 March 1983, p 1.
135 See 'America–Israel: Cracks in the Special Relationship', *The Middle East*, March 1983, p 13.
136 ibid.
137 Andrew Wier and Jonathon Bloch, 'Mossad's Secret Rivals', *The Middle East*, December 1981, p 24.
138 Leslie H. Gelb, 'Israel, Angered at US Sanctions, Baulks at Passing Over War Data', *New York Times*, 5 September 1982, pp 1, 6.
139 Halloran, 'US Offers Israel Plan on War Data', p 1.
140 *Defense Electronics*, January 1983, p 13.
141 Winslow Peck, 'Silvermine', *Counter Spy*, Spring 1976, pp 56–60.
142 Neil Ulman, 'South Africa Over-Prepares Hoping to Lure Naval Allies', *Australian Financial Review*, 8 August 1975.
143 Gordon Winter, *Inside BOSS: South Africa's Secret Police* (Penguin, Harmondsworth, 1981), pp 36, 225; Thomas Plate and Andrea Darvi, *Secret Police: The Terrifying Inside Story of an International Network* (Abacus, London, 1983), pp 117–18, 126.
144 Winter, *Inside BOSS*, p 419.
145 See Barrie Penrose and Roger Courtiour, *The Pencourt File* (Secker and Warburg, London, 1978).
146 Alister Taylor, 'The Security Axis', *New Zealand Monthly Review*, May 1975, p 7.
147 'ASIO Under Covers', *Bulletin*, 8 June 1974, pp 6–7.
148 John Stockwell, *In Search of Enemies: A CIA Story* (W.W. Norton, New York, 1978), p 187.

8 The signals intelligence connection
1 Joint Intelligence Organization, *Fourth Annual Report, 1974, Part 2*, (Canberra, November 1974), p 6.
2 Duncan Campbell, 'Threat of the Electronic Spies', *New Statesman*, 2 February 1979, pp 140–4.

3 John Sawatsky, *Men in the Shadows: The RCMP Security Service* (Doubleday, New York, 1980) p 92; Transcript of the 'The Fifth Estate — The Espionage Establishment', broadcast by the Canadian Broadcasting Company, 1974.
4 Chapman Pincher, *Inside Story: A Documentary of the Pursuit of Power* (Stein and Day, New York, 1979) p 157.
5 Sawatsky, *Men in the Shadows*, p 92.
6 Bob Elliot, *Scarlet to Green: Canadian Army Intelligence, 1903–1963* (Hunter Rose, Toronto, 1981), p 461. For instances of such phenomena during the Second World War, see Aileen Clayton, *The Enemy is Listening* (Ballantine, New York 1982), pp 132–5.
7 Desmond Ball, *A Suitable Piece of Real Estate: American Installations in Australia* (Hale and Iremonger, Sydney, 1980) p 40.
8 House Permanent Select Committee on Intelligence, *Annual Report* (US Government Printing Office, Washington DC, 1978), p 31.
9 Deborah Shapley, 'Who's Listening?: How NSA Tunes in on Americans' Overseas Phone Calls and Messages', *Washington Post*, 9 October 1977, pp C1, C4.
10 William J. Broad, 'Evading the Soviet Ear at Glen Cove', *Science* 3 September 1982, pp 910–11.
11 Shapley, 'Who's Listening?'
12 ibid.; and James Bamford, *The Puzzle Palace: A Report on NSA, America's Most Secret Agency* (Houghton Mifflin, Boston, 1982) pp 173–4.
13 House Permanent Select Committee on Intelligence, *Annual Report* (1978), p 36.
14 On the development of radar, see J.G. Crowther and R. Whiddington, *Science at War* (His Majesty's Stationery Office, London, 1947); and R.V. Jones, *The Wizard War: British Scientific Intelligence 1939–1945* (Coward, McCann and Geohegan, New York, 1978).
15 John Prados, *The Soviet Estimate: U.S. Intelligence Analysis and Russian Military Strength* (The Dial Press, New York, 1982), p 35.
16 ibid., p 203; Farooq Hussain, *The Future of Arms Control: Part IV, The Impact of Weapons Test Restrictions* (Adelphi Paper No. 165, International Institute for Strategic Studies, London, 1980); and Robert Kaiser, 'Verification of SALT II: Arts and Science', *Washington Post*, 15 June 1979, p 1.
17 House Permanent Select Committee, *Annual Report* (1978), p 38.
18 ibid., p 28.
19 Robert Lindsey, *The Falcon and the Snowman* (Simon and Schuster, New York, 1979), p 54.
20 Frequency is a term used to describe either the number of times an alternating current goes through its complete cycle per second or the vibration rate of sound waves in air. One cycle per second is referred to as a hertz (Hz). 1 000 Hz is a kilohertz, 1 000 000 Hz is a megahertz (MHz) and 1 000 000 000 Hz is a gigahertz (GHz). Frequencies may range from 0.001 Hz to 8×10^{21} Hz. The terms used in this book and the corresponding frequency limits are given in the table below.

Terms Used	Frequency Limits
Very Low Frequencies (VLF)	3 to 30 kHz
Low Frequencies (LF)	30 to 300 kHz
High Frequencies (HF)	3 to 30 MHz
Very High Frequencies (VHF)	30 to 300 MHz
Ultra High Frequencies (UHF)	300 MHz to 3 GHz (Gc)
Super High Frequencies (SHF)	3 to 30 GHz
Extremely High Frequencies (EHF)	30 to 300 GHz

Microwave frequencies overlap the UHF, SHF and EHF bands — running from 1 to 50 GHz. See Robert L. Shrader, *Electronic Communication* (McGraw Hill, New York, 1980), pp 64–5, 627.
21 Lindsey, *The Falcon and the Snowman*, p 57.
22 Desmond Ball, 'The Rhyolite Programme', Reference Paper No. 86, Strategic and Defence Studies Centre, Australian National University, Canberra, November 1981, p 25.
23 ibid.
24 Lindsey, *The Falcon and the Snowman*, pp 345–6; Robert Lindsey, 'Soviet Spies Got Data on Satellites Intended for Monitoring Arms Pact', *New York Times*, 29 April 1979, p 1; and Clarence Robinson, 'Soviets Push Telemetry Bypass', *Aviation Week and Space Technology*, 16 April 1979, p 14
25 House Committee on Foreign Affairs, *The Role of Intelligence in the Foreign Policy Process* (US Government Printing Office, Washington, DC, 1980), p 232.
26 Philip J. Klass, 'U.S. Monitoring Capability Impaired', *Aviation Week and Space Technology*, 14 May 1979, p 18.
27 ibid.
28 Lindsey, *The Falcon and the Snowman*, p 111.
29 Ball, 'The Rhyolite Programme', p 5.
30 Duncan Campbell, 'Target Britain', *New Statesman*, 31 October 1980, pp 6–9.
31 This spacecraft was launched into orbit on an Atlas Agena D from the Eastern Test Range. The physical description in terms of shape, weight, length and diameter matches that of Rhyolite but the orbital parameters do not. However, the orbital parameters given are not necessarily final. See *Revised Table of Earth Satellites, Volume 2, 1969–1973*, (Royal Aircraft Establishment, Farnborough, Hants., 1979), p 228.
32 Lindsey, *The Falcon and the Snowman*, pp 110–11.
33 Richard Burt, 'U.S. Plans New Way to Check Soviet Missile Tests', *New York Times*, 29 June 1979, p A3.
34 Farooq Hussain, *The Future of Arms Control: The Impact of Weapons Test Restrictions* (Adelphi Paper No. 165, International Institute for Strategic Studies, London, Spring 1981), p 42.
35 House Armed Services Committee, *Department of Defense Authorization for Appropriations for Fiscal Year 1984*, (US Government Printing Office, Washington, DC, 1983), Part 3, p 904.
36 Jeffrey Richelson, 'The Satellite Data System', *Journal of the British Interplanetary Society*, (vol. 37, No. 5), 1984, pp 226–228.
37 John Pike, 'Reagan Prepares for War in Outer Space', *Counter Spy*, vol. 7, No. 1, September–November 1982, pp 17–22.
38 House Appropriations Committee, *Department of Defense Appropriations for 1980*, (US Government Printing Office, Washington, DC, 1979), Part 6, p 160; Senate Armed Services Committee, *Department of Defense Authorization for Appropriations for Fiscal Year 1979*, (US Government Printing Office, Washington, DC, 1978), Part 8, pp 2666–7.
39 US Department of Defense, *DoD C^3I Program Management Structure and Major Programs* [Sanitized Version], 10 December 1980.
40 Anthony Kenden, 'US Reconnaissance Satellite Programmes', *Spaceflight*, vol. 20, No. 7, 1978, pp 243–62.
41 ibid.
42 'Industry Observer', *Aviation Week and Space Technology*, 14 March 1977, p 11
43 'Washington Round Up', *Aviation Week and Space Technology*, 4 June 1979, p 11.

44 Walter Pincus and Mary Thornton, 'US to Orbit "Sigint" Craft From Shuttle', *Washington Post*, 19 December 1984, pp A1, A8, A9; and Jeffrey T. Richelson and William M. Arkin, 'Spy Satellites: "Secret" But Much is Known', *Washington Post*, 6 January 1985, pp. C1–C2.
45 'Reconnaissance and Special Duty Aircraft,' *Air Force Magazine*, May 1978, p 118.
46 ibid.
47 'Shaping Tomorrow's CIA', *Time*, 6 February 1978, pp 10 ff; 'Radar Detector Abroad SR-71 Alerted to Missile Attack', *New York Times*, 29 August 1981, p 3.
48 Ted Greenwood, *Reconnaissance, Surveillance and Arms Control* (Adelphi Papers No. 88, International Institute for Strategic Studies, London, 1978).
49 'SR-71 Imposes Burden on Maintenance Units', *Aviation Week and Space Technology*, 18 May 1981, pp 105–8; Brian Bennett, Tony Powell and John Adams, *The USAF Today* (West London Aviation Group Publication, London, 1981), pp 42–53.
50 Duncan Campbell, 'Spy in the Sky', *New Statesman*, 9 September 1983, pp 8–9.
51 'U-2 Facts and Figures', *Air Force Magazine*, January 1976, p 45.
52 ibid.
53 Harry F. Eustace, 'Changing Intelligence Priorities', *Electronic Warfare/Defense Electronics*, November 1978, pp 85 ff.
54 Dennis MacShane, 'Spy Stations in Cyprus', *New Statesman*, 30 June 1978, p 870.
55 'Reconnaissance and Special Duty Aircraft', *Air Force Magazine*, May 1979, p 124.
56 ibid.; Charles W. Corddry and Albert Schlstedt, Jr., 'Planes' Covert Role is to Monitor Soviet Space Flights, Missile Tests', *Baltimore Sun*, 7 May 1981, p 1.
57 Philip Taubman, 'U.S. Intelligence Plane Was on Routine Mission', *New York Times*, 5 September 1983, p 4.
58 House Committee on Appropriations, *Department of Defense Appropriations for 1984, Part 8*, (Government Printing Office, Washington, DC, 1983), p 384.
59 Bennett, et al., *The USAF Today*, pp 42, 49, 51, 53.
60 George C. Wilson, 'U.S. RC-135 was Assessing Soviet Air Defenses', *Washington Post*, 7 September 1983, p A12.
61 Michael Getler, 'Soviets Held Test of New Missile Three Days After Jet Downed', *Washington Post*, 16 September 1983, p A28; and John P. Wallach, 'Soviets trying to hide missile test the night jet was shot', *San Francisco Examiner*, 25 September 1983, p 1.
62 Duncan Campbell, 'Target Britain', *New Statesman*, 31 October 1980, pp 6–9.
63 'Reconnaissance and Special Duty Aircraft', *Air Force Magazine*, May 1979, p 121.
64 Philip J. Klass, 'USAF Tracking Radar Details Disclosed', *Aviation Week and Space Technology*, 25 October 1976, pp 41 ff.
65 ibid.
66 Dr. E. Michael del Papa, *Meeting the Challenge: ESD and the Cobra Dane Construction Effort on Shemya Island*, (Electronic Systems Division, Bedford, 1979), p 3.
67 Klass, 'USAF Tracking Radar Details Disclosed'.
68 This description of the AN/FLR-9 is from *Cryptologic Collection Equipments* (Naval Education and Training Command, Pensacola, 1977); and Bamford, *The Puzzle Palace*, p 162.
69 Bamford, *The Puzzle Palace*, p 162.
70 J. Hockley, 'A Goniometer for Use with High Frequency Circularly Disposed

Aerial Arrays', *Radio and Electronic Engineer*, vol. 43, No. 8. August 1973, pp 475–85.
71 The description of Rhombic array is based on Bamford, *The Puzzle Palace*, p 163.
72 Klass, 'U.S. Monitoring Capability Impaired', *Aviation Week and Space Technology*, 14 May 1979, p 18.
73 ibid.
74 Richard Burt, 'Technology is Essential to Arms Verification', *New York Times*, 14 August 1979, pp C1, C2.
75 Klass, 'U.S. Monitoring Capability Impaired', *Aviation Week and Space Technology*, 14 May 1979, p 18.
76 See House Committee on Armed Services, *Inquiry into the U.S.S. Pueblo and EC-121 Plane Incidents* (US Government Printing Office, Washington, DC, 1969).
77 Richard Halloran, 'U.S. Says Navy Surveillance Ship is Stationed off Central America', *New York Times*, 25 February 1982, pp 1, 6.
78 Kenneth J. Stein, 'Cobra Judy Phased Array Radar Tested', *Aviation Week and Space Technology*, 10 August 1981, pp 70–3.
79 Loring Wirbel, 'Somebody is Listening', *The Progressive*, November 1980, pp 16–22.
80 See Appendix 1 for a full list of US SIGINT facilities.
81 Bamford, *The Puzzle Palace*, p 172.
82 ibid., pp 170–2.
83 Senate Committee on Armed Services, *Military Construction Authorization FY1983* (US Government Printing Office, Washington, DC, 1972), p 287.
84 See Appendix 1.
85 'Military Spy Station May Remain in Virginia', *Washington Star*, 28 July 1981, p B-3.
86 Duncan Campbell, 'Thatcher Bugged by Closest Ally', *New Statesman*, 25 July 1980, p 4.
87 See Appendix 1.
88 Bamford, *The Puzzle Palace*, pp 177–8.
89 See Appendix 1.
90 See Appendix 1.
91 House Committee on Appropriations, *Military Construction Appropriations for 1981* (US Government Printing Office, Washington, DC, 1989), Part 1, p 826.
92 Campbell, 'Thatcher Bugged by Closest Ally', p 4; Captain Mike R. Ehrlick, 'See you at the Credit Union', *INSCOM Journal*, February 1982, p 6.
93 See Appendix 1.
94 'Memorandum to Bill Moyers, Subject: President's Weekly Report' (Department of Defense, Washington, 12 May 1964).
95 See Appendix 1.
96 Andriana Ierodiaconou, 'Greek Socialists Reportedly Seeking Closure of 1 of 4 US Bases', *Washington Post*, 13 December 1982, p A24.
97 Stockholm International Peace Research Institute (SIPRI), *World Armaments and Disarmament, SIPRI Yearbook 1980* (Taylor and Francis Ltd., London, 1980), p 296.
98 Owen Wilkes and Nils Peter Gleditsch, *Intelligence Installations in Norway: Their Number, Location, Function and Legality* (International Peace Research Institute, Oslo, 1979), p 24; Senate Committee on Appropriations, *Military Construction Appropriations FY1977* (US Government Printing Office, Washington, DC, 1976), p 341.

99 House Committee on Appropriations, *Military Construction Appropriations for 1978* (US Government Printing Office, Washington, DC, 1977), Part 1, p 548.
100 SIPRI, *SIPRI Yearbook 1980*, p 296.
101 Prados, *The Soviet Estimate*, p 103; and Wilkes and Gleditsch, *Intelligence Installations in Norway*, p 10.
102 R.W. Apple Jr., 'Norwegians Ardent Neutralists Also Want their Defense Strong', *New York Times*, 5 August 1978, p 2.
103 SIPRI, *SIPRI Yearbook 1980*, p 296.
104 House Committee on International Relations, *United States Military Installations and Objectives in the Mediterranean* (US Government Printing Office, Washington, DC; 1977) pp 37–9.
105 SIPRI, *SIPRI Yearbook 1980*, p 296.
106 House Committee on International Relations, *United States Military Installations and Objectives in the Mediterranean*, p 39.
107 SIPRI, *SIPRI Yearbook 1980*, p 296.
108 ibid.
109 Robert C. Toth, 'U.S. and China Jointly Track Firing of Soviet Missiles', *Los Angeles Times*, 19 June, 1981, pp 1, 9; Philip Taubman, 'U.S. and Peking Jointly Monitor Russian Missiles', *New York Times*, 18 June, 1981, pp 1, 14; and Murrey Marder, 'Monitoring: Not so Secret Secret', *Washington Post*, 19 June, 1981, p 10.
110 See Appendix 1.
111 Senate Committee on Foreign Relations, *United States Security Agreements and Commitments Abroad* (US Government Printing Office, Washington, DC, 1971), p 1504.
112 'How the US Listened In', *Newsweek*, 12 September 1983, p 25.
113 Prados, *The Soviet Estimate*, p 103; and Harvey Yale, *Close-out of the 6937th Communications Group Peshawar Pakistan* (Air Force Office of History, Washington, DC, 1970).
114 Victor Marchetti and John Marks, *The CIA and the Cult of Intelligence* (Dell, New York, 1981), p 175.
115 Elliot, *Scarlet to Green*, p 461.
116 Notes by the Secretaries to the Joint Communications–Electronics Committee, *Revision of the Interim Outline Plan for Telecommunications Support of National Security Agency* (JCEC 1971/1, 19 July, 1956), Appendix C to Enclosure A.
117 *Global Autovon Defense Communications System Directory* (Defense Communications Agency, Washington, DC, March 1981), pp 7, 12, 20.
118 ibid., p 115.
119 ibid., p 10, 21, 22.
120 ibid., p 23.
121 Colin Gray, *Canadian Defence Priorities: A Question of Relevance* (Clarke, Irwin and Co., Toronto, 1972), inset.
122 *Global Autovon* p 21.
123 Private information.
124 Private information.
125 *Global Autovon* p 96.
126 Desmond Ball, *A Suitable Piece of Real Estate*, p 45.
127 'Cipher', *Defense Electronics*, March 1982, p 30.
128 Joint Intelligence Organization, *Fourth Annual Report, 1974*, Part 2, p 7; and Desmond Ball, 'The US Naval Ocean Surveillance System (NOSIS) — Australia's Role', *Pacific Defence Reporter*, June 1982, p 42.
129 Senate Armed Services Committee and Senate Appropriations Committee, *Military Construction Authorization Fiscal Year 1973*, (US Government Printing

Office, Washington, DC, 1972), p 299. See also 'Uncle Sam and His 40 000 Snoopers', *Nation Review*, 5–11 October 1972, p 1613. According to this article, written by a former NSA officer, the NSG operation at North West Cape 'intercepts traffic in the Sunda Straits and in the Indian Ocean'. However, the existence of NSG at North West Cape is officially denied by the Australian Department of Defence.

130 Dr. J.F. Ward, 'A Low Delta, Surface Wave Interferometer Array for High-Frequency Radio Communication', *Nature*, vol. 205, 13 March 1965, p 1062; and '6 Signal Regiment', *Signalman*, No. 5, 1980, pp 19–22.
131 'Direct Tap of US Satellites', *Australian Financial Review*, 8 August 1979; 'Project Sparrow Satellite Terminal Progresses', *Signalman*, No. 6, 1980, p 49; and 'Official Opening and Handover of Watsonia Satellite Terminal', *Signalman*, No. 8, 1981, p 31.
132 Commander J.B. Newman, 'Memorandum for Discussion at Singapore', (no date but probably October 1942), Australian Archives Accession, No. MP 1185/8 File MP 1973/415.
133 Ball, *A Suitable Piece of Real Estate*, pp 42–4; 'Embassies Messages Taped', *Nation Review*, 20–26 April 1978, p 4.
134 J.T. Starbuck, 'A High Frequency Direction Finding Equipment for the 1.5MHz to 30MHz Band', *Communications Equipment and Systems* (IEE Conference Publication 139), June 1976, pp 5–8.
135 Ball, *A Suitable Piece of Real Estate*, p 44.
136 R.N. Thompson, 'Sigint Presence in Singapore and New Station at Darwin', (memorandum to the Secretary, Department of Defence, 23 February 1973).
137 *Northern Territory News*, 12 March 1970, p 1.
138 Desmond Ball, 'The Rhyolite Programme'.
139 ibid., pp 27–8.
140 ibid., p 28.
141 ibid., p 31.
142 Roger Foley, 'Spying on Radio Waves', *New Zealand Times*, 8 April 1984; and David Young, 'Secret Circles', *New Zealand Listener*, 21 April 1984.
143 Duncan Campbell, 'The Spies Who Spend What They Like', *New Statesman*, 16 May 1980, pp 738–44.
144 Nick Anning, 'A Battery of Hearing Aids Listening to the World', *The Leveller*, No. 37, April 1980, pp 18–19; and 'On Watch in Berlin', *INSCOM Journal*, vol. 5, No. 5, May 1982, p 13.
145 Nick Anning, 'A Battery of Hearing Aids Listening to the World', p 19; and Dennis MacShane, 'Spy Stations in Cyprus', *New Statesman*, 30 June 1978, p 870.
146 'Britannia Scorns to Yield', *Newsweek*, 19 April 1982, pp 41–6.
147 Nick Anning, 'A Battery of Hearing Aids Listening to the World', p 19; and information provided by Duncan Campbell.
148 Seymour Hersh, 'Iran Signs Rockwell Deal for Persian Gulf Spy Base', *New York Times*, 1 June 1975, pp 1, 39.
149 Nick Anning, 'A Battery of Hearing Aids Listening to the World', pp 18–19; Duncan Campbell, 'Secrecy for Its Own Sake', *New Statesman*, 23 July 1982, pp 6–8; 'Britain's World Spy Network', *Sunday Times*, 18 July 1982; and information provided by Duncan Campbell.
150 'Diplomacy by Satellite: Foreign Office Link With Embassies', *The Times*, 2 February 1967; Bamford, *The Puzzle Palace*, p 333; and information provided by Duncan Campbell.
151 'Memorandum to Bill Moyers . . .'
152 'The Eavesdroppers', *Time Out*, May 1975, p 21.

372 The Ties That Bind

153 House Committee on Appropriations, *Military Construction Appropriations for 1981* (US Government Printing Office, Washington, DC, 1980), p 1123.
154 Duncan Campbell and Linda Malvern, 'America's Big Ear on Europe', *New Statesman*, 18 July 1980, pp 10–14.
155 ibid.
156 ibid.
157 ibid.
158 ibid.
159 Duncan Campbell, 'Target Britain', *New Statesman*, 31 October 1980, pp 6–9; and 'Second SR-71 Deployed to England', *Aviation Week and Space Technology*, 31 January 1983, p 59.

9 Ocean surveillance

1 See F.H. Hinsley, *British Intelligence in the Second World War: Its Influence on Strategy and Operations* (Her Majesty's Stationery Office, London, 1979); Patrick Beesly, *Very Special Intelligence: The Story of the Admiralty's Operational Intelligence Centre in World War II* (Sphere Books Limited, London, 1977), Chapter 1; Richard Deacon, *The Silent War: A History of Western Naval Intelligence* (Sphere Books Limited, London, 1980); Edward Van Der Rhoer, *Deadly Magic: A Personal Account of Communications Intelligence in World War II in the Pacific* (Charles Scribner's Sons, New York, 1978); Ronald W. Clark, *The Man Who Broke PURPLE: The Life of the World's Greatest Cryptologist Colonel William F. Friedman* (Weidenfield & Nicolson, London, 1977); David Kahn, *The Codebreakers* (Weidenfield & Nicolson, London, 1966); and Clay Blair Jr., *Silent Victory: The US Submarine War Against Japan* (J.B. Lippincott Company, Philadelphia, 1975).
2 Jim Bussert, 'Computers Add New Effectiveness to SOSUS/Caesar', *Defense Electronics*, October 1979, p 64.
3 Senate Appropriations Committee, *Department of Defense Appropriations for Fiscal Year 1978*, (US Government Printing Office, Washington, DC, 1977), Part 5, pp 600–1.
4 See, for example, on the Naval Security Group Detachment at Rota, Spain, the Hearings before a Subcommittee of the House of Representatives Committee on Appropriations, *Military Construction Appropriations for 1978* (US Government Printing Office, Washington, DC, 1977), Part 1, pp 546–50.

The NSG facility at Rota is described in this testimony as being part of 'the SISSZULU project'. The monitoring system is 'a circularly-disposed antenna array (CDAA)'.

On the NSG Activity at Kami Seya, Japan, see the Hearings before the Special Subcommittee on the U.S.S. *Pueblo* of the House Committee on Armed Services, *Inquiry Into the U.S.S. Pueblo & EC-121 Plane Incidents* (US Government Printing Office, Washington, DC, 1969), pp 670–1.
5 Testimony of Admiral Metzel, Senate Armed Services Committee, *Department of Defense Authorization for Appropriations for Fiscal Year 1980*, (US Government Printing Office, Washington, DC, 1979), Part 6, p 2925.
6 Owen Wilkes, 'Strategic Anti-Submarine Warfare and its Implications for a Counterforce First Strike', *SIPRI Yearbook 1979* (Taylor and Francis Ltd., London, 1979), p 430.
7 House Foreign Affairs Committee and Senate Foreign Relations Committee, *Fiscal Year 1981 Arms Control Impact Statements* (US Government Printing Office, Washington, DC, 1980), p 239; and Norman Friedman, 'SOSUS and US ASW Tactics', *US Naval Institute Proceedings*, March 1980, pp 120–2.
8 House Appropriations Committee, *Department of Defence Appropriations for*

Fiscal Year 1977, (US Government Printing Office, Washington, DC, 1976), Part 5, p 1255; Drew Middleton, 'Expert Predicts A Big US Gain in Sub Warfare', *New York Times*, 18 July 1979, p A5; and Chapman Pincher, 'US to Set Up Sub Spy Station', *Daily Express*, 6 January 1973.
9 Harvey B. Silverstein, 'Caesar, SOSUS and Submarines: Economic and Institutional Implications of ASW Technologies', *Oceans '78* (Proceedings of the Fourth Annual Combined Conference sponsored by the Marine Technology Society and the Institute of Electrical and Electronics Engineers, Washington, DC, 6–8 September 1978), p 407.
10 ibid.; and Defense Market Survey (DMS), 'Sonar–Sub-surface–Caesar', *DMS Market Intelligence Report* (DMS Inc., Greenwich, Connecticut, 1980), p 1.
11 *New York Times*, 18 July 1979, p A5; and Bernhard Kovit, 'New Anti-Sub Aircraft', *Space/Aeronautics*, vol. 45, No. 2, February 1966, pp 58–71.
12 Harvey Silverstein, 'Caesar, SOSUS and Submarines', p 407; Clyde W. Burleson, *The Jennifer Project*, (Prentice-Hall, Inc., Englewood Cliffs, New Jersey, 1977), pp 16–17, 24–25; and Sven Hirdman, 'The Militarization of the Deep Ocean', in Stockholm International Peace Research Institute (SIPRI), *SIPRI Yearbook of World Armaments and Disarmament 1969/70* (Almqvist & Widsell, Stockholm, 1970), p 150.
13 DMS, 'Sonar Technology — AUTEC', *DMS Market Intelligence Report* (DMS Inc., Greenwich, Conn., 1981).
14 Howard B. Dratch, 'High Stakes in the Azores', *The Nation*, 8 November 1975, pp 455–6; 'NATO Fixed SONAR Range Commissioned', *Armed Forces Journal*, August 1972, p 29; 'Atlantic Islands: NATO Seeks Wider Facilities', *International Herald Tribune*, June 1981, p 7S; and Richard Timsar, 'Portugal Bargains for US Military Aid with Strategic Mid-Atlantic Base', *Christian Science Monitor*, 24 March 1981, p 9.
15 DMS, 'Sonar — Sub-surface — Caesar', p 1.
16 Senate Appropriations Committee, *Department of Defense Appropriations, Fiscal Year 1975* (US Government Printing Office, Washington, DC, 1974), Part 3, p 444.
17 'Militarisering av Haven: USAs Vapen Utvekling Rubbar Grunden for "Terrorbalansen"', *Kommentar*, October 1980, p 22; and Joel S. Wit, 'Advances in Antisubmarine Warfare', *Scientific American*, vol. 244, No. 2, February 1981, pp 36–7. The facility in the northeastern Indian Ocean is described in these and other sources as being located off Christmas Island. However, the Australian Minister for Defence, Mr Killen, has officially stated that 'there is no underwater sensor system at Christmas Island'. See *Hansard (House of Representatives)*, 5 May 1981, p 2004; and *Hansard (House of Representatives)*, 19 August 1981, p 522. However, there could well be such a system located in Australian waters elsewhere in this area.
18 Senate Armed Services Committee, *Department of Defense Authorization for Appropriations for Fiscal Year 1980*, Part 6, pp 2947–9; Owen Wilkes, 'Strategic Anti-Submarine Warfare and its Implications for a Counterforce First Strike', p 431; and House Committee on International Relations, *Evaluation of Fiscal Year 1979 Arms Control Impact Statements: Toward More Informed Congressional Participation in National Security Policymaking*, (US Government Printing Office, Washington, DC, 1978), p 112.
19 Kosta Tsipis, 'Antisubmarine Warfare: Fact and Fiction', *New Scientist*, 16 January, 1975, p 147.
20 DMS, 'ASW', *DMS Market Intelligence Report*, (DMS Inc., Greenwich, Conn., 1980).
21 Larry L. Booda, 'Antisubmarine Warfare Reacts to Strategic Indicators', *Sea*

Technology, November 1981, p 12.
22 House Foreign Affairs Committee and Senate Foreign Relations Committee, *Fiscal Year 1981 Arms Control Impact Statements*, pp 347–8.
23 See, for example; 'British Say Soviet Lags in Sub Detection', *Baltimore Sun*, 31 December 1980, p 4.
24 Senate Armed Services Committee, *Department of Defense Authorization for Appropriations for Fiscal Year 1980*, Part 6, p 2984; and Senate Armed Services Committee, *Department of Defense Authorization for Appropriations for Fiscal Year 1979*, (US Government Printing Office, Washington, DC, 1978), Part 8, p 6350.
25 House Committee on International Relations, *Evaluation of Fiscal Year 1979 Arms Control Impact Statements*, p 111.
26 ibid.
27 Senate Armed Services Committee, *Department of Defense Authorization for Appropriations for Fiscal Year 1980*, Part 6, pp 2947–9; Larry L. Booda, 'SURTASS, RDSS Augment Ocean Surveillance', *Sea Technology*, November 1981, pp 19–20; Norman Polmar, 'SURTASS and T-AGOS', *US Naval Institute Proceedings*, March 1980, pp 122–4; and House Committee on Foreign Affairs and Senate Committee on Foreign Relations, *Fiscal Year 1981 Arms Control Impact Statements*, p 342.
28 DMS, 'FLR-15', *DMS Market Intelligence Report*, (DMS Inc., Greenwich, Conn., May 1977).
29 Don Oberdorfer, 'Behind a New Policy: Oil, Crises and a Year of Deliberations', *Washington Post*, 24 January 1980, p 1; Oswald Johnston, 'US Talks with Britain, Portugal on Use of Bases', *Los Angeles Times*, 25 January 1980, p 1. See also 'New Listening Post?', *Defense Electronics*, November 1979, p 25.
30 Anthony Cave Brown, *Bodyguard of Lies*, (Harper & Row, New York, 1975), pp 356–7; and David Kahn, *The Codebreakers*, p 274.
31 Statement of Ambassador Edward Korry, Former Ambassador to Ethiopia, in Hearings before the Subcommittee on African Affairs of the Senate Foreign Relations Committee, *Ethiopia and the Horn of Africa* (US Government Printing Office, Washington, DC, 1976), p 35.
32 ibid., p 113.
33 ibid; see also Hearings before the Subcommittee on the Near East and South Asia of the House of Representatives Committee on Foreign Affairs, *Proposed Expansion of US Military Facilities in the Indian Ocean* (US Government Printing Office, Washington, DC, 1974), pp 1, 15, 38, 47.
34 House Armed Services Committee, *Report of the Delegation to the Indian Ocean Area*, (US Government Printing Office, Washington, DC, 1980), pp 11–12; House Foreign Affairs Committee, *Proposed Expansion of US Military Facilities in the Indian Ocean*, pp 1, 5, 15, 26, 33, 38, 64; Commander Daniel W. Urish, 'To Build a Link — the Seabees at Diego Garcia', *US Naval Institute Proceedings*, April 1973, pp 101–4; Petty Officer Kirby Harrison, 'Diego Garcia: the Seabees at Work', *US Naval Institute Proceedings*, August 1979, pp 53–5; 'Diego Garcia Assumes New Strategic Role', *Aviation Week and Space Technology*, 25 February 1980, p 19.
35 House Foreign Affairs Committee, *Proposed Expansion of US Military Facilities in the Indian Ocean*, p 33.
36 House Appropriations Committee, *Hearings on Military Construction Fiscal Year 1978*, (US Government Printing Office, Washington, DC, 1977), Part 2, p 183.
37 'Classic Wizard Reporting System', 26 May 1981, in *CINCPAC Fleet Note 5215*, 11 February 1983, Enclosure 1, p 10.

38 House Appropriations Committee, *Military Construction Appropriations for 1965* (US Government Printing Office, Washington, DC, 1964), Part 1, pp 462–3.
39 Senate Foreign Relations Committee, *United States Security Agreements and Commitments Abroad* (USGPO, Washington, DC, 1971), p 1504; and Peter Laurie, *Beneath the City Streets* (Granada, London, 1979), p 258.
40 'Classic Wizard Reporting System', 26 May 1981, in *CINCPAC Fleet Note 5215*, 11 February 1983, Enclosure 1, p 10.
41 Senate Foreign Relations Committee, *United States Security Agreements Abroad*, pp 1455, 1485. See also 'Narrowband Assignment and Reporting Instructions for the Pacific High Frequency Direction Finding Net', 17 February 1982, in *CINCPAC Fleet Note 5215*, 11 February 1983, Enclosure 1, p 10.
42 Senate Armed Services Committee, Subcommittee on Military Construction and Stockpiles, *Military Construction Authorization Fiscal Year 1980* (USGPO, Washington, DC, 1979), p 229; House Appropriations Committee, *Military Construction Appropriations for 1980* (USGPO, Washington, DC, 1979), Part 4, pp 1002–3; and House Appropriations Committee, *Military Construction Appropriations for 1982* (USGPO, Washington, DC, 1981), Part 1, pp 1231–5.
43 *CINCPAC Fleet Note 5215*, 11 February 1983, Enclosure 1, p 10.
44 Senate Armed Services Committee and Senate Appropriations Committee, *Military Construction Authorization Fiscal Year 1973*, (USGPO, Washington, DC, 1972), p 287.
45 Richard Deacon, *The Silent War*, p 157; and DMS, *Code Name Handbook*, p 68.
46 Desmond Ball, *A Suitable Piece of Real Estate*, p 30.
47 *Air Force Magazine*, May 1979, p 97; and R.T. Pretty and D.H.R. Archer, (eds), *Jane's Weapon Systems 1973–74* (Sampson Low, Marston & Co., Ltd, London, Fifth Edition, 1973), p 250.
48 'Alternative Snooping', *Far Eastern Economic Review*, 18 June 1976.
49 Senate Foreign Relations Committee, *United States Security Agreements and Commitments Abroad*, pp 92, 103.
50 R.T. Pretty, (ed.), *Jane's Weapon Systems 1979–80* (Macdonald & Jane's, London, Tenth Edition, 1979), pp 638–9; J. Hockley, 'A Goniometer for Use With High Frequency Circularly Disposed Aerial Arrays', *Radio and Electronic Engineer*, vol. 43, No. 8, August 1973, pp 475–85; and J.T. Starbuck, 'A High Frequency Direction-Finding Equipment for the 1.5 MHz to 30 MHz Band', *Communications Equipment & Systems*, (IEE Conference Publication 139); June 1976, pp 15–18.
51 F.J. Hatch, 'Developments in H.F. Direction-Finder Shore Stations Using Adcock Aerials', *Journal of the Institute of Electronic Engineers*, (vol. 94, Part III), 1947, pp 683–92; and P.J.D. Gething, 'High-Frequency Direction-Finding', *Proceedings of the Institute of Electronic Engineers*, vol. 113, No. L, January 1966, pp 49–61. (At the time of writing this article Dr Gething was with GCHQ at Cheltenham.)
52 Desmond Ball, *A Suitable Piece of Real Estate*, p 41.
53 Brigadier R.M. Bremner, 'My Visit to the Australian Intelligence Corps, December 1971', *The Rose and the Laurel*, vol. 8, No. 34, December 1972, pp 57–8.
54 Richard V. Hartman (ed.), *The International Countermeasures Handbook* (EW Communications, Inc., Palo Alto, California, 9th Edition, 1984), p 116.
55 *Aviation Week and Space Technology*, 18 February 1968, p 1.
56 *Space/Aeronautics*, February 1970, p 23.
57 *Aviation Week and Space Technology*, 10 September 1973, p 12.

376 The Ties That Bind

58 ibid.
59 *Aviation Week and Space Technology*, 10 September 1973, pp 12–13; 19 August 1974, p 22; and 23 June 1975, p 19.
60 *Aviation Week and Space Technology*, 10 September 1973, p 13.
61 *Defense Electronics*, January 1982, p 62.
62 'The War Beneath The Seas', *Newsweek*, 8 February 1982, p 35.
63 John W.R. Taylor and David Mondey, *Spies in the Sky*, (Charles Scribner's Sons, New York, 197), p 118.
64 ibid., pp 118–19.
65 House Armed Services Committee, *Hearings on Military Posture and H.R. 5068*, (US Government Printing Office, Washington, DC, 1977), Book 1 of Part 3, p 751; and *Defense Electronics*, July 1981, p 78.
66 'Navy Ocean Surveillance Satellite Depicted', *Aviation Week and Space Technology*, 24 May 1976, p 22; and 'Expanded Ocean Surveillance Effort Set', *Aviation Week and Space Technology*, 10 July 1978, pp 22–3.
67 *Aviation Week and Space Technology*, 20 June 1977, p 11; and 10 July 1978, pp 22–3.
68 'Ocean Surveillance System Launched', *Aviation Week and Space Technology*, 10 March 1980, p 18.
69 'Expanded Ocean Surveillance Effort Set', *Aviation Week and Space Technology*, 10 July 1978, pp 22–3.
70 ibid.; and *Aviation Week and Space Technology*, 24 May 1976, p 22.
71 SIPRI, *World Armaments and Disarmament: SIPRI Yearbook 1979* (Taylor and Francis Ltd., London, 1979), p 267.
72 ibid., p 268.
73 *Aviation Week and Space Technology*, 10 July 1978, p 23; and 'Interference With Radio Astronomy', *Science*, vol. 195, 11 March 1977, pp 932–3.
74 Defense Marketing Survey (DMS), *Code Name Handbook*, (DMS Inc., Greenwich, Conn., Ninth Edition, 1979), p 68.
75 See House Committee on Appropriations, *Military Construction Appropriations for 1981*, (USGPO, Washington, DC, 1980), pp 1474–7, 1504–9 and 1516–19; House Appropriations Committee, *Military Construction Appropriations for 1982* (USGPO, Washington, DC, 1981), pp 1231–6 and 1301–6; Senate Armed Services Committee, Subcommittee on Military Construction and Stockpiles, *Military Construction Authorization Fiscal Year 1980* (USGPO, Washington DC, 1979), p 229; and House Armed Services Committee, *Military Construction Authorization Fiscal Year 1980* (USGPO, Washington, DC, 1979), p 474.
76 Senate Armed Services Committee, *Military Construction Authorization Fiscal Year 1980*, p 229.
77 On the AN/FSQ-111 and AN/FYK-11A CLASSIC WIZARD Collection and Processing Systems, see US Navy, Naval Military Personnel Command, *Catalog of Navy Training Courses*, various pages on CLASSIC WIZARD training courses.
78 *Newsweek*, 21 April 1969, p 57.
79 Senate Armed Services Committee, *Department of Defense Authorization for Appropriations for Fiscal Year 1979*, (US Government Printing Office, Washington, DC, 1978), Part 8, pp 6268–70.
80 Colonel E.A. Bates, 'National Technical Means of Verification', *RUSI Journal*, vol. 123, No. 2, June 1978, p 65; and Philip J. Klass, *Secret Sentries in Space* (Random House, New York, 1971), pp 170–1.
81 Bhupendra M. Jasani, 'Military Uses of Outer Space', in SIPRI, *World Armaments and Disarmament: SIPRI Yearbook 1979* (Taylor and Francis Ltd., London, 1979), p 270.
82 'SEASAT: An Ocean-Dedicated Satellite', *Sea Technology*, May 1978, p 33.

83 Senate Committee on Commerce, Science and Transportation, *NASA Authorization for Fiscal Year 1978* (US Government Printing Office, Washington, DC, 1977), p 1616; and Lee-Lueng Fu and Benjamin Holt, *SEASAT Views Oceans and Sea Ice With Synthetic-Aperture Radar*, (JPL Publication 81–210, Jet Propulsion Laboratory, California Institute of Technology, Pasadena, California, 15 February 1982), p 1.
84 *Aviation Week and Space Technology*, 21 February 1977, p 9.
85 *Aviation Week and Space Technology*, 10 July 1978, p 23.
86 House Armed Services Committee, *Hearings on Military Posture and H.R. 5068*, p 751.
87 Senate Armed Services Committee, *Department of Defense Authorization for Appropriations for Fiscal Year 1979*, Part 8, pp 6268–9.
88 House Appropriations Committee, *Hearings on Military Posture and H.R. 5068*, (1977), Book 1 of Part 3, p 751.
89 DMS, 'Integrated Tactical Surveillance System (ITSS)', *DMS Market Intelligence Report*, (DMS Inc., Greenwich, Conn., 1983), pp 1–2.
90 House Armed Services Committee, *Hearings on Military Posture and H.R. 5968*, (US Government Printing Office, Washington, DC, 1982), Part 5, p 573.
91 Cited in Joel S. Wit, 'Advances in Anti-submarine Warfare', *Scientific American*, vol. 244, No. 2, February 1981, p 33.
92 DMS, 'Lockheed P-3 Orion', *DMS Market Intelligence Report*, (DMS Inc., Greenwich, Conn., 1982), pp 1–7.
93 ibid.
94 Owen Wilkes, 'Strategic Anti-Submarine Warfare and its Implications for a Counterforce First Strike', pp 432–5; *Aviation Week and Space Technology*, 14 January 1980, pp 37, 45; and *Aviation Week and Space Technology*, 11 February 1980, pp 85, 99.
95 'A Face-lift for the Nimrod', *Air International*, July 1981, pp 7–16.
96 DMS, 'Program 749', *DMS Market Intelligence Report*, (DMS Inc., Greenwich, Conn., 1977), pp 1–2.
97 See Ross Babbage, *Rethinking Australia's Defence* (University of Queensland Press, St Lucia, Qld, 1980), pp 20–1.
98 DMS, 'Program 749', p 3.
99 *Hansard (House of Representatives)*, 11 March 1981, pp 664–5.
100 'Protesters Greet the First B-52 as it Lands in Darwin', *Australian*, 6 May 1981, p 1.
101 *House of Representatives*, Answer to Question No. 2155, 16 February 1982.
102 Senate Armed Services Committee, *Department of Defense Authorization for Appropriations for Fiscal Year 1980*, Part 6, p 2927.
103 ibid.
104 ibid., p 2928.
105 House Committee on International Relations, *Evaluation of Fiscal Year 1979 Arms Control Impact Statements*, pp 109–10.
106 Seymour M. Hersh, 'Submarines of US Stage Spy Missions Inside Soviet Waters', *New York Times*, 25 May 1975, pp 1, 42; and Seymour M. Hersh, 'A False Navy Report Alleged in Sub Crash', *New York Times*, 6 July 1975, pp 1, 26.
107 *New York Times*, 25 May 1975, p 42; and George B. Kistiakowsky, *A Scientist at the White House: The Private Diary of President Eisenhower's Special Assistant for Science and Technology* (Harvard University Press, Cambridge, Mass., 1976), p 153.
108 *New York Times*, 25 May 1975, p 42.
109 ibid.

378   *The Ties That Bind*

110 *New York Times*, 6 July 1975, pp 1, 26.
111 ibid., p 26.
112 *New York Times*, 20 January 1976, p 1.
113 See James Coates, 'Special Report: Undersea Warfare', *Chicago Tribune*, 4 December 1977.
114 See Michael Drosnin, 'Desktop: A Military Mystery Story', *New York Times*, 2 April 1976, p 32.
115 Senate Appropriations Committee, *Department of Defense Appropriations Fiscal Year 1978*, (US Government Printing Office, Washington DC, 1977), Part 4, p 750.
116 ibid.
117 ibid., p 751.
118 Clyde W. Burleson, *The Jennifer Project* (Sphere Books Limited, London, 1979), pp 28–9; and Roy Varner and Wayne Collier, *A Matter of Risk* (Coronet Books, Hodder and Stoughton, 1980), p 36.
119 ibid., pp 30–2.
120 ibid., pp 18–19; and 'Deep-Sea Salvage: Did CIA Use Mohole Techniques to Raise Sub?', *Science*, 16 May 1975, pp 710–13.
121 Seymour Hersh, 'CIA Salvage Ship Brought Up Part of Soviet Sub Lost in 1968, Failed to Raise Atom Missiles', *New York Times*, 19 March 1975, pp 1, 52.
122 Varner and Collier, *A Matter of Risk*, pp 18–19; Burleson, *The Jennifer Project*, pp 18–23.
123 ibid., pp 30–3.
124 Hersh, 'CIA Salvage Ship Brought Up Part of Soviet Sub', *New York Times*, 19 March 1975, p 52; and Burleson, *The Jennifer Project*, p 57.
125 ibid., pp 80–6.
126 ibid., pp 121–6.
127 ibid., pp 35–9, 125–6.
128 ibid., p 51.
129 ibid., pp 150–2.

10 Other areas of cooperation
1 Duncan Campbell and Clive Thomas, 'BBC's Trade Secrets', *New Statesman*, 4 July 1980, pp 13–14.
2 ibid.
3 ibid.
4 ibid.
5 ibid.
6 Ray Cline, *The CIA Under Reagan, Bush and Casey* (Acropolis, Washington, DC, 1981), p 189.
7 Leonard Mosley, *Dulles: A Biography of Eleanor, Allen and John Foster Dulles and Their Family Network* (Dial Press/James Wade, New York, 1978), p 278.
8 ibid., p 279.
9 M. Richard Shaw, 'British Intelligence and Iran', *Counter Spy*, May–June 1982, pp 31–3.
10 ibid.
11 Kermit Roosevelt, *Countercoup: The Struggle for Control of Iran* (McGraw Hill, New York, 1979), p 3.
12 ibid., p 107.
13 ibid., p 119; Shaw, 'British Intelligence and Iran', pp 31–3.
14 ibid.
15 Roosevelt, *Countercoup*, p 121.
16 Shaw, 'British Intelligence and Iran'.

17 Roosevelt, *Countercoup*, p 120.
18 ibid., p 46.
19 Mosely, *Dulles*, p 49s.
20 Duncan Campbell, 'Green Berets Come to Stay in UK', *New Statesman*, 12 February 1982, pp 3–4.
21 ibid.
22 ibid.
23 ibid.
24 ibid.; Richard Halloran, 'Military Is Quietly Rebuilding Its Special Operations Forces', '*New York Times*, 19 July 1982, pp 1, 9.
25 Campbell, 'Green Berets Come to Stay in UK', pp. 3–4.
26 Cited in Denis Freney, *The CIA's Australian Connection* (privately printed, Sydney, 1977).
27 Brigadier F.P. Serong, interviewed in *Allies* (A Grand Bay Film, Directed by Marian Wilkinson and Produced by Sylvie Le Clezio, Sydney, 1983), transcript of interview.
28 Major Ian McNeill, *The Team: Australian Army Advisers in Vietnam 1962–1972* (Australian War Memorial, Canberra, 1984), p 411.
29 ibid.
30 Testimony of William E. Colby before a Subcommittee of the Committee on Government Operations, US House of Representatives, cited in McNeill, *The Team*, p 407.
31 ibid., p 409.
32 Brigadier F.P. Serong, interviewed in *Allies*, transcript of interview.
33 Private interviews with members of the AATTV.
34 Royal Commission on Intelligence and Security, *Fifth Report* (Australian Government Printer, Canberra, 1977), Appendix 5-D, paragraph 215.
35 Mosley, *Dulles*, p 369.
36 ibid.
37 ibid.
38 ibid., pp 417–18.
39 ibid., p 418.
40 John Prados, *The Soviet Estimate: U.S. Intelligence Analysis and Russian Military Strength* (Dial Press, New York, 1982), p 176.
41 Duncan Campbell, 'How We Spy on Argentina', *New Statesman*, 30 April 1982, p 5.
42 House Committee on Armed Services, *Hearings on Military Posture and HR 1872* (US Government Printing Office, Washington, DC, 1979), Book 1, Part 3, p 1375.
43 *Defense Electronics*, October 1982, p 154.
44 Royal Commission on Intelligence and Security, *Fifth Report*, paragraph 210. All the material in this section on clandestine human intelligence collection activities is derived from this source.
45 Prados, *The Soviet Estimate*, p 57.
46 *A Summary of Soviet Guided Missile Intelligence* (Central Intelligence Agency, Washington, 1953) in *DDRS* 1975–81, cover page.
47 ibid., Table of Contents.
48 *Soviet Capabilities and Probable Courses of Action Against North America in a Major War Commencing During the Period 1 January 1958 to 31 December 1958* (JIC 491/122 Report ACAI 42, Canadian–US Joint Intelligence Committee, Central Intelligence Agency, Washington, 1 March 1957), in *DDRS* 1981–169A; *Soviet Capabilities and Probable Courses of Action Against North America in a Major War Commencing During the Period of 1 July 1958 to 30 June 1954*, (JIC

491/131 Report ACAI 46, Canadian–US Joint Intelligence Committee), in *DDRS*, 1981–169B.
49 Ray Cline, 'A CIA Reminiscence', *Washington Quarterly*, Autumn 1982, pp 88–92.
50 Joint Intelligence Organization, *Fourth Annual Report, 1974, Part 1*, (Canberra, November 1974), p 36.
51 ibid.
52 ibid.
53 ibid.
54 Cline, *The CIA Under Reagan, Bush and Casey*, p 149.
55 Seymour Hersh, 'The President and the Plumbers: A Look at 2 Security Questions', *New York Times*, 9 December 1973, pp 1, 78.
56 'RCMP Demystified', *Counter Spy*, November 1981–January 1982.
57 Royal Commission on Intelligence and Security, *Fifth Report*, Appendix 5–D, paragraph 213.
58 B.R. Hancock, 'The New Zealand Security Intelligence Service', *Auckland University Law Review*, vol. 1, No. 2, 1973, pp 1–34.

11 Discord, non-cooperation and deceit within the UKUSA community

1 M.R.D. Foot and J.M. Langley, *M19: Escape and Evasion 1939–1949* (The Bodley Head, London, 1979), p 40.
2 See Victor Marchetti and John D. Marks, *The CIA and the Cult of Intelligence* (Dell Books, New York, 1974), p 96.
3 ibid.
4 William Sullivan, with Bill Brown, *The Bureau: My Thirty Years in Hoover's FBI*, (Pinnacle Books, Inc., New York, 1979) p 208.
5 Interview with Desmond Ball, 15 July 1979.
6 William Sullivan, *The Bureau*, pp 40–1.
7 ibid., p 270; and John Sawatsky, *Men in the Shadows: The RCMP Security Service* (Doubleday, New York, 1980), p 6.
8 Royal Commission on Intelligence and Security, *Third Report* (Australian Government Publishing Service, Canberra, 1977), p 25.
9 Sir Arthur Tange to Mr A.P. Renouf, 21 January 1975.
10 See Fedor Mediansky, 'The JIO–ONA Tug-of-War for Intelligence Supremacy', *Australian Financial Review*, 8 August 1978.
11 ibid.
12 Richard Hall, *The Secret State: Australia's Spy Industry* (Cassell, Australia, Sydney, 1978), p 29.
13 ibid., p 12.
14 John Sawatsky, *Men in the Shadows*, p 18.
15 ibid., p 19.
16 John Sawatsky, *For Services Rendered: Leslie James Bennett and the RCMP Security Service*, (Doubleday, New York, 1982), p 5.
17 Sir Guy Powles, *Security Intelligence Service: Report by Chief Ombudsman* (New Zealand Government Printer, Wellington, 1976), pp 69–70.
18 Chapman Pincher, *Inside Story: A Documentary of the Pursuit of Power* (Sidgwick and Jackson, London, 1978), p 24.
19 Marchetti and Marks, *The CIA and the Cult of Intelligence*, pp 206–7.
20 See Miles Copeland, *Without Cloak or Dagger: The Truth About the New Espionage* (Simon & Schuster, New York, 1974), pp 181–2.
21 See J.C. Masterman, *The Double-Cross System in the War of 1939 to 1945* (Ballantine Books, New York, 1982).
22 Sullivan, *The Bureau*, pp 187–8.

23 Andrew Tully, *Inside the FBI* (McGraw-Hill, New York, 1980), p 57.
24 Patrick Seale and Maureen McConville, *Philby: The Long Road to Moscow* (Penguin, Harmondsworth, 1978), p 173.
25 Chapman Pincher, *Their Trade is Treachery* (Sidgwick & Jackson, London, 1981), p 11.
26 Chapman Pincher, *Inside Story*, p 84.
27 Tully, *Inside the FBI*, p 44.
28 See David C. Martin, *Wilderness of Mirrors* (Harper and Row, New York, 1980).
29 Hall, *The Secret State*, p 161.
30 *Nation Review*, 2–8 December 1976, p 148.
31 ibid.; and *Bulletin*, 20 November 1976, p 16.
32 David Broadbent, 'ONA Men "Aided Russian Cause"', *Age*, 15 April 1982; Laurie Oakes, 'China Trade Agents "Given ONA Secrets"', *Age*, 14 April 1982; and David Broadbent, 'Other ONA Leaks "Revealed Soon"', *Age*, 12 April 1982.
33 Statement by Mr R.W. Furlonger, Director-General, Office of National Assessments, Canberra, 4 April 1980. See also Dennis Shanahan, 'Secret Security Paper Missing', *Sydney Morning Herald*, 3 April 1980.
34 See Dennis Shanahan, 'ASIO Report Criticises ONA', *Sydney Morning Herald*, 14 June 1980.
35 See Robert C. Toth, 'White House to Put Limits on Army's Secret Spy Unit', *Los Angeles Times*, 15 May 1983, Part 1, pp 10–11.
36 See George C. Wilson, 'Secret Army Intelligence Unit Lived on After 1980 Iran Mission', *Washington Post*, 23 August 1983, p A6.
37 For the full text of General George C. Marshall's 'Eyes Only' Top Secret Letter to Thomas E. Dewey, see George A. Brownell, *The Origin and Development of the National Security Agency* (Aegean Park Press, Laguna Hills, California, 1981), pp 87–9.
38 Victor Marchetti, interviewed in *Allies* (A Grand Bay Film, Directed by Marian Wilkinson and Produced by Sylvie Le Clezio, Sydney, 1983), transcript of interview.
39 Brian Toohey, 'CIA Funded Covert Action Against Australian Opponents of Vietnam War', *National Times*, 29 June–5 July 1980.
40 ibid.
41 'Vesco Redux', *Time*, 19 September 1983, p 25.
42 George A. Brownell, *The Origin and Development of the National Security Agency*, p 35.
43 ibid., pp 48, 53.
44 Lieutenant General Marshall S. Carter, cited in James Bamford, *The Puzzle Palace: A Report on America's Most Secret Agency* (Houghton Mifflin, Boston, 1982), p 75.
45 ibid., p 209.
46 ibid.
47 Interview, 24 January 1978.
48 *Sydney Morning Herald*, 17 April 1974 and 18 April 1974.
49 Royal Commission on Intelligence and Security, *Third Report*, pp 30–1.
50 Brownell, *The Origin and Development of the National Security Agency*, p 11.
51 ibid.
52 ibid., pp. 38, 48.
53 *Electronic Warfare/Defense Electronics*, January 1979, pp 19–22.
54 US Department of Justice, *Report on Inquiry Into CIA-Related Electronic Surveillance Activities* (SC–05078–76, June 1976), p 78.

55 Sullivan, *The Bureau*, pp 97, 187; and Bamford, *The Puzzle Palace*, pp 375-6.
56 ibid., p 278.
57 Lawrence Freedman, *US Intelligence and the Soviet Strategic Threat* (Macmillan, London, 1977), p 32.
58 ibid., pp. 32-3.
59 See Graham T. Allison, *Essence of Decision: Explaining the Cuban Missile Crisis* (Little, Brown and Company, Boston, 1971), pp 121-3.
60 See John Prados, *The Soviet Estimate: US Intelligence Analysis and Russian Military Strength* (The Dial Press, New York, 1982), pp 108-9; and Jeffrey T. Richelson, *United States Strategic Reconnaissance: Photographic/Imaging Satellites* (ACIS Working Paper No 38, Center for International and Strategic Affairs, University of California, Los Angeles, May 1983), pp 5-10.
61 ibid., pp. 13-16.
62 Marchetti and Marks, *The CIA and the Cult of Intelligence*, p 112.
63 ibid., pp. 111-112.
64 William Colby, *Honourable Men: My Life in the CIA* (Simon and Schuster, New York, 1978), p 370.
65 See Philip J. Klass, 'US Monitoring Capability Impaired', *Aviation Week and Space Technology*, 14 May 1979, p 18; and Bamford, *The Puzzle Palace*, pp 198-9.
66 *Australian Financial Review*, 8 August 1978.
67 *National Times*,
68 *Australian*, 19 February 1979, pp 1, 4.
69 Prados, *The Soviet Estimate*, pp 42-9.
70 ibid., pp. 76-89 and 112-19; and Desmond Ball, *Politics and Force Levels: The Strategic Missile Program of the Kennedy Administration* (University of California Press, Berkeley, 1980), pp 53-5, 95-102.
71 Prados, *The Soviet Estimate*, pp 155-64.
72 ibid., pp 208-18.
73 US Senate, Select Committee to Study Governmental Operations with Respect to Intelligence Activities, *Foreign and Military Intelligence* (US Government Printing Office, Washington, DC, 1976), Book 1, pp 77-9.
74 Prados, *The Soviet Estimate*, pp 257-9.
75 Clarence A. Robinson, 'Soviets Push for Beam Weapon', *Aviation Week and Space Technology*, 2 May 1977, pp 16-23.
76 See Steven Rosefielde, *False Science: Underestimating the Soviet Arms Buildup: An Appraisal of the CIA's Direct Costing Effort, 1960-80* (Transaction Books, New Brunswick, New Jersey, 1982).
77 Prados, *The Soviet Estimate*, p 246.
78 Royal Commission on Intelligence and Security, *Third Report*, p 16.
79 Leonard Mosley, *Dulles: A Biography of Eleanor, Allen and John Foster Dulles and Their Family Network* (Dial Press/James Wade, New York, 1978), p 279.
80 Philip Taubman, 'US Aides Say British Spy Gave Soviet Key Data', *New York Times*, 24 October 1982, pp 1, 15.
81 Sullivan, *The Bureau*, p 183.
82 John Sawatsky, Men in the Shadows, p 12.
83 Sullivan, *The Bureau*, p 184.
84 ibid.
85 ibid., pp 185-6.
86 Philip Agee, *Inside the Company: CIA Diary* (Penguin, Harmondsworth, 1975), p 62.
87 See Alan Stretton, *Soldier in a Storm* (Collins, Sydney, 1977), pp 76-7; *Hansard (House of Representatives)*, 30 September 1948, p 1037; and Sir Arthur

Fadden, *They Called Me Artie: The Memoirs of Sir Arthur Fadden* (The Jacaranda Press, Sydney, 1969), p 97.

88 The three known occasions when the US threatened to cut off the intelligence flow during 1972–75, were, first, in December 1972, when Australian and American security agencies were worried that the Prime Minister had exempted his personal staff from the requirement to undergo security clearances; second, in March 1973 following Attorney-General Murphy's 'raid' on ASIO headquarters in Melbourne; and, third, in November 1975 when the CIA feared that Prime Minister Whitlam might 'blow the lid off' the operations at Pine Gap and Nurrungar. For discussion of these three incidents in this context, see Henry S. Albinski, *Australian External Policy Under Labor* (University of Queensland Press, St Lucia, 1977), pp 168–9; Richard Hall, *The Secret State*, pp 1–5; *Canberra Times*, 19 December 1972; and 'The CIA, Labor and ASIO', *Bulletin*, 5 June 1976, pp 14–16.

89 Joint Intelligence Organisation, *Fourth Annual Report, 1974* (Canberra, November 1974), Part 1, p 29.

90 See interview with James Angleton on the ABC program 'Correspondent's Report', 12 June 1977, transcript.

91 'The CIA, Labor and ASIO', *Bulletin*, 5 June 1976, p 16.

92 Frank Snepp, interviewed in *Allies*, transcript.

93 'Information Withheld by CIA: Boyce', *Canberra Times*, 24 May 1982. See also Julie Flynn, 'Government Ignores Spy's Claims of CIA Role in Australia', *National Times*, 30 May–5 June 1982, p 7. Boyce's allegations were made under oath in United States of America versus Christopher John Boyce, US District Court No. CR 77–121–RJK), Los Angeles, 26–27 April 1977, reporter's transcript of proceedings, pp 34–8, 182–92.

94 Confidential interviews.

95 See, for example, Dennis Shanahan, 'ONA Faces New Row: Some CIA Papers Now Withheld', *Sydney Morning Herald*, 3 May 1980.

96 Cited in Robert Sheppard, 'Canada, US Study Reopening DEW Line', *Globe and Mail*, 5 August 1983, p 2.

97 Martin, *Wilderness of Mirrors*, pp 72–5.

98 See Allen Dulles (ed.), *Great True Spy Stories*, (Ballantine Books, New York, 1982), p 82; and Bamford, *The Puzzle Palace*, pp 130–3.

99 'Briton Says US Solved Secret Code of Allies', *New York Times*, 23 November 1956, p 22.

100 Winslow Pick, 'US Electronic Espionage: A Memoir', *Ramparts*, August 1972, p 44.

101 Cited in Wayne G. Barker and Rodney E. Coffman, *The Anatomy of Two Traitors: The Defection of Bernon F. Mitchell and William H. Martin* (Aegean Park Press, Laguna Hills, California, 1981), pp 51, 77, 80.

102 See Bamford, *The Puzzle Palace*, pp 153–4.

103 Charles A. Babcock and Scott Armstrong, 'Ethics Unit to Summon 4 Officials', *Washington Post*, 9 June 1977, pp A1, A11; Jack Anderson and Les Whitten, 'US Intercepted Seoul's Messages', *Washington Post*, 7 October 1977, p D29; and Bamford, *The Puzzle Palace*, pp 366–7.

104 'US Spies on Germans', *Chicago Tribune*, 7 October 1982, p 5; and 'US Said to Tap Phones in West Germany', *International Herald Tribune*, 7 October 1982, p 5.

105 Seymour M. Hersh, *The Price of Power: Kissinger in the Nixon White House* (Summit Books, New York, 1983), p 101.

106 Peck, 'US Electronic Espionage', p 45.

107 ibid.

108 ibid.
109 Ronald W. Clark, *The Man Who Broke PURPLE: The Life of the World's Greatest Cryptographer, Colonel William F. Friedman* (Weidenfield & Nicholson, London, 1977), p 162.
110 ibid., p 187.
111 ibid., pp ix, 189.
112 Cited in Duncan Campbell, 'Thatcher Bugged by Her Closest Ally', *New Statesman*, 25 July 1980, p 4; and 'Report Says the US is Spying on British', *New York Times*, 30 September 1982, p 8.
113 'British MP Accuses US of Electronic Spying', *New Scientist*, vol. 71, No. 1012, 5 August 1976, p 268.
114 Duncan Campbell and Linda Malvern, 'America's Big Ear in Europe', *New Statesman*, 18 July 1980, pp 10–14.
115 'The Fifth Estate: The Espionage Establishment', (Canadian Broadcasting Corporation, 1974), transcript of CBS Special Broadcast, pp 6–7.
116 ibid., p 12.
117 Don Sellar, 'Foolproof Code Leak Riles Ottawa', *Vancouver Sun*, 23 January 1982, p 1.
118 'Hushed Words', *Sun-Herald*, (Sydney), 29 April 1979, p 152.
119 See *Australian Financial Review*, 1 May 1979.
120 'Pine Gap and the Intelligence Link', *National Times*, 8 July 1978, p 27.
121 Philip J. Klass, 'U.S. Monitoring Capabilities Impaired', *Aviation Week and Space Technology*, 14 May 1979, p 18.
122 'United States of America versus Christopher John Boyce' (Reporter's transcript of proceedings), 27 April 1977, p 2121.
123 'Former Agent Accuses FBI', *Washington Post*, 30 July 1983, p A4.
124 CBS Special, 'The Fifth Estate: The Intelligence Establishment', transcript of broadcast, p 8.
125 See Duncan Campbell, 'Big Brother's Many Mansions', *New Statesman*, 8 February 1980, p 196.
126 Christopher Andrew, 'The British Secret Service and Anglo–Soviet Relations in the 1970's, Part I: From the Trade Negotiations to the Zinoviev Letter', *The Historical Journal*, vol. 20, No. 3, 1977, pp 673–706.
127 See H. Montgomery Hyde, *Secret Intelligence Agent* (Constable, London, 1982), p 179.
128 Gordon Winter, *Inside BOSS: South Africa's Secret Police* (Penguin, Harmondsworth, 1981), p 620.
129 'CIA Helped 2 Socreds Win in Election, Committee Told', *Toronto Globe and Mail*, 27 May 1981, p 8.
130 Robert Sheppard, 'Ottawa Investigated Claims that RCMP Infiltrated by CIA', *Toronto Globe and Mail*, 20 May 1982, pp 1, 2; and 'Is the CIA Intervening in Canada's Elections?' *Counter Spy*, September–November 1982, p 4.
131 'CIA Helped Socred', *Toronto Globe and Mail*, 27 May 1981, p 8.
132 Sheppard, *Toronto Globe and Mail*, 20 May 1982, pp 1–2.
133 ibid.
134 ibid.
135 Milton Viorst, 'An Analysis of American Intervention in the Matter of Quebec', *McLean's*, November 1972, pp 22 ff.
136 Robert Sheppard, 'Kaplan May Convene a Closed Probe on CIA', *Toronto Globe and Mail*, 21 May, 1982, p 3.
137 'Dirty Work North: Now the CIA Keeps Tabs on Canada', *McLean's*, 9 October 1978, p 27.

138 'PM Talks of CIA Links', *Australian*, 3 November 1975, p 1; and 'CIA Money in Australia — PM', *Australian*, 7 November 1975, p 3.
139 *Hansard (House of Representatives)*, 4 May 1977, p 1522.
140 Interview with James Angleton, ABC Television, 'Correspondent's Report', 12 June 1977, transcript.
141 See Brian Toohey, 'Anthony's CIA Connection', *Australian Financial Review*, 3 November 1975, pp 1, 5; Brian Toohey, 'CIA Man's Wide Contacts', *Australian Financial Review*, 4 November 1975, pp 1, 4; and 'Stallings — Most Successful Agent', *Nation Review*, 7–13 November 1975, p 79.
142 Paul Kelly, *The Unmaking of Gough* (Angus & Robertson, Melbourne, 1976), p 32.
143 See William Pinwill, in 'November 11 1975: The Pieces Fall Into Place', *National Times*, 9–15 November 1980, p 11.
144 For the full text of the ASIO telex of 8 November 1975, see Desmond Ball, *A Suitable Piece of Real Estate: American Installations in Australia*, (Hale & Iremonger, Sydney, 1980), pp 169–71.
145 Sir John Kerr, Letter to the Editor, *Foreign Policy*, No. 51, Summer 1983, pp 198–9.
146 See James A. Nathan, 'Dateline Australia: America's Foreign Watergate?', *Foreign Policy*, No. 49, Winter 1982–83, pp 168–85.
147 Cited in William Pinwill, 'Just Who Betrayed Whom?: The Real Question of the Boyce Affair', *Australian*, 19–20 September 1981, Weekend Magazine, p 1.

12 Organization and performance
1 Commission on the Organization of the Government for the Conduct of Foreign Policy, *Report* (US Government Printing Office, Washington, DC, 1975).
2 Royal Commission on Intelligence and Security, *Third Report* (Australian Government Printing Service, Canberra, 1977).
3 Commission of Inquiry Concerning Certain Activities of the Royal Canadian Mounted Police, *Freedom and Security Under the Law, Volumes 1 and 2* (Canadian Government Publishing Centre, Ottawa, 1981).
4 For example see, Peter Szanton and Graham Allison, 'Intelligence: Seizing the Opportunity' *Foreign Policy*, vol. 22, 1976, pp 183–214; Robert Ellsworth and Kenneth L. Adelman, "Foolish Intelligence", *Foreign Policy*, vol. 36, 1979, pp 147–59.
5 Senate Select Committee on Intelligence, *National Intelligence Act of 1980* (US Government Printing Office, Washington, DC, 1980), p 356.
6 See Robert L. Galluci, *Neither Peace Nor Honor: The Politics of American Military Policy in Vietman* (Johns Hopkins University Press, Baltimore, 1975), pp 65–8; Patrick J. McGarvey, 'The Culture of Bureaucracy: DIA, Intelligence to Please', *Washington Monthly*, July 1970.
7 House Permanent Select Committee on Intelligence, *U.S. Intelligences Performance on Central America: Achievements and Selected Instances of Concern* (US Government Printing Office, Washington, DC, 1982).
8 See Gordon W. Prange, *At Dawn We Slept: The Untold Story of Pearl Harbor* (McGraw Hill, New York 1981); Stewart Steven, *The Spymasters of Israel* (Macmillan, New York, 1980); Barton Whaley, *Codeword Barbarossa* (MIT Press, Cambridge, 1973); and Richard Betts, *Surprise Attack* (Brookings Institution, Washington, 1982).
9 John Bruce Lockhart, 'The Relationship Between Secret Services and Government in a Modern State', *RUSI Journal*, vol. 119, 1974, pp 3–8.
10 House Permanent Select Committee on Intelligence, *Iran: Evaluation of U.S.*

Intelligence Performance (US Government Printing Office, Washington, DC, 1979).
11 Szanton and Allison, 'Intelligence: Seizing the Opportunity'; Ray S. Cline, *Secrets, Spies and Scholars* (Acropolis, Washington, 1976).
12 George Carver, 'Comment on Intelligence: Seizing the Opportunity', *Foreign Policy*, vol. 22, 1976, pp 206–11.
13 Szanton and Allison, 'Intelligence: Seizing the Opportunity'.
14 'Coordination of Intelligence Production', National Security Council Intelligence Directive (NSCID) Number 3, 13 January 1948, in *Declassified Documents Reference System (DDRS)*, 1976–165F.
15 Peter Wyden, *Bay of Pigs: The Untold Story* (Simon and Schuster, New York, 1979).
16 R.W. Furlonger, 'The Role of the Office of National Assessments', *Pacific Defence Reporter*, September 1978, p 63.
17 Justin Galen, 'Intelligence: The Reagan Challenge', *Armed Forces Journal International*, January 1981, pp 72 ff.
18 Carl Bernstein, 'C.I.A.'s Secret Arms Aid to Afghanistan', *Chicago Sun-Times*, 6 September 1981, p 1.
19 This is not to say that simple knowledge that there is a leak inevitably leads to *identification* of the source or *immediate* closing of the leak.
20 Cline, *Secrets, Spies and Scholars*; and 'Shaping Tomorrow's C.I.A.', *Time*, 6 February 1978, pp 10–26.
21 'Shaping Tomorrow's C.I.A. ...', pp 10–26.
22 See E.H. Cookridge, *Inside S.O.E.: The Story of Special Operations Executive in Western Europe 1940–1945* (Arthur Barker, London, 1966); and Nigel West, *MI6: British Secret Intelligence Operations 1909–1945* (Weidenfield and Nicholson, London, 1983).
23 Senate Select Committee to Study Governmental Operations with Respect to Intelligence Activities, *Supplementary Detailed Staff Reports on Foreign and Military Intelligence, Book IV* (US Government Printing Office, Washington, DC, 1976), pp 25–41.
24 Lockhart, 'The Relationship Between Secret Services and Government in a Modern State'.
25 The President's Board of Consultants on Foreign Intelligence Activities, 'Letter of December 20, 1956', *DDRS*, 1976–204C.
26 William Carson, *The Armies of Ignorance: The Rise of the American Intelligence Empire* (Dial Press, New York, 1977), p 422.
27 David Binder, 'Intelligence Services Reorganized with Tighter Rules on Surveillance', *New York Times*, 23 January 1978, pp 1, 11.
28 Joseph Fromm, 'Inside Story of Battle to Control Spying', *U.S. News and World Report*, 8 August 1977, p 27.
29 ibid.
30 'Major Intelligence Shifts Set', *Aviation Week and Space Technology*, 8 August 1977, pp 14–17.
31 David Binder, 'Intelligence Services Reorganized with Tighter Rules on Surveillance', pp 1, 11.
32 *Office of National Assessments Act of 1977* (Australian Government Printing Service, Canberra, 1977).
33 Fedor Mediansky, 'The Selling of ONA: The Battle for Acceptance in Canberra's Power Play', *Australian Financial Review*, 7 August 1978.
34 Senate Select Committee on Intelligence, *National Intelligence Act of 1980*, p 356.
35 See, for example, David S. Sullivan, 'Evaluating U.S. Intelligence Estimates', in

Roy Godson (ed.), *Intelligence Requirements for the 1980's* (Transaction, New Brunswick, 1980) pp 49–73; Daniel O. Graham, 'Analysis and Estimates', in Roy Godson (ed.), *Intelligence Requirements for the 1980's: Elements of Intelligence* (Transaction, New Brunswick, 1979) pp 23–9.
36 Samuel. T. Francis, 'The Intelligence Community', in Charles L. Heatherly (ed.), *Mandate for Leadership: Policy Management in a Conservative Administration* (Heritage Foundation, Washington, 1980), pp 903–53.
37 Senate Select Committee on Intelligence, *National Intelligence Act of 1980*, p 373.
38 ibid., p 371 (testimony of Paul Nitze).
39 Lockhart, 'The Relationship Between Secret Services and Government in a Modern State'.
40 House Permanent Select Committee, *U.S. Intelligence Performance on Central America*, p 7, emphasis added.
41 In any case, competing centres do not necessarily guarantee that one will produce the 'correct' estimate. See Steve Chan, 'The Intelligence of Stupidity: Understanding Failures in Strategic Warning', *American Political Science Review*, vol. 73, 1979, pp 171–80.
42 Royal Commission on Intelligence and Security, *Third Report*, pp 9–11.
43 Fedor Mediansky, 'The JIO–ONA Tug-of-War for Intelligence Supremacy', *Australian Financial Review*, 8 August 1978.
44 Commission of Inquiry, *Freedom and Security Under the Law*, vol. 2, p 1098.
45 Lockhart, 'The Relationship Between Secret Services and Government in a Modern State'.
46 Senate Select Committee on Intelligence, *National Intelligence Act of 1980*, p 37 (testimony of Admiral Stansfield Turner).
47 See Galen, 'Intelligence: The Reagan Challenge'.
48 Michael Tenzin, 'New Security Forces Could Be Like C.I.A., McMurty Aide Says', *Toronto Globe and Mail*, 5 October 1981, p 10.
49 At least this is the justification given. See the following chapter.

13 Dissent and the UKUSA security services
1 For example, see G. Crowder, 'The Security Intelligence Service Amendment Act of 1977 and the State Power to Intercept Communications', *Victoria University of Wellington Law Review*, vol. 9, February 1978, pp 145–64; and Richard Gruner, 'Government Monitoring of International Electronic Communications: National Security Agency Watch List Surveillance and the Fourth Amendment', *Southern Californian Law Review*, vol. 51, March 1978, pp 420–66.
2 Richard Hall, *The Secret State: Australia's Spy Industry* (Cassell Australia, North Melbourne, 1978), p 45.
3 Richard G. Fox, 'The Salisbury Affair: Special Branches, Security and Subversion', *Monash Law Review*, vol. 5, 1979, pp 251–70.
4 *Special Branch Security Records: Initial Report to the Honourable Donald Allen Dunstan Premier of South Australia* (Government of South Australia, Adelaide, 1977).
5 Hall, *The Secret State*, p 71.
6 *Australian Security Intelligence Organization Annual Report 1979/1980*, p 11.
7 Tony Bunyan, *The Political Police in Britain* (St Martin's, New York, 1976), p 125.
8 Carol Ackroyd, Karen Margolis, Jonathan Rosenhead and Tim Shallice, *The Technology of Political Control* (Pluto Press, London, 1977), p 127.
9 Harold Wilson, *The Labour Government 1964–1970* (Penguin, Harmondsworth, 1971), p 311.

10 'MI5 Spy on Unionist', *State Research Bulletin*, October—November 1980, p 11.
11 Bunyan, *The Political Police in Britain*, pp 123—9.
12 ibid., pp 136—7.
13 ibid., p 149.
14 Duncan Campbell, 'The Monster that Just Grows', *New Statesman*, 5 March 1982, pp 6—8.
15 Athan Theoharis, 'FBI Surveillance During the Cold War Years: A Constitutional Crisis', *Public Historian*, vol. 3, 1981, pp 4—14.
16 Roxanne Arnold, 'FBI Tailed, Sought Arrest of Lennon, U.S. Files Show', *Los Angeles Times*, 22 March 1983, pp 13, 14.
17 Frank J. Donner, *The Age of Surveillance* (Knopf, New York, 1980).
18 ibid., p 152.
19 Canadian Civil Liberties Association, *Toward a Charter for the Royal Canadian Mounted Police* (CCLA, Ottawa, 1980).
20 Michael Parker, *The S.I.S.: The New Zealand Security Intelligence Service* (Dunsmore Press, North Palmerston, 1979), p 136.
21 Sir Guy Powles, *Security Intelligence Service: Report by Chief Ombudsman* (Government Printer, Wellington, 1976), p 27.
22 Roger Boshier, 'Footsteps Up Your Jumper: The Activities of the New Zealand Security Service', *Perspective*, vol. 6, 1969, p 17.
23 Powles, *Security Intelligence Service*, p 27.
24 ibid.
25 Parker, *The S.I.S.*, p 103.
26 Harry Orsman, 'The Image of Security', *Comment*, June 1962.
27 B.R. Hancock, 'The New Zealand Security Intelligence Service', *Auckland University Law Review*, vol. 1, No. 2, 1973, pp 1—34.
28 ibid.
29 See David J. Garrow, *The FBI and Martin Luther King Jr: From 'Solo' to Memphis* (W.W. Norton, New York, 1981).
30 Christine M. Marwick, 'The Government Informer: A Threat to Political Freedom', *First Principles* 2, March 1977, pp 1—10.
31 Senate Select Committee to Study Government Operations with Respect to Intelligence Activities, *Intelligence Activities and the Rights of Americans Final Report, Book II* (US Government Printing Office, Washington, DC, 1976), p 175.
32 ibid.
33 John Sawatsky, *Men in the Shadows: The RCMP Security Service* (Doubleday, New York, 1980), p 260.
34 ibid., p 275.
35 Robert Sheppard, 'Greater Parliamentary Scrutiny of RCMP to be Urged', *Toronto Globe and Mail*, 24 August 1981, p 4.
36 ibid.
36 ibid.
38 Commission of Inquiry Concerning Activities of the Royal Canadian Mounted Police, *Freedom and Security under the Law Second Report — Volume I* (Canadian Government Publishing Centre, Hull, 1981), pp 112—13.
39 Richard Cotter, 'Notes Towards a Definition of National Security', *Washington Monthly*, December 1975, pp 4—14.
40 Senate Select Committee, *Supplementary Detailed Staff Reports on Intelligence Activities and the Rights of Americans* (US Government Printing Office, Washington, DC, 1976), p 639.
41 Richard Morgan, *Domestic Intelligence: Monitoring Dissent in America* (University of Texas Press, Austin, 1980), p 98.

42 Commission of Inquiry, *Freedom and Security under the Law, Volume 1*, pp 149–54.
43 Garrow, *The FBI and Martin Luther King, Jr.*, and Senate Select Committee, *Supplementary Detailed Staff Reports*, pp 81–184.
44 Senate Select Committee, *Supplementary Detailed Staff Reports*, pp 271–353.
45 'ASIO's Lawless Years', *Nation Review*, 2–8 December 1976, pp 147 ff.
46 Hall, *The Secret State*, p 71.
47 Mark Plunkett, 'ASIO's Annual Report: Australian Spooks Trail Unemployed and Chinese', *National Times*, 28 June 1981, p 3.
48 Tony Reid, 'A Chic Escort to the Chief: A Close Look at New Zealand's Security Service', *New Zealand Weekly News*, 16 June 1969.
49 Margaret Howard, *Diary of the Kirk Years* (A.W. Reed Limited, Wellington, 1981) p 142.
50 Boshier, 'Footsteps Up Your Jumper', p 21.
51 Duncan Campbell, Bruce Page and Nick Anning, 'Destabilizing the Decent People', *New Statesman*, 15 February 1980, pp 234–6.
52 Sheppard, 'Greater Parliamentary Scrutiny of RCMP to be Urged', p 4.
53 Commission of Inquiry, *Freedom and Security under the Law, Volume 1*, p 113.
54 ibid.
55 Sawatsky, *Men in the Shadows*, p 238.
56 Richard French and Andre Beliveau, *The R.C.M.P. and the Management of National Security* (Institute for Research on Public Policy, Halifax, 1978), p 77.
57 'Worried about Soviet Agents, Former Mountie tells Theft Trial', *Toronto Globe and Mail*, 21 April 1982, p 3; 'Mistrial Declared in Case Against Quebec Mountie', *New York Times*, 10 May 1982, p 5.
58 French and Beliveau, *The RCMP and the Management of National Security*, p 71.
59 Sawatsky, *Men in the Shadows*, pp 247–51.
60 French and Beliveau, *The RCMP and the Management of National Security*, p 25.
61 Donner, *The Age of Surveillance*, p 131.
62 ibid.
63 John M. Crewdson, 'Details on FBI's Illegal Break-ins Given to Justice Department' and 'Ex-FBI Informant says Agents Ordered 2 Oregon Break-ins in '74', *New York Times*, 27 January 1979, p 9 and 15 September 1976, p 14.
64 ibid.
65 'ASIO's Lawless Years', pp 1 ff.
66 ibid.
67 Boshier, 'Footsteps Up Your Jumper', p 22.
68 Hancock, 'The New Zealand Security Intelligence Service'.
69 Hall, *The Secret State*, p 74.
70 Commission of Inquiry, *Freedom and Security under the Law, Volume 1*, pp 267–8.
71 ibid., p 268.
72 ibid., p 272.
73 Sheppard, 'Greater Parliamentary Scrutiny ...'.
74 Sawatsky, *Men in the Shadows*, p 264.
75 Sheppard, 'Greater Parliamentary Scrutiny ...'; Robert Dion, *Crimes of the Secret Police* (Black Rose, Montreal, 1982), pp 68–9.
76 See Garrow, *The FBI and Martin Luther King, Jr.* For an account of FBI dirty tricks directed against actress Jean Seberg, see David Richards, *Played Out: The Jean Seberg Story* (Houghton-Mifflin, Boston, 1981).
77 Garrow, *The FBI and Martin Luther King Jr.*, pp 21–77.

78 Donner, *The Age of Surveillance*, p 215.
79 Garrow, *The FBI and Martin Luther King Jr.*, back cover.
80 Donner, *The Age of Surveillance*, p 178.
81 Sanford J. Ungar, *The FBI* (Little, Brown, Boston, 1975), p 634.
82 Senate Select Committee, *Supplementary Detailed Staff Reports*, pp 187–224.
83 Ungar, *The FBI*, p 470.
84 Senate Select Committee, *Supplementary Detailed Staff Reports*, pp 187–9.
85 Jay Peterzell, *Nuclear Power and Political Surveillance* (Center for National Security Studies, Washington, 1981), p 47.
86 Jack Anderson, 'FBI Smear Tactics in the Silkwood Case', *Washington Post*, 4 February 1980, p E25; and Richard Rashke, *The Killing of Karen Silkwood* (Houghton-Mifflin, Boston, 1981).
87 Peterzell, *Nuclear Power and Political Surveillance*, pp 38–46.
88 Anderson, 'FBI Smear Tactics ...', p E25.
89 Sir Harold Scott, *Scotland Yard* (Penguin, Harmondsworth, 1957), p 219.
90 Commission of Inquiry, *Freedom and Security under the Law, Volume I*, p 65.
91 See Andrew Boyle, *The Climate of Treason* (Hutchinson, London, 1980).
92 Donner, *The Age of Surveillance*, p 171.
93 Powles, *Security Intelligence Service*, p 30.
94 Hayward, *Diary of the Kirk Years*, p 127.
95 Theoharis, 'FBI Surveillance during the Cold War Years'.
96 Robert Sheppard, 'The Bottom Line on the RCMP Inquiry: Ottawa Weak Willed', *Toronto Globe and Mail*, 28 August 1981, p 7; and John Gray, 'Trudeau knew Mounties Broke the Law, Report Says', *Toronto Globe and Mail*, 26 August 1981, p 12.
97 Ungar, *The FBI*, p 468.
98 Commission of Inquiry, *Freedom and Security under the Law, Volume I*, p 503.
99 Dennis Phelps quoted by Boshier, 'Footsteps Up Your Jumper', p 32.
100 'Submission of the Public Service Association', in Powles, *Security Intelligence Service*, p 97.
101 Quoted by Boshier, 'Footsteps Up Your Jumper', pp 17–18.
102 ibid., p 16.
103 Donner, *The Age of Surveillance*, p 225.
104 See John Barron, *KGB: The Secret Work of Soviet Secret Agents* (Reader's Digest, New York, 1974); Gordon Winter, *Inside BOSS: South Africa's Secret Police* (Penguin, Harmondsworth, 1981); and Thomas Plate and Andrea Darvi, *Secret Police* (Doubleday, New York, 1981).
105 John T. Elliff, *The Reform of FBI Intelligence Operations* (Princeton University Press, Princeton, 1978).
106 Ungar, *The FBI*, p 198.
107 'Guidelines for F.B.I.'s Surveillance of Political Groups Being Released', *New York Times*, 25 June 1982, p 10.
108 Senate Committee on the Judiciary, *Attorney General's Guidelines for Domestic Security Investigations (Smith Guidelines)* (US Government Printing Office, Washington, DC, 1983), p 9.
109 Powles, *Security Intelligence Service*, p 30.
110 ibid., p 31.
111 Ungar, *The FBI*, p 601.
112 ibid., p 466.

14 Conclusion
1 Brigadier Herbert E. Gilbert, cited in Marvyn Cull, 'Goodbye Cloak and Dagger', *New Zealand Herald*, 17 July 1976, Section 2, p 1.

Notes   391

2 William Stevenson, *A Man Called Intrepid: The Secret War 1939–1945* (Sphere Books, London, 1977), p 110.
3 Royal Commission on Australia's Security and Intelligence Agencies, *Report on Terms of Reference (C)* (Australian Government Publishing Service, Canberra, December 1983), p 14.
4 *Hansard (House of Representatives)*, 1 June 1976, p 2738.
5 Royal Commission on Intelligence and Security, *Third Report* (Australian Government Publishing Service, Canberra, April 1977), p 17.
6 *Newsweek*, 19 April 1982, pp 14–15; Duncan Campbell, 'How We Spy on Argentina', *New Statesman*, 30 April 1982, p 5; 'Electronics Give "Unfair Edge"', *Australian*, 6 May 1982; and Christopher Dobson, John Miller and Ronald Payne, *The Falklands Conflict* (Coronet Books, Hodder and Stoughton, London, 1982), Chapter 12.
7 Alfred Price, *Instruments of Darkness* (William Kimber, London, 1967), p 206; and Anthony Cave Brown, *Bodyguard of Lies* (Harper and Row, New York, 1975), p 521.
8 ibid., pp 102–4.
9 See Desmond Ball, 'Soviet Strategic Planning and the Control of Nuclear War', *Soviet Union/Union Sovietique* (vol. 10, Parts 2–3), 1983, pp 201–217.
10 See Desmond Ball, *A Suitable Piece of Real Estate: American Installations in Australia* (Hale & Iremonger, Sydney, 1980), Chapter 12; and Desmond Ball, 'Limiting Damage From Nuclear Attack', in Desmond Ball and J.O. Langtry (eds), *Civil Defence and Australia's Security in the Nuclear Age* (Strategic and Defence Studies Centre, Australian National University, Canberra, and George Allen & Unwin Australia, Sydney, 1983), pp 148–53.
11 See Stewart Cockburn, *The Salisbury Affair* (Sun Books, Melbourne, 1979), p 279; and *National Times*, 17 June 1978, pp 8–9. Salisbury was dismissed as Police Commissioner by the South Australian Government on 17 January 1978 for having misled it about the activities of the Special Branch of the South Australian Police Force. A central point in Salisbury's subsequent defence was that 'Special Branch was collecting intelligence for ASIO and was receiving intelligence from it ... I believed that I did owe a duty to ASIO not to jeopardise its work by throwing open Special Branch to persons not authorised by ASIO'. See Cockburn, *The Salisbury Affair*, p 278.
12 Letter from Sir Leonard Hooper to Lt.-Gen. Carter, 27 July 1969, cited in James Bamford, *The Puzzle Palace: A Report on America's Most Secret Agency* (Houghton Mifflin Company, Boston, 1982), p 336.
13 ibid., p 333.
14 See US Department of Justice, *Report on Inquiry Into CIA-Related Electronic Surveillance Activities* (SC–05078–76, 30 June 1976), p 160.
15 Royal Commission on Intelligence and Security, *Third Report* (April 1977), p 17.
16 Senate Select Committee to Study Governmental Operations With Respect to Intelligence Activities, *Final Report: Foreign and Military Intelligence* (US Government Printing Office, Washington, DC, 1976), Book 1, p 425.
17 ibid., p 429.
18 ibid., p 432.
19 Sir Guy Powles, *Security Intelligence Service: Report by Chief Ombudsman* (New Zealand Government Printer, Wellington, 1976), p 56.
20 Royal Comission on Intelligence and Security, *Third Report* (April 1977), p 16.
21 Comission of Inquiry Concerning Certain Activities of the Royal Canadian Mounted Police, *Second Report: Freedom and Security Under the Law* (Canadian Government Publishing Centre, Ottawa, August 1981), Volume 2, p 859.

22 ibid., Volume 1, p 93; and Volume 2, pp 845−6 and 868.
23 The Rt Hon. The Lord Franks (Chairman), *Falkland Islands Review: Report of a Committee of Privy Counsellors* (Her Majesty's Stationery Office, London, January 1983), pp 84−6.
24 Duncan Campbell, 'Big Brother's Many Mansions', *New Statesman*, 8 February 1980, p 197; and 'Watchdog Wanted', *Economist*, 4 December 1982, p 18.
25 Senate Select Committee to Study Governmental Operations With Respect to Intelligence Activities, *Final Report: Foreign and Military Intelligence*, Book 1, p 16.
26 ibid., pp 11−16, 423−6.
27 Powles, *Security Intelligence Service*, pp 75−6.
28 Royal Commission on Intelligence and Security, *Third Report*, p 17.
29 Commission of Inquiry Concerning Certain Activities of the Royal Canadian Mounted Police, *First Report: Security and Information* (Canadian Government Publishing Centre, Hull, Quebec, 1979), p 41.

Index

ABCA Agreement, 155–7
Acorn, Project, 77
Acoustical Intelligence (ACOUSTINT), 177
Adak, Alaska, 207, 216
Ad Hoc Ministerial Group on Security, 26, 28, 29
Adcock DF system, 192, 209
Afghanistan, 36, 115, 274
Africa, 42, 170, 173
airborne warning and control systems (AWACs), 159
aircraft, 180, 182, 183, 187, 189, 197, 220, 221, 222, 231; see also Strategic Reconnaissance aircraft; U-2 aircraft
Air Force Electronic Security Command (ESC), 106
Air Force Intelligence Service (AFIS), 123, 124
Air Force Security Service (AFSS), 144, 250
Air Force Technical Applications Center (AFTAC), 123, 125
Albania, 229–30
Aldridge, Edward C., 99
Allied Intelligence Bureau (AIB), 3, 30, 141
AN/FLR-9 antenna system, 184–5, 186, 187, 188, 195, 207
AN/FSC-78 antenna system, 192
Angleton, James, 110, 163–4, 246, 259, 266
Angola, 274
Annual Land Warfare Intelligence Conference, 237
Antarctica, 34
antenna systems, 160, 183, 184–5, 186, 187, 188, 192, 193, 195, 197, 206, 207, 209
anti-ballistic missile (ABM) systems, 176, 254
Arab-Israeli conflict, 42, 103, 115

Argentia Naval Station, Newfoundland, 189, 200, 201
Argentina, 110, 118, see also Falklands/Malvinas War
ARGUS satellites, 131, 253–4, 260
Arlington, Virginia, 187
array antenna systems, 183, 184–5, 186, 188, 192, 193, 195, 197, 206, 207, 209
Ascension Island, 19, 150, 194, 201, 220
Association of South East Asian Nations (ASEAN), 35, 169, 170, 172
Atkins, R.B., 75
Atlantic Undersea Test and Evaluation Center (AUTEC), 200, 248
Atomic Energy Detection System (AEDS), 125
AUS-CAN-UK-US Military Communications-Electronics Board (MCEB), 157
Australia: exports, 35; cooperation, 7, 155, 156, 236–7, 263–4, 266–8; police, 60, 61, 62, 65; and Second World War, 3–4, 135, 137–8, 192; security, 34–6, 48; service intelligence, 30, 48, 56–9, 65, 140; and UKUSA, 5–6, 8; see also individual organisations
Australian Federal Police (AFP), 61, 62, 65
Australian Secret Intelligence Service (ASIS), 30, 31, 32, 37, 52, 63, 65; and CIA, 153–4, 161, 168–9, 234–5; operations of, 151, 161, 234–5, 273, 275, 304; organisation of, 42–7; and other nations, 75, 171, 172; and SIS, 152–3, 168, 232, 234, 235, 238
Australian Security Intelligence Organisation (ASIO), 30, 31, 35, 37, 47, 52, 61, 63, 65, 66, 155, 242, 282; and JIO, 246; and ONA, 246–7; operations of, 60, 285, 286, 291,

393

292–3, 303; and other nations, 68, 71, 161, 173, 237, 258–9, 267
AUTODIN system, 161
AUTOVON system, 161, 190
Azores, 220
Azores Fixed Acoustic Range (AFAR), 200, 201
AZORIAN, Project, 225

Bahamas, 160, 200, 201, 248
Ballistic Missile Early Warning System (BMEWS), 158
Bangladesh, 46
Barbados, 201
Barbour, Peter, 50
BARNACLE, Project, 223
Barnett, Sam, 68
Barnett, T.H., 50
Barrier, Project, 200
Beale Air Force Base, California, 158, 182
Bennett, Leslie James, 163
Bermuda, 190, 201, 220
B-52 aircraft, 220, 222
'Big Bird' satellites, 97, 167, 181, 217, 253
Blackford, J., 78
Blake, George, 13
Blakehill, Wiltshire, 195
Bletchley, UK, 137, 302
Blunt, Anthony, 13
BOLLARD, Project, 223
'bomber gap', 254–5
Borneo, 40
Botterill, R.D., 37
Boyce, Christopher, 178, 260, 264
Brawdy, Wales, 159, 195, 200, 201, 305
Brazil, 118
break-ins, 51, 284, 291–3
Bricole, Operation, 292
Britain: cooperation, 7–8, 140, 155, 156, 236–7; intelligence community, 13–29; and Second World War, 135–41; 198; and US, 1–3, 136–41, 228–38 *passim*, 261, 262–3; *see also* individual organisations
Britain-United States Agreement (BRUSA), 2, 137, 138–9, 142, 143, 144, 161, 165, 311
British Broadcasting Corporation's (BBC) Monitoring Service, 6, 25–6, 228–9
British Security Coordination (BSC) 136, 137, 139, 140, 141, 264
Bronco, Project, 200
Brookes, Alfred D., 42–3, 47, 152
Brora, Scotland, 195
Brunei, 55
Buckley, Colorado, 158
BULLSEYE, 202, 206
Bureau of Economic Intelligence, 82, 90, 95
Bureau of Intelligence Assessments, 280
Bureau of Intelligence and Research (INR), 96, 115–17, 129, 255, 256, 280
Burgess, Guy, 245
Burma, 44, 45
BYEMAN, 167

Cabarlah, Queensland, 40, 190, 192, 208, 209, 210
Caesar hydrophone arrays, 200
Cambodia, 74, 123, 234, 235; *see also* Kampuchea
Camp Peary, Virginia, 110
Canada: intelligence, 31–2, 36, 264, 280, 281–2; intelligence community, 82–95; intelligence cooperation, 140, 155, 156, 236–7; and Second World War, 3–4, 88, 135, 137, 139, 189; and UKUSA, 6, 8; *see also* individual organisations
Canadian Security Intelligence Service (CSIS), 82, 83, 86–7, 95, 282
CAN-UK-US Naval Communications (NAVCOMMs) Board, 157
CANUSA Agreement, 143
Cape Hatteras, North Carolina, 201
Carp Canadian Forces Station, Ottawa, 189
Carter, Lieutenant-General Marshall S., 150, 163
Casey, William J., 109, 112
Caversham, Park UK, 229
Cawthorn, Walter, 31
Central Bureau, 30, 37, 141
Central Intelligence Agency (CIA), 6, 96, 122, 123, 129, 130, 139, 141, 222; and Australia, 45, 46, 47, 50, 62, 153–4, 161, 168–9, 192, 193–4, 231–2, 234–5, 237, 248, 259–60, 264, 266–8, 305; and cooperation, 15, 75, 151–4, 161, 169, 173, 230–2, 237, 238, 260–1; and FBI, 240–1, 243–5, 246, 248; intelligence results, 36, 270, 279–80; operations of, 99, 110, 151, 177, 225, 230–2, 272, 276, 290; organisation of, 102, 106–15, 270–1, 272–3, 276–7; and UKUSA, 260–1, 265–6; and other US agencies, 97, 98, 247, 251–3, 255–7
Central Intelligence Group (CIG), 106
Central Security Service (CSS), 105–6, 124
CHALET, 167, 179–80, 181
CHAOS, Operation, 108
Charged Particle Beam Weapons (CPBWs), 254
Charyk, Dr Joseph, 97
Chayes, Antonia, 99
Cheadle, Staffordshire, 195
CHECKMATE, Operation, 293
Chicksands, UK 144, 146, 161, 184, 195, 262, 263
Chile, 45, 118, 234–5
China: and Australia, 45, 46, 47, 51; assess-

Index 395

ments of, 56, 114, 237; cooperation with, 170, 171–2, 188, 251; monitoring of, 84, 176, 177, 190, 206, 233
Church Committee, 308
Circularly Disposed Antenna Array (CDAA), 184, 185, 188, 192, 193, 195, 197, 206, 207, 209
civil-military conflict, 248–50, 251–3, 255–6
Clark, Captain S.R.I., 139
CLASSIC OUTBOARD system, 210
CLASSIC WIZARD satellites, 127, 159, 186, 206, 207, 214, 216, 305
classifications, 164–7
Clear, Alaska, 158
CLIPPER BOW satellites, 214, 217, 218–19
COBRA DANE radar, 183–4, 186
COBRA JUDY radar, 186
COBRA TALON radar, 189
codewords, 143, 166–7; *see also* individual words
Colby, William, 232, 234, 253, 271
Colossus hydrophone arrays, 200
Combat Talon aircraft, 231
Combe, David, 52
Combined Communications Board (CCB), 156
Combined Communications-Electronics Board (CCEB), 157
COMINT Communications Relay Centers (CCRCs), 144, 171
Committee on Imagery Requirements and Exploitation (COMIREX), 130–1
Committee on Overhead Reconnaissance (COMOR), 130, 252
Commonwealth Investigation Branch (CIB), 48, 135–6, 140
Commonwealth Investigation Service, 48
Commonwealth Security Service (CSS), 136, 140
Commonwealth SIGINT Organisation (CSO), 7, 142–3, 144
Communications Branch, National Research Council (CBNRC), 89, 143, 144, 189
Communications Intelligence (COMINT), 39, 175–6, 182, 221, 224; Canadian, 88; co-operation, 138–9, 143, 144; distribution systems, 145–7; indoctrination, 5, 148–9; security, 144; Soviet, 166; stations, 144, 171, 187, 197; US 101, 103, 104, 130
Communications Security (COMSEC), 37, 38, 39, 77, 88, 102, 105, 106, 131, 156, 207, 262, 263
Communications Security Establishment (CSE), 82, 88–9, 95, 142, 143, 189, 194, 202
COMSAT/INTELSAT stations, 186

C-130 aircraft, 189
Cook, Michael, 33
Coonawarra, Northern Territory, 36, 40, 138, 192, 193
Coordinator of Information (COI), 139–40, 141
Coordinator of Intelligence and Security, 26, 27, 29
Corona satellites, 167, 253, 255
Corral (codeword), 143
covert intelligence: action, 110, 229–32, 264–8, 270–1, 273–6, 293–6; collection, 151–4, 271, 273–6
Crisis Policy Centre (CPC), 61
cryptanalysis, 21, 39, 124, 137, 302
cryptography, 104, 105, 106, 127
Cuba, 84, 182, 233, 252
Culmhead, Somerset, 195
Cummings, Admiral Sir Mansfield, 15
Current Intelligence Unit, 34
Curtin, Brigadier General Richard B., 98
Cyprus, 19, 162, 182, 194
Czechoslovakia, 84, 229, 244

Dahlgren, Virginia, 127
Darwin RAAF Base, 222
Data Encryption Standard (DES), 104
Debert Canadian Forces Station, Nova Scotia, 189
deep sea recovery, 225
Defence Intelligence Estimates Staff (DIES), 54, 55, 241
Defence Intelligence Staff, 13, 22–4, 29, 120, 280
Defence Security Branch (DSB), 59–60, 65
Defence Signals Bureau (DSB), 31, 37, 141, 143
Defence Signals Directorate (DSD): budget, 32; facilities, 175, 190–2, 202, 206, 208–9; operations, 36, 46, 57, 304; organisation of, 36–42, 63, 64, 65; and other agencies, 7, 31, 77, 142, 143, 150, 161, 194
Defence Signals Division (DSD), 30, 31
Defense Intelligence Agency (DIA), 96, 117, 119–22, 129, 161, 255–7, 270, 280
Defense Intelligence Division, Energy Department, 97, 128
Defense Investigative Service, 128
Defense Mapping Agency, 128–9
Defense Satellite Communications System (DSCS), 102, 104, 161, 201, 202, 206
Defense Support Program 125, 158, 180, 181, 190
DELTA codewords, 166
Denmark, 170, 171, 187, 188, 201
Denning Report, 17
DESKTOP, Project, 127, 167, 222, 224
DEXTER (codeword), 143

396   Index

Diego Garcia, 150, 159, 162, 194, 201, 202, 205–6, 216, 220
Digby RAF Base, Lincolnshire, 195
Digital Network Defense Special Security Communications System (DIN/DSSCS), 104
DINAR (codeword), 166
Diplomatic Telecommunications Maintenance Service, 19
Direction-Finding (DF): stations, 3, 202–10; systems, 1, 88, 137, 160, 192, 207, 209
Director of Central Intelligence (DCI), 256, 277–8, 308
Directorate of Air Force Intelligence and Security (DAFIS), 57, 58, 59, 65
Directorate of Military Intelligence (DMI), 30, 48, 56–7, 59, 65, 140
Directorate of Naval Intelligence and Security (DNIS), 30, 57, 58, 59, 65
Directorate of Service Intelligence (DSI), 54, 55, 57
Distant Early Warning (DEW) radar, 159, 189
Donovan, Colonel, 139, 140
Drake, Lieutenant-Colonel Edward M., 139
Duff, Sir Anthony, 27
Dulles, Allen, 163–4, 230, 271

early warning systems, 157–8, 159, 170, 176, 180, 189, 256
Easton, Sir Edward, 47
EC-135 aircraft, 182
Edinburgh, South Australia, 220–1
Edzell, Scotland, 159, 195, 216, 263, 305
Egypt, 15, 44, 45, 46, 114, 233, 261, 262, 304
Eichelburger, James, 15
El Salvador, 186
Electronic Security Command (ESC), 123, 124, 125, 171, 187, 188, 189, 207
Electronic Security Committee, 28, 29
electronic surveillance, 51, 290–1
Electronic Warfare (EW), 171
Electronics Intelligence (ELINT), 88, 101, 103, 104, 130, 176–7; 182, 187, 189, 214, 221, 224, 233, 304
Elgin Air Force Base, Florida, 158
Ellis, Colonel C.H., 42–3, 152, 162–3
Elmendorf Air Force Base, Alaska, 144, 187
Enforcement Branch, 83, 92, 95
ENIGMA, 2, 195
Ethiopia, 189, 202–5, 262
Eveland, Wilbur Crane, 15
External Intelligence Bureau (EIB), 67, 73–5, 78, 81, 161

Fairbanks, Alaska, 218
Falklands/Malvinas War, 77, 233, 304
Far Eastern Combined Bureau (FECB), 137

Fauer, Lieutenant-General Lincoln G., 105
Federal Bureau of Investigation (FBI), 96, 129, 102, 117–19, 287–8, 289, 290, 292, 294–6, 297, 298, 299, 300; and CIA, 240–1, 243–5, 246, 248; and NSA, 251; and UKUSA, 136, 140, 141, 161, 258–9, 281
Ferret satellites, 180–1
Figures, Colin, 15
Finn, Ted D'Arcy, 86
Fleet Ocean Surveillance Information Centers (FOSICs), 199
Fleet Satellite Communications (FLTSATCOM), 127, 201, 202
Fleming, A.P., 30–1
Folkes, Major Kenneth, 68
Foreign Broadcast Information Service (FBIS), 6, 115, 152, 229
Foreign Instrumentation Signals Intelligence (FISINT), 177
Foreign Science and Technology Center, 122, 123
Foreign Technology Division (FTD), 123, 124–5, 256, 280
Fort Belvoir, 124
Fort Bragg, 123
Fort Devens, Massachusetts, 186
Fort Knox, Kentucky, 186
Fort Meade, Maryland, 40, 101, 104, 121, 144, 145, 161, 187, 189, 191, 194
Fort Monkton, 16
Fort Richardson, Alaska, 186
Fort Shafter, Hawaii, 186
Fort Sheridan, Illinois, 186
France, 56, 261
Franks, Sir Arthur, 15
Franks Report, 309
Furlonger, R.W., 31, 33, 66, 247
Furner, Brigadier Jim, 43
Fyfe, Sir David Maxwell, 17
Fylingdales, UK, 158

GAMMA codewords, 166
Gander Canadian Forces Station, Newfoundland, 189
George, Clair E., 112
Germany: cooperation with, 170, 171; East, 151; and Second World War, 137, 302; stations in, 19, 125, 144, 162, 171, 184, 187, 194, 262, 305
Ghana, 229
Gibraltar, 194, 201, 202
Gibson, Frederick E., 86
Gilbert, Brigadier Herbert E., 68–9, 70, 75
Gilnahirk, Northern Ireland, 195
Giroux, J.B., 84
Goldstone, California, 218
Golitsin, Anotili, 246, 303
Goodfellow Air Force Base, Texas, 158

Index 397

Gouzenko, Igor, 303
Government Code and Cipher School (GCCS), 20, 136, 137, 141, 206
Government Communications Headquarters (GCHQ), 13, 19–22, 29, 141, 143, 198, 258, 279, 309; activities, 40, 138, 142, 143, 144, 173, 190, 194–5, 202, 206, 264, 304; and other nations, 39, 150, 161, 190, 262–3, 305–6
Government Communications Security Bureau (GCSB), 39, 67, 76–8, 80, 81, 142, 143, 150, 194
Grand Prairie, Alberta, 189
Greece, 187, 262
Greenland, 158
Greer, Brigadier-General, 97
Guam, 201, 207, 216, 220, 222

Halliday, Vice-Admiral Sir Roy, 24
Ham, Operation, 292
Hamblen, D., 68
Hanley, Sir Michael, 18
Hansen, C.M., 78
Hanslope Park, 195
Harry, R.L., 47
Hawklaw, Scotland, 195
Hearder, Lieutenant-Colonel R.D., 43
Helms, Richard, 244, 271, 277
Hensley, G.C., 80
Hermann, Robert J., 98
high frequency (HF) antenna, 160, 194, 191, 207
High Level Intelligence (HILEV), 118
HMAS Harman, 36, 39, 138, 190, 192, 193, 208, 209
HMNZS Irirangi, 77
Hollis, Sir Roger Henry, 18
HOLYSTONE, Project, 127, 131, 167, 222, 223–4
Homestead Air Force Base, Florida, 184, 187
Hong Kong, 18, 19, 22, 40, 44, 45, 110, 143, 150, 153, 162, 190, 191, 194, 206
Hooper, Sir Leonard, 27, 139, 150, 163
Hooton, Brigadier J.G., 250
Hoover, J. Edgar, 240–1, 244, 245, 251, 258–9
Hope, Mr Justice, 43, 44, 45, 46, 153; *see also* Royal Commission on Intelligence and Security
HTLINGUAL program, 108
human intelligence (HUMINT), 121, 234–5, 247, 272
Hungary, 229
Hunt, P.R., 89
hydrophone arrays, 199–200, 202

Iceland, 127, 187, 199, 201, 220
India, 46
Indonesia, 34, 39, 40, 42, 44, 45, 46, 55, 172, 190, 193, 234
Information Research Department (IRD), 25
INR *see* Bureau of Intelligence and Research
Integrated Tactical Surveillance System (ITSS), 217–19, 222
intelligence: analysis, 271, 279–80; cooperation, 1–6, 160; estimates, 235–7; quality of, 36, 270; priorities, 276–9; separation, 270–6, 281–2
Intelligence Center Pacific, 76
Intelligence Division, Office of Export Enforcement, 128
Intelligence and Security Command (INSCOM), 103, 106, 122, 143, 171, 186, 188, 207
Intelligence Support Activity (ISA), 122–3
Intelligence Support Agency (ISA), 247
INTELSAT, 102, 195, 306
Intercontinental Ballistic Missiles (ICBMs), 125, 157, 158, 178, 183, 254, 255, 256
International Regulations on SIGINT (IRSIGs), 5, 144, 148–9
Inuvik, Canada, 189
Iran: covert action in, 14–15, 122, 230, 247, 271; reports on, 42; stations in, 185, 188, 189, 195, 251, 262
Iraq, 15, 42, 45
Irian Jaya, 40, 42
Irish Republican Army (IRA), 25
Irish Special Branch, 24
Irton Moor, Yorkshire, 195
Island Hill, Northern Ireland, 195
Israel, 7, 42, 103, 115, 169, 170, 173, 261, 271, 304
Italy, 137, 184, 187, 201, 220, 261
Ivanov, Valeriy, 52, 66, 303
Ivory Coast, 229

James, T., 37
Japan: and Australia, 44, 45; cooperation with, 142, 170, 171, 220, 221; and Second World War, 1–2, 77, 137, 138, 248, 302; stations in, 122, 127, 144, 182, 184, 188, 199, 201, 206–7
Java, 138
Jaynes, V.E., 75
JENNIFER, Project, 222, 225–7
Jensen, Major Selwyn, 69, 72, 75
Jockel, Gordon, 246
Joint Communications-Electronic Committee (JCEC), CAN-UK-US, 156
Joint Intelligence Bureau (JIB) (Aus), 30, 31, 52, 55, 74
Joint Intelligence Bureau (Can), 90
Joint Intelligence Bureau (JIB) (UK), 22–3
Joint Intelligence Committee (JIC) (Aus), 31, 52–3, 192
Joint Intelligence Committee (JIC) (UK), 26, 27–8, 29, 273, 279, 280, 309

398 Index

Joint Intelligence Organisation (JIO), 30, 31, 32, 43, 52–6, 63, 64, 65, 170, 171, 172, 249–50, 259, 273, 280; and ONA, 33, 35–6, 241–2, 254, 278; and other nations, 75, 120, 161; and other Australian services, 39, 45, 46, 57, 59, 246
Joint Intelligence Staff (JIS), 30, 31, 55
Joint Surveillance System (JSS), 159
Jones, Sir Edward M. Furnival-, 18
Jones, Lieutenant Colonel H.E., 135, 136
Jones, Sir John Lewis, 18

Kampuchea, 42, 45, 46, 114, 254; see also Cambodia
Kell, Vernon, 18
Kent Island, 187
KGB, 68, 71, 151, 303
KH satellites, 97, 99, 107, 167, 180, 181, 246, 253, 304; see also 'Big Bird', Corona, SAMOS
Kingston, Ontario, 189
Kinloss RAF Base, 221
'Kinsfolk' system, 188, 207
'Kittiwake', Project, 40
Korea: North, 144, 182; South, 42, 142, 144, 169, 170, 171, 188, 206, 262
Kowandi, Northern Territory, 153, 161
Kuzichkin, Vladimir, 303

Langley, Virginia, 109
Laos, 123
LARSWOOD, Project, 193
Lebanon, 110
Lee, Andrew Daulton, 178
Leitrim, Ontario, 150, 162, 189
Lochore, Dr R.A., 68
Lockhart, Bruce, 14
London Signals Intelligence Board (LSIB), 26, 28, 29
Long Range Technical Search (LRTS), 21
Loop Antenna Array, 195
Loughborough, UK, 195

McClellan Air Force Base, California, 125
MacDonald Commission, 309
Machrihanish, Scotland, 231
Mackenzie Commission, 83, 86, 87
Maclean, Donald, 245
McMahon, John, 109
MAGNUM satellites, 181
mail surveillance, 51, 108, 284, 290–1
Makalapa, Hawaii, 199
Malaya, 40, 44, 45, 46
Malaysia, 7, 45, 46, 55, 170, 172, 190, 232
Malta, 19
Manned Orbital Laboratory (MOL), 253
Marconi-Adcock HF-DF system, 1, 137
Mark, Hans, 98

Masset Canadian Forces Station, British Columbia, 189
MATADOR, Project, 225
Mauritius, 19
Mehuron, Dr William, 102
Menwith Hill, Yorkshire, 150, 162, 195–7, 249, 263
Menzies, Major-General Sir Stewart, 15
MERRIMAC, Project, 108
Merritt Island, Florida, 218
Mexico, 118
Meyer, Cord, 152
Middle East, 14, 15, 34, 42, 103, 115; see also individual countries
MI-5 see Security Service
Mildenhall RAF Base, 182, 197
Military Intelligence Advisory Group (MIAG), 57, 58
Military Intelligence Section 9 (MI-9), 4
military intelligence: Australia, 30, 48, 56–9, 65, 140; NZ, 67; UK, 4, 14, 19, 25, 26, 198; US, 96, 99, 103, 106, 122–7, 139, 143, 171, 186, 188, 207, 216, 250, 251–2
military rivalries, 250–1, 255–6
MINARET, Operation, 103, 306
MI-6 see Secret Intelligence Service
'missile gap', 255
Missile Intelligence Agency, 122, 123
missiles, 125, 157, 158, 176, 178, 183, 184, 252, 254, 255, 256
MKULTRA, 108
Moffett Field, California, 201
Molineaux, Paul Loxton, 69
Montgomery, Hugh, 115
Morocco, 144, 189, 262
Morwenstow, Cornwall, 195, 306
Moscow, Maine, 158
Mosley, Leonard, 230
Murphy Commission, 269
Mutual Balanced Force Reduction (MBFR), 120

National Assessments Staff (NAS), 31, 53, 241
National Foreign Intelligence Board (NFIB), 129–30, 273, 278
National Foreign Intelligence Program (NFIP), 120, 130
National Intelligence Authority, 106
National Intelligence Committee (NIC), 31, 53, 63–4
National Intelligence Council, 129
National Intelligence Tasking Center (NITC), 278
National and International Security Committee (NISC), 65, 66
National Photographic Interpretation Center (NPIC), 114–15, 121

Index 399

National Reconnaissance Office (NRO), 62, 96, 97–9, 129, 131, 181, 182, 214, 225, 253, 277–8
National Security Agency (NSA), 7, 39, 96, 99–106, 120, 121, 124, 127, 129, 130, 152, 171, 225; activities, 138, 142, 143, 144, 150, 173, 174, 187, 188, 189, 190, 192, 194, 195, 197, 222, 249, 251, 277–8; and UKUSA, 161, 261–3, 305–6
National Security Council, 129, 253
Naval Electronics Systems Command (NAVALEX), 127, 216
Naval Intelligence, 19, 198
Naval Intelligence Command (NIC), 126–7
Naval Ocean Surveillance Information System (NOSIS), 6, 77, 160, 171, 206, 207, 208, 209
Naval Ocean Surveillance Satellite (NOSS) system, 214
Naval Research Laboratory, 214, 216, 217
Naval Security Group Command (NSG), 106, 127, 143, 144, 186, 187, 188, 189, 190, 195, 198, 202, 206, 207, 216; and other services, 125, 126–7, 214, 216, 217, 255
Naval Space Surveillance (NAVSPASUR) system, 127
Nave, Commander T.E., 30, 137
Navstar GPS satellites, 127
Navy Space Project of the Naval Electronics Systems Command (NAVALEX), 99
Need-to-Know (NTK) principle, 168, 239, 257
Netherlands, 220, 221, 261
New Zealand, 3–4, 32, 67–81, 135, 155, 156, 237; *see also* individual organisations
New Zealand Directorate of Defence Intelligence (NZDDI), 67, 75–6, 78, 81
New Zealand Intelligence Council (NZIC), 67, 77, 78, 79–80
New Zealand Security Intelliegence Service (NZSIS), 67, 68–73, 78, 79, 81, 173, 237, 238, 243, 282, 288–9, 291, 293, 297, 298, 300, 308, 311
New Zealand Joint Intelligence Bureau (NZJIB), 73–4
Nicaragua, 186
Nimrod aircraft, 220, 221
Norfolk, Virginia, 199
North American Air Defense Agreement (NORAD), 82, 157–9, 170, 183, 260
North American Space Administration (NASA), 218
North Atlantic Treaty Organisation (NATO), 7, 82, 142, 157, 165, 170, 200
North West Cape Naval Communications Station, 190, 206
Norway, 127, 170, 171, 188, 199, 201, 220, 221
Nurrungar, South Australia, 158, 162, 190

Nutmeg hydophone arrays, 200

Oakhanger, UK, 162, 218, 233, 305
Oakley, Gloustershire, 23
ocean surveillance, 88, 192, 198–227; airborne, 220–2; cooperation in, 1, 3–4, 6, 159–60, 302; satellites, 97, 127, 210–19
Ocean Surveillance Information System (OSIS), 199, 202
ODDBALL, Operation, 293
Odom, Major General William, 123
Office of the Assistant Chief of Staff for Intelligence (OACS/I), 122, 123, 124
Office of Current Intelligence (OCI), 53, 63, 241
Office of Intelligence, Drug Enforcement Administration, 97, 128
Office of Intelligence Liaison, Commerce Department, 128
Office of Intelligence Support, Treasury Department, 96, 128
Office of the Joint Chiefs of Staff (OJCS), 120
Office of Microwave Space and Mobile Systems, 99
Office of National Assessments (ONA), 31, 32–6, 39, 53, 55, 65, 66, 75, 161, 169–70, 171, 241–2, 246–7, 250, 254, 260, 273, 278–9, 280
Office of Naval Intelligence (ONI), 125, 126, 255
Office of Policy Coordination (OPC), 275–6
Office of Special Operations (OSO), 275–6
Office of Strategic Services (OSS), 2–3, 106, 115, 139, 140, 141, 151, 247–8
Office of War Information (OWI), 140
Offut Air Force Base, Nebraska, 187
Oldfield, Sir Maurice, 15
O'Malley, Edward J., 117
Oman, 143, 150, 162, 194, 202, 204
Orion aircraft, 220–1
Otis Air Force Base, Massachusetts, 158
Overseas Economic Intelligence Committee (OEIC), 26, 27, 28, 29
Overseas Information Department, 25
Over-the-Horizon (OTH) radars, 183, 210

Pakistan, 42, 46, 114, 189
Panama, 201
Papua New Guinea, 40, 42, 44, 45, 56, 169, 170, 172, 190, 232
Park Orchards, 36, 40
Pearce Air Force Base, Perth, 40, 190, 192, 208–9, 210
Pearl (codeword), 143, 166
Pearl Harbor, 137, 138, 139, 140–1, 187, 270
Penkovsky, Colonel Oleg, 151
Permanent Under Secretaries Committee on Intelligence Services (PSIS), 26, 27, 29

Petrie, David, 18
Petrov, Vladimir, 68, 163, 258, 303
phased-array radar, 158, 159, 183−4, 186, 189
Philby, H.A.R. (Kim), 13, 151, 230, 245
Philippines: cooperation with, 7, 153, 172, 199; monitoring at, 44, 45, 46; stations at, 137, 138, 144, 184, 188, 201, 206, 207−8, 220
photographic reconnaissance, 97, 182, 232−4, 304
Pine Gap, Northern Territory, 50, 62, 162, 178, 179, 190, 193−4, 197, 248, 251, 260, 263, 266−7, 304, 305
PINNACLE, Project, 223
Pinup (codeword), 143, 166
police, 60, 61, 62, 65, 68; *see also* Royal Canadian Mounted Police, Special Branch, Metropolitan Police
Police and Security Branch, Solicitor General's Office, 82, 90−3, 95
Portugal, 229, 248
Poundon, Buckinghamshire, 195
Powles report, 69−70, 71−2, 73, 78, 79, 164, 243, 288, 297
PRAIRIE SCHOONER, Project, 222, 224
Prime, Geoffrey, 22, 258
Proctor, Edward, 152
Project No. 980 satellite, 181
Protective Services Coordination Centre (PSCC), 30, 31, 32, 60, 61, 65
Puerto Rico, 201, 220
Punnett, B.M., 78
PURPLE code, 1, 137, 302
PYRAMIDER-type satellites, 110, 167

Quadripartite Agreements, 155−6
Quadripartite Working Groups (QWGs), 156, 237
Quebec Agreement, 155

Rabid (codeword), 143
radar systems, 158, 183−4, 188; *see also* antenna systems, early warning systems, hydrophone arrays, ocean surveillance satellites, Over-the-Horizon radar, phased array radar, synthetic aperture radar
Radford-Collins Agreement, 160
Radar Intelligence (RADINT), 102, 103, 176−7
radio broadcast monitoring, 6, 25−6, 228−9
Rae, John, 26
Rapidly Deployable Surveillance System (RDSS), 127, 201
RC-135 aircraft, 182−3, 187, 197
RED code, 137
Reed, Mr Justice, 50
Reilly, Sidney, 14
Rennie, Sir John, 15

'Reprieve' system, 40
RESISTANCE, Project, 108
REWSON, Project, 127
RF-4C Phantom aircraft, 183
Rhombic array antenna system, 185, 186
RHYOLITE satellite system, 62, 97, 99, 107, 131, 167, 177−9, 180, 181, 184, 190, 193, 248, 253, 260, 263−4, 266−7, 305
Robertson W.T., 31, 43, 152
Robins Air Force Base, Georgia, 158
Rockbank, Melbourne, 190, 191
Royal Canadian Mounted Police (RCMP) Security Service, 82, 83−7, 90, 91, 140, 141, 242−3, 258, 265, 282, 289, 290, 291−2, 293−4, 296, 297, 298, 309, 311
Royal Commission on Intelligence and Security, 32, 36, 42, 52, 62−3, 64, 235, 250, 257, 273, 303, 307, 308
RUFF (codeword), 167

SAC-PAV, 60−1
St Mawgan RAF Base, 221
SAMOS satellites, 97, 98, 167, 253
San Antonio, Texas, 187
San Diego, California, 207
SAND DOLLAR, Project, 127, 167, 222, 225
Satellite Data System (SDS), 102, 180, 195
satellite systems, 97, 98, 99, 102, 104, 125, 127, 161, 167, 201, 202, 206, 217; uses, 176, 210−19, 233−4; *see also* individual satellite names
Saudi Arabia, 15
Schlesinger, James, 111
Scotland Yard *see* Special Branch, Metropolitan Police
Sea Reconnaissance Unit, 4
Sea Spider hydrophone arrays, 200, 201, 226
SEASAT-A satellite, 217−18
Second World War, 1−4, 135−41
Secret Intelligence Australia (SIA), 4, 30
Secret Intelligence Service (SIS), 2, 13, 14−16, 18, 30, 136, 198, 245; and Australia, 31, 42−3, 45, 47, 152−3, 154, 161, 168, 232, 234, 235, 238; operations of, 14−15, 18, 20, 151, 161, 230, 304; organisation of, 15−16, 270, 272, 273, 275, 279, 280, 282, 309; other cooperation, 140, 141, 173, 237, 260−1
SECRET SPOKE, 166
security, domestic, 50, 51, 71−2, 282, 283−5
Security Branch, Department of Supply and Services, 83, 92, 95
Security Intelligence Bureau (SIB), 68, 140
Security Service, 13, 17−19, 29, 136, 243, 245, 286, 291; and Australia, 48, 50, 136, 237, 303; other cooperation, 68, 140, 161, 173, 237
Seek Skyhook balloon, 159

SHAMROCK, Operation, 103
Shemya Island, Alaska, 159, 183
Shenley Church End, Buckinghamshire, 195
Shetland Islands, 201
Shoal Bay, Northern Territory, 40, 190, 192–3, 208, 209
Shoe Cove, Newfoundland, 218
Signal Intelligence Service (SIS), 139, 250
signals intelligence: airborne, 174; Australian, 30, 36, 37, 38, 39, 142–3, 174–5, 190–4; Canadian, 89, 142–3, 174–5, 180–90; cooperation in, 135, 137, 138, 141–3, 149, 156, 302, 304; facilities, 186–7, 305; NATO, 170–1; NZ, 67, 77, 143, 174–5, 194; personnel, 22, 149; responsibilities for, 5, 7, 174, 248–9, 251; and Second World War, 1–4; ship-based, 185–6; systems, 177–8, 202, 307; types of, 175–7; UK, 20–2, 141–4, 174–5, 194–7, 198; US, 99, 101, 102, 104, 105, 106, 121, 122, 124, 127, 230, 141–4, 171, 172, 174–5, 186–9, 247–8
Sillitoe, Sir Percy, 18, 48, 68
Simmonds, Robert, 83
Sinclair, Admiral Sir Hugh, 15
Sinclair, Major-General John, 15
Singapore: cooperation with, 7, 44, 45, 153, 170, 172; stations at, 40, 63, 137, 138, 190, 192–3, 302, 304; studies on, 55
SISSZULU HF-DF system, 207
Skaggs Island, 186, 207
SLBW Phased Array Warning (PAVE PAWS) radar, 158
Smith, Sir Howard Trayton, 18
Smith, Brigadier John Lindsay, 69
Smith, General Walter Bedell, 140, 151, 241
Sound Surveillance System (SOSUS), 26, 127, 159, 199–202, 305
Space Detection and Tracking System (SPADATS), 251
Space Surveillance (SPASUR) system, 159, 250
Spain, 187–8, 199, 220, 221, 229
'Sparrow', Project, 40, 192
Special Air Service (SAS), 25, 26
Special Boat Squadron (SBS), 25, 26
Special Branch, Metropolitan Police, 13, 24–5, 29, 243, 286–7, 291, 296, 298
Special Interdepartmental Committee on Protection Against Violence (SIDC-PAV), 61
Special Investigation Unit, Department of National Defense, 82–3, 92, 95
Special Operations Australia, 4
Special Operations Executive (SOE), 2–3, 4, 136, 140, 141, 275
Spry, Brigadier Sir Charles, 48, 50, 163–4, 258–9

S-3A anti-submarine aircraft, 220
Stolz, Richard F., 152
Strategic Arms Limitation Talks (SALT), 24, 34, 103, 120, 177
Strategic Reconnaissance (SR) aircraft, 182, 197, 220, 233, 253, 304
Stretton, Major General Alan, 30
Strong, Kenneth, 22
Submarine-Launched Ballistic Missiles (SLBMs), 125, 158, 184
submarines: attack, 223–4, 225–6; detection: 211–14, 302
Sugar Grove, West Virginia, 186
Sullivan, William, 258, 294
surface-to-air missiles (SAMs), 252, 255
surveillance, domestic, 285–300, 306, 307
Surveillance Towed Array Sensor Systems (SURTASS), 127, 201–2
Swan Island, Victoria, 44
Switzerland, 110
synthetic aperture radar (SAR), 217–18
Syria, 15

Tactical Assault Group (TAG), 62, 65
T-AGOS ships, 202
Taiwan, 170, 171
'Talent-Keyhole' (TK) material, 166–7
Tangimoana, NZ, 77, 194, 209–10
Target Data Inventory (TDI), 120
Telemetry Intelligence (TELINT), 102, 103, 177
telemetry interception, 185, 187
telephone interception, 51, 103, 284
TEMPEST operations, 39
terrorism, 60–2, 73, 118, 281, 282
TEXTA, 39
Thailand, 7, 44, 45, 46, 114, 172, 189, 190, 234
Thompson, R.N., 37
Thumb (codeword), 143, 166
Tiltman, Colonel John H., 139
Timor, 40, 42, 45, 234
Tordella, Dr Louis, 103
Travis, Commander Edward, 139
TRINE (codeword), 166
Tripartite Agreements, 155
Tripartite Defense Intelligence Estimates Conference, 237
Truong, David, 245
Turkey, 19, 122, 143, 144, 150, 184, 188, 194, 201, 233, 261, 262
Turner, Admiral Stansfield, 111, 178, 247, 275, 277–8

UKUSA Agreement, 4–8, 135, 137, 141–4 *passim*, 174; and Australia, 5–6, 30, 302; and Canada, 6, 82, 88, 89; community, 160–1, 239, 301; consequences of, 301–11;

and NZ, 67, 75, 302; non-cooperation in, 168–70, 257–68; operations, 22, 39, 164–5, 170–3; and UK, 302
ULTRA (codeword), 2, 7, 143, 166
UMBRA (codeword), 5, 22, 166
Underseas Surveillance Project, 127, 223
underwater surveillance, 127, 199–202, 223, 225
Union of Soviet Socialist Republics (USSR): monitoring, 45, 50, 51, 84, 102–3, 176, 177, 180, 183, 188, 189, 190, 192, 195, 206, 223–4; reconnaissance of, 182, 183–4; studies on, 114, 124, 169, 170, 236, 280; weapons systems, 46, 56, 125, 219, 225–7, 235–6, 254–7, 302; *see also* KGB
United Kingdom *see* Britain
United States: bases in Australia, 5–6, 34, 175, 193–4; cooperation, 1–3, 7–8, 136–41, 155, 156, 198, 228–38 *passim*; intelligence community, 96–131, 239–40; *see also* individual organisations
U-2 aircraft, 107, 125, 182, 185, 197, 220, 221–2, 233, 252

Vale, B.R., 39
Vela satellites, 125
VHF intercepts, 197, 207
VHF-UHF-SHEF receivers, 183, 184, 185, 187, 188
Victoria Barracks, Melbourne, 37, 190, 191
Vietnam, 45, 46, 123, 231–2, 254
Vint Hills Farm Station, Virginia, 186–7, 263

Wahiawa, Hawaii, 144, 147, 184, 186, 207
Watsonia Barracks, Melbourne, 40, 190, 191
WESTWING, Project, 99
Wheeler Air Force Base, Hawaii, 125, 187
Whenapui, NZ, 221
White, Sir Dick Goldsmith, 15, 18, 27
WHITE CLOUD satellites, 97, 99, 127, 159, 214–16, 304, 305
Whitehorse, Canada, 189
'Wideband Extraction', Project, 186–7
Wigg, George, 27
Williams, Lieutenant-General James A., 121
Wilton, General J., 53
Winter Harbor, Maine, 186, 216
Woodward, Mr Justice, 50
Woomera, South Australia, 155, 160
Wullenweber antenna system, 184–5
Wymeswold, Leicestershire, 195
Wyton RAF Base, 195

Yardley, Herbert O., 88
Yemen, 15, 274
Young, George Kennedy, 15